THE CONCISE A to Z GUIDE TO FINDING IT IN THE Bible

A Quick-Scripture Reference

Compiled by
Seth Ehorn and Linda Washington

a division of Baker Publishing Group
Grand Rapids, Michigan

Condensed from *The A to Z Guide to Finding It in the Bible,* published in 2010 by Baker Publishing Group.

Published by Baker Books
a division of Baker Publishing Group
P.O. Box 6287, Grand Rapids, MI 49516-6287
www.bakerbooks.com

Printed in the United States of America

Library of Congress Cataloging-in-Publication Data

Ehorn, Seth.
The concise A to Z guide to finding it in the Bible / compiled by Seth Ehorn and Linda Washington.
pages ; cm.
Includes bibliographical references and index.
ISBN 978-0-8010-1527-4 (alk. paper)
1. Bible—Indexes. I. Washington, Linda M. II. Title.
BS432.E463 2013
220.3—dc23 2012032057

Produced by The Livingstone Corporation (www.LivingstoneCorp.com). Project staff include Betsy Schmitt, Linda Washington, Ryan Taylor, Linda Taylor, Lois Jackson, Andy Culbertson, Dana Niesluchowski. Interior designed by Larry Taylor. Typeset by Joel Bartlett and Tom Shumaker.

13 14 15 16 17 18 19 7 6 5 4 3 2 1

Table of Contents

▶ Abandoned *(forsaken, friendless, left alone, orphaned, rejected)*

When you are left to your own resources or devices and feel as if no one cares about you; when you withdraw your support from a person or a cause

Deuteronomy 4:31. He will never abandon you.

Deuteronomy 31:6. He goes ahead of you wherever you go.

Joshua 1:5. He will never abandon you.

Joshua 24:20. A warning against abandoning the Lord

Psalm 27:10. A place to go, even if those closest to you abandon you

▶ Abase/Abasement *(humbled, rejecting prestige, giving up pride)*

A lowering of rank; voluntarily humbling yourself for the sake of someone greater

Genesis 18:1–2. Abraham's abasement

Ezra 9:5. Ezra's self-abasement

Philippians 4:12. Paul knew how to abase himself.

▶ Abhorrence *(disgust, hatred, repugnance)*

A feeling of disgust or repugnance for a person or object

Leviticus 26:11. God will not abhor His people.

1 Chronicles 21:6. Joab's abhorrence for David's command

Job 19:19. Job's friends' abhorrence for him

Psalm 119:163. Lying is an abhorrence to God.

Isaiah 66:24. What happens to the disobedient

▶ Ability(ies) *(gift, talent)*

The quality of being able to do something

Exodus 28:3. God gives people abilities.

Deuteronomy 8:17–18. Don't count on your abilities; count on God.

1 Chronicles 26:8. Our abilities help us serve.

Proverbs 18:20. Abilities help provide for your life

Daniel 5:12. Some abilities are special.

Matthew 25:15. Given money according to abilities

▶ Abolish *(destroy, do away with, end, set aside)*

When you annul or end something, i.e., a law, a kingdom

Isaiah 2:18. God promises one day to abolish idols.

Daniel 11:31. A prophecy of the future describes the end of daily sacrifices.

Hosea 2:18. God will one day abolish war.

Micah 5:14. God will abolish sites dedicated to idols.

Matthew 5:17. What Jesus did not come to do

▶ Abomination *(disgusting, unclean, unholy)*

An item of disgust

Genesis 43:32. Some food is an abomination to others.

Exodus 8:26. An abomination to the Egyptians

Leviticus 11:10. What not to eat

Daniel 9:27. Abomination of a future ruler

Matthew 24:15. Jesus confirms Daniel's message.

▶ Abortion *(killing, life, murder)*

The termination of a pregnancy that results in the death of the fetus

Genesis 1:26. Made in God's image

Genesis 4:8–10. Innocent blood calls to God.

Exodus 1:16. Murder is the same before or after birth.

Exodus 21:22. It is a crime to destroy life before birth.

2 Chronicles 28:3. God judges nations that kill children.

Psalm 139:13–16. Alive and loved in the womb

Isaiah 49:1, 5. Called and known by God

Jeremiah 1:5. God forms the child.

A

▶ Abound *(abundant, increase)*

To flourish; to increase in number
Genesis 1:20. Let the creatures increase.
Psalm 4:7. Joy comes when resources abound.
Psalm 72:7. Increase of peace
2 Corinthians 9:8. Grace abounds.
Philippians 1:9. Let love abound.

▶ Abrahamic covenant *(promise)*

A series of promises God made with Abraham and his descendants
Genesis 12:2. First promise
Genesis 12:7. Second promise
Genesis 13:15. Third promise
Genesis 15:4–5. Fourth promise
Genesis 17:2–8. Fifth promise
Genesis 18:10. Sixth promise

▶ Absent *(away, dead, not present)*

The state of being away from a group; dead or imprisoned
Proverbs 10:19. Sin is not absent.
2 Corinthians 10:11. Paul's defends his actions when present and absent.
2 Corinthians 13:2. Warnings during absence
Philippians 2:12. Paul reminds the Philippians to remain obedient—not just when Paul is present.
Colossians 2:5. Absent in body, present in spirit

▶ Absolute *(unlimited, unrestricted)*

Not limited or restricted
Psalm 147:5. Unlimited understanding
Song of Solomon 7:6. Absolute beauty
Ezekiel 43:12. Absolute holiness
Matthew 20:25. Absolute power
John 5:22. Absolute authority to judge

▶ Absolutes *(moral thinking, complete in itself, perfect, set apart, ultimate)*

A belief system that adheres to a moral code; the ultimate basis of thought; something completely independent of something else
Genesis 18:19. Do what is right.
Deuteronomy 5:20. There is truth.
John 14:6. Jesus is truth.
1 Timothy 5:1–2. Morally pure
1 John 4:8. God is love.

▶ Absolution *(seek or grant forgiveness, make peace)*

To absolve a wrongdoing; seeking forgiveness through an offering made
Exodus 29:14. Seek absolution with an offering
Exodus 30:10. Aaron seeks absolution for Israel's sins.
Leviticus 4:3. Absolution for a priest
Numbers 19:17. Red cow as absolution for sin
1 Samuel 15:25. Saul begs Samuel for absolution.

▶ Abstinence *(avoidance of indulging, resistance)*

To abstain from sex, drinking, or drugs
Exodus 19:15. Abstinence is a must when preparing to go before the Lord.
Numbers 6:3. Nazirites must abstain from wine.
1 Samuel 1:14. Eli warns Hannah to abstain from drinking.
Song of Solomon 3:5. Keep away from premarital sex.
Acts 15:20. Warnings from the apostles

▶ Abundance *(plentiful)*

Something that is great in number; an increase
Genesis 41:29. Abundant harvest in Egypt
Deuteronomy 33:19. Abundance God promises
1 Chronicles 29:16. Offering abundance to God
Psalm 49:6. Wealth in plenty
John 10:10. The abundant life

▶ Abuse *(mistreatment)*

Hurting or injuring someone with words or actions

Deuteronomy 28:33. Promise of abuse to come
Proverbs 9:7. When offering correction
Proverbs 22:10. How to stop abuse
Amos 4:1. Amos rebukes abusive women.
1 Corinthians 4:12. What to do when verbally abused

▶ Abyss *(bottomless pit)*

The pit reserved for Satan and demons
Luke 8:31. Where demons are sent
Revelation 9:1. Key to the abyss
Revelation 9:1–11. A vision of dark times to come
Revelation 11:7. The beast from the bottomless pit
Revelation 17:1–8. The beast from the bottomless pit
Revelation 20:1–3. The power of one angel over the abyss

▶ Acacia *(tree)*

A tree the wood of which was often used in building
Exodus 25:10. Making the ark of the covenant
Exodus 26:37. Making the tabernacle
Exodus 30:1. God's plan for the altar of incense
Exodus 35:24. Contributions for the tabernacle
Exodus 36:20. Building the tabernacle
Exodus 37:1. Craftsmen shape the acacia.
Deuteronomy 10:3. Moses remembers
Isaiah 41:19. A promise of restoration

▶ Acceptable *(adequate, pleasing, satisfactory)*

Worthy of being accepted
Exodus 5:8. Unacceptable in brick making
Exodus 30:15. Acceptable lives
Judges 6:17. Gideon inquires about his acceptability.
1 Samuel 18:26. An acceptable son-in-law
1 Chronicles 6:49. Acceptable to God
2 Chronicles 36:21. Acceptable land
Psalm 19:4. Acceptable words

▶ Acceptance *(approval, inclusion, recognition)*

Having favor or approval; coming to a point of belief
Leviticus 23:11. Waiting for acceptance
Isaiah 60:7. Acceptance at God's altar
Romans 11:15. Acceptance of Gentiles
1 Timothy 1:15. A statement worthy of acceptance
1 Timothy 4:8–9. Paul urges Timothy to accept the truth of godly living.

▶ Access *(admission, approach, entrance)*

A way of approaching
2 Kings 25:19. Access to the king
Esther 1:3. Access to Xerxes
Jeremiah 52:25. Taking the people with access to the king
Amos 5:12. Denial of access
Zechariah 3:7. Free access

▶ Accident(s) *(calamity, collision, mishap, mistake)*

An unexpected event that causes problems
Exodus 21:13. A place to go in case of an accidental slaying
Joshua 20:6. A place to go in the event of an accidental slaying
1 Samuel 6:9. God's doing or an accident?
2 Kings 1:2. A terrible accident
1 Corinthians 4:9. How bearers of the gospel sometimes feel

▶ Acclaim/Accolades *(approval, applause, fame, praise)*

Public praise
1 Chronicles 29:2. Solomon's acclaim
Psalm 89:15. People are blessed who acclaim the Lord.
Isaiah 24:14. The Lord's acclaim
Luke 4:15. Approving Jesus

A

▶ Accommodate/ Accommodation(s) *(lodging)*

Something that meets a need; providing room for someone

Genesis 24:23. Abraham's servant seeks the right accommodations.

Genesis 26:22. God accommodates Isaac and Abimelech.

Genesis 34:21. The men of Shechem are fooled by the accommodating Israelites.

Isaiah 26:15. Stretching the borders

▶ Accomplishment(s) *(achievement, success, triumph)*

Something completed successfully

1 Kings 10:6–7. The queen of Sheba praises Solomon's accomplishments.

2 Kings 10:34. Jehu's heroic acts

Ecclesiastes 2:11. Nothing gained from accomplishments

Ecclesiastes 9:1. People and accomplishments are in God's hands.

2 Corinthians 10:16. Not boasting in another man's accomplishments

Galatians 6:4. Proud of accomplishments

▶ Accountability *(answering to, liability, responsibility)*

Taking account of one's actions; answerable to another party for one's actions

Ezekiel 3:18. Held accountable for failure to warn

Ezekiel 33:6. Watchman accountable

Daniel 6:2. Satraps accountable

Matthew 23:35. Pharisees and teachers of the law held accountable

Matthew 23:36. Others held accountable

▶ Accountants *(auditors, bookkeepers)*

Those who keep or audit records

Esther 6:1. A king consults his staff about the records.

Matthew 18:24. Servants give an account.

Matthew 25:19. Settling accounts

▶ Accuracy *(correctness, exactness, precision)*

Being careful or exact; not making mistakes

Deuteronomy 25:15. Use accurate weights

Proverbs 11:1. Accuracy is pleasing to God.

Proverbs 22:21. Give an accurate report.

Acts 18:25. Accurate teaching

Acts 23:15. Faking a need for accuracy

▶ Accusation *(allegation, charge, indictment)*

A charge of wrongdoing

Ezra 4:6. Enemies' accusations against the Israelites

Psalm 52:4. An enemy who loves to accuse

Matthew 18:16. What to do when accused

Matthew 27:37. An accusation against Jesus

John 18:29. Pilate demands to know the Jews' accusation of Jesus.

Acts 22:30. The Jews' accusation of Paul

▶ Accuser *(allegation, charge, indictment)*

Someone who accuses someone of wrongdoing or shortcoming

Job 1:6. Satan accuses Job.

Job 31:35. Job defends himself against his accuser.

Psalm 109:6. What to do when accused

Isaiah 50:8. Vindication before accusers

Zechariah 3:1. Satan seeks to accuse Joshua the priest.

▶ Achievements *(accomplishments, feats, triumphs)*

Results gained by effort; great or heroic deeds

1 Kings 15:23. Asa's achievements

1 Kings 16:5. Baasha's achievements

2 Kings 10:34. Jehu's achievements

Proverbs 31:31. Reward for achievements

Ecclesiastes 4:4. Meaningless achievements

▶ Acknowledgment *(credit, greeting, recognition)*

Admitting the rightness of or praising the actions of someone

Deuteronomy 33:9. Lack of acknowledgment from the tribe of Levi

1 Samuel 11:14. Acknowledgment of Saul as king

Hosea 4:1. Failure to acknowledge God

Hosea 6:6. God wants to be acknowledged.

Titus 1:1. Paul acknowledges the truth.

Philemon 6. Acknowledgment of good

▶ Acquiescing *(agreeing, complying, yielding)*

To agree with or yield to someone without protest

2 Samuel 12:12–13. David acquiesces to Nathan's accusation.

Matthew 5:40. Jesus preaches acquiescence.

Matthew 26:42. Jesus acquiesces to the Father's plan.

▶ Acquittal *(discharge, exoneration, freedom, release)*

Setting free from the charge of an offense

Exodus 23:7. No acquittal for the guilty

Isaiah 53:11. We are acquitted, thanks to God's righteous servant.

Jeremiah 26:16. Jeremiah is acquitted.

Micah 6:11. No acquittal for a dishonest man.

Romans 3:27. We are acquitted by faith.

▶ Acrostic *(poem)*

A poem with lines the first letters of which form a word or name or follow a pattern (i.e., the Hebrew alphabet)

Psalm 25. An acrostic prayer for mercy

Psalm 34. An acrostic of praise to God for His help

Psalm 37. An acrostic of wisdom

Psalm 119. An acrostic on the value of God's Word

Psalm 145. An acrostic of praise for God's character and deeds

Proverbs 31:10–31. An acrostic to a virtuous woman

▶ Action(s) *(achievement, battle, deed, work)*

Performing an act or engaging in battle; usually a plea for God's assistance or for people to obey God in some way

1 Kings 8:31–32. A call to take action against the guilty

Ezra 10:4. A call to righteous action

Ezekiel 8:18. God will act against idol worshipers.

Daniel 11:28. A prophecy of a future war

Luke 12:35. Be ready when Jesus returns.

1 Peter 1:13. Peter urges believers to be ready to act according to their faith.

▶ Adapting *(changing, conforming, modifying)*

To change one's behavior according to a situation, climate, or to obey a rule; a hereditary change

Genesis 3:17–19. Because of the curse, Adam and Eve's descendants will be forced to adapt.

Leviticus 25:1–2. Festival adaptations

Deuteronomy 18:19. God warns against changing in the way of the Canaanites.

Judges 2:10–12. An evil adaptation

▶ Adequacy *(competence, satisfactoriness, sufficiency)*

Sufficiency to meet a need

Deuteronomy 1:15. The adequacy of officials

1 Samuel 6:4. Adequate compensation

Ecclesiastes 5:18. Tools for an adequate life

1 Corinthians 2:3–4. Paul is totally inadequate?

2 Corinthians 2:16. Who is adequate?

▶ Adhesive *(glue)*

A substance providing adhesion

A

Genesis 11:3. Tar used as mortar
Exodus 2:3. To seal a water vessel
Daniel 2:43. Lack of adhesion

▶ Administration *(government, management, organization)*

Management of business affairs; the activity of a sovereign state in the exercise of its powers or duties
1 Kings 4:1–28. Solomon's administration
Nehemiah 2:16. Nehemiah bypasses the administration.
1 Corinthians 12:28. The gift of administration
2 Corinthians 9:12. The administration of this service
Ephesians 3:2–3. Administration of God's grace

▶ Admirable *(estimable, venerable, worthy)*

Something or someone deserving admiration
Genesis 32:10. Jacob doubts that he's worth admiring.
Esther 1:19. Vashti is replaced by someone more admirable.
Psalm 106:2. The Lord is admirable.
Matthew 6:16. Is fasting admirable?
Philippians 4:8. Think about what is admirable.

▶ Admonish *(caution, rebuke, reprimand)*

Gently reprove
Psalm 81:8. God admonishes His people.
Romans 15:14. Admonish one another.
Colossians 3:16. Admonish one another.
1 Thessalonians 5:12. Respect those who admonish you.
2 Thessalonians 3:15. Respect those who admonish you.

▶ Admonitions *(advice, reproofs, warnings)*

Advice or warning
Malachi 2:1. Admonition for priests
1 Corinthians 10:11. Paul's admonition
Ephesians 6:4. Warning for fathers
Titus 3:10. Reject a divisive man.

▶ Adolescence *(childhood, puberty, youth)*

The period of development from puberty to maturity
Genesis 21:8–10. Problems during Isaac's adolescence
Genesis 37:3. Joseph reaps trouble with his brothers during his adolescence.
2 Kings 2:23. Elisha jeered by adolescents.
Ecclesiastes 12:1. Adolescence is a time to remember God.
Luke 2:52. Jesus' adolescence
1 Corinthians 10:1–11. What Paul gave up as he grew older

▶ Adoption *(acceptance, embracing)*

Taking someone into your family
Romans 8:15. God's adopted children
Romans 8:23. Waiting for adoption
Romans 9:4. Adoption as sons
Galatians 4:4–5. What Jesus did to bring about our adoption
Ephesians 1:5. Jesus freely chose to adopt us.

▶ Adoration *(adulation, love, worship)*

The act of worshiping or honoring God; the act of regarding someone with love and devotion
1 Chronicles 29:11. David's adoration of God
Psalm 45:11. Adore your king—the Lord
Psalm 139:14. Worship in adoration
Song of Solomon 1:4. Adoration of the bridegroom

▶ Adornment *(clothing, embellishment, raiment)*

To clothe or adorn a person or thing
Job 40:10. God challenges Job to adorn himself.

Psalm 144:12. Children are adornments.
Proverbs 1:9. Wisdom as an adornment
Isaiah 60:13. Adorning the sanctuary

▶ Adulterer(s) *(adultery, sinner, unfaithful)*

One who commits adultery
Leviticus 20:10. What the law says about adulterers
Job 24:15. Adultery under cover of night
Proverbs 5:3–4. An adulterous woman
John 8:3–4. Woman caught in adultery
Romans 7:3. Who is an adulterer?
Hebrews 13:4. Judging the adulterer

▶ Adultery *(disloyalty, infidelity, sexual sin)*

A relationship between a married person and a person to whom he or she is not married
Exodus 20:14. One of the Ten Commandments
2 Samuel 11:2–5. David and Bathsheba
Psalm 50:18. God rebukes the wicked.
Proverbs 6:32. The destruction of adultery
Proverbs 30:20. The way of an adulterous woman
Jeremiah 3:8. The adultery of Israel and Judah

▶ Advantage *(benefit, gain, profit)*

Benefiting or profiting, sometimes at the expense of another
Exodus 22:22. Avoid taking advantage of widows and orphans.
Leviticus 25:14. Sellers to avoid taking advantage
Leviticus 25:17. Fear God, instead of taking advantage.
Nehemiah 5:15. Using power to take unfair advantage of others
Job 24:21. Men who take advantage
Proverbs 16:26. Hunger works to your advantage.

▶ Advent *(arrival, beginning, coming)*

A coming or arrival; the four Sundays before Christmas commemorating Jesus' arrival
Isaiah 7:14. The Savior will be born of a virgin.
Isaiah 9:6. A child will come—the Prince of Peace.
Isaiah 53:2–4. A Savior born to die
Micah 5:2. The Savior will be born in Bethlehem.
Luke 2:10. Angels announce Jesus' advent.

▶ Adversity *(calamity, hardship, trouble)*

Hardship or affliction
Deuteronomy 29:21. Separated for adversity
2 Samuel 4:9. Redeemed from adversity
2 Samuel 12:11. Adversity is the result of adultery.
Proverbs 17:17. A friend in adversity
Isaiah 30:20. Bread of adversity

▶ Advice *(counsel, guidance, recommendation)*

An opinion given about what could be done to solve a problem
Exodus 18:19. Jethro's advice for Moses
Numbers 24:14. Balaam's advice for Balak
Judges 20:7. A Levite seeks advice.
2 Samuel 15:31. Ahithophel's advice
1 Kings 12:6. Rehoboam seeks advice.
2 Kings 1:3. Consequences of seeking the wrong advice

▶ Advocate *(backer, helper, supporter)*

Someone who pleads the case of someone else.
1 Samuel 24:15. God as David's advocate
Job 16:19. Job's advocate
John 14:26. The Holy Spirit as Advocate
1 John 2:1. Our Advocate—Jesus

▶ Affectation *(artifice, mannerism, pretentiousness)*

A pretense; artificial behavior
Isaiah 29:13. Wrong worship is really an affectation.
Jeremiah 3:10. Judah's return is an affectation.

Matthew 6:1–2. Good deeds as affectations
Matthew 23:5. Affectations of the Pharisees

▶ Affection *(fondness, love)*

Tender feeling toward someone
Deuteronomy 7:7. The Lord's affection
Esther 2:9. Esther wins the king's affection.
2 Corinthians 9:14. Affection of the Christian community
2 Timothy 3:2–4. In the last days, some people will lack affection for others.
2 Peter 1:5–7. Add affection.

▶ Affirmation *(avowal, encouragement)*

The act of affirming someone; a positive statement or judgment; a solemn declaration
2 Kings 23:3. The people affirm God's Word.
Romans 3:8. The wrong thing to affirm
1 Corinthians 15:31. Paul's affirmation
1 Timothy 1:7. What false teachers affirm
James 1:25. Where affirmation can be found

▶ Affliction *(see Disease; Sickness)*

▶ Affluence *(see Prosperity; Wealth)*

▶ Agape *(communion, love)*

Greek word for "unconditional love"
John 15:13. The greatest love
John 21:15–16. Jesus asks about Peter's love
1 Corinthians 11:21, 33. The love feast
2 Peter 2:13. False teachers wrongly take part in the love feasts.
1 John 2:5. Agape perfected

▶ Age *(era, epoch, time; mature, old)*

The length of one's existence; a period of time in history
Genesis 15:15. God promises that Abraham would live to an old age.
Genesis 25:7–8. God keeps his promise.
Leviticus 19:32. Respect the aged.
Judges 2:8. Joshua dies of old age.
1 Samuel 2:32. Living to old age is a privilege that God can revoke.
Esther 9:28. Purim to be celebrated through the ages
Psalm 71:18. Praising God in one's old age
Luke 1:36. An elderly woman is pregnant.
Titus 1:2–3. A message for every era

▶ Agony *(anguish, pain, suffering)*

Intense mental or physical pain
Nehemiah 9:36–37. The Levites express the agony of their people.
Psalm 116:3–5. A psalmist praises God for deliverance from agony.
Jeremiah 51:54. A prophecy about the future suffering of the Babylonians
Matthew 24:30. Agony at the second coming
Matthew 27:45–46. The Savior in agony on the cross
Revelation 12:1–2. Prophecy of the end times

▶ Agreement *(accord, harmony, union)*

A union of opinions; acting with one accord; a legally binding contract
Genesis 21:27. Abraham's agreement with Abimelech
Genesis 31:43–44. Laban and Jacob agree to part peacefully.
Deuteronomy 32:31. Even enemies should agree that God is dependable.
Joshua 24:24–25. The people of Israel agree to serve God.
Ruth 3:13. Naomi cautions waiting for Boaz to agree to become Ruth's kinsman-redeemer.
Matthew 1:19. Engagement is an agreement as binding as a marriage.

▶ Agriculture *(cultivation, farming, gardening)*

The act of farming
Genesis 26:12. Isaac's crops blessed by God
Genesis 41:5–7. Pharaoh's dream about a rich harvest before a famine
Exodus 9:31–32. Crops in Egypt destroyed by the plague of hail
Exodus 23:16. Harvest festival

Leviticus 19:9–10. Grain to be left in fields for the poor

▶ Air *(atmosphere, sky, space)*

The atmosphere; mixture of nitrogen and oxygen

Genesis 1:6–8. God creates the sky.

Genesis 2:7. The first breath in man's lungs came from God.

Job 38:29. God reminds Job that he created all things.

Psalm 144:4. The fleeting life of a human compared to air

2 Corinthians 2:14. Christians are like a fragrance in the air

▶ Alarm(s) *(fear, danger signal, warning)*

A warning of danger; a sudden fear

Nehemiah 4:18. Alarm system used when rebuilding the wall of Jerusalem

Hosea 5:8–9. Prophecy of future alarm

Joel 2:1. Alarms will sound on the day of the Lord.

Amos 3:6. God responsible for the sound of alarms

2 Corinthians 7:11. Alarm due to godly sorrow

▶ Alcohol *(liquor, wine)*

Intoxicating liquor

Proverbs 20:1. The influence of alcohol

Proverbs 31:6–7. Drinking to forget

Isaiah 5:22. Sorrow for those who indulge in alcohol

1 Timothy 3:8. Deacons to avoid alcohol addiction

Titus 2:3. Older women to avoid drunkenness

▶ Alcoholic *(drunkard)*

Person who suffers from alcoholism

Genesis 9:20–21. Noah's drunkenness causes problems.

1 Samuel 1:13–14. Eli mistakenly believes that Hannah is drunk.

1 Samuel 25:36. Nabal gets drunk.

Proverbs 26:9. A proverb about an alcoholic

Isaiah 5:11. The sad life of an alcoholic

▶ Alien(s) *(see Foreigner[s])*

▶ Alive *(animate, breathing, living)*

Having life

Genesis 6:19–20. God's instructions for keeping animals alive during the flood

Genesis 43:7–8. Joseph's brothers report on Joseph's inquiries about their father.

Numbers 16:31–33. Korah and other rebels swallowed up alive.

Joshua 14:10–11. Caleb marvels how God kept him alive while many others died in the wilderness.

Mark 16:14. Jesus appears to his disciples to show that he is alive.

Romans 6:13. From death to life

Romans 8:10. Spirits are alive.

▶ Allegories *(fables, metaphors, parables, stories)*

Using characters or events to represent ideas or principles

2 Samuel 12:1–4. Nathan uses a story to rebuke David's adultery.

Ezekiel 23. An allegory for Samaria and Jerusalem

Hosea 1:2. Hosea's marriage is a living allegory.

John 16:21–25. Jesus uses an allegory to explain his understanding of the disciples' upcoming grief and joy.

Galatians 4:21–31. Paul uses an allegory to explain the difference between enslavement to the law and the freedom of grace.

▶ Alliance *(association, coalition, union)*

An association of nations or groups

Psalm 83:5–7. A psalm pleading for God's help against an alliance of enemy nations

Isaiah 7:2. Aramean alliance

Jeremiah 50:9–10. An alliance against Babylon

Daniel 11:6. Daniel's vision of an alliance

A

▶ Almighty, the *(all-powerful, invincible, omnipotent)*

A name for God

Genesis 17:1. God names himself to Abraham.

Genesis 35:11. God names himself to Jacob.

Deuteronomy 3:23–24. Moses discusses God.

2 Samuel 7:18–19. David talks to the Almighty.

Job 13:3. Job argues his case before the Almighty.

▶ Alms *(charity, gifts)*

Money or goods given to the poor

Luke 11:41. Alms to the poor

Luke 12:33. Jesus preaches about giving.

Acts 3:2–3. A lame man asks for alms.

Acts 10:1–2. Cornelius, a centurion, gave alms to the poor.

Acts 24:17. Paul gives alms to the poor.

▶ Alone *(lonely, solitary, unaccompanied)*

Apart from others

Genesis 2:18. Not good for man to be alone

Genesis 32:24. Jacob alone before he met with God

Exodus 18:14. Moses alone had the responsibility for judging the disputes of the people.

Ruth 1:3–5. Naomi alone

Ecclesiastes 4:8. Sadness of being alone

▶ Alpha and Omega *(beginning and end)*

The Greek letters of the alphabet (the beginning and end respectively) used as a name for God

Revelation 1:8. Jesus is the beginning and the end.

Revelation 1:10–11. John hears from the Alpha and the Omega.

Revelation 21:6. Jesus is the Alpha and the Omega.

Revelation 22:13. Jesus is the Alpha and the Omega.

▶ Altar(s) *(table of worship)*

A structure, usually a table, used in the worship of God

Genesis 8:20. Noah's altar

Genesis 12:7. Abram's altar

Genesis 26:25. Isaac's altar

Exodus 20:24–26. God's requirements for building an altar

Exodus 27:1–8. The altar for the tabernacle

Lamentations 2:7. God rejects an altar.

▶ Amazement *(astonishment, surprise, wonder)*

Great wonder or astonishment

Genesis 43:33. Joseph's brothers show amazement at Joseph's knowledge of them.

Daniel 3:24. Nebuchadnezzar is amazed that Shadrach, Meshach, and Abednego lived after being tossed into the furnace.

Matthew 8:10. Jesus is amazed at the faith of a centurion.

Matthew 27:14. Jesus amazes Pilate.

Luke 24:41. The disciples are amazed that Jesus is alive.

▶ Ambidextrous *(right-handed or left-handed)*

Able to use both hands equally well

1 Chronicles 12:1–2. Ambidextrous warriors

Psalm 74:11. Psalmist urges God to use both hands to help.

Psalm 89:25. Ambidextrous metaphor to show God's promotion of David

Micah 7:3. Both hands involved in wrongdoing

Matthew 6:3. Jesus uses a hand metaphor.

▶ Ambiguity *(haziness, uncertainty, vagueness)*

Uncertainty as to interpretation

Numbers 23:25–27. Balaam is ambiguous about cursing the Israelites.

Job 31. Job tries to process what he sees as God's ambiguous punishment.

Daniel 5. Belshazzar was puzzled when a mysterious hand wrote an ambiguous message on the wall.

Habakkuk 2:2. God desires clarity, rather than ambiguity.

Luke 9:45. The disciples find Jesus' words ambiguous.

▶ Ambition *(aim, goal, objective)*

Desire for rank, fame, or power; desire to achieve a particular result

2 Samuel 15:9–11. Absalom's ambition—to usurp the kingdom from David

1 Kings 1:7–8. Adonijah's ambition—to become king after David

Romans 15:20. Paul's ambition—to preach the gospel

Galatians 5:19–21. Selfish ambition is part of the corrupt nature.

Philippians 2:3. Be humble not selfishly ambitious.

▶ Ambivalence *(hesitance, indecision, in two minds)*

Having contradictory feelings toward a person or object

Joshua 24:14–15. Joshua refuses to be ambivalent about God.

2 Samuel 13–14. David's ambivalence in regard to Absalom

1 Kings 18:21. Israelites criticized for ambivalence

Matthew 6:24. Jesus cautions against ambivalence.

James 1:8. Doubts show ambivalence.

▶ Ambush *(ensnare, trap, waylay)*

A sneak attack

Joshua 8. Ambush at Ai

Judges 9:25. Abimelech ambushed

Judges 20. Benjamites ambushed during the war between Israel and the tribe of Benjamin

1 Samuel 15:5. Saul and troops ambush the Amalekites.

1 Peter 5:8. Satan seeks to ambush believers.

▶ Amen *(agree)*

A solemn ratification or statement of assertion; in other words, "let it be done"

Numbers 5:21–22. Say amen to an oath

Deuteronomy 27:16. Agreeing to a curse

Nehemiah 5:13. Giving an amen to a promise

Psalm 41:13. An eternal amen

Jeremiah 28:5–6. A false prophet's amen

▶ Amends *(atonement, compensation, reparation)*

To compensate for a loss

2 Samuel 21:1–14. David seeks to make amends to the Gibeonites.

2 Kings 8:1–6. A king makes amends to a woman of Shunem.

Nehemiah 5:1–13. Amends made to the poor

Job 20:4–29. Amends of the wicked

Proverbs 14:9. Fools mock making amends for sin.

Luke 19:1–10. Zacchaeus makes amends.

▶ Amillennialism *(end times, second coming)*

The thousand-year reign of Christ

2 Samuel 7. God promises David that his kingdom would last forever.

2 Samuel 23:5. A lasting promise

Psalm 89:3–4. Praising God for the promise of an unending kingdom

Daniel 12. An angel interprets Daniel's vision of the end times.

Revelation 20:1–7. Christ's thousand-year reign

▶ Amputation *(deducting, cutting off, excluding)*

Removing, excluding, or cutting off a limb or a person

Isaiah 38:12. When faced with a life-threatening illness, Hezekiah feels amputated.

Jeremiah 48:25. Figurative amputation of Moab

Matthew 5:29–30. Amputation to avoid sin

Matthew 18:8. Amputation to save faith

Acts 3:23. Amputated from the community

▶ Analogy *(likeness, similarity, parallel)*

Comparison based on the similarity of two or more objects

A

Genesis 13:16. Descendants like the dust

1 Samuel 17:36. Analogy of the lion and bear

Psalm 80. Analogy of the vine

Proverbs 9. Wisdom analogy

John 15:1–8. Jesus' analogy of the vine

▶ Anarchy *(chaos, disorder, rebellion)*

State of lawlessness or political disorder

Judges 10:6. Anarchy of Israel

1 Kings 11:26–40. Anarchy of Jeroboam

Isaiah 3. Anarchy in a time of judgment

Galatians 5:13. Antidote for anarchy

2 Peter 2:10. Anarchy of false teachers

1 John 3:4. Anarchy of sin

▶ Anatomy *(composition, framework, makeup)*

Structural makeup of an organism

Genesis 2:7. What we're made of

Job 39:13. Anatomy of an ostrich versus the anatomy of a stork

Job 40:15–18. Anatomy of the behemoth

Psalm 139:13, 15. God knows our anatomy.

1 Corinthians 12:12–31. Anatomy of the body of Christ

▶ Ancestor(s) *(antecedent, forebear, forefather)*

One from whom a person is descended

Genesis 10:21. Shem as ancestor

Joshua 17. Land allotments in Canaan according to ancestry

Matthew 1:6–17. David was an ancestor of Jesus.

Hebrews 7:9–10. Abraham was an ancestor of the tribe of Levi.

James 2:21. James writes of his ancestor Abraham.

▶ Anchor(s) *(affix, fasten, secure)*

A principal support; something that holds an object firmly; a device on a ship that serves to hold the ship firmly

Deuteronomy 11:18. Anchor God's Word firmly to your heart.

Acts 27:13. Weighing anchor off Crete

2 Corinthians 4:18. Anchor your eyes to the unseen.

Hebrews 3:1. Anchor your gaze on Jesus.

Hebrews 6:19. Faith in Christ is an anchor for our lives.

▶ Ancient of Days *(God)*

A name for God

Daniel 7:9. Daniel's vision of the Ancient of Days

Daniel 7:13. Appearing before the Ancient of Days

Daniel 7:22. Judgment of the Ancient of Days

▶ Anesthesia *(God)*

Loss of consciousness; drug used to put the body to sleep

Genesis 2:21. The first need for anesthesia

Genesis 15:12. Deep sleep of Abram

Matthew 27:34. Gall used as an anesthetic

▶ Angels *(archangels, cherubim, messengers)*

Spiritual beings created by God often used as messengers; the word *angel* means "messenger"

Genesis 3:24. Angels guard the tree of life.

Exodus 25:18. Cherubim sculpture on the ark of the covenant.

Ezekiel 1:4–21. Ezekiel sees cherubim.

Luke 1:26–38. An angel appears to Mary.

Luke 2:8–15. Angels announce the good news.

Revelation 8. John sees angels in his vision of heaven.

▶ Anger *(annoyance, fury, rage)*

To make angry or become angry

Genesis 4:6–7. God urges Cain to master his anger.

Numbers 14:18. God is slow to anger.

Proverbs 15:1. Antidote for anger

Proverbs 27:4. Cruel anger, but jealousy worse?

Ephesians 4:26. Rules for anger

▶ Anguish *(agony, pain, suffering)*

In extreme pain, agony, or distress

Exodus 15:14. Prediction of anguish

1 Samuel 1:16. Hannah wants Eli to know that she's in anguish.

Job 3:26. Job's anguish

Jeremiah 4:19. Jeremiah is in anguish at the coming destruction of Jerusalem.

Matthew 26:37. The Savior in anguish in the Garden of Gethsemane

▶ Animals *(creature, fauna, mammal)*

Any of the organisms classified as single-celled or multi-celled and differing from plants; members of the animal kingdom

Genesis 1:24–25. God creates animals.

Genesis 3:1. The craftiest animal

Genesis 7:14–16. Animals saved during the flood.

Numbers 18:15. Priests and Levites own firstborn animals.

1 Kings 4:33. King Solomon classifies plants and animals.

▶ Animism *(belief system, philosophy, worship)*

The belief that all created things (including animals, rocks, and rivers) have souls and can be worshiped

Exodus 12:12. The last plague is a strike against Egyptian animism.

Exodus 20:3–4. God condemns animism.

Deuteronomy 17:2–3. Moses warns the Israelites against animism.

1 Kings 20:23. The Arameans believe their god is stronger than the God of Israel.

1 Corinthians 8:5–6. Paul discusses animism in his letter.

▶ Annals *(chronologies, histories, records)*

A chronological record of the kings of Israel

1 Kings 14:19. Jeroboam's reign

1 Kings 15:31. Nadab's reign

1 Kings 16:5. Baasha's reign

1 Kings 16:27. Omri's reign

2 Kings 1:18. Ahaziah's reign

▶ Anniversary(ies) *(date, celebration, yearly event)*

The annual recurrence of a notable event

Exodus 12:14. Israelites to celebrate the anniversary of Passover

Leviticus 16:34. Anniversary of atonement

Deuteronomy 16:5–6. More instructions on the Passover anniversary

Joshua 5:10. A sacred anniversary

Esther 9:20–21. Purim anniversary

Hosea 2:11. God threatens to end some anniversary celebrations.

▶ Announcement(s) *(declaration, proclamation, statement)*

A public notification

Leviticus 23:4. Festival announcements

Judges 13:2–20. Announcement of Samson's birth

Isaiah 48:12–22. An announcement of freedom

Luke 1:5–22. An angel announces the birth of John the Baptist to his father Zechariah.

Luke 1:26–38. Gabriel announces the birth of Jesus.

▶ Annul *(cancel, invalidate, nullify, withdraw)*

To make legally invalid

Numbers 30:13. A husband can nullify a wife's vow.

Deuteronomy 22:13–19. No annulment or divorce possible in this situation.

Matthew 1:19. Joseph considers an annulment.

Mark 7:13. Pharisees' actions nullify the Word of God.

Romans 3:31. Is the law nullified?

▶ Anoint *(daub, oil, rub)*

To apply oil in a sacred rite

Exodus 28:41. Aaron and sons to be anointed as priests

Exodus 29:7. Method of anointing

1 Samuel 10:1. Saul anointed as Israel's king

1 Samuel 16:12–13. David anointed as king

2 Kings 9:3. A hurried anointing

A

▶ Anonymity *(mystery, obscurity)*

One who is anonymous; remaining nameless

Psalm 100. Anonymous psalm

Acts 17:23. An anonymous god

Galatians 1:22. Paul is anonymous to the churches in Judea.

Hebrews. Anonymous epistle writer

Revelation 19:11–12. Rider has a name no one knows.

▶ Answer(s) *(reply, respond, response)*

Something spoken or written in response to a question

Genesis 41:16. Through Joseph, God answers Pharaoh's request.

Numbers 22:8. Balaam answers Balak's request.

1 Samuel 14:41. Saul complains that God hasn't answered.

1 Samuel 28:6. God refuses to answer Saul.

Jeremiah 33:3. God promises to answer.

▶ Ant(s) *(social insect)*

A hymenopteran insect of the Formicidae family

Proverbs 6:6. The lesson of the ant

Proverbs 30:25. The wise ant

▶ Anthems (see *Music*)

▶ Anti-Semitism *(hatred)*

Hostility or hatred toward the Jews

Exodus 1. Egyptians oppress the Israelites.

Numbers 22. Balak wants the Jews cursed.

Judges 6. Israelites overpowered by the Midians

Esther 3:5–6. Haman's hatred

Nehemiah 4. Anti-Semitism of Sanballat and others

▶ Anthropomorphism *(human characteristics, humanization)*

Attributing human traits or actions to nonhuman things

Exodus 15:8. The nostrils of God

Job 38:35. Communicating with lightning

Isaiah 55:12. Nature worships God.

Habakkuk 2:11. Stones and beams speak of crime.

Luke 19:39–40. Stones will worship if people don't.

▶ Antichrist *(beast, man of lawlessness)*

The great antagonist who will be opposed by Christ in the end times; those who claim to be the Messiah, but aren't

Matthew 24:5. Antichrists' claims

2 Thessalonians 2:3–4. Antichrist will oppose anything worshiped.

1 John 2:18. Antichrists here already

1 John 4:3. Spirit of the antichrist

2 John 7. Mark of the antichrist

▶ Antinomianism *(against the law, lawlessness)*

A heretical belief that a Christian is above the law because of Jesus' death on the cross

Romans 3:31. Paul denounces antinomianism.

Romans 6. Not controlled by laws? Unthinkable!

Romans 7. The purpose of the law

Romans 13:8. How to fulfill the law

Jude 4. Jude condemns lawless behavior.

▶ Anxiety *(apprehension, fear, worry)*

A fearful concern

Deuteronomy 28:65. Anxiety due to being cursed

Psalm 94:19. Soothing anxiety

Ecclesiastes 11:10. Banish anxiety

Ezekiel 4:16. Famine anxiety

1 Peter 5:7. Give God your anxiety.

▶ Apathy *(ennui, indifference, lack of interest)*

Lack of interest or feeling

Proverbs 21:13. Don't be apathetic to the poor.

Jonah 1. Jonah's apathy

Romans 12:11. Don't be apathetic; serve God instead.

Hebrews 12:25. Apathy of the Israelites
Revelation 3:14–22. Apathy of the Laodiceans

▶ Aphorisms *(adages, principles, proverbs, sayings)*

Concise statements of truth or sentiment
Proverbs 3:15. Aphorism about wisdom
Proverbs 11:3. Aphorism about integrity
Proverbs 12:1. Aphorism about discipline
Proverbs 25:11. Aphorism about words
1 Corinthians 13:1. Paul's use of an aphorism

▶ Apocalypse *(catastrophe, disaster, Judgment Day)*

A prophesied battle during end times when God destroys the power of evil
Daniel 10:1. Daniel's vision of the apocalypse
Daniel 12:1. A time of trouble
Revelation 6. Riders of the apocalypse
Revelation 19:14–16. The rider who will conquer
Revelation 19:19–20. Apocalyptic war

▶ Apocalyptic literature *(Daniel, Zechariah, Revelation)*

Revelatory books describing end times activity and also with a view to encourage God's people
Ezekiel 38–39. Ezekiel's prophecy
Daniel 8–12. Daniel sees the end.
Joel. Joel's vision of judgment
Zechariah 1:7–6:8. Zechariah sees the end.
The book of Revelation. John's vision

▶ Apocrypha *(3 and 4 Esdras, Tobit, Judith, I and II Maccabees)*

Books not adopted as part of the biblical canon
Numbers 21:14–15. The Book of the Wars of the Lord
Joshua 10:13. The book of Jasha
2 Chronicles 12:14–15. Book of Shemaiah
Nehemiah 12:23. The Book of Chronicles
Jude 14–15. The Book of Enoch

▶ Apologetics *(convincing argument, defense)*

Systematic argument in defense of a doctrine
Romans 3:5. Paul's apologetic
Titus 3:3–8. Apologetic on everlasting life
Hebrews 6:16–18. Convincing argument
1 Peter 1:10–12. The apologetic of the prophets

▶ Apostasy *(falling away)*

Renunciation of faith
Mark 4:17. Falling away from the faith
Luke 7:23. Those who avoid apostasy are blessed.
1 Timothy 4:1–4. Believers who fall away
2 Timothy 3:1–9. People of apostasy
Hebrews 6:4–6. Deserters of Christ
2 Peter 3:17. Don't fall away.

▶ Apostle *(disciple, messenger, missionary)*

One sent on a mission, particularly to carry the Gospel of Christ; one of Jesus' twelve disciples sent with authority after the death and resurrection of Christ
Matthew 10:1–4. Jesus chooses the apostles.
Acts 1:26. Matthias replaces Judas.
Acts 2:14. Peter and the apostles
Romans 1:1. Paul the apostle
Ephesians 1:1. Apostle by God's will

▶ Appearance *(form, exterior, look)*

External manifestation of a being or object
1 Samuel 16:7. God cares about the heart, rather than the appearance.
2 Samuel 14:25. Absalom's unblemished appearance
Isaiah 53:2. The suffering servant's unassuming appearance
Ezekiel 40:3. Bronze appearance of the man at the temple
Joel 2:4. The soldiers of Joel's vision

▶ Appeasement *(conciliation, peace making, sacrificing)*

To bring to a state of peace; buy off an aggressor through a sacrifice

Judges 3:15. Tribute money as an appeasement

Proverbs 16:14. Appeasing a king's wrath

Micah 6:7. Is God appeased by sacrifices?

Acts 16:39. Appeasement of the officials of Philippi

1 Thessalonians 5:9. The ultimate appeasement of God's anger

▶ Appetite *(craving, desire, hunger)*

A strong wish or urge, especially for food and drink

Numbers 11:5–6. Israelites complain about appetite loss.

Proverbs 13:4. Appeasing an appetite through work

Proverbs 13:25. Appetites of the wicked

Ecclesiastes 6:7. An appetite never satisfied

Isaiah 5:14. Appetite of the grave

▶ Appoint *(assign, choose, select)*

Select or designate to fill a position

Genesis 41:34. Joseph suggests the appointment of supervisors in Egypt.

Numbers 3:10. Aaron and sons appointed as priests

Deuteronomy 16:18. Appointment of judges

1 Kings 14:14. Appointment of a king

1 Chronicles 15:16. Appointment of musicians

▶ Appraising *(assessing, evaluating, judging)*

Estimating the quality of something

Genesis 30:33. Jacob submits to a wage appraisal

Leviticus 27:11–12. Priest's appraisement

Leviticus 27:14. House appraisal

Leviticus 27:18. Field appraisal

1 Kings 20:22. Appraising an army

▶ Appreciation *(approval, gratitude, recognition)*

Recognition of the quality or value of people and things

2 Chronicles 17:5. Appreciation for Jehoshaphat

Job 12:5. No appreciation for misfortune?

Acts 24:3. Paul's appreciation for Felix, the Roman governor

1 Corinthians 16:18. Show appreciation for those who comfort others.

1 Thessalonians 5:12. Appreciation for leaders

▶ Apprentice *(beginner, novice, trainee)*

One legally contracted to work in return for instruction

Exodus 24:13–14. Joshua—Moses' apprentice

2 Kings 2:2–3. Elisha's brief apprenticeship

Daniel 1:4–6. Daniel's apprenticeship

Matthew 10:42. A true apprentice

2 Timothy 3:10. Timothy—an apprentice of Paul

▶ Appropriation *(authorized usage, taking possession of)*

Setting apart for a specific use

Exodus 3:22. Appropriation of Egyptian wealth

Exodus 13:1–2. Appropriation of firstborn

Exodus 29:27–28. Appropriation of a ram

Exodus 32:2–4. Appropriation of gold for a golden calf

Leviticus 24:9. Bread of the presence appropriated for priests

▶ Approval *(acceptance, consent, endorsement)*

Official sanction; favorable regard

Genesis 6:8. God approves of Noah.

Genesis 15:6. God's approval of Abram

Deuteronomy 6:25. How to gain the Lord's approval

Matthew 5:6. Thirsting for God's approval

Romans 5:1–2. Why we have God's approval

2 Timothy 2:22. Seek activities that have God's approval.

2 Timothy 3:16. Training for a life with God's approval

▶ Approximating *(estimating, figuring, guessing)*

Estimating based on previous information or no information

Matthew 16:2–3. Approximating the weather

Matthew 24:36. No one can approximate the return of Christ.

Matthew 27:46. Approximate time Jesus fulfilled yet another Scripture

Luke 14:28. Approximating the cost

John 6:5–7. Philip approximates the cost of food for over 5,000 people.

▶ Arab *(Middle Eastern)*

A member of the Semitic people inhabiting Arabia

Genesis 25:13–18. Arab ancestors

1 Kings 10:14–15. Gold from Arabian kings

Nehemiah 2:19. Ridicule of Geshem

Isaiah 13:20. Prophecy against Babylon

▶ Aramaic *(language)*

Semitic language begun by the Arameans

2 Kings 18:26. Speaking in Aramaic

Ezra 4:7. Enemies of Judah write in Aramaic

Daniel 2:4. Language of the astrologers in Persia

Mark 14:36. Jesus speaks in Aramaic.

Mark 15:34. Jesus cries out in Aramaic from the cross.

John 5:2. Bethesda—an Aramaic word

▶ Arbitration *(adjudication, mediation, negotiation)*

The process of settling or judging a matter between two parties in dispute through the use of an arbitrator

1 Kings 3:16–28. Solomon's arbitration

Job 9:33–34. Job seeks arbitration.

Isaiah 47:3. God will not arbitrate.

Ezekiel 44:24. Priests act in matters of arbitration.

Luke 12:13–14. Jesus asked to be an arbitrator.

▶ Archaeology *(science)*

The study of material remains from past life and culture

Isaiah 58:12. Ancient ruins restored

Isaiah 61:4. Renewing the ancient ruins

Jeremiah 49:13. Ruins of Bozrah

Ezekiel 26:20. Among the ancient ruins

Zephaniah 2:9. Just like Gomorrah

▶ Archangels *(angel)*

High-ranking angels

Daniel 10:20–21. Archangels in battle

Daniel 11:1. Helping an archangel

Daniel 12:1. Michael will act during the end times.

1 Thessalonians 4:16. Voice of the archangel

Jude 9. Michael the archangel

▶ Archery *(bow and arrow)*

Skill of shooting with a bow and arrow

Genesis 21:20. Ishmael skilled at archery

2 Samuel 22:33–35. God helps with archery

Psalm 46:9. End of archery?

Jeremiah 51:3. Archers against Babylon

▶ Architecture *(building, structural design)*

The art and science of designing and erecting buildings; buildings and other large structures

Genesis 11:5. Tower of Babel

1 Kings 6:2. Solomon's temple

Ezra 6:16. Zerubbabel's temple

Acts 3:10–11. Temple architecture

Acts 17:19. City court of Athens

▶ Arid *(dry, parched, waterless)*

Lacking moisture

Deuteronomy 8:15. God led Israel through arid lands.

Psalm 107:35. What God does to arid places

Isaiah 58:11. Guidance in arid places

Joel 3:18. Arid valleys watered

Matthew 12:43. An evil spirit's journey

A

▶ Ark *(ark of the covenant, Noah's ark)*

The sacred chest of the Israelites; large boat Noah built to save his family and animals from the Flood

Genesis 6–8. Noah's ark
Exodus 25:10–22. Ark of the covenant
Exodus 40:21. Ark of the covenant placed in the tabernacle
Joshua 3:14. Carrying the ark of the covenant through the Jordan
Joshua 6:2–4. The ark goes into war.

▶ Armageddon *(final battle)*

The final battle between good and evil

Daniel 12:1. Armageddon—time of trouble
Revelation 16:16. The place called Armageddon
Revelation 19:19. War with the beast

▶ Armor *(breastplate, chain mail, protective covering)*

Defensive covering worn to protect the body against weapons

1 Samuel 17:5. Goliath's armor
1 Samuel 17:38–39. Saul's armor is not a good fit for David.
1 Samuel 31:10. Philistines dishonor Saul by displaying his armor.
1 Kings 22:34. Ahab wounded even while wearing armor.
2 Chronicles 26:14. Armor of Uzziah's army

▶ Armor of God *(breastplate, sword of the Spirit, truth)*

Metaphor Paul used for the tools of spiritual warfare

Ephesians 6:11. Put armor on.
Ephesians 6:14. Belt of truth and the breastplate of righteousness
Ephesians 6:15. Shoes of the Good News
Ephesians 6:16. Shield of faith
Ephesians 6:17. Helmet of salvation and the sword of the Spirit

▶ Army(ies) *(armed forces, military, soldiers)*

Large body of people organized and trained for land battle

Exodus 14:4. Pharaoh's army will pursue the Israelites during the Exodus
Exodus 17:13. Joshua's army beats the Amalekites
Numbers 2. Armies of the tribes of Israel
Joshua 5:13–14. Commander of the Lord's army
Judges 4. Sisera's army defeated by God

▶ Aroma(s) *(fragrance, odor, smell)*

A pleasant odor

Genesis 8:20–21. Soothing aroma
Exodus 29:41. Aroma that pleases God
Leviticus 6:15. The aroma of a grain offering
Leviticus 23:13. Firstfruits aroma
Numbers 28:1–2. Offering a soothing aroma
2 Corinthians 2:15. Aroma of Christ

▶ Aromatherapy *(fragrances, oils)*

A term coined in 1928 by Henri Maurice Gattefosse to define the essential oils used to promote healing

Exodus 30:34–36. Fragrant spices
Psalm 51:7. Hyssop
Proverbs 7:17. Myrrh, aloes, and cinnamon
Matthew 2:11. Frankincense and myrrh
John 12:3. Nard
John 19:39. Myrrh and aloe

▶ Arrogance *(see **Pride**)*

▶ Arrow(s) *(barbed word, dart, projectile)*

Thin shaft with a pointed head used for fighting or hunting; metaphor for malicious comments

1 Samuel 20:35–36. Arrows as a signal
2 Kings 13:17. Arrow of the Lord's victory
Job 20:23–24. Arrow of suffering
Psalm 91:5–6. Don't fear the arrows.
Jeremiah 9:8. Tongues like arrows

▶ Arson *(combustible, fire-starting, inflammable)*

Willfully setting fire to one's own or someone else's property

Joshua 8:19. Arson at Ai
Joshua 11:13. Hazor razed
Judges 15:4–5. Foxes used in arson
2 Kings 25:8–10. Setting Jerusalem on fire
Isaiah 1:7. A prophecy of arson

▶ Art *(drawing, painting, pottery, sculpture)*

Human effort to imitate or supplement the works of nature; producing or arranging sounds, colors, forms to affect the sense of beauty
1 Kings 6:29. Art in the temple
Psalm 74:6. Vandals destroy art.
Isaiah 29:16. Pottery
Ezekiel 8:10. Ezekiel's vision of bad art
Ezekiel 4:1–3. Instructive art

▶ Ascension *(ascending, climbing, rising)*

The act or process of ascending; the bodily rising of Jesus into heaven after His resurrection
Judges 13:20. Ascension of the Messenger of the Lord
Psalm 47:5. God has ascended.
Mark 16:19. Jesus returning to heaven
Acts 1:3–11. Jesus ascends.
Ephesians 4:7–10. Christ's triumphal ascension

▶ Asceticism *(plainness, severity, starkness)*

Self-denial and austerity
Matthew 9:14. Jesus challenged about non-ascetic lifestyle
Colossians 2:21–23. Asceticism rebuked
1 Timothy 4:1–4. Warning Timothy about asceticism

▶ Ashamed *(embarrassed, humiliated, mortified)*

A feeling of shame, guilt, or inadequacy
2 Samuel 19:3. Troops ashamed of David's mourning
2 Kings 8:10–11. Hazael ashamed
Ezra 8:22. Ezra ashamed
Isaiah 24:23. Shame of the moon and sun
Mark 8:38. Ashamed of Jesus?
Romans 1:16. Not ashamed of the gospel
2 Timothy 2:15. How to avoid shame

▶ Asherah *(goddess, Ishtar, queen of heaven)*

Canaanite goddess often paired with Baal
1 Kings 18. Elijah challenges the prophets of Baal and Asherah.
2 Kings 23:4. Ridding the temple of the worship of Asherah
2 Chronicles 15:16. Removing the aspects of Asherah worship
Jeremiah 7:18. Worshiping Asherah
Jeremiah 44:17–18. Consequences of Asherah worship

▶ Asherah pole *(grove, tree)*

Sacred tree honoring Asherah, the Canaanite goddess
Exodus 34:13. God warns the Israelites to tear down Asherah poles in Canaan.
Deuteronomy 16:21–22. Avoid Asherah poles.
Judges 6:25–26. Asherah pole to be cut
1 Kings 14:15. Ahijah the prophet condemns the use of Asherah poles.
1 Kings 16:33. Ahab's Asherah poles

▶ Asia Minor *(southwestern Asia, peninsula, Roman province)*

Peninsula also known as Anatolia (part of modern-day Turkey); Roman province
Acts 6:9. Stephen faces opposition from men of Asia Minor.
Acts 9:30. Saul (Paul) is sent to his hometown of Tarsus in Asia Minor.
Acts 16:6. Paul prevented from going to Asia Minor.
Acts 19:10. Paul preaches in Asia Minor.
Acts 20:16. Paul bypasses Asia Minor.

▶ Ask/Seek/Knock *(make request, pray, seek)*

Phrase uttered by Jesus containing metaphors for communicating with God

A

2 Chronicles 7:14. Seek him.
Matthew 7:7–8. Ask, seek, and knock.
John 14:12–14. Ask in Jesus' name.
John 15:7. Yours for the asking
John 15:16. Chosen to ask
Revelation 3:20. Jesus knocks.

▸ Assassination *(elimination, killing, murder)*

Murder of a prominent person
Judges 3:12–30. Assassination of Eglon
2 Samuel 3:27. Assassination of Abner
2 Samuel 4:5–6. Assassination of Ishbosheth
2 Kings 11:1–3. Joash saved from assassination
2 Kings 12:19–20. Joash assassinated by servants
2 Chronicles 32:21. Sennacherib assassinated

▸ Assembly *(assemblage, gathering, meeting)*

A group gathered for a common purpose (i.e., sacred or social)
Genesis 49:5–6. An assembly to avoid
Exodus 12:16. Passover assembly
Leviticus 4:14. Sacrifice of the assembly
Leviticus 23:7. Festival assembly
Numbers 29:35. Assembly on the eighth day

▸ Assertive individuals *(forceful, pushy, self-confident)*

Aggressively self-assured people who didn't end well
Genesis 49:3–4. Reuben
1 Samuel 17. Goliath
1 Kings 1:5–53. Adonijah
1 Kings 21. Jezebel
2 Kings 19. Sennacherib

▸ Assets *(belongings, possessions, resources)*

Useful or valuable qualities or people; valuable items owned
Genesis 13:2. Abram's assets
Exodus 19:5. Israel is an asset.
2 Kings 20:12–21. Hezekiah foolishly shows his assets.
Proverbs 31:10–11. A wife who is an asset to her husband
1 Corinthians 11:15. Hair as an asset

▸ Assistance *(aid, help, support)*

Aiding or helping
Numbers 8:26. Assisting Levites
2 Chronicles 8:14. System of assistance
Ezra 8:36. Official assistance
Job 29:12. The assistance of Job
Romans 15:24. Paul's need for assistance

▸ Assurance *(confidence, guarantee, pledge)*

A statement that inspires confidence
Esther 9:30. Mordecai's assurance
Ephesians 1:14. Holy Spirit: a believer's assurance
1 Timothy 3:13. Assured faith
Hebrews 10:22. Approach with assurance
Hebrews 11:1. Assurance of faith

▸ Assyrians *(conquerors, Sennacherib, Shalmaneser, Tiglath Pileser)*

Ancient empire who conquered the Israelites; name comes from Asshur, a city-state
2 Kings 15:29. Territories captured by Assyria
2 Kings 17:3. Israel defeated by Assyria again
Isaiah 10:24. Isaiah's prophecy: don't fear the Assyrians.
Isaiah 19:23. Assyrians and Egyptians will worship together.
Ezekiel 23. An alliance with Assyria angers God.

▸ Astrology *(reading the stars, zodiac signs)*

Study of the positions of the celestial bodies and the belief that they influence human matters
Deuteronomy 4:19. Don't worship or serve the celestial bodies.

Isaiah 47:13–14. Consequences of astrology

Jeremiah 10:2. Don't be caught up in astrology.

Daniel 2. Nebuchadnezzar's astrologers fail him.

Daniel 4. Nebuchadnezzar's astrologers again fail him.

▶ Astronomy *(stars, planets)*

Scientific study of stars and planets

Job 26:7. God made astronomy possible.

Job 38:31–33. Laws of the sky

Psalm 8:3–4. Star gazing

Psalm 19:1–6. Display of the sky

Isaiah 13:10. Disaster in the sky

▶ Atheism *(agnosticism, skepticism, unbelief)*

Disbelief in the existence of God

Psalm 14. There is no God?

Psalm 53. Godless fools

Romans 1:19–20. No excuse for unbelief

2 Timothy 3:1–9. Unbelief in the last days

▶ Athletes *(competitors, contestants, participants)*

Persons with the natural abilities to participate in physical exercise

Judges 20:16. Athletic soldiers of the tribe of Benjamin

1 Samuel 17. David's athletic prowess matched with the strength of God

1 Corinthians 9:24–26. Athletic advice

Philippians 3:12–14. Athletic metaphor for the Christian life

2 Timothy 2:5. Athletes who win

Hebrews 12:1. Christians as athletes

▶ Atonement *(amends, appeasement, reparation)*

Reconciliation between God and man brought about by the continual sacrifice of animals in Old Testament times and once and for all by Jesus Christ

Exodus 30:10. Day of Atonement (Yom Kippur today)

Leviticus 4:3–21. Atonement for wrongs

Leviticus 23:27. A special day for atonement

Numbers 29:7–11. Atonement offerings

Hebrews 9:23–28. Christ's once-for-all atonement

▶ Attitudes *(feelings, mindsets, outlooks, thoughts)*

A state of mind or a feeling

Genesis 31. Laban's attitude change toward Jacob

Ezra 6:22. Changing a king's attitude

Daniel 3. A change in attitude

Philippians 2:5–11. Have the attitude of Jesus.

▶ Attributes of God *(characteristics, qualities, traits)*

Qualities or characteristics inherent in God as revealed by God

Exodus 3:15. God is eternal.

Exodus 15:7. God's anger

Exodus 33:19. God's mercy

Exodus 34:6–7. God reveals His attributes to Moses.

Deuteronomy 7:9. God's faithfulness

Matthew 9:35–38. Jesus' compassion

1 John 4:7–21. God's love

▶ Aurora Borealis *(lights, northern lights)*

Bands of light visible in the northern skies

Job 37:22. A golden light

Job 38:19. Where does light live?

▶ Authenticity *(genuineness, legitimacy, validity)*

The quality of being authentic, genuine, or trustworthy

Isaiah 29:13. Lack of authenticity in worship

Matthew 11:18–19. Jesus' authenticity

2 Corinthians 6:8–9. Paul's authenticity

Philippians 2:20. Timothy—a model of authenticity

1 Peter 1:7. Trials help develop authentic faith.

A

▶ Authority *(clout, influence, power)*

The power to enforce laws, judge, or exact obedience

Numbers 27:20–21. Moses passes some of his authority to Joshua.

Esther 9:29. Esther and Mordecai's authority

Isaiah 22:20–21. God gives authority.

Matthew 7:28–29. Jesus' authority

Matthew 10:1. Jesus gives authority.

▶ Authorization *(approval, endorsement, permission)*

The act of authorizing or sanctioning

Genesis 41:44. Nothing to be done without Joseph's authorization

Ezra 3:7. Authorized to rebuild the temple

Ezra 4. The Israelites' authorization to rebuild the temple is stripped away.

Nehemiah 2. Nehemiah gains the king's authorization to travel to Jerusalem.

Acts 15:24. Lacking authorization

▶ Autumn *(fall)*

The season of the year between summer and winter

Deuteronomy 11:14. God promises rain in autumn.

Jeremiah 5:24. What the rebellious don't notice about autumn

Joel 2:23. Give thanks for autumn rain

James 5:7. Waiting patiently for autumn rain

▶ Avenger *(nemesis, punisher, righter of wrongs)*

One who takes vengeance or inflicts punishment

Numbers 35:12. Avengers halted at cities of refuge

Deuteronomy 19:5–6. Avenger of blood

Joshua 20:5. Avengers cannot harm.

2 Samuel 14. The woman of Tekoa pleads against revenge.

Psalm 8:2. Protection from the avenger

▶ Awaken *(rouse, stir, wake up)*

To cause to wake up; to resurrect from death; to acknowledge an act of God

Psalm 57:8. David awakens to praise.

Psalm 80:2. Awaken and help.

Song of Songs 2:7. Don't awaken love.

Romans 13:11. Time to awaken

Ephesians 5:13–14. Awaken and rise.

▶ Awareness *(alertness, consciousness, responsiveness)*

Having cognizance or knowledge

Genesis 19:30–38. Lot's lack of awareness

Genesis 28:10–22. Jacob now aware of God's presence

Exodus 34:29. No awareness of glory

Nehemiah 4:15. Awareness of plot

Matthew 16:8. Jesus' awareness of his disciples' lack of faith

▶ Awe *(admiration, astonishment, fear, wonder)*

A mixed emotion of reverence, respect, and dread

1 Samuel 12:18. In awe of God

1 Kings 3:28. In awe of Solomon

Job 25:2. Bildad speaks of awe.

Psalm 119:120. In awe of God's laws

Jeremiah 2:19. No awe of God

▶ Ax *(tool)*

The quality of being authentic, genuine, or trustworthy

Deuteronomy 19:5. Accident with an ax

Judges 9:47–49. Abimelech urges ax usage.

2 Kings 6:1–7. Elisha makes an ax head float.

Ecclesiastes 10:10. As sharp as an ax?

Luke 3:9. John the Baptist uses an ax metaphor to warn the people of Israel.

▶ Baal *(Canaanite god, fertility god, idol)*

Head god in the Canaanite pantheon who is believed to have command over fertility, agriculture, and animals

Deuteronomy 4:3–4. Consequences of Baal worship

Judges 2:11–14. A generation of Baal worshipers

1 Kings 16:29–33. Ahab worships Baal.

2 Kings 10:18–28. Jehu's war against Baal worship

2 Kings 11:17–18. Cleansing the land of Baal worship

▶ Babylonian Chronicles *(historiography)*

Ancient Mesopotamian tablets discussing the events of Babylonian history from the time of the Sumerian kings through the Seleucid dynasties

2 Kings 25:8–10. Fall of Jerusalem mentioned in the *Babylonian Chronicles*

Nahum 2:6. Event mentioned in the *Babylonian Chronicles*

Nahum 2:10. Event mentioned in the *Babylonian Chronicles*

▶ Backbiting *(bad-mouthing, spite, unkind remarks)*

Speaking spitefully about someone or something

Psalm 15:3. A tabernacle dweller does not backbite.

Proverbs 25:23. A backbiting tongue

Ephesians 4:32. Stop the backbiting.

▶ Backsliding *(falling away, turning back)*

Sliding away from commitment to God

Jeremiah 2:19. Consequences of backsliding

Jeremiah 3:22. A cure for backsliding

Jeremiah 14:7. Backsliding Judah

Jeremiah 15:6. Backsliding Judah

▶ Bad bosses *(arrogant kings, cheating leaders, cruel overseers)*

Leaders who take advantage of those under their rule

Genesis 30:25–31:55. Laban tries to cheat Jacob out of his wages.

Exodus 1:8–14. Egyptian overseers act with cruelty.

Exodus 2:11–15. Moses kills a cruel Egyptian overseer.

Exodus 22:21. Good advice bad bosses refused to heed.

1 Kings 12:1–24. Rehoboam vows to be harsh.

▶ Baking *(bread, cakes)*

Goods baked in an oven

Genesis 18:6. Sarah bakes bread.

Genesis 19:3. Lot bakes bread for angels.

Genesis 27:17. Rebekah bakes.

Genesis 40. A baker's dream of baked goods

▶ Balanced life *(favor, meaningful, stable)*

A life in which a person has favor with God and with people

Numbers 6:24–26. The blessing of balance

Micah 6:8. The results of a balanced life

Luke 2:52. Jesus exemplified the balanced life.

Acts 2:46–47. New Christians achieve balance.

Romans 14:18. How to have a balanced life

▶ Baldness *(hairlessness, hair loss)*

Loss of hair

Leviticus 13:40–44. Rules concerning baldness

Leviticus 21:5. Don't make yourself bald!

2 Kings 2:23–25. Elisha's baldness is mocked.

Isaiah 3:24. Baldness as a result of sin

Ezekiel 29:18. Bald soldiers of Babylon

Micah 1:16. Sorrow and baldness

B

▶ Balm *(medicinal oil, perfume)*

Resin used to make medicine

Genesis 37:25. Ishmaelites bring balm.

Genesis 43:11. The gift of balm

2 Chronicles 28:15. Balm provided

Jeremiah 46:11. Balm in Gilead

Ezekiel 27:17. Balm for soldiers of Babylon

▶ Bandit(s) *(cutthroat, robber, thief)*

A robber

Ezra 8:31. Protected from bandits

Proverbs 6:11. Poverty will come like a bandit.

Hosea 7:1–2. Bandits robbing

Luke 10:30. Bested by bandits

2 Corinthians 11:26. Paul and bandits

▶ Banishment *(deportation, exile, expulsion)*

Using an official decree to force someone to leave a place

Genesis 3:22–24. Banishment of Adam and Eve

2 Samuel 13–14. Absalom banished after murdering Amnon

2 Kings 13:23. Israel not banished

Psalm 5:10. A request for banishment

Psalm 125:5. The Lord will banish.

Jeremiah 7:34. Sounds of joy banished

▶ Bankruptcy *(economic failure, liquidation, ruin)*

Legal insolvency

Judges 14:15. Will Samson bankrupt the Philistines?

Micah 6:16. Forced into bankruptcy

Galatians 4:9. Bankrupt principles

▶ Banner *(flag, standard, streamer)*

Cloth on a staff used as a standard by a monarch or military commander

Exodus 17:15. "The Lord Is My Banner"

Psalm 60:4. Raise a banner

Song of Songs 2:4. His banner over me

Isaiah 5:26. The Lord lifts up a banner.

Isaiah 11:10–12. Root of Jesse as a banner

Isaiah 13:2. Banner against Babylon

▶ Banquet *(dinner, feast, formal meal)*

Ceremonial dinner honoring a special guest

1 Samuel 9:22. Samuel's banquet

1 Samuel 25:36. Nabal's banquet

Esther 1. Xerxes's banquet

Psalm 23:5. The Shepherd's banquet for His sheep

Ecclesiastes 7:2. What's better than a banquet?

Isaiah 25:6. God's banquet

Luke 14:16–24. God's banquet

▶ Baptism *(dip, immerse, initiation)*

Christian sacrament with water as a symbol shows a person's belonging to the Christian community

Mark 1:4. Baptism of repentance

Mark 1:9–11. Jesus' baptism

Mark 10:35–45. A special baptism

Acts 10:48. Peter baptizes Cornelius and his household

Acts 18:25. Apollos's limited knowledge about baptism

Acts 19:1–7. Paul preaches about baptism.

Ephesians 4:5–6. One baptism

Colossians 2:12. Relating to Christ through baptism

▶ Barbers *(hair cutting, shaving)*

Those who cut hair or shave beards

Leviticus 19:27. Don't be your own barber.

Judges 16. Barbering Samson

Isaiah 7:20. Metaphorical barber

Ezekiel 5. Ezekiel the barber

▶ Barren (see *Childless*)

▶ Barrier(s) *(blockade, obstacle, wall)*

Something that blocks, separates, or hinders

Joshua 22:25. A barrier to worship

Song of Songs 8:9. A barrier of protection for an engaged woman

Ezekiel 40:11–12. Barrier at the temple

Ephesians 2:14–15. Christ broke the barrier between God and us.

▶ Bartering *(exchanging, negotiating, trading)*

An exchange of goods and services in lieu of money

Genesis 30:25–43. Jacob barters with Laban.

Job 6:27. Barter a friend?

Job 41:6. Can you barter with leviathan?

Lamentations 1:11. Bartering for food

▶ Basics of belief *(doctrine, foundation, milk)*

The essential elements of belief in Christ

John 3. You must be born again.

Acts 16. Just believe

Hebrews 5:12. Elementary truths

Hebrews 6:1. Back to the basics

1 Peter 2:2. As basic as milk

▶ Bathing *(dipping, soaking, swimming)*

Soaking or cleansing the body in water

Leviticus 15:16. Bathing rules

2 Samuel 11:1–5. David catches Bathsheba bathing.

2 Chronicles 28. Prisoners allowed to bathe after mistreatment

Song of Songs 5:12. Metaphorical bathing

▶ Battle(s) *(combat, fights, skirmishes)*

Encounters between opposing forces

Genesis 14. Battle of the five kings

Exodus 13:18. Readying the people for battle

Exodus 17:8–13. Israel's battle with the Amalekites

Numbers 14. Disobedience brings death in battle.

Joshua 8. Battle at Ai

Joshua 11. Battle with the northern kings of Canaan

Judges 20. Battle with the Benjamites

1 Samuel 28:1. Battle with the Philistines

▶ Beaches *(sand)*

Shore of a body of water

Isaiah 17:13. Like breakers on a beach

Ezekiel 27. Tyre abandons ship

John 21. Breakfast on the beach with the risen Christ

Acts 21:5–6. Praying on the beach

Acts 27–28. From shipwreck to shore

▶ Bear(s) *(animals)*

Omnivorous mammal in the *Ursidae* family

1 Samuel 17:36. David the bear killer

2 Samuel 17:8. David and his men compared to bears

2 Kings 2:23–25. Bears and baldness

Isaiah 11:7. Cows and bears—a sign of peace

Isaiah 59:11. The metaphor of the bear—impatience and frustration

▶ Beard(s) *(facial hair, men, shaving)*

Hair on a man's chin, cheeks, and throat

Leviticus 14:1–32. Beards and infectious diseases

1 Samuel 21:13. David pretends insanity

2 Samuel 10:4–5. Humiliation of a shaved beard

Ezra 9:3. Ezra tears his beard in mourning.

Jeremiah 41:4–5. Shaving beards in mourning

▶ Beasts *(antichrists, evil leaders)*

Metaphorical beasts mentioned in the Bible who stand for evil leaders to come

Revelation 11. The beast at end times

Revelation 13:1–10. Beast from the sea

Revelation 13:11–18. Beast from the earth

Revelation 14:9–11. Worship the beast at your peril.

Revelation 15:2–3. Victory over the beast

Revelation 17. Red beast of Babylon the Great

▶ Beatitudes *(blessedness, blessings, sayings)*

Declarations of blessing made by Jesus during the Sermon on the Mount

Matthew 5:1–3. The blessing of spiritual helplessness
Matthew 5:4. The blessing of mourning
Matthew 5:5 The blessing of gentleness
Matthew 5:6. The blessing of thirst for righteousness
Matthew 5:7. The blessing of being merciful
Matthew 5:8. The blessing of purity
Matthew 5:9. The blessing of peacemakers
Matthew 5:10–12. The blessing of persecution

▶ Beautiful Gate *(gate, Nicanor Gate, Herod's temple)*

Gate at Herod's temple leading into the women's court
Acts 3. The lame man at the Beautiful Gate

▶ Beauty *(attractiveness, good looks, loveliness)*

Quality associated with the harmony of form or color; something beautiful
2 Chronicles 20:21. Beauty of God's holiness
Esther 1:10–12. Xerxes wants to show off Vashti's beauty.
Psalm 27:4. David writes of God's beauty.
Proverbs 6:20–35. Don't be led astray by the beauty of the adulterous woman.
Proverbs 31:30. Beauty evaporates.

▶ Beauty contest *(beauty treatments)*

Contest instigated by Xerxes's staff to replace Vashti as queen
Esther 2. A beauty contest proposed

▶ Bed(s) *(sleep)*

A place to recline and sleep
Genesis 19:1–11. Trouble at bedtime
Genesis 47:31. Prayer at bedtime
Genesis 49:33. Bed as a euphemism for death
Exodus 8:3. Frogs in the bed
Leviticus 15:5. A bed not to touch
Deuteronomy 3:11. An iron bed
1 Samuel 19:13–16. Idols in the bed

▶ Bees *(insects)*

Winged, hairy insects of the *Apoidea* family
Deuteronomy 1:44. Amorites like bees
Judges 14:8. Samson and the bees
Psalm 118:12. Enemies like bees
Isaiah 7:18. Assyrian bees

▶ Begging *(alms, pleading, petitioning)*

Asking earnestly for something; soliciting alms
Psalm 37:25. No beggars?
Proverbs 18:23. Timidity while begging
Mark 10:46–52. Bartimaeus begs, but receives a miracle.
John 9. Begging for a miracle
Acts 3:2. Begging at Beautiful Gate

▶ Beginning(s) *(creation, foundation, inauguration)*

The process of bringing something into being; a start
Genesis 1:1. The beginning of everything
Genesis 11:5–6. A bad beginning
Exodus 9:18. Worst plague since the beginning of Egypt's history
Numbers 13:20. Grapes beginning to ripen
Joshua 8:33. Blessing at the beginning
1 Samuel 10:1. Kingship in Israel begins
2 Samuel 21:9. Death at the beginning of harvest
1 Kings 16:11. Murder at the beginning of a reign

▶ Behavior *(actions, conduct, deeds)*

The manner in which one behaves
1 Samuel 21:12–13. David behaving insanely
Job 13:15. Job defends his behavior.
Proverbs 1:3. Purpose of the proverbs
Proverbs 8:13. Hateful behavior

Proverbs 21:16. Wandering from wise behavior

Ezekiel 28:15. Perfect behavior until . . .

▶ Behead *(decapitate, guillotine, execute)*

To cut off someone's head

1 Samuel 17:51. Goliath's beheading

1 Samuel 31:8–9. Saul's beheading

Matthew 14:1–12. John the Baptist's beheading

Acts 12:1–2. James put to death

Hebrews 11:36–37. Persecution of Christians

Revelation 20:4. Beheading of martyrs

▶ Belief *(conviction, faith, principle)*

Placing confidence or trust in someone or something

Exodus 4:8–9. Signs to inspire belief in God

Numbers 14:1–3. Israel's lack of belief in God's ability to take them into the Promised Land

Psalm 78:21–22. Israel's unbelief revisited

Psalm 119:66. A belief in God's commands

2 Thessalonians 2:13. A belief in truth

▶ Believer *(advocate, Christian, supporter)*

Someone who has Christian faith or a belief in the goodness of someone or something

1 Kings 18:3. Obadiah

Acts 16:1. Timothy's mother

Acts 16:15. Lydia

1 Corinthians 7:12. Believers and unbelievers in marriage

1 Timothy 5:16. Believers helping widows

▶ Bells *(decoration, high priest)*

Hollow metallic devices that reverberate when struck; golden bells used on the fringe of the high priest's robe

Exodus 28:33–35. Bells on Aaron's priestly garment

Exodus 39:25–26. The bell at the hem

Zechariah 14:20. Written on the bells

▶ Belonging *(community, family, fitting in)*

Close or intimate relationship; a possession of someone

Genesis 32:17–18. Those belonging to Jacob

Genesis 45:9–11. Joseph vows to provide for those who belong to Jacob's family.

Exodus 13:11–12. Firstborn belong to God.

1 Kings 14:11, 13. Prophecy affecting those who belong to Jeroboam

1 Peter 2:9. Belonging to God

▶ Beloved *(adored, favorite, much loved)*

One dear to the heart

Deuteronomy 33:12. Beloved of God

Song of Songs 1:4. Song of the beloved

Song of Songs 2:3. Song of the beloved continues.

Jeremiah 11:15. Wickedness of the beloved

▶ Benediction(s) *(approval, blessing, sanction)*

Short blessing at the conclusion of public worship; invoking a blessing

Genesis 1:28. Creation benediction

Genesis 14:18–20. Melchizedek benediction

Numbers 6:22–26. Priestly benediction

2 Samuel 24:23. Araunah's benediction

1 Kings 8:55–59. Solomon's benediction at the temple's dedication

▶ Benefactor *(backer, patron, sponsor)*

One who makes a gift or bequest

Nehemiah 5:8. Nehemiah and the returning exiles

Luke 7:3–5. Roman centurion

Luke 19:8. Zacchaeus

Luke 22:25. Kings

Acts 4:36–37. Joseph (Barnabas)

2 Timothy 1:16. Onesiphorus

▶ Beneficiary *(receiver, recipient, the needy)*

Person designated to receive an inheritance or gift

B

Genesis 15:2. Abram assumes that Eliezer will be his beneficiary.
Leviticus 20:22–24. The people of Israel
Numbers 27:8–9. Daughters and brothers
Psalm 41:1–2. The helpless
Ephesians 1:14. Believers

▶ Benevolence *(see Alms, Compassion)*

▶ Bereans *(believers, Gentiles)*

Christians living in Berea (near Thessalonica)
Acts 17:10–14. Paul and the Bereans
Acts 20:3–4. Bereans with Paul

▶ Bereavement *(see Grief)*

▶ Besetting sin *(sin, temptation, weakness)*

Habitual wrongdoing; sin that one finds difficult to overcome
Numbers 20:11–12. Consequences of Moses' besetting sin
Judges 4:1. Israel's besetting sin
2 Samuel 12:7–10. Consequences of David's besetting sin
Romans 7:18–20. Paul's besetting sin
Hebrews 12:1. Besetting sin of the believer

▶ Betrayal *(disloyalty, infidelity, treachery, unfaithfulness)*

Using treachery to deliver someone to an enemy
Genesis 37. Joseph's brothers' betrayal
1 Samuel 22:9–10. Doeg betrays David.
2 Samuel 19:24–30. Ziba's betrayal of Mephibosheth
Psalm 41:9. Betrayal of a friend
Jeremiah 12:6. Jeremiah's family betrays him.
Luke 22:1–6. Judas betrays Jesus.

▶ Betrothal *(see Engagement)*

▶ Bible *(Holy Spirit)*

Written by people, the Bible is believed to be the inspired Word of God.
2 Samuel 23:2. Inspired psalms
John 20:30–31. Inspired to believe
Acts 1:15–16. The Holy Spirit and the Scriptures
2 Timothy 3:16. Every Scripture inspired
2 Peter 1:20–21. Inspiration of the Holy Spirit

▶ Bible study *(learn, read, study)*

Effort expended to read and learn Scriptures in order to apply them to one's life
Deuteronomy 6:6–9. Study God's commands.
Ezra 7:10. Ezra studies.
Nehemiah 8:7–8. The returning exiles study the Scriptures.
John 5:39–40. Jesus rebukes the Jews about the hypocrisy of their Scripture study.
2 Timothy 2:15. Study and teach

▶ Biers/Coffins *(death, funeral)*

Coffins and stands used to bury someone
Genesis 50:26. Joseph's death
2 Samuel 3:31. Abner's coffin
2 Chronicles 16:13–14. Asa entombed
Luke 7:11–17. Man raised to life while in the coffin

▶ Binding and loosing *(freedom, guilt, innocence)*

The authority to pronounce someone guilty or innocent; constrained by legal authority
Nehemiah 10:29. Bound to a curse
Matthew 16:19. Binding and loosing
Matthew 18:18. Binding and loosing

▶ Bingeing *(drunkenness, gorging, overindulgence)*

Going on a drunken spree or revel; overeating
Deuteronomy 21:20. Bingeing and rebellion
1 Samuel 25:36. Nabal binges.
Proverbs 25:16. Don't binge on honey.

▶ Biology *(ecology, natural science, nature)*

Study of living organisms and processes; plants and animals in an environment

Genesis 1:1–2. Creation makes biology possible.
Job 38:14. Earth changes
Job 38:25–27. Rain patterns
Job 39:26. Understanding bird migration
Psalm 24:1–2. God—the founder of the earth

▶ Bird(s) *(dove, eagle, pigeon)*

Winged, warm-blood invertebrates
Genesis 1:20–23. Creation of birds
Genesis 7:8–9. "Clean" birds taken on the ark
Genesis 15:9–11. Abram's sacrifice
2 Samuel 21:10. Rizpah keeps away the birds
Matthew 6:26. Look at the birds.
Mark 4:31–32. Look at the birds.

▶ Birth control *(contraceptives, pregnancy prevention)*

Methods used to prevent pregnancy
Genesis 20:18. God controls births.
Genesis 38:9–10. Onan's method of birth control

▶ Birthright *(firstborn, inheritance, legacy)*

Privilege or possession to which one is entitled to by birth; inheritance of the firstborn
Genesis 21:10. Sarah refuses to allow Ishmael to have the birthright.
Genesis 25:29–34. Jacob desires Esau's birthright.
Genesis 27:36. Esau mourns the loss of his birthright.
1 Chronicles 5:1. Reuben loses his birthright.
1 Chronicles 26:10. Shimri's birthright

▶ Bishop *(church leader, elder, overseer, presbyter)*

One with spiritual or ecclesiastical supervision
Acts 20:28. Advice for bishops
1 Timothy 3:1–7. Rules for bishops
Titus 1:6–7. A bishop's family and character

▶ Bitterness *(hostility, resentment, sullenness)*

Acrid or astringent; an attitude of animosity
Genesis 49:23. Joseph attacked with bitterness
Ruth 1. Naomi's bitterness
1 Samuel 1:10. Hannah's bitterness
1 Samuel 15:32. Bitterness of death
Job 7:11. Job's bitterness

▶ Blaming others *(censuring, condemning, passing the responsibility)*

Finding fault with or placing the responsibility on someone else
Genesis 3. Adam blames Eve; Eve blames the snake.
Exodus 16:2–3. Israel blames Moses.
1 Samuel 22. Saul blames Ahimelech and the priests for David's escape.
2 Samuel 3:29–30. David blames Joab for Abner's death.
Colossians 1:22. We are without blame, because of Christ.

▶ Blaspheme *(curse, profane, swear against)*

To speak of God in an irreverent or erroneous manner
Exodus 22:28. Do not blaspheme.
Acts 26:11. Paul confesses that he once forced others to blaspheme.
1 Timothy 1:18–20. Avoiding blasphemy
2 Peter 2:10–13. Blasphemy of false teachers
Revelation 13:1–10. Blasphemy of the beast from the sea

▶ Blemish *(fault, flaw, imperfection)*

Imperfection that mars or renders a person, animal, or thing unusable as a sacrifice or unclean
Leviticus 22:21. An offering without blemish
2 Samuel 14:25. Unblemished Absalom
Song of Songs 4:7. An unblemished bride
Ephesians 5:26–27. An unblemished church

B

▶ Blessed *(approved, consecrated, favored)*

To invoke divine favor upon or convey well-being upon; something consecrated

Genesis 2:3. Blessing the seventh day
Genesis 5:1–2. Blessed humans
Genesis 28:6. Jacob blessed
Deuteronomy 33:1. Blessing Israel
Joshua 14:13. Blessing Caleb

▶ Blessing of God *(divine favor)*

Divine favored experienced

Genesis 39:5. Potiphar experiences God's blessing.
Exodus 32:29. A blessing today
Leviticus 25:21. A blessing in the jubilee year
Deuteronomy 28:1–14. God's blessing
2 Samuel 7:29. David seeks God's blessing.
Psalm 3:8. Where His blessing rests
Psalm 24:3–5. The person who receives God's blessing

▶ Blindness *(lacking understanding, sightlessness)*

Unable to see physically or conceptually; lack of awareness

Genesis 19:11. Struck with blindness
Deuteronomy 28:28. The curse of blindness
2 Kings 6:18. Elisha's blindness request
Luke 4:18–19. The call of the Messiah
John 9:1–7. Curing blindness
John 9:41. Spiritual blindness

▶ Blood *(family relationship, life blood, payment)*

Plasma, platelets, and blood cells; payment for sin

Genesis 4:10. Abel's blood
Genesis 9:4–6. Bloodshed
Exodus 24:8. Promise sealed in blood
Leviticus 1:4–5. Blood payment
Hebrews 9. Blood sacrifice of Christ
1 Peter 1:2. Sprinkled with His blood

▶ Boast *(assertion, brag, showing off)*

Glorify oneself; excessive pride

1 Samuel 2:3. Don't boast.
Psalm 20:7. Appropriate boasting
Isaiah 3:9. Boasting of sins
Isaiah 61:6. Boasting of splendor
Amos 4:5. A challenge to boast

▶ Boat(s) *(craft, ship, vessel)*

Crafts used for sailing

Job 9:26. Metaphorical boats
Isaiah 2:16. Boats of Tarshish
Isaiah 18:1–2. Sudanese boats
Mark 4:35–41. Boats in a storm
Luke 5:1–11. Fishing boats
John 6:23–24. Boats from Tiberias

▶ Body *(cadaver, human body, organization)*

Material or physical structure of an organism, particularly a human

Genesis 9:23. Noah's unclothed body
Exodus 2:12. Moses hides the body of the Egyptian.
Numbers 5:1–2. Don't touch dead bodies.
Deuteronomy 28:35. Results of curses on the body
Psalm 84:2. Praising with the body
Psalm 139:13–15. Body made by God

▶ Body of Christ *(believers, the church, the family of God)*

Universal church; the physical body of Christ; representation of Christ's broken body used in communion

1 Corinthians 6:15. Part of Christ's body
1 Corinthians 10:16–17. Sharing His body
1 Corinthians 12:27. Each a part of Christ's body
Ephesians 4:12. Building up the body of Christ
Ephesians 5:23. Christ—the head of the body
Colossians 1:24. Suffering on behalf of the body
Colossians 2:9–10. All of God in the body

▶ Boils *(carbuncles, sores, ulcers)*

Pus-filled inflammation of the skin

Exodus 9:8–12. Plague of boils

Deuteronomy 28:27, 35. Curse of boils

Job 2:7–8. Struck with boils

Job 30:30. Results of having boils

Revelation 16:2. Painful results of worshiping the beast

▶ Boldness *(bravery, confidence, courage)*

Showing courage/confidence; exhibiting bravery

Exodus 14:8. Israelites leaving Egypt with boldness

Psalm 138:3. Boldness from God

Proverbs 28:1. Righteous boldness

Luke 11:8. Good results of boldness

Acts 4:29. Asking for boldness

▶ Bondage *(burden, oppression, recurrent sin)*

Enslavement or subjection to someone or something

Genesis 47:19. In bondage to Pharaoh

Exodus 2:23. Cries of those in bondage

Exodus 6:9. Bondage of the Israelites

Ezra 9:8–9. Relief in bondage

Romans 8:21. Liberated from bondage

▶ Bone(s) *(dead body, remains, skeleton)*

Calcified connective tissue forming the skeletons of many vertebrates

Genesis 2:23. Eve is bone of Adam's bones.

Genesis 50:25. Carry Joseph's bones away

Leviticus 22:22. No broken bones in sacrificial animals

1 Samuel 31:11–13. Bones of Saul and his sons

Ezekiel 37. Valley of dry bones

Luke 24:39. The risen Christ has flesh and bones.

▶ Book of Life *(papyruses, parts of the Bible)*

Written sheets or scrolls with records of events

Exodus 32:31–34. Don't blot them out of the book

Psalm 69:28. Erased from the book

Psalm 139:16. Days of life recorded

Philippians 4:3. Names in the Book of Life

Revelation 3:5. Listed in the Book of Life

Revelation 13:8. Not listed in the Book of Life

Revelation 21:27. The Lamb's Book of Life

▶ Book(s) *(papyruses, parts of the Bible)*

Written sheets or scrolls with records of events

Exodus 24:7. Book of the Lord's Promise

Numbers 21:14. Book of the Wars of the Lord

Deuteronomy 28:58, 61. Book of Teachings

Joshua 8:31. Book of Moses' Teachings

Joshua 10:13. Book of Jashar

Joshua 24:26. Book of God's Teachings

2 Kings 23:21. Book of the Promise

▶ Booths, Feast of *(see Feast(s); Tabernacles, Feast of)*

▶ Boredom *(ennui, monotony, tedium)*

A sense of tedium

Proverbs 4:23. Boredom can lead to trouble so be careful to guard your heart.

Proverbs 14:14. A heart that turns from God becomes bored.

▶ Born again *(born of the Spirit, Christianity, regeneration, second birth)*

Spiritual rebirth of someone who professes faith in Christ

John 3:1–21. You must be born again.

Galatians 4:28–29. Spiritual birth

1 Peter 1:23. Born again through God's Word

B

▶ Botany *(plants, seeds)*

The study of plants

Genesis 1:11. The plant cycle begins.

Genesis 3:17–18. Plant cycle changes

1 Kings 4:32–33. Solomon the botanist

Isaiah 17:10. Concentrating on plants instead of God

Matthew 13:32. Study the mustard seed.

▶ Boundaries *(borders, landmarks, limits)*

Indications of borders or limits

Exodus 19:12, 21. Boundary around Mount Sinai

Deuteronomy 19:14. Don't move boundary markers.

Deuteronomy 27:17. Result of moving a boundary marker

Psalm 16:6. Pleasant boundary

Jeremiah 5:22. Boundary for the sea

Ezekiel 45:7. Boundaries of the holy area

▶ Bowing *(curtseying, sign of obeisance)*

Inclining the body or head as a sign of courtesy

Genesis 24:26, 48. Bowing before God

Genesis 37:9. Bowing before Joseph, Part 1

Genesis 43:28. Bowing before Joseph, Part 2

Exodus 12:27. Bowing in agreement

Exodus 34:8. Bowing before the presence of God

Numbers 22:31. Bowing before the Messenger of the Lord

▶ Bowls of wrath *(consequences of evil, judgment)*

Signs of God's judgment on the earth and humanity

Revelation 15:7. Seven bowls of wrath

Revelation 16:1, 8. Bowls of wrath poured out

Revelation 17:1. Judgment of Babylon

Revelation 21:9. Hope in the midst of the bowls of wrath

▶ Boy(s) *(child, son, young man)*

Male child

Genesis 48:16. Blessing Joseph's boys

Exodus 1:15–22. Killing Hebrew boys

Numbers 31:17. Killing Midianite boys

Isaiah 3:4. Prophecy of judgment—boys as leaders

Joel 3:3. Trading boys and girls

Matthew 2:16–18. Killing Hebrew boys

▶ Bracelet *(armlet, bangle, jewelry)*

Ornamental band or chain worn on the wrist

Genesis 24:22, 30. Bracelets for Rebekah

Numbers 31:50. Bracelets for peace

2 Samuel 1:10. Saul's bracelet

Isaiah 3:16. Ankle bracelets

Ezekiel 16:11. Metaphorical bracelets

Ezekiel 23:42. Other metaphorical bracelets

▶ Bragging *(arrogance, boasting, pride)*

Saying pompous or boastful statements

Psalm 12:3–4. Cutting off the bragging tongue

Jeremiah 9:24. Best kind of bragging

Romans 3:27. Eliminating bragging

1 Corinthians 4:7. Why brag?

1 Corinthians 9:15. Paul's bragging

2 Corinthians 7:14. Bragging to Titus

James 4:16. Arrogant bragging

▶ Brain *(see Mind)*

▶ Branch *(bough, Messiah)*

Sprout of a tree; also a metaphor for the Messiah and other aspects of the spiritual life

Exodus 12:22. Branch of hyssop

Numbers 13:23. Branch from a vineyard in Canaan

Job 15:32. Metaphor of the wicked

Isaiah 4:2. Branch of the Lord

Isaiah 11:1. Branch of Jesse—the Messiah

Isaiah 14:19. A rejected branch

Jeremiah 1:11. Jeremiah's vision of the almond branch

▶ Bravery (see *Courage*)

▶ Bread *(Bread of the presence, loaves, manna)*

Food made from dough

Genesis 14:18. The bread of hospitality

Genesis 18:5. Abraham offers bread to angels.

Exodus 12. Unleavened bread

Exodus 25:30. Bread of the presence

Exodus 29:2–25. Bread as a sacrifice

Numbers 6:15. Rings of bread and unleavened bread

Judges 7:13. A dream of bread

Matthew 4:3–4. You can't live on bread alone.

▶ Bread of life *(Jesus, name of Jesus, manna)*

A messianic metaphor comparing Jesus to the manna provided by God for the people of Israel during their wilderness sojourn

John 6:32–33. Bread from heaven

John 6:35. Bread of life

John 6:48–51. Bread that brings life

▶ Breakfast *(mealtime, morning)*

First meal of the day

Genesis 21:14. Providing breakfast

Genesis 49:27. Metaphorical breakfast

Exodus 16:8. God provides breakfast

Judges 19:8. A long breakfast

Psalm 90:14. Mercy for breakfast

John 21. Breakfast with the risen Jesus

▶ Breastplate of righteousness (see *Armor of God*)

▶ Breath *(air, inhalation, respiration)*

Air inhaled and exhaled

Genesis 2:7. Breath of life

Genesis 25:7–8. Abraham's last breath

Exodus 15:10. God's breath controls the Red Sea.

Numbers 16:22. Everyone has the breath of life.

2 Samuel 22:16. The Lord's breath

Job 7:7. Life as short as a breath

▶ Breeding *(birth, procreation, reproduction)*

The production of offspring

Genesis 30:37–39. Jacob's animal breeding scheme

Genesis 31:10. Breeding season

Leviticus 19:19. Rules about animal breeding

Deuteronomy 32:14. Giving Israel the best breeding stock

Job 21:10. The wicked seem blessed, even in animal breeding.

▶ Bribery *(gift, pay-off, subornment)*

The process of offering money, goods, or other items in order to gain favor or persuade someone

Exodus 23:8. Never take a bribe.

Deuteronomy 10:17. God does not take bribes.

Deuteronomy 16:19. Don't pervert justice by taking bribes.

1 Samuel 12:3. Samuel didn't take bribes.

Job 6:22–23. Job didn't take bribes.

Proverbs 18:16. According to some, however, a bribe opens doors.

▶ Brick(s) *(block, clay, stone)*

Block of baked clay used for building or paving

Genesis 11:3. Bricks for a tower

Exodus 1:14. Brutal brick-making

Exodus 5. Pharaoh makes brick-making difficult.

Isaiah 9:10. Replacing bricks with stones

Nahum 3:14. The people of Nineveh will try to shore up their defenses during a siege, but will be defenseless.

▶ Bride *(the church, newly married woman, wife)*

A woman about to be or recently married; also a metaphor for the church

Song of Songs 1:2. Song of a bride
Isaiah 49:18. A bride's display
Jeremiah 2:2. Loving God with the love of a bride
Jeremiah 2:32. A bride's veils
Revelation 19:7. Bride of the Lamb

▶ Bridegroom *(husband, Jesus, newly married man)*

A man about to be or recently married; also a metaphor for Jesus' relationship with the church

Exodus 4:25–26. Moses: a bridegroom of blood
Isaiah 62:5. God rejoices like a bridegroom.
Matthew 9:14–15. Jesus is the bridegroom.
Matthew 25:1–13. The bridegroom comes.
John 2:9–10. A groom is credited with wine Jesus produces.
John 3:29. The bride belongs to the groom.

▶ Brimstone *(burning stone, fire, sulfur)*

Divine retribution in the form of burning sulfur

Genesis 19:24. God destroys Sodom and Gomorrah with brimstone and fire.
Deuteronomy 29:23. Brimstone is the result of disobedience.
Job 18:15. Brimstone on the home of the wicked
Psalm 11:6. The wicked are punished with brimstone.
Isaiah 30:33. God's breath is like brimstone.

▶ Broken/Brokenness *(embarrassed, humiliated, shattered)*

Fractured, sundered, or violated; crushed by grief

Leviticus 6:28. Broken pottery
Leviticus 26:13. Egypt's power is broken.
Numbers 15:31. A broken commandment
2 Kings 18:21. Trusting a broken stick
Isaiah 53:5. The Suffering Servant will be broken.
John 19:36. Jesus' legs were not broken after crucifixion.

▶ Bronze Age *(period of history, weapons)*

Period of human culture between the Stone Age and the Iron Age in which weapons made of bronze were used

Genesis 4:22. Bronze tools
Exodus 26:11. Bronze used in the tabernacle.
Numbers 21:4–9. Bronze snake
Joshua 6:24. Bronze for the treasury
1 Samuel 17:5–6. Goliath's bronze armor and weapons
2 Samuel 21:16. More bronze weapons

▶ Brother *(fellow Christian, kinsman, male sibling)*

Male having the same parent or parents as another; also a kinsman, fraternity member, or close male friend

Genesis 4:1–16. Cain's brother Abel
Genesis 24:29. Brother of Rebekah
Exodus 4:14. Moses' brother, Aaron
1 Samuel 17:18. David's brothers
Mark 3:35. A brother to Jesus
Romans 16:23. A brother in the faith

▶ Brotherhood *(fellow Christians, fraternity, siblings)*

State of being brothers

Zechariah 11:14. The brotherhood of Judah and Israel
Amos 1:9–10. Treaty of brotherhood
1 Peter 2:17. Brotherhood of believers
1 Peter 5:9. Suffering with the brotherhood of believers

▶ Brutality *(cruelty, violence, viciousness)*

Ruthless, cruel, or harsh treatment of someone

Genesis 34:25–27. Brutality of Simeon and Levi
Exodus 6:9. Brutality of slavery
Proverbs 20:30. Brutal beatings
Ezekiel 21:31. Promise of brutality to come
2 Timothy 3:1–3. Brutality in the last days

▶ Budgets *(accounts, financial plan, resources)*

Summary of expenditures

Proverbs 31:13, 16–18. The wise wife works within a budget.

Luke 14:28. Make out a budget.

▶ Building projects *(pyramid, temple, tower)*

Buildings or other edifices constructed by the Israelites and others

Genesis 6:13–16. Noah is told to build an ark.

Genesis 11:1–9. Tower of Babel

Exodus 1:11. Egyptian cities

Exodus 37:25. Altar of incense

1 Kings 6. Solomon's temple

1 Kings 7:1–12. Solomon's palace

Nehemiah 3. Rebuilding the wall of Jerusalem

1 Peter 2:5. Building a spiritual house

▶ Bull(s) *(male cow)*

Adult male bovine

Exodus 22:9. Who owns the bull?

Exodus 29:1–14. Bull as an offering

Exodus 21:28–32. When gored by a bull

Leviticus 4:3–12. Bull as an offering

Numbers 15:8–11. Bull as an offering

Hosea 4:16. Israel as stubborn as a bull

▶ Burden(s) *(load, problem, sin, weight, yoke)*

Something emotionally difficult to bear; a difficult task or responsibility

Genesis 49:15. Issachar's burden

Numbers 11:10–11. Moses' burden

Deuteronomy 28:48. Heavy burden

1 Kings 12:4. The people beg for their burdens (taxes) to be reduced.

Matthew 11:29–30. Jesus' burden

▶ Bureaucracy *(government, organization, procedure, red tape)*

Administration of a government through bureaus or non-elected officials

1 Samuel 8:15–17. Bureaucracy to come

1 Kings 10:4–5. Breathless at bureaucracy

2 Kings 12:19–20. Plotting bureaucrats

Ecclesiastes 5:8. Bureaucracy in action

Daniel 6:1–2. Bureaucracy of Darius's court

▶ Burial *(entombment, funeral, interment)*

Process of burying the dead

Genesis 23:19. Sarah's burial

Ecclesiastes 6:3. Lacking an honorable burial

Jeremiah 22:19. A donkey's burial

Jeremiah 26:23. Uriah's burial

Ezekiel 39:11. Gog's burial

John 19:40–42. Jesus' burial

▶ Burning *(ablaze, flaming, smoldering)*

Marked by flames or intense heat

Genesis 22:6. Burning coals for a sacrifice

Exodus 3:2–4. Burning bush

Exodus 15:7. God's burning anger

Exodus 30:1. Burning incense

Psalm 140:10. Burning coals on enemies

Proverbs 6:27–28. The burn of temptation

▶ Business *(commerce, industry, trade)*

A person's occupation, work, or trade

1 Samuel 21:8. David pretends to be about the king's business.

1 Samuel 25:2–3. Nabal—a successful businessman

Job 20:18. The business of the wicked

Psalm 107:23–24. Business on the high seas

Ecclesiastes 5:14. Bad business deals

Acts 16:14. Lydia—an astute businesswoman

▶ Busybodies *(bad-mouthing, spite, unkind remarks)*

Speaking spitefully about someone or something

2 Thessalonians 3:11. Paul rebukes busybodies

1 Timothy 5:13. The business of busybodies

1 Peter 4:15. Don't be a busybody.

▶ Calendar *(almanac, dates, time)*

A system for reckoning time

Exodus 23:15. In the month of Abib

Leviticus 23:27. A date to mark

Numbers 1:1. Keeping track of time

Numbers 9:2–3. On the fourteenth day

Numbers 33:3. On the fifteenth day

▶ Calf worship *(idols)*

Using calf-shaped idols in worship

Exodus 32. Gold calf

Deuteronomy 9:16–21. Moses recaps the calf incident.

Nehemiah 9:17–18. God didn't abandon his people, even when they made the gold calf.

1 Kings 12:28–31. Jeroboam encourages calf worship.

Psalm 106:19. Worshiping the calf

▶ Called/Calling *(election, ministry, occupation)*

The selection of a leader for a purpose; those who are the elect or chosen by God

Matthew 4:18–20. Calling the first disciples

Romans 1:6–7. Called to belong to Jesus

Romans 8:28–30. Those who are called

Hebrews 3:1. Heavenly calling

2 Peter 1:10. Make your calling secure.

▶ Camel(s) *(domestic animals, herds)*

Domesticated, humped ruminant mammal

Genesis 12:16. Plenty of camels for Abram

Genesis 24:17–19. Rebekah provides water for Abraham's camels.

Genesis 32:13–15. Jacob gives camels to appease Esau.

Leviticus 11:4. Don't eat camels.

Judges 7:12. Many camels

Jeremiah 2:23. Judah is like a young camel.

Mark 10:25. Camel through a needle

▶ Candle(s) *(light, wax, tallow, wick)*

Cylindrical mass of tallow or wax used to provide light

Isaiah 42:3. Flickering candle

Isaiah 43:17. Snuffed like a candle wick

Matthew 12:20. Jesus—the chosen servant

▶ Cannibalism *(curse, siege behavior)*

Eating the flesh of another human being

Leviticus 26:29. The covenant curse of cannibalism

Deuteronomy 28:53. Cannibalism as a result of the curse

2 Kings 6:28–29. Cannibalism during a famine

Jeremiah 19:9. Fulfillment of a covenant curse

Lamentations 4:10. Cannibalism in the midst of a siege

John 6:51–52. Jesus accused of cannibalism

▶ Canon *(Bible, books, Scriptures)*

The books of the Bible officially accepted as Scripture

Deuteronomy 4:2. Commandment to avoid adding to Scriptures

Deuteronomy 31:26. Law—part of the canon

Mark 12:26. Jesus discusses the book of the law

2 Peter 3:16. Paul's letters accepted as part of the Scriptures.

▶ Capability *(see Ability[ies]), Talent)*

▶ Capital punishment *(execution)*

Killing a person by judicial process

Genesis 26:11. Penalty for touching Isaac or Rebekah

Genesis 40:19. Chief baker to be hanged

Exodus 21:12. Capital offenses

Leviticus 20:9. Curse leads to death.

Deuteronomy 13:9. Punishment for idolatry

Esther 7:8–10. Haman is put to death.

Daniel 3:6. Penalty for refusal to bow to the statue set up by Nebuchadnezzar

C

▶ Capital(s) *(headquarters, hub, main city)*

The town or city that is the official seat of government; also the upper part of a pillar

Genesis 36:32, 35. Edom capitals
Joshua 13:9–10. Capital of Heshbon
1 Chronicles 1:50. A capital city of Edom
Isaiah 7:8–9a. Capital cities of Israel and Judah

▶ Captive *(hostage, prisoner, slave)*

One forcibly confined, enslaved, or taken prisoner as a result of war

Deuteronomy 21:10. Rules about taking captives
Judges 18:30. Priests until captivity
1 Samuel 30. The captives of Ziklag
2 Kings 6:22. Handling the captives during a siege
2 Kings 24:15. Capturing Jehoiakin
2 Corinthians 10:5. Taking thoughts captive
Ephesians 4:7–8. Rescuing captives of sin

▶ Caravan(s) *(convoy, group, parade)*

A group of travelers journeying together

Genesis 37:25. Caravan of Ishmaelites
1 Kings 10:2. Queen of Sheba's caravan
Isaiah 21:13. Caravan of Arabians
Isaiah 30:6. Caravan through the Negev
Luke 2:43–44. Jesus travels in Passover caravan

▶ Careers (see *Trade, Work*)

▶ Carnal *(earthly, self-centered thoughts, sexual desires)*

Relating to the physical or sexual appetite

Romans 7:14. Spiritual versus carnal
Romans 8:7. Hostile toward God
Romans 15:27. Using earthly materials
1 Corinthians 3:1. Not spiritual but carnal

▶ Carnivorous animals *(bears, lions, vultures, wolves)*

Flesh-eating predators

Genesis 31:39. Flocks killed by wild animals
Leviticus 7:24. Law against eating an animal killed by another
Leviticus 26:22. The curse of the carnivores
1 Samuel 17:34–35. Rescuing the flock from carnivores
Job 39:30. Carnivorous birds

▶ Carpenter *(wood worker)*

A worker who makes finished wooden products

Exodus 38:22–23. Bezalel
2 Samuel 5:11. Hired carpenters
2 Kings 12:11–12. Contributions to pay carpenters
Isaiah 41:7. Encouraging carpenters
Isaiah 44:13. Work of carpenters
Matthew 13:55. Jesus and Joseph

▶ Catastrophe *(calamity, disaster, tragedy)*

A great and sudden calamity

Genesis 19:29. Catastrophe at Sodom and Gomorrah
Jeremiah 11:23. Catastrophe God allows
Revelation 8:13. Catastrophe, catastrophe, catastrophe
Revelation 9:12. More and more catastrophes
Revelation 11:14. Second and third catastrophes

▶ Cattle/Cow *(bulls, oxen, steers)*

Mammals of the genus *Bos*

Genesis 13:5. Lot's cattle
Genesis 24:35. Abraham's cattle
Exodus 9:1–7. Plague on cattle
Leviticus 1:2. Offering of cattle
Deuteronomy 2:35. Cattle as spoils of war
Psalm 50:10. All cattle belong to God
Jeremiah 5:17. Cattle taken as a result of Judah's disobedience

▶ Caught in the act *(accused, convicted)*

Individuals caught in the middle of a wrongdoing

Deuteronomy 22:22. The adulterers
Joshua 7. Achan
Psalm 10:2. The wicked
Mark 14:72. Peter
John 8:1–11. Woman caught in adultery

▶ Cause and effect *(cycles, triggers)*

The cycle of events or actions and the effects produced by them
Deuteronomy 28:1. Cause: obedience; effect: blessing
Deuteronomy 28:15. Cause: disobedience; effect: curses
Judges 4. Cause: Israel's sin; effect: conquered by the Canaanites
Judges 9. Cause: Abimelech's murders; effect: punishment from God and ambushes
Isaiah 3. Cause: arrogance/oppression of the women of Zion; effect: punishment from God

▶ Cautions *(see Admonitions, Warning[s])*

▶ Cave *(cavern, grotto, tomb)*

Hollow or natural passage into the earth
Genesis 19:30. Taking shelter in a cave
Genesis 23:7–19. Abraham buries Sarah in a cave.
Joshua 10:16–27. Hiding in a cave
Judges 15:8. Samson in a cave
1 Samuel 22:1. Escape to a cave

▶ Cedars of Lebanon *(trees)*

Trees indigenous to the mountains of Lebanon
Judges 9:15. An allegory involving the cedars of Lebanon
1 Kings 5:6. Cedars used in building the temple
1 Kings 10:27. Plentiful cedars
2 Kings 19:23. Sennacherib threatens deforestation
Psalm 92:12. The righteous are like the cedars.
Psalm 104:16. The Lord's trees
Isaiah 2:12–13. A prophecy against the cedars of Lebanon

▶ Celebrate *(commemorate, honor, remember)*

To observe special days or events with ceremonies of respect
Exodus 5:1. A festival to celebrate
Exodus 12. Celebrate Passover
Exodus 23:14. Celebrate three times a year
Leviticus 23:39. Celebrate for seven days.
Numbers 9:4–5. Celebration in the desert
Matthew 26:18. Jesus celebrates Passover

▶ Celibacy *(see Abstinence)*

▶ Censer *(incense)*

Vessel for burning incense
Leviticus 10:1. Censers of Nadab and Abihu
Numbers 16. Challenge with censers
1 Kings 7:50. Temple furnishings
2 Kings 25:15. Babylonians loot the censers.

▶ Census *(poll, population count, survey)*

An official enumeration of a population, often for taxation or military purposes
Exodus 30:11–12. Ransom after a census
Numbers 1. Moses takes a census.
Numbers 4:1–2. Census of the Levites
Numbers 26:52–53. Census of the Levites
2 Samuel 24. A bad census

▶ Centurion *(Roman soldier)*

Commander in the Roman army with authority over 100 soldiers
Matthew 8:5–13. A centurion believes
Matthew 27:54. The centurion at the cross
Mark 15:44–45. The centurion's report
Acts 10. Cornelius the centurion
Acts 22:25. Paul appeals to a centurion.

C

▶ Ceremony *(observance, ritual, service)*

A formal act as prescribed by a ritual or custom

Genesis 50:10. Ceremony for Jacob

Exodus 12:25. Passover ceremony

Numbers 9:14. Passover ceremony

Acts 21:24. Purification ceremony

Acts 24:18. Paul talks of the purification ceremony.

▶ Chaff *(leftovers, hay, straw, winnowing)*

Finely cut straw or hay used as fodder

Job 13:25. Dry chaff

Job 21:18. Swept away like chaff

Psalm 1:4. Wicked are like chaff.

Psalm 35:5. Enemies treated like chaff

Isaiah 17:13. Chased away like chaff

▶ Chain(s) *(bonds, fetters, links, shackles)*

Connecting links used for binding or for ornamentation

Exodus 28. Chains for the high priest

Judges 8:26. Chains on camels

Judges 16:21. Chaining Samson

1 Kings 6:21. Chains at the temple

Isaiah 28:22. Chains in Jerusalem

Mark 5:4. Chains of a demon-controlled man

▶ Challenge *(confront, dare, test)*

A call to engage in a contest, fight, or competition

Numbers 16. Korah challenges Moses and loses.

1 Samuel 17:8–11. Goliath challenges Israel.

1 Kings 18. Elijah challenges the prophets of Baal.

Job 38. God challenges Job.

Jeremiah 49:19. God challenges Edom.

▶ Change *(alteration, conversion, transformation)*

To cause to be different; to have a different form or appearance

Numbers 23:19. God never changes.

1 Kings 8:48–49. A change of heart

1 Kings 13:33. Jeroboam didn't change.

Psalm 7:12. Change or be shot.

Jeremiah 7:3. Judah—change!

▶ Chaos *(confusion, disorder)*

Condition or place of great disorder or confusion

Exodus 8:24. Chaos in Egypt

Isaiah 34:11. Chaos in Edom

Habakkuk 3:2. Mercy in chaos

Acts 21:30. Chaos in Jerusalem

▶ Character *(personality, qualities, temperament)*

The combination of qualities that distinguish a person

Ruth 2:1. Boaz's outstanding character

Proverbs 31:10. Wife of strong character

Romans 5:3–4. Endurance produces character.

2 Corinthians 5:12. Prouder of appearance than of character

Ephesians 5:13–14. Light exposes true character.

▶ Chariot *(conveyance, transport)*

Two-wheeled, horse-drawn conveyance used in war or for ceremony

Genesis 41:43. Joseph's chariot

Exodus 14:5–31. Pharaoh pursues Israel with chariots.

Judges 4:15. Sisera and his chariots

2 Samuel 10:18. The Arameans and their chariots

2 Samuel 15:1. Absalom's chariot

1 Kings 4:26. Solomon's chariots

1 Kings 18:44–45. Ahab's chariot

▶ Chastity (see *Purity*)

▶ Cheating *(deception, dishonesty, trickery)*

Deceiving by trickery

Genesis 27. Esau is cheated out of his birthright.

Genesis 30:27–43. Laban tries to cheat Jacob out of his wages.

Malachi 3:8–9. Cheating God by withholding tithes

Mark 7:20–23. Cheating makes a person unclean.

▶ Cheerfulness *(brightness, exuberance, jollity)*

Having good spirits; being merry

1 Kings 8:66. Cheerful hearts at the temple dedication

Esther 8:16. Cheerfulness after deliverance

Proverbs 15:13, 15. Cheerful face and heart

Proverbs 16:15. Cheerful king

Ecclesiastes 3:12. Be cheerful.

2 Corinthians 9:7. Cheerful givers

▶ Chemistry *(science)*

The science of the composition, structure, properties, and reaction of matter

Exodus 30:34–35. Instructions on mixing incense

Job 38:29–30. Formation of ice

John 1:3. Chemistry possible because of God's creation

▶ Cherubim *(angels, living creatures)*

Winged celestial beings

Genesis 3:24. Cherubim guard the Garden of Eden

Numbers 7:89. Cherubim on the ark

2 Samuel 6:2. God enthroned between cherubim

1 Kings 6:23. Cherubim in the temple

Ezekiel 1. Ezekiel's vision of cherubim

▶ Child abuse *(mistreatment)*

The mistreatment of children

Genesis 37. Abusing Joseph

Exodus 1:15–16. Murdering children

Joel 3:3. Children not cherished

▶ Child sacrifice *(human sacrifice)*

Killing children to appease a god

Genesis 22. Isaac's sacrifice as test for Abraham

Leviticus 18:21. Never sacrifice children.

Leviticus 20:2–5. Death punishment for sacrificing children

2 Kings 23:10. Stopping child sacrifices

Jeremiah 32:35. Sites for child sacrifices

▶ Childbirth *(having children, reproduction)*

The process of giving birth

Genesis 35:16–18. Rachel dies in childbirth.

Exodus 1:15–16. Orders to kill during childbirth

Leviticus 12:1. Childbirth makes a woman ritually unclean.

Isaiah 21:3. Fall of Babylon is like childbirth.

Luke 2:2–7. Birth of Jesus

Romans 8:22. Creation groans like a woman in childbirth.

▶ Childless *(barren, infertile)*

Unable to have children

Genesis 16:1. Sarai was childless.

Genesis 25:21. Praying for a childless wife

1 Samuel 2:5. The prayer of a formerly childless woman

1 Samuel 15:33. Agag's mother soon to be childless

2 Samuel 6:23. Michal is childless

Psalm 113:9. Turning a childless woman into a joyful mother

Isaiah 54:1. Song of a childless woman

▶ Children *(blessings from God, daughter, son, youth)*

A son or daughter; an offspring

Genesis 29:31. Children for the unloved wife

Genesis 30:1–2. Desperate for children

Deuteronomy 6:6–7. Teach God's laws to children.

1 Samuel 2:20. Children dedicated to the Lord

Psalm 127:3–5. Children as an inheritance

Jeremiah 38:23. Children exiled to Babylon

Matthew 11:16–17. Jesus compares adults to children.

Matthew 19:13–15. Jesus blesses children.

▶ Choice(s) *(alternatives, options, selections)*

The act of choosing

Exodus 17:8–9. Choosing fighting men

Numbers 14:3–4. The Israelites rebel and want to choose another leader.

Deuteronomy 1:13. Choosing good leaders

Joshua 24:15. Choose who you will serve.

1 Chronicles 21:11–12. Choosing between punishments

▶ Choir *(chorale, music, singers)*

Organized company of singers

1 Chronicles 15:16. David chooses a choir.

2 Chronicles 5:13. The choir at the temple dedication

2 Chronicles 29:28. The choir at the temple rededication

Nehemiah 12:28–29. Choirs at the dedication of the rebuilt wall of Jerusalem

Psalm 68:26. Thanking God with choirs

▶ Choir directors *(leaders, singers)*

People chosen to lead a choir

1 Chronicles 15:22. Chenaniah is chosen to direct.

Psalm 4, direction. Notes for the choir director

Psalm 59, direction. Notes for the choir director

Psalm 60, direction. Notes for the choir director

▶ Christ *(Messiah, Suffering Servant the Chosen One)*

Greek translation of the Hebrew word *Messiah*—the Savior foretold in the Old Testament

Matthew 1:1. History of the Christ

Matthew 11:2–3. Jesus—the chosen servant

Matthew 24:24. False Christs

Matthew 26:67–68. The Christ mocked

John 1:41. Christ found

Acts 16:18. Speaking in the name of the Christ

▶ Christianity *(Christian faith, the church, the Way)*

Belief system based on the teachings of Jesus; embracing the belief that Jesus is the Son of God who died for the sins of all and was resurrected

Acts 11:26. First mention of Christians

Acts 26:10. Paul—the enemy of Christianity at one point

Acts 26:27. Can Paul persuade Agrippa to become a Christian?

Romans 9:1. The truth of a Christian

Romans 12:6. Agreeing with the Christian faith

1 Peter 4:16. Pride in being a Christian

▶ Christmas *(Advent, birth of Jesus, holiday)*

Holiday that celebrates the birth of the Savior, Jesus

Isaiah 7:14. Prophecy of Christmas to come

Micah 5:2. Setting of the first Christmas

Matthew 1:18. The Holy Spirit's part in Christmas

Luke 1:25–38. The promise of Christmas

Luke 2:1–20. The birth that started Christmas

▶ Church *(believers, community, congregation)*

Christians all over the world; the body of Christ; also a building where a congregation meets

Matthew 16:18. Building the church

Acts 2. Birth of the church

Acts 5:11. Fear sweeps the church

Acts 8:1. Persecuted church

Romans 16:1. A deacon of the church

1 Corinthians 7:17. Guidelines for the church

1 Corinthians 10:32. Don't mislead church members.

▶ Church discipline *(admonishing, reproving)*

Following biblical guidelines in order to reprove those within the community

Matthew 18:15–17. A model for church discipline

1 Corinthians 5:11. Paul calls for discipline.

1 Corinthians 6:9–10. Conduct that calls for church discipline

2 Corinthians 2:6–7. Don't over-discipline.

Ephesians 4:25. Speak the truth in church discipline.

▶ Cinnamon *(spice)*

Dried bark of tropical trees that is ground to make a spice

Exodus 30:23. Cinnamon in oil

Proverbs 7:17. A bed perfumed with cinnamon

Song of Songs 4:13–14. A love like a paradise with cinnamon

Revelation 18:12–13. No one to buy cinnamon

▶ Circumcision *(rite of inclusion, symbol of God's promise)*

The surgical removal of the foreskin of the male reproductive organ

Genesis 17:9–14. Covenant of circumcision

Exodus 4:25. Moses' son circumcised

John 7:22–23. Jesus discusses circumcision.

Acts 7:8. Continuing circumcision

Romans 2:25–29. Value of circumcision

▶ Circumstances *(conditions, situations, status)*

Determining or modifying factors; the results of events

1 Chronicles 29:29–30. Circumstances of David

Romans 4:10. The circumstances of faith

1 Corinthians 7:15. The circumstances that break a marriage vow

Philippians 4:11. Contentment regardless of the circumstances

Colossians 4:8. Reporting on circumstances

▶ Cistern *(container, reservoir, tank)*

Receptacle for holding water

Genesis 37:21–22. Joseph thrown into a cistern

Leviticus 11:35–36. Clean cistern

1 Samuel 19:22. Saul searches for David at the cistern in Secu

2 Kings 18:31. Sennacherib uses the analogy of a cistern to mock Hezekiah.

Proverbs 5:15. Drink from your own cistern.

Jeremiah 38. Jeremiah is imprisoned in a cistern.

▶ Cities of refuge *(Bezer, Ramoth, Golan, Kedesh, Shechem, Hebron)*

Six designated cities where those who commit accidental manslaughter can escape those seeking revenge

Numbers 35:6–34. Cities of refuge

Deuteronomy 4:41–42. Cities of refuge east of the Jordan

Deuteronomy 19:1–10. Places of refuge

Joshua 20. Cities chosen as places of refuge

▶ Citizen *(inhabitant, national, resident)*

Person entitled by birth or naturalization to the protection of a state or nation

Acts 16:37. Paul is a Roman citizen.

Acts 21:39. Citizen of Tarsus

Ephesians 2:19. Citizens together

Philippians 3:20. Citizens of heaven

▶ Citizenship *(nationality, residency)*

The status of a citizen with rights and privileges

Acts 22:28. The price of citizenship

Ephesians 2:12. Excluded from citizenship

▶ City walls *(fortification, reinforcement, strengthening)*

Fortifications used to protect a city and its citizens from danger

Joshua 2:15. A house in the wall

Joshua 6. Wall of Jericho falls

1 Samuel 31:12. Wall of Beth Shan

2 Kings 14:13. Wall of Jerusalem

Nehemiah 1:3. Wall of Jerusalem destroyed
Nehemiah 6:15. Wall of Jerusalem rebuilt

▶ City(ies) *(capital, metropolis, municipality)*

Center of population, commerce, and culture; a large town
Genesis 4:17. Cain's city
Genesis 33:18. The city of Shechem
Joshua 6:3. The city of Jericho
Joshua 8:1. The city of Ai
Judges 1:16. The City of Palms (Jericho)
1 Samuel 15:5. The city of Amalek
2 Samuel 5:7. The City of David
Isaiah 62:12. The City Not Deserted
Revelation 21:10. The holy city of Jerusalem

▶ Civil disobedience *(insurrection, revolt, rebellion)*

Refusing to obey laws without resorting to violence
Exodus 1:16–17. Civil disobedience of the midwives
Esther 4. Civil disobedience of Esther
Daniel 6. Civil disobedience of Daniel
Matthew 12:1–2. Civil "disobedience" of Jesus' disciples
Matthew 12:9–10. Jesus disobeys the rules.
Acts 5:29. Civil disobedience of the apostles

▶ Civil war *(war)*

War between regions of the same country
Judges 20. War between Israel and Benjamin
2 Samuel 1–4. War between David's house and Saul's
1 Kings 12:1–24. Jeroboam versus Rehoboam
1 Kings 15:16–17. Asa, king of Judah, versus Baasha, king of Israel

▶ Civility *(courtesy, graciousness, politeness)*

Courteous behavior
Genesis 18. Civility of Abraham
Genesis 24. Civility of Abraham's servant and Rebekah
Ruth 2. Civility of Boaz
1 Samuel 25. Civility of Abigail
Luke 17:11–19. Civility of a leper

▶ Clans *(kin, family, tribe)*

Tribal divisions
Genesis 24:37–38. Abraham's clan
Exodus 6. Clan divisions of the Levites
Leviticus 25:10. Returning to the clan
Joshua 7:14. Presenting clans for judgment

▶ Clapping *(applauding, praising, sign of joy or derision)*

The act or sound of clapping the hands
Psalm 47:1. Clap your hands
Psalm 98:8. Rivers clapping
Isaiah 55:12. Trees clapping
Lamentations 2:15. Derisive clapping

▶ Clay *(earth, soil, mud)*

Material used to make pottery, bricks, and tiles; it hardens when fired
Leviticus 6:28. Break the clay pot
Leviticus 14:5, 50. Cleansing and clay bowls
Job 10:9. Made from clay
Isaiah 45:9. Inquiries from clay
Isaiah 64:8. We are the clay.

▶ Clean/Cleanliness *(ritually pure, unsoiled)*

Ceremonially or morally able to approach God or to be used in the worship of God, based on prescribed rules and regulations having been met
Genesis 7:2. Clean animals on the ark
Leviticus 6:10–11. A clean place
Leviticus 7:19. If you're clean, you can eat.
Leviticus 13. Declared clean of a skin disease
Psalm 24:3–4. Clean hands
Psalm 51:7. Clean with hyssop
Matthew 8:2–3. Be clean!

▶ Cleanse *(clean, purify, wash)*

To restore someone to ritual purity; to purge the sin of someone

Leviticus 16:30. Cleansed on the day of Atonement
Psalm 51:2. Cleanse me from sin.
Jeremiah 33:8. God cleanses sin.
Ezekiel 36:25. A promise of cleansing
Matthew 10:8. Commissioned to cleanse
Hebrews 10:22. Cleansed from guilt

▶ Clergy *(see Levites; Priest)*

▶ Clothing *(attire, garments)*

Garments worn by people
Genesis 24:53. A gift of fine clothing
Genesis 45:21–22. Joseph provides clothing.
Leviticus 13:47–50. Clothing and mildew
Leviticus 19:19. Clothing regulation
Deuteronomy 22:5. Gender-related clothing

▶ Clothing mishaps *(crime of fashion, mistake, slip up)*

Clothing choices which reflect poor planning and/or immodest values
Genesis 3:7. Makeshift clothing
Proverbs 23:20–21. Picking out clothes when drunk
Nahum 3:5. Threat of exposure
Matthew 22:10–12. Not dressed for the occasion
Mark 1:6. A strange look
1 Timothy 2:9. Appropriate and modest clothing

▶ Cloud *(cumulonimbus, nimbus, pillar of cloud)*

A body of water droplets visible in the atmosphere miles above sea level; also a manifestation God used when leading Israel out of Egypt
Exodus 13:21. Pillar of cloud
Exodus 19:9. Coming in a cloud
Luke 21:27. Jesus will return in a cloud.
Acts 1:9. A cloud at Jesus' ascension

▶ Cobra *(snake)*

Venomous hooded snake native to Asia and Africa
Psalm 58:4–5. Like cobras
Psalm 91:13. Stepping on cobras
Isaiah 11:8. Sign of peace: an infant near a cobra's hole

▶ Code of Hammurabi *(laws)*

Ancient codes of law ratified by Hammurabi, a Babylonian king; similarities between the code and biblical commandments have been found.
Exodus 21:18–19. The code: accidental injuries
Exodus 21:23–25. The code: an eye for an eye
Matthew 5:38–39. Jesus responds to the code

▶ Coin(s) *(currency, denarii, drachma, silver)*

Pieces of metal with specific weights used as currency
Matthew 17:24–27. Coin in a fish's mouth
Matthew 26:14–16. Judas betrays Jesus for 30 coins.
Mark 12:42. A widow's coins
Luke 10:35. The good Samaritan's coins
Luke 15:8–10. Parable of the lost coin
John 2:15. Scattered coins

▶ Collaboration *(see Cooperation)*

▶ Collateral *(guarantee, security)*

Property used as security for a loan
Exodus 22:26–27. Clothing as collateral
Deuteronomy 24:10–13. Rules about collateral
Deuteronomy 24:17. Don't take collateral from widows.

▶ Collateral damage *(casualties, damages)*

Unintentional damage as a result of a situation (usually in a military setting)
Judges 11:29–40. The harm of a vow

Judges 21. Death of women as a result of war with Benjamin

2 Samuel 4:4. Crippled as a result of bad news

▶ Color(s) *(hue, shade)*

Specific colors mentioned in the Bible, some of which are symbolic

Exodus 24:9–10. Sapphire blue

Exodus 26. Colors used for the tabernacle

Exodus 28:15. Breastplate colors

1 Chronicles 29:2. Colors in the temple

Ezekiel 17:2–3. Riddle of the colorful eagle

▶ Comfort *(reassurance, relieve, soothe)*

To soothe in a time of affliction

Ruth 2:13. The comfort of Boaz

Psalm 71:21. Built up and comforted

Isaiah 12:1. Comforted by God

Isaiah 28:12. A place of comfort

Isaiah 40:1–2. Comfort my people

Isaiah 61:2. The comfort of God's chosen servant

2 Corinthians 1:3–7. The God of comfort

▶ Comforter(s) *(advocate, helper, Holy Spirit)*

One who offers comfort; a name for God or the Holy Spirit

Ecclesiastes 4:1. No comforter

Jeremiah 8:18. A Comforter in sorrow

Lamentations 1:16. A distant comforter

John 14:26. A comforting helper

▶ Commandment(s) *(law, regulation, Ten Commandments)*

A law or order; one of the Ten Commandments

Exodus 20:1–17. The Ten Commandments

Joshua 22:5. Follow the commands.

Matthew 22:37–40. The greatest commandment

Luke 23:56. Obeying the Sabbath commandment

Romans 7:7–13. What the commandments show

Ephesians 6:2–3. A commandment with a promise

▶ Commemorate *(see Memorial)*

▶ Commerce *(business, selling, trade)*

The buying and selling of goods

Genesis 23. Abraham buys a tomb.

Ruth 4. Boaz conducts business.

2 Samuel 24:19–25. David buys a threshing floor.

1 Kings 10:22. The king's commerce

Ezekiel 27:17, 33. Tarshish commerce

▶ Commission *(assign, hire, order)*

Granting power or authority to carry out a task

Numbers 27:18–20. Joshua is commissioned.

Deuteronomy 3:28. Reminded to commission

Matthew 28:19. The Great Commission

Acts 26:12. Paul's old commission

Colossians 1:25–26. Paul's new commission

▶ Commitment *(pledge, promise, vow)*

Something pledged, for instance, an engagement or a vow; being bound to someone emotionally or intellectually

Joshua 24:27. A stone of commitment

Jeremiah 30:22. A statement of commitment

Jeremiah 31:36–37. God's commitment to his people

John 6:66. Lack of commitment

Romans 12:1–2. Actions of commitment

▶ Committees *(board, team, working group)*

A group of people delegated for a particular function

Numbers 16. A rebellious committee

Acts 6. Committee to help Greek widows
Acts 15. Decided by committee
Acts 25:12. Festus's advisory committee

▸ Common sense *(good judgment)*

Having or exhibiting native good judgment
Job 12:24. Common sense taken away
Proverbs 12:15, 21. Common sense proverbs
Proverbs 15:5. How to show good sense
Proverbs 17:18. Lacking common sense
Proverbs 19:8. It's common sense to love yourself.
Micah 6:8. A common sense approach to life
Romans 1:20. Belief in God is simply common sense.

▸ Common-law wife *(see Concubine[s])*

▸ Communication *(announcement, message, speech)*

The exchange of thoughts, messages, or information
Genesis 34:6. Communicating to settle a problem
Exodus 20:22. What Moses was to communicate to the Israelites
Deuteronomy 6:7. Communicating God's laws
Matthew 6:9–15. Communicating with God
2 Timothy 4:2. Communicate the gospel

▸ Communion *(see Lord's Supper)*

▸ Community *(body, fellowship, group)*

A group of people living in the same locality
Exodus 12:3–11. Tell the whole community.
Exodus 16:1. Moving a community
Exodus 35:20–21. Community contributions
2 Chronicles 31:18. Those the community depend on
Jeremiah 30:20. An established community

▸ Companionship *(see Friendship; Husband[s]; Wife[ves])*

▸ Comparison(s) *(assessment, contrast, evaluation)*

Comparing or evaluating; estimating the similarities or differences
Job 28:17–18. No comparison
Job 39:13. Wings of an ostrich can't compare with a stork.
Psalm 86:8. God is incomparable.
Psalm 89:6. God is incomparable.
Proverbs 8:11. Nothing compares with wisdom.
Romans 5:15–16. No comparison between grace and sin

▸ Compassion *(concern, kindness, sympathy)*

Deep awareness of the suffering of another
Exodus 33:19. God's compassion
Deuteronomy 13:17. God will have compassion.
Judges 2:18. Moved to compassion
1 Kings 3:26. A mother's compassion
Matthew 9:36. Jesus' compassion

▸ Compatibility *(attuned, like-mindedness, well-suited)*

The capability of existing together in harmony
1 Samuel 13:14. A heart compatible with God's
2 Corinthians 6:15. Incompatibility
1 Thessalonians 5:13. Peace: the secret to compatibility
1 Peter 3:8. How to be compatible

▸ Compensation *(see Wages)*

▸ Competition *(contest, rivalry, struggle, war)*

A contest between rivals
Genesis 30. Competition for having children
1 Kings 18:22–24. Competition on Carmel
Jeremiah 12:5. How can you compete?
1 Corinthians 9:24–27. Compete to win.

▶ Complacency *(self-satisfaction)*

Contented to a fault; self-satisfied and unconcerned

Proverbs 1:32. Complacency of fools
Isaiah 32:9, 11. Complacent women
Ezekiel 30:9. Frightened out of complacency
Amos 6:1. Complacency in Zion
Zephaniah 1:12–13. Consequences for complacency

▶ Complaining *(see Grumbling)*

▶ Complete *(finished, full, total, whole)*

Having all the necessary parts, components, or steps; bringing to a finish

Deuteronomy 16:15. Complete joy
Esther 2:12. Completing a beauty treatment
Zechariah 4:9. Zerubbabel will complete the temple.
Luke 6:49. Complete destruction
Luke 14:28. Be sure you can complete a task.
John 15:11. Having Jesus' complete joy
Acts 20:24. Paul wants to complete his mission.

▶ Compliment *(admiration, affirmation, praise)*

An expression of praise, admiration, or gratitude

Genesis 12:10–11. Abraham compliments Sarai.
Ruth 2:11–12. Boaz compliments Ruth.
1 Kings 10:1–9. The queen of Sheba compliments Solomon.
Song of Songs 1:10, 16. Compliment for a bride and groom
Luke 7:9. Jesus compliments the faith of a centurion.

▶ Composure *(calm, poise, self-possession)*

A calm or tranquil state of mind

1 Samuel 25:17–19. Abigail keeps her composure in the face of death threats.
Proverbs 15:1. Why it's best to keep one's composure
Isaiah 7:3–4. Isaiah tells Ahaz to keep his composure.
Isaiah 26:3. The secret to keeping one's composure

▶ Comprehension *(see Understanding)*

▶ Compromise *(conciliation, give and take, negotiate)*

A settlement of differences in which each side makes concessions; a settlement to something pejorative or detrimental

Genesis 13:8–9. Abram and Lot compromise
Luke 12:58. Compromise before court
2 Corinthians 4:2. Paul refuses to compromise.
James 4:4. Compromising behavior
1 John 2:15. John warns against compromising.

▶ Compulsive behavior *(habits, obsession, uncontrollable)*

Behavior patterns governed by compulsion

Mark 5:5. Compulsive behavior of a demon-possessed man
Romans 7:18–20. Compulsive sin
2 Corinthians 12:6–9. Paul's compulsion

▶ Comrades *(see Friendship)*

▶ Conceit *(see Pride)*

▶ Concubine(s) *(common-law wives, secondary wives)*

A woman contracted to a man as a secondary wife

Genesis 22:24. Nahor's concubine
Genesis 35:22. Jacob's (Israel's) concubine
Judges 8:30–31. Gideon's concubine
2 Samuel 3:7. Saul's concubine
1 Kings 11:3. Solomon's concubines
1 Chronicles 1:32. Abraham's concubine

▶ Condemn/Condemnation *(criticize, denounce, disapprove)*

To express strong disapproval of; to find someone guilty

Job 9:20. Self-condemnation
Job 40:8. Condemning God
Psalm 109:31. Condemned to death
Matthew 12:42. Condemned by the queen from the south
Romans 3:8. They are condemned.
Romans 8:1. No condemnation

▶ Condition *(circumstance, situation, state)*

State of being

Genesis 34:15. On one condition
1 Samuel 11:2. Compromising condition
Proverbs 27:23. Condition of a flock
Matthew 12:45. A bad condition
John 5:6. Do you want to change your condition?

▶ Condolences *(commiseration, pity)*

A formal declaration of sympathy with a person who has experienced grief or misfortune

2 Samuel 10:1–2. David's condolences
2 Kings 20:12. King Merodach's condolences
Job 2:11. Condolences of Job's friends
John 11:19. Condolences upon the death of Lazarus

▶ Conduct *(behavior, manner, ways)*

To comport oneself in a specific way

Esther 1:17–18. The queen's conduct
Job 21:31. Conduct of the wicked
Proverbs 20:11. A child's conduct
Jeremiah 4:18. Israel's conduct
Jeremiah 32:19. God sees the conduct of Adam's descendants.

▶ Confession *(admission of guilt, acknowledgment)*

To admit a wrongdoing; to acknowledge faith

Leviticus 5:5. If you're guilty, confess.
Numbers 5:5–7. Confess your sin.
Nehemiah 1:6. Nehemiah confesses.
Romans 10:9. Confession of faith
Philippians 2:10–11. Confession about Jesus
1 John 1:9. Confess sins.

▶ Confidence *(assurance, belief)*

Trust or faith in a person or thing

2 Kings 18:19. Hezekiah's confidence questioned
Nehemiah 6:16. Self-confidence of enemies
Psalm 71:5. My confidence
Proverbs 3:26. Your confidence
Micah 7:5. An expression of woe
2 Corinthians 3:4. Confidence from Christ

▶ Confirmation *(authentication, proof, verification)*

Something that confirms or verifies

Genesis 17:2. God provides confirmation.
Deuteronomy 29:13. Confirming that God is God
1 Kings 1:14. Confirmation from the prophet Nathan
Daniel 9:27. Confirmation of the Messiah
Acts 15:27. Confirmation by Judas and Silas

▶ Conflict *(argument, disagreement, quarrel)*

Open or prolonged fighting; a battle or war

2 Samuel 2:14–17. Conflict between Abner and Joab
Habakkuk 1:3. Conflict abounds.
2 Corinthians 7:5. Conflicts
Galatians 5:17. Conflict between the corrupt nature and the spiritual nature
Philippians 4:2. Conflict between Euodia and Syntyche
3 John 9–10. Conflict between John and Diotrephes

▶ Conformity *(agreement, conventionality, submission)*

Action or behavior that corresponds with customs, rules, or styles

Romans 12:2. Avoid conformity.
Ephesians 2:1–2. You once conformed.
Colossians 2:8, 20. Encouraged to conform
1 Peter 1:14. An apostle's advice about conformity

▶ Confrontation *(argument, conflict, disagreement)*

A meeting face-to-face in order to confront someone; discord or a clash of opinions
Exodus 8:20–21. Confronting Pharaoh
1 Samuel 12:7. Samuel confronts the people of Israel.
Job 38:1–2. God confronts Job.
Psalm 17:13. A wish for confrontation
Matthew 18:15–17. Rules for confrontation

▶ Confusion *(bewilderment, perplexity, misunderstanding)*

The state of being confused; a disturbed mental state
Genesis 11:6–7. Language confusion
Exodus 14:24. An army in confusion
Deuteronomy 28:28. Confusion God allows
Joshua 10:10. Confusion at Gibeon
1 Samuel 14:20. Confusion among the Philistines

▶ Congregation *(flock, parishioners, worshipers)*

A body of assembled people, especially for religious worship
Leviticus 4:13–14. Shared guilt of a congregation
Leviticus 8:3. Gathering the congregation
Psalm 22:22. Praise within the congregation
Acts 13:43. Dismissing the congregation
Hebrews 2:11–12. Jesus repeats the call to praise God within the congregation.

▶ Conqueror(s) *(defeater, overcomer, subjugator, vanquisher)*

One who overcomes by force of arms
2 Kings 25. Arrival of the conquerors
Isaiah 14:12. Fall of a conqueror
Isaiah 49:24. Prisoners of conquerors
Micah 1:15. God will send a conqueror.
Romans 8:37. More than conquerors

▶ Conquest *(capture, invasion, takeover)*

The act of conquering
Judges 3:8. Conquest of Cushan
Judges 6:2–4. Conquest of Midian
Amos 6:13. Conquest of Lo Debar
Revelation 6:2. A rider bent on conquest

▶ Conscience *(ethics, principles, scruples)*

Awareness of a moral or ethical aspect to one's conduct
Genesis 20:5–6. Abimelech's conscience
1 Samuel 24:4–5. David's conscience
1 Samuel 25:30–31. Abigail reminds David of his conscience.
Job 27:6. Not accused by conscience
1 Corinthians 4:4. A clear conscience

▶ Consecrate *(make holy, sanctify, set apart)*

To declare or set apart as sacred
Exodus 19:10. Set yourselves apart.
Exodus 28:38. Consecrated gifts
Exodus 29:27. Set this apart.
Leviticus 8:11. Consecrated altar and utensils
Leviticus 16:19. Consecrated altar and utensils
Numbers 6:11. Consecrated head

▶ Consensus *(agreement, harmony)*

A view or stance reached by the whole group
Deuteronomy 27:15. Group consensus
1 Samuel 8:4–5. Consensus of the people
2 Chronicles 18:12. A consensus demanded
Nehemiah 10:30. Reaching a consensus about intermarriage
1 Corinthians 1:10. A consensus encouraged

▶ Consent *(assent, blessing, permission)*

To give assent as to the proposal of another

Genesis 34:8. Hamor seeks Jacob's consent to a marriage between Shechem and Dinah.
Job 39:9. Will the wild ox consent?
Hosea 8:4. Israel fails to seek God's consent.
1 Corinthians 7:5. Mutual consent
Philemon 14. Seeking Philemon's consent

▶ Conservation *(maintenance, preservation)*

The controlled use of and systemic protection of natural resources, particularly forests
Genesis 2:15. Adam appointed as conservator of Eden
Leviticus 19:23–25. Controlled use of fruit trees
Deuteronomy 20:19. Conservation law in a time of war

▶ Consideration *(contemplation, deliberation, thought)*

Careful thought
1 Samuel 26:21. Saul considers his behavior.
1 Kings 16:31. Ahab's lack of careful consideration
Job 1:8. For Satan's consideration: Job
Psalm 119:59. Considering one's life
Matthew 1:20. Joseph considers the matter of Mary's pregnancy.

▶ Consistency *(constancy, dependability, steadiness)*

Agreement or coherence; reliability or uniformity of results or events
Nehemiah 5:9. Nehemiah pleads for consistent behavior.
Luke 16:13. Inconsistent service
Romans 14:22. Just be consistent.
1 Corinthians 10:21. Can't be consistent

▶ Conspiracy(ies) *(plot, scheme, secret plan)*

Agreeing with someone to perform an illegal or subversive act
2 Samuel 15:12. Absalom's conspiracy
2 Kings 15:15. Shallum's conspiracy
Esther 2:21. The conspiracy of Bigthan and Teresh
Psalm 64:2. Hide me from conspiracies.
Isaiah 8:11–12. Don't call everything a conspiracy.
Jeremiah 11:9. Conspiracy in Judah

▶ Constellation(s) *(stars)*

Arbitrary formation of stars perceived as a figure or a design
Job 9:9. Creator of the constellations
Job 38:31–32. Connector of the constellations
Amos 5:8. God made the constellations.

▶ Contamination *(contagion, infectivity, pollution)*

The state of being contaminated or made impure
Leviticus 13:49–59. Contamination in clothing
2 Corinthians 6:17. Avoid that which contaminates.
2 Corinthians 7:1. Cleanse self from contaminants
James 1:27. Avoid contamination by the world.

▶ Contemplate *(see Meditate/ Meditation)*

▶ Contempt *(condescension, derision, disdain)*

Disparaging or haughty disdain
Leviticus 22:9. Treated with contempt
Numbers 14:11, 23. Israel's contempt for God
Numbers 16:30. Consequences of treating God with contempt
Deuteronomy 17:12. Consequences of treating leaders with contempt
Psalm 31:18. Contempt of the wicked.
Proverbs 18:3. Contempt comes with the territory

▶ Contentment *(ease, satisfaction)*

The state of being satisfied; content
Joshua 7:7. Joshua bewails a lack of contentment.

Proverbs 19:23. Fear of the Lord brings contentment.
Ecclesiastes 4:8. Not content with wealth
Philippians 4:11–12. Paul's contentment
Hebrews 13:5. Be content

▶ Contract *(binding agreement, pact, treaty)*

An agreement between two or more parties enforceable by law
Genesis 21:27. Abraham contracts with Abimelech.
Genesis 26:26–31. Isaac contracts with Abimelech.
1 Kings 5:8–11. Solomon's contract with Hiram
Isaiah 16:14. Moab's contracts
Isaiah 21:16. Kedar's contracts

▶ Contrast *(difference, disparity, dissimilarity)*

To set in opposition in order to show or emphasize differences
Proverbs 15:13. Joyful heart and heartache
Proverbs 15:20. Wise and foolish sons
Proverbs 16:8. Honest acquisition versus unjust gain
Proverbs 17:1. Dry bread versus a family feast
John 1:5; 3:19. Light and dark

▶ Contrite/Contrition *(remorseful, repentant, sorrow)*

Sincere remorse for wrongdoing
Psalm 51:17. Contrite heart
Isaiah 57:14–15. Metaphor for contrition
Isaiah 66:2. God notices contrition.

▶ Controversy *(argument, debate, disagreement)*

A public dispute
Exodus 4:24–25. Controversy over circumcision
Joshua 9:15–16, 18. A controversial decision
1 Samuel 25:10–11. Nabal's controversial decision
2 Samuel 6:20. Michal's controversial stance
Acts 10–11. Peter stirs up controversy by visiting Gentiles.

▶ Conversation *(discussion, talk)*

A spoken exchange of thoughts and opinions
Exodus 13:9–10. Passover: part of your conversation
Numbers 12:8. God and Moses conversed.
1 Samuel 19:7. Conversation between Saul and Jonathan
Jeremiah 38:24, 27. Secret conversation
Colossians 4:6. Season your conversation.

▶ Conversion *(born again, change, renewal)*

Adopting a new religion, faith, or belief
Acts 2:41. Three thousand converted
Acts 8:26–39. An Ethiopian's conversion
Acts 9. Saul's conversion
Acts 10. Cornelius and his household are converted.
Acts 13:16. Paul addresses converts to Judaism.
Acts 16:29–33. A Philippian jailer's conversion
Acts 17:4, 17. Converted to Judaism

▶ Conviction *(awareness, knowledge of guilt, certainty)*

An awareness that one is guilty of a crime; the state of being convinced; finding someone guilty of a crime
Proverbs 24:25. Convicting the guilty
John 8:46. Can anyone convict Jesus?
John 16:8–9. Holy Spirit convicts
1 Thessalonians 1:5. Deep conviction
Jude 15. The Lord convicts

▶ Convince *(encourage, persuade, talk into)*

To bring to firm belief by the use of an argument or evidence
Acts 16:15. Lydia convinces Paul.
Acts 19:8. Speaking boldly to convince
Acts 28:23. Trying to convince the Jews
2 Timothy 1:5, 12. Paul is convinced.
Hebrews 6:9. Better things in store: we are convinced.

▶ Convocation *(holy assembly)*

An assembly of the clergy and laity

Leviticus 23:4, 37. Assigned holy assemblies
Numbers 10:7. Fanfare at the convocation
Numbers 29:1, 7, 35. Hold these convocations.
Deuteronomy 9:10. Recalling the convocation at Mount Sinai

▶ Cooking *(food preparation)*

Preparing food
Genesis 18:7. A meal cooked for special guests
Genesis 25:29–30. Jacob cooks
Genesis 27:14. Rebekah cooks a meal to deceive Isaac.
Jeremiah 1:13. Jeremiah's vision of a boiling pot
Ezekiel 4:9. Cooking as an example
Ezekiel 24:3–5. Cooking metaphor

▶ Cooperation *(assistance, collaboration, support)*

Working together toward a common end
Exodus 36. Cooperating to build the tabernacle and its utensils
2 Chronicles 24. Cooperating to repair the temple
Nehemiah 2:17–18. Calling for cooperation to rebuild the wall of Jerusalem
Ecclesiastes 4:9. Better to cooperate
3 John 8. We must cooperate.

▶ Copper *(ore, tools, utensils, weapons)*

Malleable metallic element used for making utensils and weapons
Deuteronomy 8:9. Mining for copper
Job 28:1–2. Melting rocks for copper
Ezekiel 22:17–18, 20. Smelted copper
Ezekiel 24:11. Copper pot
Matthew 10:9. Copper coins

▶ Corban *(gift, offering)*

Greek word that means "given"; a vow declaring an item as dedicated to God
Exodus 20:12. Why *corban* violates this commandment
Numbers 30:1–2. Justification for *corban*
Mark 7:11–12. Jesus rebukes the Pharisees about *corban* items.

▶ Cornerstone *(bridging stone, Jesus)*

Stone at the corner of a building that unites two intersecting walls; a metaphor for Jesus
Job 38:6–7. Cornerstone of creation
Isaiah 28:16. A precious cornerstone
Jeremiah 51:26. No cornerstones to be found
Zechariah 10:4. Judah's cornerstone
Ephesians 2:20–21. Jesus is the cornerstone.
1 Peter 2:6–8. The stone rejected becomes the cornerstone.

▶ Coronation *(crowning)*

The act of crowning a sovereign
1 Samuel 10. Saul's coronation
2 Samuel 5:3–4. David's coronation
1 Kings 1:38–40. Solomon's coronation
2 Kings 11:12. Joash's coronation
1 Chronicles 12:38–39. Feast in celebration of David's coronation

▶ Corporal punishment *(discipline, spanking)*

Pain used as a disciplinary measure
Proverbs 13:24. Refusing to spank
Proverbs 22:15. Spanking and foolishness
Proverbs 23:13–14. Spanking and discipline
Proverbs 29:15. Wisdom through spanking

▶ Corpse *(cadaver)*

A dead body
Leviticus 22:4. Skin disease and touching a corpse
Judges 14:9. Honey from a lion's corpse
2 Kings 9:37. Jezebel's corpse
Isaiah 14:19. Corpse metaphor of rejection
Isaiah 26:19. Corpses will rise.
Isaiah 34:2–3. The stench of corpses
Isaiah 37:36. Many, many corpses
Jeremiah 34:19–20. Corpses for food for wild animals
John 11:39. The corpse of Lazarus

▶ Correction *(discipline, modification)*

Disciplinary measures or punishment intended to rehabilitate or improve

Leviticus 26:23–24. God's corrective measures

Job 36:10. Corrective warnings

Proverbs 5:12. Despising correction

Proverbs 10:17. Ignoring correction

Proverbs 12:1. Loving correction

▶ Correspondence *(communication, letters, messages)*

Communication by the exchange of letters

2 Kings 20:12. Letters from Babylon

Ezra 4:6–22. Letters to and from Artaxerxes

Jeremiah 29:1. Jeremiah's letter to the captives in Babylon

Romans 1:1. Letter from Paul to the Roman believers

1 Corinthians 1:1. Letter from Paul to the Corinthian believers

Galatians 1:1–2. Letter from Paul to the believers in Galatia

▶ Corruption *(bribery, death, dishonesty, distortion)*

The state of being corrupt

2 Kings 23:13. The Hill of Corruption

Ezra 9:11. Corrupting the land

Isaiah 1:4. A corrupt nation

Hosea 9:9. Deep into corruption

▶ Cosmetics *(eye shadow, makeup, women)*

Preparations designed to beautify the body

2 Kings 9:30. Jezebel applies eye shadow.

Jeremiah 4:30. Judah's cosmetics

Ezekiel 23:40. Metaphorical makeup

1 Peter 3:3. Beauty does not come from makeup

▶ Cost(s) *(charge, price, rate)*

An amount paid or requirement in payment of a debt or purchase

Joshua 6:26. Frightening cost in the curse on Jericho

2 Samuel 24:24. David insists on paying the cost of the threshing floor.

1 Chronicles 12:19. A high cost

Proverbs 7:23. The cost of following the adulterous woman

Isaiah 55:1. No cost

Luke 14:28, 33. Count the cost of following Jesus.

▶ Counsel *(advice, direction, guidance)*

Advice given as a result of consultation; a plan of action or behavior

2 Samuel 15:31. Unwise counsel

2 Chronicles 18:4. Seeking God's counsel

2 Chronicles 22:5. Following bad counsel

2 Chronicles 25:16. Consequences of avoiding wise counsel

Job 12:13. Wise counsel comes from God.

Job 38:2. Who darkens God's counsel?

▶ Counselor *(advocate, Holy Spirit, lawyer)*

Person who counsels; another name for the Holy Spirit

2 Samuel 15:12. David's counselor

1 Chronicles 26:14. A chosen counselor

1 Chronicles 27:32. A chosen counselor

John 14:16, 26. Sending the Counselor

John 15:26. When the Counselor comes

▶ Coups *(overthrow, rebellion, takeover)*

Brilliantly executed stratagem; the prize is usually a kingdom

2 Samuel 15–18. Absalom's failed coup

2 Kings 9–10. Jehu's successful coup

2 Kings 11–12. Jehoiada's coup

2 Chronicles 22:10–23:21. Jehoiada's coup on behalf of Joash

▶ Courage *(bravery, confidence, valor)*

Quality of mind that enables one to face danger or fear with resolution

Joshua 1:1–9. God tells Joshua to have courage.

2 Samuel 4:1. Ishbosheth loses courage.

Ezekiel 22:14. Will Jerusalem have courage?

1 Corinthians 16:13. Be courageous.
Hebrews 3:6. Be courageous.

▸ Courts *(judges, temple courts)*

Open ground partially enclosed by walls; person or body of persons whose task is to hear and render decisions on cases submitted
Exodus 21:22. The court decides.
2 Kings 23:11. In the temple courtyard
1 Chronicles 26:18. Temple courts
Job 11:10. God's court
Matthew 5:25. Settle before going to court.
James 2:6. Dragged into court

▸ Courtship *(love)*

The period of courting
Genesis 29. Jacob courts Rachel.
Judges 14:1–2. How Samson courted
Ruth 3. Courtship of Ruth and Boaz
Song of Songs 4:1. Courting phrases

▸ Covenant *(agreement, contract, promise)*

A binding agreement based on obligations; usually between God and people
Exodus 6:2–4. God remembers His covenant with the patriarchs.
Exodus 34:10. A covenant made
Leviticus 2:13. Salt of God's covenant
Deuteronomy 7:12. If Israel is faithful, God will keep His covenant.
2 Kings 23:3. A covenant renewed
1 Chronicles 16:15. A covenant forever

▸ Covet *(crave, desire, yearn for)*

Blameworthy desire for what someone else has
Exodus 20:17. You shall not covet.
Deuteronomy 7:25. Don't covet idols of other nations.
Romans 7:7. Paul reviews the commandment against coveting.
Romans 13:9. Instead of coveting, love.
James 4:2. Coveting and murder

▸ Cowards *(fearful, deserters)*

Those who show cowardice
Genesis 3. Adam shows cowardice.
Genesis 12:10–13. Abram shows cowardice.
Joshua 7:4–5. Cowardice at Ai
1 Samuel 17:11. Saul and his army
Psalm 78:9. Cowardice of the men of Ephraim
Matthew 8:25–26. Cowardice during a storm
John 9:21–22. Cowardice of the parents of the man born blind

▸ Craftsman *(artisan, skilled worker)*

A man who practices a craft with great skill
Genesis 4:22. Tubalcain—a tool maker
Exodus 35:30–35. Bezalel—master artist
1 Kings 7:14. Hiram—skilled craftsman
1 Chronicles 4:14. Valley of Craftsmen
Proverbs 8:29–30. Wisdom—a master craftsman
1 Corinthians 3:10. Paul—a skilled craftsman at sharing the gospel

▸ Craftsmanship *(artistry, skill)*

Work produced by skilled labor
Genesis 1:31. God is pleased with His craftsmanship.
Exodus 36:8–9. Craftsmanship at work
1 Chronicles 22:15–16. Craftsmanship encouraged
2 Chronicles 4:18. Craftsmanship for the temple
Hosea 13:2. Craftsmanship for idols

▸ Cravings *(hunger, passion, thirst)*

To have an intense desire for something
Numbers 11:4. Craving for food other than manna
Job 20:20. The wicked have no respite from cravings.
Psalm 106:14. Unreasonable desire
Proverbs 10:3. Unreasonable desire
1 John 2:16. Some cravings come from the world.

▸ Creation *(conception, formation, establishment)*

The world and all the creatures and things in it; the act of making the world
Genesis 1–2. The creation story

Job 38:4–5. God created the earth.
Matthew 13:34–35. Truth hidden since creation
Romans 1:20. God's qualities seen since the creation of the world
Romans 8:19–23. All creation waits for the second coming.
2 Corinthians 5:17. A new creation
Ephesians 1:4. Chosen before creation

▶ Creativity *(imagination, inventiveness, vision)*

The ability to create
Genesis 1–2. God is creative.
Exodus 31:1–5. Bezalel is creative.
Deuteronomy 4:32. Heavens show God's creativity.
Psalm 33:3. Be creative in praise.
Hebrews 13:21. God equips us to be creative.

▶ Creator *(Author, God, Maker of heaven and earth)*

One who creates; usually used in reference to God
Genesis 14:19, 22. God the Creator
Ecclesiastes 12. Remember your Creator.
Isaiah 27:11. For the rebellious, the Creator is pitiless.
Isaiah 40:28. Untiring Creator
Matthew 19:4–5. Male and female made by the Creator

▶ Creature(s) *(being, mortal, person)*

Something created
Genesis 1:28. Rule over every living creature.
Genesis 6:17–20. Creatures saved in the flood
Genesis 9:2. Creatures under the control of people
Leviticus 11. Creatures under the control of people
Psalm 136:25. God gives food to his creatures.
Ezekiel 1. Ezekiel's vision of the four living creatures

▶ Credentials *(qualifications, testimonial)*

That which entitles one to confidence, credit, or authority
Exodus 34:6–7. God's credentials
Ruth 2:1. Boaz's credentials
Matthew 16:13–16. Jesus' credentials
John 16:13–15. Holy Spirit's credentials
Philippians 3:4–6. Paul's ministry credentials

▶ Credibility *(authority, reliability, trustworthiness)*

The quality or capability of eliciting belief
Deuteronomy 19:15. Two witnesses required for credibility.
John 5:34–36. Jesus does not rely on humans for credibility.
John 8. Jesus' credibility questioned
Acts 2:12–41. The credibility of the apostles and Christ
2 Corinthians 6. Paul's credibility as a minister

▶ Credit *(acknowledgment, recognition)*

Official certification or recognition; approval for an act; influence based on the good opinion of others
Genesis 15:6. Belief credited to Abram.
Esther 2:22. Esther credits Mordecai for the discovery of a plot against Xerxes.
Luke 6:32. No credit given for loving those who love you
Romans 4:24. Faith credited to us
1 Peter 2:20. Credit deserved?

▶ Creed *(article of faith)*

A formal statement of religious belief
Deuteronomy 6:4–9. The Shema
1 Kings 18:39. Declaring that God is God.
Acts 16:31. A simple creed
1 Corinthians 15:3–8. Paul's creed
Philippians 2:6–11. Creed affirming Jesus is God

▶ Cremation *(death custom)*

Incinerating a corpse
Genesis 38:24. Cremation as an execution
Leviticus 20:14. Cremate them.
Numbers 16:35. God chooses to cremate.
Joshua 7:25. Cremation of Achan and his family

1 Samuel 31:11–12. Cremation of Saul and his sons

Amos 2:1. Anger of God due to cremation

▶ Crime solvers *(detective, police)*

Those who took an active part in solving crime or administering justice

Joshua 7. Joshua

1 Samuel 15. Samuel

1 Kings 3:16–28. Solomon

1 Kings 21. God

Acts 5:1–11. Peter

▶ Crime(s) *(law breaking, felony, offense, sin)*

An act committed in violation of a law

Genesis 31:36. What is Jacob's crime?

Deuteronomy 19:16. Witnesses to a crime

1 Samuel 20:1. What is David's crime?

Psalm 69:27. The crimes of the persecutor

Ecclesiastes 8:11–12. Encouraged to commit crimes?

Matthew 27:23. What is Jesus' crime?

▶ Criminal(s) *(felon, offender, sinner)*

One who commits a crime

Exodus 2:11–15. Moses

2 Samuel 11. David

Matthew 27:38. Jesus is crucified with two criminals.

John 18:30. The Jews insist that Jesus is a criminal.

1 Peter 4:15–16. No suffering for being a criminal.

▶ Crises *(disasters, predicaments)*

Crucial or decisive points or situations; an emotionally stressful event or a traumatic change in a person's life

Numbers 14. Crisis point after the return of the twelve spies

1 Samuel 25. Crisis averted in David's life

1 Kings 19. Elijah in crisis

Psalm 77. A soul in crisis

1 Corinthians 7:26. Corinthian crisis

▶ Criticism *(censure, condemnation, disapproval)*

Critical comment or judgment

Genesis 37:10. Joseph is criticized for his dream.

Numbers 12:1–2, 8. Miriam and Aaron's criticism

Numbers 21:4–5. The criticism of the people of Israel

2 Samuel 6:20. Michal's criticism

Romans 14:3–4. Don't criticize.

2 Corinthians 8:20. Avoiding criticism

▶ Crocodile *(see Leviathan)*

▶ Crooked *(bent, curved, twisted)*

Marked by bends, curves, or angles

2 Samuel 22:27. How God reveals himself to the crooked

Psalm 125:5. When people become crooked

Proverbs 2:12, 14–15. Crooked paths

Proverbs 8:8. There is nothing crooked in wisdom.

Isaiah 59:8. Crooked paths of rebellious people

Luke 3:5. Crooked ways made straight

▶ Cross, the *(crucifixion of Christ)*

The instrument upon which Jesus was crucified; the central point of Christianity

Mark 8:34. Pick up your cross.

Mark 15:29–30. Come down from the cross!

1 Corinthians 1:17–18. Message of the cross

Galatians 5:11. Offense of the cross

Galatians 6:12–14. Boasting in the cross

Colossians 2:14. What Christ did on the cross

Hebrews 12:2. Enduring death on the cross

▶ Crowds *(groups, multitude, people, populace)*

Large groups of people

Matthew 4:25. Large crowds follow Jesus.

Matthew 7:28. Jesus amazes the crowds.

Luke 3:7. Crowds of vipers?

John 7:12. Crowds are split about Jesus.

Acts 5:15–16. Crowds desire healing from Peter

Acts 8:6. Crowds listen to Philip.

▶ Crown *(honor, Christian's prize, wreath)*

The symbol of a king or queen's honor or office; metaphor for royalty

2 Samuel 1:10. Saul's crown

2 Samuel 12:29–30. Crown of the king of Rabbah

Esther 1:10–11. Vashti's crown

Proverbs 12:4. The crown of a husband

John 19:2. The crown of thorns

1 Corinthians 9:25. The believer's crown

James 1:12. The crown of life

▶ Crucifixion *(cross, death)*

Execution on a cross; the metaphor for the death of the old nature

Matthew 27:31–56. Jesus crucified

Mark 15:20–41. Mocked then crucified

Luke 23:33–49. Crucified at the place called The Skull

John 19:4–17. The people want Jesus crucified.

Acts 2:36. The crucified Lord

Romans 6:6. We also were crucified.

Galatians 2:19. I have been crucified.

▶ Cubit *(measurement)*

Measurement equal to the length of the forearm—from the tip of the middle finger to the elbow (about 17 to 22 inches)

Genesis 6:16. Measurements for the ark

Exodus 25:10. A chest two and a half cubits long

Exodus 26:13. Cubits of the tent curtains

1 Kings 7:23–24. Cubits used in making the temple furnishings

Ezekiel 40:5. Cubits of the temple wall

▶ Cults *(factions, sects)*

Religious sects considered to be extremists

Matthew 24:24. The false messiahs

Acts 15. The Judaizers

1 Timothy 6:20–21. Gnostics

▶ Culture *(civilization, social mores)*

The behavior patterns, beliefs, and institutions of society

Genesis 17:9–13. Circumcision is a necessity in the Jewish culture.

Deuteronomy 18:9. Don't adapt the culture of the other nations.

Matthew 5:10. Countercultural thinking of Jesus.

Matthew 6:2. Hypocrites hope to be seen in the synagogues

Luke 2:41. Passover—a part of the culture

John 4:9. Samaritans ostracized

▶ Cumin *(spice)*

A Mediterranean herb of the parsley family

Isaiah 28:24–25, 27. Beating black cumin

Matthew 23:23. Tithing cumin

▶ Cuneiform *(writing)*

Wedge-shaped characters used by the Sumerians, Akkadians, Assyrians, Babylonians, and Persians from 3500 BC until AD 75

Ezra 1:8. List written in cuneiform

Esther 10:1–2. Recorded in cuneiform

Daniel 1:4. Daniel would have learned cuneiform.

Daniel 4:1. Nebuchadnezzar would have used cuneiform.

▶ Cupbearer *(butler, wine steward)*

One who fills and distributes wine in a royal household

Genesis 40. Pharaoh's cupbearer

2 Chronicles 9:3–4. Solomon had cupbearers.

Nehemiah 2:1. Nehemiah was a cupbearer.

▶ Cups *(fortune-telling, goblets, metaphorical)*

Various types of cups used throughout the Bible

Genesis 44. Joseph's silver cup

Esther 1:7. Golden cups

Matthew 20:22. Jesus' cup of suffering

1 Corinthians 10:16. Cup of blessing

1 Corinthians 11:25. Cup of the new promise

▶ Curds *(cheese)*

Coagulating part of the milk used in cheese making

Genesis 18:8. Abraham serves curds.

Deuteronomy 32:14. A description of God's care for his people

2 Samuel 17:28–29. A description of God's care for his people

Isaiah 7:15, 22. Curds and honey

Ezekiel 34:3. Bad shepherds eat the curds, but neglect the flock

▶ Curiosity *(inquisitiveness, interest)*

A desire to know or learn

Genesis 3:6. Eve's curiosity led to sin.

Genesis 18:16–33. Abraham is curious about God's plans for Sodom and Gomorrah.

Genesis 32:29. Jacob is curious about the man with whom he wrestled.

1 Samuel 6:19. Curiosity led to death.

John 21:21. Peter is curious about John's future.

▶ Currency (see *Coin[s]; Money)*

▶ Curse(s) *(misfortune)*

The misfortune that came as the result of disobedience to one of God's commandments

Genesis 3:14. The snake is cursed.

Exodus 22:28. Never curse a leader.

Numbers 22. Balak tells Balaam to curse the Israelites.

Deuteronomy 28:15–68. Curses to come with sin

2 Kings 2:24. Elisha calls a curse upon mocking youths.

Nehemiah 10:29. An oath with a curse

▶ Curtain(s) *(drapery)*

Material which served as coverings and sectioning aids in the temple and tabernacle

Exodus 27:9–10. Curtains for the tabernacle court

Exodus 35:17. Curtains made by craftsmen

Leviticus 16:2. Curtains hide the ark of the covenant

Numbers 4:25–26. Gershonites in charge of the curtains

Matthew 27:51. Temple curtain tears at Jesus' death.

Hebrews 6:19–20. Jesus went behind the curtain for us.

▶ Customs *(mores, society, traditions)*

Practices followed by a people group

Leviticus 20:23. Customs of other nations

2 Kings 17:34. Following other customs

John 19:40. Burial customs

Acts 6:14. Stephen is accused of wanting customs changed.

Acts 21:21. Has Paul abandoned Jewish customs?

▶ Cyrus cylinder *(clay cylinder, cuneiform text)*

Document written by Cyrus the Great, the Persian king (now housed in the British Museum)

2 Chronicles 36:22–23. Scripture confirmed in the Cyrus cylinder

Ezra 6:10. Scripture inscribed on the Cyrus cylinder

Isaiah 44:23–45:8. Scripture confirmed on the Cyrus cylinder

▶ Dairy products *(cheese, curds, milk)*

Food produced from milk

Genesis 18:8. Abraham gives cheese to his guests.

Genesis 49:12. Milk comparison

Numbers 16:13–14. A land flowing with milk and honey

1 Samuel 17:17–18. Cheese for the captain

Job 10:10. Poured out like milk

▶ Damnation *(condemnation, eternal punishment, hell)*

Being condemned to eternal punishment

Psalm 88:11. Places of eternal punishment

Matthew 13:50. Cries of the condemned

Matthew 23:14. The greater damnation

2 Peter 2:4. Condemned angels

Revelation 20:15. Eternally condemned

▶ Dancing *(at feasts, in celebration, in worship)*

Rhythmic movement to music

Exodus 15:20. Dancing after the victory at the Red Sea

Exodus 32:19. Dancing while worshiping the golden calf

Judges 11:34. Jephthah's daughter dances.

2 Samuel 6:16. David dances.

Psalm 30:11. From sobbing to dancing

Matthew 14:6–7. The dance that led to John the Baptist's death

▶ Danger *(hazard, menace, threat)*

Exposure to harm or risk

1 Samuel 20:21. Signal for danger

Proverbs 14:25. Danger of a liar

Proverbs 27:12. Seeing danger

Matthew 8:28. Dangerous and demon-possessed

Luke 8:23. Disciples in danger

▶ Darkness *(absence of light, gloom, night)*

Lack of light; metaphor for sin

Genesis 1:2–6. Darkness in the beginning

Exodus 10:21–29. Plague of darkness

Deuteronomy 5:23. Voice out of the darkness

2 Samuel 22:29. The Lord turns darkness into light.

Matthew 6:23. Full of darkness

▶ Dating (see *Courtship*)

▶ Daughter(s) *(child, young woman)*

Female child; female descendant

Genesis 5:4. Daughters of Adam

Judges 11:35. Jephthah's daughter is caught in her father's vow.

Song of Songs 2:7. Advice to daughters of Jerusalem

Isaiah 16:2. Moab's daughters

Isaiah 43:6. Exiled sons and daughters

Joel 2:28. Daughters will prophesy.

Mark 5:21–43. Two daughters healed

Mark 6:3. Daughters of Mary and Joseph

▶ Daughter-in-law *(daughter by marriage)*

The wife of one's son

Genesis 6:18. Noah's daughters-in-law

Genesis 8:15–16. Leaving the ark

Genesis 46:5. Jacob's daughters-in-law

Ruth 1. Naomi's daughters-in-law

Hosea 4:13–14. Daughters-in-law of Israel

▶ Davidic covenant *(promise)*

Covenant made between God and King David

2 Samuel 7:12–16. The covenant

1 Kings 2:4. David remembers the covenant.

1 Kings 6:12–13. Solomon remembers God's covenant with David.

1 Kings 8:25. Solomon remembers God's covenant with David.

1 Kings 11:11–13. Although Solomon sins, God remembers his covenant with David.

D

▶ Dawn *(daybreak)*

When daylight first begins

Genesis 19:15. Destruction begins at dawn.

Genesis 32:24. Wrestling until dawn

Exodus 14:24. Panic before dawn

Judges 16:2. Murder at dawn

Nehemiah 4:21. Spears at dawn

Job 3:9–10. Job curses the dawn of the day of his birth.

Job 38:12–13. God questions Job about the dawn.

▶ Day *(daylight hours, daytime)*

Period of light between dawn and nightfall

Genesis 1. Creation of day

Exodus 16:23. A day of worship

Exodus 20:8–10. Remember the seventh day.

Leviticus 23:27. Day of Atonement

Numbers 14:14. How God led the Israelites by day

Joshua 10:13–14. The longest day ever

Matthew 4:2. Jesus fasted for 40 days.

▶ Day of Atonement *(see Atonement; Day)*

▶ Day of the Lord *(judgment)*

The time in which God judges the earth

Isaiah 13:5–22. Day of the Lord's anger

Lamentations 2:22. Day of the Lord's anger

Joel 2:1–11. The day of the Lord is coming.

Zephaniah 1–3. Day of the Lord

Malachi 4:5. Elijah to come before the terrible day of the Lord

▶ Deacon *(church leader)*

Cleric ranking below a priest in the Anglican or Catholic church; lay leader in the Protestant church who assists the minister

Acts 6:1–7. Seven men chosen as deacons

Romans 16:1. Phoebe the deacon

Colossians 4:7. Tychicus the deacon

1 Timothy 3:8–13. Deacon requirements

▶ Dead Sea *(lake, Salt Sea)*

Saltwater lake between Israel and Jordan

Genesis 14:3. Battle at the Dead Sea

Numbers 34:3–4. Boundary of Israel's land to the Dead Sea

Deuteronomy 3:17. The Sea of Plains

Joshua 3:15–16. Cutting off the flow of water all the way to the Dead Sea

2 Kings 14:25. Restoring land boundaries to the Dead Sea

▶ Dead Sea Scrolls *(manuscripts)*

Scrolls found in Khirbet, Qumran between 1947–1956.

Exodus. Most of Exodus was found among the Dead Sea Scrolls.

Numbers. Most of Numbers was found among the Dead Sea Scrolls.

1 Samuel 1:23–24. Scripture found in the Dead Sea Scrolls

Isaiah. One of the books found among the Dead Sea Scrolls

Jeremiah 42–49. Scripture found among the Dead Sea Scrolls

▶ Deafness *(hearing loss)*

Partial or complete inability to hear

Exodus 4:11. Unable to hear

Leviticus 19:14. Never curse the deaf.

Psalm 28:1. Don't turn a deaf ear.

Isaiah 29:18. The deaf will hear.

Matthew 11:4–5. Jesus heals the deaf.

Mark 7:32–35. Jesus heals a deaf-mute man.

▶ Death *(bereavement, loss, passing away)*

Termination of life

Genesis 5:5. Death of the first man

Genesis 23:1–2. Sarah's death

Judges 15:6. A revenge death

2 Samuel 8:2. Moabites put to death

Psalm 22:15. Dust of death

Psalm 23:4. Dark valley of death

Proverbs 16:25. Way of death

Romans 6:23. Payment for sin

▶ Death penalty *(law)*

A sentence of punishment by execution

Leviticus 20. Death penalty for crimes

Leviticus 24:16. Death penalty for cursing the Lord's name

Numbers 1:51. Death penalty for going near the tabernacle without authorization

Numbers 3:10. Death penalty for performing priestly duties

Numbers 15:32–36. Death penalty for gathering wood on the Sabbath

Numbers 25:5. Death penalty for worshiping Baal

Deuteronomy 19:6. Undeserved death penalty

John 8:3–5. Death penalty for adultery

▶ Deathbed words *(blessings, curses, promises)*

Words spoken just before a person dies

Genesis 48:21–49:33. Jacob/Israel's deathbed words

Genesis 50:24–25. Joseph's deathbed words

Deuteronomy 33. Moses' deathbed words

1 Kings 2:1–9. David's deathbed words

John 19:30. Jesus' deathbed words

▶ Debates *(arguments, discussions)*

Arguments engaged through the discussion of opposing views

Acts 15:1–35. Circumcision debate

Acts 17:15–34. Paul's debates in Athens

Acts 18:4. Paul debates in synagogue

Acts 19:8–9. Debates in Ephesus

Acts 25:20. King Agrippa discusses Paul's debate with Jewish leaders.

▶ Debauchery *(decadence, depravity, dissipation, sin)*

Extreme indulgence in sensual pleasures

Exodus 32:6. Idolatry and debauchery

Romans 13:13. Avoid debauchery.

2 Corinthians 12:20–21. Grieving over debauchery

Galatians 5:19. Acts of the sinful nature

Ephesians 5:18. Drunkenness leads to debauchery.

1 Peter 4:3. Past debauchery

▶ Debt *(arrears, balance due, liability)*

Something owed (money, goods, services)

Deuteronomy 15:3. Rules about collecting debts

1 Samuel 22:1–2. Those in debt went to David.

2 Kings 4:7. Elisha helps a widow pay her debt.

Matthew 18:23–35. Jesus' parable about forgiveness and debts

Luke 7:41–43. A parable about debt

Romans 13:8. Debt of love

▶ Decay *(decompose, fester, putrefy)*

Break down into composite parts; rot

Psalm 16:9–10. The body of the holy one will not decay in the grave.

Proverbs 12:4. Decay in the bones

Isaiah 5:24. Decay of the rebellious

Acts 2:25–27. Peter confirms that David's words were said about Jesus.

Acts 13:34. Jesus' body did not decay in the grave.

Romans 8:20–21. Creation set free from slavery to decay

▶ Deceit (see *Lying; Pretense*)

▶ Decision (see *Choice[s]*)

▶ Decorating *(beautifying, embellishing, furnishing)*

Furnishing or adorning something

Exodus 25:33–35. Adorning the lamp stand in the tabernacle

Exodus 39:32–43. Furnishing the tabernacle

1 Kings 6. Building and decorating the temple

1 Kings 7:40–42. More decorations for the temple

Matthew 23:29. Decorating monuments

D

▶ Decree *(command, law, order)*

An authoritative order having the force of law

Esther 1:13–22. How Xerxes made decrees

Esther 2:8. Enactment of Xerxes' decree

Esther 3:8. Haman lies about the Jews' disobedience of Xerxes' decrees.

Daniel 2:12–13. Death decree

Daniel 6:7–9. Darius's decree

▶ Dedication *(ceremony)*

A rite or ceremony of dedicating; also selfless devotion

1 Kings 8. Dedication of the temple

1 Kings 14:15. A wrong dedication

1 Kings 16:33. Poles dedicated to Asherah

Ezra 6:16. Dedication of the rebuilt temple

Nehemiah 3:1. Dedication of the rebuilt Sheep Gate

Nehemiah 12:27. Dedication of the rebuilt wall of Jerusalem

▶ Deeds *(actions, feats)*

A praiseworthy act or feat; also a document sealed as an instrument of bond, contract, or conveyance in regard to property

Deuteronomy 3:23–24. Deeds of God

Deuteronomy 34:12. Deeds of Moses

Ezra 9:13. Evil deeds

Psalm 17:7. Miraculous deeds

Psalm 20:6. Mighty deeds

Psalm 99:8. God punishes sinful deeds.

Isaiah 1:16. Get rid of evil deeds.

Jeremiah 32. Jeremiah signs a deed for a field.

▶ Deer *(doe, hind, stag)*

Hoofed ruminant of the *Cervidae* family

Deuteronomy 12:15. Deer meat?

Deuteronomy 14:4–5. Deer on the menu

Psalm 18:33. Feet like those of a deer

Psalm 42:1. The longing of a deer

Isaiah 35:6. Leaping like deer

Habakkuk 3:19. Walking like a deer

▶ Defeat *(crush, overpower)*

To win victory over

Genesis 14:14–15, 17. Defeating Lot's captors

Exodus 17:13. Defeat of the Amalekites, Part 1

Joshua 8:15–16. Pretending defeat at Ai

2 Samuel 1:1. Defeat of the Amalekites, Part 2

2 Samuel 2:17. Abner's defeat

1 Kings 5:2–3. Defeating David's enemies

▶ Defection *(abandonment, disloyalty, treason)*

Disowning allegiance to one's country and taking up residence in another; switching from one belief system to another

1 Samuel 27. David appears to defect.

John 17:12. Judas's defection

Jude 6. Defection of angels

▶ Defense *(guard, protection, security)*

The act of defending someone or something against attack

Exodus 2:15–17. Moses comes to the defense of the daughters of Jethro.

Psalm 18:18. The Lord's defense

Isaiah 22:7–8. Judah's defenses removed

Isaiah 34:8. In defense of Zion

Jeremiah 41:9. Cistern defense plan

▶ Defenseless *(exposed, unprotected, weak)*

Having no means of protection; vulnerable

Judges 3:13–15. Israel is defenseless against various enemies.

Judges 6:14–15. Gideon feels defenseless.

Psalm 116:6. Protector of the defenseless

Psalm 141:8. Left defenseless?

Jeremiah 4:31. Defenseless

▶ Defiant *(disobedient, insubordinate, rebellious)*

Full of resistance

Nehemiah 9:26. Israel's defiance
Isaiah 3:8. Defiance in the presence of God
Jeremiah 5:23. God's defiant people
Ezekiel 2:4. Ezekiel sent to a defiant people.

▶ Defile/Defilement *(unclean)*

To render ceremonially unclean
Exodus 20:25. Defiled altar
Leviticus 11:43. Defiled by what is eaten
Leviticus 18:20, 23. Defiled by an unlawful relationship
Leviticus 21:15. The offspring of a priest must not be defiled.
Numbers 18:32. Avoid defiled offerings.
Numbers 35:34. Do not defile the land.
2 Kings 23:16. Defiling the altar

▶ Degenerate *(corrupt, deteriorate, worsen)*

Sunk to a lower, more corrupt state; also someone immoral or perverted
Isaiah 2:9. Degenerate Israel
Isaiah 3:9. Degenerate Sodom
Jeremiah 2:21. A degenerate plant
Ezekiel 16:30. A degenerate heart

▶ Degradation *(deprivation, humiliation, squalor)*

Declining to a low, destitute, or demoralized state
Leviticus 19:29. Don't degrade a daughter.
Deuteronomy 25:2–3. Avoiding the degradation of a criminal
2 Samuel 6:21–22. David is willing to be degraded.
Ezekiel 16:25. Degradation of unfaithful Israel

▶ Deity *(God, idol)*

God; also refers to any of the pantheon of gods worshiped by other nations surrounding Israel
Colossians 2:9. Christ has the fullness of the Deity
2 Chronicles 15:16. Removing the statue of a Canaanite deity
Isaiah 65:11. Worshiping pagan deities
Amos 5:26. Statues of pagan deities

▶ Delay *(postponement, setback, wait)*

To stop, detain, or hinder for a while
Genesis 24:56. Wishing to avoid a delay
Psalm 40:17. Do not delay!
Ezekiel 12:25. Consequences will not delay.
Daniel 9:19. Daniel pleads for the Lord to avoid delay.
Hebrews 10:37. He's coming without delay.
Revelation 10:6. No more delay.

▶ Delegate *(assign, designate, pass on)*

Person acting for another; also, to entrust to another
Ezekiel 23:24. God delegates judgment to Israel's enemies.
Acts 6:2–4. Problem of food distribution is delegated to seven men.
1 Corinthians 16:3. Choosing a delegate to bring a gift

▶ Delicacies *(luxuries, treats)*

Something pleasing to eat that is considered rare or luxurious; also, precise or refined perceptions
Genesis 49:20. Delicacies fit for a king
Numbers 11:8. Manna is like a delicacy.
Psalm 141:4. Delicacies of troublemakers
Proverbs 23:6. Delicacies of the stingy
Jeremiah 51:34. Metaphorical delicacies
Lamentations 4:5. From delicacies to destitution

▶ Delight *(enjoyment, relish, satisfaction)*

High degree of gratification
Deuteronomy 30:9. What God will delight in doing
2 Samuel 1:26. A friend in whom David delighted
1 Chronicles 29:17. Delighted with honesty
Proverbs 29:17. Correction brings delight.
Song of Songs 3:11. Delight in the king

Isaiah 5:7. Garden of his delight

Isaiah 32:14–15. A delight for wild donkeys

▶ Deliverance *(escape, liberation, rescue)*

Liberating someone or something

Genesis 45:7. Joseph sent to Egypt to bring about a great deliverance.

Exodus 14:13–31. Deliverance at the Red Sea

Judges 5. Deborah and Barak's song of deliverance

Judges 13:5. Samson to begin Israel's deliverance

1 Samuel 2:1. Hannah's song of deliverance

2 Samuel 22. David's song of deliverance

▶ Deliverer *(Savior)*

Someone who makes freedom or rescue possible for someone else

Judges 3:9, 15. Israel's deliverers

2 Kings 13:4–5. Delivered from Aram's power

Psalm 18:2. God—the ultimate deliverer

Psalm 70:5. Pleading for the deliverer to act

Acts 7:35. Moses the deliverer

▶ Demands *(anxiety, weight)*

To claim as just or due; an urgent requirement or need

Genesis 9:4–5. What God demands

Exodus 21. Other demands

1 Kings 20. Benhadad's demands

Nehemiah 5:18. No demands from Nehemiah

Micah 7:3. Gifts demanded

▶ Demon possession *(influence, inhabitation)*

Inhabitation or influence by demons

Matthew 8:28–34. Possessed by a legion of spirits

Matthew 9:32–34. Rendered mute by a demon

Matthew 11:18. John accused of demon possession

Matthew 12:22. Jesus helps a demon-possessed man.

Mark 1:23–27. Jesus helps another demon-possessed man.

Acts 16:16–40. Paul and the demon-possessed servant girl

▶ Demons *(evil spirits, former angels)*

Evil spirits

Deuteronomy 32:17. Sacrificing to demons

Psalm 106:37. Children sacrificed to demons

Matthew 4:24. Curing people of demon possession

Matthew 7:22. Forcing out demons in Jesus' name

Matthew 8:16. Helping those possessed by demons

Matthew 12:24. Jesus is accused of working with demons.

▶ Demonstration(s) *(display, exhibition, show)*

Showing the merits of a product or service; showing conclusive evidence

Genesis 24:12. Abraham's servant asks God to demonstrate his kindness.

Exodus 4:21. A demonstration of God's power

Acts 17:2–3. Paul's demonstration

1 Corinthians 2:4. Demonstration of the Spirit's power

2 Corinthians 6:3–4, 7. Enduring many things

2 Corinthians 8:24. Demonstration of love

▶ Denarius *(coin, money)*

A silver coin equal to one day's wage

Matthew 18:28. Owing a hundred denarii

Matthew 20:1–16. Everyone given one denarius

Matthew 22:19–21. Who is on the denarius?

Mark 6:37. Will 200 denarii feed over 5,000 people?

Luke 7:41–42. Five hundred denarii debt

▶ Denial *(disavowal, repudiation, renunciation)*

Refusal to admit the truth or reality; also, the refusal to satisfy a request

Exodus 23:6. Denial of justice
Proverbs 30:8–9. Denial of God
Isaiah 29:21. Wrongdoers who deny justice will come to an end.
Matthew 26:33–35, 69–75. Peter's denial of Jesus
Acts 4:16. Can't deny the miracle of Peter and John
Titus 1:16. Denying God

▶ Departures *(leave-takings)*

Leave takings expressed throughout the Bible
Genesis 31:53–55. Jacob's departure from Laban
Deuteronomy 16:6. Anniversary of the departure from Egypt
2 Kings 2:1–14. Elijah's departure
Acts 1:9. Jesus' departure from earth
Acts 20. Paul's departure from Ephesus

▶ Depend *(rely, trust)*

Place reliance or trust in
2 Chronicles 16:7. Consequences of not depending on God
Psalm 62:7. Glory depends on God
Psalm 118:8–9. Better to depend on God
Psalm 123:2. As servants depend on masters
Isaiah 31:1. The horror of depending on Egypt or war horses
Matthew 22:40. The whole basis of the law depends on two commandments.
1 Corinthians 7:31. Don't depend on the things of this world

▶ Dependability *(see Integrity; Reliability)*

▶ Deposit *(credit, place, security)*

To place for safekeeping or as a pledge
Genesis 38:16–18. Leaving a deposit with Tamar
Deuteronomy 24:10–12. Rules for collecting a deposit on a loan
Ezra 5:14–15. Depositing articles in the temple
Ezekiel 24:6. Metaphorical deposit

▶ Depravity *(decadence, immorality, evil)*

Corrupt practice or act
Ezekiel 16:47. Taking time to be depraved
Ezekiel 23:11. Even more depraved
Romans 1:29. Filled with depravity
2 Timothy 3:8. The depraved leading the depraved
2 Peter 2:19. The depraved leading the depraved

▶ Depression *(despair, gloominess, misery)*

Feelings of dejection and hopelessness
Leviticus 26:14–16. Depression: a consequence of disobedience
1 Samuel 1:15–16. Hannah's depression
Proverbs 15:13. Heartache and depression
Proverbs 17:22. Depression: a drain on strength
Isaiah 65:14. Depression is what those who disobey God can expect.

▶ Descendant(s) *(offspring, progeny, successor)*

One who proceeds from an ancestor
Genesis 3:15. Eve's descendant
Genesis 22:17–18. Blessing on Abraham's descendants
Leviticus 6:18. Aaron's descendants can eat some of the grain offerings.
Numbers 26:59. Levi's descendants
Matthew 1:20. David's descendant, Joseph
Romans 4:16. A promise for every descendant

▶ Desecrate/Desecration *(defile, despoil, profane)*

To violate the sanctity of someone or something
Leviticus 21:11–12. The high priest must not desecrate the sanctuary.
Leviticus 22:15. Priests must not desecrate the offerings.
Ezekiel 24:21. God will desecrate the sanctuary.

Daniel 11:31. God will desecrate the temple fortress.

Acts 24:6. Paul accused of desecrating the temple.

▶ Desert of Sin *(wilderness)*

Wilderness lying between Elim and Mt. Sinai

Exodus 16–17:1. The desert of Sin

Numbers 33:11–12. Camping and moving in the Desert of Sin

▶ Desert(s) *(wilderness)*

Arid land with sparse vegetation

Genesis 14:5–6. Defeat of the Rephaim in the desert

Genesis 16:6–7. Hagar flees to the desert.

Genesis 21:20–21. Ishmael lives in the desert.

Exodus 3–4. Moses meets God in the desert.

Numbers 3:4. The Desert of Sinai

Numbers 13:3. Spies sent from the Desert of Paran

▶ Deserter *(apostate, fugitive, traitor)*

One who abandons military service without leave; one who leaves others in the lurch

Judges 7:3. Twenty-two thousand deserters

Psalm 78:9. Deserters of Ephraim

Ezekiel 7:14. Everyone will be a deserter.

Matthew 26:56. The disciples become deserters.

▶ Deserve *(earn, justify, warrant)*

To be worthy of or suitable for

Genesis 40:15. A punishment Joseph didn't deserve

Leviticus 20:11. A crime deserving of death

2 Samuel 3:39. What evildoers deserve

1 Kings 2:26. A priest deserving of death

Ezra 9:13. Punished less than what was deserved

Psalm 28:4. A punishment equal to what is deserved

▶ Desires *(requirements, wants, wishes)*

What one longs or hopes for

2 Samuel 3:21. Everything David desires

Job 20:20. Desires of the godless

Psalm 37:4. Giving you the desires of your heart

Proverbs 3:15. Your desires can't equal wisdom.

Matthew 23:25. Uncontrolled desires

Romans 6:12. The body's desires

Romans 7:7–8. The body's desires

▶ Despair *(depression, despondency, misery)*

To lose all hope or confidence

Leviticus 26:36. Despair in the land of enemies

Numbers 14:6. Despair of Joshua and Caleb at the complaints of Israel

Deuteronomy 28:65. Despair for Israel

Esther 6:12. Haman in despair over Mordecai's promotion

Psalm 88:15. A psalmist's despair

Ecclesiastes 2:20. Despair for hard work

▶ Desperate *(distressed, frantic, worried)*

Having lost hope; moved by despair

2 Samuel 24. A desperate situation

2 Samuel 12:18. A desperate act?

Job 6:26. Desperate words

Psalm 60:3. Desperate times

Psalm 142:6. A desperate cry

▶ Despise *(hate, spurn)*

To regard with contempt or scorn

1 Samuel 2:30. Insignificance of those who despise the Lord

2 Samuel 6:16. Michal despises her husband David.

2 Samuel 12:9–10. God's message to David: Why did you despise my word?

Esther 1:17. Wives will despise their husbands.

Job 5:17. Don't despise discipline.

Psalm 51:17. What God does not despise

Proverbs 1:7. What stubborn fools despise

Isaiah 60:14. Those despised bow

▸ Destiny *(fate, fortune)*

The fate to which a particular person is destined

Job 8:13. Destiny of the godless

Psalm 73:16–17. Destiny of oppressors

Ecclesiastes 7:2. Everyone's destiny?

Ecclesiastes 9:2–3. All share the same destiny

Isaiah 65:11. Goddess of destiny

▸ Destruction *(annihilation, devastation, obliteration)*

The act of destroying

Genesis 19:29. Lot and his daughters escape the destruction of Sodom and Gomorrah.

Leviticus 27:28. Dedicated for destruction

Numbers 21:3. Claimed for destruction

Deuteronomy 7:9–10. God sends destruction

Deuteronomy 30:15. Choose: life or destruction?

Joshua 6:18. Stay away from things marked for destruction

1 Kings 13:34. Jeroboam's family: marked for destruction

▸ Details *(information, particulars)*

Particulars considered individually or in relation to the whole

Exodus 30:11–14. Details for the census and ransoms

2 Samuel 11:18. Details of the battle

1 Kings 6:38. Details of building the temple

1 Chronicles 28:19. Making the details clear

▸ Determination *(fortitude, resolve, willpower)*

Firmness of purpose; resolve

1 Samuel 1:9–10. Hannah's determination

1 Samuel 20:33. Saul's determination

1 Kings 21:7–10. Jezebel's determination

Acts 20:22. Paul's determination

Acts 21:13–14. Paul is determined to go to Jerusalem.

▸ Detestable *(loathsome, repugnant, vile)*

Inspiring abhorrence or scorn

Genesis 43:32. What's detestable to Egyptians

Leviticus 7:21. Touching what's detestable

Deuteronomy 7:26. Idols are detestable.

Ezekiel 5:9, 11. Detestable actions of the people of Jerusalem

Ezekiel 7:3–4. Punishment for detestable actions

▸ Devil, the (see *Satan*)

▸ Devoted items *(forbidden items, taboo)*

Items or animals that God forbids Israel to have

Leviticus 27:28–34. Can't redeem devoted items

Joshua 6:18. Avoid devoted things.

Joshua 7. Achan's theft of devoted items

Joshua 22:20. Wrongfully claiming devoted items

1 Chronicles 2:7. The harm of claiming devoted items

▸ Devotion *(dedication, love, worship)*

Religious fervor

2 Chronicles 32:32. Hezekiah's devotion

2 Chronicles 35:26. Josiah's devotion

Psalm 69:9. David's devotion

Psalm 119:39. Devotion for God's Word

Jeremiah 12:3. Jeremiah's devotion

John 2:17. Jesus' devotion

▸ Devout *(devoted, dedicated, pious)*

Devoted to religion or religious duties

1 Kings 18:3. Obadiah was devout.

Luke 2:25. Simeon was devout.

Acts 2:5, 12. Devout Jewish men in Jerusalem

Acts 8:2. Devout mourners bury Stephen.

Acts 10:1–2. Devout Gentiles

Acts 13:50. Devout women persecute Paul.

▸ Diets *(regimen, weight maintenance)*

Habitual nourishment; regimens to lose weight

Exodus 16. Diet of manna and quails

Job 20:16. Diet of the godless person

D

Psalm 42:3. A diet of tears
Daniel 1:11–16. The diet of Daniel, Hananiah, Mishael, and Azariah
Matthew 3:4. John the Baptist's diet

▶ Differences *(disparity, diversity)*

The quality of being different; disparity in opinions
Leviticus 10:10. Knowing the difference between clean and unclean
Leviticus 15:3. It makes no difference.
Deuteronomy 1:39. Knowing the difference between good and evil
1 Kings 3:9. Solomon desires wisdom to know the difference between good and evil.
2 Chronicles 12:7–8. Knowing the difference between serving God and serving foreign kings
Romans 14:1. Differences of opinion

▶ Difficulty *(see Hardship)*

▶ Dignity *(poise, pride, self-respect)*

The quality or state of being worthy, honored, or esteemed
Exodus 28:2. Clothes to enhance the dignity of the priests
Job 40:9–10. Dignity like God's
Proverbs 30:29–31. Who or what moves with dignity?
Titus 2:7. Be an example of dignity.

▶ Diligence *(attentiveness, meticulousness, thoroughness)*

Being conscientious and showing care about performing a task
Ezra 5:8. Building the temple with diligence
Ezra 6:12–13. Do the work with diligence.
Ezra 7:21, 23. Do the work with diligence.
Proverbs 4:23. Keep your heart with diligence.
Hebrews 6:11. Show diligence.

▶ Dimensions *(extent, size, scope)*

Range over which something extends; the quality of spatial extension
Job 38:4–5. Dimensions of the earth
Ezekiel 42:11. Temple dimensions
Psalm 102:25. God set the dimensions of the earth long ago.
Proverbs 8:27–29. Wisdom helped establish the earth's dimension and that of the seas.
Isaiah 48:13. Dimensions established by God

▶ Direction *(advice, management, path)*

Guidance or supervision of action or conduct; an explicit instruction; also, the line or course on which something is moving or is aimed to move
Genesis 13:10. Looking in the direction of Sodom
Genesis 24:48. Led in the right direction
Exodus 38:21. Directed by Ithamar
Deuteronomy 27:18. Leading the blind in the wrong direction
Psalm 36:4. Going in the wrong direction
Proverbs 1:5. Gaining direction

▶ Dirges *(funeral songs)*

Songs or hymns of grief or lamentation
2 Samuel 3:33–34. A dirge for Abner
2 Chronicles 35:25. A dirge for Josiah
Jeremiah 9:10. Chanting dirges
Lamentations. Jeremiah's dirge for the fall of Jerusalem and for his people
Ezekiel 19:1. A dirge for the princes of Israel
Matthew 11:17. Dirge of children

▶ Disability *(disadvantage, disqualified, restricted)*

Inability to pursue an occupation due to a physical or mental impairment
2 Samuel 4:4. Disability of Jonathan's son
2 Samuel 19:26. Mephibosheth talks of his disability.
Matthew 15:30–31. Curing disabilities
Matthew 18:8. Better disabled than eternally punished
Luke 13:11–12. Jesus helps a disabled woman.

▶ Disagreement *(argument, dispute, misunderstanding)*

A conflict of opinions; a dispute

Exodus 18:15–16. Settling disagreements
Exodus 24:13–14. Aaron and Hur to settle disagreements
Deuteronomy 21:5. Priests have a say in settling disagreements.
Deuteronomy 25:1. Disagreements brought to court
Acts 15:36–41. The disagreement of Paul and Barnabas

▶ Disappointment *(discontent, displeasure)*

The state of being defeated in expectation or hope
Genesis 4:3–6. Cain's disappointment
Psalm 119:116. Avoiding disappointment
Jeremiah 12:13. Harvest disappointment
Jeremiah 14:4. Lack of rain leads to disappointment

▶ Disaster *(calamity, catastrophe, tragedy)*

A sudden calamitous event bringing great damage or destruction
Genesis 19:18–19. Disaster at Sodom
Exodus 32:12. Moses hopes to avoid disaster.
Deuteronomy 29:19–21. A disastrous attitude
Deuteronomy 32:23. One disaster after another
Joshua 7. Disaster at Ai
Judges 11:35. Jephthah's vow brings disaster.
2 Kings 14:9–10. Why invite disaster?

▶ Discernment *(acumen, insight, judgment, shrewdness)*

The quality of being able to grasp or understand what is obscure
Deuteronomy 32:28. No discernment
1 Kings 3:11–12. God gives Solomon discernment.
2 Chronicles 2:12. Huram acknowledges Solomon's discernment.
Psalm 119:125. Give me discernment.
Proverbs 17:10. A man of discernment

▶ Disciple *(believer, follower, pupil)*

One who accepts and assists in spreading the doctrines of another; one of the 12 apostles
1 Kings 20:35–43. A disciple of prophets
2 Kings 4:1. Helping the wife of a disciple
Amos 7:14. Not a prophet or a disciple
Matthew 8:19–22. The cost of being a disciple of Jesus
Matthew 10:1–4. Jesus' twelve disciples

▶ Discipleship *(see Disciple)*

▶ Discipline *(control, correction, obedience)*

Training that corrects, molds, or perfects the mental faculties or moral character
Leviticus 26:18, 23–24. Seven times the discipline
Deuteronomy 8:5. Disciplining children
Deuteronomy 11:2. Discipline from God
Psalm 6:1. Discipline, but not anger
Psalm 94:12. Disciplined, but blessed
Proverbs 1:8–9. Listen to discipline
Proverbs 4:13. Listen to discipline

▶ Discontent *(dissatisfaction, restlessness, unhappiness)*

Showing dissatisfaction or restless longing
1 Samuel 22:2. David gathers the discontent.
Acts 6:1. Discontent among the believers

▶ Discord *(conflict, disagreement, dissension)*

Lack of agreement or harmony
Esther 1:18. Discord expected due to Vashti's behavior
Proverbs 6:14. Sowing discord
Proverbs 6:16, 19. God hates discord.
Galatians 5:19–21. Discord—a product of the sinful nature

▶ Discouragement *(despair, disappointment, dismay)*

Being deprived of courage or confidence

D

Exodus 6:9. Discouragement of the Israelites

Numbers 32:6–9. Discouragement of the spies

1 Samuel 17:32. Discouragement of the Israelite army

Psalm 43:5. Discouragement of the soul

Isaiah 42:4. The Lord's servant will not be discouraged.

2 Corinthians 2:6–7. Don't discourage the wrongdoer.

▶ Discretion *(diplomacy, foresight, good judgment)*

Ability to make responsible decisions

1 Chronicles 22:12. Discretion from God

Proverbs 1:4. Purpose of the proverbs

Proverbs 2:11. Protected by discretion

Proverbs 5:1–2. Acting with discretion

Proverbs 8:12. Wisdom acquires discretion.

▶ Discrimination *(favoritism, intolerance, prejudice)*

Having a prejudiced or a prejudicial outlook

John 4:7–9. Discrimination toward Samaritans

Acts 15:9. God doesn't discriminate.

1 Timothy 5:21. Avoid discrimination.

James 2:4. Discriminating against people

▶ Disease *(leprosy, sickness, skin problems)*

A condition of the living animal or plant body or of one of its parts that impairs normal functioning and is typically manifested by distinguishing signs and symptoms

Leviticus 13–14. Skin diseases

Leviticus 22:4. Disease renders a person unclean.

Numbers 12:10. Miriam contracts a disease after criticizing Moses.

Deuteronomy 28:22. Diseases: one result of disobedience

1 Kings 15:23. Asa's foot disease

2 Chronicles 21:8–20. Jehoram's intestinal disease

Luke 5:12–13. Jesus cures a skin disease.

▶ Disgrace *(humiliation, out of favor, shame)*

A sense of shame or loss of favor

Genesis 30:22–23. Rachel's disgrace

Deuteronomy 22:30. Avoiding a father's disgrace

Joshua 5:9. Removing disgrace

1 Samuel 11:2. Trying to disgrace Israel

Job 10:15. Job's disgrace

▶ Disguise *(camouflage, concealing outfit, mask)*

To furnish with a false appearance or an assumed identity

Genesis 38:13–16. Tamar's disguise

1 Samuel 28:8. Saul's disguise

1 Kings 14:1–4. Disguise of Jeroboam's wife

1 Kings 22:30. Disguise of King Ahab

2 Corinthians 11:13–15. Disguise of false apostles

▶ Dishonesty *(deceitfulness, falsehood, lying)*

Lack of honesty or integrity

Proverbs 4:24. Remove dishonesty

Proverbs 13:11. Dishonest gain

Jeremiah 9:3. Dishonesty of God's people

Jeremiah 22:17. Dishonest profits

Luke 16:1–9. Jesus' parable of a dishonest but shrewd manager

▶ Disloyalty *(betrayal, treachery, unfaithfulness)*

Lacking in loyalty; unfaithful

Joshua 7:1. Achan's disloyalty

Psalm 78:57. Disloyal ancestors and descendants

Daniel 9:7. Daniel prays about disloyalty

▶ Disobedience *(defiance, sin, waywardness)*

Refusal or neglecting to obey

Exodus 34:7. God forgives disobedience.

Job 7:21. Job pleads for forgiveness for disobedience.

Psalm 32:1. The blessing of forgiveness for disobedience
Psalm 107:17. Suffering for disobedience
Isaiah 24:20. Disobedience of the earth
Romans 5:19. Disobedience passed down through Adam
Romans 11:30–32. Disobedience of the Jewish people

▶ Dispensation *(allowance, indulgence, special consideration)*

A general state or ordering of things; a particular arrangement or provision especially of providence or nature
Deuteronomy 4:5–31. Dispensation of the law
Ephesians 1:10. Dispensation of the fullness of time
Ephesians 3:1–2. Dispensation of God's grace

▶ Disqualifications *(disadvantages, ineligibility, prohibitions)*

Items that disqualify or incapacitate
Exodus 19:15. Avoid disqualification
Leviticus 21:18. Disqualified from approaching the altar
Leviticus 22:4. Disqualification from eating the offerings
Judges 7:5–8. Disqualified from military service
Colossians 2:18. Worship of angels disqualifies.

▶ Disrespect *(contempt, disregard, insolence)*

Showing contempt
Exodus 22:28. Avoid disrespecting God
Esther 1:18. Disrespect of Persian women
1 Corinthians 11:4. Disrespect for God

▶ Dissatisfaction *(see Discontent)*

▶ Diversity *(assortment, mixture, variety)*

The inclusion of people of different races or cultures in a group or organization
Acts 2:5–6. Diversity in Jerusalem
Acts 10:35–36. Diversity in God's kingdom
Revelation 7:9–10. Diversity in heaven

▶ Divination *(forecasting, fortune-telling)*

Seeking to foresee or foretell future events
Genesis 30:27. Laban's divination
Genesis 44:5. Joseph's divining cup
Leviticus 19:26. Avoid those who practice divination.
Numbers 22–24. Balaam's divination
Deuteronomy 18:10–11. Avoid divination.
1 Samuel 15:23. Rebellion is like divination.

▶ Divisions *(family groups, groups, tribes)*

The process of dividing
Genesis 36:30. The Horite divisions
Exodus 6:26. Israel divided into family groups
Exodus 12:17. Brought out of Egypt in divisions
Numbers 1:3. Numbering the divisions
Numbers 2:3. The divisions of Judah
Joshua 18:10. The divisions of Canaan

▶ Divorce *(annulment, break up, separation)*

The dissolution of a marriage
Leviticus 21:7. Priest can't marry a divorced woman.
Numbers 30:9. Vows are binding for the divorced.
Deuteronomy 22:13–19. No divorce for a false charge
Deuteronomy 24:1–4. Certificate of divorce
Jeremiah 3:8. God divorces Israel.
Malachi 2:16. God hates divorce.
Matthew 5:31–32. Jesus preaches about divorce.
Matthew 19:1–12. Jesus is questioned about divorce.

D

▶ DIY *(Do It Yourself) projects*

Projects or activities (often spontaneous) that people have to do themselves or do because someone else should have done them

Genesis 28:18–19. Jacob builds an altar.

Numbers 25:6–9. Phinehas stops a plague.

1 Samuel 15. Samuel does what Saul should have done.

Ezra 4:1–3. Building the second temple

▶ Doctor *(see Physician)*

▶ Doctrine *(dogma, guidelines)*

Principle or system for acceptance or belief as by a religious or philosophic group

1 Timothy 1:3. False doctrine

1 Timothy 6:3–4. Teaching false doctrine

2 Timothy 4:3. Sound doctrine

Titus 2:1. Teach according to sound doctrine.

Titus 3:10. Avoid those who teach false doctrine.

▶ Documents *(credentials, papers)*

Written papers bearing the original, official, or legal form of something and which can furnish evidence or information

Nehemiah 9:38. Document professing obedience to God's law

Esther 1:21–22. Documents sent to the provinces

Esther 3:13. Documents granting property seizure

Esther 8:10. Documents granting peace

Jeremiah 32:14. Documents in a clay jar

Daniel 6:10. Document forbidding prayer

▶ Dog(s) *(canine)*

Domestic mammal related to the gray wolf; also a euphemism for a worthless person

Exodus 11:7. Not even a dog will be disturbed by the last plague

1 Samuel 17:43. Is Goliath a dog?

2 Samuel 9:8. A dead dog like Mephibosheth?

1 Kings 14:11. Dogs to eat Jeroboam's relatives

1 Kings 21:17–19, 23–24. Dogs to eat Ahab's relatives

Psalm 22:16, 20. Surrounded by dogs

Matthew 15:21–28. A conversation about dogs

▶ Domination *(control, power, tyranny)*

Supremacy or preeminence over another; exercise of mastery or ruling power

Genesis 1:17–18. The sun and moon dominate the sky.

Judges 4:1–3. The domination of the Canaanites

Daniel 11:12. The southern king will dominate.

John 11:48. Under Rome's domination

1 Peter 5:8. Under Satan's domination

▶ Donkeys *(Equus asinus)*

Domestic animals of the horse family

Genesis 16:11–12. Ishmael: like a wild donkey

Exodus 13:12–13. Redeeming a donkey

Exodus 20:17. Donkey mentioned in the Ten Commandments

Numbers 22:21–35. Balaam's talking donkey

Zechariah 9:9. The Messiah will enter Jerusalem on a donkey.

Matthew 21:1–11. Jesus enters Jerusalem on a donkey.

Luke 13:15–16. Wouldn't you help a donkey on the Sabbath?

▶ Door *(access, entrance, gate)*

A barrier by which an entry is closed or open; a means of access

Genesis 4:6–7. Sin at the door

Genesis 6:16. Door in the ark

Deuteronomy 3:5. Double doors of the fortified cities of Canaan

Deuteronomy 15:16–17. Piercing a slave at the door

Psalm 141:3. The door of the lips

Proverbs 5:8. Avoid the door of the adulterous woman.

Ezekiel 10:19. Angels at the door

Revelation 3:20. Jesus stands at the door.

▶ Double portion *(birthright, inheritance)*

Provision in the law of Moses according the firstborn with a double portion of the inheritance; also, an extra blessing or an extra curse

Deuteronomy 21:15–17. A double portion

1 Samuel 1:4–5. Hannah receives a double portion.

2 Kings 2:9. Elisha asks for a double portion.

Isaiah 61:7. A double portion, instead of shame

Revelation 18:6. Babylon will receive a double portion of grief.

▶ Double-mindedness *(ambivalence, in two minds)*

A state of ambivalence

1 Timothy 3:8. Deacons should not be two-faced.

James 1:6–8. Double-minded man

James 4:8. The hearts of the double-minded

▶ Doubt(s) *(misgivings, skepticism, uncertainties)*

To lack confidence in someone or something

Matthew 14:28–31. Peter walks on water, then doubts.

Matthew 21:20–22. Have faith, rather than doubt.

Matthew 28:16–17. Some had doubts.

Luke 24:38–39. Why do you doubt?

Romans 14:13, 21. Don't cause others to doubt.

James 1:6. Ask, but don't doubt.

Jude 22. Show mercy to doubters.

▶ Dove *(pigeon)*

A small, wild pigeon

Genesis 8:6–12. Noah sends a dove to search for land.

Genesis 15:9–10. A dove as a sacrifice

Leviticus 1:14. The command to sacrifice a dove

Psalm 55:6. Wings of a dove

Hosea 7:11. Ephraim, the dove

Matthew 3:16. The Holy Spirit is like a dove.

▶ Downhearted *(see Discouragement)*

▶ Dowry *(bride price, gift, offering)*

Money, goods, or estate that a woman brings to her husband in marriage; a price paid for a bride

Genesis 24:52–53. Gifts for Rebekah and her family

Genesis 34:12. Shechem's willingness to pay any price for Dinah

Exodus 22:16–17. Dowry for seduction

1 Samuel 18:25. Dowry for Michal

1 Kings 9:16. Dowry for a princess

▶ Doxology *(praise)*

A liturgical expression of praise to God

Isaiah 6:3. Doxology in heaven

Luke 2:14. Doxology at the birth of the Savior

Romans 16:27. Paul's doxology

Ephesians 3:21. Paul's doxology

Jude 25. Jude's doxology

▶ Drachma *(coin)*

Ancient Greek silver coin

Matthew 17:24. Two-drachma tax

Luke 15:8. Woman with ten silver coins

▶ Dragon *(the devil, Satan)*

Huge serpent; metaphor for Satan

Revelation 12. Attack of the dragon

Revelation 13. Authority of the dragon

Revelation 20:1–3. The dragon defeated

▶ Dread *(alarm, dismay, fear)*

Great fear; extreme reluctance to face someone or something

D

Exodus 15:16. Terror and dread of the Egyptians

Psalm 119:39. Dreaded insults

Proverbs 1:33. Dread of disaster

Proverbs 10:24. Dread of the wicked

Isaiah 57:11. Dread of Israel

Jeremiah 42:16. Dreaded famines

▶ Dream interpretation *(prophecy)*

Explanations from God as to the meaning of dreams

Genesis 40. Joseph interprets the dreams of Pharaoh's servants.

Genesis 41:25–32. Joseph interprets Pharaoh's dreams.

Daniel 2:16–45. Daniel interprets Nebuchadnezzar's first dream.

Daniel 4:19–33. Daniel interprets Nebuchadnezzar's second dream.

▶ Dream(s) *(communication, revelation, vision, warning)*

Series of thoughts, images, or emotions occurring during sleep; one of the ways in which God spoke to prophets

Genesis 20:1–7. Abimelech's dream

Genesis 28:10–15. Jacob's first dream

Genesis 31:10–13. Jacob's second dream

Genesis 37:5–11. Joseph's dreams

Genesis 40. The dreams of Pharaoh's cupbearer and baker

Genesis 41. Pharaoh's dreams

Numbers 12:5–6. God speaks about dreams.

Daniel 2. Nebuchadnezzar's dream

Matthew 1:20–23. Joseph's dream

▶ Drink offering *(offering of wine, sacrifice)*

One of the daily sacrifices for sin; often accompanied animals given as sacrifices

Exodus 29:40–41. Drink offering with lamb

Numbers 6:17–21. Drink offering with a Nazirite vow

Numbers 15:1–5. Two quarts of wine

Numbers 28:7, 9. A quart of wine with lamb

▶ Drinking *(drunkenness)*

The consumption of alcoholic beverages

1 Samuel 30:16. Drinking in celebration

2 Samuel 13:28. Absalom plots to kill Amnon while Amnon drinks.

1 Kings 1:25. Drinking with Adonijah

1 Kings 20:12. Benhadad drinking with his allies

Esther 1. Drinking at Xerxes's banquet

Ecclesiastes 2:3. Drinking to feel better

Matthew 11:18–19. Jesus accused of drunkenness

▶ Dropsy *(edema, swelling)*

Swelling of the soft tissues

Deuteronomy 8:4. No dropsy in the wilderness

Luke 14:2–4. A man with dropsy

▶ Drought *(lack of rain)*

Period of dryness due to a lack of rain

Deuteronomy 28:22. Drought is a curse.

1 Kings 17:1–18:46. Three-year drought

Job 12:15. God allows drought.

Job 24:19. Drought, the water stealer

Jeremiah 2:6. Drought in the desert

Jeremiah 14:1. Drought to come

▶ Drug(s) *(homeopathic medicines, pharmaceuticals)*

A substance used as a medication or in the preparation of medication; often an illegal substance that causes addiction, habituation, or a marked change in consciousness

Matthew 27:34. Jesus is offered a sedative.

Galatians 5:20–21. Taking drugs: an act of the corrupt nature

▶ Dung *(excrement, Dung Gate, manure, offal, waste)*

Offal of an animal or person

Exodus 29:14. Burning the dung of a bull

1 Kings 14:10. Burning like dung

Nehemiah 2:13. The Dung Gate

Job 20:7. Wicked perish like dung
Ezekiel 4. Baking bread with dung

▶ Duty *(job, obligation, responsibility)*

Obligatory task, conduct, service, or function that arises from one's position; active music, military, or priestly service

Genesis 38:8. A man's duty to brother's widow
Leviticus 5:14. Failing one's duty
Numbers 1. Military duty
Deuteronomy 24:5. Discharged from military service
2 Kings 11:4, 7. Guards on duty
1 Chronicles 9:33. Musicians on duty
Luke 1:8–9. Priest on duty

▶ Dysentery *(diarrhea)*

A disease characterized by severe diarrhea with passage of mucus and blood and usually caused by infection

2 Chronicles 21:14–19. Jehoram will be struck, possibly with dysentery
Acts 28:8. Publius's father suffering from dysentery

▶ Eagerness *(enthusiastic, fervor, zeal)*

Enthusiastic or impatient desire or interest

2 Samuel 21:2. Saul's eagerness

Acts 17:11. The Bereans' eagerness

2 Corinthians 7:11. The Corinthians' eagerness

2 Corinthians 8:19. Paul's eagerness

▶ Eagle *(bird)*

Any of various large diurnal birds of prey (family Accipitridae) noted for their strength, size, keenness of vision, and powers of flight

Deuteronomy 28:49. Swooping like an eagle

Deuteronomy 32:11–12. Like an eagle in a nest

Job 39:27–30. Who orders the eagle?

Isaiah 40:31. Renewed strength like that of eagles

Jeremiah 49:16. Edom is like the eagle.

Ezekiel 1:10. The face of an eagle

▶ Ear *(hearing)*

The organ of hearing and equilibrium

Exodus 21:5–6. Piercing a slave's ear

Exodus 29:19–20. Blood on the ear lobe

Leviticus 14:17. Oil on the ear lobe

Numbers 11:19–20. Meat coming out of the Israelites' ears

1 Samuel 7:8. Don't turn a deaf ear.

2 Kings 19:16. Hezekiah pleads: Turn your ear to me.

Matthew 26:51. Cutting off the ear of the chief priest's servant

Mark 4:23. Got ears? Listen!

▶ Earrings *(jewelry, ornamentation)*

Jewelry worn on the ears

Genesis 35:4. Giving Jacob earrings

Exodus 32. A calf made out of earrings

Exodus 35:22. Gifts of earrings for the tabernacle

Judges 8:22–35. Gideon makes a gold idol out of earrings.

Ezekiel 16:12. Earrings from God

▶ Earth *(dirt, planet, soil)*

The planet on which we live, as well as a fragment of the material composing part of the surface of the globe

Genesis 1:1. God created the earth.

Genesis 2:7. Man is formed from the earth.

Genesis 7:17. The earth flooded.

Job 38:14. The earth changes.

Psalm 24:1–2. The earth belongs to God.

Psalm 47:7. The king of the earth

Matthew 6:10. In heaven and on earth

▶ Earthquake(s) *(eruption, tremor)*

Shaking or trembling of the earth that is volcanic or tectonic in origin

1 Samuel 14:15. Philistines panic during an earthquake.

1 Kings 19:11–12. Elijah and the earthquake

Ezekiel 38:19. An earthquake to come

Amos 1:1. Amos prophesies before the earthquake.

Zechariah 14:5. Flee from the earthquake.

Matthew 27:51–54. The earthquake during Jesus' crucifixion

Acts 16:26. The earthquake in Philippi

▶ East *(compass direction)*

To or toward the east

Genesis 2:8. Eden in the east

Genesis 3:24. Angels east of Eden

Genesis 4:16. Cain wanders east of Eden.

Exodus 14:21–22. The east wind and the Red Sea

Numbers 2:3. Judah at the east

Joshua 14:3. Inheritance east of the Jordan River

1 Kings 7:25. Bulls facing east

Matthew 24:27. Second coming is like lightning from the east.

▶ Easter *(Christ's resurrection, holiday)*

A feast that commemorates Christ's resurrection and is observed with variations of date due to different calendars on the first Sunday after the paschal full moon

E

Matthew 28. Why Easter is celebrated
Mark 16:1–8. Back to life on Sunday
Luke 24:1–12. An empty tomb
John 20. The first Easter

▶ Ebenezer *(campsite, victory site)*

Campsite for the Israelites where they were defeated but later achieved victory over the Philistines

1 Samuel 4:1. Defeat at Ebenezer
1 Samuel 5:1. Ark taken from Ebenezer
1 Samuel 7:10–12. A rock named Ebenezer

▶ Eclipse *(conceal, overshadow)*

The total or partial obscuring of one celestial body by another

Job 5:14. Eclipse for the wicked?
Isaiah 13:10. Eclipse on the day of the Lord
Joel 2:10. Eclipse and earthquake on the day of the Lord
Amos 8:9. God will cause an eclipse.
Matthew 24:29. Jesus predicts a cataclysmic eclipse.

▶ Economics *(finances, money matters)*

The social science concerned chiefly with description and analysis of the production, distribution, and consumption of goods and services

1 Kings 9:11. Supply-side economics
Ezekiel 27. Tyre's economic situation before its predicted fall
Matthew 6:24. Jesus preaches on economics.

▶ Eden *(garden, paradise)*

Place in which God created a garden and placed Adam and Eve

Genesis 2:8–9, 15. A garden in Eden
Genesis 3:6, 23. First sin happens in Eden.
2 Kings 19:12. The people of Eden
Ezekiel 28:13, 16. The fall in Eden
Joel 2:3. The fall in Eden

▶ Edification *(benefit, learning, understanding)*

Intellectual, moral, or spiritual enlightenment

Romans 14:19. Do what leads to mutual edification.
1 Corinthians 12:7. For our mutual edification
1 Corinthians 14:12–13. Gifts for the edification of all
Ephesians 1:17–18. Paul's desire for the edification of the Ephesian believers

▶ Education *(instruction, learning, teaching)*

The act or process of educating; the learning that comes through that process

Deuteronomy 11:18–19. Parents to educate children about God's laws
2 Chronicles 17:9. Education for all
Daniel 1:4–6. The education of Daniel and his friends in Babylon
Acts 7:22. Moses' education
Acts 22:2–3. Paul's education

▶ Effectiveness *(efficiency, success, usefulness)*

Power to be effective; the quality of being able to bring about an effect

1 Kings 18. Elijah chides the Baal prophets for not being effective.
Acts 14:1. Paul and Barnabas are effective.
1 Corinthians 16:9. Paul's effectiveness
James 5:16. Effective prayers

▶ Effort *(exertion, struggle, work)*

The use of physical or mental energy to do something

Ecclesiastes 4:4. Pointless effort?
Ecclesiastes 6:7. Wasted efforts
Luke 13:6–9. Parable about the effort needed to produce fruit (to live the Christian life)
Romans 3:27–28. Gaining God's approval is not due to our efforts but God's grace.
Romans 9:16. Not dependent on our effort
Hebrews 4:11. Make effort to enter God's place of rest.

▶ Egnatian Way *(road)*

The Roman-built road across northern Greece, one Paul would have taken when he visited Neapolis, Philippi, Amphipolis, Apollonia, and Thessalonica. The Romans built the road to allow their military to travel easier.

Acts 16:11–12. Traveling the Egnatian Way

Acts 17. Back down the Egnatian Way

Philippians 4:15–16. On the Egnatian Way to Philippi

1 Thessalonians 2:1–2. On the Egnatian Way to Thessalonica

▶ Egocentric *(pride, self-worth)*

Confined in an attitude or interest in one's own needs or affairs

Genesis 37:5–8. Joseph's dream seems egocentric.

Daniel 4. Nebuchadnezzar's egocentric behavior

Matthew 2. Herod's egocentric behavior

Romans 2:8. Wrath for the egocentric

▶ Egyptian(s) *(citizen of Egypt)*

One native to Egypt

Exodus 1:11–14. Egyptian slave drivers

Exodus 8:26–27. Israelite sacrifices are an abomination to the Egyptians.

Exodus 14:23, 27–28. Pursuing Egyptians are killed in the Red Sea.

Isaiah 19–20. Punishment of the Egyptians

Isaiah 23:5. Fall of Tyre will hurt the Egyptians.

Isaiah 30:3. The Egyptians are not all powerful.

▶ Elder(s) *(leader)*

Head of a family group (Old and New Testament); leaders who led church congregations in the first century (New Testament)

Joshua 24:1. Summoning the elders

Judges 11:8. The elders seek a leader.

Acts 24:1. The elders build a case against Paul.

1 Timothy 5:17. Honor the elders.

Titus 1:5–6. Blameless elders

▶ Elect *(the chosen ones)*

The notion that the choice of who will be saved is ultimately up to God

Matthew 24:31. Gathering the elect

Romans 8:33. A charge against the elect

Colossians 3:12. The elect of God

1 Thessalonians 1:4. God chose you.

1 Timothy 5:21. Elect angels

▶ Election *(selection)*

The state of being chosen by God or predestined to be among the elect

Romans 11. Enemies of the elect, but loved by election

1 Thessalonians 1:3–4. Your election by God

2 Peter 1:10. Make your election sure.

▶ Elephant *(see Ivory)*

▶ Eloquence *(expressiveness, fluency, persuasiveness)*

Persuasive, powerful discourse

Exodus 4:10. Moses downplays his eloquence.

Acts 2. Peter's eloquence

Acts 7. Stephen's eloquence leads to his death.

Acts 17:22–31. Paul's eloquence in Athens

Acts 26. Paul's eloquence before Festus and Agrippa

▶ Embalm *(preserve, protect)*

Preservatives used to prevent a corpse from decaying

Genesis 50:1–3. Embalming Jacob (Israel)

Genesis 50:26. Embalming Joseph

▶ Embarrassment *(discomfiture, humiliation, shame)*

Feeling self-conscious or ill at ease

Leviticus 19:29. Avoid embarrassing a daughter through prostitution.

Judges 3:25. The embarrassment of waiting for Eglon

1 Corinthians 11:22. Embarrassing those who have less

2 Corinthians 7:14. Paul not embarrassed

2 Corinthians 9:3–4. Avoid mutual embarrassment about the collection.

▶ Embroidery *(needlework)*

Ornamentation of fabric with needlework

Genesis 37:3. Joseph's embroidered robe

Exodus 26:1, 36. Embroidery on the tabernacle fabric

Exodus 27:16. An embroidered screen

Exodus 28. Embroidered clothes for Aaron

Psalm 45:13. Embroidered clothes of the princess

Ezekiel 16:10. Embroidered dress of Jerusalem

Ezekiel 26:16. Embroidered clothes of princes

▶ Emotion *(feeling, passion, sentiment)*

A strong feeling

Genesis 45:1–2. Joseph shows a lot of emotion when he reveals his identity to his brothers.

Exodus 32:19–20. Moses' strong emotion at the discovery of the golden calf

2 Samuel 12:5, 16. David has a mixture of emotions at the aftermath of the discovery of his sin.

Psalm 30:11. Emotions can change.

John 11:35–36. Jesus shows emotion at the tomb of Lazarus.

▶ Employment *(occupation, service, work)*

The work in which one is engaged

Judges 11:3. Not gainfully employed

Ezekiel 39:14. Employed to cleanse the land

Matthew 20:1–16. Employment offered at a vineyard.

Acts 18:2–3. Employed as tentmakers

Acts 19:24. Employed as a silversmith

▶ Emptiness *(barrenness, meaninglessness, void)*

Containing nothing

Genesis 1:2. Emptiness at creation

Genesis 31:42. Empty-handed

Genesis 37:24. An empty cistern

Psalm 4:2. Loving emptiness

Ecclesiastes 5:7. Empty words

Isaiah 5:9, 18. Empty houses and promises

Isaiah 19:5. Empty river

▶ Emulation *(see Imitate/Imitation)*

▶ Enable *(allow, facilitate, permit)*

To supply with the means, knowledge, or opportunity

Leviticus 26:13. Enabled to walk with dignity

2 Samuel 22:34. Enabled to stand on the heights

Luke 1:74–75. Enabled to serve without fear

John 6:65. Enabled to come to Jesus

Acts 2:4. Enabled to speak in other languages

Philippians 4:13. Enabled to do all things

▶ Encouragement *(heartening, inspiration, uplift)*

Inspiring with hope, courage, or confidence

Acts 4:36. His name means encouragement.

Acts 13:15. Is there any encouragement?

Acts 15:31–32. Encouragement received

Acts 20:1–2. Paul's encouragement

Romans 12:8. The gift of encouragement

Romans 15:4–5. Encouragement and endurance through the Scriptures

1 Corinthians 14:3. Encouragement through revelation

▶ End times *(eschatology)*

The events predicted to occur in the last days

Daniel 12. End times events

Matthew 24. Jesus talks about the end times.

1 Thessalonians 4:16–17. The rapture at end times

Revelation 15. The seven plagues at end times

Revelation 19. The lamb's wedding banquet at the end

▶ Endurance *(fortitude, stamina)*

The power to withstand hardship or stress

2 Corinthians 1:6, 8. Enduring suffering

2 Corinthians 6:3–5. Enduring many things

Colossians 1:11. Endurance with joy

1 Thessalonians 1:3. Endurance of faith

1 Timothy 6:11. Pursue endurance

2 Timothy 3:10. Paul's endurance

Titus 2:2. Examples of endurance

▶ Enemy(ies) *(adversary, opponent, rival)*

One who opposes another or intends injury toward

Exodus 15. God dealt with Israel's enemies.

Exodus 23:4–5. Help an enemy.

Numbers 10:9. Rescued from enemies

Deuteronomy 28:25. Curse of disobedience: defeated by enemies

Judges 3:12–30. Moab—the enemies of Israel

1 Kings 21. Ahab's enemy

Matthew 5:38–48. Love your enemies.

▶ Engagement *(betrothal, commitment, promise of marriage)*

Promising to marry someone; a conflict in which one is involved

Genesis 29:18–20. Jacob and Rachel are engaged.

Deuteronomy 22:23–25. Consequences of a man having sex with an engaged woman

Judges 12:2. Engaged in a great struggle

Matthew 1:18–19. Joseph considers ending his engagement to Mary.

1 Corinthians 7:36. Rules of engagement

▶ Entertainment *(amusement, distraction, leisure activity)*

Something that amuses, pleases, or diverts, particularly a performance or a show

Judges 16. A blinded Samson to entertain the Philistines

1 Samuel 18:10. David entertains Saul.

Esther 1. One hundred and eighty days of entertainment

Matthew 14:6–7. Herodias's daughter provides entertainment at a party.

Hebrews 13:2. Entertaining angels (hospitality)

▶ Enthusiasm *(eagerness, fervor, zeal)*

Great excitement or interest in a subject or cause

Ecclesiastes 9:10. Work with enthusiasm.

Matthew 22:37. Love God with enthusiasm.

2 Corinthians 8:17. Titus's enthusiasm

2 Corinthians 9:2. Enthusiasm of the Corinthian believers

Philippians 2:28. Paul is enthusiastic about sending Epaphroditus.

▶ Environment *(atmosphere, location, surroundings)*

The totality of circumstances around an organism; the social and cultural conditions altering an individual or a community

Genesis 2:15. Man's first task was to care for the environment.

Genesis 3:17–18. Curse brings a change in the environment.

Genesis 13:10. A pleasing environment

Leviticus 19:23–25. Caring for the fruit trees is a way of caring for the environment.

Isaiah 5:5–6. Bad environmental changes

Isaiah 35. Good environmental changes

▶ Envy *(covet, desire, jealousy)*

Feeling of discontent or resentment aroused by the desire for the possessions or qualities of another

Job 5:2. Envy slays.

Psalm 68:16. Envy of the mountain peaks

Proverbs 3:31. A person not to envy

Proverbs 23:17. Don't envy sinners.

Matthew 27:18. Envy of the Jewish leaders caused them to hand Jesus to Pilate.

Mark 7:21–23. Envy is one of the characteristics that make a person unclean.

Galatians 5:19–21. Envy: an effect of the corrupt nature

▸ Epicureans *(followers of Epicurus)*

Those who adhere to a philosophy devoted to the pursuit of pleasure

Ecclesiastes 2:1–10. Description of the Epicurean lifestyle

Luke 7:33. John was no Epicurean.

Acts 17:18–33. Debates with Epicureans

1 Corinthians 15:32–33. Don't be deceived by the Epicurean mindset.

▸ Epidemic *(disease, outbreak, plague)*

Spreading rapidly by infection and affecting many people

Leviticus 13. Cleansing rituals and isolation helped avoid an epidemic.

Leviticus 14:33–57. Scraping a house to avoid an epidemic

Deuteronomy 32:24. Deadly epidemics

2 Samuel 24. An epidemic due to David's disobedience

Romans 5:19. An epidemic of disobedience

▸ Equality *(fairness, impartiality, parity)*

Having the same privileges, status, or rights

John 5:17–18. Jesus' equality with the Father

Acts 10:34–35. All equally acceptable to God

1 Corinthians 12:13. The Holy Spirit given equally to all

Philippians 2:6. Jesus did not flaunt his equality with God.

Colossians 3:9–11. Grace breeds equality.

▸ Equip/Equipment *(furnish, provide, supply)*

To supply with necessities such as provisions

Genesis 27:2–3. Hunting equipment

Exodus 39:33, 40. Moses inspects all of the equipment for the tent of meeting.

Numbers 1:50. Levites in charge of the equipment for the tent of meeting

Deuteronomy 23:12–13. Equip yourself with a stick.

1 Samuel 8:11–12. A king will require equipment.

Hebrews 13:20–21. May God equip you.

▸ Error *(fault, inaccuracy, mistake)*

An act or belief that deviates from what is correct

Job 4:18–19. Error of angels

Ecclesiastes 10:5. An error of rulers

Isaiah 32:6. Error of a fool

Daniel 6:4. No error in Daniel

Matthew 22:29. Sadducees in error

James 5:20. Correcting the error of a person's ways

▸ Escape *(avoid, flee, freedom)*

Break loose from confinement; to succeed in avoiding

Genesis 19. Lot and his family escape the destruction of Sodom and Gomorrah.

Genesis 27:41–43. Jacob needs to escape from Esau's wrath.

Joshua 2. Two spies escape from Jericho with the help of Rahab.

1 Samuel 19. David escapes from Saul.

1 Samuel 21–23. More of David's escapes

Acts 12. Peter escapes from prison with the help of an angel.

▸ Espionage *(see Spy[ies]/Spying)*

▸ Essenes *(sect)*

Ascetic Jewish sect that existed from the second century B.C. to second century A.D.

Acts 4:32. Essenes believed in sharing possessions.

Acts 15:5. Essene belief

▸ Established *(launched, recognized, set up)*

Set up; placed in a secure position

Genesis 9:17. A covenant established

Exodus 23:31. Borders established

Numbers 28:6. Burnt offerings established

1 Samuel 13:13. Saul's kingdom would have been established.

2 Samuel 3:9–10. Abner confirms God's promise to establish David's kingdom.

1 Kings 2:12. Solomon is firmly established.

▶ Esteem *(regard, respect, value)*

Regard with respect; prize

Esther 10:3. In high esteem

Proverbs 4:8. Wisdom to be held in high esteem

Isaiah 53:3. God's servant will not be held in high esteem.

Isaiah 66:2. The one whom God esteems

Daniel 10:10–11. Daniel was held in high esteem.

▶ Estrangement *(alienation, separation)*

Hostility that leads to separation; removal from an accustomed association

Judges 14:20. Estrangement of Samson and his wife

2 Samuel 14. The estrangement of David and Absalom

Job 19:13. Job's estrangement from his family

Romans 8:38. No estrangement between God and us

▶ Eternal *(everlasting, never ending, perpetual)*

Having no beginning or end; existing outside of time

Matthew 25:46. Eternal punishment

Romans 1:20. God's eternal power

2 Corinthians 4:17. Eternal glory

2 Corinthians 5:1. Eternal house in heaven

Hebrews 5:9. Eternal salvation

Hebrews 6:2. Eternal judgment

Hebrews 9:14. The eternal Spirit

▶ Eternal life *(immortality, life after death)*

Unending life

Matthew 19:16–30. Inheriting eternal life

John 3:14–16. Eternal life comes through believing in the Son of God.

John 4:13–14. The spring of eternal life

1 John 1:1–2. Jesus' eternal life

1 John 2:25. Promise of eternal life

▶ Eternity *(forever, perpetuity, time without end)*

An immeasurable amount of time; forever

Psalm 93:2. From all eternity

Proverbs 8:23. Wisdom exists in eternity

Ecclesiastes 3:11. Eternity in the heart

John 12:34. The forever Messiah

John 14:16. The Holy Spirit will be with us throughout eternity.

▶ Ethics *(code, morals, principles)*

Set of principles for right conduct

Exodus 20. Ethics established at Mount Sinai

Matthew 5–7. Jesus' code of ethics

Matthew 22:37–40. The ethics of love

Romans 12:9–21. Ethical behavior

1 Timothy 3. Ethical behavior of leaders

▶ Eucharist *(see* ***Lord's Supper****)*

▶ Eunuchs *(castrated males)*

Castrated men serving in harems

2 Kings 9:32. Eunuchs at Jezreel

2 Kings 24:12. Jehoiakin's eunuchs

Esther 1. Eunuchs serving Xerxes

Esther 2:21–23. Eunuchs plotting against Xerxes

Esther 4:4. Eunuchs tell Esther about Mordecai.

Matthew 19:12. Eunuchs and celibacy

▶ Euphemisms *(sayings, substitutions)*

Substituting mild or indirect terms for harsher or offensive terms; referring to something else by the use of another term

Genesis 3:19. Euphemism for *death*

Exodus 20:7. Avoid euphemisms for God's name.

Matthew 5:34–37. Avoid euphemisms.

▶ Evaluation *(assessment, estimate, valuation)*

The assessment of value or worth; examining or judging carefully

E

Numbers 13. Twelve spies sent to evaluate Canaan

1 Samuel 20. Jonathan agrees to evaluate Saul's behavior toward David.

1 Corinthians 4:1–5. Evaluation of the work of Paul and other apostles

Titus 1:5–9. Evaluate church leaders by examining their families and their behavior.

1 John 4:1. Evaluate whether someone has the Spirit of God.

▶ Evangelism *(gospel message)*

Spreading the gospel of Christ

Matthew 4:19. Work of evangelism is like fishing.

Matthew 10. Disciples are sent to evangelize.

Matthew 28:19. Evangelism is the Great Commission.

Acts 17. Paul's evangelism in Thessalonica

Philippians 1:18. Evangelism is primary; motives are secondary.

2 Timothy 4:2. Be ready to evangelize.

▶ Evangelist *(spreader of the gospel, teacher)*

One who practices evangelism

Acts 8:26–40. Philip the evangelist

Acts 13. Barnabas and Saul set aside as evangelists

Ephesians 3:8. The work of an evangelist

Ephesians 4:11. Some are evangelists.

1 Thessalonians 3:2. Timothy the evangelist

▶ Evidence *(confirmation, facts, proof, verification)*

Items helpful in the formulation of a conclusion or judgment

Exodus 22:10–13. Dead body as evidence

Matthew 26:59. False evidence

John 14:11. Jesus' actions are evidence of His being the Messiah.

2 Thessalonians 1:5. Evidence of God's right judgment

James 2:20. Evidence of the uselessness of faith without deeds

▶ Evil *(immorality, vice, wickedness)*

Morally reprehensible; arising from bad character or behavior

Genesis 2:9. Tree of the knowledge of good and evil

Genesis 8:21. Evil in the heart

Exodus 32:21–22. Aaron's excuse: the people are evil.

Deuteronomy 21:18–21. Purge the evil.

Judges 4:1. Israel's evil

Matthew 5:39. Don't oppose an evil person.

Matthew 7:11. Even evil parents give good gifts to children.

▶ Evolution *(development, growth, progression)*

A gradual process in which something changes into a different and usually more complex or better form

Genesis 1:1. Major argument against a theory of evolution

Genesis 6:5. Evolution of evil

Exodus 20:11. The earth was made, instead of gradually evolving.

Romans 1:25. Another argument against a theory of evolution

▶ Exaggeration (see *Hyperbole*)

▶ Exalt *(acclaim, laud, praise)*

To glorify, praise, or honor; to raise in rank, character, or status

Exodus 15:1–2. God is highly exalted.

Joshua 3:7. Joshua exalted

2 Samuel 22:47. Let God be exalted.

Psalm 89:24. Exalting David

Psalm 99:5. Exalting the Lord

▶ Examination *(assessment, inspection, investigation)*

The study or analysis of something; testing or checking the condition or health of someone

Leviticus 13. Examinations by priests

Leviticus 14:1–7. Examinations outside the camp

Leviticus 14:48. Mildew examination

Psalm 26:2. Examine me.

Matthew 8:3–4. Report to the priest for an examination.

▶ Example *(model, pattern)*

One who represents a group; one that serves as a pattern

2 Kings 16:2–3. Bad examples of the kings of Israel

Ecclesiastes 9:13–15. An example of wisdom

Ezekiel 14:7–8. Making an example

John 13:15. Jesus sets an example to follow.

1 Corinthians 10:6. Negative examples to avoid

1 Corinthians 16:15–16. Follow this example.

Philippians 3:17. Live by this example.

1 Peter 2:21. Following an example of suffering

▶ Excellence *(brilliance, distinction, merit)*

State, quality, or condition of excelling; superiority

Exodus 15. God's excellence

Ezra 5:8. Excellent work

1 Timothy 3:1, 13. Aspiring to excellence

1 Peter 2:9. Excellent qualities

▶ Exclusivity *(exceptionality, uniqueness)*

The state of being exclusive; excluding some or most

Genesis 12:2–3. God's promise is exclusive to one man, through one family.

Leviticus 20:26. God's exclusive people

Numbers 16. Exclusivity in a rebellious situation

Deuteronomy 4. God dealt exclusively with Israel.

Matthew 15:24. Exclusive to Israel

John 14:6. The only way to the Father

Acts 4:10. Exclusivity of salvation

▶ Excommunication *(exclusion)*

Ecclesiastical censure; being thrown out of the synagogue

John 9. Fear of excommunication

John 12:42. More fear of excommunication

John 16:1–2. Jesus warns of excommunication.

Acts 26:11. Paul had authority to excommunicate.

▶ Excuses *(justifications, pretexts)*

Explanations offered to justify or obtain forgiveness

Exodus 4:10–11. Moses offers an excuse.

Exodus 5:20–21. An excuse to kill

Ecclesiastes 5:6. Don't make excuses.

Matthew 8:21–22. Offering an excuse, instead of discipleship

Luke 14:16–21. Please excuse me.

▶ Execution *(see Capital Punishment)*

▶ Executioners *(killers, lawful murderers)*

Those who execute the condemned

Numbers 15:32–36. A community of executioners

1 Samuel 15:32–33. Samuel acts as an executioner.

Job 33:22. A life drawn near to the executioners

Ezekiel 21:11. A sword in the hand of executioners

Mark 6:27–28. The executioner and John the Baptist

▶ Exegete/Exegesis *(textual interpretation)*

Providing a critical interpretation or explanation of Scripture

Luke 24:44–48. Jesus' exegesis

Acts 2:14–36. Peter's exegesis

Acts 8:34–35. Philip's exegesis

Acts 17:11. The exegesis of the Bereans

Acts 18:4. Paul's exegesis

Romans 4. Paul's exegesis

▶ Exhibitionism *(public exposure)*

Behaving in a way so as to attract attention; something on display

E

Genesis 2:25. When exhibitionism wasn't a problem
Genesis 9:20–23. Noah's exhibitionism
1 Samuel 19:24. Saul's exhibitionism
2 Samuel 6:20. Michal mocks what she believes is David's exhibitionism.
Esther 1:10–12. Vashti avoids exhibitionism.

▶ Exhumation *(disinter, dig up, unearth)*

Removal of a dead body from the grave
Exodus 13:19. Exhumation of Joseph
2 Samuel 21:10–14. Exhumation of Saul and his sons
Matthew 27:51–52. Exhumation at the death of Jesus
1 Thessalonians 4:14. Mass exhumation

▶ Exile *(banishment, explusion)*

Enforced removal from one's native country (most often refers to Israel's exile in Babylon); one who lives in exile
Ezra 2. Those returning to Jerusalem from exile in Babylon
Ezra 3:8. Exiles rebuild the temple.
Isaiah 5:13. The promise of exile
Lamentations 4:22. Exile won't last forever.
Ezekiel 12. Acting out Israel's exile
Amos 5:27. Exile beyond Damascus

▶ Exodus *(evacuation, mass departure, migration)*

A departure of a large number of people
Exodus 13. The exodus
Exodus 16:1. The time of the exodus
Joshua 24:5–7. Joshua discusses the exodus.
Judges 2:1. Brought out of Egypt
Amos 2:10. Remembering the exodus

▶ Exorcism *(expulsion)*

The act, practice, or ceremony of expelling evil spirits
Mark 1:23–26. Exorcism in a synagogue
Mark 5:1–20. Exorcism of a man who lived among the tombs
Mark 9:14–29. Exorcism of a demon-possessed boy
Luke 11:24–26. A short-lived exorcism
Acts 16:16–18. Exorcism at Philippi

▶ Experience *(knowledge, occurrence)*

Active participation in events or activities, leading to the accumulation of knowledge or skill
Deuteronomy 11:2. Experiencing God's power
Judges 2:10. No experience with God
Job 32:7. Age and experience
Psalm 60:3. Experiencing hardship
Psalm 119:100. Years of experience
Ecclesiastes 1:16. The experience of wisdom and knowledge

▶ Expertise *(knowledge, proficiency, skill)*

Expert advice; skill or knowledge in a particular area
Genesis 25:27. Esau's expertise
Exodus 31:1–3. Expertise of Bezalel
Exodus 35:31. Crafts expertise
Ezra 7:6. Ezra's expertise
Matthew 22:34–36. Expertise in the law
Acts 5:34. Gamaliel's expertise

▶ Exploitation *(misuse, taking advantage)*

Utilization of another selfishly
Esther 1:10–11. Exploitation of Vashti
Proverbs 22:22–23. Don't exploit the poor.
1 Thessalonians 4:6. Don't exploit believers.
2 Peter 2:10–12. Exploitation of false prophets

▶ Exploration *(adventure, discovery, traveling)*

Searching into or traveling in for the purpose of discovery
Numbers 13–14. Exploring Canaan
Joshua 14:7–8. Caleb's exploration summary

Judges 18:1–2. Exploration of the land
Job 28:9–11. Exploration of rivers
Ecclesiastes 7:25. Study and exploration

▶ Extortion *(extract, falsely obtaining)*

Illegal use of one's official position or powers to obtain property, funds, or patronage
Leviticus 6:1–5. Restitution for extortion
2 Kings 5:19–27. Gehazi's extortion
Psalm 62:10. Don't count on extortion.
Isaiah 33:15. Getting rich by extortion
Luke 3:14. Don't extort money.

▶ Eyes *(eyesight)*

The organ of vision or of light sensitivity
Genesis 29:17. Attractive eyes
Exodus 21:24, 26. An eye for an eye
Leviticus 26:14–16. Curse of eye trouble
Judges 16:21. Samson loses his eyesight.
1 Samuel 11:1. Eye poker
2 Kings 6:16–17. Open their eyes.
Mark 8:22–26. Healing a blind man's eyes

▶ Faction(s) *(groups, parties, sections)*

Group forming cohesive, often contentious, minority within a larger group

1 Kings 16:21. Two factions

1 Corinthians 11:19. The need for factions

2 Corinthians 12:20. Factions among the Corinthian church

Galatians 5:19–20. Factions—a product of the corrupt nature

▶ Facts *(details, information, specifics)*

Information presented as objectively real

1 Samuel 23:23. Come back with the facts.

Acts 19:35–36. Undeniable facts?

Acts 21:34. Difficult fact-finding

Romans 4:19. Abraham knew the facts.

1 Corinthians 10:7, 14. Look at the facts.

▶ Failure *(catastrophe, fiasco, sin)*

Not having achieved one's desired end or ends; one that fails

Judges 2:1–5. Consequences of Israel's failure

Acts 5:35–36. Theudas's failure

Romans 5:15–17. One person's failure affects all.

Romans 11:11–12. Israel's failure

▶ Fainthearted *(cowardly, nervous, timid)*

Deficient in conviction or courage; timid

Deuteronomy 20:3–8. Don't be fainthearted.

Joshua 2. The fainthearted in Jericho

Judges 7:3. An out for the fainthearted

Isaiah 7:3–4. A command to avoid faintheartedness

Jeremiah 49:23. Fainthearted Hamath and Arpad

▶ Fairness *(equality, impartiality, justice)*

Exhibiting a disposition free of favoritism or bias; impartiality

Psalm 98:8–9. Judging with fairness

Psalm 99:4. God established fairness

Proverbs 1:1–3. Acquiring fairness

Proverbs 29:14. Judging the poor with fairness

Isaiah 32:1. Ruling with fairness

▶ Faith *(assurance, confidence, conviction, trust)*

Confident belief in the truth, value, or trustworthiness of a person, an idea, or a thing

Genesis 15:6. The faith of Abram

1 Samuel 2:12. No faith

1 Samuel 23:16. Strengthening David's faith

Matthew 8:10. Amazing faith

Matthew 8:23–27. Little faith during a storm

Matthew 11:6. Keeping the faith

Luke 8:48. The faith that leads to healing

Hebrews 11:1. A definition of faith

▶ Faithfulness *(constancy, loyalty, steadfastness)*

Exhibiting a steadfast adherence to a faith or cause

Genesis 32:9–10. God's faithfulness

Joshua 24:14. Serve God with faithfulness.

1 Chronicles 9:26. Resume of faithfulness

Psalm 36:5. Praising God's faithfulness

Psalm 100:5. Enduring faithfulness

Isaiah 11:5. Messianic faithfulness

▶ Fall *(autumn, sin)*

The season of autumn; the loss of innocence after Adam and Eve ate the forbidden fruit in the Garden of Eden; also, to experience defeat or ruin

Genesis 3. The fall

Deuteronomy 11:14. Rain in the fall

2 Kings 17. The fall of Samaria

2 Kings 25. The fall of Jerusalem

Psalm 66:8–9. Not allowed to fall

Romans 11:12. The fall of the Jewish people

▶ False god(s) (see *Idol[s]*)

F

▶ False messiah(s) *(antichrist, false leaders)*

Anyone falsely claiming to be the Messiah

Matthew 24:23–24. False messiahs

2 Thessalonians 2:9. A false messiah

1 John 2:22. The false reject God.

Revelation 13:13. Power of a false messiah

▶ False prophet(s) *(false messengers)*

Spokesmen or messengers who claimed to speak for God but were not sent by God

Numbers 31:16. Balaam the false prophet

1 Kings 22. Four hundred false prophets

Nehemiah 6:14. False female prophet

Isaiah 44:25. Signs of false prophets

Jeremiah 6:13–14. Message of false prophets

Jeremiah 14:14. Lies of false prophets

Ezekiel 13:8–9. God acts against false prophets.

Matthew 7:15–16. Beware of false prophets.

▶ False teacher(s) *(false doctrine, heresy)*

Teachers who teach heresy, rather than truth

1 Timothy 1:3–4. Teaching a false doctrine

1 Timothy 6:3–4. The conceit of false teaching

2 Timothy 4:3. The desire to hear false teaching

Titus 1:10–11. False teachers ruin families.

2 Peter 2:1–3. False teachers

2 John 7–11. Don't even greet a false teacher.

▶ False witness(es) *(liar)*

A person or persons who provide false testimony; liar

Exodus 20:16. Don't be a false witness.

Deuteronomy 19:18–19. Punish a false witness.

1 Kings 21:8–10. Finding false witnesses

Psalm 27:12. False witnesses

Proverbs 6:16, 19. God hates false testimony.

Proverbs 12:17. Deceitful witness

▶ Falsehood (see *Lying*)

▶ Fame *(prominence, notoriety, recognition)*

Great renown; public estimation

Deuteronomy 26:18–19. God will provide fame in exchange for obedience.

Joshua 6:27. Joshua's fame

1 Samuel 18:6–7. David's fame eclipses Saul's.

1 Kings 4:30–31. Solomon's fame

1 Chronicles 14:17. David's fame

2 Chronicles 26:15. Uzziah's fame

Isaiah 66:19. God's fame

▶ Familiarity *(acquaintance, informality, intimacy)*

Enthusiastic or impatient desire or interest

Numbers 11:4–6. Desire for familiar foods

Psalm 139:3. God is familiar with our ways.

Isaiah 53:3. Familiar with suffering

Acts 26:26. Agrippa's familiarity

Romans 7:1. Familiar with Moses' teachings (the law)

▶ Family *(kin, relations, relatives)*

Parents and offspring; people sharing a common ancestry; believers united by the Holy Spirit

Genesis 7:1. Noah's family

Exodus 12:3. One Passover lamb per family

Leviticus 27:22. Family property

Psalm 68:6. God makes families.

Proverbs 27:27. Promise of provision for a family

Galatians 6:10. Family of believers

1 Peter 4:17. Judgment starts with the family of God.

▶ Famine *(deprivation, scarcity, starvation)*

Drastic wide-reaching food shortage

Genesis 12:10. Abram faces a famine.

Genesis 41. Pharaoh dreams of a famine.

Deuteronomy 32:24. Starved by famines

Ruth 1:1. Fleeing to Moab due to a famine

2 Samuel 24:13. David's choice: fleeing, famine, or plague
1 Kings 8:37–38. Famine in the land; prayers for mercy
2 Kings 6:24–25. A severe famine
Romans 8:35. Even famine can't separate us.
Revelation 6:7–8. Wars and famines to come

▶ Fanatic *(extremist, zealot)*

Person marked by extreme unreasoning enthusiasm as for a cause

John 2:16–17. After driving out the moneychangers, Jesus' zeal might have seemed like fanaticism to some.
Acts 26:9–11. Paul's fanaticism against Christianity
Romans 10:2. Devoted but misguided
Galatians 4:17–18. Avoid fanatics.

▶ Farmer *(cultivator, grower, planter)*

One who works on or operates a farm; one who cultivates crops

Genesis 4:2–3. Cain—the first recorded farmer
Isaiah 28:24. Questions about farmers
Jeremiah 14:4. Disappointed farmers
Amos 5:16. Mourning farmers
Zechariah 13:4–5. False prophets will admit to being farmers.
Mark 4:3–20. Parable of the farmer sowing seeds
James 5:7. Have the patience of farmers.

▶ Fashion *(make, form, style)*

The make or form of something; a distinctive or peculiar and often habitual manner or way; a prevailing custom, usage, or style

Exodus 28:15. Fashioning a breastpiece for a high priest
Job 10:8. Would He destroy what He fashioned?
Psalm 33:15. God fashions each heart.
Isaiah 40:19. Fashioning silver chains for an idol
Isaiah 45:18. He who fashioned the earth

▶ Fasting *(abstain)*

Partial or total abstinence from food as to show humility and submission before God

2 Samuel 12:15–17. David fasts and pleads for his child's life.
2 Chronicles 20:3. Jehoshaphat proclaims a fast.
Ezra 8:21. Ezra proclaims a fast.
Esther 4:15–16. Esther proclaims a fast.
Matthew 6:16–18. Jesus preaches about fasting.
Matthew 9:14–15. Does Jesus fast?

▶ Father *(God, man with children)*

Man who has offspring; also, a name for God or a respected leader

Genesis 2:24. Leaving father and mother
Genesis 17:5. The father of many nations
Ruth 4:18–22. David's forefathers
Matthew 6:9. God the Father in heaven
Romans 8:15. Abba Father
Ephesians 1:2. God our Father

▶ Father-in-law *(the father of one's spouse)*

The father of a man's wife

Genesis 30:25–31:55. Jacob is cheated by his father-in-law
Genesis 38. Tamar and her father-in-law, Judah
Genesis 41:50. Joseph's priestly father-in-law
Exodus 18. Moses' father-in-law, Jethro
1 Samuel 18:19–21. David's father-in-law, Saul
John 18:12–13. Annas, the father-in-law of Caiaphas

▶ Fault *(blemish, error, mistake)*

Character weakness or defect

Genesis 16:5. Abram's fault
Exodus 5:15–16. Pharaoh's fault
1 Samuel 29:3. No fault in David
Job 15:14. Faultess mortal?
Colossians 1:22. Entering God's presence without fault
Jude 24. Standing without fault

▶ Faultfinding *(blaming, nagging, nitpicking)*

Petty or nagging criticism; carping

Job 40:2. Will you find fault with God?

Romans 9:19. Why does God still find fault?

2 Corinthians 6:3. You can't fault us.

James 1:5. God doesn't find fault.

Jude 16. Complaining and finding fault

▶ Faultless *(see Fault)*

▶ Favor *(approval, esteem, partiality)*

The state of being held in high regard

Genesis 30:6. Favor with God

Genesis 32:5. Trying to win Esau's favor

Numbers 6:22–26. The blessing of God's favor

Deuteronomy 33:23. Naphtali enjoys God's favor.

Zechariah 11:7. Favor and Unity

Matthew 22:15–16. Jesus' favor

Luke 1:28. Highly favored

Luke 2:40. Jesus has God's favor.

▶ Favoritism *(bias, partiality, preference)*

A display of partiality toward a favored person or group

Genesis 25:27–28. Isaac and Rebekah show favoritism.

Exodus 23:2–3. Don't show favoritism.

Leviticus 19:15. Don't play favorites in situations requiring justice.

Acts 10:34. God doesn't play favorites.

Romans 2:11. Again, God doesn't play favorites.

Ephesians 6:9. Be like your Master in heaven: don't play favorites.

▶ Fear(s) *(anxiety, concern, worry)*

A feeling of agitation or anxiety caused by present or imminent danger; also, to be in awe of, revere

Genesis 9:1–2. Fear of man

Genesis 22:12. Fear God.

Genesis 31:42. The Fear of Isaac

Exodus 19:16. Shaking with fear

Leviticus 25:17. The only kind of fear to have

2 Chronicles 20:29–30. The fear of the Lord falls on other nations.

Psalm 55:4–5. Fear and trembling

▶ Feast(s) *(banquet, holiday)*

A large, elaborate meal for many guests; a periodic religious festival

Genesis 21:8. Abraham holds a feast.

Leviticus 23:2. Required feasts

2 Samuel 3:20–21. David holds a feast.

2 Kings 6:22–23. A feast for enemies

Proverbs 17:1. Dry bread is better than a feast.

Jeremiah 51:37–39. A feast for Babylon

▶ Feelings *(manner, point of view, thoughts)*

Susceptibility to emotional response; sensibilities

Numbers 5:12–15. Feelings of jealousy

Psalm 17:10. The wicked and their feelings

Proverbs 29:11. A fool and his feelings

Habakkuk 3:16. A rotten feeling

John 12:27. Jesus—too troubled to express His feelings

2 Corinthians 7:13–15. Titus's feelings

▶ Feet *(measurement, movement, steps)*

The lower extremities of the vertebrate legs; also, a unit of measurement

Genesis 6:15. How many feet?

Genesis 18:3–4. Washing feet

Genesis 49:33. Pulled in his feet

Exodus 12:11. Sandals on your feet

Exodus 26:7–8. Tent measurements in feet

Ruth 3:6–7. Uncovering Boaz's feet

2 Samuel 19:24. Untended feet

2 Samuel 22:37. A wide path for David's feet

▶ Fellowship *(companionship, friendship, partnership)*

Relating to God and with fellow believers

Exodus 20:24. Fellowship offerings

2 Chronicles 31:2. Priests assigned to the fellowship offerings

1 Corinthians 1:9. Called into fellowship

Galatians 2:9. Right hand of fellowship

Philippians 2:1–2. Fellowship of the Spirit

▶ Female *(girl, woman)*

A member of the sex that produces ova or bears young

Genesis 1:27. Created male and female

Genesis 15:9. Sacrificing a female animal

Genesis 21:28–30. Using female lambs as a sign

Judges 21:10–11. Claim these females.

Luke 22:56. A female slave confronts Peter

Acts 16:16. A demon-possessed female slave

▶ Fermentation *(making alcohol)*

Chemical reaction that turns a complex organic compound into a simple substance, i.e., alcohol is converted by yeast

Leviticus 10:9. Priests to avoid fermented drinks while on duty

Numbers 28:7. Fermented drink offering

Deuteronomy 14:26. Fermented drink

Deuteronomy 29:6. No wine in the wilderness

Isaiah 63:2. Wine-making metaphor

▶ Fertility *(childbearing, fruitfulness, productiveness)*

The quality or state of being fertile; birthrate of a population; also, capable of bearing or producing crops abundantly

Genesis 1:22. Birds, be fertile.

Genesis 29:31–35. Leah's fertility

Genesis 30:14–15. Fertility superstition: mandrakes will cause pregnancy

Genesis 35:9, 11. The command to be fertile

1 Kings 14:23. Worshiping a fertility goddess

▶ Festival *(assembly, celebration, feast)*

Required holiday or celebration where Israel commemorated an event or a person

Exodus 5:1. A festival in God's honor

Exodus 12:14–17. Festival of Unleavened Bread

Exodus 12:21–27. Passover

Leviticus 23:5. Passover festival date

Leviticus 23:33–34. Festival of Booths

Leviticus 25:3–5. Festival for the land

▶ Fever(s) *(temperature)*

Abnormally high body temperatures; a disease characterized by a high fever

Leviticus 26:14–15. Fever as a result of disobedience

Deuteronomy 28:20–22. Curses and fevers

Job 30:30. Job's fever

Matthew 8:14–15. Curing a fever

John 4:46–53. Curing another fever

▶ Field(s) *(land, pasture)*

A broad, level, open expanse of land

Genesis 4:8. Killing fields

Genesis 23. Abraham buys Machpelah's field.

2 Samuel 2:15–17. Field of Enemies

2 Samuel 14:28–30. Destroying Joab's barley field

Jeremiah 4:3. Unplowed fields

Jeremiah 32. Jeremiah buys a field.

Matthew 27:6–10. Field of blood

▶ Fig tree *(shrub, tree)*

Tree or shrub that produces the common fig

Genesis 3:7. First clothes made from the leaves of a fig tree

1 Samuel 25:18. Fruit of the fig tree

Jeremiah 24. Figs as a metaphor

Hosea 2:12. Destroyed fig trees: punishment for God's unfaithful wife

Joel 1:7, 12. Other prophecies of destroyed fig trees

Micah 4:4. Prophecy of peace: sitting under fig trees

Matthew 21:18–22. Jesus curses the fig tree.

F

▶ Fight (see *Battle[s]*)

▶ Figures of speech *(hyperbole, metaphor, simile)*

Expressions in which words are used in a nonliteral way (metaphor or simile) or in which certain phrases are repeated through a device like anaphora (repeating the same word at the beginning of each sentence) or epistrophe (repetition of a word or expression at the end of each sentence or phrase)

Psalm 7:14. Metaphor
Psalm 10:9. Simile
Psalm 118. Epistrophe
Matthew 5:3–11. Anaphora
John 10:6. Jesus uses a figure of speech.
John 16:29–30. Without figures of speech

▶ Financial planning *(investing, planning, using wisely)*

Money management

Exodus 22:25. Don't charge interest on loans.
Ecclesiastes 2:8–9. Building a nest egg
Ecclesiastes 2:20–21. Estate planning woes
Luke 12:13–15. Jesus' advice about financial planning
2 Corinthians 9:6–7. Give wisely and cheerfully.

▶ Finger(s) *(digits, hand)*

One of the five digits of the hand

Genesis 41:42. A sign of Joseph's authority: a signet ring on Joseph's finger
Exodus 29:12. Aaron and sons' commissioning: blood on the finger
2 Samuel 21:20. Six-fingered man
Psalm 8:3–4. God's fingers
Psalm 144:1. He trained my fingers.
Isaiah 2:8. Idols Israel's fingers molded
Matthew 23:1–4. Pharisees don't lift a finger to help.

▶ Finishing well *(ending)*

Coming to the end of one's task or life in a God-pleasing way

Deuteronomy 34:10–12. A life well spent
2 Kings 23:25. Josiah works to finish well.
Philippians 1:6. God wants you to finish well.
2 Timothy 4:6–8. Finishing well
Revelation 7:9–10, 13–14. People who finished well

▶ Fire *(blaze, flames, inferno)*

Chemical change that produces heat and light and is composed by flame

Exodus 3:2. Fire on a bush
Exodus 13:21–22. Column of fire
Leviticus 1:10–13. An offering made by fire
Leviticus 10:1–2. Unauthorized fire leads to death by fire.
Psalm 50:3. A devouring fire
Proverbs 26:20. No wood, no fire; no gossip, no quarrel
Daniel 3:22. An extremely hot fire

▶ Firstborn *(born first)*

First in order of birth, whether people or animals

Genesis 4:4. Abel offers firstborn animals.
Genesis 27:32. Isaac's firstborn son, Esau
Exodus 11–12. Death of the firstborn
Exodus 22:29–30. God wants the firstborn.
Luke 2:6–7. Mary's firstborn son
Romans 8:29. Firstborn among many

▶ Firstfruits *(first, best, more to come)*

The firstborn child or the best part of a crop offered to God

Exodus 23:16, 19. Firstfruits
Exodus 34:22, 26. Bring the first and the best.
Leviticus 2:12. Firstfruit offerings are not burned on the altar.
Numbers 18:12. Firstfruit offerings are gifts for the priests and Levites.
2 Chronicles 31:5. A tithe of firstfruit offerings

▶ Fish *(go fishing, big fish)*

Any of the cold-blooded aquatic vertebrates

Genesis 1:26. Humans to rule over the fish of the sea

Exodus 7:20–21. Plague of blood affected the fish.

Nehemiah 13:16. Selling fish on the Sabbath

Job 12:7–8. Fish as teachers

Jonah 1:17–2:10. Big fish swallows Jonah.

Matthew 14:13–21. Jesus feeds over 5,000 people with five loaves and two fish.

John 21:1–11. The miraculous catch of fish

▶ Fisherman *(occupation)*

One who fishes as an occupation

Isaiah 19:8. Mourning fishermen

Ezekiel 29:4. God as a fisherman, trawling for Egypt

Matthew 4:18, 21. Fishermen at the Sea of Galilee

Luke 5:1–11. Fishermen on task

▶ Fishing for people *(conquer, witnessing)*

Metaphor for sharing the Good News of Jesus with people and also for enemy nations sent to conquer Israel

Jeremiah 16:16. Enemies fishing for Israel

Matthew 4:19. Fishing for people

Matthew 13:47–50. Parable of the fishing net: throwing back the wicked

Luke 5:10. Catching people

▶ Flattery *(adulation, sycophancy)*

Excessive or insincere praise

Job 32:21–22. Job avoids flattery.

Psalm 5:9. Flattery of the wicked

Daniel 11:32. Flattery of a conqueror

1 Thessalonians 2:5. Paul never used flattery.

Jude 16. Flattery of the sinful

▶ Flesh *(body, nature)*

The soft tissue of the body of a vertebrate; also, a metaphor for human existence

Genesis 2:21–24. Flesh of his flesh

Genesis 6:3. Flesh and blood

Leviticus 13. Disease of the flesh

Job 41:23. The flesh of Leviathan

Luke 24:38–39. Jesus in the flesh

1 Corinthians 15:50. Flesh and blood cannot inherit the kingdom of God.

▶ Flies *(insects)*

Any of the two-winged insects of the *Diptera* order

Exodus 8:20–32. Plague of flies

Psalm 105:31. Recalling the plague of flies

Ecclesiastes 10:1. Dead flies

Isaiah 7:18–19. Whistling for flies

Isaiah 51:6. Dying like flies

▶ Flirt *(play, seduction)*

To make playfully romantic sexual overtures without serious intent

Song of Songs 1. Flirting with the groom

Isaiah 3:16. Flirting of the women of Zion

Ezekiel 23. Metaphor of a flirting, adulterous nation

James 4:4. Flirting with the world

▶ Flock(s) *(animals, Christians)*

Group of animals that live, travel, or feed together; also, a metaphor for Israel or a group of Christians in the same church

Genesis 27:9. Rebekah sends Jacob to the flock.

Deuteronomy 16:2. An animal from the flock

1 Samuel 17:15. David tended the family flock.

Psalm 79:13. God's flock

Isaiah 40:10–11. He takes care of his flock.

Matthew 26:31. Scattered flock

Luke 12:32. Little flock

1 Peter 5:2–3. Be examples for the flock.

▶ Flogging *(punishment, whipping)*

A severe beating with a whip or a rod

Deuteronomy 25:3. Flogging limit

Psalm 89:32. Punished with flogging

Matthew 10:17. Flogging in the synagogue

Matthew 27:26. Jesus was flogged.

Acts 22:24. Paul was flogged.
2 Corinthians 11:23–24. Catalogue of flogging
Hebrews 11:36. Flogged for the faith

▶ Flood *(deluge, inundation, torrent)*

An overflowing of water onto land that is normally dry
Genesis 6–8. The great flood
Genesis 49:4. Reuben is like a flood.
Joshua 4:18. Seasonal flood level of the Jordan
Job 20:28. The wicked punished with a flood
Proverbs 15:28. A flood of stupidity
Malachi 3:10. A flood of blessings
Matthew 24:37–29. Caught unawares by the flood

▶ Flow *(current, pour)*

To move or run smoothly with unbroken continuity
Exodus 14:26. Flow of the Red Sea
Numbers 24:7. Prophecy of plenty: flowing water
Nehemiah 9:15. Water flowing from a rock
Psalm 147:18. God causes water to flow.
Proverbs 5:16. Water flow—metaphor for promiscuity
Ecclesiastes 1:7. Water cycle starts with flowing water.

▶ Flower(s) *(blossom, bloom, lily, rose)*

The reproductive structure of some seed-bearing plants
Exodus 25:31–34. Flower-shaped cups of the lamp stand
Psalm 103:15–16. Like a flower
Isaiah 28:1. Like a withered flower
Nahum 1:4. The flowers of Lebanon
Matthew 6:28–29. God cares for flowers and people.
James 1:10–11. Rich people and flowers

▶ Focus *(center, concentration, hub)*

Center of interest or activity
Psalm 86:11. Focus my heart.
Isaiah 26:3. A mind focused on God is kept in perfect peace.
Romans 12:17. Focus your thoughts.
Colossians 3:1. Focus on things above.
1 Timothy 4:16. Focus on what you do.
Hebrews 12:2. Focus on Jesus.

▶ Follow through/Follow up *(going along with, continuing on with)*

The instance of following up, as to review new developments
Matthew 18:15–16. How to follow up on a confrontation
Romans 1:8–13. Paul's follow-up to ministry
2 Corinthians 2:1–4. Paul's follow-up to a painful letter
Galatians 5:16. You won't have to follow through.
Philippians 2:25–28. Ephaphroditus's follow-up visit

▶ Follower *(disciple)*

One who subscribes to the teachings and methods of another
Numbers 16. Korah and his followers
Psalm 106:17–18. Abiram's followers
Matthew 23:15. Followers of the Pharisees and scribes
Acts 9. A murderer of followers becomes a follower of Christ
Acts 24:14. A follower of the way
2 Corinthians 12:2. A follower of Christ

▶ Folly *(foolishness, madness, stupidity)*

A lack of good sense, understanding, or foresight
1 Samuel 25:25. Folly goes with him.
Job 42:8. Folly of Job's friends
Psalm 38:5. My folly
Psalm 69:5. God sees all folly.
Proverbs 5:23. Folly can lead to death.

▶ Food *(sustenance, Word of God)*

Material (plants or animals) that contains or consists of essential body nutrients, such as carbohydrates, fats, proteins, etc.

Genesis 1:29. Green plants for food

Genesis 3:17–19. Food by the sweat of your brow

Genesis 41:29–31. Plenty of food before the famine

Leviticus 26:26. One of the curses of disobedience: destroyed food supply

Mark 6:41. Jesus gives thanks for the food before performing a miracle.

▶ Food preparation *(baking, cooking, frying)*

Any of the various ways that food is prepared

Genesis 18:7. Servant prepares food for visiting angels.

Genesis 19:3. Lot prepares a meal.

Genesis 27:30–31. Esau prepares a meal.

Leviticus 7:9. Various ways to prepare a grain offering

Joshua 5:11. Roasting—one way of preparing food

Judges 6:19. Gideon prepares a meal.

John 12:2. A prepared meal at the home of Mary, Martha, and Lazarus

▶ Foolishness *(folly)*

Lacking good judgment

Ecclesiastes 2:12–13. An advantage over foolishness

Ecclesiastes 7:25. The foolishness of wickedness

Ecclesiastes 10:13. Foolish talk from a fool

Isaiah 9:17. Foolishness of those who reject God

Mark 7:20–22. Foolishness starts within.

▶ Foot washing *(cleansing the feet)*

Washing the grime off a person's feet—a task usually performed by servants in Bible times

Genesis 19:2. Lot offers to wash the feet of visiting angels.

Genesis 24:32. Washing the feet of Abraham's servant

Exodus 30:17–21. Bronze basin for foot washing

1 Samuel 25:41. Foot washing as a metaphor for an acceptance of a marriage proposal

John 12:3. Washing Jesus' feet

John 13:1–20. Jesus washes His disciples' feet.

▶ Forbearance *(patience, restraint, self-control)*

Tolerance and restraint in the face of provocation

1 Samuel 25:23–31. Abigail encourages forbearance.

Proverbs 25:15. A ruler's forbearance

Romans 2:3–4. God's forbearance

Romans 3:25–26. God's forbearance

▶ Forbidden *(banned, illegal, prohibited)*

An act or item one is commanded to avoid

Genesis 2:15–17. The forbidden fruit

Leviticus 4. When you do what's forbidden . . .

Deuteronomy 2:37. Forbidden to go to the Ammonites

Ezra 7:24. Forbidden to demand tolls or fees from temple workers

Lamentations 1:10. Forbidden to enter the congregation

1 Peter 4:3. Forbidden worship

▶ Forefather *(ancestor)*

A person from whom one is descended

Numbers 26:58. Amram's forefather

Joshua 19:47. Dan the forefather

1 Chronicles 24:19. Aaron, the priests' forefather

Romans 4:1. Our forefather Abraham

▶ Foreigner(s) *(alien, stranger)*

One who is from outside a particular group or community; an outsider

Genesis 17:12. Circumcise every male child, even those of foreigners.

Exodus 2:22. His name is Foreigner.

Exodus 12:43–44. Foreigners excluded from the Passover

Exodus 22:21. Never oppress foreigners.

Leviticus 24:21–22. Same rule for Israelites or foreigners

Deuteronomy 23:20. Foreigners can be charged interest.

Ruth 2:10. "I'm only a foreigner."

▶ Foreknowledge *(awareness)*

Awareness of something before its existence or occurrence

Acts 2:23. God's set purpose and foreknowledge

Romans 8:29. Foreknowledge and predestination

Romans 11:2. Foreknowledge and predestination

1 Peter 1:1–2. God's foreknowledge

▶ Forerunner *(forbear, precursor, predecessor)*

One that precedes, as in time

Malachi 4:5–6. Elijah was the forerunner of John the Baptist

Matthew 3:1–4. John the Baptist: the forerunner of Jesus

Romans 8:29. Jesus is our forerunner.

Hebrews 6:19–20. Our forerunner behind the veil

▶ Forget *(fail to remember)*

Unable to remember something

Genesis 41:51. He Helps Me Forget—Manasseh, son of Joseph

Deuteronomy 4:9–10. Don't forget, Israel.

Deuteronomy 8:11. Don't forget God.

Deuteronomy 14:27. Don't forget the Levites.

Psalm 10:12. Don't forget, God.

Psalm 45:10. Forget your people.

Psalm 119:16. I never forget your Word.

▶ Forgiveness *(absolution, clemency, pardon)*

The act of forgiving

Psalm 130. Forgiveness from God

Proverbs 14:9. Forgiveness among decent people

Mark 1:4. Forgiveness of sins

Luke 1:77. Saved through forgiveness of sins

Luke 4:18–19. Jesus proclaims the forgiveness of sins.

Luke 7:47. Forgiving a sinful woman

▶ Fornication *(sexual sin)*

Sexual intercourse between partners who are not married to each other

Isaiah 23:17. Tyre's fornication

John 8:41. Not born of fornication

2 Corinthians 12:21. Repenting of fornication

Galatians 5:19. Fornication: a work of the flesh

Ephesians 5:3. Fornication should not be named among you.

▶ Forsake *(abandon, give up, renounce)*

To give up something held dear

Deuteronomy 31:6, 8. He won't forsake you.

Joshua 1:5. Joshua would not be forsaken.

2 Kings 21:14. A forsaken remnant

Psalm 27:9–10. Forsaken by parents, but taken by God

Psalm 37:28. Saints are not forsaken.

Psalm 71:18. Even when I'm old and gray, please don't forsake me.

Proverbs 4:2. Don't forsake my teaching.

▶ Fortress *(bastion, fortification, stronghold)*

A fortified place, particularly a military stronghold

2 Samuel 5:7, 9. The fortress Zion

2 Samuel 12:26–27. The fortress of Rabbah

2 Kings 15:23–25. Capture of a royal fortress

Nehemiah 1:1–2. The fortress at Susa

Psalm 18:2. The ultimate fortress: God

▶ Fortune *(destiny, luck, wealth)*

The chance happening of fortunate or adverse effects; extensive amounts of material possessions or financial wealth

Genesis 30:11. What good fortune!

Isaiah 65:11. God of good fortune
Hosea 12:8. Ephraim's fortune

▶ Fortune-telling *(see Divination)*

▶ Forty *(number)*

The cardinal number equal to 4 times 10
Genesis 7:4. Forty days and nights of rain
Genesis 8:6–7. Forty days later
Exodus 16:35. Forty years of manna
Exodus 24:18. Forty days and nights on Mount Sinai
Exodus 26:19–21. Forty silver sockets (tabernacle furnishings)
Numbers 14:34. Forty years of wandering
Matthew 4:1–2. Forty days of fasting

▶ Foul language *(see Profanity)*

▶ Foundational truths *(basic beliefs)*

Truths that are the basis for Christianity
Matthew 7:24–29. Building on a foundation of truth
John 3:16. Truth to build on: Jesus died for you.
John 14:16. Truth to build on: The Holy Spirit is with you forever.
Acts 10:34. Truth to grow on: God doesn't play favorites.
Romans 1:4. Truth to build on: Jesus is the Son of God who rose from the dead.
Romans 10:9–10. Truth to build on: God's approval comes through Jesus.
1 Thessalonians 4:14. Truth to build on: Jesus will return to earth.

▶ Fountain *(cascade, spray, spout)*

An artificially created jet or stream of water
Nehemiah 2:13–14. Fountain Gate
Psalm 36:9. God: The fountain of life
Proverbs 16:22. Understanding: A fountain of life
Proverbs 18:4. The fountain of wisdom
Jeremiah 2:13. God: The fountain of life-giving water
Jeremiah 9:1. A fountain of tears
Revelation 21:6. The fountain of the water of life

▶ Four horsemen *(apocalypse, end times)*

The four horsemen described in the book of Revelation
Zechariah 1:8–11. The four horsemen patrol.
Zechariah 6:1–7. The four horsemen patrol.
Revelation 6:1–8. The four horsemen ride.

▶ Fox(es) *(the animal, deceitful person)*

Carnivorous mammals of the genus *Vulpes*, and related to dogs and wolves
Judges 15:4–5. Foxes and fire
Nehemiah 4:3. Sarcastic comments about a fox and the wall of Jerusalem
Song of Songs 2:15. Catch the little foxes.
Ezekiel 13:4. Prophets like foxes
Luke 13:31–32. Herod the fox

▶ Fragrance *(aroma, perfume, scent)*

The state or quality of having a pleasing odor
Song of Songs 1:2–3, 12. The fragrance of cologne and perfume
Song of Songs 2:13. The fragrance of the grapevine
Song of Songs 4:10–11. A fragrant bride
Song of Songs 7:8, 13. Pleasing fragrances
John 12:3. The fragrance of nard
2 Corinthians 2:14–16. The fragrance of the believer

▶ Frankincense *(oil, perfume)*

Aromatic gum resin obtained from African and Asian trees
Exodus 30:34–35. Pure frankincense
Numbers 5:15. Frankincense for jealousy test
Matthew 2:11. Frankincense: a gift for a king
Revelation 18:11–13. Cargo of frankincense

▶ Freedom *(choice, independence, liberty)*

Liberty of a person from slavery, detention, or oppression

Genesis 27:40. Esau will eventually gain his freedom.

Exodus 21:2. Freedom from slavery in the seventh year

Acts 7:25. Freedom for Israel from God

Romans 8:20–21. Freedom of God's children

1 Corinthians 8:9. Don't use freedom to cause a person to sin.

Galatians 4:5. Jesus paid for our freedom.

▶ Freewill *(autonomy, freedom)*

Offerings made voluntarily

Exodus 35:29. Freewill offerings

Leviticus 7:16. Freewill offerings eaten

Leviticus 22:21. Bring freewill offerings to the Lord.

Leviticus 23:37–38. In addition to freewill offerings

Deuteronomy 12:6. The freedom to bring freewill offerings

▶ Friction *(resistance, tension)*

The rubbing of one object or surface against another; also, conflict

Genesis 27:40–41. Jacob's trickery and Isaac's blessing create friction.

1 Samuel 17:26–29. Friction between David and Eliab

1 Timothy 6:4–5. Constant friction

▶ Friend *(acquaintance, companion, comrade)*

A person whom one knows, likes, and trusts

Genesis 26:26. Abimelech's friend

Exodus 33:11. God's friend, Moses

Deuteronomy 13:6. Tempted by your best friend?

Job 2:11. Job's friends come to comfort him.

Proverbs 17:17–18. What a friend does

Proverbs 18:24. A loving friend

Proverbs 27:6. Wounds by a friend

Colossians 4:14. Paul's friend, Dr. Luke

James 2:23. Abraham, the friend of God

▶ Friendship *(relationship)*

The relationship between friends

Deuteronomy 23:3, 6. Never offer friendship

1 Samuel 20:42. David and Jonathan's friendship

2 Samuel 16:17–18. No loyalty in friendship

Psalm 109:4–5. When friendship goes bad

John 11:1–12:11. Jesus' friendship with Mary, Martha, and Lazarus

John 15:13–15. Jesus' friendship with his disciples and other believers

▶ Frog(s) *(amphibian)*

Any of the numerous tailless amphibians of the order *Anura*

Exodus 8:1–15. The second plague: frogs

Psalm 78:45. Rehashing the plague of frogs

Psalm 105:30. Frogs in Egypt

Revelation 16:13. Like frogs

▶ Frugality *(see Stewardship)*

▶ Fruit *(fruit of the vine, results)*

The ripened ovary or ovaries of a seed-bearing plant; also, the result of an activity

Genesis 1:11–12. The creation of fruit

Genesis 2:9, 16–17. Fruit of the garden

Genesis 3. Fruit that leads to a fall

Leviticus 19:23–25. Fruit trees

Proverbs 11:30. Fruit of the righteous

Matthew 7:17–20. Good and bad fruit

Luke 3:9. Produce good fruit or be cut down.

▶ Fruit of the Spirit *(characteristics)*

The characteristics developed by the Holy Spirit

2 Corinthians 6:6–7. Fruit you can see

Galatians 5:22–23. Fruit of the Spirit

Ephesians 4:2. Show the fruit of the Spirit

Ephesians 5:9. Fruit in goodness, righteousness, and truth

Colossians 3:12. God's people have this kind of fruit.

▶ Fuel *(add to, encourage, fire)*

Something consumed to produce energy

Isaiah 9:5. Boots and garments as fuel

Isaiah 9:19. People like fuel

Isaiah 44:15. Trees used as fuel

Ezekiel 4:12. Excrement for fuel

Ezekiel 15:1–4. Vine as fuel

▶ Fugitive *(deserter, escapee, renegade)*

Running away or fleeing as from the law

Genesis 4:12–14. Cain the fugitive

Judges 12:5. Fugitives from Ephraim

Proverbs 28:17. A fugitive with a murder charge

Isaiah 15:9. Fugitives from Moab

Jeremiah 50:28. Fugitives and refugees from Babylon

Ezekiel 24:25–26. A fugitive messenger

▶ Fulfillment *(accomplishment, completion, satisfaction)*

An action that brings something to an end or completes it

2 Chronicles 36:21. Fulfillment of God's words spoken through Jeremiah

Psalm 119:123. The fulfillment of God's promise

Daniel 11:14. Fulfillment of Daniel's vision

Luke 22:15–16. The Passover fulfilled

Luke 22:37. A prophecy to be fulfilled

▶ Full *(filled, packed)*

Containing all that is possible; complete in every particular

Genesis 6:11–13. Full of violence

Genesis 41:1. Two full years of imprisonment for Joseph

Exodus 16:20. Manna full of worms

Deuteronomy 23:24. Eat until you're full.

Acts 11:24. Full of the Holy Spirit

Acts 13:9–10. Full of the Holy Spirit versus full of dirty tricks

1 Peter 3:10. A full life

▶ Fundraising *(collecting, soliticiting)*

Collecting money for a cause

Romans 15:26–28. The fundraiser for the poor

1 Corinthians 16:1–3. Paul's fundraising suggestions

2 Corinthians 8:10–12. Matching donations for the fundraiser

2 Corinthians 9:1–3. Workers to help with the fundraising

▶ Funeral *(ceremony, interment, memorial)*

Ceremonies held in connection with the burial or cremation of a dead person

Genesis 50:11. Jacob (Israel's) funeral

2 Samuel 3:33–34. Abner's funeral

2 Chronicles 35:25. Song at Josiah's funeral

Jeremiah 34:4–5. Funeral fires

Ezekiel 19:1. Funeral song for princes

Ezekiel 27. Funeral song about Tyre

Amos 8:10. Festivals into funerals

▶ Furniture *(equipment, furnishings)*

The movable articles in a room or an establishment that make it fit for living or working

Genesis 48:2. Jacob's bed

Exodus 27. Furnishings for the tabernacle

Exodus 30:1–10. More furnishings

Exodus 31:7. Furniture of the tabernacle

2 Samuel 9:7. David's table

Matthew 21:12. Jesus turns over the furniture of the moneychangers.

▶ Futility *(ineffectuality, pointlessness, uselessness)*

No useful result

Job 7. The futility of life

Job 9:1–3. Arguing with God is futile. (Part 1)

Job 38–41. Arguing with God is futile. (Part 2)

Psalm 89:47. Created for futility?

Ephesians 4:17. Futility of their thinking

F

▶ Future *(forthcoming, impending, upcoming)*

The indefinite time yet to come

Genesis 44:15. Joseph knows the future?

Exodus 12:17. Future generations

Deuteronomy 6:20. In the future

2 Samuel 7:19. The future of David's dynasty

Psalm 31:15. The future of David's dynasty

Proverbs 23:18. There is a future.

Jeremiah 29:11. Plans for a hope-filled future

▶ Gain *(acquire)*

To come into possession or use of

Genesis 37:26. What will we gain?

2 Kings 15:19. Gaining support

Job 11:12. What an empty-headed person gains

Psalm 44:3. Who gained the victory?

Ecclesiastes 1:3. What do people gain?

Matthew 19:16. Gaining eternal life

1 Timothy 6:6. Great gain

Titus 3:5. Gaining God's approval

▶ Gall *(bitter herb)*

Bitter herb; liver secretion

Psalm 69:21. Gall—metaphor for bitterness

Lamentations 3:15, 19. Sated with gall

Matthew 27:34. Wine mixed with gall

▶ Gallows *(hanging)*

Device with two upright posts supporting a crossbeam from which a noose is suspended and used for execution by hanging

Esther 2:22–23. Hung on the gallows

Esther 5:14. Setting up the gallows

Esther 6:4. To the gallows with Mordecai?

Esther 7:10. Haman is hung on his own gallows.

Esther 8:7. Aftermath of being hung on the gallows

Esther 9:25. Joining their father on the gallows

▶ Gambling *(betting, dicing, gaming)*

To bet on an uncertain outcome

Job 6:27. Gambling for an orphan

Psalm 22:18. Gambling for garments

Proverbs 16:33. You can gamble, but God determines the outcome.

Joel 3:3. Gambling for a nation

Jonah 1:7. Gambling for blame

Luke 23:34. Gambling prophecy fulfilled

▶ Game(s) *(entertainment, pastime, sport)*

An activity providing entertainment or amusement; also, wild animals, birds, or fish hunted for sport or food

Genesis 27:2–7. Hunt wild game.

Job 21:11. Children of the wicked still happily play games.

Matthew 11:16–17. Children's games

1 Corinthians 9:25. Competing in the games

▶ Gang(s) (see *Mercenary[ies]*)

▶ Garden(s) *(Eden, Gethsemane, vegetable)*

Plot of land for the cultivation of flowers, vegetables, herbs, or fruit

Genesis 2:8–25. The Garden of Eden

Genesis 3. Fall in the Garden of Eden

Genesis 13:10. Like the Lord's garden

Deuteronomy 11:10. Vegetable garden

2 Kings 21:18. The garden of Uzza

Jeremiah 39:4. Escape through the king's garden

Matthew 26:36. In the Garden of Gethsemane

▶ Gardener *(tender)*

One who works or tends a garden for pleasure or hire

Genesis 2:15. The first gardener

Amos 7:14. Fig grower

Luke 13:6–9. Parable with a gardener

John 20:15. Is he the gardener?

▶ Garment *(clothing)*

An article of clothing

Ruth 3:8–9. Spread your garment.

1 Samuel 19:13. Covered with a garment

1 Kings 11:30–31. Torn garment; torn kingdom

Proverbs 20:16. Hold that garment.

Proverbs 31:24. Linen garments

Isaiah 50:9. Wearing out like a garment

G

▶ Gate(s) *(Beautiful Gate, city gate, Sheep Gate)*

A structure that can be swung, drawn, or lowered to block an entrance or a passageway

Genesis 34:20. At the city gate

Joshua 2:5. Gate of Jericho

1 Samuel 23:7. A gate with a double door

1 Chronicles 26:16. Shallecheth Gate

2 Chronicles 23:5. Foundation Gate

2 Chronicles 25:23. From gate to gate

2 Chronicles 33:14. Fish Gate

Nehemiah 3:1. Sheep Gate

Acts 3:2. Beautiful Gate

▶ Gather *(assemble, collect, group)*

To cause to come together; convene

Genesis 29:7. Gather the livestock.

Genesis 49:2. Gather around.

Exodus 5:6–8. Gathering their own straw

Exodus 16. Gathering manna

Leviticus 8:3. Gather at the tent.

Leviticus 23:22. Don't gather all of the grain.

▶ Gehenna *(hell, valley)*

English transliteration of the phrase, "the valley of Hinnom"

Joshua 15:8. Valley of Hinnom

2 Kings 23:10. Making Gehenna unclean

2 Chronicles 28:3. Sacrifices in Gehenna

Jeremiah 7:32. From Gehenna to Slaughter Valley

Mark 9:43. Better a cut-off hand than to end up in Gehenna

▶ Gem(s) *(jewel)*

Pearl or mineral that has been cut and polished for use as an ornament

Exodus 28:17–30. Gems on Aaron's breastplate

1 Chronicles 29:2. Gathering gems

2 Chronicles 3:6. Beautifying with gems

Job 28:18. More valuable than gems

Ezekiel 28:13. Covered with gems

Revelation 4:3. Gems on God's throne

Revelation 21:11, 17–21. Gems in heaven

▶ Gender *(femininity, masculinity, sex)*

Sexual identity, especially in relation to society or culture

Genesis 24:11. Task of women—drawing water

Exodus 1:16. Task of women—help in childbirth

Exodus 18:21. Task of men—leadership

Exodus 38:8. Task of women—serving at the entrance to the tabernacle

Numbers 4:35. Task of men—serving at the tabernacle

Numbers 36:8. Gender-based rule

Psalm 1:1. Not gender-specific

Titus 2:5. Gender-specific task

▶ Genealogy *(family record, family tree)*

Record or table of the descent of a person, family, or group from an ancestor or ancestors

1 Chronicles 1. Genealogy of Isaac's descendants

1 Chronicles 2:3–55. Genealogy of Judah's descendants

1 Chronicles 3. Genealogy of David's descendants

1 Chronicles 4. Genealogy of Judah's descendants (continued)

Matthew 1:1–17. Jesus' genealogy

▶ Generation *(age group)*

All of the offspring that are at the same stage of descent from a common ancestor

Genesis 15:16. The fourth generation

Exodus 1:6. Joseph's generation

Numbers 32:13. Death of a generation

Judges 2:10. Sin of a generation

Matthew 8:38. Sinful generation

Matthew 17:7. Corrupt generation

▶ Generation gap *(values)*

A broad difference in values and attitudes between one generation and another

1 Kings 12. Generation gap

2 Kings 2:23. Older prophet mocked by youths

1 Timothy 5:1–2. Intergenerational conversations
Titus 2:3–5. Bridging the gap

▶ Generosity *(liberality)*

Liberality in giving
Exodus 12:36. Generosity of the Egyptians
1 Kings 10:13. Solomon's generosity
Esther 1:7. Xerxes's generosity
Matthew 20:15. Generosity of a vineyard owner
2 Corinthians 9:11, 13. Generosity inspires thanksgiving.

▶ Genetics *(heredity, related characteristics)*

The branch of biology that deals with heredity; inherited characteristics among similar or related organisms
Genesis 1:11–12. Producing seed according to genetic makeup
Genesis 1:20–21. Fish and birds doing what they're genetically created to do
Genesis 1:24–25. Animals created to keep within a genetic code

▶ Genocide *(murder)*

The systematic and planned extermination of an entire nation, racial, political, or ethnic group
Numbers 31:17. Genocide of Midianites
Deuteronomy 7:1–2. Prepare for genocide.
Deuteronomy 20:13. Kill every man.
Joshua 8:24–25. Genocide at Ai
Esther 3:6. Haman turns to genocide.

▶ Gentile *(Greek, Roman, other nations)*

A non-Jewish person
Ezra 6:21. Unclean practices of the Gentiles
Acts 10. Associating with a Gentile
Acts 21:25. Gentiles not to eat food sacrificed to idols
Romans 2:9–10. Trouble for Jews and Gentiles
Romans 10:12. No difference between Jews and Gentiles

▶ Gentleness *(mildness, tenderness)*

Kindness or consideration; not showing harshness or severity
Psalm 18:35. God's gentleness
Proverbs 15:1. A gentle answer
Matthew 5:5. The blessing of gentleness
2 Corinthians 10:1. The gentleness of Christ
Galatians 5:22–23. One of the fruit of the Spirit
1 Timothy 6:11. Pursue gentleness
1 Peter 3:15. A gentle defense

▶ Genuine *(authentic, valid)*

Not spurious or counterfeit; authentic
1 Corinthians 11:19. Genuine believers
2 Corinthians 8:8. Genuine love
2 Corinthians 9:13. Genuine act of service
Philippians 2:20. Genuine interest
1 Timothy 1:2. A genuine child in the faith
James 2:22. Genuine faith

▶ Geometry *(measurement relationships)*

The mathematics of the properties, measurement, and relationship of points, lines, angles, surfaces, and solids
1 Kings 6. Geometry of the temple
Nehemiah 3:19–20. At the Angle
Job 38:5. Geometry of the earth
Ezekiel 42. Geometry of the temple in Ezekiel's vision

▶ Gethsemane *(garden)*

Place near the Mount of Olives; possibly a grove of olive trees
Matthew 26:36. Praying in the Garden of Gethsemane
Mark 14. Betrayed in the Garden of Gethsemane
Luke 22:39. Going to the garden near the Mount of Olives

▶ Ghost *(phantom, specter, spirit)*

The spirit of a dead person
1 Samuel 28:11–20. Saul seeks the ghost of Samuel.

Matthew 14:26. A ghost?
Matthew 28:19. Holy Ghost
Luke 24:36–37. Seeing a ghost?

▶ Giant(s) *(huge, massive)*

Person or thing of great size
Genesis 6:4. Giants in the land
Numbers 13:33. Giant descendants of Anak
Deuteronomy 2:20–21. Land of the giants
Deuteronomy 3:11. Last of the giants
1 Samuel 17. Goliath the giant
2 Samuel 21:16, 18. Son of a giant

▶ Gift(s) *(ability, bequest, present)*

Something bestowed voluntarily and without compensation
Genesis 32:13–15. A gift for Esau
Genesis 43:11. Gifts for Joseph
Numbers 18:6–7. Levites and priests: Gifts from God
Deuteronomy 33:13–16. The best gifts
1 Corinthians 12:28–31. Spiritual gifts
1 Corinthians 13:8. The gift of languages
Ephesians 3:16. The gift of the wealth of God's glory

▶ Girl(s) *(female)*

Female child
Genesis 24:13–14. Searching for the right girl for Isaac
Exodus 1:16. Girls allowed to live
Leviticus 12:5. Uncleanness after giving birth to a girl
2 Kings 5:2–4. A servant girl helps Naaman.
Ezekiel 23. A tale of two girls: Oholah and Oholibah
Matthew 9:18–26. A dead girl returns to life

▶ Giving *(bestowing, charitable)*

According or tendering to another
Genesis 9:12. Giving the rainbow
Genesis 17:8. Giving the land
Exodus 23:1. Giving false testimony
Numbers 18. Giving the best to the priests
Deuteronomy 1:21. Giving them the land

▶ Giving up *(quitting, surrendering)*

Stopping; ceasing from doing something
Numbers 20:7–8. Rock, give up your water.
1 Kings 19. Elijah gives up.
Nehemiah 6:9. Nehemiah and the people persist, instead of giving up.
Luke 18:1–8. Never give up on prayer.
Galatians 6:9. We'll reap if we don't give up.
Hebrews 12:1. Run and never give up.

▶ Gladness *(cheerfulness, delight, happiness)*

The experience of joy and pleasure
Psalm 51:8. Joy and gladness
Isaiah 51:3. Gladness will return to Zion.
Isaiah 65:14. Singing for gladness
Jeremiah 48:33. Gladness is gone.

▶ Gleaner *(gather grain)*

A person who picks up the leftover grain or other crops in a field after the reapers have gathered it
Deuteronomy 24:19. Leaving wheat for gleaners
Ruth 2. Ruth becomes a gleaner.
Job 24:6. Gleaners in the vineyard of the wicked
Jeremiah 6:9. The gleaners of Benjamin

▶ Gleaning *(gathering)*

Gathering leftover grain or other crops from a field
Leviticus 19:9–10. Allow the poor to glean.
Deuteronomy 24:20–21. Leave olives for others to glean
Isaiah 24:13. Gleaning of grapes
Jeremiah 49:9. Gleaning grapes

▶ Glorify *(exalt, praise)*

Give glory, honor, or praise
Psalm 22:23. Glorify God.
Psalm 34:3. Glorify God when gathered for worship.
Psalm 63:3. Glorify God with the lips.
Psalm 107:32. Glorify God when gathered for worship.

John 13:32. Glorify the Son of Man.

▶ Glory *(honor, magnificence, renown)*

Great honor, praise, or distinction accorded by common consent

Exodus 15:6. God's glory

Exodus 16:7. Glory of the Lord

Exodus 33:18. Moses asks to see God's glory.

1 Samuel 4:21–22. The glory is gone.

1 Kings 8:11. Filling the temple with glory

Mark 10:37. Jesus' glory

Romans 2:10. Glory for everyone

▶ Glossolalia *(see Language[s]; Tongue[s])*

▶ Gluttony *(excess, greed)*

Excessive eating or drinking

Deuteronomy 21:20. Our son the glutton

Proverbs 23:2. Given to gluttony? Put a knife to your throat.

Proverbs 23:20–21. Gluttons will be poor.

Matthew 11:19. Accusing Jesus of gluttony

▶ Gnashing of teeth *(agony)*

Metaphor for physical agony; grinding the teeth in fear or sorrow

Matthew 8:12. Weeping and gnashing of teeth

Matthew 13:42. Gnashing in the furnace

Matthew 22:13. Gnashing in the darkness

Matthew 24:51. Hypocrites gnash

Matthew 25:30. Worthless servant joins the weepers and gnashers.

▶ Gnat(s) *(bugs, flies, pests)*

Any of various small, biting two-winged flies

Exodus 8:16–19. A plague of gnats

Psalm 105:31. God spoke and gnats came.

Matthew 23:24. Straining gnats

▶ Gnostic(s) *(heretic)*

Adherents of Gnosticism

Colossians 2:10–15. We're complete in Christ, unlike what Gnostics believe.

1 Timothy 6:20. Beware Gnostics.

2 Peter 2:12. Gnostics are false teachers.

Jude 19. Gnostics cause divisions.

▶ Gnosticism *(knowledge)*

Belief system centered around secret knowledge and the soul's imprisonment

Colossians 1. Truth to combat Gnostic beliefs

Colossians 2:3. Real knowledge versus secret, Gnostic knowledge

1 John 1:10. Deception of Gnosticism

2 John 7–11. Another deception of Gnosticism

▶ Goals *(objectives)*

The purposes toward which one's efforts are directed

Job 6:11. What goal do I have?

Psalm 146:9. Goal of the wicked

Habakkuk 2:3. Hurrying toward the goal

Romans 15:6. Having the same goal

Romans 15:20. Paul's goal

1 Corinthians 9:26. A clear goal

▶ Goat(s) *(animal)*

Any of the various hollow-horned, bearded ruminants of the genus *Capra*

Genesis 30:32–33. Jacob's wages: speckled goats

Exodus 12:3. For Passover, use a lamb or a goat.

Exodus 26:7. Sheets made of goats' hair

Leviticus 3:12. Offering of a goat

Matthew 25:31–46. Parable of the sheep and the goats

▶ God *(Almighty, Creator, God of Israel, Yahweh)*

The Triune God and Creator; the one who revealed Himself to various individuals and interacted through the lives of the people He created

Genesis 1. God creates.

Genesis 6:9. God approves.

Exodus 3. God reveals himself to Moses and his plans for his people.

Jeremiah 23:24. God is immense.
Mark 10:18. God is good.
John 4:24. God is a spirit.
Hebrews 13:8. God is unchanging.

▶ Goddess *(idols)*

A female being of supernatural powers or attributes believed in and worshiped by people

Exodus 34:13. Goddess Asherah
1 Kings 11:5. Solomon turns to the goddess of the Sidonians.
Isaiah 65:11. Goddess of destiny
Jeremiah 7:18. Worshiping the queen of heaven
Acts 19:27. Greek goddess Artemis

▶ Gods *(idols)*

Being of supernatural powers or attributes and worshiped by people

Genesis 31:30–32. Household gods
Genesis 35:2. Get rid of the foreign gods.
Exodus 12:12. Punishing the gods of Egypt
Exodus 20:3–5. Commanded to avoid worshiping other gods
2 Kings 17:29. Making their own gods
2 Kings 17:31. The gods of Sepharvaim

▶ God's will *(choice, decision, determination)*

God's choice

Jeremiah 29:11. God's plans
Acts 18:21. If it is God's will
2 Corinthians 8:5. In keeping with God's will
Ephesians 1:5–6, 11. God chose.
Ephesians 1:8–9. God revealed.
Colossians 1:1. An apostle by God's will

▶ Going "Green" *(conservation)*

Environmentalism

Genesis 1:29. Green plants given for food
Genesis 2:15. The call to take care of the earth
Leviticus 19:23. Plant trees, but avoid overworking the fruit trees.
Deuteronomy 22:6–7. Caring for the animals in the environment
Psalm 8:6–8. The task of caring for the environment

▶ Gold *(metal)*

A soft, yellow malleable metallic element occurring in veins and alluvial deposits

Genesis 2:11–12. Where gold is found
Genesis 13:2. Abram's gold
Exodus 3:22. Take the Egyptians' gold.
Exodus 25:10–13. An ark covered in gold
1 Kings 6:20–22. Gold in the temple
Acts 3:6–7. We don't have gold, but we have a miracle.

▶ Golden rule *(law of reciprocity)*

The biblical teaching on treating others as one would be treated

Matthew 7:12. The golden rule and Moses' teachings
Luke 6:27. One aspect of the golden rule
Luke 6:31. The golden rule

▶ Good *(excellent, high-quality)*

Being positive or desirable in nature; not bad or poor

Genesis 1. God's good creation
Genesis 3:6. Good fruit, bad choice
Genesis 39:21. On good terms
Exodus 3:8. A good land
Psalm 25:8. The Lord is good.
Matthew 12:35. Good people do what is good.
Mark 10:17–18. Good Teacher; good God

▶ Good housekeepers *(busy wife, entrepreneur, follower of Christ)*

A woman who exemplifies the characteristics of a successful wife, mother, businesswoman, or chef

Judges 4. Deborah—wife, prophet, and judge
Proverbs 31:10–31. Wife in Proverbs 31
Luke 10:38–42. Martha of Bethany
Acts 16:13–15. Lydia of Thyatira
Acts 18:1–3, 24–26. Priscilla—tentmaker and teacher

▶ Good News *(see Gospel)*

(see Gospel)

▶ Good Shepherd *(God, Jesus)*

A name Jesus assigned to Himself as a metaphor for His role in the life of His people; a parallel to God's being called a shepherd in the Old Testament

Psalm 23:1. The Lord is my shepherd.

John 10:11. The Good Shepherd gives His life.

John 10:14. The Good Shepherd knows His sheep.

▶ Good works *(charitable deeds, God-pleasing work)*

Charitable deeds, emotionally satisfying work, or actions that reveal one's faith

Matthew 6:1–4. Don't announce good works.

2 Corinthians 9:8. Abound in every good work.

Ephesians 2:10. God created us to do good works.

Ephesians 4:28. Thieves should turn to good works.

Philippians 1:6. You are God's good work.

▶ Goodness *(decency, integrity, kindness)*

The state or quality of being good

Exodus 33:19. All of God's goodness

Psalm 23:6. Goodness and mercy will follow me.

Psalm 25:7. God's goodness and mercy

Romans 15:14. Filled with goodness

Galatians 5:22. Goodness: a fruit of the Spirit

Hebrews 6:4–5. The goodness of God's Word

▶ Gospel *(good news, Jesus, salvation)*

The good news of Jesus Christ

Matthew 24:14. The gospel will be preached.

Mark 8:35. Losing your life for the gospel

Mark 13:10. Gospel preached to all nations

Romans 1:15–16. Not ashamed of the gospel.

Ephesians 1:13. The gospel of your salvation

▶ Gospels, the *(Matthew, Mark, Luke, John)*

The books describing the life and times of Jesus Christ

Matthew. The Gospel of the Messiah

Mark. The Gospel of the Suffering Savior

Luke. The Gospel of the Savior of Jews and Gentiles

John. The Gospel of the Light of the World

▶ Gossip *(hearsay, rumor)*

Rumor or talk of personal, sensational, or intimate nature; a person who spreads gossip

Leviticus 19:16. Never gossip.

Psalm 41:6. Gossip collector

Proverbs 16:28. Hazard of gossip

Proverbs 18:8. Where gossip goes

Proverbs 26:20. Gossip and quarrels

▶ Government *(administration, regime, rule)*

The act or process of government, particularly the control and administration of public policy in a political unit

Isaiah 9:6–7. Government of the Messiah

Micah 4:8. Former government

Luke 23:13–14. Jesus: a rebel against the government?

John 4:46–54. Jesus heals a government official's son.

Romans 13:1–7. Obey the government.

▶ Grace *(clemency, kindness, mercy)*

Unearned mercy and salvation extended to a people from God through the Savior, Jesus

Romans 4:16. The gift of grace

Galatians 5:4. Fallen away from grace

Ephesians 2:8–9. Saved by grace

Philippians 1:2. Grace to you

2 Thessalonians 2:16–17. Learn about grace.

2 Timothy 1:8–10. Grace in Christ

Titus 2:11. Grace for all people

▶ Grace and truth *(characteristics)*

Statement used about Jesus describing attributes Christians are to model

John 1:14. Full of grace and truth

2 John 3. Grace will be with you in truth and love.

▶ Grain *(barley, wheat)*

The one-seeded fruit of a cereal grass

Genesis 27:28. Fresh grain

Genesis 37:6–7. Joseph's grain dream

Genesis 41:5–7. Pharaoh's grain dream

Judges 15:5. Burning grain

Ruth 2:17. Gathering grain

Mark 2:23. Picking and eating grain on the Sabbath

▶ Grain offering *(bread, firstfruits, crushed grain)*

A sacrificial offering to God given with burnt offerings

Exodus 29:41. Evening grain offering

Leviticus 2. Rules for grain offerings

Leviticus 6:14–15. The people's grain offering

Numbers 18:9. Grain offerings given to priests and Levites

2 Kings 16:15. Grain offerings of the king

▶ Grandchildren *(children)*

The children of one's children

Genesis 31:43. Laban's grandchildren

Genesis 45:10. Bring the grandchildren to Egypt.

Exodus 10:2. Something to tell the grandchildren

Deuteronomy 4:25. When you have grandchildren

2 Kings 17:41. Setting a bad example for grandchildren

Jeremiah 2:9. Charges against grandchildren

Joel 1:3. Pass on messages to grandchildren.

1 Timothy 5:4. Repaying a debt to grandparents

▶ Grandparent(s) *(parents of parents)*

The parents of a person with offspring

Genesis 50:22–23. Joseph the grandfather

Job 42:16–17. Job the grandfather and great-grandfather

Proverbs 17:6. A grandparent's crown

▶ Grapes *(berries, wine)*

Any of numerous woody vines of the genus *Vitis* bearing edible berries

Genesis 40:9–11. Cupbearer's dream about grapes

Leviticus 19:10. Leave fallen grapes.

Leviticus 25:11. Don't pick grapes in the year of jubilee.

Numbers 6:3–4. No grapes for Nazirites.

Numbers 13:23–24. The spies bring back grapes.

Matthew 21:34. Grapes in Jesus' vineyard parable

▶ Grasshopper *(insect)*

Any of numerous orthopteran insects of the families *Locustidae* and *Tettigoniidae*

Leviticus 11:22. Grasshopper—a clean food

Numbers 13:33. Feeling as small as grasshoppers

1 Kings 8:37. Curse of the grasshoppers

Psalm 105:34–35. God calls the grasshoppers.

Psalm 109:23. Shaken off like a grasshopper

Ecclesiastes 12:5. The dragging grasshopper

Isaiah 33:4. Gathering like grasshoppers

▶ Gratitude *(appreciation, gratefulness, thanksgiving)*

The state of being grateful

Leviticus 7:11–12. Gratitude offering

Nehemiah 11:17. Gratitude prayer

Romans 16:3–4. Paul shows gratitude.

Colossians 3:15–16. Show gratitude.

2 Timothy 3:2–3. No gratitude

Hebrews 12:28. Gratitude for an unshakable kingdom

▶ Grave *(death, tomb)*

A place of burial; often a euphemism for death

Genesis 35:19–20. Rachel's grave

Genesis 44:29–31. Driven to the grave
Numbers 19:16. Unclean if a grave is touched
Deuteronomy 34:5–6. Unknown location of Moses' grave
Psalm 30:3. Up from the grave
Psalm 55:15. The grave of the wicked

▶ Grazing *(foraging)*

Feeding on growing grasses and herbage
Genesis 29:7. Let the livestock graze.
Genesis 41:2. Pharaoh's dream: well-fed cows graze
Exodus 22:5. When grazing animals damage a field
1 Chronicles 27:29. Grazing herds
2 Chronicles 14:14–15. Capturing grazing animals
Job 1:13–15. Looting Job's grazing animals

▶ Greater *(better, larger, superior)*

Larger in size; more powerful or superior
Genesis 39:8–9. No one is greater.
Genesis 49:26. A father's blessings are greater.
Numbers 24:7. A king greater than Agag
Deuteronomy 4:38. Greater nations
1 Kings 1:37. A greater king than David?
Matthew 11:11. No one is greater than John.
John 1:50. Greater things than that
John 3:30. He must become greater.

▶ Greatness *(magnitude, prominence)*

The state of being powerful or remarkable; outstanding in magnitude
Deuteronomy 32:3. God's greatness
1 Chronicles 29:11. God's greatness
Esther 1:4. Xerxes's greatness
Esther 10:2. Mordecai's greatness
Psalm 34:3. Praise God's greatness.
Psalm 49:16–17. Greatness of the wealthy
Psalm 69:13. Greatness of God's mercy

▶ Great tribulation *(persecution)*

Intense suffering or persecution; the period during the end times when Christians suffer for their faith
Daniel 9:27. A coming tribulation that brings destruction
Daniel 12:1. Rescued from the tribulation
Matthew 24:15–22. A period of great tribulation
Revelation 7:14. Out of the great tribulation

▶ Great white throne *(final judgment, seat of judgment)*

A scene in the vision of John the apostle when God judges the earth
Revelation 20:11–15. Judgment at the Great white throne

▶ Greed *(avarice, gluttony, materialism)*

An excessive desire to acquire or possess more than one needs or deserves
Psalm 52:7. Strength through greed
Proverbs 1:19. Greed takes away life.
Proverbs 11:6. Trapped by greed
Isaiah 57:17. Sinful greed
Luke 12:15. Beware of greed
Romans 1:29. Lives full of greed

▶ Greek *(Gentile, language)*

A person of Greek ancestry; language in which the New Testament was written and to which the Hebrew Scriptures were translated
Mark 7:25–30. Faith of a Greek woman
John 19:20. Notice written in Greek
Acts 6:1–7. Greek-speaking Jews
1 Corinthians 10:32. Whether Jewish or Greek
Revelation 9:11. A king with the Greek name Apollyon

▶ Greetings *(compliments, good wishes)*

Salutations usually given in a letter or upon meeting someone
1 Samuel 16:5. Samuel brings greetings.
Luke 1:28. Angelic greetings
Acts 15:33. Friendly greetings
Romans 16:22. Greetings from Tertius

1 Corinthians 16:19. Christian greetings
Philippians 4:21. Greetings to you

▶ Grief *(anguish, heartache, sorrow)*

Deep mental anguish as from bereavement
Genesis 26:34–35. Isaac and Rebekah's grief
Genesis 37:29. Reuben's grief
Joshua 7:6. Grief over sin
Judges 11:35. Jephthah's grief
2 Samuel 13:30–31. David's grief
Matthew 2:18. Grief in Bethlehem
1 Timothy 6:10. Causing themselves grief

▶ Growth *(see Spiritual Growth)*

▶ Grudge *(begrudge, ill-will, resentment)*

A deep-seated resentment or rancor
Genesis 50:15. Will Joseph hold a grudge?
Leviticus 19:18. Never hold a grudge.
Jeremiah 3:5. God won't hold a grudge forever, will he?
Nahum 1:2. God holds grudges.
Mark 6:19. A grudge against John the Baptist
Luke 11:53–54. A grudge against Jesus

▶ Grumbling *(complaining)*

To complain in a surly manner
Exodus 16. Grumbling of Israel
Numbers 14:27. God hears the grumbling.
Numbers 17:5. Silencing the grumbling
Matthew 20:11. Grumbling at a landowner
John 6:41. Grumbling about Jesus
James 5:9. Condemnation for grumbling

▶ Guarantee *(assurance, promise, security)*

Something that assures a particular outcome or condition
Genesis 43:8–9. Judah makes a guarantee.
Deuteronomy 24:6. Guarantee on a loan
Job 17:3. Bail guarantee
Psalm 33:17. Horses are no guarantee of victory.
Ephesians 1:14. The Holy Spirit is our guarantee.

▶ Guarding *(protecting, safeguarding)*

Protecting from harm
Genesis 3:24. Angels guard the tree of life.
Deuteronomy 24:8. Guard against outbreaks.
Joshua 10:18–19. Post a guard.
Psalm 17:8. Guard me.
Psalm 138:7. You guard my life.

▶ Guerilla tactics *(raiding parties)*

Tactics used by small forces to undermine the enemy
Judges 9:33–34. Abimelech's guerilla tactics
Judges 15:4–5. Samson's guerilla tactics
1 Samuel 30. Guerilla tactics at Ziklag
2 Samuel 14:28–30. Absalom's guerilla tactics get attention.

▶ Guests *(visitors)*

Those who receive the hospitality of another
Judges 19:23. Protecting a guest
Esther 5:12. An invited guest
Psalm 5:4. Evil is not God's guest.
Matthew 9:15. Wedding guests
Matthew 22:1–14. Guests at the great banquet

▶ Guidance *(advice, counsel)*

Guiding someone, giving counsel or advice
1 Samuel 24:20. Under David's guidance
1 Chronicles 10:13–14. The wrong guidance
2 Chronicles 24:13. The foremen's guidance
Proverbs 11:14. Lack of guidance
Proverbs 20:18. Guidance and war

▶ Guile *(craftiness, cunning, deviousness)*

Treacherous cunning; skillful deceit
Exodus 21:14. Slaying with guile
Psalm 32:2. Blessed to have no guile
Psalm 34:13. Avoid speaking guile.
Psalm 55:11. Deceit and guile
John 1:47. A man with no guile

▶ Guilt *(blame, fault, responsibility)*

Responsible for committing an offense
Genesis 44:16. Guilt uncovered
Deuteronomy 21:8–9. Getting rid of guilt
1 Samuel 26:9. Free of guilt
Lamentations 2:14. Guilt exposed
Ezekiel 24:23. Wasting away due to guilt
John 16:8–11. Convicting the world of guilt

▶ Guilt offerings *(sacrifices)*

Offerings given for unintentional sin or for causing loss to someone
Leviticus 5. Guilt offerings
Leviticus 6:1–7. Repay and bring a guilt offering.
Leviticus 7:1–10. Rules for guilt offerings
Leviticus 14:17. Blood of the guilt offering
1 Samuel 6:17. The Philistines' guilt offering

▶ Habit(s) *(custom, routine, tendency)*

Recurrent, often unconscious pattern of behavior

Exodus 21:29. A bad habit
Numbers 22:30. A donkey's habit
Zechariah 8:21. Make a habit of asking.
1 Corinthians 15:33. Good habits corrupted
1 Timothy 5:13. A habit of idleness

▶ Hades *(see Hell; Sheol)*

▶ Hail *(ice pellets, sleet)*

Precipitation in the form of spherical pellets of ice; also, to summon someone

Exodus 9:13–35. Plague of hail
Job 38:22–23. Storehouses for hail
Psalm 78:47–48. Recalling the plague of hail
Isaiah 28:17. Sweeping away lies with hail
Haggai 2:17. Struck by hail
Revelation 8:7. Hail, fire, and blood

▶ Hair *(locks, mane, tresses)*

Any of the filaments characteristically growing out of the epidermis of a mammal

Exodus 25:3–4. Goats' hair
Leviticus 10:6. Uncombed hair as a sign of mourning
Judges 13:5. Don't cut Samson's hair.
2 Samuel 14:25–26. Absalom's hair
1 Timothy 2:9. Beauty is not about hairstyles.

▶ Hallelujah *(praise, worship)*

An acclimation that means "Praise the Lord"

Psalm 104:35. Praise the Lord! Hallelujah!
Psalm 106:1. Hallelujah! Give thanks.
Psalm 111:1. Hallelujah! I will give thanks.
Psalm 146:10. The Lord rules. Hallelujah!
Revelation 19. Hallelujah in heaven

▶ Hallowed *(consecrated, holy, sacred)*

Something sacred or sanctified

Exodus 20:11. Hallowing the Sabbath
Exodus 29:21. Hallowed garments
Leviticus 12:4. Women forbidden to touch hallowed items after childbirth
Leviticus 19:8. Hallowed offerings
Matthew 6:9. His name is hallowed.

▶ Hand(s) *(fingers, furnish)*

The part of the human arm below the forearm and consisting of the wrist, palm, four fingers, and a thumb; also, physical help

Genesis 19:16. Grabbing Lot and his family by the hands
Genesis 27:22–23. Faking Esau's hairy hands
Exodus 17:10–13. Lifting Moses' hands
Luke 13:13. Healing with hands
Luke 23:46. Into God's hands
Luke 24:38–40. Touching the hands of the risen Christ
Acts 6:6. Hands placed on the called

▶ Handicap *(see Disability)*

▶ Handsome *(attractive, good looking, striking)*

Pleasing and dignified in form and appearance

Genesis 39:6. Handsome Joseph
1 Samuel 9:2. Handsome Saul
1 Samuel 16:12. Handsome David
2 Samuel 23:20–21. Handsome Egyptian
1 Kings 1:5. Handsome Adonijah
Psalm 45:2. A handsome descendant

▶ Handwriting *(scrawl, script, writing)*

Writing done with the hand

Exodus 32:16. Handwriting on tablets
Numbers 17:2–3. Handwriting on staffs
Isaiah 8:1. Handwritten on a tablet
Daniel 5. The handwriting on the wall
Colossians 2:13–14. Handwriting of requirements

H

▶ Hanukkah *(festival of dedication, festival of lights)*

Eight-day Jewish festival commemorating the victory in 165 B.C. of the Maccabees over Antiochus Epiphanes

John 10:22–42. Jesus attends the Festival of the Dedication.

▶ Happiness *(delight, gladness, glee)*

A state of enjoyment marked by pleasure or satisfaction

Job 21:13. Happiness of the wicked

Psalm 106:4–5. Happiness of people

Proverbs 17:20. Happiness eludes the twisted.

Proverbs 23:26. Find happiness in obedience.

Isaiah 9:3. Happiness to come

▶ Harass *(annoy, bother, pester)*

Irritate or torment persistently

Numbers 25:17. License to harass

Numbers 33:55. Drive them out or face harassment.

Deuteronomy 2:9. Don't harass the Moabites.

Psalm 56:2. Harassed by enemies

Matthew 9:36. Harassed people

▶ Hard-heartedness *(callousness, pitilessness)*

Lacking in feeling or compassion

Deuteronomy 15:8. Never be hard-hearted.

Proverbs 28:14. Disaster for the hard-hearted

Ezekiel 3:7. Hard-hearted Israel

▶ Hardship *(suffering)*

Extreme privation

Deuteronomy 15:18. No hardship if you free a slave

Psalm 119:143. Trouble and hardship

Isaiah 30:6. Israel's hardship

Lamentations 3:5. A lament of hardship

2 Corinthians 12:10. Paul's acceptance of hardship

▶ Harlot *(see Prostitution)*

▶ Harmless *(not detrimental, safe)*

Incapable of causing harm

Proverbs 1:11. Thugs out to hurt the harmless

Matthew 10:16. Harmless as doves

Philippians 2:14–15. Be blameless and harmless.

Hebrews 7:26. Harmless high priest

▶ Harmony *(accord, agreement, concord)*

Agreement in feeling or opinion

Job 22:21. In harmony with God

Psalm 133:1. Living in harmony

Acts 4:32. Believers in harmony

Romans 12:16. Live in harmony.

Romans 15:5. Encouragement to live in harmony

▶ Harp *(musical instrument)*

An instrument consisting of an upright, open triangular frame with strings played by plucking with the fingers

Genesis 4:21. The first to play the harp

1 Samuel 10:5. Prophets led by music of the harp, flute, and lyre

Psalm 33:2. Praise God with the harp.

Psalm 57:8. Wake up, harp and lyre!

Psalm 71:22. Giving thanks with a harp

Psalm 144:9. Singing a new song with a harp

▶ Harvest *(gather, reap, season)*

Act or process of gathering crops

Genesis 30:14. Wheat harvest

Genesis 41:34. Collecting the harvest in readiness for a famine

Genesis 47:24. Tithe from the harvest

Exodus 23:16. Festival of the Harvest

Exodus 34:22. Celebrate with grain from the wheat harvest.

Leviticus 19:10. Don't harvest everything in the field.

Leviticus 23:9–10. Give the first harvested grain.

▶ Haste *(alacrity, speed)*

Rapidity of action or motion

Genesis 19:14. Hasten out of Sodom and Gomorrah.

Exodus 12:11. Eat it in haste.

Deuteronomy 16:3. Left in haste

Judges 13:10. Ran in haste

1 Samuel 20:38. Make haste.

▶ Hat(s) *(head covering, turban)*

A covering for the head

Exodus 28:4, 37. Hat for the high priest

Job 29:14. Putting on justice and righteousness as one puts on a hat

Isaiah 3:18–23. Hats will be taken away.

Ezekiel 24:17. Put on your hat and don't grieve.

Daniel 3:21. Thrown into the furnace wearing hats

Zechariah 3:5. A clean hat for God's servant

1 Corinthians 11:4. Hats not to be worn while praying

▶ Hatred *(abhorrence, loathing, revulsion)*

Intense animosity or hostility

2 Samuel 13:15. Hatred for the abused

Psalm 25:19. Hatred of enemies

Proverbs 10:18. Hiding hatred

Galatians 5:19–20. Hatred—a product of the corrupt nature

Colossians 3:8. Get rid of hatred.

James 4:4. Hatred toward God

▶ Haughty *(see Pride)*

▶ Hawk(s) *(bird of prey)*

Any of the various birds of prey of the order *Falconiformes*

Leviticus 11:13–16. Hawk—an unclean bird

Job 28:7. The hawk can't find wisdom.

Job 39:26. Who controls the hawk's flight?

▶ Healing *(curing, relieving)*

Curing someone of an affliction

Proverbs 12:18. Wise words bring healing.

Proverbs 13:17. A dependable envoy brings healing.

Isaiah 53:5. Healing from the wounds of God's servant

Jeremiah 8:15. Terror instead of healing

Luke 13:14. Healing on the Sabbath

John 5:16. Persecuted for healing on the Sabbath

▶ Health *(physical condition, soundness, wellness)*

The overall condition of an organism

Psalm 41:3. The Lord will support.

Psalm 90:10. If health allows

Proverbs 1:12. Like those in good health

Isaiah 38. Hezekiah returns to health after an illness

Jeremiah 8:22. Spiritual medicine for an unhealthy people

Mark 3:4. Restore someone to health or let him die?

▶ Hearing *(hear, perceive)*

The sense by which sound is perceived; the capacity to hear

Genesis 29:33. His name means Hearing.

1 Samuel 4:14–15. A cry heard

Amos 8:11. A famine of hearing God's Word

Matthew 13:15. Hard of hearing

Luke 9:9. Hearing about Jesus

▶ Hearsay *(see Gossip)*

▶ Heart *(compassion, feelings, sympathy)*

The chambered muscular organ that pumps blood; also, the repository of one's deepest beliefs and feelings

Exodus 28:29. Carrying the names over his heart

Deuteronomy 4:29. Searching for God with all your heart

Deuteronomy 6:5–6. Love God with all your heart.

Deuteronomy 7:7. God's heart

Judges 16:15. Your heart isn't mine.

1 Samuel 1:15. Pouring out my heart

H

▸ Heartache *(anguish, grief, sorrow)*

Emotional anguish

Proverbs 10:10. When a wink causes heartache

Proverbs 15:13. Heartache and depression

Proverbs 17:25. A parent's heartache

Ecclesiastes 1:18. Heartache and wisdom

Romans 9:2. Paul's heartache over his people

▸ Heathen *(pagan)*

One who adheres to a religion that does not acknowledge God

Matthew 6:7. Vain repetition like the heathen

Matthew 18:17. Dealing with a heathen

1 Thessalonians 4:3–5. Heathens who don't know God

▸ Heaven *(paradise)*

The abode of God, angels, and souls granted salvation

Matthew 6:10. God's will is done in heaven.

Matthew 6:20. Treasure in heaven

Matthew 8:11. The kingdom in heaven

Luke 6:23. Reward in heaven

Revelation 8:1. Silence in heaven

Revelation 12:7. War in heaven

▸ Heavens *(sky, space, and the planets)*

The sky or universe as seen from Earth; the firmament

Genesis 1:1, 6–8. The heavens created.

Genesis 49:25. Blessings from the heavens

Deuteronomy 28:12. Opening the heavens

Deuteronomy 33:26. Riding through the heavens

1 Samuel 2:10. Thundering from the heavens

1 Chronicles 16:26. Maker of the heavens

▸ Hebrew *(language, person)*

A member or descendant of Abraham, Isaac, and Jacob; an Israelite; also, the Semitic language

Genesis 14:13. Abram the Hebrew

Genesis 39:13–14. Complaints about Joseph the Hebrew

Exodus 1:15–16. Hebrew midwives and childbearing women

John 5:2. *Bethesda* in the Hebrew language

John 19:13. *Gabbatha* in the Hebrew language

Acts 22:2. Speaking in the Hebrew language

▸ Hedonism *(pagan)*

Pursuit or devotion to pleasure

Proverbs 21:17. Poverty of the hedonist

Ecclesiastes 2:1–3. Study of hedonism

Luke 15:11–32. Hedonism of a son

1 Timothy 5:6. Hedonism deadens a life.

▸ Heirs *(inheritors)*

Those who inherit

1 Kings 14:8. David's heirs

2 Kings 10:1. Ahab's heirs

Acts 3:25. Heirs of the promise

Romans 8:17. God's heirs

Galatians 3:29. Abraham's heirs

▸ Hell *(Hades, Sheol, torture)*

Place of punishment for unbelievers

Deuteronomy 32:22. The depths of hell

Psalm 49:14–15. Driven and brought back from hell

Psalm 139:8. A bed in hell

Proverbs 7:27. The way to hell

Matthew 5:30. Maimed in life is better than hell

Matthew 16:18. Gates of hell

▸ Help/Helping *(aid, assist)*

Offering assistance; gift of service

Exodus 2:23. Cries for help

Leviticus 11:47. Instructions to help you understand

Deuteronomy 22:4. Help out.

Psalm 28:2. Calling to God for help

Mark 9:24. Help my lack of faith.

1 Corinthians 4:17. Timothy will help.

1 Corinthians 12:28. A gift for helping

▶ Helpless *(frail, powerless, weak)*

Unable to manage by oneself; lacking power or strength

Deuteronomy 32:10. Helping the helpless
Job 6:13. Completely helpless
Psalm 41:1. Those who help the helpless
Matthew 5:3. Spiritually helpless
Matthew 9:36. Helpless crowd

▶ Herald *(messenger)*

Person who announces important news

Daniel 3:4–6. The herald proclaims the furnace consequence.
Habakkuk 2:2. Heralding the revelation
1 Timothy 2:7. Appointed as a herald

▶ Heredity *(genetics, inherited traits)*

The genetic transmittal of traits from parent to offspring

Genesis 1:27. Starting the chain of heredity
Genesis 5:3. A son in his own image
Exodus 20:5. A heredity of punishment or mercy
Psalm 51:5. A heredity of sin
Jeremiah 31:29–30. No longer responsible for what's passed on

▶ Heresy *(dissent, sacrilege, unorthodoxy)*

An opinion or doctrine at variance with established religious beliefs

Acts 24:14. Christians believed to be heretical
1 Corinthians 11:19. A warning about heretical beliefs
Ephesians 4:14. No longer swayed by heresy
Titus 3:10. Avoid those who teach heretical beliefs.
2 Peter 2:1. Heresy of false teachers

▶ Heritage *(birthright, inheritance, legacy)*

Property that can be inherited; a tradition passed on from preceding generations

Job 20:29. An appointed heritage
Job 27:13. A ruthless man's heritage
Job 31:2. A man's heritage
Psalm 127:3. Children are a heritage.
Isaiah 54:17. A heritage of protection

▶ Hermeneutics *(interpretation, study)*

The study of interpretations or explanations of Scripture

Matthew 2:15. Interpreting the prophets in reference to Jesus
Matthew 5:21–22. Hermeneutics in the Sermon on the Mount
Matthew 19:3–6. Jesus teaches hermeneutics.
Luke 3:4–6. The hermeneutics of John's advent
2 Timothy 2:15. Proper hermeneutics

▶ Heroes *(champions, the courageous)*

Persons noted for feats of courage or nobility of purpose

1 Samuel 17:51. Death of a Philistine hero
Psalm 52:1. An evil hero
Proverbs 16:32. What's better than being a hero?
Zephaniah 3:17. The ultimate hero
Hebrews 11:4–40. Heroes of the faith

▶ Hesitate *(falter, vacillate)*

To be slow to act, speak, or decide

Judges 18:9. Don't hesitate.
Job 30:10. No hesitation
Proverbs 23:13. Don't hesitate on discipline.
Acts 10:19–20. Don't hesitate, Peter.

▶ Hide/Hidden *(conceal, mystery, secret)*

To keep out of sight; something kept out of sight

Genesis 3:7–8. Trying to hide from God
Genesis 18:17. Nothing to hide from Abraham
Exodus 2:1–3. Keeping Moses hidden
Deuteronomy 29:29. Some things are hidden.
Joshua 2. Hiding two spies
Psalm 139:15. Nothing is hidden from God.

H

▶ High Places *(worship place)*

Translated from the Hebrew word *ramah,* which means "to be high"; places where idols were worshiped

Deuteronomy 12:2. Destroy the high places.

1 Kings 11:7. Solomon builds a high place.

1 Kings 13:2–3. Judgment on those who worship at the high places

1 Kings 14:22–24. People of Judah built worship sites for themselves.

1 Kings 15:14. Committed, but did not destroy the high places

▶ High Priest *(priest)*

The chief of the priests

Exodus 28:11–12. Stones worn by Aaron the first high priest

Leviticus 16:32–33. The high priest makes atonement.

Leviticus 21:10. Rules for the high priest

Numbers 35:25. Stay in the city of refuge until the death of the high priest.

2 Kings 12:10. High priest collects the contributions for the temple.

▶ Hindrance *(barrier, impediment, obstacle)*

Something that gets into the way of something else

1 Samuel 14:6. Nothing is a hindrance for God.

Matthew 19:14. Don't be a hindrance to children coming to Jesus.

1 Corinthians 9:12. Avoiding hindering the Good News

Acts 28:31. Preaching with hindrance.

▶ History *(account, record, the past)*

Chronological record of events

Exodus 9:18. Worst hailstorm in history

2 Chronicles 13:22. A written history

Ezra 4. The Samaritans' view of history

Esther 10:2. History of the kings of the Medes and Persians

Isaiah 41:4. God determined the course of history.

▶ Hoard/Hoarding *(accumulate, cache, stockpile)*

A hidden fund or supply stored for future use

Proverbs 11:26. Grain hoarding

Ecclesiastes 5:13. Hoarding riches

Amos 3:10. Hoarding plunder

▶ Holiday(s) *(feast days, festivals)*

A religious feast day to commemorate or celebrate a particular event

Esther 2:18. A holiday

Esther 8:17. Enjoying a holiday

Esther 9:19, 22. Holiday in Adar

▶ Holiness *(consecration, set apart)*

Attribute of God that signifies his transcendence; also a quality in the people of God

Genesis 2:3. Holiness of the seventh day

Exodus 3:5. Holy ground

Exodus 19:10. Set apart as holy

Exodus 22:31. God's holy people

Isaiah 6:1–3. God is holy.

1 Thessalonians 5:23. May God make you holy.

▶ Holy kiss *(greeting)*

Christian greeting

Romans 16:16. A holy kiss

1 Corinthians 16:20. Everyone greet with a holy kiss.

2 Corinthians 13:12. Holy people, greet with a kiss.

1 Thessalonians 5:26. Greet with a holy kiss.

▶ Holy Land *(Palestine)*

The biblical region of Palestine and the cities and places that can be found there

Genesis 17:8. The promise given to give Abraham's descendants a permanent home

Joshua 16:5–10. Ephraim

Ruth 1:1. Bethlehem

1 Kings 3:15. Jerusalem

Matthew 3:13. Galilee

Matthew 16:13. Casesarea Philippi

▸ Holy Place(s) *(tabernacle, temple, places of worship)*

Places made holy by the presence of God or by the order of God

Exodus 3:5. Mount Horeb—holy ground

Exodus 15:17. The holy place built by God

Exodus 25:8. A holy place made for God

Exodus 26:33–34. Holy places in the tabernacle

Exodus 29:43. God makes a place holy.

Leviticus 16:2, 17. Rules for the holy place

▸ Holy Spirit *(God, Spirit of God)*

Third person of the trinity; God in active form

Genesis 1:2. The Spirit of God

Psalm 51:11. Don't take away the Holy Spirit.

Luke 1:15. Filled with the Spirit before birth

Luke 4:1–2. Led the Holy Spirit

John 14:16–17. Promise of the Holy Spirit

Acts 2. Arrival of the Holy Spirit

Romans 5:5. The gift of the Holy Spirit

1 Corinthians 6:19. The temple of the Holy Spirit

2 Corinthians 6:6–7. The Holy Spirit's presence

▸ Holy war *(jihad)*

A war deemed to have religious or high moral purpose

Exodus 17:15–16. God goes to war.

Numbers 21:14. History of the wars of the Lord

Deuteronomy 20. Rules about holy war

Joshua 6. Carrying the ark into a holy war

1 Samuel 11. Holy war against the Ammonites

1 Samuel 25:28. The Lord's battles

▸ Home *(abode, house, residence)*

A place where one lives

Genesis 12:1. Abram leaves home.

Leviticus 25:29. Rule for selling a home

Deuteronomy 6:7. Teach children at home.

Mark 10:29–30. Giving up one's home for the Good News

Romans 16:3–5. Greet the church in this home.

Revelation 21:3. God's home is with humans.

▸ Homeless *(dispossessed)*

Having no home or haven

Genesis 23:3–4. No permanent home for Abraham

Job 20:9. Homeless plight of the wicked

Isaiah 58:7. Share with the homeless.

Matthew 8:20. No permanent home for Jesus

1 Corinthians 4:11. Paul is homeless.

▸ Homeopathic medicine *(alternative medicine, herbal medicines)*

Treating diseases based on the administration of small doses of a drug; using herbal medicines

2 Kings 20:7. Boiled figs for illness

Luke 10:34. Treating wounds with oil and wine

1 Timothy 5:23. Wine for a stomach ailment

Revelation 3:18. Eye ointment

▸ Homosexuality *(lesbian, same sex)*

Sexual orientation to persons of the same sex

Genesis 19. Homosexuality leads to destruction of Sodom and Gomorrah.

Romans 1:26–27. Indecent acts with men and women

1 Corinthians 6:9–10. Those who won't inherit

1 Timothy 1:10. Laws intended for homosexuals

Jude 7. Homosexual activities

▸ Honesty *(candor, sincerity, truthfulness)*

The quality or condition of being honest

Genesis 30:33. Jacob's honesty

1 Chronicles 29:17. God delights in honesty.

Psalm 25:21. Protected by honesty

Proverbs 29:14. Judging with honesty

Isaiah 59:14. Honesty can't come in.

H

▶ Honey *(product of bees)*

Yellowish viscid fluid produced by bees
Genesis 43:11. A gift of honey
Exodus 3:8. Flowing with milk and honey
Exodus 16:31. Like wafers made with honey
Leviticus 2:11. Never burn honey.
Deuteronomy 8:8. Honey in the promised land
Judges 14:8–20. Samson finds honey.

▶ Honor *(admiration, respect, reputation)*

High respect
Genesis 30:20. Hoping for honor
Exodus 5:1. A festival in God's honor
Exodus 14:4. God will receive honor.
Exodus 15. Moses and the people honor God with a song.
Exodus 20:12. Honor your father and your mother.

▶ Honorable *(admirable, praiseworthy, respectable)*

Deserving or earning honor and respect
Deuteronomy 32:4. God is honorable.
Deuteronomy 33:21. Gad does what is fair and honorable.
1 Kings 1:42. An honorable man
Proverbs 20:3. An honorable action
Philippians 4:8. Whatever is honorable

▶ Hope *(anticipation, expectation, optimism)*

To wish for something with the expectation of its fulfillment
Genesis 49:18. Waiting with hope
Job 4:6. Do you have hope?
Psalm 9:18. Hope of the oppressed
Psalm 27:14. Wait with hope.
2 Thessalonians 2:16. Hope from God

▶ Hopeless *(despondent, forlorn, in despair)*

Having no hope
1 Chronicles 29:15. No hope.
Job 13:15. Hopeless
Isaiah 57:10. You didn't think it was hopeless.
Acts 27:31. There's no hope if you leave.
Ephesians 2:12. Without God, without hope

▶ Horoscope *(see Astrology)*

▶ Horse(s) *(animal)*

Large hoofed mammal having a short-haired coat, a long mane, and a long tail
Genesis 49:17. Like a viper that bites a horse
Exodus 14:9. Pharaoh's horse-drawn chariots
1 Kings 9:19. Cities for horses
1 Kings 10:28–29. Imported and exported horses
1 Kings 20:20–21. Escaping on a horse

▶ Hospitality *(kindness, warmth, welcome)*

Cordial and generous reception of or disposition toward guests
Genesis 18. Abraham's hospitality
Genesis 19:1–11. Lot's hospitality
Romans 12:13. Practice hospitality.
Romans 16:23. Practice hospitality.
Hebrews 13:2. Show hospitality.
1 Peter 4:9. Offer hospitality.
3 John 8. Be hospitable to missionaries.

▶ Hostage situations *(captives, prisoners)*

Capturing a person in a conflict as security that specified terms will be met by the opposing party
Genesis 14. Lot taken captive
1 Samuel 30. Hostages taken at Ziklag.
2 Kings 14:13–14. Hostages of Jehoash

▶ House arrest *(imprisoned)*

Confinement to one's quarters, rather than prison
Jeremiah 37:14–16. A house turned into a prison
Acts 28:15–16, 30–31. Paul under house arrest
Philemon 1. Writing while under house arrest

▶ House church *(believers, church)*

A body of Christian believers meeting in a home

Acts 1:13–14. Waiting for the Holy Spirit together

Acts 20:20. Paul mentions house church meetings.

1 Corinthians 16:19. The church in the home of Aquila and Prisca (Priscilla)

Colossians 4:15. The church in the home of Nympha

Philemon 1–2. The church in the home of Philemon

▶ Household gods *(idols, teraphim)*

Idols kept in the home

Genesis 31. Rachel steals Laban's household gods.

Judges 18:14, 17–18. Other household gods

1 Samuel 19:12–13. Michal uses idols to help David escape.

2 Kings 23:24. Josiah disposes of idols.

Ezekiel 21:21. Household gods of the king of Babylon

▶ Households *(families, homes)*

Domestic unit consisting of the members of a family who live together along with non-relatives

Genesis 12:17. Pharaoh's household

Exodus 12:3–4. One Passover animal per household

Leviticus 22:11. A slave born in a priest's household

Numbers 1:4. The head of a household

Joshua 7:14. Checking household by household

▶ Humanity *(civilization, humankind, people)*

Human beings considered as a group

Job 34:11. God's judgment on humanity

Psalm 22:6. Scorned by humanity

Proverbs 3:4. Favor with God and humanity

Proverbs 29:26. Justice for humanity

Proverbs 30:14. Oppression of humanity

Isaiah 49:26. All humanity will know.

▶ Humiliation *(degradation, disgrace, shame)*

A lowering of pride, dignity, or self-respect

Psalm 69:7. Humiliation endured

Psalm 71:13. Disgrace and humiliation

Proverbs 25:9–10. Humiliation from a neighbor

Proverbs 29:23. Humiliation due to pride

Isaiah 23:9. Humiliation of honored people

▶ Humility *(meekness, modesty)*

Being humble; lacking in pride

2 Samuel 22:28. The humble and the proud

Psalm 138:6. God's care for humble people

Proverbs 15:33. Humility before honor

Proverbs 22:4. Humility before riches

Zephaniah 2:3. Search for humility.

Philippians 2:3. Consider others as better.

Colossians 2:18. False humility

1 Peter 5:5. Serve with humility.

▶ Humor *(absurdity, comedy, wittiness)*

The quality that makes something laughable or amusing

Psalm 2:4. Humor at presumption

Psalm 37:13. A joke with no punch line

Proverbs 11:22. Beauty and the beast—a humorous aphorism

Habakkuk 1:10. Laughing at kings

▶ Hunger *(desire, famine, starvation)*

A strong desire or need for food; strong desire or craving

Deuteronomy 8:3. Suffering from hunger

Psalm 147:14. Satisfying hunger

Lamentations 2:19. Fainting from hunger

Ezekiel 7:19. Failing to be rescued from hunger

Matthew 5:6. Hungering for God's approval

Romans 8:35. Staying with God even while hungry

▶ Hunting *(pursuing, searching, tracking)*

The sport of pursuing game; conducting a search for someone

Genesis 27:3. Go hunting, Esau.

Leviticus 17:13. When you hunt, pour out the blood.

1 Samuel 26:17–18, 20. Why are you hunting for me, Saul?

Psalm 140:11. Let the evil hunt the evil.

Lamentations 4:19. Hunted by enemies

▶ Hurt *(damage, harm, injure)*

To cause physical damage or pain

Genesis 37:22. Don't hurt Joseph.

Proverbs 3:21–23. Wisdom helps keep from hurt.

Proverbs 9:7. Hurt by the wicked

Isaiah 27:7. Will the Lord hurt Israel?

Matthew 26:22. Hurt at the pronouncement of imminent betrayal

Ephesians 4:29. Hurt with words

▶ Husband(s) *(male spouse)*

A man joined to a woman in marriage

Genesis 3:6. Sinning with her husband

1 Samuel 1:8. Hannah's husband, Elkanah

2 Samuel 3:14–16. A woman with two husbands

Isaiah 54:4–5. Your Maker is your husband.

John 4. A woman with five husbands

Ephesians 5:25–28. Husbands, love your wives.

▶ Hygiene *(cleanliness, sanitation)*

The promotion and preservation of health

Leviticus 14:8. Washing to be clean

Numbers 19:14–16. Hygiene rules about dealing with a dead body

Deuteronomy 23:12–13. A rule for keeping the camp hygienic

Matthew 23:25–26. Hygiene and hypocrisy

John 13:10. Physical and spiritual hygiene

▶ Hymn(s) *(sacred song)*

Song of praise or thanksgiving to God

Nehemiah 12:8, 46. Hymns of thanksgiving

Psalm 26:6–7. A hymn of thanksgiving

Matthew 26:30. Singing a hymn after the Last Supper

Acts 16:25. Singing hymns in prison

Ephesians 5:18–19. Instead of being drunk, sing hymns.

Colossians 3:16. Use hymns as instruction.

▶ Hyperbole *(exaggeration)*

Figure of speech in which exaggeration is used for emphasis or effect

Deuteronomy 1:28. Hyperbole in the wilderness

1 Samuel 18:7. Hyperbole with Saul and David

Matthew 5:29. Hell and hyperbole

Matthew 19:24. Hyperbole about salvation

Matthew 23:24. Camels and hyperbole

▶ Hypocrisy *(duplicity, insincerity, pretense)*

The practice of professing beliefs, feelings, or virtues that one does not hold or possess

Proverbs 11:3. Hypocrisy leads to ruin.

Matthew 23:28. Full of hypocrisy

Mark 12:15. Recognizing hypocrisy

Luke 12:1. Watch out for hypocrisy.

1 Peter 2:1. Get rid of hypocrisy.

▶ Hypocrites *(fraud, phonies)*

People given to hypocrisy

Psalm 26:4. Not found among the hypocrites

Hosea 10:1–2. They are hypocrites.

Matthew 6:5. Don't be like the hypocrites.

Matthew 7:5. Hypocrite, remove that beam.

Matthew 23:13–15. Hypocritical scribes and Pharisees

Acts 23:2–3. God will strike you, you hypocrite!

▶ Hyssop *(perfume, plant)*

Woody Eurasian plant with spikes of small blue flowers and aromatic leaves used in perfumery

Exodus 12:22. Branch of hyssop

Leviticus 14. Hyssop and cleansing

Numbers 19:1–6. Take a hyssop sprig.

Psalm 51:7. Purified with hyssop

John 19:29. Vinegar on hyssop

Hebrews 9:19. Sacrifices and hyssop

▶ "I Am" *(name of God)*

Statements by which Jesus declared Himself; name of God

Exodus 3:14. I Am Who I Am.
John 6:35. I am the bread of life.
John 8:12. I am the light of the world.
John 8:57–58. Before Abraham was, I am.
John 10:7–9. I am the gate.
John 10:11. I am the good shepherd.

▶ Ichabod *(name)*

A word meaning "no glory"; a name given to the son of Phinehas after the Philistines took the ark of the covenant

1 Samuel 4:19–22. Ichabod is born.
1 Samuel 14:2–3. Ichabod's nephew

▶ Identity *(character, personality, uniqueness)*

Characteristics by which a person or thing is recognized or known

Genesis 10:5. An identity for each nation
Genesis 27:23. Faking Esau's identity
Genesis 45. Joseph reveals his identity.
1 Peter 2:10. No identity at first

▶ Idleness *(lazy, unemployment, without substance)*

Not employed or busy; insubstantial

Deuteronomy 32:47. Idle talk
Proverbs 31:27. Bread of idleness
Ecclesiastes 10:18. Idleness of hands
1 Timothy 5:13. A habit of idleness

▶ Idol(s) *(false god)*

An image used as an object of worship

Exodus 34:17. Don't make idols.
Deuteronomy 7:26. A disgusting idol
Judges 8:27. Gideon's idol
Judges 17:3–6. Micah's idol
2 Kings 21:7. Manasseh's idol
Psalm 106:19. Worshiping an idol

▶ Idolatry *(worshiping false gods)*

Idol worship

Exodus 20:3–5. Idolatry is forbidden.
Joshua 24:2. Idol worship long ago
1 Kings 12:28–31. Jeroboam ushers in idolatry.
Jeremiah 44:5–6. Israel's idolatry
Hosea 13:1–2. Guilty of idolatry

▶ Ignorance *(lacking in knowledge, unawareness)*

The condition of being unaware, uninformed, and uneducated

Ezekiel 45:20. Sins of ignorance
Acts 3:17. Acting in ignorance
Acts 17:30. Acting in ignorance of people in the world
Ephesians 4:17–18. Ignorance of people in the world
1 Peter 2:15. Silence the ignorance of foolish people

▶ Ignore *(disregard, overlook)*

Refuse to pay attention to

Leviticus 5:2–4. Ignore and be guilty.
Leviticus 20:4–5. Ignore them at your peril.
Joshua 23:16. Ignore God and face His anger.
Nehemiah 4:4–5. Don't ignore their guilt, God.
Esther 3:3. Why do you ignore this?

▶ Illegitimacy *(unlawful)*

A birth out of wedlock

Deuteronomy 23:2. Illegitimate son
Hosea 5:7. Illegitimate births
John 8:41. Jews claim they are not illegitimate.

▶ Illness (see *Disease; Sickness)*

▶ Illumination *(clarification, enlightenment, explanation)*

Enlightening intellectually or spiritually

Psalm 119:18. Asking for illumination

Luke 24:45. Jesus provides illumination on the Scriptures.

John 14:26. The Holy Spirit will bring illumination.

Ephesians 1:16–17. Praying for illumination

Hebrews 4:12. Scriptures pierce and illuminate.

▶ Image *(copy, idol, likeness)*

To make or produce a likeness of; a reproduction of an object; a mental picture of something real

Genesis 5:3. In Adam's image

Job 4:16. A vague image

Jeremiah 44:19. Image of the queen of heaven

Acts 17:29. Images made from gold, silver, or stone

1 Corinthians 13:12. A blurred image

2 Corinthians 3:18. Changed into Christ's image

▶ Image of God *(likeness)*

Something created with the characteristics of God or bearing His likeness

Genesis 1:26–27. Made in God's image

Genesis 9:6. In the image of God

Romans 5:14. An image of the one to come (Jesus)

Romans 8:29. In the image of God's Son

1 Corinthians 11:7. God's image and glory

2 Corinthians 4:4. Christ is God's image.

▶ Imitate/Imitation *(custom, routine, tendency)*

Recurrent, often unconscious pattern of behavior

Luke 10:37. Imitate a good example.

1 Corinthians 4:16. Imitate Paul.

1 Corinthians 11:1. Imitate Christ.

Ephesians 5:1–2. Imitate God.

2 Thessalonians 3:7. Imitate a disciplined life.

Hebrews 13:7. Imitate the faith of leaders.

▶ Immanuel *(name)*

Hebrew name meaning "God with us"

Isaiah 7:14. God with us

Isaiah 8:8. O Immanuel

Matthew 1:20–23. Name him Immanuel.

▶ Immaturity *(childishness, irresponsibility)*

Not fully grown or developed

Isaiah 3:12. Oppressed by the immature

1 Corinthians 13:11. We were once immature.

1 Corinthians 14:20. Don't be spiritually immature.

Ephesians 4:14. No longer immature

Hebrews 5:11–13. Still babies

▶ Imminence *(nearness, proximity)*

Something about to occur

Matthew 24:2–3. Wondering about the imminence of Jesus' prediction

John 21:22–23. Mistaking the imminence of Jesus' return

Philippians 4:5. The imminence of God

2 Timothy 4:1. The imminence of Jesus' return

2 Peter 3:11–12. The imminence of the day of God

▶ Immolation *(death, fire, sacrifice)*

Death by fire

Genesis 19:24–26. Immolation of Sodom, Gomorrah, and their inhabitants

Leviticus 10:1–2. Immolation of Nadab and Abihu

Psalm 106:18. Immolation of the wicked

Matthew 3:11–12. Immolation of the old life

2 Peter 3:7. Immolation of heaven, earth, and the ungodly

▶ Immorality *(decadence, sin, wickedness)*

Living in a manner contrary to established moral principles

Judges 19. Immorality of worthless men

Psalm 12:8. When immorality increases

Jeremiah 3:9. Israel's immorality

Romans 13:13. Outing immorality

▶ Immortality *(living forever)*

Endless life or existence

Proverbs 12:28. The pathway to immortality

Romans 2:7. God gives immortality.

1 Corinthians 15:53–54. Clothed with immortality

1 Timothy 6:15–16. God's immortality

▶ Immunity *(invulnerability, protection, resistance)*

Resistance to infection; exemption from legal duties, penalties, or liabilities

Numbers 5:19. An immunity to ill effects

Romans 1:28–32. An immunity to God

2 Corinthians 4:3. An immunity to the gospel

▶ Impatience *(haste, hurry, rashness)*

An inability to tolerate delay

Numbers 21:4–5. Impatience leads to criticism.

Job 4:2, 5. Impatience and panic

Job 21:4. Shouldn't I be impatient?

Micah 2:7. Is God impatient?

Zechariah 11:8. Impatient with the sheep

▶ Imperfection *(see Blemish)*

▶ Impetuous *(hasty, impulsive, reckless)*

Marked by sudden forceful energy or emotion; impulsive and passionate

2 Samuel 11:2–4. Impetuous behavior

Job 6:3. Impetuous words

Habakkuk 1:6. Imminent invasion of an impetuous nation

▶ Importance *(significance, value, worth)*

Someone or something of significance

Genesis 48:19. The importance of Ephraim and Manasseh

Exodus 18:22. Moses to judge only cases of importance

Leviticus 16:31. Atonement: the most important festival

Esther 9:28. Importance of these days

John 3:30. Increasing in importance

1 Corinthians 15:3. The gospel is of first importance.

▶ Impossible *(impracticable, unattainable)*

Incapable of existing or occurring; not capable of being accomplished

Genesis 20:18. Impossible to have children

Exodus 32:9. They are impossible.

Exodus 34:8–9. Acknowledging the impossibility of dealing with Israel

Psalm 142:4. Escape is impossible.

Matthew 19:26. Impossible to save themselves

Luke 1:37. Nothing is impossible for God.

Romans 8:3. Impossible to meet God's standards

▶ Impostor(s) *(fake, fraud)*

One who engages in deception under an assumed name or identity

Joshua 9. The Gibeonites are impostors.

1 Kings 14:1–6. An impostor

Matthew 7:15. False prophets are impostors.

2 Corinthians 6:8. Regarded as an impostor

2 Timothy 3:12–13. Evil impostors

▶ Impotence *(helplessness, powerlessness, weakness)*

Lacking physical strength; incapable of sexual intercourse

1 Kings 1:4. Concern and impotence

Ecclesiastes 12:5. Signs of old age and impotence

▶ Imprecation *(see Curse[s])*

▶ Impressions *(name)*

Effects, feelings, or images retained as consequences of an experience

Deuteronomy 6:7. Cause God's commandments to have an impression on your kids.

1 Kings 10. Solomon makes a deep impression on the queen of Sheba.

Ecclesiastes 9:13. Wisdom's impression

I

▶ Impulsive behavior *(impetuous, reckless, spontaneous acts)*

Hasty, thoughtless behavior that sometimes leads to bad consequences

Judges 14. Samson's impulsive behavior

1 Samuel 25. David's impulsive behavior, part 1

2 Samuel 11. David's impulsive behavior, part 2

2 Samuel 13. Amnon's impulsive behavior

Proverbs 14:29. Impulsive behavior exalts folly.

▶ Impurity *(contamination, pollution, uncleanness)*

In a state of ritual uncleanness; contaminated

Leviticus 14:19. Cleansed from an impurity

Leviticus 15:19. Monthly impurity

Leviticus 20:21. An act of impurity

Ezra 9:10–11. Impurity affects the land.

Matthew 23:27. Full of impurity

▶ In the war room *(battle plans)*

Discussions between leaders about troops, strategy, and war

Numbers 21:21–35. God's counsel about soldiers marching ahead of the Israelites

Joshua 1. God's counsel about the upcoming wars in Canaan

Judges 4. Counsel of war between Deborah and Barak

1 Samuel 15. Counsel of war between Samuel and Saul

Ephesians 6:10–20. Paul's advice about spiritual war

▶ Inadequacy *(insufficiency, lack, shortage)*

Not adequate to fulfill a need or requirement

Exodus 4:10. Moses feels inadequate.

Judges 6:1–15. Gideon feels inadequate.

Isaiah 6:5. Isaiah feels inadequate.

Jeremiah 1:6–7. Jeremiah feels inadequate.

Hebrews 10:1–14. Animal sacrifices were inadequate to take away sin.

▶ Incarceration *(imprisoned)*

Confined; placed in prison

Genesis 39:19–23. Joseph is incarcerated.

Genesis 42:14–17. Joseph's brothers are incarcerated.

Matthew 11:2–3. John is incarcerated.

Acts 4:1–3. Peter and John are incarcerated.

Acts 12. Peter is incarcerated again.

Acts 16:22–40. Paul and Silas are incarcerated.

▶ Incarnation *(in flesh)*

God taking on human flesh

Luke 1:30–33. Incarnation announcement

John 1:1–18. Incarnation of the Word

1 Corinthians 15:45–47. Jesus as a second Adam

Galatians 4:4. Incarnation of God's Son

Philippians 2:7. Jesus' willingness to be human

▶ Incense *(spices and oils)*

Aromatic spices burned in the temple and tabernacle to produce a pleasant odor

Exodus 25:3–6. Contributions for incense

Exodus 30:1–10. An altar for burning incense

Exodus 30:34–38. Recipe for incense

Leviticus 2:1–2. An offering with incense

Leviticus 16. Atonement offering with incense

▶ Incest *(sexual sin)*

Sexual relations between persons closely related

Genesis 19:30–38. Lot and his daughters

Leviticus 18:6–18. Rules against incest

Leviticus 20:11–12. Death penalty for incest

Deuteronomy 27:22. Cursed for incest

1 Corinthians 5:1. Paul writes about incest in the church.

▶ Inclination(s) *(leaning, penchant, proclivity)*

A tendency toward a certain condition

Genesis 6:5. Evil inclinations

Genesis 8:21. Man's inclinations
Deuteronomy 31:21. Inclination of their behavior
Jeremiah 7:24. Stubborn inclinations

▸ Income *(profits, salary, wages)*

Amount of money received during a period of time for labor or services or for the sale of property or goods
Genesis 47:22. Priests' income
Numbers 18:21, 25–26. A tithe from every income
Deuteronomy 12:6. A tithe from every income
Ezra 4:13. Will rebuilding the wall of Jerusalem hurt the king's income?
Ecclesiastes 5:10. Craving a bigger income?

▸ Incompetence *(ineptitude, lacking skill, useless)*

Not qualified; inadequate or unsuited
1 Kings 18:26–27. Elijah mocks the incompetence of the Baal prophets.
Psalm 107:27. Disaster inspires incompetence.
Daniel 2. Nebuchadnezzar's anger over the incompetence of his astrologers
Acts 19:13–16. Incompetent at exorcism

▸ Inconsistent *(conflicting, incompatible)*

Displaying or marked by a lack of consistency
John 7:40–43. Inconsistency in a crowd
Acts 5:1–10. Peter calls Ananias on his inconsistency.
1 Corinthians 1:12–13. An inconsistency
Galatians 1:6–8. An inconsistent gospel
James 1:6. Doubting and inconsistency

▸ Indecisiveness *(irresolution, vacillation, wavering)*

Prone to or characterized by indecision
Joshua 24:15. Joshua makes a decision, even if the people don't.
1 Kings 18:21. Indecision of Israel
Matthew 27:18–21. Pilate's indecision
Acts 4:21. Indecision of the authorities

▸ Independence *(autonomy, liberty, self-determination)*

The state or quality of being independent; self-governance
Judges 18:7. Totally independent
Judges 21:25. Independent ways
2 Chronicles 21:8–10. A fight for independence
1 Corinthians 11:11. Not totally independent

▸ Indescribable *(beyond words)*

Someone or something beyond description
Ezekiel 1. Ezekiel's nearly indescribable vision
2 Corinthians 9:15. God's grace is indescribable.
2 Corinthians 12. Paul's indescribable vision
Revelation 15:1–2. John's vision is almost beyond description.
Revelation 21:1–2. A city of indescribable beauty

▸ Indictment *(condemnation, denunciation)*

A written statement charging a person with committing an offense
Job 42:7–10. God's indictment of Job's friends
Isaiah 13:11. God's indictment against the wicked
Jeremiah 3:6–7. God's indictment against Israel and Judah
Ezekiel 16:1–2. God's indictment against Jerusalem
Matthew 23:33, 35–36. Jesus' indictment against the Pharisees and scribes

▸ Indifference *(lack of interest, unconcern)*

Not mattering one way or another; having no marked feeling for or against
Proverbs 1:32. Indifference destroys.
Isaiah 13:17–18. The Medes and Persians will be indifferent to Babylon's plight.
Isaiah 49:14–16. God cannot be indifferent to his children.

Jeremiah 6:23. Judah will be invaded by an indifferent nation.

Jeremiah 13:14. God will show indifference, rather than compassion.

▶ Indigestion *(acid stomach, digestive disorder, dyspepsia)*

Discomfort of illness resulting from an inability to digest something

Jeremiah 30:6. Fear and indigestion

Lamentations 1:20. Distress and indigestion

Nahum 2:10. Upset stomachs

1 Timothy 5:23. A cure for Timothy's indigestion

Revelation 10:9–10. The scroll that gave John indigestion

▶ Indignation *(annoyance, righteous anger)*

Anger roused by something unjust

Genesis 31:36–42. Jacob's indignation at Laban's accusation of theft

Psalm 78:49. God's wrath and indignation

Psalm 119:53. Indignant over the wicked

Jeremiah 15:17. Jeremiah's indignation

Nahum 1:6. Who can withstand God's indignation?

▶ Indolence (see *Idleness, Laziness)*

▶ Indulgence *(extravagance, lenience, treat)*

Giving in to the desires and whims of someone

Exodus 32:6. Indulging in sin

Numbers 25:1. Indulging in immorality

Matthew 23:25. Self-indulgence

Galatians 5:13. Don't use freedom to indulge in sin.

Colossians 2:23. Indulging the flesh

▶ Industrious *(diligent)*

Assiduous in work or study

1 Kings 11:28. Industrious Jeroboam

2 Kings 23. Josiah is industrious.

Ezra 7:10. Industrious Ezra

Nehemiah 4:7. Anger at the industrious workers

Proverbs 6:6–8. The industrious ant

▶ Inebriation (see *Drinking)*

▶ Inequity (see *Sin[s])*

▶ Inexperience *(naiveté, immaturity, rawness)*

Lack of knowledge gained from experience

Judges 2:10. Inexperience with the ways of the Lord

1 Samuel 3:7. Samuel is inexperienced about God.

1 Samuel 17:38–39. Inexperienced with battle armor

2 Kings 12:2. Helping an inexperienced king

▶ Infallible *(flawless, perfect)*

Incapable of error

2 Samuel 22:31. Infallible God

Psalm 19:7. Infallible teachings

Acts 1:3. Infallible proofs

2 Timothy 3:16. Scriptures point out our fallibility.

▶ Infant *(baby, child, toddler)*

A child in infancy

Numbers 11:12. As a nurse carries an infant

Numbers 12:12. Like a stillborn infant

Isaiah 11:8. Infants and cobras

Isaiah 65:20. No longer a premature death for infants

Luke 2:12. An infant in a manger

▶ Infanticide *(abortion, death, murder)*

Killing an infant

Exodus 1. Infanticide in Egypt

Leviticus 20:1–2. Condemning infanticide by sacrifice

2 Kings 6:28–30. Infanticide in Samaria

Lamentations 2:20. Confronting God about infanticide during a famine

Matthew 2:16–18. Infanticide in Bethlehem

▶ Infatuation *(fascination, obsession, passion)*

An unreasoning or extravagant passion

Genesis 34. Shechem's infatuation

Genesis 39:7–20. The infatuation of the wife of Potiphar

Judges 14:1–2. Samson's infatuation

2 Samuel 13. Amnon's infatuation

Ezekiel 23. Metaphor of the infatuation of Samaria and Jerusalem

▶ Inferiority *(inadequacy, lowliness, weakness)*

Second-rate; persistent sense of inadequacy or a tendency toward self-diminishment

Judges 6:14–15. Gideon feels inferior.

1 Samuel 9:19–21. Saul feels inferior.

Job 12:3. Job is not inferior.

Daniel 2:39. An inferior kingdom

2 Corinthians 11:6. Paul doesn't feel inferior.

▶ Infertility *(barren, childlessness, unproductiveness)*

Inability to have a child

Genesis 16:1–2. An infertile Sarai tries to gain children another way.

Genesis 30. Rachel's infertility

Exodus 23:25–26. No infertility

1 Samuel 1. Hannah's infertility

2 Kings 2:20–21. A cure for infertility

Luke 1:7. Elizabeth's infertility

▶ Infidelity *(betrayal, disloyalty, unfaithfulness)*

Unfaithfulness to a sexual partner, particularly a spouse

Numbers 5:11–19. Infidelity test

Numbers 14:33. Israel's infidelity

Judges 19:2–3. Infidelity of a concubine

2 Chronicles 30:7. Infidelity of ancestors

Ezekiel 23. Metaphor of Israel's infidelity

▶ Infinite *(endless, inestimable, vast)*

Having no boundaries or limits; immeasurably great or large

Job 36:26. God's infinite years

Psalm 147:5. God's infinite understanding

Romans 11:33. God's infinite riches, wisdom, and knowledge

Ephesians 3:10. God's infinite wisdom

Philippians 3:8. Infinite value of knowing Christ

▶ Infirmity (see *Disease; Sickness*)

▶ Influence *(authority, power)*

The ability to affect indirectly or intangibly

Proverbs 20:1. Under the influence

Romans 3:19. Influenced by Moses' Teachings (the Law)

Romans 6:2. Sin's influence

Romans 7:5. Influence of the corrupt nature

Colossians 2:20. The world's influence

▶ Inform *(enlighten, tell)*

To impart information to; make aware

Ruth 4:3–4. Just to inform you

1 Samuel 22:17. Uninformed Saul

Ezra 4:14–15. A letter to inform the king

Esther 4:8. Informing Esther

Jeremiah 51:31. Informing the king

▶ Ingratitude *(thanklessness, ungratefulness)*

Lack of gratitude

Numbers 14. Israel's ingratitude

Psalm 109:4–5. Attitude of ingratitude

Ezekiel 16:17–18. Ingratitude and adultery of the people of Jerusalem

Luke 17:11–18. Ingratitude of nine lepers

2 Timothy 3. Ingratitude in the last days

▶ Inheritance *(bequest, birthright, heritage, legacy)*

Something inherited or regarded as a heritage

Genesis 21:10. Isaac's inheritance

Deuteronomy 18:2. The Lord is the Levites' inheritance.

Joshua 13:6–7. Land as an inheritance

Psalm 2:8. Inheriting nations

Luke 12:13–14. Jesus not the judge of inheritances

▶ Iniquity *(see Evil; Sin[s])*

▶ Initiative *(ingenuity, plan, resourcefulness)*

The power or ability to begin or follow through energetically with a plan or task

Numbers 25:6–13. Rewarding Phinehas's initiative

1 Corinthians 9:17. Not from Paul's own initiative

2 Corinthians 8:17. Titus's initiative

2 Peter 1:20–21. Human initiative

▶ Injure *(damage, harm, hurt)*

To cause physical harm to someone or something

Exodus 21:22–25. Injuring a pregnant woman

Proverbs 8:36. If you sin, you injure yourself.

Zechariah 12:3. Injure Jerusalem, injure yourself.

Luke 10:18–19. You won't be injured.

Revelation 9:19. Horses that injure

▶ Injustice *(bias, inequality, unfairness)*

Violation of another person's rights or of what's right

Job 6:29–30. Don't permit injustice.

Psalm 7:3–5. Consequences of injustice

Proverbs 13:11. Wealth and injustice

Proverbs 22:8. Planting injustice

Amos 5:10. On the side of injustice

▶ Inn(s) *(public house)*

Public lodging house serving food and drink to travelers

Genesis 42:27. Before there were established inns

Luke 2:6–7. No room in the inn

Luke 10:33–34. Taking an injured man to the inn

Acts 28:15. Three Inns

▶ Innocence *(blamelessness, purity, virtue)*

The state of being uncorrupted by evil, malice, or wrongdoing

Genesis 18:23–33. The innocent and the guilty

Genesis 20:4–5. Abimelech's innocence

Exodus 23:7. Don't kill the innocent.

1 Samuel 25:26. Kept from shedding innocent blood

Psalm 17:2. Verdict of innocence

Psalm 26:6. Washing hands in innocence

▶ Inquire *(ask, query, question)*

To seek information by asking a question

Genesis 25:22. Rebekah inquires of the Lord.

Deuteronomy 17:9–10. Inquire of the priests and judge.

Joshua 9:14. Failure to inquire of God

Judges 18:5. Inquiring about a journey

1 Samuel 9:9. Prophets inquire of God.

▶ Insanity *(madness, mental illness)*

Persistent mental disorder or derangement

Deuteronomy 28:15, 28. Curse of insanity

1 Samuel 21:12–15. David fakes insanity.

Ecclesiastes 2:12. Studying insanity

Zechariah 12:4. Struck with insanity

2 Peter 2:15–16. Balaam's insanity

▶ Insect(s) *(ant, bug, creature, pest)*

Any of the numerous small arthropod animals of the class Insecta

Leviticus 11:20–23. Clean and unclean insects

Deuteronomy 14:19. Swarming, winged insects

Malachi 3:11. Stopping the insects

▶ Insecurity *(anxiety, lacking confidence, timidity)*

Lacking emotional stability; inadequately guarded

Psalm 37:9–11. The hope of the insecure

Psalm 94:18. A place of insecurity

Proverbs 27:24. Insecurity of wealth

John 15:7. Help for the insecure
1 John 4:1–3. Help for discernment insecurity

▶ Insensitive *(inconsiderate, unfeeling, unsympathetic)*

Lacking in sensitivity to the feelings or circumstances of others
Genesis 38:8–10. God ends the life of an insensitive man.
Exodus 5:6–11. Pharaoh is insensitive to the Israelites.
Deuteronomy 15:9. Insensitivity to the poor is condemned.
1 Samuel 1:13–14. Eli is insensitive to Hannah's plight.
Psalm 119:69–70. Cold and insensitive
Lamentations 1:2. Insensitivity to Jerusalem's plight
Luke 13:14–16. Jesus is appalled at the insensitivity of a synagogue leader.

▶ Insincerity *(see Hypocrisy)*

▶ Insomnia *(restlessness, sleeplessness)*

Chronic inability to fall asleep or remain asleep for a length of time
Esther 6:1. Xerxes's insomnia
Psalm 22:2. Unable to sleep
Psalm 77:2. Up all night
Ecclesiastes 2:22–23. No rest at night
Daniel 6:18–19. Darius's insomnia

▶ Inspiration of Scriptures *(see Bible)*

▶ Instinct *(feeling, impulse, nature)*

An inborn characteristic of a species that is often a response to specific environmental stimuli
Proverbs 1:17. A bird's instinct
Proverbs 30:27. Instinct of locusts
Isaiah 1:3. Animal instincts
2 Peter 2:12–13. Creatures of instinct
Jude 10. Watch out for the instincts of the destructive.

▶ Instruction *(education, teaching, training)*

Imparted knowledge
Exodus 24:12. For the people's instruction
2 Chronicles 17:7–9. Instruction in Judah
Job 22:21–22. Accept God's instruction.
Proverbs 19:27. A father's instruction
Lamentations 2:9. No instruction
Malachi 2:7. Seek instruction from a priest.

▶ Instrument(s) *(equipment, musical, tool)*

A tool for making music or performing a task
Psalm 92:2–3. Ten-stringed instrument
Isaiah 8:7. Assyria is God's instrument.
Acts 9:15–16. God's chosen instrument
2 Timothy 2:21. An instrument for a noble purpose

▶ Insubordination *(defiance, disobedience, rebelliousness)*

Lack of submission to authority
1 Timothy 1:8–9. The lawless and the insubordinate
Titus 1:6. Children accused of insubordination
Titus 1:10–11. Insubordinate, idle talkers

▶ Insult(s) *(affront, offend, upset)*

To treat with gross insensitivity
Psalm 4:2. You insult my honor.
Psalm 44:15–16. Those who insult and slander us
Psalm 69:9. Insults from the enemy
Psalm 74:22. Insults of godless fools
Ezekiel 8:17. Judah insults God.
Matthew 5:11. Blessed are you when people insult you.

▶ Insurrection *(anarchy, civil disobedience, rebellion)*

An attempt to overthrow the ruling authorities
2 Samuel 20. Sheba's insurrection

Ezra 4:19. A history of insurrection?

Psalm 55:9–11. Insurrection in the city

Psalm 64:2. Hide me from insurrectionists.

Luke 23:18–19, 25. In prison for insurrection

▶ Integration *(amalgamation, assimilation, incorporation)*

Making a whole by bringing all parts together; unifying

Acts 2. The Holy Spirit causes integration.

1 Corinthians 12:12–13. Integrated in one body

Revelation 7:9–10. Integration in heaven

▶ Integrity *(honesty, honor, reliability)*

Steadfast adherence to a strict ethical code

Genesis 6:9. Noah: a man of integrity

Genesis 17:1. Live with integrity.

Deuteronomy 18:13. Have integrity.

Joshua 24:14. Serve God with integrity.

Job 1:1. Job's integrity.

Psalm 25:21. Protected by integrity

2 Peter 1:3–5. Add integrity.

▶ Intelligence *(aptitude, cleverness, intellect)*

The capacity to acquire and apply knowledge

Genesis 41:33, 39. Joseph's intelligence

Deuteronomy 1:13. Choose intelligent men.

Job 34:2. Listen, intelligent men.

Proverbs 17:28. Silence and intelligence

Daniel 1:3–4. Looking for intelligent men

▶ Intemperance *(see Drinking, Gluttony)*

▶ Intentions *(goals, purposes, plans)*

Courses one intends to follow; aims that guide action

Deuteronomy 31:21. Knowing their intentions

1 Kings 8:18–19. Good intentions

Proverbs 12:2. Wicked intentions

Proverbs 14:17. Wicked intentions

Hebrews 4:12. Judging a person's intentions

▶ Intercession *(prayer)*

Petitioning God

Isaiah 53:12. God's servant intercedes for the rebellious.

Jeremiah 7:16. Don't make intercession.

Jeremiah 27:18. Prophets should intercede.

Romans 8:26–27. The Holy Spirit makes intercession.

▶ Interim activities *(intervening, short-term, temporary)*

Activities taking place in the interim between major events

1 Samuel 16–2 Samuel 5:5. In the interim between being anointed king and taking the throne, David was on the run from Saul.

Amos 8:11. In the interim between the present and the coming judgment of God, there will be silence from God.

Malachi 4:5–6. In the interim of waiting for the Messiah, a new Elijah will come.

2 Corinthians 2:1–3. In the interim between the writing of 1 and 2 Corinthians, Paul elects not to visit.

▶ Intermarriage *(endogamy, marriage)*

Marrying someone from another clan or nation

Genesis 34:8–9. Hamor suggests intermarriage.

Deuteronomy 7:2–4. Never intermarry with the nations in the Promised Land.

Joshua 23:12–13. Intermarriage is forbidden.

1 Kings 11:1–2. Solomon breaks God's commandment against intermarriage.

Ezra 9:14. Ezra prays about intermarriage.

Ezra 10:18–19. Vowing to right the wrong of intermarriage

▶ Intermediary *(liaison, mediator)*

Acting as a mediator or an agent between persons or things

Exodus 18:15–16. Moses acts as an intermediary.

1 Samuel 19:1–3. Jonathan acts as an intermediary for David.

2 Samuel 3:12. Messengers act as intermediaries for Abner.

Esther 10:3. Mordecai acts as an intermediary.

Proverbs 31:8–9. Act as an intermediary.

▶ Interpretation *(analysis, explanation, understanding)*

An explanation of a work; an exegesis

Genesis 40:22. Reality of Joseph's interpretation

1 Corinthians 12:10. Interpretation of tongues

1 Corinthians 14:13. Language interpretation

1 Peter 1:10. The prophets' own interpretation?

▶ Intimacy *(closeness, familiarity, relationship)*

The condition of being intimate; marked by close acquaintance, association, or familiarity

Proverbs 3:32. Intimate advice

Job 19:19. Job's intimate friends

Job 29:4. God's intimate friendship

Hosea 3:3. Avoid intimacy.

John 15:14. Intimacy with Christ

▶ Intimidation *(bullying, pressure, threats)*

Making someone timid by the use of threats or coercion

1 Samuel 17:4–9. Goliath's intimidation

2 Kings 18:28–35. Assyrian intimidation

Nehemiah 6:9, 13–14. Intimidation of the enemies to the wall-building effort

Isaiah 41:23–24. Intimidation from idols

Philippians 1:28. Intimidation from opponents

▶ Intoxication *(see Drinking)*

▶ Introspection *(self-examination)*

Contemplation of one's own thoughts, feelings, and sensations

Psalm 7:9. Let God examine thoughts, rather than self-examining.

Psalm 19:14. Let thoughts be God pleasing, rather than introspective.

1 Corinthians 4:3. Paul avoids introspection.

2 Corinthians 10:5. Corral thoughts, rather than giving in to introspection.

Philippians 4:8. The cure for morbid introspection

▶ Invasion *(attack, foray, offensive)*

The act of invading, especially the entrance of an armed force into a territory to conquer

Exodus 10:1–20. Invasion of locusts

Deuteronomy 28. Invasion—one of the curses of disobedience

Joshua 6. The invasion of the Promised Land begins at Jericho.

1 Samuel 30:14. An invasion of the southern area

2 Kings 25. Invasion and destruction of Jerusalem

▶ Invention *(creation, discovery, finding)*

A new device, method, or process developed from study and experimentation

Psalm 58:2. Inventing new crimes

Daniel 11:23–24. Invention of the invading ruler

Amos 6:1, 5. Inventing musical instruments

Micah 2:1. Inventing trouble

Romans 1:29–31. Inventing ways of doing evil

▶ Inventory *(account, list, record)*

A detailed itemized record of things in one's possession; a periodic survey of all goods and materials in stock

Exodus 25:3–7. Inventory of items needs for the tabernacle

Exodus 38:21. Inventory of materials used for the tabernacle (tent of meeting)

1 Kings 10:14–29. An inventory of Solomon's wealth

2 Kings 20:13. Hezekiah shows off his inventory.

Ezra 1:7–11. Inventory of temple utensils

▶ Investigation *(analysis, examination, study)*

A detailed inquiry or systematic examination

Deuteronomy 13:13–15. Make a thorough investigation.

Deuteronomy 17:2–4. Investigate thoroughly.

Deuteronomy 19:16–19. Investigate false witnesses.

Ezra 10:10, 16. Investigate the problem of intermarriage.

Proverbs 25:2. Kings must investigate.

▶ Investment *(asset, outlay, time)*

An amount invested; a commitment, as of time

Matthew 6:20. A heavenly investment

Matthew 16:24. Investing in Jesus

Luke 19:11–27. A parable about investments

▶ Invisible (see *Unseen*)

▶ Invitation *(call, request, summons)*

A request for someone's presence or participation

Exodus 2:20–21. An invitation to supper

Exodus 34:15. Refuse this invitation.

1 Chronicles 13:1–3. An invitation to bring back the ark

Matthew 22:8–10. Invitation in a parable

Luke 11:37. An invitation to the home of a Pharisee

Revelation 3:20. An invitation to open the door

▶ Iraq *(country)*

Country of southwest Asia with Baghdad as its capital

Genesis 10:11–12. Building cities in what is now Iraq

Genesis 11:31. Leaving Ur (Iraq)

Genesis 29:1. Jacob travels east (Iraq).

Daniel 1. Daniel and the Israelites are taken captive to Babylon (Iraq).

Jonah 3:1–2. Jonah is sent to Nineveh (Iraq).

▶ Iron *(metal)*

Malleable, ductile, magnetic or magnetizable metallic element occurring abundantly in ores

Genesis 4:22. Iron tools

Numbers 31:22–23. Put iron through the fire.

Numbers 35:16. Use of iron weapons constitutes murder.

Deuteronomy 3:11. An iron bed

Proverbs 27:17. Iron sharpens iron.

Isaiah 44:12. Blacksmiths shape iron.

▶ Irony *(biting wit, mockery, sarcasm, satire)*

The use of words to express something different from and often opposite to their literal meaning

2 Samuel 6:20. Michal's use of irony

Job 12:1–2. Job's use of irony

Ezekiel 16:17. The irony of a gift misused

Ezekiel 28:3–5. Irony about the king of Tyre

Matthew 22:15–16. The Pharisees' use of irony

▶ Irresponsible *(careless, immature, reckless)*

Not reliable or trustworthy

Exodus 16:19–20. Irresponsibility leads to problems.

Judges 16. Samson's irresponsibility leads to tragedy.

1 Samuel 15. Saul's irresponsible behavior causes regret in God.

2 Samuel 11. One irresponsible act leads to another.

Luke 15:11–13. An irresponsible lifestyle

▶ Irreverent *(disrespectful, satirical)*

Lacking proper respect or seriousness for what is sacred

Exodus 20:7. Irreverent use of God's name is prohibited.

Leviticus 10:1–2. Irreverence leads to death.

2 Samuel 6:6–7. Uzzah's irreverence

John 8:48–49. The Jews' irreverence

▶ Irrevocable *(final, immutable, irreversible, unalterable)*

Impossible to retract or revoke

Esther 1:19. An irrevocable law ousts Vashti.

Esther 8:8. An irrevocable edict

Daniel 6:8–9. Irrevocable law of the Medes and Persians

Romans 11:29. Irrevocable gifts and calling

Galatians 3:15. An irrevocable agreement

▶ Irrigation *(watering)*

Supplying dry land with water by means of ditches or streams

Genesis 2:5–6. Natural irrigation

Deuteronomy 11:10. Irrigated like a vegetable garden

Ecclesiastes 2:6. Irrigation for the trees

Isaiah 58:11. Irrigation as a figure of speech

1 Corinthians 3:6–8. Metaphorical irrigation

▶ Irritation *(annoyance, frustration, pain, vexation)*

A condition of inflammation, soreness, or irritability of a body organ or part

Leviticus 13. Skin irritation

1 Samuel 1:6. Hannah's irritation

Proverbs 10:26. Irritation caused by lazy workers

Proverbs 12:16. Irritation of a stubborn fool

Proverbs 27:3. Irritation caused by a stubborn fool

▶ Islam *(nation, religion)*

The monotheistic religion based on the doctrine of submission to God and of Muhammad as the last prophet of God; the civilization based on Islam

Genesis 25:17–18. Ishmael is the ancestor of practitioners of Islam.

Galatians 4:22–26. Judeo-Christian beliefs and a precursor to Islamic beliefs

▶ Isolation *(seclusion, separation)*

The act of isolating

Leviticus 13. Isolation and skin disease

Leviticus 15:31. Necessary isolation

Numbers 12:14–15. Miriam is kept in isolation.

▶ Israel *(nation, person)*

The descendants of Jacob regarded as the chosen people of God

Genesis 32:28. Jacob's name is changed to Israel.

Exodus 1. Jacob's family becomes the nation of Israel.

Numbers 1. Numbering the people of Israel

1 Kings 11:30–33. The nation of Israel splits into two kingdoms.

Ezekiel 14. Israel's idolatry

Matthew 10:23. Persecuted in Israel

Matthew 15:24. The lost sheep of Israel

Revelation 7:4–8. The sealed tribes of Israel

▶ Ivory *(tusks)*

Hard, smooth, yellowish-white substance obtained from the tusks of elephants

1 Kings 10:18. Solomon's ivory throne

1 Kings 10:22. Bringing back ivory

1 Kings 22:39. Ahab's ivory palace

Psalm 45:8. Ivory palaces

Song of Songs 5:14. A chest like ivory

Ezekiel 27:6. A deck with ivory

▶ Jail breaks *(escape, release)*

An escape from jail

Genesis 41. Joseph is released from prison to interpret Pharaoh's dream.

Acts 12. An angel helps Peter escape from jail.

Acts 16:27–28. A Philippian jailer fears a jail break

▶ Jealousy *(covetousness, protectiveness, suspicion)*

A jealous attitude or disposition; fear of losing the affection of another person

Exodus 20:5–6. A jealous God

Numbers 5:11–29. A fit of jealousy

Job 5:2. Jealousy murders.

Proverbs 6:33–34. Jealousy arouses fury.

Proverbs 14:30. Cancerous jealousy

Proverbs 27:4. Who can survive jealousy?

▶ Jehovah *(Adonai, God, Lord)*

Translation of a misreading of the word *Yahweh*

Genesis 22:14. The Lord Will Provide (Jehovah-Jireh)

Genesis 49:18. Waiting in hope for the Lord (Yahweh/Jehovah)

Exodus 34:5–6. The Lord (Yahweh/Jehovah) reveals Himself.

Judges 5:3. A song to the Lord (Yahweh/Jehovah)

Psalm 104:35. Praise the Lord (Yahweh/Jehovah)

▶ Jericho *(city)*

Ancient city of Palestine near the northwest shore of the Dead Sea

Numbers 22:1. Camping near Jericho

Joshua 6. Destruction of Jericho

1 Kings 16:34. Rebuilding Jericho

2 Kings 2:4–5. Sent to Jericho

Luke 18:35. On the road to Jericho

▶ Jerusalem *(city, fortress)*

The capital city of Israel

Joshua 10. War with King Adoni Zedek of Jerusalem and other kings

1 Samuel 17:54. Taking Goliath's head to Jerusalem

2 Samuel 5:6–7. David captures Jerusalem.

2 Kings 25. Fall of Jerusalem

Matthew 21:1–11. Jesus' triumphal entry into Jerusalem

Matthew 23:37. Jesus mourns over Jerusalem.

▶ Jesus *(Savior, Son of God, Son of Man)*

The second member of the trinity; founder of Christianity

Matthew 1:18–25. Jesus—born of a virgin

Matthew 5–7. Jesus preaches the Sermon on the Mount

Mark 1:9–11. Jesus is baptized by John the Baptist.

Luke 2:6–7. Jesus is born in a stable.

John 19:17–37. Jesus is crucified.

Romans 5:17. The gift of righteousness through Jesus

Romans 8:11. Christ brought back to life

1 Corinthians 1:5. Rich through Jesus

2 Corinthians 4:5. Servants of Jesus

Ephesians 1:5–6. Adopted through Jesus

Philippians 2:8. Jesus humbled himself.

Revelation 22:20. Jesus will return to earth someday.

▶ Jew *(Hebrew, Israelite, person)*

A member by birth or conversion of the people tracing their descent from the ancient Hebrews

Ezra 3:8. The Jews return from exile.

Esther 2:5. Mordecai

Matthew 2:1–2. The one born king of the Jews

John 1:19. The Jews query John the Baptist.

John 2:18–20. The Jews question Jesus.

John 11:45. Many Jews believe in Jesus.

J

▶ Jewelry *(bracelets, necklaces, rings)*

Ornaments such as bracelets, rings, necklaces

Genesis 24:52–53. Gift of jewelry

Exodus 3:22. Ask for jewelry.

Exodus 33:5–6. Take off your jewelry.

Jeremiah 2:32. A woman can't forget her jewelry.

Ezekiel 16:11–13. God gave jewelry.

▶ Jobs *(duties, tasks, work)*

Specified duties or responsibilities

Exodus 36:7. More than enough to do the job

Judges 8:21. A man's job

2 Chronicles 19:11. Do your job.

Ezra 5:8. An excellent job

Luke 15:15. The lost son finds a job.

▶ Jordan River *(river)*

River in southwest Asia rising in Syria and flowing to the Sea of Galilee

Numbers 13:29. Nations along the Jordan River

Numbers 32. Asking for land east of the Jordan River

Joshua 3. Crossing the Jordan River

Joshua 16:1. Joseph's territory near the Jordan River

Matthew 3:13. Baptized in the Jordan River

John 10:39–40. Jesus escapes over the Jordan River.

▶ Journey *(travel, trip, voyage)*

Traveling from one place to another

Numbers 10:33. Three days' journey

Deuteronomy 8:2. Israel's 40-year journey through the desert

1 Kings 19:7–8. Elijah's journey

Ezra 8:21. Praying for a safe journey

Proverbs 16:9. You can plan your journey, but God directs your steps.

▶ Joy *(delight, happiness, pleasure)*

Intense, ecstatic happiness; one of the fruit of the Spirit

1 Samuel 2:1. Joy in the Lord

2 Samuel 6:14–15. Joy in the Lord

Psalm 13:5. Joy in salvation

Psalm 21:1. Joy in God's strength

Psalm 71:23. Singing with joy

Ezekiel 7:7. No joy in the mountains.

Galatians 5:22. Joy—a fruit of the Spirit

Colossians 1:11. Endure everything with joy.

▶ Jubilee *(see Year of Jubilee)*

▶ Judge *(adjudicator, arbitrator, determine, moderator)*

To hear and decide on in a court of law; to form an opinion or estimation of after careful consideration

Genesis 18:25. God: The judge of the whole earth

Deuteronomy 1:16–17. Judges, be impartial.

Deuteronomy 25:1–2. Judges to decide on punishment

Judges 2:15–16. God sent judges.

Judges 11:27. The Lord is the judge.

1 Chronicles 26:29. Judges appointed

▶ Judgment of God *(justice, punishment)*

God's response to the actions of humans

Exodus 6:6. God's mighty acts of judgment

1 Samuel 3:11–13. A permanent act of judgment

1 Kings 11:10–11. A judgment against Solomon

Ezekiel 7. Judgment against Israel

Ezekiel 25:16–17. Further judgment against Israel

▶ Judgment of people *(discernment, mediation)*

The act or process of judging; forming an opinion after consideration or deliberation

1 Samuel 29:9. Achish's judgment

1 Kings 3:16–28. Solomon's wise judgment

2 Chronicles 22:8. Jehu executes judgment.

Job 12:20. Good judgment

Daniel 2:14. Daniel's shrewd judgment

▶ Justice *(fairness, impartiality, rightfulness)*

The principle of moral rightness; upholding what is just

Exodus 23. Rules for justice

Leviticus 19:15. Administering justice

Deuteronomy 10:17–18. Justice for orphans and widows

Deuteronomy 16:20. Strive for justice.

Psalm 72:1–2. Give the king justice.

Luke 18:1–8. Parable of an unjust judge and a widow's cry for justice

▶ Justification *(rightness with God)*

The state of being right with God through God's action in forgiving sins; also, the fact of being justified or validated

Ezekiel 16:52. Justification for actions

Acts 13:38–39. Justification through Jesus

Romans 4:25. Handed over for our justification

Romans 5:16. The gift of justification

Romans 8:30. Predestined and justified

Galatians 2:16. Justification does not come through human effort.

▶ Key(s) *(enter, lock, solution)*

A notched and grooved device that is turned to open or close a lock

Deuteronomy 32:34. Under lock and key

Judges 3:25–26. The key to a dead man's room

Matthew 16:18–19. Keys of the kingdom

Luke 11:52. Key that unlocks knowledge

Revelation 3:7–8. Key of David

▶ Kidnap *(abduct, ransom, take hostage)*

To seize and detain unlawfully and usually for a ransom

Deuteronomy 24:7. Penalty for kidnapping

2 Samuel 19:41. Why were you kidnapped, David?

▶ Kindness *(compassion, consideration, thoughtfulness)*

The quality or state of being kind; one of the fruit of the Spirit

Genesis 24:11–12. A prayer for kindness

Ruth 2:13. Boaz's kindness

1 Samuel 20:14–15. A covenant of kindness

2 Samuel 9. David's desire to show kindness

Psalm 90:17. Kindness of God

Galatians 5:22. Kindness: a fruit of the Spirit

▶ King(s) *(ruler, sovereign)*

A male sovereign

Genesis 14. An alliance of kings

Genesis 36:31–34. Kings of Edom

Deuteronomy 31:4. King Sihon and King Og

1 Samuel 8. Israel demands a king.

2 Kings 25. Nebuchadnezzar, king of Babylon

▶ King of Israel *(House of David, ruler, sovereign)*

The male ruler of Israel; title given to Jesus

1 Samuel 10:1. Anointing the first king of Israel

2 Samuel 2:10. Ishbosheth, the king of Israel

2 Samuel 5:4–5. David, the king of Israel

1 Kings 2:12. Solomon, the king of Israel

1 Kings 16:29–30. Ahab, one of the worst of the kings of Israel

Mark 15:31–32. The Messiah, the king of Israel

John 1:49. You are the king of Israel!

▶ Kingdom *(empire, monarchy, realm)*

A political or territorial unit ruled by a sovereign

Genesis 10:8–10. The kingdom of Cush

Genesis 20:9. Trouble in Abimelech's kingdom

Exodus 19:6. God's kingdom of priests

Deuteronomy 3:3–4. The kingdom of Og

1 Samuel 18:8. Saul begrudges David his kingdom.

▶ Kingdom of God *(dominion, rule)*

God's rule through the actions of Christ

Matthew 3:1–2. John the Baptizer announces the kingdom of heaven.

Matthew 5:10. The kingdom of heaven belongs to the persecuted.

Matthew 21:43. The kingdom of God taken away

Mark 4:30–32. What is the kingdom of God like?

Mark 10:14–15. Little children are part of the kingdom of God.

Acts 1:3. Jesus talked about the kingdom of God.

▶ Kinsman-redeemer *(relative)*

A person who reclaimed the property of a debtor kinsman

Ruth 3:9. Boaz is Ruth's kinsman-redeemer.

Ruth 4. Settling the matter of the kinsman-redeemer

▶ Kissing *(sign of affection)*

Touching with the lips as an expression of affection

Genesis 27:26–27. A kiss between father and son

Genesis 31:28. Laban is prevented from kissing his family.

2 Samuel 15:5. A kiss from Absalom to steal a kingdom

2 Samuel 20:9–10. A kiss from an assassin

Song of Songs 1:2–3. A kiss from a bride

Mark 14:44. A kiss from a traitor

▶ Kneeling *(bowing, showing respect)*

Going down on or resting on one's knees; a common way of showing respect in Bible times

1 Kings 1:31. Bathsheba kneels.

1 Kings 8:54. Solomon kneels.

Esther 3:2. Kneeling and bowing

Isaiah 45:23. Everyone will kneel before God.

Mark 15:16–19. The soldiers mock Jesus by kneeling in front of him.

Philippians 2:10–11. Everyone will kneel before Christ.

▶ Knowledge *(information, skill, wisdom)*

The state or fact of knowing; familiarity, awareness, or understanding gained through experience

Genesis 2:9. The tree of the knowledge of good and evil

1 Samuel 2:3. A God of knowledge

2 Chronicles 1:9–10. Solomon asks for wisdom and knowledge.

Ezra 7:11. Ezra: a man of knowledge

Proverbs 1:7. Knowledge begins with fear of the Lord.

Proverbs 2:1, 5–6. Knowledge of God

▶ Kosher *(dietary laws)*

Conforming to dietary laws; ritually pure

Exodus 34:26. Kosher law concerning goat's milk

Leviticus 3:17. Never eat fat or blood.

Leviticus 11. Kosher and non-kosher animals

Leviticus 20:25–26. Unclean animals and birds

Deuteronomy 12:23–24. A reminder to never eat blood

▶ Labor *(childbirth, toil, work)*

Physical or mental exertion; the physical efforts of childbirth

Genesis 3:16. An increase in labor pain

Genesis 35:16. Rachel's labor pains

Exodus 1:11. Forced to labor

Joshua 16:10. Forced labor of the Canaanites

Matthew 11:28. Relief for those who labor

1 Corinthians 4:12. Physical labor

▶ Lack *(need, shortage)*

A deficiency or an absence

Genesis 27:39. Esau will experience a lack of fertile land.

Job 39:13. An ostrich's lack of feathers

Proverbs 5:22–23. Lack of discipline

Proverbs 31:11. This husband won't lack anything.

Isaiah 34:16. Not lacking a mate

Mark 9:24. Lack of faith

1 Corinthians 1:7. Not lacking any gift

▶ Laity *(laypeople, congregation)*

The non-ordained people in a congregation

Romans 16. Paul greets the laity of the churches in Rome.

1 Corinthians 12:4–31. The same Spirit equips ministers and the laity.

Philippians 4:2–3. Lay leaders

1 Peter 2:9. Lay priests

▶ Lamb *(sheep)*

A young sheep

Genesis 22:7–8. The lamb for a burnt offering

Genesis 30:34–35. Laban tries to cheat Jacob by taking away the black lambs asked for as wages.

Exodus 12. Passover lamb

Exodus 29:38–39. A regular offering of a lamb

Leviticus 4:32–33. Lamb as a sin offering

Jeremiah 11:19. Like a trusting lamb

▶ Lamb of God *(conqueror, Jesus, sacrifice)*

Term used by John the Baptist to denote a sacrifice for sin; many believe the term refers to Jesus.

Isaiah 53:7. Led like a lamb to the slaughter

John 1:29, 36. Lamb of God

1 Corinthians 5:7. Our Passover lamb

1 Peter 1:19–20. Christ—the lamb with no defects

Revelation 5—6. The lamb that was slaughtered

Revelation 19:7. The marriage of the lamb

Revelation 21:22–23. The lamb in New Jerusalem

▶ Lame *(disability)*

Disabled so that movement is difficult

Leviticus 21:18. The lame could not go near the altar.

Deuteronomy 15:21. Lame animals could not be sacrificed.

2 Samuel 5:6. The blind and the lame

Matthew 15:30–31. Healing the lame

Mark 9:45. Go lame and avoid hell.

▶ Lamp *(light)*

Clay or pottery vessel that contains oil and burned with a wick for illumination; also a metaphor for the continuation of a life, prosperity in a life, or revelation and guidance

1 Kings 15:4. A lamp in Jerusalem

Job 18:5–6. Lamp of the wicked

Job 29:2–3. Lamp of God

Psalm 119:105. A lamp for my feet

Proverbs 20:27. Person's soul as a lamp

Matthew 25:1–13. Parable of bridesmaids and their lamps

Mark 4:21–22. A lamp in a room

▶ Lamp stand *(candelabrum, menorah)*

A seven- or nine-branched candelabrum used in worship and as a symbol of Judaism

Exodus 25:31–39. Lamp stand for the tabernacle
Exodus 31:8. Pure gold lamp stand
Exodus 37:17. Making the lamp stand
Leviticus 24:4. Keeping the lamps on the lamp stand lit
Hebrews 9:2. The lamp stand in the tent
Revelation 2:5. The lamp stand of the church at Ephesus

▶ Land *(earth, ground, soil, territory)*

The solid ground of the earth
Genesis 1:9–10. Creation of land
Genesis 15:7. A gift of land
Deuteronomy 30:5. The land of your ancestors
1 Kings 14:15. Uprooted from the land
Nehemiah 9:25. A rich land
Job 31:38–40. The witness of the land

▶ Landmark(s) *(familiar sights, markers)*

A prominent identifying feature; fixed marker that indicates a boundary line
Deuteronomy 19:14. Don't remove landmarks.
Deuteronomy 27:17. Remove a landmark and be cursed.
Proverbs 23:10. Ancient landmark
Hosea 5:10. Like those who remove a landmark
John 4:4–6. A local landmark

▶ Language(s) *(verbal communication, words, speech)*

The use of human voice sounds and written symbols representing these sounds
Genesis 10:5. Different languages
Genesis 11:6–7. A confusion of languages
Genesis 31:47. Laban's language
2 Kings 18:28. Judean language
Acts 2:4. Speaking other languages
1 Corinthians 12:10. Speaking and interpreting languages

▶ Laodiceans *(people)*

Of or relating to Laodicea (ancient city in what is now west Turkey)
Colossians 2:1. Working for the people of Laodicea
Colossians 4:15–16. The church at Laodicea
Revelation 1:11. A scroll for Laodicea
Revelation 3:14–16. Warning to the Laodiceans

▶ Large families *(church, nuclear family)*

Families with numerous members
Genesis 17:1–2. Abraham's large family
Exodus 1:5–7. Jacob's large family grows larger.
Leviticus 26:8–9. Promise of large families
1 Chronicles 4:27. A large family, but not as large as Judah
Nehemiah 5:1–2. "We have large families!"
Revelation 7:9–10. God's large family

▶ Lashes (see *Flogging*)

▶ Lascivious behavior *(lecherous behavior)*

Actions that express lust
Genesis 19:4–5. Lascivious behavior of the men of Sodom
Genesis 39:7–12. Lascivious behavior of Potiphar's wife
Ezekiel 16:25–26. Lascivious behavior of Jerusalem
Ezekiel 23. Lascivious behavior of Oholah and Oholibah
2 Peter 2:17–18. Lascivious behavior encouraged by false teachers

▶ Last days (see *End times*)

▶ Last Supper *(Passover)*

The last meal Jesus had with his disciples before his crucifixion
Matthew 26:17–30. The Last Passover with the disciples

Matthew 26:26–28. The Lord's Supper is introduced at the last supper.

Mark 14:18. At the last supper, Jesus declares that he will be betrayed.

Luke 22:24–26. At the last supper, the disciples argue over greatness.

John 13:4–5. Jesus washes his disciples' feet at the last supper.

▶ Laughter *(amusement, hilarity, mirth)*

The sound produced by laughing

Genesis 21:5–7. A son whose name means "laughter"

Job 8:20–21. God fills mouths with laughter.

Proverbs 10:23. The laughter of a fool

Ecclesiastes 2:1–2. Experimenting with laughter

Jeremiah 30:19. Laughter will be heard.

James 4:9–10. Laughter into mourning

▶ Law *(commandment, decree, rule)*

The rule of conduct or procedure established by custom, agreement, or authority; also, books of Moses' Teaching (the Law)

Exodus 12:24. A permanent law

Exodus 29:28. Aaron's portion—a permanent law

Leviticus 16:29–30. Atonement—a permanent law

Deuteronomy 17:12–13. Never defy God's law.

Acts 25:8. Jewish law

Romans 2:14. A law to themselves

▶ Lawful *(allowable)*

Being within the law; allowed by law, particularly the law of Moses

Ezekiel 18:19. What is lawful and right

Matthew 12:3–4. David did what was not lawful.

Matthew 12:9–15. Is it lawful to heal on the Sabbath?

Matthew 14:3–4. Herod's marriage is not lawful.

Matthew 19:3. Is divorce lawful?

▶ Lawsuit(s) *(complaint, court case, grievance)*

An action or a suit brought before a court

Exodus 23:2–3. Don't show favoritism in lawsuits.

2 Samuel 15:1–6. Absalom discusses lawsuits.

Hosea 10:4. Lawsuits spring up.

Micah 6. God's lawsuit against his people

1 Corinthians 6:7. Lawsuits among believers

▶ Lawyer *(attorney, legal representative, law expert)*

One whose profession is to give legal advice and represent clients in legal matters; an expert in the law of Moses

Matthew 22:34–36. Tested by a lawyer

Luke 10:25–26, 29. Questions from a lawyer

Acts 24:1. Tertullus the lawyer

Titus 3:13. Zenas the lawyer

▶ Lay-offs/Firings *(job loss)*

Suspension or dismissal of employees

Genesis 3:23. Adam is fired from his job as gardener in Eden.

Numbers 20:12. Moses is dismissed from the job of taking the Israelites into the Promised Land.

1 Samuel 15. God plans to replace Saul as king.

1 Kings 11. Demoted to king over one job, rather than all of Israel

▶ Laying on of hands *(identification, transference of guilt)*

Identifying with the animal to be sacrificed; also, commissioning someone for an office

Leviticus 1:4. Place your hand on the animal.

Numbers 27:18–23. Moses lays hands on Joshua.

Acts 6:5–6. Laying hands on the new deacons

Acts 13:2–3. Laying hands on Barnabas and Saul

1 Timothy 4:14. Laying hands on Timothy

L

▸ Laziness *(idleness, sluggishness, slothfulness)*

Resistance to work; a disposition to idleness

Exodus 5:6–8. The Israelites are accused of laziness.

Proverbs 12:24. Lazy hands

Proverbs 19:15. The problem of laziness

Ecclesiastes 4:4–6. Is laziness better than hard work?

Ecclesiastes 10:18. The results of laziness

▸ Leadership *(direction, guidance, management)*

The position or office of a leader

Genesis 25:16. Leaders of tribes

Exodus 3:16. Assemble the leaders.

Numbers 33:1. Moses' and Aaron's leadership

1 Samuel 12. The people reject Samuel's leadership in their desire for a king.

Acts 24:2. Wise leadership

Romans 12:8. If you're a leader, lead.

▸ Learning *(culture, education, knowledge, wisdom)*

The act or process of gaining knowledge

Leviticus 23:42–43. Future generations will learn of this custom.

Deuteronomy 5:1. The necessity of learning God's laws

Proverbs 4:3–4. Learning from parents

Proverbs 23:12. Learning from a father

2 Corinthians 7:7. Learning about comfort

▸ Leaven *(yeast)*

An agent, such as yeast, that causes batter or dough to rise, especially by fermentation

Exodus 12:15. Remove the leaven.

Leviticus 2:11. Don't use leaven with a grain offering.

Leviticus 6:17. Don't bake with leaven.

Matthew 16:6. Beware the leaven of the Pharisees.

▸ Left-handed *(blessing with the hands, use of the hands)*

Using the left hand more skillfully than the right; a lesser blessing given with the left hand

Genesis 48. Left-handed blessing

Judges 3:15–30. Ehud is left-handed.

Judges 20:16. Left-handed troops

▸ Legalism *(nitpicky)*

Strict literal adherence to the law or a particular code

Isaiah 29:13. A definition of legalism

Matthew 15:1–20. Pharisees' legalism

John 1:17. Law versus grace

Romans 14:1. Be welcoming, rather than legalistic.

Galatians 3:24–25. Legalism is not necessary after Christ's coming.

Colossians 2:20–22. Avoid legalism.

▸ Legend(s) *(folklore, inscriptions, myths, traditions)*

An unverified story handed down from an earlier time; an inscription

Job 26:12. Job discusses a legend.

Daniel 5:24–25. The legend on the wall

Zechariah 3:9. Engraving a legend

Acts 17:22–24. The legend of the unknown god

▸ Legion *(crowd, many, multitude)*

Major unit of the Roman army consisting of 3,000 to 6,000 infantry troops; a large number

Matthew 26:53. Twelve legions of angels

Mark 5:1–20. The legion of demons

▸ Leisure *(free time, freedom, holiday)*

Freedom from time-consuming duties, responsibilities, or activities

Genesis 2:2–3. A day to not work

Psalm 46:10. While you're at leisure . . .

Ecclesiastes 2:1. Experimenting with leisure activities

Mark 6:31. Jesus suggests leisure time.

▸ Lent *(Lenten season, preparation and repentance before Easter)*

The forty weekdays from Ash Wednesday until Easter; these days represent the forty days Jesus spent in the wilderness before his temptation.

Genesis 3:19. Ash Wednesday pronouncement (Lent begins)

Matthew 3:2. A time to repent

Matthew 4:1–2. The forty days of Jesus' fast

Matthew 6:16–18. A season of fasting; rules for fasting during the season

▶ Leper *(person with leprosy)*

A person suffering from leprosy

Leviticus 13:45–46. Rules for lepers

Leviticus 22:4. Priests who are lepers

2 Kings 5. Naaman the leper

Matthew 26:6–7. Simon the leper

Mark 1:40–42. Healing a leper

▶ Leprosy *(disease)*

Chronic contagious disease characterized by ulceration of the skin, loss of sensation, paralysis, gangrene, and deformation

Leviticus 13:24–25. Identifying leprosy

Numbers 12:10–12. Miriam's leprosy

2 Samuel 3:29. May leprosy never leave his house.

2 Kings 5:26–27. Gehazi gains leprosy after lying to Naaman and Elisha.

2 Kings 7:3–11. The four men with leprosy

2 Kings 15:1–7. Jeroboam becomes leprous.

Luke 17:11–19. Healing ten men of leprosy

▶ Lesbians (see *Homosexuality*)

▶ Letter writing (see *Correspondence*)

▶ Leviathan *(sea serpent, monster)*

An ancient monster which lives in the sea, sometimes a metaphor for God's power

Job 3:8. Dangerous, dragon-like monster

Job 41:1–34. Poetic description of Leviathan's strength compared to the Lord

Psalm 74:13–14. God's power over Leviathan

Psalm 104:26. God created Leviathan

Isaiah 27:1. The monster in the sea

▶ Levirate marriage *(marriage, family relationships)*

Law delivered by Moses which states that a brother is to marry his deceased brother's widow and name the first son after the deceased brother

Genesis 38:8. Production of progeny

Deuteronomy 25:5–10. Providing a legacy

Ruth 3:1–18. Responsibility of family

Ruth 4:10. Maintaining a family name

▶ Levites *(priests, tribe of Levi, sons of Aaron)*

Designation given to descendents of the tribe of Levi who are best known for their priestly services in the tabernacle and temple

Exodus 28:1. Members of the family of Aaron

Exodus 32:26–29. Cost of being God's priests

Numbers 3:45. Set apart for the Lord

Numbers 18:21. Israel gives one-tenth to the Levites

1 Kings 8:4. Performing the duties of the priesthood

Hebrews 7:5–11. The priesthood of Melchizedek

Hebrews 8:6. Jesus' priesthood is greater

▶ Liar *(deceiver, false witness)*

Someone who doubts God's promises, rejects sound teaching, and presents false witness

Genesis 20:2. Abraham lies to save Sarah.

Job 24:25. Liar's words are worthless.

Psalm 26:4–5. The righteous avoid being with liars.

Psalm 58:3. Liars go astray.

John 8:44. The devil is the father of lies.

Acts 5:1–6. God's judgment upon liars.

1 John 1:10. Denying sin makes God a liar.

1 John 2:22. Liars reject the Messiah.

1 John 4:20. Love God and hate others.

▶ Liberality *(free, lavish, openly)*

Giving to and caring for those who are less fortunate

Deuteronomy 15:4. God blesses the poor.
Esther 1:7. The king lavishes food upon guests.
Hosea 2:8. The Lord's provision is misused.
Matthew 6:26. God provides for animals and humans.
Galatians 2:10. Caring for the poor
Ephesians 1:8. God gives wisdom.
James 1:5. God gives to those who ask.

▶ Liberate *(set free, release, save)*

To free from political structures, social groups, and even personal sin
Exodus 3:10. God freed Israel from bondage in Egypt.
Psalm 102:20. Set free from the power of death
Isaiah 51:14. Prisoners will be set free.
Matthew 16:19. Heaven and earth liberated
Matthew 27:20. Barabbas released instead of Jesus
Galatians 3:13. Christ frees us.
1 Timothy 2:6. Christ died to free us from sin.
Titus 2:14. Freed in order to do good things
James 1:25. God's teaching brings freedom.

▶ Liberty *(freedom, release)*

Being free to believe, act, and think; freedom from sin
Leviticus 25:54. The year of jubilee
Isaiah 61:1. Freedom for the captives
Jeremiah 34:8–11. Freedom given, freedom taken
John 8:32. The truth brings freedom.
John 8:36. Freedom in the Son
Romans 6:1–2. Freed from sin
Galatians 5:13. Serve one another with freedom.
1 Peter 2:16. Use freedom appropriately.
Jude 4. Grace is not a warrant for unchecked freedom.

▶ License *(permit, authorization, credentials)*

Permission or decree which authorizes or prevents certain actions
Exodus 3:14. God authorizes leaders.
Acts 22:25–29. Citizenship
Hebrews 6:3. God allows actions.

▶ Licentious *(immoral, promiscuous, sinful)*

Sinful actions which bring about God's judgment
2 Samuel 11:1–13. Sexual immorality
Micah 7:18. God forgives the sins of his people.
Romans 1:18. God's anger revealed against immorality
Ephesians 5:3. Avoid even the mention of sinfulness.
Colossians 3:5. Stop sinful lifestyles.
1 Thessalonians 4:7. Called to be holy
James 1:21. Accept the word, reject immorality.
2 Peter 2:9. Immorality punished
Jude 8. Sin contaminates the body.

▶ Lie *(deception, falsehood, half-truth)*

Intentionally misrepresenting the truth
Deuteronomy 19:18–19. Expel falsehood.
1 Samuel 15:29. God does not lie.
Job 15:6. Lies condemn.
Psalm 5:9. Lies come from the heart.
Proverbs 19:5. Liars will be punished.
John 8:44. Satan is the father of lies.
Romans 1:25. Exchanged God's truth for a lie
2 Thessalonians 2:9. Deception occurs through lies.
Revelation 22:15. Liars remain outside the gates of heaven.

▶ Life *(eternal life, kingdom of God, human life)*

Gift of God, creator of all life; eternal life initiated and offered through faith in Christ
Genesis 2:7. Life comes from God.
Genesis 3:24. Tree of life
Ecclesiastes 12:7. God gives life and death.
Luke 12:20. Life demanded

John 1:3–5. Jesus is the source of life.
John 3:16. Eternal life
John 10:10–11. Jesus gave his life.
John 17:3. Eternal life is knowing God.
Romans 5:17. Life in Christ
1 Corinthians 8:6. All life is because of Christ.
Philippians 2:30. Risking your life
James 4:14. Brevity of life

▶ Lifestyle *(behavior, conduct, way of life)*

Manner of conduct which demonstrates one's commitments and outlooks in life
Psalm 1:1–6. Lifestyles of unbelievers
Psalm 84:11. Blessings for the blameless
Ecclesiastes 8:15. Recommended lifestyle
Ezekiel 18:5–9. Lifestyle of the righteous person
Micah 6:8. The lifestyle God requires
Romans 6:21. Deadly lifestyle
Galatians 5:16. Follow your spiritual nature.
Ephesians 4:1–2. Live worthy of your calling.
1 Thessalonians 3:13. Prepared for Christ's return
1 Timothy 4:12. Lifestyle of younger Christians
Jude 7. Results of bad lifestyle

▶ Light *(life, eternal life, holiness)*

Absence of darkness, biblical metaphor with life, death, joy, blessing, rescue, and sorrow
Genesis 1:3. The beginning of creation
Psalm 27:1. God's presence and favor
Isaiah 9:2. Deliverance
Amos 5:18. Judgment
John 3:19. Jesus is light.
2 Corinthians 4:6. Light of knowledge
Colossians 1:12. Eternal life
1 Timothy 6:16. God's holiness
1 Peter 2:9. Called into light

▶ Light of the world *(Jesus, light)*

Image applied to Jesus, underscoring his self-revelation in the world. His followers, in turn, are themselves to be light and spread light among the world.
Matthew 5:14. Disciples shine the light.
Matthew 28:19–20. Command to spread the light
John 1:9. Jesus came into the world.
John 8:12. Jesus is the light.
John 9:5. The mission of Jesus
Ephesians 5:14. Christ converts us.

▶ Lightning *(bright, glittering, judgment)*

Sign of God's presence, His revelation, and judgment
Exodus 19:16–17. God's presence
2 Samuel 22:15. Sign of judgment
Job 28:23–28. God's control of weather
Psalm 135:7. God's creation of weather
Matthew 28:3. Angel bright like lightning
Luke 17:24. The coming of God's kingdom
Revelation 4:5. God's majesty revealed
Revelation 20:9. Judgment from heaven

▶ Likeness *(archetype, image, image of God)*

Lines of continuity between a source and its extension
Genesis 1:26. Created in God's image
Genesis 5:3. Children in their parent's image
Romans 6:5. Made like Christ in life and death
1 Corinthians 15:49. God's likeness passed on
Hebrews 1:3. Jesus is God's likeness.
Hebrews 10:1. Old Testament sacrifices only a likeness of Christ's sacrifice
James 3:9. Avoid cursing people made in God's image.

▶ Lily *(flower, plant, scent)*

Flower known for its beauty, image of God's people for whom God supplies the sustenance needed to grow and bloom
Song of Songs 2:1–2. An image of beauty
Isaiah 35:2. God's people will bloom again.
Hosea 14:5. God (re)establishes his people.
Luke 12:27. God's provision

L

▶ Limitation(s) *(humility, limit, restraint)*

Boundaries set by God's creative decrees and through His revelatory Word

Exodus 7:3. God limits human hearts.

Psalm 119:96. God's commandments are without limit.

Psalm 147:5. No limit to God's knowledge

Ecclesiastes 5:2. Limit your words.

John 3:34. God's unlimited gift of the Spirit

2 Corinthians 12:7. Humility through limitation

Philippians 2:6–11. Divine self-limitation

▶ Lineage *(ancestry, descent, family)*

Group of individuals tracing descent from a common ancestor

Genesis 25:17. Ancestry and death

Exodus 3:6. God of your fathers

Deuteronomy 1:8. Promise made to Abraham's lineage

Judges 2:17. Refusing to live like ancestors

Matthew 1:1. The lineage of Jesus

Luke 2:4. David's lineage

Romans 11:28. Jews loved by God

Galatians 1:14–16. Leaving behind traditions of ancestry

▶ Linen *(cloth, garment, sheet)*

Material made of flax, often used in reference to the temple and its officials

Genesis 41:42. Joseph's robe

Exodus 26:31. The veil in the tabernacle

Exodus 28:39. Priestly garments

Ezekiel 44:17. Used for coolness of material

Matthew 27:59. Tomb clothes

Revelation 19:8. The bride wears linen.

Revelation 19:14. God's army clothed in white linen

▶ Linguistics *(language, speech, tongue)*

Use of unique languages for the purpose of communication

Genesis 10:5. Nations have their own languages.

Genesis 11:1–9. Languages confused by God

Deuteronomy 28:49. Foreign language

Nehemiah 13:24. Israel learning other languages

Mark 15:34. Jesus spoke Aramaic.

Acts 2:6. God enlightens language through the Spirit.

1 Corinthians 14:11–19. Pray for the gift of interpretation.

Revelation 5:9. God saves people from every language.

▶ Lion(s) *(animal, powerful, royal)*

Most powerful of animals known in the ancient world, personification of courage, ferocity, and royalty

Genesis 49:9. Royal status

Numbers 23:24. Powerful like a lion

Judges 14:6. Samson's Spirit-empowered strength

1 Samuel 17:36. David's victories

1 Kings 13:24. Lion attacks human.

Job 10:16. Preying like a lion

Daniel 6:22. God shuts the lions' mouths.

Revelation 4:7. Heavenly creature like a lion

Revelation 5:5. Christ, the Lion of Judah

▶ Lion of Judah *(Christ, Jesus, Messiah)*

Messianic title for Jesus alluding to Genesis 49:9, where Judah is depicted as a lion

Genesis 49:9. Judah the lion cub

Hosea 5:14. Judgment from God

1 Peter 5:8. The devil is only like a lion

Revelation 5:5. Messianic title

▶ Lion's den *(cave, den, lair)*

Lion's lair representing its home

Psalm 10:9. Hiding place

Daniel 6:16. Punishment for disobedience to king

Daniel 6:22. God's protection of Daniel

Amos 3:4. Poetic description of God announcing judgment

Nahum 2:11. Feeding place

▶ Lips/Mouth *(speech, sing, tongue)*

Used generally referring to how one uses lips/mouth for praise or blame, truth or lies, wisdom or folly

Job 27:4. Speaking the truth
Psalm 71:23. Singing with joy
Habakkuk 3:16. Showing fear
Matthew 15:8. Lip service, but not heart service
Luke 4:22. Wisdom from Jesus' lips
Romans 3:13. The danger of deceitful talk
James 3:10. Lips that praise and curse
1 Peter 3:10. Do not say evil things.

▶ Listening *(hearing, obey, paying attention)*

Paying close attention to what is said; to hear and obey God's commands

Genesis 17:20. God listens.
Genesis 49:2. Listening to your elders
Deuteronomy 6:4. Command to listen
Joshua 10:14. God listens to a man.
Psalm 34:15. God hears the righteous.
Psalm 102:1. Plea for God to listen
Ephesians 6:1. Listen to your parents.
Hebrews 13:17. Listening to leaders
1 John 2:3. Listening is indicator of knowing Christ.

▶ Literature *(narrative, literary, writing)*

All writings and literary forms included as Scripture, representing various genres, such as poetry, history, prophecy, and so forth

Ecclesiastes 12:9–10. Written carefully
Daniel 1:4. Daniel learned literature.
Daniel 1:17. Understanding given by God
2 Peter 1:21. God inspired literature.
Revelation 1:19. God's revelation through literature

▶ Litigation *(indictment, lawsuit, legal action)*

The process of filing a lawsuit; a legal dispute or complaint between two parties

Exodus 18:13. Leaders discern disputes.
Lamentations 3:33–36. The Lord does not deny justice.
Matthew 5:25. Settling out of court
Luke 11:46. Some lawyers unhelpful
Acts 26:1. Self-defense
Romans 3:26. God's justice in Christ
1 Corinthians 6:1. Settle Christian complaints in the church.
Colossians 2:14. Christ's death canceled our debt.

▶ Livestock *(animal, cow, farm animal)*

Asset used for food, labor, and sacrifice

Genesis 1:28. Humanity's care of the animals
Genesis 2:20. Named by man
Genesis 4:20. Earliest livestock
Genesis 13:2. Sign of wealth
Psalm 66:15. Used in sacrifices
Acts 10:9–16. Eating of animals

▶ Living water *(Holy Spirit, temple, water)*

Metaphor for life, most often associated with God's temple in the Old Testament; in the New Testament, related to the gift of the Spirit in believers

Genesis 2:10. Flowing from Eden
Song of Songs 4:15. Running water
Jeremiah 17:13. Spiritual sustenance
Zechariah 14:8. Waters flowing from God's temple
John 4:10–11. The Holy Spirit indwelling
John 7:38. Outward effects of God's inner work
Revelation 22:1. Flows from God
Revelation 22:17. A gift from God

▶ Loan(s) *(borrowing, lending, sharing)*

Borrowed money which needs to be repaid

Exodus 21:2. Forgiving debts in the year of jubilee
Exodus 22:25. Lend money without interest to God's people.
Deuteronomy 23:19–20. Fair interest may be charged to outsiders.

Psalm 15:5. Lending fairly to all
Proverbs 11:15. Warning against cosigning a loan
Matthew 18:34–35. Forgiving debts
Luke 19:23. Squandering a loan

▶ Locust(s) *(bugs, insects, swarm)*

Common bug in the ancient world which brought devastation to crops; sometimes used as a metaphor for judgment and destruction
Exodus 10:4. Sent as judgment
Exodus 10:14. Plague of locusts
Leviticus 11:22. Types of food
Matthew 3:4. Food of God's prophet
Revelation 9:3. Persecution and pain
Revelation 9:7. Spiritual battle

▶ Logic *(argument, maturity, thinking)*

Disciplined thought that is honoring to God and represents Christian maturity
1 Kings 3:16–28. Solomon's logic reunites a mother and son.
Job 13:6. Good logic is worth listening to.
Proverbs 29:9. Fools are illogical.
Matthew 22:37. Loving God with the mind
Mark 12:28. Jesus' use of logic
Romans 1:21. Lack of logic in the sin-plagued mind
1 Corinthians 13:11. Leaving aside childish ways of thinking
1 Corinthians 14:20. Maturity in thinking
James 1:5. Asking for wisdom in thinking

▶ Lonely/Loneliness *(alone, solitude)*

Being isolated from God or from other humans, longing for community
Deuteronomy 31:6. God will not leave his people.
Job 19:13–14. Lack of friends in times of trouble
Psalm 13:1. When God seems absent
Psalm 102:7. Insomnia and loneliness
Ecclesiastes 4:8. No immediate family
Matthew 28:20. Jesus will never leave his people.
Mark 15:34. Jesus' loneliness at the cross
2 Timothy 1:4. Longing for a friend
Revelation 1:9. Exiled and lonely

▶ Longevity *(duration, lifespan, lifetime)*

Length of one's life
Genesis 5:1–32. Long lifespan
Genesis 6:3. God limits the human lifespan
Genesis 15:15. God promises Abraham old age.
Ruth 4:15. Child nourishes old age.
Matthew 10:39. Preservation of life in Christ
Luke 1:36. A child of old age

▶ Longing *(burning, desire, yearning)*

Earnest desire for something, either good or bad
Deuteronomy 5:21. Sinful desires
2 Samuel 11:3–4. Sexual longing
Psalm 107:9. God satisfies the soul.
Psalm 119:20. Longing for God's law
Proverbs 13:12. Goodness of fulfilled longings
Isaiah 63:15. Longing for the new creation
Luke 15:16. Longing for sustenance
Romans 8:19. Creation longing for the children of God
1 Corinthians 14:1. Earnestly desire spiritual gifts.
2 Corinthians 5:2. Longing for heaven
Philippians 2:26. Longing for friends
Hebrews 11:16. Longing for heavenly country

▶ Looting *(contraband, plunder, stealing)*

Acquiring of goods which do not belong to you, generally after warfare
1 Samuel 23:1. Looting during a raid
2 Chronicles 21:16–17. Judgment from God
Lamentations 1:10. Looting the temple
Ezekiel 26:12. Destruction from looting
Obadiah 13. Warning against looting
Zechariah 2:8. Looters will be looted.

▶ LORD *(Christ, God, master)*

In the Old Testament, the unutterable name of Israel's God; in the New Testament, designation applied directly to Jesus. Can also mean any master.

Genesis 2:4. The creator God
Exodus 6:6. The God of the exile
Psalm 110:1. The Lord speaks to the king.
Psalm 115:11. Fear and trust the Lord.
Psalm 116:5. Merciful and righteous
Psalm 118:29. Give thanks for the Lord's goodness.
Proverbs 19:23. Fear the Lord.
Isaiah 33:22. Judge, lawgiver, king, and savior
Matthew 4:10. Worship the Lord only.
Matthew 8:25. Jesus is called "Lord."
Romans 10:9. Confessing Jesus as Lord
1 Corinthians 8:6. Only one Lord, Jesus Christ
1 Corinthians 12:3. Spirit-empowered confession of Christ as Lord.
Philippians 2:10–11. One day all will confess that Jesus is Lord.

▶ Lord's Day (see *Sabbath*)

▶ Lord's Supper *(breaking bread, Eucharist, last supper)*

Jesus' final meal shared with his disciples involved the breaking of bread and sharing of wine on/near the Passover.

Mark 14:12–15. Passover meal
Luke 22:19–20. Bread and cup
1 Corinthians 10:16. Union with Christ
1 Corinthians 11:25. Repeat the sacrament.
Hebrews 13:10. Eating the sacrifice

▶ Lord's table (see *Lord's Supper*)

▶ Loss(es) *(stealing, suffer loss, taking away)*

Losing something or someone whether through misplacement, theft, death, or other means

Job 1:13–21. Job's response to loss
Job 27:19. Possessions gone overnight
Luke 15:1–7. Lost sheep
1 Corinthians 3:15. Painful loss of work of the church
Philippians 3:7. Loss of worldly things for Christ
Hebrews 10:34. Cheerful response to loss of possessions

▶ Lost *(unsaved, wandering)*

Referring to people who are wandering from true belief and repentance

Matthew 10:6. Jews who are lost
Luke 15:32. Celebrate a lost person now found.
Luke 19:10. Jesus' purpose is to save the lost.
John 18:9. Jesus lost none of his own.
Hebrews 4:11. Lost because of bad examples
1 Peter 2:25. Like lost sheep, cared for by the shepherd

▶ Lots *(dice, divination, magic)*

Commonly practiced means of gaining knowledge in circumstances during biblical times

Leviticus 16:8. Lots used for discernment
Joshua 18:6. Lots done in the presence of God
Nehemiah 10:34. Priests draw lots.
Psalm 22:18. Lots using dice
Jonah 1:7. Lots show that Jonah is responsible for the storm.
Luke 23:34. Jesus' clothes were divided by lots.

▶ Loud noises *(clamor, sound, thundering)*

Associated with both the actions of humanity and of God, highlighting everything from acts of judgment to senseless chatter

Genesis 19:13. Complaints of God's people
Exodus 12:30. Cries of death
Joshua 6:20. The broken wall
1 Samuel 7:10. Loud noise causing confusion
Psalm 150:5. Praising God out loud

Isaiah 29:6. Loud sounds as judgment
Jeremiah 51:55. Silencing a city's livelihood
Ezekiel 3:12. God's thundering voice
Matthew 24:31. A gathering trumpet call
1 Corinthians 13:1. Language without love is nothing but loud noise.
Revelation 19:1. The cries of heaven

▶ Love *(affection, care, desire)*

Feelings of great affection toward another person or God; a steady quiet decision of the will to care for another person
Genesis 22:2. A beloved son
2 Samuel 1:26. Platonic love
Psalm 33:18. The Lord's steadfast love
Isaiah 43:4. Precious to God
Matthew 5:44. Love your enemies.
John 3:16. God loved the world.
John 5:42. No love for God
John 13:35. Love as indicator of true discipleship
Romans 5:8. God's love demonstrated in Christ
Romans 12:9–10. Genuine familial love
Romans 14:15. Caring for the opinions of others
1 Corinthians 13:1. The necessity of love
1 Corinthians 13:13. The greatest is love.
1 Corinthians 14:1. Pursue love.
1 Corinthians 16:22. Those who do not love the Lord are accursed.
Galatians 5:6. Faith working through love
Galatians 5:22. Love produced by the Spirit
Ephesians 5:2. Love sacrificially.
Ephesians 6:24. God's favor is upon those who love him.
Colossians 3:19. Husbands should love their wives.
2 Timothy 2:22. Pursue love.
1 Peter 4:8. Love extinguishes the sins of God's people.
1 John 2:15. Do not love the world.
1 John 4:7. Love comes from God.
1 John 4:11. Imitate God's love.
1 John 5:3. Loving God means obeying God.
Jude 21. Remain in God's love.

▶ Love stories *(accounts, narratives)*

Stories of love won and love lost in the Bible; greatest love story of all is between God and His people
Genesis 29:9–30. Jacob and Rachel
Ruth 3:6–14. Boaz and Ruth
Song of Songs 1:1–4. Two young lovers
Isaiah 62:5. God rejoices over his bride.

▶ Loyalty *(allegiance, faithfulness, obedience)*

Remaining true to someone or something in the face of opposition or opportunity
Genesis 12:1–4. Abram's loyalty to God
Numbers 32:11. Lacking loyalty
Deuteronomy 13:6–10. Breaking family loyalties
Joshua 1:16–17. Loyalty to leadership
1 Samuel 19:1–2. Losing and gaining loyalty
Psalm 119:113. Loyalty divided
Jeremiah 2:11. Loyalty to the gods
Matthew 10:37–39. Loyalty to God above family
Luke 16:13. Serving two masters
John 14:21–24. Obedience to God
1 Corinthians 15:30–31. Loyalty to Christ in spite of danger

▶ Lucifer (see *Satan*)

▶ Lukewarm *(apathetic, indifferent, tepid)*

Moderately warm; neither hot nor cold
Proverbs 1:32. Folly of indifference
Revelation 3:16. A lukewarm church

▶ Lumber *(timber, tree, wood)*

Wood used to construct altars, buildings, walls, or boats
Genesis 6:14. A boat of cypress wood
Genesis 22:3. Altar for burnt offering
Exodus 26:15. Construction lumber
Leviticus 1:7. Lumber for sacrifices
Nehemiah 13:31. Nehemiah's building plan

▶ Lust *(desire, passion, sexual appetite)*

Impetuous sexual desire which is contrary to God's will

Genesis 19:4–8. Lot offers his daughters
Numbers 25:1–2. Lust and syncretism
2 Samuel 11:1–27. David takes Bathsheba.
1 Kings 11:1–13. Solomon's weakness leads to other immorality.
Job 31:1. Choosing not to look
Psalm 141:4. Prayer to remove temptation
Proverbs 6:25–26. Desiring only beauty
Isaiah 57:5. Burning with lust
Jeremiah 5:8. Lustful men are wild.
Ezekiel 6:9. Lust committed in heart and mind
Ezekiel 22:11. Abominations
Amos 2:7. Dishonoring to God
Matthew 5:27–28. Looking with lust is adultery.
Romans 1:24–26. Given over to perversion
Romans 7:5. Lust results in death.
Ephesians 4:19. Continual lust
Colossians 3:5. Put lust to death.
2 Timothy 2:22. Put aside youthful lusts.
Titus 2:11–12. God's grace helps us avoid lust.
1 Peter 2:11. Lust attacks.
2 Peter 2:14. Stay away from lust.
1 John 2:16. Lust is not from God.

▶ Luxury *(comfort, extravagance, opulence)*

Lavish state of affairs

Genesis 1:28–31. Paradise
1 Kings 4:22–23. Diet fit for a king
Esther 1:5–6. Royal banquet
Proverbs 19:10. Fools do not live in luxury.
Amos 6:3–4. Warning to those who are pampered
Matthew 26:6–13. Luxury for Jesus
Luke 7:25. Luxury under a king
1 Timothy 2:9–10. Modest luxuries
James 5:5. The danger of luxury

▶ Lying *(dishonesty, falseness, white lies)*

Misleading someone with falsified, malicious, or otherwise incorrect information

Genesis 12:12–13. Lying about family
Psalm 31:18. Silence lying lips.
Psalm 120:2. Deliverance from lies
Proverbs 12:22. God disgusts in lying lips.
Acts 5:3. Lies originate from Satan.
Romans 1:25. Truth exchanged for a lie
Colossians 3:9. Living as a new person
1 Timothy 2:7. God's apostles tell the truth.
Hebrews 6:18. Impossible for God to lie
1 John 1:6. Do not lie about your relationship with God.
1 John 2:21. Lies cannot come from the truth.
Revelation 14:4–5. God's people do not lie.

▶ Lyre *(harp, instrument, strings)*

A stringed musical instrument used in worship and celebration

Genesis 31:27. Used in celebrations
1 Samuel 10:5. Carried by prophets
Psalm 33:2. Instrument of praise
Daniel 3:15. Call to worship

▶ Magi *(astrologers, interpreters, wise men)*

A class of wise men or astrologers who interpret dreams and messages
Daniel 1:20. Wise and insightful
Daniel 2:10–12. Interpreters, not manufacturers
Daniel 5:15. Limited capabilities
Matthew 2:1–12. Following the astral sign
Acts 13:6. Astrologer and prophet?

▶ Magic *(divination, sorcery, tricks)*

Magic attempts to gain information from the gods and manipulate an outcome
Leviticus 19:31. Magic is unclean.
Deuteronomy 18:10. Magic forbidden
1 Samuel 28:11–12. Calling up the dead
2 Kings 9:22. Folly of witchcraft
Daniel 1:20. Earthly wisdom
Ephesians 6:11. Armor of God protects us.
Revelation 22:15. Magic involves deception

▶ Magicians *(enchanter, sorcerer, witch)*

Workers of magic, including sorcerers and witches
Exodus 22:18. Destroying evil artisans
1 Samuel 28:11–12. The medium at Endor
Ezekiel 13:17–23. False prophets
Daniel 1:20. Earthly wisdom
Acts 8:9–11. Simon the magician
2 Timothy 3:8. Magicians of Egypt
Revelation 21:8. Judgment upon magicians

▶ Magnificat *(magnify, praise, song)*

Mary's song in Luke 1, following the Latin translation of "praise"
Luke 1:46–55. Mary's praise-filled song

▶ Majesty *(beauty, dignity, royal)*

God's dignity, glory, and power are often associated with His majesty
Exodus 15:7. God's majestic power
Deuteronomy 33:26. Israel's unique God
Job 13:11. God's terrifying majesty
Psalm 93:1. Clothed in majesty
Isaiah 35:2. God's majestic glory
Lamentations 1:6. Majesty departed from Jerusalem
2 Peter 1:16. The majesty of Christ

▶ Majority *(group, large party, superiority)*

A dominant or superior group
Exodus 23:2. Avoiding peer pressure
2 Chronicles 30:18. A majority group
Matthew 26:55. Masses come for Jesus.
Acts 21:34. Mob mentality
Acts 27:12. Groups of merchants
1 Corinthians 11:17–34. Haves exclude the have nots.
2 Corinthians 2:6. Majority excommunicates someone

▶ Makeup *(cosmetics, face, mask)*

Cosmetic products used to enhance one's appearance
Genesis 37:25. Cosmetic ingredients
Ruth 3:3. Freshening up
2 Samuel 12:20. Ointments
2 Kings 9:30. Eye shadow
Esther 2:9, 12. Extensive beauty treatment
Isaiah 3:24. Replacing self-indulgence with judgment
Jeremiah 4:30. Vain efforts toward beauty

▶ Male *(boy, human, man)*

God's creation of humanity is reflected in the distinct creation of both male and female.
Genesis 1:27. Maleness created by God
Genesis 3:6. Man's culpability in the fall
Exodus 12:29. Loss of first-born males
Mark 10:7. Uniting male and female
Galatians 3:28. Unity in Christ
Titus 2:2. Instructions for mature men
Titus 2:6–8. Instructions for young men

M

▶ Malice *(enmity, evil, spite)*

A quality or foundation of a person's actions which are evil, vengeful, or overtly sinful

Genesis 50:20. What humans meant for evil, God meant for good.
Psalm 41:5. Malice of enemies
Ezekiel 25:15. Revenge
Matthew 16:1. Maliciously testing Jesus
Titus 2:3. Show your dedication to God.
James 1:21. Accepting the saving word
1 Peter 2:1. Putting away malice

▶ Mammon *(see Money)*

▶ Management *(administration, leadership, overseeing)*

A position of stewardship wherein the manager is entrusted with responsibility and duties

Nehemiah 3:1–32. Nehemiah delegates work
Proverbs 6:6–8. Self-motivation
Jeremiah 22:13. Bad leadership
Mark 10:42. Absolute power
Luke 7:3. Concern for those you manage
1 Corinthians 12:28. Appointed by God
1 Timothy 3:4–5. Qualified leaders

▶ Mandate *(authorization, command, sanction)*

An official authorization or command to act a certain way

Genesis 1:28. God's mandate to humanity
Exodus 20:1–17. The Ten Commandments
John 15:17. Mandate to love one another
Romans 16:25–26. God's order for the nations
2 Corinthians 8:8. Love better than commands
2 Thessalonians 3:6. Do not associate with undisciplined believers.
1 Timothy 4:10–11. Command to teach truth

▶ Mandrake(s) *(flower, plant, love-plant)*

A native plant in the Mediterranean known for its pungent fragrances and narcotic properties, particularly as an aphrodisiac

Genesis 30:14–16. Infertility remedy
Song of Songs 7:13. Fragrant flower

▶ Manipulate *(exploit, influence, control)*

Controlling a situation, people, or persons unfairly and usually with an aim toward personal gain

Genesis 39:16–18. Lying about exploitation
Isaiah 36:15. Do not be fooled.
Galatians 2:4. False Christians
Ephesians 6:9. Warning against manipulating a slave
1 Thessalonians 4:6. The Lord will punish exploitation.
2 Peter 2:3. Trickery
1 John 5:19. World controlled by evil one

▶ Manna *(bread, food, sustenance)*

The sustenance which God supplied to Israel during their wandering in the desert

Exodus 16:4. God-given food
Numbers 11:6. Complaining about God's provision
Joshua 5:12. Manna stopped in Canaan
Matthew 4:3–4. Resisting temptation and living on God's words
John 6:48–49. Bread of life, bread of death
Hebrews 9:4. Manna stored in the ark
Revelation 2:17. Spiritual sustenance

▶ Manners *(actions, conduct, habits)*

One's public behavior or habits

Exodus 23:9. Treating foreigners well
Proverbs 3:27–28. Not holding back
Matthew 25:35. Caring for others
Luke 10:5–9. A courteous guest
Romans 12:13. Sharing
Galatians 6:10. Caring for God's family
1 Thessalonians 2:7–8. Being gentle

▶ Manslaughter *(death, homicide, killing)*

The crime of killing someone in an instance that is not deemed to be murder

Exodus 17:3. Exaggerated complaints of thirst
Exodus 21:22–25. Eye for an eye

Exodus 21:29. Culpable for an animal's actions
Numbers 35. Cities of refuge
Numbers 35:27. Avenging manslaughter
Deuteronomy 4:42. Unintentional killing
2 Samuel 1:1–16. Assisted suicide

▶ Manufacture *(build, make, produce)*

The skill of building or producing items using natural substances
Exodus 35:35. Skilled artisans
Isaiah 44:13. Manufacturing idols
Mark 6:3. Carpentry
Mark 14:58. Manufacturing another kind of temple
Acts 18:3. Tent making
Acts 19:24–25. Idol makers
Hebrews 3:3. Jesus, the builder

▶ Map *(chart, plan, guide)*

A visual representation of an area which marks out features such as cities and roads
Numbers 32:13. Lost because of sin
Job 19:23. Written directions
Ezekiel 4:1. Clay tablet

▶ Marathon *(long-distance, race, running)*

Primarily metaphorical in the NT referring to running in the Greek games
Ecclesiastes 9:11. Life as a race
1 Corinthians 9:24–27. Running to win
Philippians 2:16. Unwasted effort
Philippians 3:14. Running for the prize
2 Timothy 4:7. Finishing the race
Hebrews 12:1. Great examples in the race

▶ March/Marching *(advance, stride, tramp)*

To walk in rhythm and in physical formation with others
Numbers 32:17. Battle formation
Joshua 6:3. Marching around the city walls
Nehemiah 12:31. Celebration march
Jeremiah 46:9. Marching warriors
Nahum 2:5. Stumbling
Habakkuk 1:6. Judgment comes marching
Revelation 20:9. Satan's last march

▶ Market *(agora, assembly, marketplace)*

A place for purchasing life's necessities, public gathering, and social interaction
Matthew 20:3. Idle standing
Matthew 23:7. Pride in the market
Mark 6:56. Sick and beggars
Mark 7:4. Flaunting social standing
Luke 7:32. Children shouting
Acts 16:19. Place for being tried for (in) justice
Acts 17:17. Place for public discussion

▶ Marriage *(matrimony, union, wedlock)*

The union before God of man to woman
Genesis 2:18–24. First marriage
Proverbs 5:18–20. The joys of marital fidelity
Jeremiah 2:1–3. Israel, God's bride
Mark 12:25. No marriage in heaven
1 Corinthians 7:10–16. One unbelieving spouse
Colossians 3:18–19. Marital behavior
Revelation 19:7–8. The marriage of the lamb

▶ Marriages in trouble *(conflict, divorce, immorality)*

Marriages which are "at risk" due to one or both partners giving up on each other, setting aside the bond of the covenant of marriage
Genesis 15:2. Dealing with childlessness
1 Chronicles 15:29. Michal despises David.
Job 2:9–10. Religious disagreement
Jeremiah 44:16–19. Mutual rebellion
Hosea 3:1. Loving an unfaithful wife
Matthew 5:31–32. Instructions regarding divorce
Matthew 19:3–9. When to divorce

M

▶ Martyr *(sufferer, testimony, witness)*

One who bears witness for a cause; someone who testifies (in court), is persecuted, or is killed

1 Samuel 22:17–18. Priests murdered
Matthew 14:1–12. John the Baptist
Acts 7:1–60. Stephen is stoned.
Acts 12:2. James killed by the king
Acts 21:13. Prepared for martyrdom
Hebrews 11:35. Gaining eternal life
Revelation 20:4. Martyred saints

▶ Martyrdom *(martyr, persecution, suffering)*

Suffering for a cause or purpose

Matthew 10:21. Trouble coming
Luke 12:4–5. Not fearing death
Acts 20:24. Witnessing to the Good News
Romans 8:17. Heirs with God
Galatians 5:11. Persecuted for the cross
Colossians 1:24. Filling up what is lacking
Revelation 2:13. Living in a divided kingdom

▶ Masonry *(building, stonework)*

The craft of working with stone

Exodus 1:11. Building cities
Joshua 10:18. Covering a cave
2 Samuel 5:11. Skilled builders
1 Kings 5:17–18. Building the temple
1 Corinthians 3:11. Christ the foundation
1 Peter 2:6. God as a mason

▶ Massacre *(annihilation, mass killing, slaughter)*

The slaughtering of human life as an act of judgment, vengeance, or warfare

Genesis 7:23. The flood devastates.
Exodus 14:27. Egyptians drown.
Exodus 32:28. Punishment for idolatry
Joshua 6:15–21. God orders destruction.
2 Samuel 18:7. David defeats Israel's army.
2 Chronicles 21:4. Consolidating power
2 Chronicles 21:17. Judgment

▶ Master(s) *(Lord, ruler, teacher)*

An overseer who possesses the power to command

Exodus 1:11. Brutal masters
Luke 16:13. Cannot serve two masters
John 15:20. Servant is not greater than master.
Romans 6:16. Mastered by sin or obedience
Ephesians 6:9. One ultimate master
Colossians 3:22. Obeying masters
Revelation 6:10. The holy Master

▶ Matchmaking *(arranged marriage, playing cupid)*

The act of arranging a relationship

Genesis 2:23–24. Suitable for one another
Genesis 21:21. Chosen by the mother
Genesis 24:58. A woman's consent
Genesis 38:6. Chosen by the father
Judges 14:2. Parents' role
Ruth 3:1–2. Mother-in-law as matchmaker
Hosea 1:2–3. An unlikely match

▶ Materialism *(money, riches, vanity)*

The valuing of material possessions in disproportion to valuing the things of God

1 Kings 3:11–13. Asking for the right things
Psalm 49:10. Riches will be left behind.
Psalm 62:10. Warnings against misuse of wealth
Ecclesiastes 5:13. Riches lead to downfall.
Mark 4:19. Desiring things
Luke 12:21. Rich in wealth, poor in relationship with God
1 Timothy 6:17. Confidence in God's riches

▶ Mathematics *(counting, math, numbers)*

The science of working with numbers

Genesis 15:5. Promise of innumerable offspring
Leviticus 25:8. Multiplication
Numbers 23:10. Growing population

Deuteronomy 1:11. Proverbial multiplication
Matthew 10:30. Tedious arithmetic
Luke 12:52. A divided family
John 19:23. Applied mathematics

▶ Matricide *(death, kill, mother)*

Killing of one's mother
Exodus 21:15. Hitting one's mother
Leviticus 20:9. Cursing one's mother
2 Chronicles 15:12–13. Killing all non-believers
1 Timothy 1:9. Laws for killers of mothers

▶ Maturity *(developed, responsible, sophisticated)*

Growing to adulthood; growing in one's spiritual life and disciplines
1 Corinthians 2:6. Mature wisdom
1 Corinthians 13:11. Put aside childish things.
1 Corinthians 14:20. Childish in evil, mature in thinking
Ephesians 4:11–13. God-given means to grow to maturity
Hebrews 5:14. Discerning good and evil
James 1:4. Maturity through testing

▶ Meaning of life *(basis, purpose, reason)*

The reason(s) human beings were created by God
Deuteronomy 6:13. Fearing and serving God
Ecclesiastes 12:13. Reflection on life
Matthew 5:16. Demonstrating God's goodness
Matthew 22:37–38. Greatest commandment
Mark 1:38. Spreading the Good News
John 10:10. Abundant life
1 Corinthians 10:31. All things for God's glory

▶ Meaninglessness *(futility, uselessness, vanity)*

Having a false or absent purpose, hope, or direction in life
1 Samuel 12:21. Following empty things
Proverbs 30:8. Avoiding vanity
Ecclesiastes 1:14. Reflecting on vanity
Ecclesiastes 2:1. Failed attempts at light-heartedness
Isaiah 49:4. Failed attempts
1 Corinthians 15:17. Meaningless without Christ
1 Peter 1:18–19. Freed from meaninglessness

▶ Measurement *(assessment, evaluation, quantification)*

The calculation of a distance, quantity; evaluation of person or persons
Exodus 16:18. Measuring manna
Leviticus 19:35. Measuring fairly
Psalm 39:4. Measuring one's life
Isaiah 40:12–13. A measurement of God's greatness
Jeremiah 33:22. Metaphorically unmeasurable
Matthew 7:2. Measuring others carefully
Revelation 21:15–17. The new creation

▶ Meat *(animal, flesh)*

The flesh of an animal, used for food and sacrifices
Genesis 25:28. Wild game
Exodus 12:8. Flame-roasted Passover lamb
Exodus 16:3. Israel desires to eat meat.
Deuteronomy 12:15. Eating meat is condoned.
Deuteronomy 14:8. Keeping kosher
2 Chronicles 4:6. Meat used in priestly service
Romans 14:21. Avoiding meat for a weaker person

▶ Meat of the Word *(solid food, steak)*

A metaphor for Christian maturity and the need to be fed in proportion to that maturity
1 Corinthians 3:1–2. Basic teaching instead of advanced teaching
Hebrews 5:12. Advanced truths
Hebrews 5:14. Solid food is for the mature

M

▸ Mediator/Mediation *(advocate, intercessor, reconciliation)*

Intervention between two persons/groups for the purpose of bringing about reconciliation which was not otherwise possible

Exodus 28:1. Priests
Exodus 32:30–32. Moses
John 1:17. Kindness and truth mediated
2 Corinthians 5:18. Restored so that we can restore
Ephesians 2:12–17. Brought near by the cross
1 Timothy 2:5. One mediator between God and humanity
Hebrews 9:15. Mediating the new covenant

▸ Medicine *(balm, treatment, remedy)*

A product or mixture used in aiding wellness or curing ailments

Genesis 37:25. Imported medicine
Genesis 43:11. A fine gift
Proverbs 17:22. A joyful heart
Ezekiel 27:17. Valuable commodity
Matthew 10:8. Curing diseases
Luke 8:43. Failed medication
Luke 9:1. Divine medicine given to apostles

▸ Meditate/Meditation *(cogitation, contemplation, reflection)*

Thinking deeply or focusing one's mind on something

Joshua 1:8. Meditating on God's law
Psalm 1:2. Reflecting day and night on the Lord's teachings
Psalm 77:12. Considering God's deeds
Psalm 119:148. Reflecting during the night
Matthew 26:36. Jesus meditates and prays on his final night.
Philippians 4:8. Thinking about good things
2 Timothy 2:7. Thinking with God's help

▸ Medium(s) *(fortune teller, necromancer, spiritualist)*

Someone who seeks knowledge regarding the present and future circumstances through consultation with a deceased person

Leviticus 19:31. Warning against seeing mediums
Leviticus 20:6. Judgment against those who use mediums
2 Kings 23:24. Getting rid of mediums
1 Chronicles 10:13. Death for using a medium
Isaiah 8:19. Asking God for help
Isaiah 19:3. Desperate measures
Jeremiah 29:8. The tricks of mediums

▸ Meekness *(gentle, humble, lowly)*

Approaching others with a spirit of humility and gentleness without the use of coercion to attain a desired end

Psalm 37:11. Blessing of the meek
Zechariah 9:9. The humble Messiah
Matthew 5:5. The meek shall inherit the earth.
Matthew 11:29. Learning humility from Jesus
Ephesians 4:2. Dealing with others
2 Timothy 2:25. A meek rebuke
1 Peter 3:15. Be prepared with a gentle defense.

▸ Melancholia *(depression, gloomy, sadness)*

A deep sadness or gloom which one experiences

1 Samuel 1:8. Having no children
Ezra 3:12. Weeping for God's temple
Ecclesiastes 7:3. Sorrow is sometimes better than laughter.
Luke 18:23. Learning of a difficult task
John 16:20. Sorrow turned to joy
2 Timothy 1:4. Longing to see a friend
Revelation 21:4. God will wipe every tear.

▸ Membership *(belonging, group)*

The reality of being a part of a larger group or community than oneself

Genesis 15:3. Choosing membership
Romans 11:1. Tribal membership
1 Corinthians 1:10. Appeal for unity among members

1 Corinthians 5:9–13. Some are to be excluded

1 Corinthians 12:27. Membership in the body of Christ

Ephesians 2:19. Members of God's family

1 Timothy 5:8. Household membership

▶ Memorable entrances *(making an entrance, putting on a show)*

An unusual, unexpected, or fanciful entrance which generates excitement

1 Samuel 18:6. Of damsels and tambourines

1 Chronicles 15:28. Rejoicing over the ark

Matthew 21:9–10. A triumphant entry

Luke 2:1–20. Angels celebrate Christ's incarnation.

John 2:13–17. Clearing the temple

Acts 2:2–4. Coming of the Spirit

Acts 12:16. An unexpected visitor

▶ Memorial *(monument, remembrance, statue)*

A monument, statue, or other means of reminder which honors someone no longer present

Genesis 31:44–45. Reminder of an agreement

Genesis 35:20. Rachel's gravestone

1 Samuel 15:12. Honoring the king

2 Samuel 18:18. Preserving a family name

Isaiah 56:5. Promise of a lasting name

Matthew 23:29. Monuments of folly

1 Corinthians 11:24. Lord's Supper as memorial

▶ Memorize *(commit to memory, learn, remember)*

The discipline of committing something to memory

Deuteronomy 6:4. Memorizing the Shema

Deuteronomy 11:19. Knowing God's commands

Judges 2:12. Forgetting God

Ezra 7:10. Diligent study

Nehemiah 8:13. Studying God's teaching

Ecclesiastes 12:12. Growing weary

▶ Men *(humanity, male, mankind)*

Generically, humankind; specifically, the male gender and particularly adults

Genesis 1:27. Maleness created by God

Genesis 17:23. Men were to be circumcised.

Leviticus 6:9. Males and the priesthood

1 Corinthians 16:13. Act like men.

1 Timothy 2:8. The praying man

1 Timothy 3:1–7. Aspiring to be an overseer

1 Peter 3:7. Husbands are to honor their wives.

▶ Menopause *(see Menstruation)*

▶ Menstruation *(menstrual cycle, period)*

The once-monthly flow of blood and discharge from the lining of the uterus in a woman

Genesis 31:34–35. Rachel sits on idols during menstruation.

Leviticus 12:2. Menstruation represented loss of (potential for) life.

Leviticus 15:19–24. Sitting on things makes unclean

Leviticus 20:18. Sex during menstruation

Ezekiel 36:17. Unclean

Mark 5:25–34. Chronic bleeding

▶ Mental health *(health, [in] sanity, wellness)*

The condition or stability of one's mind in relation to lucidity, sanity, and society

1 Samuel 21:13. Pretending to be insane

Psalm 38:3. Unhealthy on account of sin

Proverbs 3:1–2. Sound teaching brings peace of mind.

Hosea 9:7. Misjudging spiritual people

Mark 5:15. Sanity after demon possession

Acts 26:24–25. Too much education

2 Corinthians 5:13. Being sane for the sake of others

M

▶ **Mercenary(ies)** *(hired, professional, soldier)*

A person interested in personal gain at the expense of ethics

Judges 11:3. Jephthah's gang

2 Samuel 11:1. David's mercenaries go to war.

2 Samuel 15:18. Bodyguards

2 Chronicles 25:5–6. Amaziah hires Israelites.

1 Corinthians 9:7. Motivation for working

▶ **Mercy** *(compassion, forgiveness, peace)*

God's compassionate disposition toward those whom He wills

Exodus 25:17–21. The mercy seat for the ark

Deuteronomy 30:3. Mercy upon the exiled

Matthew 9:13. God desires mercy.

Romans 3:25. Christ the throne of mercy

Ephesians 2:4. The richness of God's mercy

James 2:13. Mercy for the merciful

Jude 22–23. Showing mercy to doubters

▶ **Message** *(gospel, word)*

Metonymy for the gospel of salvation in Christ

Acts 13:26. The message of salvation

1 Corinthians 1:18. Power to those being saved

1 Corinthians 2:4. How to deliver the message

2 Corinthians 5:19. The message of reconciliation

2 Timothy 4:17. Strengthened to share the Good News

1 John 1:5. God is light.

1 John 3:11. Love one another.

▶ **Messenger** *(courier, go-between, prophet)*

One who brings a message

Genesis 32:6. Bringing information

Haggai 1:13. Prophets are God's messengers.

Malachi 2:7. Priests as God's messenger

Matthew 11:10. John the Baptist, God's promised messenger

2 Corinthians 12:7. Paul's thorn in the flesh

Galatians 4:14. Welcoming God's messenger

2 Timothy 1:11. Appointed by God

▶ **Messiah** *(anointed one, deliverer, savior)*

An anointed one, especially God's anointed Messiah in the Second Temple period; the Christ

Matthew 11:2–5. Are you the Messiah?

Mark 14:61–62. Jesus affirms that He is the Messiah

John 4:25. Messianic expectation

Acts 2:36. Crucified Messiah

1 Corinthians 15:1–7. Messiah died for sins.

Hebrews 9:28. The Messiah's second coming

1 John 5:1. New birth

▶ **Metal worker(s)** *(artisan, idol maker, silversmith)*

An artisan skilled in preparing and working with metal

Exodus 35:35. Skills given by God

Numbers 16:38. Fashioning a new cover for the altar

1 Kings 7:23. Temple furnishings

2 Kings 24:16. Weapon makers

Jeremiah 6:29. Metal working metaphor

Habakkuk 2:18. Making worthless idols

Acts 19:24. Silversmith

▶ **Metaphor(s)** *(figure of speech, symbol, trope)*

Metaphors communicate something that is unknown by using an image or idea that is already known.

Psalm 23:1. God is a shepherd

Psalm 94:22. God is a rock

Matthew 5:13. Salt of the earth

John 6:35. Bread of life

John 8:12. Light of the world

John 15:5. The true vine

1 Thessalonians 5:3. Labor pains

▶ Meteorology *(atmosphere, storm, weather)*

The study of atmospheric conditions

Jonah 1:4–16. Futile to ask the gods concerning weather

Matthew 8:24. A sudden, unexpected storm

Matthew 16:2–3. Red night, sailor's delight

Luke 12:56. Predicting the weather

Acts 27:9–10. Dangerous time for sailing

▶ Middle age *(best days, prime)*

Period of time between young adult life and later life

1 Samuel 2:33. Judgment upon descendants in their prime

Job 29:4. The prime of life

Psalm 102:24. An early death

Isaiah 38:10. Robbed of life

▶ Midnight *(dark, late hour, night)*

A late hour of the night when it is still dark

Exodus 11:4. Judgment executed

Judges 7:19. Changing of the guard

Judges 16:3. In bed with a prostitute

Ruth 3:8. Chill of the night

Psalm 119:62. Nocturnal meditation

Acts 16:25. Late night singing

Acts 20:7. Filibuster

▶ Midwife(ves) *(assistant, helper, woman)*

An assistant trained in aiding in process of childbirth

Genesis 35:17. Comforting in the midst of pain

Genesis 38:28. Keeping track of twins at birth for the birthright

Exodus 1:15–22. Midwives obey God and not an evil king.

Ezekiel 16:4. Birth without a midwife

▶ Migration *(moving, relocation, settling)*

Moving from one place of habitation to another

Genesis 11:2. Settling in a new area

Genesis 12:1. Abram called to leave his land (and therefore his local gods)

Exodus 12:50–51. Out of Egypt

Numbers 32:13. Constantly moving

Jeremiah 8:7. Missing the signs of migration

Acts 7:2–4. Reflection on Abraham's migration

▶ Mildew *(fungus, mold, unclean)*

A type of fungus which grows on damp organic materials

Leviticus 13:49–59. Mildew makes things ceremonially unclean

Leviticus 14:34–39. Mildew in the home

Leviticus 14:54–57. Instructions for dealing with mildew

Deuteronomy 28:22. The Lord judges the land.

2 Chronicles 6:28. Famine conditions

Amos 4:9. Crop killer

Haggai 2:17. Judgment

▶ Military *(army, service, soldiers)*

Personnel related to warfare who are trained in the art of war

Numbers 1:47–49. Priests excluded from military service

Judges 1:19. Winning some battles, losing others

Judges 3:1–2. Learning about war

Psalm 68:17. The army of God

Isaiah 31:1–3. Trusting in God for strength

Acts 21:34. Military compound

2 Timothy 2:1–4. Soldiers of Christ

▶ Milk *(basics, drink, nourishment)*

Literally, the filling and fattening milk of an animal for drinking; metaphorically, wealth and luxury or basic teachings or instructions which are essential for growing to maturity

Judges 4:19. Kindness

Isaiah 7:22. Decadence

Isaiah 55:1. Metaphor for God's law

Isaiah 60:16. Sign of prosperity

Ezekiel 25:4. Meal drink

Hebrews 5:12. Elementary truths
1 Peter 2:2. Desiring God

▶ Milk and honey *(food, luxury, wealth)*

A symbol of the fecundity of the Promised Land
Exodus 3:8. Land of vitality
Exodus 13:5. Promised Land
Leviticus 20:24. Reassigning the land
Numbers 16:13. Egypt
Deuteronomy 6:3. Instructions for living well in the land of milk and honey
Jeremiah 11:5. Promise renewed
Ezekiel 20:15. The most beautiful land

▶ Millennial rule of Christ *(kingdom rule, millennium, reign)*

A period of rule, whether literally one thousand years or symbolically, wherein Christ will rule and reign over all things
Revelation 20:2. Satan bound
Revelation 20:3, 7. Satan set free for a while
Revelation 20:4. Christ and the saints ruling
Revelation 20:5. Resurrection of the dead
Revelation 20:6. Blessing being counted among Christ's priests

▶ Millennium *(see Millennial Rule of Christ)*

▶ Millstone(s) *(equipment, stone, tool)*

A large stone used for grinding grain in the process of preparing food
Exodus 11:5. Often worked by slaves
Deuteronomy 24:6. Means for preparing food
Judges 9:53. Used as a weapon
Jeremiah 25:10. Symbol of well-being and health
Matthew 18:6. Used as a weight to drown someone
Matthew 24:41. Job of women
Revelation 18:22. Sign of impending death

▶ Mind *(soul, intellect, heart)*

The intangible part of a human being that reasons, imagines, and experiences emotion
Psalm 139:1–4. God examines our minds
Romans 8:6–9. Hostile to God
Romans 11:34. The Lord's unsearchable mind
1 Corinthians 2:16. We have the mind of Christ.
Philippians 4:8. Worthy of our thought
Hebrews 12:2. Fixing our thoughts on Jesus
1 Peter 1:13. Prepared to act

▶ Mineral(s) *(gems, precious stones, rocks)*

A carbon-based substance obtained through mining the earth, typically precious stones
Exodus 39:10–13. Precious stones
Job 28:1–2. Taken from the ground
Proverbs 3:15. Wisdom over jewels
Jeremiah 17:1. Diamonds
Ezekiel 28:13. Precious stones in God's garden
Revelation 4:3. Emerald
Revelation 21:18–20. The new Jerusalem

▶ Mining *(extracting, digging, harvesting)*

Finding and extracting materials from the earth
Genesis 2:11. A land where there is gold
Job 28:2. Taken from the ground
Job 28:4. Working in a mineshaft
Job 28:10. Looking for precious things

▶ Minister *(clergy, pastor, servant)*

One who serves others, especially in a religious setting
Psalm 104:4. Angels are servants of God.
Jeremiah 33:21. Priests
Acts 6:2–3. Meeting physical needs
Ephesians 4:12. Purpose of ministers
1 Thessalonians 3:2. Servant of the Good News
Hebrews 8:2. Christ as minister

▶ Ministry *(healing, preaching, teaching)*

Performing works of service to God's people through teaching, preaching, prayer, and caring for physical needs

Luke 3:23. Beginning ministry in your 30s

2 Corinthians 5:18. Ministry of reconciliation

2 Corinthians 9:12. Caring for needs

Ephesians 4:12. Building up the body of Christ

Colossians 4:17. Complete the ministry

2 Timothy 4:5. Devoted to ministry

Hebrews 8:6. Jesus' priestly ministry

▶ Miracles of Jesus *(miraculous, sign, wonder)*

A supernatural or inexplicable event meant to demonstrate who Jesus is and encourage faith in Jesus

Matthew 9:33. Healing a mute

Matthew 16:7–10. Miraculous feeding

Mark 6:5. Deciding to move on

Luke 7:21–23. Curing various ailments

Luke 8:22–25. Calming the storm

John 2:11. Demonstrated Jesus' glory

John 20:30–31. Recorded so that we will believe Jesus is Messiah

▶ Miracles of others *(miraculous, sign, wonder)*

A supernatural or inexplicable event, typically done in God's power and for the purpose of confirming the message of salvation

Exodus 4:17. Moses performs signs.

Joshua 3:5. Purity before miracles

Daniel 2:28–30. A dream and its interpretation revealed to Daniel.

Matthew 7:22. Miracles performed by unbelievers

Matthew 10:1. Disciples given authority

Romans 15:18–19. Means of spreading the Good News

2 Thessalonians 2:9. False signs and wonders

▶ Mischief *(bad behavior, disobedient, playful)*

Misbehavior which begins playfully and develops to destructive disobedience

Genesis 37:23–24. Bad brothers

Deuteronomy 8:5. God disciplines just as parents discipline.

Psalm 7:14. A vivid picture of developing mischief

Proverbs 17:4. A mischievous tongue

Proverbs 23:13. Discipline a child.

Jeremiah 31:20. A pleasant child?

▶ Miserly behavior (see *Hoard/Hoarding*)

▶ Mislead *(deceive, lie, misguide)*

Consciously lying or deceiving others by presenting false information or withholding information

Joshua 24:27. God is not deceived.

Psalm 119:118. Lies mislead from God's laws.

Isaiah 3:12. Bad leadership

Micah 3:5. Lying prophets

Ephesians 5:6. Judgment upon deceivers

2 Timothy 3:6. Deception in the last days

Hebrews 6:18. God cannot lie.

▶ Misogyny *(hate, woman hater)*

The hatred and abuse of women

Genesis 19:5–8. Lot sinfully offering his daughters

Genesis 29:31. Leah was unloved.

Deuteronomy 22:13–14. Lying about a woman's character

Deuteronomy 22:16. Disapproving of the bride

James 1:27. Taking care of widows

▶ Misrepresent (see *Mislead*)

▶ Mission *(charge, commission, task)*

The important task of sharing and spreading the message of the lordship of Jesus Christ to all peoples, tongues, and tribes

Isaiah 55:11. God's word will not return void

Matthew 28:18–20. Great Commission

John 15:16. Appointed to produce fruit

Acts 2:47. Growing numbers

Romans 1:5. Aim of missions

Romans 1:14. Obliged mission

Romans 15:30–31. Praying for other missionaries

▶ Missionary(ies) *(apostle, minister, servant)*

Those called and commissioned to do the work of spreading the gospel throughout the world

Acts 8:4. Preaching the Word

Acts 13:2. Saul/Paul set apart for mission work

Acts 21:8. Housing church leaders

1 Corinthians 9:1–12. Rights of God's servants

Galatians 2:8–9. Division of labor

Ephesians 4:11. Gifts from God to the church

2 Timothy 4:5. Charge to work as a missionary

▶ Mistaken identity *(false identity, lying, perception)*

The situation when one is mistaken for someone they are not

Genesis 20:5. Lying about identity

Genesis 29:23. Jacob is given Leah, instead of Rachel

Esther 2:10. Queen Esther hides her nationality

Mark 8:27–28. "Who do people say that I am?"

John 18:37. Political king vs. King of kings

Acts 13:6. False prophet

Acts 14:12. Barnabas and Paul mistaken for Greek gods

▶ Mistakes *(error, fault, oversight)*

Actions or judgments which are wrong

Leviticus 5:18. Unintentional mistakes

Numbers 15:25. Forgiveness for mistakes

1 Samuel 26:21. Admitting mistakes

Job 19:4. Unrecognized mistake

Ecclesiastes 5:6. Do not call a promise a mistake.

Matthew 22:29. Not knowing the Scriptures or God's power

James 3:2. Speaking mistakes

▶ Mistrust *(suspicious, skeptical, weary of)*

Expressing suspicion or lack of confidence in someone or something

Exodus 16:2–3. Longing for old ways rather than trusting God

Psalm 44:6. Not trusting in military strength

Proverbs 3:5. Put your trust in the Lord

Jeremiah 9:4. Mistrusting close companions in dire times

Micah 7:5. Not trusting others

John 2:24. Mistrusting human nature

Romans 4:20. Trusting in God's promise

▶ Misunderstanding *(false impression, misinterpret, misconstrue)*

Failure to correctly understand someone based upon a misinterpretation or a false inference of what was said or written

1 Samuel 1:14. Misunderstood for a drunkard

Psalm 56:5. Misunderstanding and twisting words

1 Corinthians 12:1. Misunderstanding spiritual gifts

1 Thessalonians 3:10. Desire to see those who have misunderstood aspects of faith

1 Thessalonians 4:13. Misunderstanding death

2 Peter 3:16. Paul's letters are difficult.

▶ Moabites *(Lot, Moab, Semitic)*

A Semitic tribe who initially settled on the southeastern border of the Dead Sea, generally hostile toward Israel

Genesis 19:37. Moab and the Moabites

Numbers 22:2–4. Tensions between Moab and Israel

Judges 11:18. The borders of Moab
1 Chronicles 18:2. David defeats Moab.
Isaiah 15:1. Predicting judgment
Jeremiah 27:3. Message sent to Moab

▶ Mockery *(contempt, derision, ridicule)*

Teasing, ridiculing, or acting in a manner which is either uncharitable or uninformed
1 Kings 18:27. Mocking false gods
2 Kings 19:16. Mocking God
2 Chronicles 36:16. The perils of mocking God's messengers
Psalm 89:50. Request for God to hear
Matthew 20:19. Mocking Jesus
Galatians 6:7. God is not mocked.
Hebrews 11:36. Suffering persecution

▶ Model *(example, leadership, pattern)*

A person, place, or thing commended as an example to imitate or follow
2 Kings 16:3. Living like an evil king
John 13:15. Following the example of Jesus
1 Corinthians 10:11. Examples in the Old Testament
Philippians 3:17. Imitate me.
1 Timothy 4:12. Model behavior
James 5:10. Suffering like the prophets
1 Peter 2:21. Following Christ's example

▶ Moderation *(restraint, self-control, temperance)*

Not given to excess or extremes in attitudes, actions, or opinions
Proverbs 25:16. Avoiding too much food
Proverbs 25:17. Bugging neighbors
Ezekiel 16:49. Ignoring the poor and needy
Romans 15:1. The strong and the weak
1 Corinthians 10:23. Using discernment
1 Timothy 3:3. Qualifications of a leader
1 Peter 4:4. Avoiding wild living

▶ Modesty *(humility, reserved, timid)*

The behavior or quality of acting in moderation, timidity, or humility
Genesis 3:7. Covering nakedness
Genesis 24:65. A modest woman
Jeremiah 13:26. Threat of immodesty
Romans 12:3. Sober self-assessment
Philippians 2:3. Thinking of and caring for others first
1 Timothy 2:9–10. Dressing modestly
1 Peter 5:5. Serving with humility, rejecting arrogance

▶ Monarchy *(government, kingdom, royalty)*

A government ruled by a monarch such as king, queen, or emperor
Deuteronomy 33:5. The Lord is king over Israel.
1 Samuel 8:5. Israel asks Samuel for a king.
2 Samuel 2:4. David anointed king
Luke 23:14. Brought before the government
Romans 13:1. Monarchy established by God
Revelation 19:16. King of kings

▶ Money *(cash, fortune, treasure)*

Commodity used as a medium of exchange or a designation of value
Numbers 31:25–54. Portion of what we have should be given to God.
Proverbs 15:27. Money gotten dishonestly causes pain.
Isaiah 55:2. Spend your resources on what is truly valuable.
Haggai 2:8. Silver and gold belong to God.
Matthew 6:19. Never put money above God.
Hebrews 13:5. Be satisfied with what God gives.
James 5:1–6. Money is gone when we die.

▶ Monotheism *(God, Trinity)*

A belief in one God
Deuteronomy 6:4–5. Monotheistic mantra
1 Samuel 26:19. Turning from God
Isaiah 45:21. All other gods are false and cannot save.
Acts 17:22–31. The true God created all things.
Romans 1:24–31. Serving the true God

1 Corinthians 8:4–6. But for us, there is one God!

Ephesians 4:5–6. Creator and sustainer of all things

▶ Monotony *(dullness, routine, tedium)*

Tedious repetition of an action with very little variety or interest

Numbers 11:4–6. Sick of the same food

Proverbs 14:14. Boredom apart from God

Ecclesiastes 1:4. Monotonous life

Ecclesiastes 1:9. Cycles of life

Luke 15:11–16. Sinfully seeking release from monotonous home life

▶ Mood(s) *(disposition, spirit, temper)*

A negative temperament or attitude which results in angry or emotional behavior

1 Samuel 16:23. Mood-soothing music

1 Kings 20:43. The king's bad mood

Nehemiah 5:6. Righteous anger

Psalm 13:2. Dealing with anxiety

Isaiah 65:14. Cheer and sadness from God

Matthew 27:3–5. Remorse

James 1:19–20. Slow to anger

▶ Moon *(orb, satellite)*

The natural satellite which orbits the earth and is visible primarily at night

Genesis 1:14–16. Night light

Deuteronomy 4:19. Idolatrous worship

2 Kings 23:5. Worshiping the moon god

Psalm 72:5. A measure of permanence

Ezekiel 32:7. Darkened moon a sign of coming judgment

Colossians 2:16. Moon festivals

Revelation 21:23. New Jerusalem does not need the moon's light.

▶ Morale *(confidence, discipline, enthusiasm)*

The level of certainty or confidence of a particular person or group

Deuteronomy 20:5–9. Keeping morale high

1 Samuel 22:2. Leading the distressed

Nehemiah 4:6. Workers' morale

Job 8:13–14. Hopeless without God

Jeremiah 38:1–6. Discouraging soldiers

2 Corinthians 1:7. Solidarity in suffering

Philippians 3:3–4. Confidence in God

▶ Morality *(ethics, righteous, virtues)*

Guidelines for discerning what is right and wrong, good and evil

Genesis 2:16–17. Knowledge of good and evil

Leviticus 11:44–45. God's holiness as our basis for holiness

Romans 13:14. Called to live like Christ

1 Corinthians 15:33. Corrupting company

1 Timothy 5:1–2. Instructions for correcting morality within Christian community

1 Peter 3:10–11. Turning from evil

▶ Morning *(AM, dawn, first light)*

The period of time from midnight through noon; daybreak, light

Genesis 1:5. Method of counting time

Exodus 7:15. Early activities of the day

Ruth 2:7. Daybreak

Psalm 30:5. God's joy comes swiftly in the morning.

Psalm 88:13. Morning prayer

Matthew 27:1. Carrying out evil plans

Luke 24:22–23. Jesus' tomb is empty in the morning!

▶ Morning star *(Christ, light, royal)*

A name figuratively given to Jesus Christ, the Promised One

Numbers 24:17. The promise of the morning star

Matthew 2:2. A symbol of royalty

2 Peter 1:19. Waiting for the morning star

Revelation 2:26–29. Gift of God

Revelation 22:16. Christ is the morning star.

▶ Mortality *(death, impermanence, loss of life)*

The situation or status of being subject to death

Genesis 3:22. Death introduced to humanity
Psalm 62:9. Vanity of all life
Ecclesiastes 8:8. Unavoidable death
Romans 8:36. Christians called to suffer and die
2 Corinthians 4:7. Although we are mortal, we contain a treasure
Philippians 3:10. Becoming like Christ in His death
Hebrews 9:15. Death of Christ

▸ Most Holy Place *(consecrated, holy of holies, separate)*

The second interior portion of the tabernacle where the ark of the covenant was kept
Exodus 26:33. Separates the ark from the rest of the tabernacle
1 Kings 6:16. Building the temple
2 Chronicles 3:10. Beautiful golden sculptures
Matthew 27:50–51. The torn veil at Jesus' death
Hebrews 9:12. The priestly sacrifice of Jesus

▸ Mother(s) *(female, mom, parent)*

Used in reference to a woman and the organic connection she has with progeny
Genesis 3:20. Archetypal motherhood
Deuteronomy 5:16. Commanded to honor mothers
Joshua 2:12–13. Arranging for family protection
Job 31:15. God's action in the womb
Proverbs 1:8. Do not neglect your mother's teachings.
Matthew 1:16. Mary the mother of Jesus
1 Thessalonians 2:7. Being gentle like a mother

▸ Mother-in-law *(family, relation, relative)*

The mother of one's husband or wife through marriage
Deuteronomy 27:23. Sexual immorality forbidden
Ruth 1:15–18. Ruth's loyalty to her mother-in-law
Micah 7:6. Trouble in the family
Matthew 8:14. The apostle Peter's mother-in-law
Matthew 10:35. Loyalty to Jesus before loyalty to family

▸ Motive *(grounds, rationale, reason)*

A (concealed) rationale for one's actions
Proverbs 16:2. God knows true motivations.
Jeremiah 20:12. God sees the motives of conquest.
John 7:18. A teacher without dishonest motives
1 Corinthians 4:5. Revealing what is hidden
Philippians 1:18. Preaching a good message with bad motivation
Colossians 3:22. Honoring earthly masters
1 Thessalonians 2:4. God tests our motives.

▸ Mount Horeb *(mountain, Mount Sinai)*

The general name for the desert mountain range in which Mount Sinai sits
Exodus 17:6. Water from the rock at Mount Horeb
Exodus 33:6. Consecrated after Mount Horeb
Deuteronomy 1:2. Traveling between distances
Deuteronomy 1:19. Desert terrain
Deuteronomy 4:10. Never forget what God did at Mount Horeb.
Psalm 106:19. Idolatry on the mountain

▸ Mount of Olives *(hill, mountain, range)*

A small range of mountains which overlooks Jerusalem from the East
2 Samuel 15:30. King David on Mount of Olives
2 Samuel 15:32. A place of worship
Zechariah 14:4. Prediction of a great earthquake
Matthew 24:3. A place of revelation
Acts 1:12. Half a mile from Jerusalem

M

▶ Mount Sinai *(see Mount Horeb)*

(see Mount Horeb)

▶ Mountain(s) *(height, hill, summit)*

A natural elevation of the earth's surface

Exodus 19:16. God's presence on the mountain

Judges 6:2. Places of refuge

Isaiah 14:13. Where the (false) gods assemble

Matthew 5:1–2. Sermon on the Mount

Matthew 17:1. Jesus transfigured on the mountain

Matthew 17:20. Faith can move mountains.

▶ Mountain of the Lord *(mountain, sacrifice)*

Originally the mountain which Abraham ascended to sacrifice Isaac where God provided a sacrifice

Genesis 22:14. The place where God provided a sacrifice

Numbers 10:33. Traveling from the mountain of the Lord

Isaiah 2:3. God's temple

Zechariah 8:3. The holy mountain at Jerusalem

▶ Mourn/Mourning *(weeping, grieving)*

To express grief over a loss

Genesis 21:16. Sobbing over a child

2 Samuel 15:30. Covering the head to mourn

2 Kings 22:19. Tearing of clothes

Ecclesiastes 3:4. A time for all things

Matthew 5:4. Mourners will be comforted.

Philippians 3:18. Weeping over enemies of Christ

▶ Moving *(active, mobile, on the move)*

The process of changing one's place of residence

Genesis 3:23. Sent out from the Garden

Genesis 12:1. Abraham called to leave his home

Exodus 12:31–32. Leaving Egypt

Ruth 1:16. Asking to stay

Acts 1:8. Worldwide witnesses

Romans 15:28. Paul the mobile missionary

Ephesians 5:31. Moving together in marriage

▶ Mugging *(assault, beat up, robbery)*

Attacking and/or robbing someone

Proverbs 22:22–23. God pleads the case of the robbed.

Isaiah 10:1–2. Woes against the unjust

Isaiah 61:8. God hates robbery.

Hosea 7:1. Robbing others in public

Matthew 27:38. Jesus crucified with criminals

Luke 10:25–37. The parable of the good Samaritan

2 Corinthians 11:26. Traveling bandits

▶ Multitude *(crowd, host, masses)*

A large or gathered group of people

Genesis 16:10. Promise of multitudes for offspring

Daniel 11:10. Commanding large forces

Mark 15:11–15. Mob mentality

Acts 5:16. Crowds come to be healed by Jesus.

Acts 21:35. Violent crowds

Revelation 7:9. A multi-ethnic crowd

Revelation 19:1. The multitudes praising God

▶ Mummy *(desiccated body, preserved)*

Preserving a body after death

Genesis 50:26. Joseph's preserved body

Luke 23:53. The tomb of Jesus

▶ Murder *(assassinate, homicide, kill)*

The premeditated killing of another human being

Genesis 9:6. Humans are made in the image of God.

Deuteronomy 17:6–12. Sentencing a murderer to death

Proverbs 28:17. Folly of murder
Matthew 14:1–12. Killing John the Baptist
Acts 5:30. Murdered Jesus brought back to life
James 4:2. Murdering to steal

▶ Murmuring *(complain, grumble, moan)*

Private or suppressed expressions of dissatisfaction and complaints
Numbers 14:27. Putting up with complaints
Joshua 9:18. Complaining about leaders
Isaiah 29:24. Rebuking murmuring
Luke 5:30. Complaining about Jesus
1 Corinthians 10:10. Condemning complaining
Philippians 2:14. Living without conflict
Jude 16. Sinful people

▶ Music *(composition, melody, song)*

An instrumental and/or lyrical composition comprised of both rhythmic and melodic elements
Genesis 4:21. First harp and flute
1 Samuel 16:14–23. David's music comforts Saul.
1 Chronicles 15:16–24. The important role of music
Proverbs 25:20. Dreadful music
Isaiah 42:10. Sing a new song to the Lord.
Colossians 3:16. Songs of instruction
Revelation 5:11–12. Song of the angels

▶ Musician(s) *(artist, instrumentalist, performer)*

One who is skilled in the performance of music
Judges 5:11. The musicians gather.
1 Chronicles 6:32. Royal musicians
1 Chronicles 15:16–24. Many, many musicians
Nehemiah 12:47. Paid musicians
Nehemiah 13:10–11. Musicians not being paid
Revelation 18:22. Musicians silenced in Babylon.

▶ Mute *(silent, speechless, taciturn)*

One who is incapable of or is refraining from oral communication
Exodus 4:11. God is in control.
Proverbs 31:8. Speaking on behalf of the mute
Ezekiel 33:22. The Lord makes the mute speak.
Matthew 15:31. Mute people talking
Luke 11:14. A silent demon
1 Corinthians 12:2. Mute idols
2 Peter 2:16. A mute donkey speaks.

▶ Mutiny *(insurrection, rebellion, uprising)*

A rebellion against a ruling party
Deuteronomy 13:5. Prophets who preach rebellion
Esther 6:2. Rebelling against a king
Matthew 26:5. Avoiding a riot
Acts 5:37. Rebellion squashed, followers scattered
Acts 17:5. A city riot
Acts 21:38. Stirring up a revolution
2 Thessalonians 2:3. A coming mutiny

▶ Myrrh *(gum, perfume, spice)*

An expensive, fragrant resin obtained from trees found in Africa and Arabia
Genesis 43:11. High-quality products
Esther 2:12. Spa treatment
Proverbs 7:17. A fragrant bed
Song of Songs 1:13. Intimate fragrances
Matthew 2:11. A gift for Jesus
Mark 15:23. A vinegar-like drink
John 19:39. Embalming fluid

▶ Mystery *(hidden, puzzle, secret)*

Anything which is hidden or secret
Ecclesiastes 7:24. Mysterious wisdom
1 Corinthians 13:2. Understanding mysteries but failing to love

1 Corinthians 15:51. Paul speaks a mystery.

Ephesians 3:9–11. God's plan for the fullness of time

Ephesians 5:31–32. The mystery of marriage

Colossians 1:25–27. Christ in you

2 Thessalonians 2:7. The mystery of sinful nature

▶ Myth(s) *(fable, legend, story)*

A false story or idea which is widely held

1 Timothy 1:4. Questing God's plan

1 Timothy 4:7. Avoiding godless myths

2 Timothy 4:4. Abandoning the truth

Titus 1:14. Commanded to avoid myths

2 Peter 1:16. A power message not based on myths

▶ Nagging *(complaining, grumbling, criticizing)*

Incessant fault-finding or criticizing which causes strained personal relationships

Proverbs 21:9. A nagging spouse
Judges 16:16. Nagging Samson
Romans 12:10. Showing love and respect within the family
Ephesians 4:29. Helping rather than hurting
Ephesians 6:4. Raising children up right
Colossians 3:21. Not nagging children
1 Peter 5:5. Submitting without complaint

▶ Nail(s) *(peg, spike, tack)*

A blunt metal object for driving into wood or other objects and fastening things together

Exodus 27:19. Bronze pegs for the tabernacle
Judges 4:21. A murder weapon
1 Chronicles 22:3. Making iron nails
Ecclesiastes 12:11. Firmly driven nails
Isaiah 41:7. Holding idols in place
Ezekiel 15:3. Object used in construction
John 20:25. Scars from nails
Colossians 2:14. Nailing charges to the cross

▶ Nakedness *(see Nudity)*

▶ Name *(label, reputation, title)*

Title by which someone is called and known; often refers to a person's reputation or renown

Genesis 2:19. Adam names animals.
Genesis 12:2. Promise of a great name
Genesis 17:5. God changes Abram's name to Abraham.
Exodus 20:7. Rightly using God's name
Deuteronomy 18:20. Speaking in God's name
2 Samuel 7:9. Promise of a great name
Psalm 7:17. Praising the name of the Lord
Psalm 102:15. Fearing the name of the Lord
Proverbs 18:10. The strong name of the Lord
Proverbs 22:1. Importance of a good name
Isaiah 7:14. A name of one to come
Isaiah 24:15. Honoring the name of the Lord
Joel 2:32. Calling on the name of the Lord
John 17:6. Christ came to reveal God's name.
Acts 4:12. Power in Jesus' name
Acts 19:5. Baptized in Jesus' name
Romans 15:20. Spreading the name of Christ
Ephesians 1:21. Name above all names
2 Timothy 2:19. Departing from iniquity

▶ Names of God *(Adonai, Elohim, God)*

Various names given to God representative of His character

Genesis 12:8. Yahweh
Genesis 14:22. Lord God Most High
Genesis 21:33. The Everlasting God
Exodus 3:14. I Am Who I Am
Exodus 17:15. The Lord Is My Banner
Deuteronomy 5:9. El is a jealous God
Judges 5:3. The Lord God of Israel
1 Samuel 17:45. The Lord of Armies
Isaiah 1:24. The Mighty One of Israel
Jeremiah 23:6. The Lord Our Righteousness
Daniel 7:9. Ancient One

▶ Names of Jesus *(Christ, Lord, Messiah)*

Various titles given to Jesus indicating His character as the anointed one of God

Isaiah 9:6. Prophecies of Jesus
Matthew 1:21. The Lord Saves
Matthew 21:11. Prophet
Mark 4:38. Teacher
Mark 8:38. Son of Man
Mark 9:5. Rabbi
Mark 12:35. Messiah
Mark 15:26. King of the Jews
Luke 22:70. Son of God
John 1:1. The Word
John 1:29. The Lamb of God

N

Acts 19:13. Lord Jesus Christ
1 Corinthians 15:21–22. Second Adam
Philippians 3:20. Our Savior
Revelation 1:8. Alpha (A) and Omega (Z)
Revelation 1:17. First and the last
Revelation 19:11. Faithful and True
Revelation 22:16. Bright morning star

▸ Naming *(heading, title)*

The action of giving a name to a person, place, or thing

Genesis 1:8. Naming creation
Genesis 2:19. Adam names animals.
Genesis 32:30. Naming a location
Exodus 2:10. Naming a child

▸ Narcissism *(egotistic, self-admiration, vanity)*

Excessive self-interest to the extent of neglecting the concerns of others

Genesis 3:1–7. Self-promoting disobedience to God
Ezekiel 16:49. Ignoring the poor and needy
Amos 6:6. Caring for self over others
Zechariah 7:4–6. Living for personal benefit
Matthew 24:12. Love growing cold
Luke 9:46–48. Who is the greatest
Luke 11:43. Desiring to be seen
Luke 18:18–25. Giving up riches
Romans 12:10. Honoring others above self
Philippians 3:19. Minds set on worldly things
2 Timothy 3:1–7. Lovers of self
James 1:9–10. God exalts the lowly.
1 Peter 5:5–6. God opposes the arrogant.

▸ Nard *(oil, perfume, scent)*

An expensive oil used as a perfume for anointing

Song of Songs 4:13–14. Description of a lover
Mark 14:3. Expensive perfume
John 12:3. Anointing Jesus

▸ Nation(s) *(land, pagans, people)*

A group of people connected together by family, culture, and traditions

Genesis 18:18. All nations blessed through Abraham
Exodus 9:24. The nation of Egypt
Exodus 32:10. Promise of a great nation
Deuteronomy 7:7–8. God chooses a nation.
Deuteronomy 32:8. Divided into nations
Job 12:23. God rules over nations.
Isaiah 37:12. Pagan nations
Isaiah 42:1. Bringing justice to the nations
Isaiah 49:6. Light unto the nations
Ezekiel 25:11. Judgment upon a nation
Amos 9:7. God cares for all nations.
Matthew 24:7. Fighting nations
Matthew 28:19. Making disciples of all nations
Acts 10:22. The Jewish nation
Romans 1:5. Making disciples from every nation
2 Timothy 4:17. Spreading Good News to the nations
1 Peter 2:9. God's people a holy nation
Revelation 2:26. Authority over the nations

▸ Nativity *(birth, genesis, origin)*

Circumstances surrounding the birth of a person

Numbers 24:17. A prophesied star
Isaiah 7:14. A virgin shall conceive.
Micah 5:2. Bethlehem prophecy
Matthew 1:18–25. Mary conceives by the Holy Spirit.
Luke 2:1–20. Baby in a manger
Revelation 12:1–5. Christ the ruler

▸ Natural resources *(land, mineral, resource)*

Materials which occur naturally and can be used for sustenance

Genesis 1:28. Called to steward creation
Genesis 2:11–12. Precious minerals
Exodus 23:10–19. Giving fields a year of rest
Numbers 35:2–3. Preserving pastureland
Psalm 24:1. Everything is the Lord's.

▸ Nature *(countryside, environment, world)*

An undeveloped and generally undisturbed piece of land or water

Exodus 3:1. The mountain of God
Numbers 13:3. Wilderness wandering
Psalm 50:10. Creatures of the forest
Psalm 107:33. God's power over nature
Isaiah 52:7. God's messenger compared with beauty of nature
Matthew 4:1. Wilderness temptation
Mark 4:39. Jesus' power over nature
Romans 11:24. Grafted olive branch
2 Corinthians 11:26. Traveling the open country

▶ Navigation *(directions, travel, traverse)*

Executing a planned route of travel
Numbers 9:23. Obeying the Lord's travel command
Numbers 21:4. Navigating around Edom
Deuteronomy 1:2. Travel directions
Isaiah 49:11. Navigating the mountains
Matthew 2:12. Divine travel plans
John 4:4. Traveling through dangerous areas
John 7:1. Navigating danger
Acts 27:1–2. Navigating the sea
2 Corinthians 1:15–17. Travel plans

▶ Nazirite *(consecrated, devoted, set apart)*

An Israelite dedicated to the service of God, taking vows of abstinence from cutting hair, drinking alcohol, and having contact with dead bodies
Numbers 6:1–4. Avoiding strong drink
Numbers 6:5. Avoid cutting hair.
Numbers 6:6–8. Avoiding dead bodies
Numbers 6:9–21. Instructions for completing Nazirite vow
Judges 13:5–7. Dedicated to God
Judges 16:17. Hair is the source of Samson's strength.
1 Samuel 1:11. Promise of dedication
Amos 2:11–12. Desecrating vows
Acts 18:18. Aquila cuts his hair in completion of a vow.
Acts 21:23. Men vowed to God.

▶ Nearness of God *(affections, closeness, intimacy)*

The immanence of God with his people; God promises to draw near to those who draw near to him.
Genesis 3:8. God walking in the garden
Exodus 16:7. Hearing the complaints of people
Numbers 16:19. Brought near to do God's work
Deuteronomy 4:7. God is near those who pray.
Psalm 28:7. Trusting in the Lord's strength
Psalm 37:4. Happiness in the Lord
Psalm 85:9. Salvation is near those who fear God.
Psalm 119:151. Comfort in God's nearness
Isaiah 58:2. Desiring for God to be near
Jeremiah 23:23. A God who is both near and far
Matthew 1:23. Jesus is "God with us."
Matthew 28:20. Jesus is always with us.
Mark 1:15. Kingdom of God is near
John 16:7. Jesus will send a helper (the Holy Spirit).
Acts 23:11. The Lord gives Paul strength.
Philippians 4:5. The Lord is near.
James 4:8. Drawing near to God

▶ Needs *(lacking, short supply, wanting)*

Essential materials of life for normal functioning and quality of life, either physical or spiritual
Exodus 16:17–20. God provides for needs.
2 Kings 6:26–27. Need for help from God
Hosea 12:8. Absence of need
Amos 4:6. Left with needs
Matthew 10:42. Meeting physical needs
Acts 16:9. Needed in Macedonia
Romans 5:6–8. Christ died for the spiritually needy.
Romans 12:13. Being hospitable with God's people.
Philippians 4:19. God will richly meet needs through Jesus Christ.

1 Timothy 6:8. Basic needs met
James 2:16. Properly caring for others
1 John 3:17. Remaining in God's love

▶ Neglect *(abandon, disregard, forget)*

The willful or fortuitous disregard of something or someone

Deuteronomy 12:19. Not neglecting God's servants
Joshua 1:5. Promise of nearness
Nehemiah 10:39. Remembering God's temple
Proverbs 1:8. Listening to the instruction of your parents
Proverbs 8:33. Hearing instruction and growing in wisdom
Jeremiah 48:10. Curse upon those who neglect the Lord's work
Luke 11:42. Judgment for ignoring justice and love
1 Timothy 4:14. Honoring God's prophetic gift
Hebrews 2:3. Ignoring salvation
Hebrews 13:2. Being mindful to care for others

▶ Negotiation *(debate, deliberation, discussion)*

An intense discussion between two or more parties aimed at reaching common ground

Genesis 29:1–20. Jacob negotiates with Laban for Rachel.
Exodus 7:1–13. Moses and Aaron negotiating with Pharaoh
Joshua 10:1–15. Joshua negotiates with God.
Matthew 26:14–16. Negotiating betrayal
Matthew 27:15–23. Negotiating the release of prisoner
Luke 14:31. Preparation for battle
Acts 15:2. Fierce dispute between the apostles

▶ Neighbor(s) *(friend, nearby)*

Individuals who live in close proximity to one another

Exodus 20:16. Telling the truth about neighbors
Exodus 20:17. Not coveting a neighbor's things
Exodus 22:5. Damaging a neighbor's property
Exodus 33:11. God speaks to Moses as a friend.
Leviticus 19:18. Love your neighbor as yourself.
Deuteronomy 19:13. Respecting a neighbor's property
Proverbs 14:21. Sin of despising a neighbor
Proverbs 17:17. A loving friend
Jeremiah 9:4–5. Pessimistic view toward others
Matthew 5:43–44. Loving neighbors and enemies
Luke 10:29–37. Who is my neighbor?
John 4:39. Witnessing toward neighbors
Romans 13:9–10. Fulfilling the Old Testament law through love
Romans 15:2. Building up your neighbor's faith
Galatians 5:14. Summing up the law
Colossians 4:5. Wise actions toward unbelieving neighbors
James 4:12. Refrain from judging your neighbor.

▶ Nephew(s) *(family, relation)*

The son of one's brother (in-law) or sister (in-law)

Genesis 12:5. Abraham brings his nephew on a trip.
Genesis 14:14. Rescuing a nephew from danger
Genesis 29:12. Keeping marriage within the family clan
1 Chronicles 5:1. Rights of the first-born given to nephews
2 Chronicles 22:8. Nephews ruling together
Acts 23:16. Paul's nephew cares for Paul.

▶ Nepotism *(bias, favoritism, partiality)*

Practice of giving preferential treatment to family and friends at the expense of others

Genesis 47:11–12. Joseph cares for his brothers.

1 Samuel 14:50. Keeping leadership in the family

2 Samuel 8:16. Royal historian

2 Samuel 19:13. Preference for trusted family

Nehemiah 7:2. Giving leadership to family

▶ Nest(s) *(home, refuge)*

Shelter constructed by birds for safely housing their young

Numbers 24:21. A solid nesting place

Deuteronomy 22:6. Sparing a nest of birds

Psalm 84:3. The swallow's nest

Proverbs 27:8. Wandering from the nest

Isaiah 16:2. Scattered from the nest

Ezekiel 17:23. A fine place for a nest

Matthew 8:20. The Son of Man has no home.

Mark 4:32. Nesting in the shade of the garden

▶ Networking *(connected, interconnected, linked)*

System of interconnected people or places

John 17:20–21. That they may be one as we are one

Romans 12:5. Christ connects believers.

Romans 16:1–16. Introducing and greeting new people

1 Corinthians 12:12. Unified body of Christ, the church

Galatians 2:1. Networking in Jerusalem

▶ New Age *(mysticism, spirituality)*

Broad-reaching religious outlook characterized by openness and mystical thought

Isaiah 41:23. Humankind as gods

Isaiah 47:10. A wicked credo

Daniel 5:11. Wiser than the king's spiritualists

Acts 8:10. Simon the magician wows the crowd.

Acts 17:23. Worshiping an unknown God

Romans 3:4. Truth belongs to God.

2 Corinthians 4:7. Power from God, not from us

Galatians 5:7. Stunted spiritual growth

Colossians 1:27. Riches of this mystery is Christ in you.

1 Timothy 6:20. Turning away from worldly discussions

1 John 1:1–2. Heard, seen, and touched

1 John 2:22. Rejecting the Messiah

1 John 4:1–2. Testing the claims of others

▶ New Covenant *(alliance, testament, will)*

The promised covenant instituted through the shedding of Christ's blood and symbolized through the cup of wine at the Lord's Supper

Jeremiah 31:31. Promise of a new covenant

Luke 22:20. Cup of the new covenant

2 Corinthians 3:6. Ministers of a new covenant

Hebrews 8:13. Superseding the old covenant

Hebrews 9:15. Receiving the promise of an eternal inheritance

Hebrews 12:24. Christ mediated a new covenant

▶ New creation *(creation, life, renewal)*

An entire re-creative act of God in the world

Isaiah 43:18–19. In breaking of new creation

2 Corinthians 5:17. Living in a new way as new creation

Galatians 6:15. What matters is new creation.

▶ New Jerusalem *(Jerusalem above, holy city)*

The heavenly Jerusalem which, in the end times, will inaugurate God's kingdom rule and a new cosmic order

Galatians 4:26. Jerusalem above and below

Hebrews 12:22–23. The heavenly Jerusalem

Revelation 3:12. The city of God

Revelation 21:2. The new city descends.

N

▶ New Moon Festival *(celebration, commemoration, festival)*

Upon the commencement of a new month, special sacrifices and instructions were to be followed in a festival ritual

Numbers 10:10. Striking up the band

Numbers 28:11–15. Instructions for the festival

1 Samuel 20:5. Eating at the king's table

2 Kings 4:23. Consulting a prophet on a festival day

Ezra 3:5. Making offerings for the New Moon Festival

Psalm 81:3. Sounding the ram's horn to mark the festival

Ezekiel 46:1. Opening the gates of the temple during the festival

Amos 8:5. Ceasing the sale of goods

▶ New Testament *(new, revelation, testimony)*

Originally written in Greek, the second half of the Christian canon of Scripture, consisting of twenty-seven books

Mark 1:1. The gospel of Jesus Christ

Acts 1:1–2. Recording the life and teaching of Jesus

2 Timothy 3:16. Inspired by God

2 Peter 3:15. Written with wisdom from God

Revelation 1:1. The revelation of Jesus Christ

▶ New year *(annual, calendar, season)*

Beginning of a new year, a tradition or holiday not bearing great significance in the Bible

Genesis 8:13. Symbolic of new creation

Exodus 40:2. Instructed to set up the tent of meeting

▶ Newborn Christians *(immature, young)*

Term referring to persons recently converted to Christianity and who (generally) need to grow in their faith and knowledge of Jesus Christ

Matthew 7:14. Entering the narrow gate

Matthew 13:44. Delighting in the kingdom of heaven

Luke 15:10. Angels rejoice over a new convert.

1 Corinthians 13:11. Putting aside childish ways

Ephesians 4:15. Growing up in Christ

Ephesians 4:22. Leaving behind old ways of living

Titus 3:5. The new birth

1 Peter 2:2. Desiring milk of the Word

1 John 2:14. Encouraging Christian growth

▶ Night(s) *(darkness, nightfall, sunset)*

The period of darkness within each twenty-four hour cycle

Genesis 1:5. Darkness called night

Deuteronomy 16:1. Brought out of Egypt at night

1 Samuel 28:8. Evil deeds done at night

Psalm 42:3. Time of anxiety

Psalm 91:5–6. Not fearing the night

Isaiah 27:3. The Lord protects during the watch of the night.

Matthew 2:14. Leaving under the cover of night

Matthew 4:2. Fasting forty days and nights

Mark 4.27. Time for sleeping

John 9:4. A coming night

1 Thessalonians 2:9. Working night and day

1 Thessalonians 5:6–7. Time of drunkenness

Revelation 22:5. Night will be no more.

▶ Nightmare *(dream, night terror, torment)*

A vision or dream which causes fear

Genesis 15:12. Dreadful, deep darkness

Genesis 41:1–8. Disturbed by a dream

Deuteronomy 28:66. Living in terror day and night

Job 4:13–14. Visions in the night

Psalm 91:5. No need to fear terrors of the night

Ecclesiastes 5:3. Caused by worrying too much

Daniel 2:1. Troubling dreams for the king

▶ Nile River *(river, snake, waters)*

A long river in Eastern Africa

Genesis 41:1. Dreaming of the Nile

Exodus 2:3. Abandoning Moses in the waters

Exodus 7:17–24. God's power of the river

Isaiah 7:18. Tributaries of the river

Amos 9:5. Flooding and receding waters

Zechariah 10:11. Drying up the deep river

▶ Noahic covenant *(mercy, salvation)*

God's promise to never bring about a catastrophic flood of this nature again

Genesis 9:8–11. God's covenant to all humanity

Genesis 9:12–16. The sign of the covenant

Isaiah 54:9. Remembering the covenant

▶ Nomad *(drifter, vagabond, vagrant)*

One who travels, wanders, or has no permanent abode

Genesis 14:13. Living in the sticks

Deuteronomy 26:5. Wandering people

Judges 19:9. Staying as a guest

Ezekiel 25:4. Threat of nomadic people

Hosea 2:14–15. Recalling the desert wandering of Israel

Hebrews 11:9. Living out of tents

▶ Non-Christian(s) *(heathen, nonbelievers, unbelievers)*

Someone who consciously or unconsciously rejects the Lord Jesus Christ as the Messiah

Matthew 9:23–24. Doubting the power of Jesus

Matthew 13:58. Hindering miracles

Romans 1:21. Minds closed toward God

1 Corinthians 1:18. The cross is foolish.

2 Timothy 3:7. Blinded toward the truth

Hebrews 4:1–2. Not believing the message heard

Hebrews 6:6. Leaving the faith

2 Peter 3:3–4. Slandering God and his promises

1 John 2:22–23. Rejecting Jesus as the Messiah

▶ Nonviolence *(diplomacy, passivity, peace)*

Using peaceful means to bring about political or social change

1 Chronicles 22:7–10. David the warrior forbidden to build God's temple

Psalm 33:16–17. Trusting in God, not military might

Isaiah 2:4. Peace among nations

Matthew 5:9. Blessed are the peacemakers

Matthew 5:43–45. Loving enemies

Luke 14:31–32. Negotiating peaceful terms

Romans 12:18. Living at peace with others

1 Peter 2:21–24. Enduring suffering without making threats

▶ North *(direction, geography, up)*

A geographical designation used for determining one's location

Exodus 26:20. On the north side

Joshua 19:27. Northern direction

1 Kings 7:25. Careful building plans

Proverbs 25:23. Wet northern wind

Isaiah 14:31. Enemies in the north

Jeremiah 3:12. Northern portion of the kingdom

Joel 2:20. Portion of the enemies' army

Amos 8:12. Symbolic of totality

▶ Nostalgia *(longing, recollection, reminiscence)*

Reminiscing about or longing for a happier past time

Exodus 16:2–3. Longing for Egypt

Haggai 2:3. Remember the former temple (house)

Luke 15:17. Remembering better days

Luke 16:25–27. Remembering a good life

▶ Nourishment *(diet, food, nutrition)*

Dietary necessities in order to assure good health

Genesis 1:29. Food given to humanity
Genesis 18:6–8. Preparing various foods
Exodus 34:15. Avoiding idol foods
Numbers 11:31. Quails covering the land
Deuteronomy 14:26. Eating well
Proverbs 3:8. A healthy body
Daniel 1:8–16. A vegetarian diet
Matthew 3:4. Strange form of nourishment
Mark 8:1–9. Feeding four thousand
John 21:9. Cooking out
Romans 11:17. Nourished from the roots

▶ Nudity *(bareness, naked, undressed)*

The state of being naked, without clothing
Genesis 2:25. Naked and unashamed
Genesis 3:7. Realizing nakedness
Genesis 9:20–25. Noah's drunken nakedness
Jeremiah 13:26. Naked and ashamed
Hosea 2:10. Judgment upon Gomer
Micah 1:8. An act of mourning
Nahum 3:5. Disgracefulness
Habakkuk 2:15. Drunken nakedness
Matthew 27:31. Stripping Jesus of his clothes
Mark 14:51–52. A naked man flees.
Luke 8:27. Demon-possessed man
Luke 10:30. Stripped and beaten
Romans 8:35. Unable to separate from the love of Christ

▶ Nuisance(s) *(annoyance, inconvenience, irritation)*

A person, place, or thing creating an inconvenience or annoyance
Deuteronomy 2:9. Leave Moab alone.
Psalm 56:2. Enemies that harass
Proverbs 6:3. Pestering a neighbor
Proverbs 27:3. A fool weighs you down.
Mark 5:35. Accused of bothering Jesus
Acts 4:2. Bothered by the apostles' teaching
Acts 16:18. Casting out a troubling spirit
2 Corinthians 11:9. Not asking for needs, counting on friends

▶ Nullify *(annul, cancel, void)*

The legal invalidation of an agreement, contract, or covenant
Mark 7:9. Rejecting God's commandments
Romans 3:3. Our unfaithfulness does not cancel God's faithfulness.
Romans 7:2. Marriage nullified at death
1 Corinthians 1:19. Nullifying the wisdom of the wise
Galatians 2:21. Accepting God's grace
Galatians 3:15. Impossible to nullify a contract
Ephesians 2:15. Creating unity through nullifying the commandments
2 Timothy 1:10. Death crushed to death
Hebrews 2:14. Destroying the devil

▶ Numbers *(numeral, symbol, unit)*

The use of numbers in the Bible can be either literal or symbolic.
Genesis 15:5. Vast number
Genesis 49:28. Twelve tribes of Israel
Exodus 20:10. Resting on the seventh day
Leviticus 25:8. Multiplication
Leviticus 27:18. Subtraction
Numbers 1:45–46. Addition
Deuteronomy 6:4. Only one God
1 Kings 17:12. Approximations
Revelation 7:9. An uncountable crowd
Revelation 13:18. Number of the beast
Revelation 14:1. The fullness of saints (12 x 12 x 1000)

▶ Nunc Dimittis *(prayer, prophecy, song)*

Latin phrase meaning "Now send forth;" used in reference to Simeon's blessing of Jesus in the temple
Luke 2:29–35. Prayer and prophecy

▶ Nutrition (see *Diets, Food, Nourishment*)

O

▶ Oath(s) *(pledge, promise, vow)*

A promise regarding future action which evokes the divine name

Genesis 22:16–18. An oath in the Lord's name

Leviticus 19:12. Misusing the name of the Lord

Deuteronomy 10:20. Sacrosanct

Deuteronomy 31:7–8. God's covenant with Israel

Isaiah 14:24. Assurance of a future

Matthew 5:34. Oaths prohibited

James 5:12. Letting yes be yes

▶ Obedience *(compliance, submission)*

Submitting to the wishes or authority of someone else

Exodus 19:5. Obeying God's promise

1 Samuel 15:22. Obedience is better than sacrifice.

Romans 5:19. Disobedience of Adam, obedience of Christ

Romans 6:17. Becoming obedient to God's teaching

Philippians 2:12. Obeying your leaders

Titus 3:1. Obeying authorities

1 John 2:4–6. Ignoring obedience

▶ Obeisance *(adoration, honor, respect)*

A gesture expressing respect, honor, or adoration typically to an authority such as a king

Genesis 49:8. Bowing down to brothers

2 Samuel 22:40. Opponents bow in respect.

Psalm 5:7. Reverence for God and His temple

Daniel 3:6. The price of refusing to honor the king

Matthew 4:9. Devil worship

1 Corinthians 14:25. Prostrate to the ground

Revelation 4:9–10. The elders bow before the throne.

▶ Obesity *(fat, overweight, stout)*

The condition of being excessively overweight

Deuteronomy 32:14–15. Forgetting God and overeating

Judges 3:22. A bulging belly

Job 15:27. Packing on the pounds

▶ Object lesson(s) of God *(example, illustration, model)*

A living, practical example of an idea or principle

Genesis 22:1–14. The sacrifice of Isaac

2 Samuel 12:1–15. Parable of David's disobedience

Isaiah 20:2–3. God tells Isaiah to wander around naked.

Hosea 1:2. Hosea ordered to marry a prostitute

Jonah 4:5–11. Jonah's lesson about compassion

Matthew 21:18–22. Cursing of the fig tree

Acts 10:9–33. Peter's lesson about clean and unclean

▶ Obligation *(commitment, duty, obligation)*

An action or responsibility one is duty-bound to accomplish

1 Samuel 21:7. Staying in the Lord's presence

Nehemiah 10:32. Caring for God's temple and priests

Romans 1:14. Obligation to minister to all

Romans 15:27. Taking care of others

1 Corinthians 9:16. Obliged to preach the Good News

Galatians 5:3. Under the obligation of the law

▶ Obstacles *(barrier, hurdle, stumbling block)*

A barrier blocking or inhibiting progress

Leviticus 19:14. Do not create obstacles for the less fortunate.

O

Isaiah 8:14. God obstructs His enemies.
Acts 15:22–35. Removing the barrier of circumcision
Romans 9:31–32. Stumbling over the law
Romans 14:13. Not creating obstacles in the faith of others
1 Corinthians 8:9. Careful exercise of freedom
1 Peter 2:8. Tripping over God's Word

▶ Obstinate *(inflexible, stubborn, unyielding)*

Stubbornly refusing to alter one's opinion or actions
Deuteronomy 2:30. God hardened a heart.
Jeremiah 11:8. Folly of ignoring God
Romans 2:5. Stirring up God's anger
Ephesians 4:18. Alienated from the life of God
Titus 1:7. Church leader must not be obstinate.
Hebrews 4:7. Command to avoid stubbornness

▶ Obstructions *(see Obstacles)*

▶ Occult *(magic, sorcery, witchcraft)*

Practices related to supernatural or magical belief and behavior
Leviticus 19:31. Magic is unclean.
Deuteronomy 18:10. Magic forbidden
Isaiah 2:6–8. God's people practicing superstition
Isaiah 44:25. Destroying the false prophets
Daniel 1:20. Wise men baffled
Acts 8:9–11. Simon amazes the crowd.
2 Thessalonians 2:9–10. False miracles
Revelation 21:8. Cast into the lake of fire

▶ Occupation(s) *(job, profession, work)*

A job performed for compensation
Genesis 46:33–34. Shepherds
Deuteronomy 18:1–2. Priestly role of the Levites
Matthew 20:2. Working in the vineyard
Acts 18:1–3. Tentmakers
2 Corinthians 6:4–6. Enduring hard things for the work of God
Colossians 3:23. Working wholeheartedly in all things
Colossians 4:14. Physicians
Titus 3:13. Lawyers

▶ Ocean *(deep, sea, waters)*

A large body of water which separates land
2 Samuel 22:16. God's power over His creation
Job 38:16. The depths of the ocean
Psalm 93:3. The rising ocean
Proverbs 8:27. Following the horizon
Isaiah 51:10. The power of God
Habakkuk 3:10. Large waves

▶ Odor *(smell, stench)*

A strong and distinctive smell
Joel 2:20. A foul odor of dead soldiers
John 11:39. The stench of a dead body

▶ Offend/Offense *(crime, hurt, transgression)*

Breaking of a rule or law which violates a legal or social norm
Genesis 31:36. What offense have I committed?
Leviticus 16:16. Atoning for offenses
1 Samuel 25:28. Asking for forgiveness
Matthew 13:57. A prophet without honor
Luke 7:23. Blessed for not being offended
Acts 25:8. Crimes against the temple or state
Galatians 5:11. The offense of the cross

▶ Offering(s) *(contribution, gifts, sacrifices)*

Something which is given or dedicated to God
Leviticus 1:3. Burnt offering
Leviticus 2:1. Grain offering
Leviticus 3:1. Fellowship offering
Leviticus 4:23. Sin offerings

Leviticus 5:6. Guilt offerings
Numbers 29:6. Regular offerings of God's people
Romans 12:1. Bodies as living sacrifices
Ephesians 5:2. Christ gave His life as an offering.
Hebrews 7:27. Once-for-all sacrifice
1 Peter 2:5. Spiritual sacrifices acceptable to God

▶ Officials *(authorities, leaders, rulers)*

Persons of authority in military service or legal and religious matters
Numbers 11:16. Moses appoints leaders.
2 Chronicles 26:11. Officials of the king
Mark 6:21. Officials of Herod
Acts 8:27. A foreign official
2 Corinthians 11:25. Troubling Roman officials
Titus 3:1. Government officials

▶ Oil *(ingredient, fuel, ointment)*

Used for cooking, trading, anointing, and medicinal purposes
Exodus 29:2. Consecration service of the priests
Leviticus 24:2. Lighting a lamp
1 Kings 5:11. Large amounts of olive oil
Esther 2:12. Oil of myrrh
Mark 6:13. Curing ailments
James 5:14. Anointing the sick with oil

▶ Old age *(aging, elderly, mature)*

The latter part of a person's life
Genesis 15:15. Promise of old age
Genesis 21:2. Having a child in old age
Genesis 24:36. Miraculous birth in old age
Ruth 4:15. Family taking care of family
Job 5:26. Time of death
Luke 1:36. Giving birth in old age

▶ Old Testament *(covenant, law, Scriptures)*

Originally in reference to the Hebrew Bible (and later Greek translations of the Hebrew Bible)
Mark 14:49. Fulfilling the Scriptures
Luke 24:27. Jesus taught through the Old Testament.
John 10:35–36. Scripture cannot be discredited.
Romans 15:4. Written to encourage us
1 Timothy 4:13. Encouraged to read publicly
2 Timothy 3:16. God-inspired

▶ Olive tree *(tree, wood)*

A tree in Palestine cultivated for olive oil
1 Kings 6:23. Construction with olive wood
Psalm 52:8. Symbol of friendship and peace
Jeremiah 11:16. A broken tree
Hosea 14:6. Beautiful trees
Luke 22:39–41. Meditating and praying on the Mount of Olives
Romans 11:17. Grafting in a wild olive branch

▶ Olivet Discourse *(apocalyptic or eschatological discourse)*

An extended eschatological teaching on the earthly situation in the latter days
Matthew 24:5–8. Exhortation to not be misled in the end
Matthew 24:9–13. Enduring persecution
Mark 13:14–20. Abomination of desolation
Mark 13:28–31. The Lord is near.
Mark 13:32–37. Being alert for the coming day

▶ Omen(s) *(portent, sign, signal)*

Signs or warnings indicating a future event or action
Genesis 24:14. Seeking information through chance
Leviticus 19:26. Interpreting omens forbidden
Numbers 24:1. Ceasing to look for omens
Joshua 10:12. Joshua asks the Lord for an omen.

▶ Omer *(ephah, measure)*

An ancient unit of measure, equivalent to half a gallon

Exodus 16:22. Four quarts
Exodus 16:36. Standard dry measure

▶ Omnipotence *(power, sovereignty, supremacy)*

In reference to God's power and sovereignty

Genesis 18:14. Is anything too hard for the Lord?
Numbers 23:19. God is able to keep His promises.
Psalm 115:3. God does whatever He wants.
Isaiah 55:11. Power of God's word
Jeremiah 32:17. Nothing is too hard for God.
Daniel 4:35. No one can oppose God.
Zechariah 8:6. Power of the Lord of Armies
Matthew 19:26. All things are possible for God.
2 Corinthians 6:18. The Lord Almighty
Galatians 4:9. False gods are weak and not powerful.
Ephesians 3:20. Doing infinitely more than we can ask

▶ Omnipresence *(boundless, everywhere, ubiquitous)*

God's unlimited presence with respect to time and space

1 Kings 8:27. God cannot be contained by space.
Psalm 139:7–10. Cannot hide from God
Isaiah 66:1–2. Present in heaven and earth
Jeremiah 23:23–24. God is both near and far.
John 4:20. Worshiping God from anywhere
Romans 8:9–10. God's Spirit lives in believers.
Colossians 1:17. God holds all things together.
Revelation 21:3. God's dwelling is with humanity.

▶ Omniscience *(all-knowing, knowledge, wise)*

The fact that God knows all things that can be known

Job 37:16. God knows everything.
Psalm 90:4. God's perfect knowledge
Psalm 139:1–2. Known by God
Psalm 147:5. No limit to the Lord's understanding
Isaiah 46:9–10. God who revealed the end from the beginning
Matthew 6:32. God's perfect knowledge
Hebrews 4:13. God sees all things.
1 John 3:20. God knows all things.

▶ Openness *(directness, honesty, vulnerable)*

Being forthright, telling the truth

Job 6:25. Painful discussions
Psalm 24:3–4. Honest before God
Psalm 32:5. Confessing sins to God
2 Corinthians 6:11. Vulnerability of the messenger
2 Corinthians 7:2. Opening hearts to trustworthy men
Galatians 4:16. Relational difficulty of being a truth-teller
1 John 1:9. Openness in confessing sin

▶ Opinion(s) *(belief, judgment, perspective)*

A view or judgment concerning something which is not necessarily based on factual information

Deuteronomy 17:9. Asking for an opinion
Job 32:6. Timid to share one's opinion
Proverbs 18:2. Fool's joy in expressing an opinion
Romans 14:1. Avoid arguments over differences of opinion
1 Corinthians 7:25. Paul gives his own perspective
2 Corinthians 8:10. A helpful opinion
2 Corinthians 10:5. Destroying lofty opinions

▶ Opportunist *(entrepreneur, pioneer, swindler)*

Taking advantage of circumstances for immediate personal gain

Mark 6:21–22. Seizing an opportunity
Luke 22:5–6. Money for betrayal

▶ Opportunity(ies) *(chance, moment, opening)*

A condition or set of circumstances that allows for the completion of something
1 Corinthians 16:9. Doing effective work
Galatians 6:10. Doing good for others
Ephesians 4:27. Preventing the devil from opportunities
Ephesians 5:16. Opportunities amidst evil days
Colossians 4:3. Praying for opportunities to share God's mystery
2 Peter 3:15. The Lord's patience

▶ Opposition *(enmity, hostility, resistance)*

Resistance expressed in action or argument against a person or idea
Job 17:2. Eyes focused on opposition
Luke 21:15. Able to stand against opposition
1 Corinthians 4:6. Wrongfully pitting believers against each other
Galatians 2:11. Paul opposes Cephas (Peter).
1 Thessalonians 2:2. Opposition to the Good News
2 Timothy 3:8. Enemies of the truth
Hebrews 12:3. Opposition which Jesus endured

▶ Oppression *(abuse, mistreat, persecution)*

Cruel or unjust treatment of people under an afflictive rule
Genesis 15:13. God's people oppressed in foreign land
Exodus 1:11. Israelites oppressed and forced to work as slaves
Deuteronomy 26:7. God hears the cries of the oppressed.
Judges 10:8. Oppression under bad leaders
Psalm 9:9. The Lord is a stronghold.
Proverbs 31:20. A righteous woman helps the oppressed.
Isaiah 1:17. Doing good
James 2:6. Rich oppressing the poor

▶ Optimism *(cheer, confidence, hope)*

Hope or confidence in the face of pending circumstances
Job 8:21. Joy which is to come
Psalm 118:24. Rejoicing and gladness
Jeremiah 29:10–11. Assurance in God's future plans
Ezekiel 13:10. False optimism
Romans 4:18. Abraham's hope in God's promise
2 Corinthians 5:6. Cheerful confidence
2 Thessalonians 2:16–17. Everlasting encouragement

▶ Option(s) *(alternative, choice(s), decision)*

A choice between two or more alternatives
Deuteronomy 11:26. Choosing between blessing or curse
Joshua 24:15. Choose who you will serve.
1 Kings 18:21. Following the Lord or false gods
1 Chronicles 21:10. The Lord gives three options.
Joel 3:14. Standing in the valley of decision
Philippians 1:23. Life with Christ preferred over present life
Hebrews 11:24–25. Making the difficult choice

▶ Opulence *(luxury, materialism, wealth)*

Extreme wealth or lavishness
Proverbs 19:10. Fools do not live in luxury.
Ecclesiastes 5:13. Riches lead to downfall.
Amos 6:4. Warning to those who are pampered
Luke 12:33. Valuing God's kingdom
1 Timothy 6:17. Confidence in God's riches
James 5:5. The danger of luxury

O

▸ Oracle *(message, revelation, word)*

A message of revelation from God given by a prophet

Numbers 24:16. The true message from God
Malachi 1:1. Divine revelation
Romans 3:2. Entrusted with God's oracles
1 Peter 4:11. Speaking God's words

▸ Orchestral music *(ensemble, music, strings)*

Music played by strings, woodwinds, and brass

Genesis 4:21. Early instrumentalist
2 Samuel 6:5. Celebrating in God's presence
1 Chronicles 15:16–24. The important role of music
Psalm 150:4. Praising God with stringed instruments
Daniel 3:5. Call to (false) worship

▸ Ordain/Ordination *(consecrate, set apart)*

The task of appointing leaders to the task of discipleship and church leadership

Mark 3:14. Apostles appointed
1 Timothy 4:14. Laying on of hands
1 Timothy 5:22. Do not hastily ordain.
2 Timothy 1:6. Developing the gifts of ministry
Titus 1:5. Appointing leaders

▸ Order *(command, commandments, instruction)*

A judgment or instruction given from a figure of authority

Deuteronomy 25:2. Authority of a judge
Joshua 4:16. Instructions for the priests
Romans 6:17. Obedience to God's teaching
Romans 15:4. Purpose of God's prior instruction
1 Timothy 5:17. Honor spiritual leaders.
Titus 1:9. Devoted to trustworthy teaching

▸ Ordinance(s) *(command, decree, instruction)*

A prescribed boundary for human behavior

Genesis 26:5. Blessed because of obedience
Deuteronomy 6:1. Teaching God's decrees
2 Chronicles 33:8. Obeying God's commands
Job 38:33. Knowing the ordinances of heaven
Ezekiel 43:18. Altar ordinances
Ephesians 2:14–15. Ordinances of the law abolished

▸ Ordinary *(common, normal, plain)*

An attitude or appearance which is normal or nondescript

Exodus 30:32. Perfume which is not for ordinary people
Amos 8:11. No ordinary famine
1 Corinthians 1:28. God worked through ordinary means.

▸ Organization *(arrangement, coordination, planning)*

A structured grouping of personnel or ideas

2 Samuel 6:1. Organizing good soldiers
1 Kings 5:12–18. Building the temple
Proverbs 15:22. Well-planned endeavors
Ezekiel 40:44–46. Organization of the priesthood
Acts 6:2–4. Organizing leadership within the body of Christ
1 Corinthians 12:28–31. Structure of church leadership
Colossians 2:5. Firm and ordered faith

▸ Original sin *(innate, guilt, sin)*

Doctrine that says all humanity is sinful on account of Adam (and Eve's) first sin

Genesis 3:1–19. The first sin by Adam and Eve
Psalm 14:3. No one is righteous.
Psalm 51:5. Born into sin
Jeremiah 17:9. The human mind is deceitful.
Romans 3:23. All have sinned.
Romans 5:12. Sin entered the world through Adam.
Romans 5:16. All condemned through one's failure

Romans 7:18. A corrupting nature

Romans 8:8. Impossible to please God with the corrupt nature

Ephesians 2:3. Following the corrupt nature

▶ Orphan *(child, fatherless)*

Parentless due to death or abandonment

Exodus 22:22–24. Commanded to care for orphans

Deuteronomy 26:12. Sharing with the less fortunate

Job 29:12. Friends caring for the helpless

Hosea 14:3. God's special concern for orphans

Malachi 3:5. Judgment against those who oppress orphans

James 1:27. Pure, unstained religion

▶ Outcast *(leper, outsider, reject)*

A person rejected or exiled from society

Exodus 29:33. Outsiders forbidden

2 Samuel 14:14. God's forgiveness toward outcasts

Psalm 147:2. The Lord gathers Israel's outcasts.

Jeremiah 30:17. Zion, the exiled outcast

Zephaniah 3:19. God's saving of the outcast

1 Corinthians 14:16. Outsiders in Christian congregations

1 Corinthians 14:24. Convincing an outsider

Ephesians 2:19. Gentiles are no longer outsiders to God's family.

▶ Outnumbered *(long shot, outmanned, weaker)*

Numerically and statistically falling short of something

Numbers 3:48. Buying back the firstborn Israelites

Deuteronomy 7:7. God chose an outnumbered nation.

Deuteronomy 7:17–18. Remembering former deliverance when presently outnumbered

Psalm 3:1. Many enemies attacking

Psalm 40:12. Sins which outnumber hairs on one's head

Philippians 3:18. Many living as enemies of the cross

▶ Outreach *(evangelism, gospel, mission)*

The act of Christian witness to the gospel of Christ in the world

Matthew 28:16–20. Called to make disciples

Acts 8:26–40. Personal evangelism

Galatians 2:7. Reaching out to circumcised and uncircumcised

Colossians 1:12. Sharing God's light

1 Peter 2:12. Living honorably among unbelievers

▶ Overconfidence *(brash, conceited, self-assured)*

Confidence or self-assurance based upon exaggerated self-opinion

Deuteronomy 1:41–42. Underestimating an enemy

Joshua 7:3–4. Overconfidence of one's strength

Isaiah 2:12. God will humble the arrogant.

2 Corinthians 12:7. Paul's affliction keeps him humble in the Lord.

Philippians 2:3. Avoid self or conceited actions.

▶ Overflowing *(bulging, overfull, spilling)*

The circumstance of having an abundance of something

Psalm 45:1. Overflowing with good news

Proverbs 18:4. Overflowing fountain of wisdom

Isaiah 66:12. Overflowing wealth

Romans 5:17. God's overflowing kindness

2 Corinthians 8:2. Joy in the midst of suffering

2 Corinthians 9:8. The gift of God's kindness

Ephesians 1:7. Forgiveness of failures because of God's kindness

O

▶ Overseer(s) *(elder, deacon, leader)*

An individual selected to serve the church in a capacity of leadership

Acts 14:23. Appointing elders

Ephesians 4:11. Multiple offices of gifts within the church

1 Timothy 3:1–2. Requirements of leaders

Hebrews 13:17. Submitting to the authority of leaders

James 5:14. Church leaders pray over the sick.

1 Peter 5:1–2. Shepherding the flock of God

▶ Ownership *(inheritance, possession, slavery)*

Possessing certain items

Exodus 22:8–12. Disputes about ownership of animals

John 13:16. Slaves and masters

Acts 16:19. Upsetting the owners

2 Corinthians 1:22. God's seal of ownership on us

Galatians 4:1. The rights of an heir

Ephesians 1:11. Receiving ownership in God's kingdom through Christ

1 Peter 2:18. Respecting an earthly owner

P

▶ Pacifism *(nonviolence, passive, peacemaker)*

Belief that violence, including war, is unwarranted and that peaceful resolution should always be sought

Isaiah 2:4. Peace which is to come
Hosea 2:18. Destroying all weapons
Romans 12:21. Conquering evil with good
1 Peter 3:9. Don't return evil with evil.

▶ Pagan *(heathen, nations, unbeliever)*

Someone who has religious practices outside of God's divine revelation to Israel and in Christ

2 Kings 23:5. Cleaning up worship practices
Proverbs 5:10. Working in a pagan household
Zephaniah 1:4. Separating out faithful priests from pagan priests
1 Corinthians 12:2. Worshiping pagan gods
1 Timothy 5:8. Actions worse than pagans

▶ Paid in full *(complete, final, whole)*

Paying a debt off once and for all

Leviticus 27:27. Getting a full refund
Ezra 6:8. Full payment made so that work is not interrupted
John 19:30. A finished payment of Jesus' life
Romans 13:7. Paying what you owe
Philippians 4:18. Repaying kindness
1 John 2:2. Payment for the sins of the world

▶ Pain *(agony, hurt, suffering)*

Physical or emotional suffering

Genesis 3:16. Pains of childbirth increased because of sin
Ecclesiastes 1:18. With knowledge comes heartache.
Isaiah 14:3. A promise of relief
Matthew 24:8. Pains of the end time
Hebrews 10:32. Keeping perspective on suffering
Hebrews 12:11. With discipline comes pain.
1 Peter 2:19. Pleasing God through enduring unjust pain
Revelation 21:4. The end of pain

▶ Palace *(citadel, stronghold, temple)*

A large residential building that houses a ruler and accompanying administration

1 Kings 3:1. Building the citadel
2 Kings 20:18. Serving in a foreign palace
Daniel 1:4. A place of learning
Amos 3:11. Destruction of the stronghold
Matthew 26:3. Gathering at the palace

▶ Panic *(anxiety, fear, hysteria)*

Sudden uncontrollable anxiety or fear

Exodus 14:24. Egyptians panic at God's coming judgment.
2 Samuel 17:2. Tired and weak, susceptible to panic
Psalm 53:5. No reason for panic
Zechariah 14:13. Panic from the Lord
Mark 16:6. Initial panic when Jesus' body is gone
1 Peter 5:7. Turning over anxiety to God

▶ Parable(s) *(allegory, fable, story)*

A normal story which is used for the purpose of illustrating a religious truth

Matthew 13:10–23. Reason for speaking in parables
Matthew 13:36–43. Jesus explains a parable.
Matthew 21:33–46. Parable of the tenants
Matthew 22:1–14. Parable of the wedding banquet
Luke 10:25–37. The good Samaritan
Luke 15:11–32. Parable of the prodigal son

▶ Parade(s) *(caravan, march/marching, procession)*

A public procession of people in a time of celebration or display of military strength

Joshua 6:15. Marching around the city walls

Judges 11:34. Dancing in the streets
2 Samuel 15:18. Marching past the king
Psalm 12:8. Parading around in wickedness
Isaiah 63:1. Announcing victory
Mark 11:1–11. A triumphal entry

▶ Paradise *(garden, glory, heaven)*

A heavenly abode where God's people ultimately dwell
Genesis 2:8. Paradise garden
Song of Songs 4:13. Bodies like paradise
Luke 23:43. Jesus promises paradise to a dying man.
2 Corinthians 12:3–4. Vision of paradise
Revelation 2:7. Promise of eating of a paradise tree

▶ Parasite(s) *(affliction, disease, sickness)*

An organism that lives by feeding off the nutrients of a host
Isaiah 51:8. Worms that devour
Isaiah 66:24. Worms and corpses
Jonah 4:7. A worm destroys a plant.
Revelation 8:11. Water turned into wormwood

▶ Parchment *(skin, surface)*

A prepared animal skin used as a writing surface
2 Timothy 4:13. Bring the parchments.

▶ Pardon *(absolve, forgive, mercy)*

Forgiving or being forgiven of an offense before God or a fellow human
Exodus 34:9. Asking the Lord for pardon
Psalm 25:11. Forgiveness for the sake of the Lord's name
Hosea 11:7. No pardon for rebellion
Micah 7:18. No one like God
Mark 11:25. Forgiving others
Luke 7:39–50. Grateful for forgiveness
Romans 4:8. No longer considered sinful
Romans 5:10. Restored relationship with God through Christ
2 Corinthians 2:5–11. Congregational forgiveness
Colossians 3:13. Forgive as the Lord forgave you.

▶ Parent(s) *(father, guardian, mother)*

The biological (or legal) guardian of a child
Exodus 20:12. Commanded to honor parents
Psalm 27:10. God's care when parents fail
Proverbs 10:1. Making parents happy
Proverbs 13:24. Disciplining a child
Joel 1:3. Generational message
2 Corinthians 12:14. Parents provide for their children.
Ephesians 6:1. Commanded to obey parents

▶ Pariahs *(lepers, outcast, rejects)*

A person or group of people who have been rejected or exiled from society
2 Chronicles 26:21. Living in a separate house due to uncleanness
Matthew 8:2–3. Jesus heals an outcast.
Luke 10:29–37. The Samaritan outcast helps a man in need.
John 4:1–26. Societal outcasts

▶ Parole *(pardon, release)*

Release of a prisoner before the full sentence has been carried out
Matthew 27:16–26. The prisoner Barabbas is freed.
Acts 16:25–35. Paul and Silas released from prison

▶ Parousia *(rapture, second coming)*

Greek term for the return of Christ
Matthew 24:44. An unexpected time
John 14:3. Jesus promises to come again.
Acts 1:11. Returning in the same way that He left
Philippians 3:20. Eagerly awaiting Christ's coming
1 Thessalonians 4:16. Coming from heaven with a command
Titus 2:12–13. Awaiting our hope
Hebrews 9:28. Appearing a second time to save those who wait

Hebrews 10:25. The day is drawing near.
James 5:8. The Lord is near.
2 Peter 3:10. Coming like a thief in the night
Revelation 1:7. Coming in the clouds
Revelation 22:20. I am coming soon.

▶ Parsimonious *(cheap, frugal, stingy)*

An attitude of unwillingness to spend one's own resources

Deuteronomy 15:9. Being careful to avoid stinginess
Deuteronomy 28:54. Frugality during a time of devastation
Proverbs 23:6. Avoiding those who are stingy
Proverbs 28:22. Warning against being cheap

▶ Partiality *(bias, favoritism, prejudice)*

A predisposition to favoring something or someone over another

Genesis 37:4. Joseph is loved more than his brothers.
Deuteronomy 10:17. No need to play favorites or take bribes
Job 32:21. Promise to avoid partiality
Proverbs 24:23. Do not show partiality when judging.
Galatians 2:6. So-called important people
Ephesians 6:9. Treating all slaves with respect
1 Timothy 5:21. Called to impartiality

▶ Participation *(association, contribution, involvement)*

One's involvement in a particular action

Joshua 23:12–13. Associating with an enemy of God
1 Corinthians 10:21. Participating at two divergent tables
2 Corinthians 8:4. Begging to participate in the ministry
2 Corinthians 8:7. Encouraged to participate in God's work
1 Timothy 5:22. Keep away from the sins of others.
Revelation 18:4. Avoiding sin

▶ Partnership *(associates, collaboration, relationship)*

A relationship between two or more of commitment, collaboration, or covenant making

Psalm 94:20. Can God associate with wicked partners?
Proverbs 29:24. Ill fate of a thief's partner
Luke 5:7. Business associates
1 Corinthians 1:9. Partnership with Christ
1 Corinthians 7:15. Dissolving a marriage
1 Corinthians 10:20. Partners with demons
Colossians 4:7. Sending a partner in my place
Hebrews 3:1. Partners in a heavenly calling

▶ Partying *(celebrating, excess, revelry)*

A social practice of celebration

Judges 14:10. Throwing a wedding party
Job 1:4. Eating, drinking, and fellowship
Ecclesiastes 10:16. Early morning parties
Galatians 5:20–21. Living under the influence of the sinful nature
1 Peter 4:3. Wild parties
2 Peter 2:13. Sinfully taking pleasure in being known for wild parties

▶ Passion(s) *(enthusiasm, sensation, strong emotion)*

Feelings which are consuming and difficult to control

Ecclesiastes 9:6. Losing the zest for life
Romans 1:26. Shameful passions which control
Romans 7:5. Sinful passions at work
Galatians 5:24. Crucifying passions of the flesh
Colossians 3:5. Putting worldly passions to death
1 Thessalonians 4:5. Blinded by passion
Revelation 14:8. Passionate sexual sins

P

▸ Passion, the *(death, suffering)*

Events surrounding the suffering and death of Jesus

Matthew 26:57–68. Jesus sentenced to death

Matthew 27:28–29. The soldiers mock Jesus.

Matthew 27:35. Jesus crucified

Mark 14:36. Jesus prays in the garden.

Luke 23:35–37. The crowds mock Jesus as He is dying.

▸ Passover *(see Festival, Lord's Supper)*

▸ Past *(former, history, previous)*

A period of time which has passed

Isaiah 43:18. Forgetting the past

Romans 3:25. God's patience for sins in the past

Ephesians 3:9. Things hidden in the past

Colossians 1:26. Mystery of the past has been revealed.

Hebrews 10:32. Remember the origins of belief.

1 Peter 4:3. A past life

2 Peter 3:2. Remember God's work in history.

▸ Pastor *(elder, bishop, overseer)*

Someone who oversees the theology and teaching of a body of believers

Acts 20:28. Watching over God's church

1 Timothy 3:2–7. Qualifications of a pastor

1 Timothy 4:14. Developing pastoral gifts

1 Timothy 5:17. Highly honoring spiritual leaders

Hebrews 13:17. Obeying church leaders

1 Peter 5:2. Shepherds of God's flock

▸ Pastoral letters *(letter writing)*

The three letters ascribed to Paul: 1 and 2 Timothy and Titus

1 Timothy 6:20. Called to guard the Good News

2 Timothy 4:2. Charged to spread the word of God

Titus 2:1. Teaching others how to live rightly

▸ Pasture *(field, grassland, meadow)*

An open area of land used for keeping and feeding animals

Numbers 35:3. Pastureland of the Levites

Joshua 21:42. Food source for large cities

1 Chronicles 6:55. Given a territory and pastureland

Isaiah 5:17. A field of lambs

Ezekiel 34:14. Promise of a good pasture

Ezekiel 34:31. Sheep of God's pasture

▸ Path(s) *(road, trail, way)*

A road which one travels

Psalm 25:10. Paths of mercy

Proverbs 2:8. Walking on the path of justice

Proverbs 3:5–6. The Lord will make your path smooth.

Acts 2:28. The path of life

2 Peter 2:15. Leaving the straight path

Jude 11. Following the wrong path

▸ Patience *(forbearance, mercy, restraint)*

Forbearance or restraint in a situation which would otherwise warrant action

Exodus 34:6. God is patient and willing to forgive.

1 Corinthians 13:7. Love is patient.

Galatians 5:22. Fruit of the spirit

Ephesians 4:2. Being patient with others

Hebrews 6:13–15. Waiting patiently for God's promises

James 5:10. Patience in the midst of suffering

2 Peter 3:9. The Lord's slowness to return is patience.

▸ Patriarch *(father, leader, ancestor, paterfamilias)*

Denotes the male head of a family

Joshua 14:1. The heads of Israel's tribes

Acts 2:29. The patriarch David

Acts 5:30. The God of our ancestors

Romans 9:5. Christ is descended from the patriarchs.

Hebrews 7:4. Abraham, father of God's chosen people

▶ Patricide *(murder, killing)*

The killing of one's father

Exodus 20:12. Honor your father and mother.

Exodus 20:13. Murder forbidden

Isaiah 37:38. Sennacherib murdered by his sons

▶ Patriotism *(jingoism, loyal, nationalism)*

Extreme and often defensive loyalty to one's country

2 Samuel 10:12. Strong on behalf of our people

2 Kings 7:9. Spreading the news

Psalm 122:6–7. Prayer for the peace of Jerusalem

Isaiah 62:1. Speaking on behalf of country

Hebrews 11:24–26. Faithful to his own people

▶ Patrolling *(guard, monitor, watch)*

Keeping guard or watching over something or someone

Genesis 3:24. Patrolling the tree of life

Exodus 12:42. God's watch over His people

Nehemiah 7:3. Standing guard

Zechariah 1:10. God's command to patrol the earth

Zechariah 6:7. Strong horses patrol the earth.

▶ Patronage *(benefaction, gift, grace)*

Support given by patron to a client

Acts 16:14–15. Lydia becomes Paul's patron.

Philippians 4:16. Providing for Paul's needs

Philippians 4:18. Paul receives gifts.

▶ Pattern *(example, image, model)*

An example which others follow

Genesis 1:26. Humans patterned after God's image

Exodus 25:9. Following the pattern

2 Kings 16:10. A model of the altar

2 Timothy 1:13. Pattern of accurate teaching

Hebrews 8:5. Temple as a pattern of what is heaven

▶ Payments *(earnings, wages, reimbursements)*

The action of paying or being paid in return for goods sold or services rendered

Exodus 21:11. Buying freedom

Isaiah 65:7. Repaying the sins of ancestors

Romans 6:23. Payment for sin is death.

1 Peter 1:18–19. Good and bad payments

1 John 2:2. Payment for the sins of the world

1 John 4:10. God's Son was a payment for sins.

▶ Peace *(completeness, soundness, well-being)*

Refers to wellness, safety, or spiritual soundness

Numbers 6:24–26. A prayer of peace

Proverbs 3:1–2. The peace of sound teaching

Matthew 5:9. Blessed are the peacemakers.

John 14:27. Offer of God's peace

1 Corinthians 14:33. The God of peace

Galatians 5:22. Produced by the spiritual nature

Philippians 4:7. God's peace guarding thoughts

Colossians 1:20. Peace through the cross

Hebrews 12:14. Living at peace with others

▶ Peace talks *(conference, discussion)*

Diplomatic conversations aimed at ending or avoiding conflict

Genesis 13:8. Making peace in the family

Genesis 37:4. Strained relationship

Deuteronomy 20:10–11. Offering peace before war

Judges 11:13. Attempts at diplomacy
1 Samuel 29:7. Avoiding displeasing an enemy
Matthew 5:9. Blessed are the peacemakers.

▶ Pearl of great price *(precious gem, kingdom of God)*

A highly valued gem; Jesus compared the value of the pearl with the kingdom of God
Job 28:18. Wisdom more valuable than pearls
Matthew 7:6. Pearls and pigs
Matthew 13:45–46. Finding a valuable pearl
1 Timothy 2:9. Outward adornment

▶ Peer pressure *(acceptance, approval, pressure)*

Social pressure exerted by one's peer group to take certain actions, adopt values, or conform in some way in order to gain acceptance
Exodus 23:2. Never follow the crowd.
Psalm 1:1–2. Leaving behind the advice of the wicked
Proverbs 1:10–19. Avoiding the path of sinners
1 Corinthians 15:33–34. Influence of bad company
Galatians 1:10. Seek only God's approval.
Galatians 2:11–13. Social pressures
Hebrews 10:24. Good peer pressure

▶ Penalty *(judgment, punishment, retribution)*

A punishment imposed for the breach of an accepted code of conduct
Leviticus 22:16. Paying the penalty for misdeeds
Numbers 35:31. Death penalty
Proverbs 13:13. Price of despising God's words
2 Thessalonians 1:9. An eternal penalty
1 John 4:18. Punishment and fear

▶ Penitence *(guilt, repentance, sorrow)*

Experiencing and admitting regret for one's actions
2 Kings 22:19. A change of heart
Job 42:5–6. Job repents for questioning God.
Psalm 78:34. Turning to God
Luke 5:32. Calling sinners to change
2 Corinthians 7:10. Changing the way one thinks and acts
2 Peter 3:9. God wants all to repent.
Revelation 2:5. Turning to righteous ways

▶ Pentecost *(fiftieth, Festival of Weeks/Harvest)*

The day when the Spirit descended on God's people
Acts 2:1. Festival gathering at Jerusalem
Acts 20:16. Trying to get to Jerusalem for Pentecost
1 Corinthians 16:8. Paul mentions Pentecost.

▶ People(s) *(humans, nations)*

Generally used to denote nationality, people(s) can refer to tribes, nations, or groups.
Genesis 1:27. Creation of people
Genesis 7:21. Destruction of peoples
Genesis 18:18. All nations blessed through Abraham
Exodus 32:10. Promise of a great nation
Job 12:23. God rules over nations.
Isaiah 49:6. Light unto the nations
Amos 9:7. God cares for all nations.
1 Peter 2:9. A chosen people
2 John 7. Deceptive people

▶ Perception *(awareness, realization, understanding)*

One's ability to use the human senses to understand something
Judges 6:22. Realization of God's messenger
Mark 4:12. Failed perception
John 4:19. Perceiving a prophet
Acts 17:22. Perceived religiosity
Ephesians 3:4. You can perceive my insight when you read this.

▶ Perfection *(betterment, improvement, refinement)*

The biblical ideal of becoming increasingly conformed into the image of God

Deuteronomy 32:4. God's faithful actions
Psalm 18:32. A straight way
Matthew 5:48. Be perfect as God is perfect.
Matthew 19:21. Difficulty of attaining perfection
1 Peter 1:18–19. A perfect sacrifice
1 John 1:8–10. Falsely claiming perfection

▶ Performing *(amusing, delighting, entertaining)*

Entertaining others with song, dance, humor, and so forth

Judges 16:25. Comedic relief
1 Samuel 10:5. Performing music
Mark 6:22. A stunning performance
Luke 15:25. Party performance

▶ Perfume(s) *(aroma, fragrance, smell)*

A fragrant substance used variously for its pleasing aroma

Exodus 30:25. Holy perfume
Ruth 3:3. Freshening up
2 Chronicles 16:14. Preparing for the deceased
Psalm 133:2. Anointed with pleasant oil
Proverbs 27:9. Warming the heart
John 12:3. Pure (expensive) nard

▶ Perjury *(deception, falsehood, lying)*

Violating an oath or vow by swearing to something untrue

Jeremiah 5:2. Lying about an oath
Jeremiah 7:9. Bad behavior
Hosea 10:4. Many bad actions
Malachi 3:5. Providing false witness
1 Timothy 1:10. Lying under oath

▶ Permanence *(abiding, endurance, stability)*

The state of being lasting or abiding

Genesis 17:8. A permanent possession
Exodus 12:14. A permanent law
Numbers 25:13. Permanent positions
1 Corinthians 9:25. A permanent crown
1 Corinthians 13:8–12. Permanence of love
Hebrews 7:24. A permanent priesthood
Hebrews 13:14. An abiding city

▶ Permission *(approval, authorization, consent)*

Giving one's consent for carrying something out

Ezra 5:13. Permission to rebuild the temple
Psalm 24:3–4. Permission to enter God's presence
Matthew 10:29. God's sovereignty over all things great and small
John 19:38. Permission to move Jesus' body
Acts 21:40. Permission to speak
Hebrews 6:3. God permitting

▶ Persecution *(martyrdom, oppression, suffering)*

Physical or verbal maltreatment for believing in the Christian message

Mark 10:30. Life now and then
John 15:20. Persecution promised
Romans 8:35. Unable to separate us from the love of Christ
2 Corinthians 12:10. Strength in weakness
Galatians 6:17. Scars of persecution which demonstrate allegiance
2 Thessalonians 1:4. Persecution which brought growth
2 Timothy 3:11. Rescued from persecutions

▶ Perseverance *(commitment, endurance, patience)*

Steadfastness and endurance in living out Christian faith

Matthew 24:13. Persevering to the end
Romans 8:25. Eagerly awaiting coming hope

Romans 12:12. Patience in times of trouble
Ephesians 6:18. Persevering in prayer
Hebrews 12:1. Running the race of faith
James 5:11. Blessed because of perseverance
1 John 2:19. Those who fail to persevere

▸ Persians *(Aryan, nations, peoples)*

A tribe of people who eventually settled on the eastern side of the Persian Gulf

2 Chronicles 36:23. Cyrus's policy of tolerance for captured people
Ezra 1:7. A Persian king
Nehemiah 12:22. Darius the Persian
Esther 1:19. Ruling over the Persians
Daniel 6:28. Prospering under Persian reign

▸ Persistence *(perseverance)*

Firm and repeated action, often in spite of opposition

Nehemiah 4:6. Working with determination
Jeremiah 7:13. Ignoring persistent talk
Romans 2:7. Persisting in goodness
1 Timothy 4:16. Persisting in faithful life
1 Timothy 5:20. Fate of those who persistent in sin

▸ Personified aspects of God *(embodiment, incarnation, representation)*

Descriptions of God's essence in ways that make sense to human beings

Genesis 3:8. God walking
Genesis 32:30. Seeing the face of God
Exodus 8:19. The hand of God
Proverbs 1:20. Wisdom
Amos 9:8. The eyes of the Lord
John 1:1. The Logos (the Word)
1 Corinthians 1:24. Christ, the wisdom of God

▸ Perspective *(opinion, position, view)*

A point of view

1 Corinthians 10:18. Judging from a human viewpoint
1 Corinthians 15:34. Returning to the right viewpoint

▸ Persuasion *(coaxing, convincing, enticing)*

The rhetorical skill of convincing others of a particular action or viewpoint

Psalm 141:4. Avoiding evil persuasions
Matthew 27:20. Crowd control
Luke 16:31. Persuasion impossible
Acts 17:4. Effective ministry
1 Corinthians 2:4. Avoiding fancy rhetoric
2 Corinthians 5:11. Persuading others

▸ Perversion *(immorality, wickedness)*

Sexual misconduct which is condemned by God and not befitting of God's people

Leviticus 18:17. Sex with multiple family members forbidden
Leviticus 19:29. Offering a daughter as a prostitute
Habakkuk 1:4. Justice perverted
Romans 6:19. Forsaking perversion
2 Corinthians 12:21. Grieved over perversion
Galatians 5:19. Corrupt nature
Ephesians 5:5. No inheritance in God's kingdom
Colossians 3:5. Put worldly ways to death.

▸ Pessimism *(despair, despondency, hopelessness)*

The propensity to focus disproportionately on negative aspects of things

Exodus 16:3. Doubting God's provision
Numbers 14:36–38. Doubting God
Job 3:25. Overtaken with fear
Job 9:25. Death is approaching.
Ecclesiastes 1:2. Meaningless life

▸ Pestilence *(epidemic, plague)*

A plague which causes physical affliction or death

Deuteronomy 32:24. Judgment

Psalm 91:3. Delivered from death
Jeremiah 21:6. To the death
Ezekiel 5:12. Pestilence in the latter days
Revelation 6:8. Famine and pestilence

▶ Petition *(intercession, prayer, requests)*

A prayer in which one presents requests to God
Nehemiah 1:11. A leader prays.
Psalm 4:1. Calling out to God
Luke 1:13. God hears the prayer of Zechariah.
1 Timothy 2:1. Interceding for others
Hebrews 5:7. God heard Jesus' prayers.

▶ Pharaoh(s) *(king, ruler, sovereign)*

The sovereign ruler of Egypt
Genesis 12:15–20. Abram before Pharaoh
Genesis 37:36. Joseph sold to Pharaoh
Exodus 1:22. Ethnic cleansing
Exodus 5:1. Moses before Pharaoh
Exodus 11:9–10. A hardened heart

▶ Pharisee(s) *(pious, separatist, zealous)*

One of several Jewish sects known for precise and minute interpretation of God's law
Matthew 3:7. Pharisees and Sadducees
Matthew 5:20. Scribes and Pharisees
Matthew 23:13. Preventing others from entering kingdom of heaven
Luke 5:17. Experts in the law of Moses
Acts 23:6. Paul was a Pharisee.

▶ Philadelphians *(people)*

Inhabitants of the Roman province of Philadelphia located in Asiatic Turkey
Revelation 3:7–13. Letter to a faithful church

▶ Philanthropy *(beneficence, generosity, welfare)*

Promotion of the welfare of others through giving of time, money, and services
Leviticus 25:35–43. Caring for your own people
Psalm 41:1. Blessing on philanthropists
Proverbs 3:27–28. Not holding back
Isaiah 58:7–12. Caring for the hungry
Matthew 5:42. Giving to those who ask
Galatians 2:10. Eager philanthropist
1 Timothy 5:8. Failure to take care of others
James 2:15–16. Meeting physical needs
1 John 3:17. Helping other believers

▶ Philistine(s) *(enemy, Goliath, sea people)*

A longstanding enemy of Israel living in Philistia (modern Lebanon) off the coast of the Mediterranean Sea
Genesis 10:14. Origin of Philistines
Judges 3:2–3. Used to punish Israel
Judges 10:6–7. Israel judged for adopting Philistine gods
1 Samuel 5:1–6:21. Philistines and the ark
1 Samuel 13:19–22. Philistine war strategy
1 Samuel 17:1–51. David kills the Philistine
2 Kings 18:8. Philistines subdued

▶ Philosophy *(belief, reason, thinking)*

Refers in Scripture to erroneous teachings that run contrary to God's truth
Isaiah 29:14. Wisdom and intelligence taken away
Acts 17:18. Paul talks with philosophers.
1 Corinthians 1:19–20. Wisdom turned into nonsense
Colossians 2:8. Careful of misleading philosophy

▶ Phoenicians *(Canaanites, people)*

People who lived on the Mediterranean coastal plain
Matthew 15:21. Coastal cities of Phoenicia
Mark 7:26. Syrophoenician woman
Acts 11:19. Scattering throughout Phoenician territory
Acts 15:3. Traveling as missionaries among Phoenician territory

P

▶ Phony *(dishonest, false, hypocritical)*

Disingenuous or misleading behavior

Daniel 2:9. Giving a phony explanation

Matthew 23:5–7. Extreme phoniness

2 Timothy 3:13. Phony preachers

1 Peter 2:1. Getting rid of hypocrisy

▶ Phylactery *(amulet, box, means of protection)*

Small leather box which contained small strips of parchment containing key teachings for God's people

Deuteronomy 6:4–9. Wearing God's words as a reminder

Deuteronomy 11:18–21. Recording words as a reminder

Matthew 23:5. Phylacteries for all to see

▶ Physician *(diviner, doctor, caregiver)*

Someone who is trained in the practice of medicine

Genesis 50:2. Doctors and morticians

2 Chronicles 16:12. Trusting doctors rather than God

Job 13:4. Worthless physicians

Jeremiah 8:11. Careless care

Matthew 9:12. Healthy people do not need a doctor.

Mark 5:25–26. Failed care

Colossians 4:14. Luke, the physician

▶ Physics *(discipline, knowledge, science)*

The scientific discipline concerned with the nature of matter and energy

Proverbs 16:33. Seemingly random outcomes controlled by God

Acts 17:28. In Him we live and move and have our being.

Colossians 1:16. All things created by God

Colossians 1:17. Christ holds all things together.

Hebrews 1:3. Upholding all things by His word

▶ Piety *(devotion, godliness, holiness)*

The quality of being religiously devout

2 Corinthians 7:1. Fear of the Lord

1 Timothy 5:4. Showing piety at home

2 Timothy 3:5. Appearance of piety

Titus 1:1. Leading others in piety

2 Peter 1:3. Power for piety

2 Peter 3:11. Holy, godly lives

▶ Pig(s) *(hog, swine, unclean)*

A domesticated animal raised for its meat, ceremonially unclean in Old Testament

Leviticus 11:7. Eating pigs forbidden

Matthew 7:6. Folly of throwing pearls to pigs

Matthew 8:30–31. Demons sent into pigs

Luke 15:15–16. Eating with the pigs

Acts 10:9–16. Peter's vision and the cleanliness of all animals

▶ Pilgrimage *(expedition, journey, mission)*

A journey to an important place of religious or social significance

Genesis 17:8. Land of pilgrimage

Genesis 47:9. Earthly pilgrimage

Luke 2:41. Pilgrimage to Jerusalem

Acts 8:27–28. Returning from a pilgrimage to Jerusalem

Hebrews 11:13. No permanent home on earth

1 Peter 2:11. Temporary residents

▶ Pillar(s) *(column, post, support)*

A tall vertical structure used in architecture for supporting a building

Genesis 19:26. Pillar of salt

Exodus 13:21. Pillars to guide the people in the wilderness

Numbers 12:5. Pillar of smoke indicating God's presence

Judges 16:25–30. Samson pushes the pillars.

1 Kings 7:2. Pillars of cedar

Job 9:6. Only God shakes the pillars of the earth.

Proverbs 9:1. Seven pillars in a house of wisdom

Galatians 2:9. Human pillars of the church
1 Timothy 3:15. Church is a pillar of truth.
Revelation 3:12. People as pillars in God's temple

▶ Pistachio(s) *(food, nut, seed)*

The delectable green seed of an Asiatic tree
Genesis 43:11. Fine products brought as a gift

▶ Pit(s) *(cistern, hole, well)*

A deep hole, either occurring naturally or dug artificially
Psalm 30:3. Called back from the pit
Psalm 40:2. Called back to fullness of life
Proverbs 1:12. The grave as a pit
Matthew 12:11. Rescuing an animal from a pit
Revelation 9:1–2. Bottomless pit

▶ Pitfall(s) *(danger, hazard, risk)*

An unsuspected or uncalculated danger
Deuteronomy 7:16. Pitfall of worshiping foreign gods
Judges 8:27. Following after an idol
Psalm 141:9. Distanced from troublemakers
Proverbs 29:6. Sin is like bait in trap.
Lamentations 3:47. Problems approaching us
2 Corinthians 11:29. Apostolic empathy
Galatians 6:1. Helping others avoid and escape pitfalls
1 Timothy 6:9. Pitfalls of wealth
James 1:14. Desires which lure and tempt

▶ Plague(s) *(affliction, disease, pestilence)*

A sickness or infestation of epidemic proportions
Exodus 7:14–25. The first of ten plagues on Egypt
Numbers 11:33. Judgment from God
2 Samuel 24:21. Stopping of a plague
1 Kings 8:37–38. Troubling disaster
Psalm 91:10. Safety from plagues
Revelation 16:21. Plagues of oversized hail

▶ Plan(s) *(goal, intention, providence)*

Planning may be used in reference to both human and divine thinking
Genesis 50:20. God's plan to bring about good
Nehemiah 4:15. God frustrates the plans of humanity.
Psalm 33:10. Plans of the nations frustrated
Proverbs 16:3. Trusting efforts to God
Jeremiah 29:11. Assurance of life in God's plan
Acts 2:23. God's definite plan for Jesus
Ephesians 1:10. Culmination of history in Christ
Ephesians 3:9. Plan of mystery which was hidden until now

▶ Planet(s) *(body, moon, star)*

A celestial body which orbits around a star
Isaiah 14:12. Venus, the morning star
Amos 5:26. Idol gods dedicated to Saturn

▶ Plant(s) *(flower, greenery, vegetation)*

Creation of God as a source of food, clothing, tools, and constructed into a writing surface
Genesis 1:11. Vegetation created
Genesis 30:14. Mandrakes
Exodus 12:22. Hyssop plant
1 Kings 19:4–5. Broom plant
Song of Songs 2:1. Roses and lilies
Matthew 6:28–29. Majesty of plants' decorum
Mark 4:31. A tiny mustard seed
John 19:29. A long reed

▶ Plea(s) *(prayers, requests, supplication)*

An emotional and often urgent request made to God
1 Kings 8:30. Pleas for mercy
Job 13:6. Pleading for God's attention
Psalm 6:9. God hears the pleas of His people.
Psalm 17:1. A plea for justice

Isaiah 1:23. Ignoring the pleas of widows
Luke 5:12. Pleading for healing
2 Corinthians 8:4. Begging to participate in God's gracious work

▶ Pleasure *(delight, happiness, joy)*

A deep feeling of satisfaction and enjoyment
Psalm 5:4. God does not take pleasure in wickedness.
Psalm 32:11. Gladness in the Lord
Psalm 37:4. Delighted in the Lord
Isaiah 57:8. Idol pleasures
Romans 7:22. Delighting in God's law
1 Corinthians 10:31. Living for God's glory
Philippians 1:25. Growing in joyful faith
James 4:3. Seeking pleasure the wrong way

▶ Pledge *(oath, promise, vow)*

A promise made or security put up for a debt
Genesis 38:17–20. Pledging payment
Deuteronomy 24:10–12. Reasonable actions for receiving pledged payment
1 Samuel 18:3. Pledge of loyalty
2 Chronicles 29:10. Pledge unto the Lord
2 Corinthians 1:22. Spirit given as a guarantee
2 Timothy 1:14. Guarding the trusted deposit

▶ Pleiades *(constellation, sky, stars)*

A well-known cluster of stars in the Taurus constellation
Job 9:9. God's creation of the heavenly bodies
Job 38:31. Human power compared with God's
Amos 5:8. God's power emphasized through creation

▶ Plenty *(affluence, prosperity, wealth)*

Generally used to refer to the condition of having a sufficient or large quantity of something
Genesis 1:28–31. Many options for food
Proverbs 19:10. Fools do not live in luxury.
Philippians 4:12. Living in plenty and want

▶ Plumb line *(measurement, rod, tool)*

A tool that checks the straightness of a wall
2 Kings 21:13. Tool used for making measurements
Isaiah 28:17. Measuring line
Isaiah 34:11. Measuring out destruction
Amos 7:7–8. Checking the "straightness" of God's people
Zechariah 4:10. Indication of judgment

▶ Poetry *(poems, rhymes, verse)*

Measured language of emotion
Psalm 23:1. Comparative poetry
Psalm 78:1. Parallelism
Psalm 107:8, 15, 21, 31. Repetition of a phrase
Psalm 119:1. An acrostic poem
Proverbs 15:2. Truth seen from two perspectives
Song of Songs 4:1. Simile
Luke 1:68–79. Magnificat
Ephesians 5:14. An early poem
Ephesians 5:18–19. Reciting psalms and hymns

▶ Poison *(pollutant, toxin, venom)*

A toxic substance which injures or kills a living organism
Numbers 21:4–9. Poisonous snakes
Deuteronomy 32:24. Judgment and poisonous animals
2 Kings 4:39. Poisonous gourd
Job 6:3–4. Poisonous arrows
Psalm 58:4. Snake venom
Hosea 10:4. Reference to hemlock
Romans 3:13. Dangerous people
James 3:8. Poisonous tongue

▶ Politics *(civics, government, state)*

Activities associated with governing of a state or country
Proverbs 24:21–22. Fearing the king
Luke 20:25. Giving what is due
Acts 19:39. Settling a matter in a legal assembly

Romans 13:1–7. Christians and government
Romans 16:23. Greetings from the city treasurer
1 Timothy 2:1–2. Praying for leaders
Titus 3:1. Submitting to government
1 Peter 2:13–14. Living under civil authorities

▶ Pollution *(contaminate, defile, impure)*

Corruption and things that defile
Genesis 1:28. Charged to steward creation well
Numbers 35:33. Actions which pollute the land
Psalm 106:38. Polluted with blood
1 Corinthians 10:26. The earth is the Lord's.

▶ Polyandry *(adultery, multiple husbands)*

A specific subset of polygamy referring to a woman with more than one husband at a single time
Genesis 12:18–19. Polyandry avoided
Romans 7:3. Polyandry condemned

▶ Polygamy *(adultery, multiple wives)*

The practice of having more than one spouse at a time
Genesis 4:19. Lamech marries two women.
Genesis 16:1–2. Women in Abram's life
Exodus 21:10. Regulating a polygamous marriage
Deuteronomy 17:16–17. Adding of many wives forbidden
1 Kings 11:3. Solomon's harem
Matthew 19:4–6. No longer two, but one
1 Timothy 3:2–3. Polygamy forbidden for church leaders

▶ Pool(s) *(cistern, reservoir, water)*

Reservoirs that collect water
2 Samuel 2:13. Pool of Gibeon
1 Kings 22:38. Bathing in the pool of Samaria
2 Kings 18:17. Israel's enemy camps out near a water supply.
Nehemiah 2:14. A king's private water supply
Ecclesiastes 2:6. Irrigation
John 9:7. Healing near the Siloam pool
James 3:12. Salt water and fresh water

▶ Poor, the *(needy, oppressed, poverty-stricken)*

Those who are economically disadvantaged and cannot meet financial or material needs
Leviticus 19:9–10. Leaving something for the poor
Deuteronomy 10:17–18. God cares for the poor.
Deuteronomy 15:11. Generosity commanded
Psalm 140:12. Promise of God's defense
Ezekiel 18:17. Character of the godly
Amos 2:6–7. A heinous crime against the poor
Matthew 26:11. There will always be poor among you.
Mark 10:21. Treasure in heaven versus treasures on earth
Luke 6:20. Blessed are the poor.
Romans 15:26. Collection for poor believers
James 2:5. God's preference for the poor
James 2:15–16. Caring for physical needs

▶ Popularity *(admired, liked, supported)*

The degree to which a person is admired or supported
2 Samuel 3:36. Approval of the king's actions
2 Samuel 15:1–6. Gaining popular appeal
Matthew 21:45–46. Fearing popular opinion
2 Corinthians 6:8–9. Popular treated poorly
Galatians 1:10. Seeking only God's approval
Colossians 3:22. Avoid mere people-pleasing

▶ Pork *(meat, pig, unclean)*

The flesh of a pig
Deuteronomy 14:8. Touching dead pigs forbidden

Isaiah 65:4. Eating pork and other unclean foods

Acts 10:9–16. Peter's vision and the cleanliness of all animals

▶ Pornography *(filth, porn, smut)*

Visual material containing explicit sexual images

Job 31:1. Looking at a virgin with lust

Proverbs 6:25. Desiring beauty in the heart

Matthew 5:27–28. Looking at a woman with lust

Mark 7:21–23. Sins which come from within

Romans 13:13–14. Forsaking desires of the sinful nature

1 Corinthians 6:9–10. Wicked will not inherit the kingdom of God.

1 Corinthians 10:8. Avoid sexual sin

Galatians 5:19–20. Effects of the corrupt nature

1 Thessalonians 4:3–8. God's will to stay away from sexual sin

1 John 2:15–17. Evil desires of the world are passing away.

▶ Portion *(inheritance, lot, share)*

A designated allotment or share

Genesis 43:34. Portions of food

Exodus 29:28. Portion given to priests

Numbers 5:26. Portions handled by the priest

2 Corinthians 6:15. Do believers share portion with unbelievers?

Revelation 22:19. Threat of a portion taken away

▶ Position *(level, place, status)*

A social, political, or religious location of status or prominence

Genesis 40:21. Restored to a position of prominence

Esther 1:19. Replacing a royal position

Psalm 62:4. Forcing a king from his position

Acts 1:25. Judas abandoned his position.

Romans 8:34. Place of interceding

James 4:10. Humble will be exalted.

1 Peter 3:22. Christ has the highest position.

Jude 6. Angels who lost their position of authority

▶ Possessions *(custody, things, ownership)*

The act of having or taking into control

Numbers 18:20. God is His people's possession.

Deuteronomy 1:8. The land God promised His people

Ezekiel 45:7. Land as a possession

Matthew 19:21. Selling of possessions

Luke 14:33. Called to give up everything

Acts 5:1–2. Withholding possessions

2 Corinthians 12:14. Not needing possessions

▶ Possessiveness *(demanding, desirous, jealous)*

The quality of demanding someone's absolute attention or allegiance

Exodus 20:5. God does not tolerate rival worship.

Joshua 24:19. God's jealousy for true followers

Zechariah 8:2. God's possessiveness of Zion

▶ Postmodern thinking *(postmodern)*

Attempts to offer a totalizing explanation of the world

Judges 17:6. Everyone did what was right in his own eyes.

John 14:6. Anti-foundationalism subverted

John 18:38. What is truth?

1 John 1:6. Importance of living rightly

▶ Postponing *(defer, delay, procrastination)*

Delaying the execution of a task to a later time

Psalm 40:17. Asking God to come without delay

James 1:19. Delaying anger
2 Peter 3:9. Postponing judgment

▶ Potential *(latent, probable, undeveloped)*

Showing the capacity for growth in the future
Exodus 18:21. Choosing capable men
Matthew 16:18. Peter's leadership potential
Mark 1:17. Utilizing potential
1 Corinthians 15:9. Recognizing potential

▶ Potter, the *(artist, clay worker)*

One who works with clay to form pottery
Isaiah 29:16. Potter better than clay
Isaiah 41:25. Controlled like an artisan with art
Isaiah 64:8. The work of the Lord's hands
Jeremiah 18:6. Like clay in the potter's hands
Romans 9:21–22. Potter's choice

▶ Poured out *(scatter, shed, spill)*

The action of pouring or emptying a vessel; can refer to death
Exodus 4:9. Water of the Nile poured out
Exodus 29:7. Oil of anointing
Leviticus 8:15. Blood poured out on altar
Isaiah 44:3. Promise of Spirit poured out
Joel 2:29. Pouring out the Spirit
Mark 14:24. Blood poured out for many
Acts 2:17. God poured out His Spirit.
Acts 10:45. Spirit poured out on Gentiles
Philippians 2:17. Impending death
2 Timothy 4:6. A sacrifice unto God
Revelation 16:2–17. Pouring out bowls of wrath

▶ Poverty *(destitution, hardship, poor)*

A position or situation of economic destitution
Deuteronomy 24:19–22. Leaving food for the poor
Psalm 73:12–14. Oppressed by the wealthy
Jeremiah 7:6. Treating poverty-stricken with dignity
Luke 2:24. Offering a sacrifice out of poverty
Luke 4:18. Preaching Good News to the poor
Acts 4:34–35. Elimination of poverty
Romans 12:13. Providing for others
2 Corinthians 6:10. Poor, but making many rich
2 Corinthians 8:1–2. Poverty inspires generosity.

▶ Power *(authority, might, strength)*

Authority or ability to do something
Psalm 62:11. Power belongs to God.
Psalm 111:6. Power of God's works
Jeremiah 32:27. Nothing too hard for God
Matthew 9:6. Power to forgive sins
Acts 1:8. Power from the Holy Spirit
Romans 1:4. Power demonstrated in resurrection
Romans 1:16. Power of the Good News
Ephesians 3:16. Power through God's Spirit
Colossians 1:16. Powers of this world
Hebrews 4:12. Power of God's word
1 Peter 1:5. Guarded by God's power

▶ Powerless *(defenseless, useless, weak)*

A state of having no power or means of influence
2 Chronicles 20:12. Powerless before an enemy
Job 14:10. Powerless after death
Isaiah 16:14. Powerlessness of oppressors
1 Corinthians 1:25. Human strength powerless against God
2 Corinthians 10:10. Powerless in person
Galatians 4:9. Powerless principles of the world

▶ Pragmatism *(immediacy, practical, simplicity)*

A philosophical approach to truth and life based upon the immediacy of the results
Hosea 6:6. Avoid mere pragmatism.
Romans 10:17. Faith comes through Christ's message.

1 Corinthians 14:20. Maturity in Christian thinking

2 Timothy 2:7. Difficult teaching

▶ Praise *(bless, thank, worship)*

An act that acknowledges, blesses, or thanks someone for who they are or what they have done

Genesis 49:8. Praise of family

Exodus 15:1–2. Moses praises the Lord for victory in Egypt.

Nehemiah 9:5. Encouraging others to praise God

Psalm 18:3. Praising God for His deliverance

Psalm 150:1. Praising God in His temple

Proverbs 31:28. Noble character praised

Acts 16:25. Singing praise while in prison

Ephesians 1:5–6. Praise and glory to the Son

Philippians 4:8. Focusing on praiseworthy things

Hebrews 13:15. Bringing a sacrifice of praise

1 Peter 1:7. Trials that result in praise

Revelation 19:5. Call to praise God

▶ Prayer *(intercession, supplication)*

To present requests to God, honor God, confess to God, or thank God for who He is and what He has done

Psalm 4:1. Answer when I call.

Proverbs 15:29. Far from the wicked, near the righteous

Matthew 6:9–13. The Lord's prayer

Luke 6:12. Spending a whole night in prayer

Ephesians 1:16–17. Prayer for other believers

Ephesians 6:18. Praying in the Spirit

Philippians 4:6. Don't worry, be prayerful.

Colossians 4:2. Exhorted to pray

James 5:17. Power of prayer

1 Peter 3:12. Hearing the prayers of the approved

Revelation 5:8. Prayers of God's people

▶ Preach *(address, proclaim, speak)*

The public announcing of the message of the Good News about Jesus

Mark 1:14. Jesus preaching the Good News

Luke 1:19. Preaching the Good News of Christ's incarnation

Luke 3:18. Sharing encouraging words

Luke 4:43. Sharing the message with many

Acts 5:42. Long ministry hours

2 Corinthians 4:5. Preaching Jesus Christ

Philippians 1:15. Preaching for the right reasons

1 Peter 3:18. The message we preach

Revelation 10:7. Good News made known

▶ Preacher *(minister, priest, teacher)*

A church leader who authoritatively teaches the Word of God

Luke 3:3. Traveling preacher

Acts 2:14–31. First Christian sermon

Galatians 1:8. Beware of false preachers.

1 Timothy 2:7. Appointed as a preacher

Titus 1:5–16. Qualifications of teaching elders

James 3:1. Teachers judged more severely

2 Peter 1:16. Eyewitnesses to Jesus

▶ Precious *(beloved, honorable, valuable)*

Something considered valuable or honorable

Exodus 28:17. Precious stones

Psalm 35:17. Rescuing a precious life

Psalm 36:7. Precious mercy

Isaiah 43:4. A precious people

1 Peter 1:7. Faith

1 Peter 1:19. The blood of Christ

1 Peter 2:4. Rejected by humans, precious to God

1 Peter 3:4. Gentle and quiet spirit

▶ Predator(s) *(animal, beast, killer)*

An organism that preys on something else

Isaiah 31:4. Predators not afraid

Jeremiah 12:9. Birds of prey

Habakkuk 1:8. Enemies prey like eagles

Acts 11:6. Animals of prey in a vision

▶ Predestine/Predestination *(choose, foreordain, plan)*

To appoint or determine ahead of time

Genesis 12:3. Blessing through Abram's family

Psalm 139:16. A life known from birth

Matthew 11:27. Revelation through the Son

Acts 4:27–28. God's plan

Acts 13:48. Appointed for belief

Romans 8:28–30. Predestined to be conformed to Christ

Romans 9:11. God's plan

Ephesians 1:4. Chosen in Christ before creation

Ephesians 1:5. Predestined for adoption in Christ

Ephesians 1:11. Obtaining an inheritance

Ephesians 2:10. Works prepared for us to do

Ephesians 3:11. God's plan for history

▶ Prediction *(anticipate, forecast, projection)*

A projected outcome or event

Leviticus 19:26. Consulting fortunetellers forbidden

Deuteronomy 18:9–14. Sin of predicting the future

1 Samuel 6:1–2. Consulting fortunetellers

1 Samuel 28:8. Seeking the future from the dead

Ezekiel 21:21. Various divination practices

▶ Preeminence *(excellence, greatness, superiority)*

A position of supremacy or distinction above other persons, objects, or gods

Exodus 20:3. No other gods

John 17:24. Glory prior to the world's creation

Acts 4:12. No other name

Colossians 1:15–16. Hymn to the preeminent Christ

Hebrews 1:2–3. Preeminence of Christ

▶ Preexistence *(Christ, logos, wisdom)*

Having a heavenly existence predating earthly, historical existence

John 1:1–4. The Word (Jesus) was with God in the beginning.

1 Corinthians 8:6. Christ as an agent in creation

1 Corinthians 15:47. Christ's descent from heaven

Galatians 4:4. Sent at the right time

Philippians 2:6–11. Jesus became like humans.

Colossians 1:15–20. Existence before all things

Hebrews 1:1–3. Christ, the image of God

▶ Pregnancy *(gestation, with child)*

A woman's condition of having life—a child—growing within her

Genesis 3:16. Labor pains increased

Genesis 21:1–7. Pregnant in old age

Genesis 25:21. Praying for pregnancy

Psalm 139:13–15. Poetic description of God's care for a child

Jeremiah 1:4–5. Appointed before pregnancy

Matthew 1:23. A pregnant virgin

John 16:21. Labor pains end.

Galatians 4:27. Spiritual children

Hebrews 11:11. Faith to become a father

▶ Prejudice *(discrimination, intolerance, prejudgment)*

A preconceived opinion which is not necessarily based upon reality

Matthew 15:21–28. Overcoming prejudiced policies

Acts 9:26. Prejudiced against a new convert

Acts 10:34–35. Nationalism overcome

Acts 14:2. Poisoning minds

2 Corinthians 7:2. Treating others well

1 John 4:5. Worldly mindset

Revelation 5:9. God saves people from every nation.

▶ Premarital sex *(immorality, infidelity, sin)*

Sexual relationship which occurs prior to marriage

P

Genesis 2:24. Two will become one flesh.
Acts 15:20. Abstaining from sexual sin
1 Corinthians 6:16. Theological problem of extra-marital sex
1 Corinthians 7:1–2. Marriage as a solution for solving sexual temptations
Ephesians 5:3. Inappropriate among God's people
1 Thessalonians 4:1–8. God's will for sex and marriage
1 Timothy 4:1–5. Sinful behavior

▶ Premeditation *(forethought, plan, plan ahead)*

The action of planning out one's future actions
Genesis 50:20. Evil plan thwarted
Exodus 21:14. Planning murder
1 Samuel 18:25. Planning evil
2 Samuel 11:14–15. Uriah's death letter
Esther 3:6. Planning a pogrom
Psalm 21:11. Failed attempts
Matthew 26:1–5. Plotting Jesus' death
Acts 20:3. Plot to kill Paul

▶ Preparation *(Passover, Sabbath)*

Used of the day of preparation for the Sabbath and once a year for Passover
Matthew 27:62. Day of Preparation
Mark 15:42. Friday as a day of preparation for Sabbath
John 19:14. Preparation for Passover

▶ Presence *(company, face)*

The status of being present in a place or thing
Genesis 27:7. Blessing in God's presence
Exodus 33:14. Promise of God's presence
Leviticus 22:3. Excluded from God's presence
1 Chronicles 16:11. Seeking the Lord's presence
Psalm 21:6. Joy of God's presence
Psalm 105:4. Always seek the Lord's presence
Isaiah 64:1. God's awesome presence
Jonah 1:3. Fleeing from the Lord
John 17:5. Glory in His presence
1 Corinthians 1:29. No boasting in God's presence
Jude 24. Before God without fault
Revelation 3:5. Acknowledged before God

▶ Present *(donation, gift, offering)*

A gift or donation given to someone
Genesis 24:53. Betrothal gifts
Genesis 25:6. Long-distance gift-giving
Genesis 43:25. Preparing gifts
Exodus 35:21. Using gifts to build the tabernacle
1 Samuel 30:26. Loot
Jeremiah 40:5. Gift for departing visitor
Micah 1:14. Farewell gifts
Hebrews 8:3. Presenting gifts to God

▶ Pressure *(compulsion, coerce, force)*

The use of social, political, or other means to compel someone to do something
Psalm 69:1. High pressure situation
Matthew 14:6–11. Social pressure
John 9:4. Pressures increasing
Acts 20:16. Pressure to reach Jerusalem
2 Timothy 4:5. Working well under pressure
Hebrews 11:24. Refusing a position of status

▶ Prestige *(honor, status, wealth)*

Respect or admiration felt for someone or something based upon their accomplishments
Job 29:7–10. Respect
Psalm 148:13. Above all others
Proverbs 25:6–7. Desiring prestige
Luke 14:8–11. A place of honor
Acts 10:25–26. Prestige mistaken
1 Timothy 5:17. Prestigious leaders

▶ Presumption *(assumption, guess, prejudgment)*

The action of assuming the correctness or truthfulness of something without hearing all the facts

Numbers 26:60–61. Presumption in offering unauthorized fire
Ephesians 3:2. Assuming that you have heard
Ephesians 4:21. No need for presumption
1 Timothy 5:21. Impartiality

▶ Pretense *(acting, faking, pretending)*

An attempt to make something that is not the case appear true
Genesis 12:10–20. False pretense discovered
2 Samuel 13:5. Pretending to be sick
2 Samuel 14:2. Pretending to be sad
1 Kings 14:6. Pretending to be someone
Jeremiah 3:10. Returning only in pretense
Mark 12:38–40. Prayer of false pretense
Philippians 1:18. Preaching under false pretense

▶ Prevention *(hinder, impede, stop)*

The stopping or hindering of an action
Genesis 38:9. Preventing a family line
1 Samuel 26:19. Preventing the Lord's inheritance
Nehemiah 4:15. Plans which God prevented
Psalm 106:23. Preventing pogrom
Ecclesiastes 8:8. No stopping death
Acts 8:36. What prevents baptism?
Romans 1:13. Prevented from visiting
Hebrews 7:23. Prevented by death from continuing office

▶ Preview(s) *(advance, sneak peek)*

A glimpse of a future reality in the present
Daniel 2:36–45. A future kingdom
Mark 9:2–8. Transfiguration
Luke 16:22–24. Lazarus's experience before being raised
2 Corinthians 12:2. Caught up into third heaven
Revelation 1:1. Things that must take place soon

▶ Pride *(arrogance, conceit)*

The attitude that is opposite of humility
Genesis 3:5. Pride in desiring God's knowledge
Proverbs 8:13. The Lord hates pride.
Proverbs 16:18. Pride precedes disaster.
Isaiah 14:12–14. Pride before a fall
Mark 7:22. Sins which come from within
Romans 3:27. No bragging in efforts
1 Corinthians 13:4. Love is not prideful.
1 Timothy 6:3–4. Prideful rejection of truth
James 4:16. Prideful bragging
1 Peter 5:5. God opposes the proud.
1 John 2:16. Pride in possessions

▶ Priest *(bishop, clergy, minister)*

One who serves as a mediator between God and humanity by performing sacrifices
Genesis 14:18. Priest of the Most High God
Exodus 19:6. A kingdom of priests
Exodus 28:1. Aaron's family to serve as priests
Nehemiah 8:1–8. Teaching responsibilities
Matthew 8:4. Jesus and the priest
Acts 14:13. Pagan priests
Hebrews 7:23–24. A priest forever
Hebrews 10:19–22. A superior priest
Revelation 1:5–6. Made priests by God

▶ Priesthood *(mediator, priest)*

Carrying out the office or duties of priesthood
Exodus 40:15. Aaron's sons anointed as priests
Hebrews 7:11–12. Another kind of priesthood
1 Peter 2:5, 9. Built into a holy priesthood

▶ Primogeniture *(birthright, firstborn)*

Refers to the rights of the firstborn
Genesis 25:31. Rights of the firstborn
Deuteronomy 21:16–17. Honoring the firstborn
Psalm 89:27. Made the firstborn
Romans 8:29. Firstborn among many children
Colossians 1:15. Firstborn of all creation
Revelation 1:4–5. Jesus, the firstborn of the dead

P

▶ Prince(s) *(governors, sovereign, rulers)*

A leader, chief, or official

Numbers 22:14. Foreign princes
Isaiah 9:6. Prince of peace
Ezekiel 37:24–25. Prince of the people
Daniel 9:25. A prince to come
Hosea 8:10. Suffering under princes
Luke 11:15. Prince of demons
Ephesians 2:1–3. Prince of the power of the air

▶ Priority *(importance, preeminence, primacy)*

Something which is understood or treated as more important than other things

Numbers 18:29. The Lord gets priority with gifts.
Proverbs 24:27. Priorities straight
Matthew 6:19–21. Earthly and heavenly priorities
Mark 16:15. Making the Good News a priority
Luke 18:18–23. One thing still needed
Acts 5:29. Obeying God
1 Corinthians 15:3. Teachings of priority
Galatians 5:6. Faith working through love
1 Timothy 6:10. Money changes priorities.

▶ Prison *(bondage, jail, lockup)*

A place of bondage for someone accused of wrongdoing

Genesis 39:20–23. Good terms with the warden
2 Chronicles 16:10. Imprisoning a prophet
Isaiah 42:7. Hope for prisoners
Jeremiah 32:2. Locking up the prophet
Matthew 14:3. Arresting John
Acts 4:3. Holding cell
Acts 5:19. Prison break
Acts 12:3–6. Guard duty
Hebrews 13:3. Remembering the imprisoned
1 Peter 3:19. Christ preaches victory.
Revelation 2:10. Suffering for Christ
Revelation 20:7. Satan temporarily freed from prison

▶ Prison letters *(communication, epistles, letters)*

Letters written from prison

Philippians 1:13–14. Result of imprisonment
Colossians 4:18. Remembering that Paul is in prison
Philemon 9. A prisoner on behalf of Jesus

▶ Prison occupations *(jobs, profession, situation)*

Actions performed by someone who is held or works in a prison

Genesis 39:22. Joseph placed in charge
Genesis 41:10. Chief baker
Matthew 11:2. Sending messengers
Acts 16:25. Praying and singing
Philippians 1:13. Bearing witness to Christ

▶ Privilege *(blessed, happy)*

A position of special status or favoritism given to a person or group

Matthew 16:17. Privileged information
Philippians 1:29. Privilege of belief and suffering
Revelation 1:3. Privilege of literacy
Revelation 2:7. Privilege to eat from the tree of life
Revelation 19:8. A beautiful garment

▶ Prize, the *(award, laurel, wreath)*

An award given for victory in a contest

1 Corinthians 9:24. Running to win
Philippians 3:14. Running toward the goal
Colossians 2:18. Deserving of a prize
1 Thessalonians 2:19. People as a prize
2 Timothy 2:5. Playing by the rules
2 Timothy 4:8. Prize from God

▶ Problem(s) *(difficulty, trouble, worry)*

A situation which presents difficulty or trouble

Leviticus 26:16. Suffering from eye problems

Deuteronomy 1:12. Requiring help during problems
Judges 9:23. Causing political problems
Ezra 2:63. Settling a problem with divination
Daniel 5:12. Problem solvers
Acts 6:3. Trusted to solve a problem
Romans 9:6. God's word has not failed, has it?
2 Corinthians 12:7. Thorn in the flesh
Philippians 4:14. Sharing in problems

▶ Procedure *(method, plan, strategy)*

An established and commended method for accomplishing a task
Leviticus 5:10. Procedures for sacrifice
Leviticus 9:16. Following procedure
1 Chronicles 24:19. Rules to follow
Matthew 18:15–20. Correcting another believer
Matthew 26:26–29. Instructions for Lord's Supper
Hebrews 13:9. Not following the rules

▶ Proclamation *(announcement, decree, edict)*

An official, public announcement of great importance
Leviticus 23:21. Announcing a holy day
2 Chronicles 24:9. Ordering contributions
2 Chronicles 36:22. Cyrus's decree
Ezra 10:7. Major proclamation
Esther 3:14. Announcing a special day
Jeremiah 34:8. Proclamation of liberty
Jonah 3:7–8. Announcing impending judgment
Luke 4:18–19. Proclaiming Good News
1 Corinthians 11:26. Lord's death proclaimed
1 Peter 3:19. Proclaiming victory over spirits in prison

▶ Procrastination *(delay, hinder, postpone)*

To delay or postpone an action
Exodus 22:29. Withholding things
Judges 19:5–6. Delaying departure
2 Chronicles 24:5. Taking time to obey
Jeremiah 7:13. Failure to listen to the Lord
Haggai 1:3–4. Waiting to rebuild the temple
Matthew 8:21–22. Excuses for delay
Luke 14:16–21. Excuses

▶ Procreation *(breed, produce offspring, reproduce)*

The production of offspring
Genesis 1:28. Be fruitful and multiply.
Genesis 4:25. A promised child
Genesis 38:8–9. Failing to procreate
1 Samuel 1:19. Remembered by the Lord
Hosea 1:3. Hosea starts a family with a prostitute.
Matthew 1:25. Miraculous procreative act
John 16:21. Painful time of birth

▶ Productivity *(effectiveness, efficiency, vocation)*

One's effectiveness and efficiency in accomplishing tasks
Genesis 3:17–18. Land's productivity slowed
Psalm 68:6. Productive lives
Proverbs 16:3. Entrusting work to God
1 Corinthians 10:31. Working for God's glory
1 Corinthians 14:14. Unproductive mind
1 Corinthians 16:9. Opportunity for effective work
Titus 3:14. Examples of productive lives
Philemon 6. Effective faith sharing
2 Peter 1:8. Increasing knowledge and productivity

▶ Profanity *(curse, obscenity, swearing)*

Language which is obscene and impulsive
Exodus 20:7. Using God's name carelessly
Psalm 109:17. Uttering curses on others
Isaiah 32:6. Speaking foolishly
Ezekiel 36:23. Revealing the holy name that has been dishonored
James 2:7. Saying a curse in the name of Jesus

P

James 3:8. Impossibility of taming the tongue
Revelation 13:6. Insulting God

▶ Profess *(confess, praise, promise)*

The affirmation of an idea or allegiance
John 9:38. Profession of faith
1 Timothy 2:10. Professing godliness
1 Timothy 6:21. Professing knowledge
Titus 1:16. Claiming to know God

▶ Profit *(advantage, earnings, proceeds)*

A benefit derived, either monetary or otherwise
Leviticus 25:36. Collecting profit from God's people
Proverbs 31:18. Working hard and earning money
Matthew 16:26. What profit is it?
Acts 19:24. Economic downturn
1 Corinthians 13:3. Profitable only through love
1 Timothy 6:5–6. Ministry and money
James 4:13–14. Folly of planning profit
Jude 11. Only seeking a profit

▶ Progress *(advance, development, improvement)*

Movement or advancement toward a desired goal
Ezra 5:8. Building progress
Ezra 6:14. Message of progress
Nehemiah 4:7. Progress on the wall
Acts 13:49. Word of the Lord making progress
Galatians 3:28. Social progress
Philippians 1:25. Making progress in Christian faith
1 Timothy 4:15. Demonstrating progress

▶ Promiscuity *(immorality, sin, wantonness)*

Refers to relationships characterized by immorality and indiscriminate sexual sin
Leviticus 18:30. Following God's standards
Romans 13:13. Living lives of holiness
Galatians 5:19. Effects of the corrupt nature
1 Thessalonians 4:3. Devoted to God
Hebrews 13:4. Judged by God
Jude 7. Recalling God's past judgment

▶ Promise(s) *(assurance, commitment, pledge)*

An assurance of continuing or future action on behalf of someone
Genesis 12:1–2. Promise given to Abraham
Deuteronomy 9:5. Confirming God's promise
Joel 2:28. Promise of the Spirit in the latter days
Matthew 28:20. Jesus' promise to be with His people
Romans 15:8. Christ's fulfillment of promises
2 Corinthians 1:20. Christ's role in promise keeping
Galatians 4:28. Children of promise
Ephesians 1:13–14. Promised Holy Spirit
Hebrews 7:22. Guarantee of a better promise
James 1:12. Promised crown of life
2 Peter 3:4. Is the Lord slow in keeping His promise?
2 Peter 3:13. Promise of new heaven and earth
1 John 2:25. Promise of eternal life

▶ Promised Land *(Canaan, inheritance)*

Canaan prior to the Israelites conquering under the leadership of Joshua
Genesis 12:1–2. "Go to the land that I will show you."
Exodus 3:8. Land flowing with milk and honey
Numbers 10:29. Place of promise
Psalm 137:4. Exile in a foreign land
Jeremiah 16:15. Promise of restoration to the land
Romans 4:13. Promise of inheriting the world
Hebrews 11:9. Country promised by God

▶ Promotion *(advancement, development, improvement)*

The advancement of one's personal or professional life

Genesis 41:40. From prison to power

Esther 3:1. Promotion after consolidating power

Daniel 3:30. Promoted for withstanding under pressure

▶ Proof/Prove *(authentication, evidence, verification)*

An argument or evidence used to help establish truth

Exodus 3:12. Proof of being sent from God

Psalm 86:17. Asking for proof

Proverbs 30:5. God's word proven true

Matthew 3:8. Proof of repentance

Matthew 25:23. Proven responsibility

Luke 1:18–19. Proof from God's messenger

Acts 25:7. Unproved accusations

Acts 26:20. Proof of changed lives

2 Corinthians 12:12. Proof of apostleship

2 Corinthians 13:3. Proof of a God-given message

Colossians 1:10. Proving you belong to the Lord

2 Thessalonians 3:17. Proof of authorship

Hebrews 6:11. Demonstrating work ethic

▶ Property *(belongings, inheritance, possessions)*

An item (or piece of land) that belongs to someone

Genesis 23:4. Asking for land

Numbers 18:20. Levites have God as a possession.

Numbers 27:8–10. Passing along family property

Luke 16:1–2. Wasting property

Luke 19:8. Donating property to the poor

Acts 2:45. Christians sharing property

Acts 5:1–2. Holding back property

2 Corinthians 11:20. Property seizure

▶ Prophecy (noun) *(information, speech)*

Authoritative speech from God mediated through a prophet, sometimes includes visions of the future

Daniel 9:24. Seal up the prophecy.

Matthew 13:14. Prophecy comes alive.

1 Corinthians 12:8, 10. Speaking what God has revealed

1 Corinthians 14:6. Need to explain prophecy

1 Thessalonians 5:20–21. Testing prophecy

1 Timothy 4:14. Gifts given through prophecy

2 Peter 1:20–21. Origin of prophecy and interpretation

Revelation 1:3. Blessed to hear prophecy

Revelation 22:19. Warning against taking away from God's prophecy

▶ Prophesy (verb) *(forecasting, foretelling, speaking)*

To speak prophetic truth from God

1 Samuel 19:20–24. Anointed with a message

Jeremiah 14:14–16. False prophecies silenced

Jeremiah 26:12. Sent to prophesy

Ezekiel 11:4. Given permission to prophesy

Joel 2:28–29. Many will prophesy.

Matthew 15:7. Correct prophecy

1 Peter 1:10. Longstanding message

Revelation 11:3. Allowing a distressing message

▶ Prophet(s) *(seer, speaker, spokesman)*

Someone who prophesies (used for a male)

Genesis 20:7. The first prophet of the Lord

Deuteronomy 13:1–3. Characteristics of a false prophet

Deuteronomy 18:15. Moses promises a future prophet.

Matthew 5:17. The Prophets

Matthew 7:15. False prophets

Luke 1:76. Prophet precursor
Ephesians 3:5. Mystery of the prophets revealed
Hebrews 1:1. God speaks through the prophets.
2 Peter 2:16. Balaam and his donkey

▶ Prophetess(es) *(seer, speaker, spokeswoman)*

Someone who prophesies (sometimes used when the prophet is a female)
Exodus 15:20. Celebration led by Miriam
Judges 4:4. The prophetess Deborah
2 Kings 22:14. Priest and prophetess
Nehemiah 6:14. Multiple female prophets
Isaiah 8:3. Isaiah's wife
Ezekiel 13:17. False prophetesses
Luke 2:36. A long-living prophetess
Acts 21:9. Philip's daughters
Revelation 2:20. Misleading prophetess

▶ Propitiation *(atonement, sacrifice)*

The action of making atonement or appeasing God's wrath
Romans 3:23–25. Christ our propitiation
Hebrews 2:17. Faithful High Priest
1 John 2:2. Payment for sins
1 John 4:10. Expression of God's love

▶ Propitious *(auspicious, disposition, favorable)*

A disposition or attitude of favor towards someone
Exodus 23:3. Avoiding auspicious behavior in court
1 Samuel 2:26. Favored by God
Psalm 26:1. Asking for favorable disposition
Matthew 22:16. Manner of favor
Romans 8:31. God is for us.
Galatians 2:20. Christ's life for believers

▶ Propriety *(correctness, decentness, respectable)*

Conforming to attitudes or behaviors befitting of one's social group and dynamic
Romans 13:13. Living in the light of day
1 Corinthians 14:40. Proper and orderly worship
1 Timothy 2:10. Proper behavior for women
1 Timothy 4:12. Setting an example of purity
Titus 2:3. Righteous living
James 1:21. Practicing moral behavior
1 Peter 2:12. Living among unbelievers

▶ Proselyte *(catechumen, convert)*

A Gentile who converts to Judaism
Exodus 12:48. Foreigners becoming like Jews
Exodus 20:10. Instructions for foreigners
1 Chronicles 22:2. Foreigners living in Israel
Isaiah 56:3. United with the Lord
Jeremiah 3:17. Nations gather in Jerusalem.
Matthew 23:15. Peril of making proselytes
Acts 6:5. Converts to Judaism
Acts 8:27. An Ethiopian proselyte
Acts 10:1–2. Devoted to God
Acts 13:43. Meeting in the synagogue

▶ Prosperity *(honor, peace, wealth)*

The condition of being financially or spiritually blessed
Genesis 39:2. Prospering in Egypt
Deuteronomy 8:10. Prospering in the Promised Land
Job 24:24. Fleeting prosperity
Psalm 90:17. Asking for success
Daniel 4:27. Prolonging prosperity
Zechariah 1:17. Coming prosperity
Philippians 4:12. Living in poverty or prosperity
3 John 2–4. Spiritual prospering

▶ Prostitute *(harlot, immoral, whore)*

Someone who exchanges sex for money or goods
Genesis 38:24. Acting like a prostitute
Leviticus 19:29. Never allow your daughter to become a prostitute.
Ezekiel 16:41. Spiritual prostitution
Hosea 1:2. Hosea's wife

Matthew 21:31–32. Faith of prostitutes
1 Corinthians 6:15–16. Do not unite with a prostitute.
Hebrews 11:31. Rahab
James 2:25. Vindicated by God
Revelation 17:1. Notorious prostitute

▶ Prostitution *(harlotry, sexual immorality, whoredom)*

The practice of engaging in sexual actions in exchange for payment
Deuteronomy 23:17–18. Prostitution forbidden
Proverbs 6:26. Low cost
Ezekiel 23:25. Coming judgment for prostitution
Hosea 4:12. Led by a spirit of prostitution
Hosea 4:14. Foolishly following prostitutes
1 Corinthians 6:18–20. Honoring God with one's body

▶ Prostrate *(bow, horizontal, sprawling)*

A physical posture of prayer or worship where one lies face down on the ground
Genesis 17:3. Abram before God
Genesis 24:26. Face to the ground
Exodus 4:31. Supplication to the Lord
Joshua 5:14. Posture of worship
Matthew 26:39. Jesus prostrate before the Father
Luke 5:12. Asking for a miracle
Acts 9:4–5. Prostrate before the Lord
1 Corinthians 14:25. Confessing God's presence

▶ Protection *(defense, preservation, security)*

Defending or shielding from harm
Genesis 39:20–21. God's protection of Joseph
Exodus 12:13. Protection during Passover
1 Samuel 30:23. Protection from military might
Psalm 16:1. Plea for protection
Psalm 25:21. Protected by honesty and integrity
Psalm 31:23. The Lord protects faithful people.
Psalm 116:6. Help for the helpless
Proverbs 4:6. Protection through wisdom
John 17:15. Protection from the evil one
2 Corinthians 11:2. Protective leaders
2 Timothy 1:12. Protecting what has been entrusted
2 Peter 2:5. Noah protected by God
1 John 5:18. Protected from sin

▶ Protesting *(complaint, dissent, objection)*

An action expressing one's disapproval or objection to a prior course of action or idea
Exodus 4:1. Protesting God's command
Judges 8:1. Protesting a man's actions
Matthew 20:1–15. Salary protest
John 7:50–51. Nicodemus protests the actions of the Sanhedrin.
Acts 13:51. Apostolic protest

▶ Protocol *(convention, formality, procedure)*

An official procedure or policy used in carrying out certain actions
Exodus 12:24. Permanent Passover protocol
Exodus 26:1–37. Instructions for building the tabernacle
Leviticus 20:23. Forsaking bad actions
Luke 10:5. Guest protocol
John 18:39. Political custom
Acts 17:2. Paul's protocol
Acts 25:16. Roman customs

▶ Proverb(s) *(adage, wisdom, saying)*

A terse wise saying
1 Samuel 10:12. Pithy saying
1 Kings 20:11. A saying before war
Proverbs 1:1. Proverbs of Solomon
Ecclesiastes 12:9. Careful arrangement of words
Luke 4:23. Quoting a proverb
John 16:25. Illustrative examples

▶ Provision *(equipping, providing, supply)*

Providing or supplying something for use

Genesis 42:25. Trip provisions
1 Kings 4:7. Provisions for the king
Psalm 18:39. Provision of strength
Ezekiel 45:25. Provision for sin offerings
Luke 12:24. God's care for His people
Ephesians 4:11–12. Provision for Christ's church
Hebrews 11:39–40. Provision in Christ

▶ Provoking *(arouse, evoke, irritate)*

The action of exciting, arousing, or producing emotion

Deuteronomy 4:25–26. Provoking the Lord to anger
Judges 2:12. Worshiping other gods
1 Kings 14:15. Judah's sin provokes God.
Acts 17:16. Stirred up
Galatians 5:26. Do not provoke others.
Colossians 3:21. Do not provoke children.

▶ Prudence *(common sense, judgment, wisdom)*

The quality of showing care or foresight for one's future

Proverbs 8:12. Wisdom and prudence dwell together.
Proverbs 15:5. Heeding correction
Jeremiah 49:7. Prudence failed
Hosea 14:9. Understanding the ways of God
Amos 5:13. Silence during an evil time
Matthew 10:16. Careful among the world
Ephesians 1:8. Prudence poured out
Ephesians 5:15. Walking with wisdom

▶ Prune *(clip, cut, trim)*

To trim dead or overgrown branches to allow for greater success of the plant

Leviticus 25:3–4. Pruning a vineyard
Isaiah 2:4. Pruning shears
Isaiah 5:6. An unkempt wasteland
Isaiah 18:5. Pruning grape shoots
Joel 3:10. Destroying tools
John 15:2–6. Pruning off the bad branches
Romans 11:17–24. Gentiles grafted in

▶ Psalm(s) *(hymn, make music, sing)*

A song or hymn to God

Psalm 8:1. Praising God's majestic name
Psalm 18:1–2. God, our protector
Psalms 19:1–2. Praising God for creation
Psalm 46:1–2. Refuge and strength
Psalm 110:1. Taking the highest position
Luke 20:42. References to Psalms
Acts 4:25. Remembering a psalm
1 Corinthians 14:26. Used in community gatherings
Ephesians 5:18–19. Making music in your hearts
Colossians 3:16. Teaching and instruction

▶ Psaltery *(harp, instrument, strings)*

A stringed musical instrument probably resembling a small harp or a lyre

Psalm 33:2. Instrument of praise
Psalm 81:2. Playing music
Psalm 144:9. Singing praises to God
Daniel 3:5. Call to worship

▶ Psychology *(mind, persona, thinking)*

The study of the human mind and brain functions, particularly those which effect behavior

Jeremiah 17:9. Deceitfulness of the human mind
Daniel 4:36. Mind returns.
Romans 12:2. Transformed by the renewal of your mind
1 Corinthians 2:16. We have the mind of Christ.
1 Corinthians 14:23. Strange behavior for outsiders
2 Corinthians 2:13. No peace of mind
Colossians 3:2. Minding heavenly matters

▶ Ptolemies *(Egypt, Macedonians, Ptolemy)*

Ptolemy's land apportioned to him after the death of Alexander the Great

Daniel 11:4. Prophecy of Alexander the Great and Ptolemy
Acts 21:17. City of Ptolemais

▶ Public opinion *(average, normal)*

A view which is prevalent or accepted by the public
Proverbs 18:2. Folly of merely expressing opinions
Matthew 6:1. Not motivated by public opinion
Mark 12:41. Only concerned with being seen
Mark 15:13–14. Public opinion of Jesus
Mark 15:43. Respected public official
Acts 17:17. Public discussions
Acts 18:28. Swaying public opinion

▶ Publican *(contractor, official, tax collector)*

Someone who works for a government collecting taxes
Matthew 5:46. Selfish
Matthew 9:9. Matthew, the tax collector, called to follow Jesus
Matthew 9:11. Spending time with Jesus
Matthew 18:17. Outcasts from society
Matthew 21:32. Tax collectors turn to God.
Luke 3:12. Repentant tax collectors
Luke 7:34. Associated with sinners
Luke 18:13–14. Justified before God

▶ Pulpit *(platform, podium, soapbox)*

A raised platform from which someone delivers a speech or sermon
Nehemiah 8:4. Ezra's raised platform

▶ Punishment(s) *(chastisement, discipline, penalty)*

A judgment and/or infliction of discipline in order to correct one's actions
Genesis 9:5–6. Death penalty
Numbers 11:1. Punished by fire
Numbers 16:31–33. Swallowed up into the earth
Psalm 51:4. Acknowledging sin, accepting punishment
Psalm 99:8. God forgives and punishes.
Luke 1:18–20. Zechariah made a mute
Acts 5:1–11. Ananias and Sapphira
Acts 12:18–19. Punished for allowing prisoners to escape
Galatians 1:4. Christ took our punishment.
1 Thessalonians 4:6. The Lord punishes.

▶ Purge *(exclude, expel, remove)*

To remove a person or persons from fellowship with a group
Deuteronomy 13:5. False prophets or dreamers
Deuteronomy 17:12. Opposing a priest
Deuteronomy 19:13. Purging murderers
2 Chronicles 34:3. Removing the land of illegal places of worship
Ezekiel 20:38. Removing rebels
Hebrews 9:14. Purging our consciences

▶ Purify *(cleanse, consecrate, purge)*

Ritual purification; personal holiness
Psalm 51:7. Request for cleansing from sin
Luke 11:39. Purifying outside and inside
John 11:55. Preparing for Passover
Acts 21:24. Ceremony of purification
Titus 2:14. Cleansed as Christ's people
Hebrews 1:3. Cleansed from sin
Hebrews 9:14. Cleansed by Christ's blood
James 4:8. Called to purify life and mind
1 Peter 1:22. Purified through the truth
1 John 3:3. Maintaining holiness

▶ Purim *(lots, Pur)*

Jewish festival; means "lot(s)" and refers to Haman's casting of lots
Esther 3:7. Throwing lots
Esther 9:24. Used to divine a day
Esther 9:26–27. Instituting a festival

▶ Purity *(clean, moral, virtuous)*

Indicates a heart condition of devotion to God

Genesis 35:2. Purified from foreign gods
Exodus 19:14. Preparing for worship
Proverbs 22:11. Purity of heart
Matthew 5:8. Blessed are the pure.
2 Corinthians 6:6. Evidence of the Holy Spirit
1 Timothy 1:5. Love from a pure heart
1 Timothy 4:12. Setting an example in purity
1 Timothy 5:2. Remaining morally pure
2 Timothy 2:22. Worshiping with a pure heart
Hebrews 13:4. Purity in marriage

▶ Purpose(s) *(basis, goal, motivation)*

The reason or basis for which life, death, and existence in general occur
Genesis 50:20. God's purpose carried out
Psalm 16:11. Joy in God's presence
Isaiah 43:7. Created for God's glory
Mark 12:30. Loving God wholly
John 10:10. Abundant life
Romans 5:2–3. Confidence in the Lord
1 Corinthians 10:31. Living for God's glory
Ephesians 1:11–12. Purpose in Christ
1 Thessalonians 1:3. Enduring faith and love

▶ Purse *(bag, carrier, money)*

A bag or special pocket to carry money or documents
Proverbs 1:14. Sharing from the same purse
Isaiah 46:6. Bags of money
Matthew 10:9. Means of carrying money
Luke 10:4. Instructions for disciples, no hindrances
Luke 22:35–36. Obeying Jesus' command

▶ Pursuit *(chase, persecute, pursue)*

Striving after someone or something
Genesis 31:23. Pursuing family
Exodus 14:4. The Lord initiates pursuit.
1 Samuel 14:22. Military pursuit
Psalm 7:1. Save me from pursuers.
Proverbs 11:19. Folly of pursuing evil
Romans 14:19. Pursuing peace
1 Corinthians 14:1. Desiring spiritual gifts, especially prophecy
1 Timothy 6:11. Pursuing a God-approved lifestyle

▶ Quail *(bird, food, meat)*

A small bird which God miraculously supplied to the Israelites in their wilderness wanderings

Exodus 16:13. God sends quails to feed Israel.
Numbers 11:31. Abundance of food
Psalm 78:27. Remembering the quails
Psalm 105:40. Asking for food

▶ Qualification(s) *(aptitude, eligibility, requirement)*

Certain accomplishments or aptitudes which make one well-suited for a particular task

Numbers 4:3. Qualified to serve as priests
Acts 1:23. Determining qualified men
1 Corinthians 12:1–11. Apostolic gifts
2 Corinthians 3:1. Demonstrating credentials
2 Corinthians 5:12. Qualified for service
Philippians 3:4. Earthly qualifications
1 Timothy 3:1–13. Qualifications of a church overseer

▶ Quality *(excellence, value, worth)*

The standard of measure for determining the value or worth of similar things

Genesis 2:12. High quality minerals
Exodus 27:20. Extra virgin olive oil
Deuteronomy 8:4. High quality garments
Psalm 45:1. Good writing
Jeremiah 6:27. Quality control
Luke 14:34–35. Quality salt
1 Corinthians 3:13. Unveiling quality work
2 Peter 1:5–8. Qualities of Christians
1 John 3:1. Divine love

▶ Quantity *(abundance, total, wealth)*

The amount or sum total of something

Genesis 16:10. Promise of many descendants
Genesis 26:4. Numerous descendants
Deuteronomy 1:10. Large population
2 Samuel 8:8. Large quantities of bronze
1 Kings 10:2. Queen of Sheba's expensive cargo
2 Chronicles 9:9. Large gift to Solomon
Luke 6:38. Giving and receiving large quantities
John 21:6. Large quantity of fish
James 5:20. Many sins forgiven
Revelation 19:6. Multitudes worshiping

▶ Quarantine *(isolate, sanitation, separate)*

A time or location of isolation from normal society. In the Bible, places of isolation were prescribed for people with various skin diseases.

Exodus 29:14. Disposing of filth
Leviticus 2:13. Disinfection
Leviticus 5:2. Cleanliness and dead bodies
Leviticus 13:2–5. Isolation for seven days
Numbers 5:2–3. Quarantine of serious skin diseases
Deuteronomy 23:10–11. Quarantine for a day
Ezekiel 16:4. Sanitizing a child after birth

▶ Quarrel(s) *(argue, disagreement, fight)*

A heated argument between two or more people

Proverbs 3:30. No-reason quarrels
Proverbs 10:12. Love versus hate
Proverbs 13:10. Produced by arrogance
Proverbs 19:13. Quarreling family
Proverbs 22:10. Driving out a quarreler
Isaiah 45:9. Folly of quarreling with God
Acts 23:10. A violent quarrel
Romans 1:29. Attitudes of unbelievers
1 Corinthians 1:11. Reports of quarrels
1 Corinthians 16:10–11. Avoid quarreling with Christian workers.
Ephesians 4:31. Abolishing harsh behaviors
1 Timothy 6:4. Unhealthy appetite for arguments
2 Timothy 2:23. Do not get involved in stupid arguments.
Titus 3:9. Worthless words
James 4:1. Caused by selfish desires

Q

▶ Queen(s) *(matriarch, royalty, ruler)*

Designation may refer to a ruling matriarch, such as queen Sheba, but also commonly refers to the mother of the king

1 Kings 10:1. The queen of Sheba and Solomon

1 Kings 11:19. Marriage arrangements

Esther 1:10–12. Beauty of the queen

Esther 2:22. Queen Esther

Isaiah 47:5. Position of honor

Jeremiah 7:18. The moon—the queen of heaven

Ezekiel 16:13. A beautiful woman

Daniel 5:10. Comforting the king

Matthew 12:42. Wisdom greater than Solomon and Sheba

Acts 8:27. Queen Candace's eunuch servant

Revelation 18:7. Babylon's boast

▶ Quench *(gratify, satisfy, slake)*

To satisfy a thirst or desire

Nehemiah 9:15. Israel's thirst quenched with water from the rock

Nehemiah 9:20. God's provision

Psalm 104:11. Waters which quench thirst

Song of Songs 8:7. Love which cannot be extinguished

Jeremiah 4:4. Unquenchable wrath

Matthew 12:20. Evil quenched and fulfilled in Jesus

Matthew 25:8. Lamps which are going out

Mark 9:48. Unquenchable fire

Ephesians 6:16. Quenching fiery arrows

1 Thessalonians 5:19. Do not quench the Spirit.

Hebrews 11:33–34. Quenching the flames

▶ Questioning *(doubt, inquiring, uncertainty)*

The expression of doubt and uncertainty regarding future actions or information

Genesis 3:1. Questioning God's commands

Numbers 14:11. Questionable faithfulness

1 Kings 10:1–3. No question too difficult

Psalm 13:1. Questioning God's presence

Psalm 60:1. Questioning God's faithfulness

Jeremiah 12:1. Questioning God's policies

Luke 2:46. Young Jesus questions leaders.

Luke 3:15. Questioning if John is the Messiah

Luke 20:39–40. Answers which silence all questions

John 18:19. Teachings questioned

Philippians 2:14. No grumbling or questioning

Colossians 2:16. Not questioning normal customs

1 Timothy 1:3–4. Questions which distract from God's plan

▶ Quicksand *(ground, sinking sand)*

Metaphorically refers to loose and unstable ground which sinks when pressure is applied

Psalm 69:2. Sinking into the ground

Acts 27:17. A large sandbank

▶ Quiet time *(devotion, prayer, solitude)*

A time of reflection and prayer on God's Word and actions

Joshua 1:8. Reflecting on God's law

Psalm 119:15. Reflecting on God's ways

Psalm 119:147. Prayer in the morning

Isaiah 33:2. Morning strength

Ezekiel 3:22. Sensing the Lord's presence

Matthew 14:23. Praying alone on the mountain

Mark 1:35. Prayer alone in the morning

Mark 6:31. Solitude and rest

Luke 4:42. Seeking to be alone

Luke 6:12. Up all night in prayer

Luke 22:41. Praying in the garden

Acts 10:9. Praying in the home

▶ Quietness *(calm, silence, still)*

The condition of being calm, still, and/or inaudible

Psalm 89:9. Quieting the sea

Psalm 131:1–2. A quiet heart

Proverbs 29:9. No peace and quiet with the fool

Ecclesiastes 4:6. Quietness preferred to busyness
Isaiah 30:15. Strength through silence
Isaiah 32:17. Effects of righteousness
1 Timothy 2:11. Keeping quiet in assembly
1 Peter 3:4. True beauty
Revelation 8:1. Silence in heaven

▶ Quota *(limit, portion, ration)*

A fixed amount of something
Exodus 5:18. Quota of bricks
1 Kings 4:28. Quota of barley
Job 14:5. Fixed number of days
Ezekiel 45:14. Quota of olive oil

▸ Rabbi(s) *(master, sir, teacher)*

A title of reverent address given to respected teachers and interpreters of the Old Testament law
Matthew 23:7. Desirous of fame
Mark 9:5. Peter's teacher
John 1:38. Rabbi explained
John 3:2. A God-sent teacher
John 3:26. John's followers address him
John 9:2. Asking questions

▸ Race *(ethnicity, nation, people)*

A division of humanity with distinct family lineage and often family traits
Genesis 25:23. Two countries in the womb
Exodus 6:7. A race forged in Egypt
1 Kings 11:1. Loving many foreign women
Ezra 9:2. Intermarriage
Psalm 87:5. All races found in Zion
Acts 2:39. Promise for all races
Acts 10:28. Associating with other races
Romans 9:5. Messiah descended from Jewish ancestry
Philippians 2:10–11. Every tribe and tongue
1 Peter 2:9. Chosen people

▸ Racism *(bigotry, chauvinism, discrimination)*

The belief that different ethnic groups have different distinguishing characteristics which make them more or less valuable as people
Genesis 21:8–10. Social and ethnic tension
Genesis 28:1. Intermarriage forbidden
Genesis 43:32. Hebrews and Egyptians eating separately
Numbers 12:1. Moses' exotic wife
Nehemiah 13:1–3. Avoiding Israelites
Esther 3:8–9. Haman's plot against the Jews
John 1:46. Racist attitude toward Nazareth
Acts 10:27–28. Unclean made clean
Acts 10:34–35. No favoritism with God
Galatians 3:28. Unity of races in Christ

▸ Rags *(cloth, old clothes, tatters)*

Old or tattered clothing material
Genesis 3:21. New clothes
Leviticus 10:6. Tearing clothes
Joshua 9:5. Tattered clothes
Proverbs 23:21. Dressed in rags
Isaiah 64:6. Righteousness like stained rags
Jeremiah 38:11–12. Old, torn clothes
Matthew 26:63–65. Alleged blasphemy

▸ Rain *(precipitation, showers, weather)*

Condensed moisture which falls from the sky
Genesis 7:11–12. Intense, prolonged rain
Deuteronomy 32:2. Teaching like rain
1 Samuel 12:18. Rain and thunder
1 Kings 18:41. Hearing rain in the distance
Job 29:23. Eager for rain
Psalm 72:6. Invoked from heaven
Isaiah 25:4. God is a shelter from the rain.
Zechariah 10:1. God supplies the rain.
Luke 12:54. Predicting weather systems
James 5:7. Patience with weather

▸ Rainbow *(arch, light, promise)*

An arch of colors in the sky caused by light refracting through moisture in the air
Genesis 9:13–14. Sign of God's promise to Noah
Genesis 9:15–16. Reminder of God's promise
Ezekiel 1:28. Appearance like a rainbow
Revelation 4:3. Glow from the throne
Revelation 10:1. Sign of splendor

▸ Ram(s) *(sheep)*

A male sheep
Genesis 22:13. God provides a sacrifice.
Exodus 19:13. Sound of the ram's horn
Exodus 26:14. Covering a tent with ram hide
2 Chronicles 29:32. Many rams offered to the Lord
Ezra 8:35. Numerous animals

Daniel 3:5. Call to (false) worship
Daniel 8:20. Ram signifies centers of power

▶ Ransom *(payment, redeem, redemption)*

The payment demanded for making appeasement or releasing a prisoner
Exodus 30:12. Ransom paid to the Lord
Numbers 3:49. Ransom (money) for the Levites
Psalm 49:7. Impossible to pay God back
Proverbs 13:8. Ransomed through riches
Matthew 20:28. Jesus' life as a ransom for many
Romans 3:24. God's approval achieved through an act of kindness.
1 Corinthians 1:30. Christ, our ransom from sin
1 Corinthians 6:20. Bought with a price
Colossians 1:14. Payment for freedom
Hebrews 9:15. A payment for sins

▶ Rape *(abuse, assault, ravish)*

The act of coercing sex, either by threats or force, out of an unwilling partner
Genesis 34:1–2. Shechem rapes Dinah.
Deuteronomy 22:25. Punishing a rapist
Deuteronomy 22:28–29. Taking care of a woman who is raped
Judges 19:24. Sinfully offering daughter to be raped
Judges 20:5. Raping a concubine
2 Samuel 13:12–14. Amnon violates his sister.
Isaiah 13:16. Judgment and destruction
Lamentations 5:11. Women are not safe after the destruction of the city.
Zechariah 14:2. Coming destruction

▶ Rapport *(affinity, empathy, understanding)*

A good faith relationship in which symbiotic respect and appreciation are exchanged
Genesis 41:39–30. Joseph's good rapport with Pharaoh
Exodus 18:6–7. Family rapport
Exodus 23:9. Good rapport with foreigners
Matthew 9:10. Jesus' relationship with sinners
Acts 17:19–21. Paul in Athens
1 Corinthians 9:22. All things to all people
Hebrews 13:2. Showing hospitality
1 Peter 4:9. Welcoming without complaint

▶ Rapture *(parousia, return, second coming)*

The time when believers will be reunited with Christ upon His triumphant return
Mark 13:32. Day and hour unknown
Luke 12:39–40. Waiting for the Lord to return
John 11:25. Resurrection life
John 14:3. Promised return
John 21:20–22. Misinformation
1 Corinthians 15:51–52. Renewed body

▶ Rationalize *(defend, explain, justify)*

An attempt to justify or explain one's actions through logical discourse, even when such actions defy logic
Job 13:2. Intelligence questioned
Psalm 14:1. Fool's credo
Proverbs 22:13. Rationalizing laziness
Luke 10:28–29. Justifying behavior
Luke 16:15. Actions known before God
Luke 21:14. Avoid defensiveness.
John 2:18. Seeking to rationalize behavior
John 7:1. Rationalizing different travel plans

▶ Raven(s) *(bird, crow)*

A large, black crow known for feeding on carrion
Genesis 8:7. Noah releases a raven after the flood.
Leviticus 11:13–15. Unfit for eating
1 Kings 17:5–6. Ravens fed Elijah.
Job 38:41. Scavenging for food
Psalm 147:9. God feeds the animals.
Proverbs 30:17. Bird of prey
Song of Songs 5:11. Hair black as a raven
Luke 12:24. Consider the ravens.

▶ Reaction(s) *(cause and effect, response)*

The response given to a prior cause

1 Samuel 3:4. Samuel responds to God's calling.

John 2:23. Reactions to Jesus' miracles

John 8:30. Reactions to teaching

John 10:27. Reacting to the shepherd

Acts 6:7. Massive response to the gospel message

Galatians 2:2. Traveling in response to a revelation

2 Thessalonians 1:8. Refusing to respond to the Good News

1 Peter 1:8. Response of faith

1 John 5:10. Bad reaction to Christian message

▶ Reading *(perform, recite, study)*

The acquired skill of learning to understand written communication

Exodus 24:7. Reading from the book of the covenant

Nehemiah 8:8. Publicly reading God's Word

John 19:19–20. The sign on Christ's cross

Acts 8:28–30. "Do you understand what you are reading?"

Acts 13:15. Reading in corporate worship

Ephesians 3:4. Insight into mystery through reading

Colossians 4:16. Reading Paul's letters

1 Timothy 4:13. Public reading of Scripture

2 Timothy 4:13. Important reading materials

▶ Ready *(organized, prepared, set up)*

The status of being prepared for an action

Exodus 12:11. State of perpetual readiness

Proverbs 21:31. Prepared for battle

Matthew 22:4. Ready for a feast

Matthew 24:44. Prepared for Christ's return

Luke 22:33. Ready to undergo persecution

2 Timothy 4:2. Ready to spread the word

Titus 3:1. Ready to help good government

1 Peter 1:5. Salvation ready to be revealed

1 Peter 3:15. Ready to defend Christian hope

▶ Reaffirm *(establish, recall, remember)*

The reiteration of something previously stated

Genesis 9:15–16. Promise reaffirmed constantly

Leviticus 26:42. Promises remembered

2 Corinthians 2:8. Reaffirming love and support

▶ Real estate purchases *(buying land, buying homes)*

Buying property such as buildings or land

Genesis 23:8–9. Buying land for burial

Genesis 33:19. Jacob buys land in Canaan.

Genesis 47:20. Buying up property in bad economic times

Ruth 4:3. Redeeming a family property

Isaiah 5:8. Folly of acquiring much real estate in bad times

Jeremiah 32:8. Buying family property

Jeremiah 32:43–44. Prosperity restored

Matthew 27:7. Purchasing land

Acts 1:18. Land for burial

▶ Realism *(common sense, practicality, pragmatism)*

Accepting the reality of a situation "as is"

Genesis 3:5. Rejecting realism

1 Kings 20:33. Taken at his word

Isaiah 53:1. Unbelieved message

Jonah 3:4–5. Jonah's message believed

Mark 6:35–37. Recognizing a material need

▶ Reap *(garner, gather, harvest)*

The cutting and gathering of a crop in harvest time

Leviticus 23:22. Remembering the poor

Ruth 2:2. Reapers of grain during harvest

Hosea 10:12. Reaping faithfulness
Micah 6:15. Unfinished work
Matthew 6:26. Things which neither sow nor reap
Matthew 25:26–27. Reaping where you have not sown
John 4:38. Some labor, others reap.
2 Corinthians 9:6. Sowing and reaping in proportion
Galatians 6:7–9. Reaping and sowing in life
Revelation 14:15. The reaping hour has come.

▶ Reason *(consider, discuss, argue)*

The cause or basis for understanding one's action
Genesis 3:1, 4. Bad reasoning
Job 12:24. Common sense taken away
Jeremiah 12:1–2. Pondering the fate of righteous and wicked
Ezekiel 33:19–20. Bad policy?
Mark 9:34. Vain argument
Acts 17:17–18. What reason demands
Acts 18:14–16. Public discussion
2 Timothy 1:12. Basis of suffering
Jude 9. Reasoning over Moses' body

▶ Rebel *(mutiny, revolt, riot)*

Rigid resistance to an established pattern or authority
Numbers 14:9. Do not rebel against the Lord.
1 Samuel 12:14. Following the Lord
Psalm 78:17. Recalling rebellion
Proverbs 17:11. Looking for evil
Isaiah 1:20. Pending destruction
Isaiah 50:5. Refusing to rebel
Daniel 11:14. Rebellion of future kingdoms
Matthew 10:21. Rebelling against family
Romans 10:21. Israel's current state of rebellion
Titus 2:9. Not rebelling against circumstances

▶ Rebellion *(offense, sin, transgression)*

A willing and conscious act of defiance toward an established rule or policy
Deuteronomy 13:5. False prophets who preach rebellion
1 Samuel 15:23. Rebellion through divination and magic
2 Kings 18:20. Finding trust during rebellion
Ezra 4:19. Many political uprisings
Esther 6:2. Plotting royal rebellion
Psalm 36:1. Rebellious heart
Psalm 106:43. Perpetual rebellion
Isaiah 53:8. Judgment for rebellion
Jeremiah 28:16. Certain death
Micah 7:18. God's forgiveness of his rebellious people

▶ Rebuke *(see Discipline, Reproach)*

▶ Receptive *(amenable, responsive, well-disposed)*

Able or willing to receive or hear something
Jonah 3:4–5. Responding to the prophet's message
Matthew 10:13. Guests and greetings
John 10:27. Receptive sheep
Acts 6:7. Many accept the faith.
Acts 16:5. Strengthened day by day
Romans 10:16. "Who has believed our message?"
1 Corinthians 1:6. Message received
2 Thessalonians 1:8. Unreceptive to the Good News

▶ Reciprocity *(benefit exchange)*

A symbiotic relationship of sharing which involves mutual benefit
Romans 15:27. Obligation to Jerusalem
1 Corinthians 9:11. Reciprocating needs
Galatians 6:6. Sharing benefits
Philippians 4:10. Relationship of reciprocity

▶ Recitation *(perform, present, repeat)*

The action of repeating an instruction or teaching aloud from memory
Exodus 17:14. Reciting a message
Deuteronomy 6:7. Reciting the law
Deuteronomy 11:29. Reciting a blessing

Deuteronomy 31:30–32:43. Reciting a song
Joshua 1:8. Continue to recite the law.
Psalm 9:14. Reciting praise in Zion
Jeremiah 23:38. A saying not worth repeating
Luke 4:23. Reciting a stale proverb
Ephesians 5:18–19. Living the Spirit-filled life

▶ Reckless *(careless, impulsive, thoughtless)*

Used of a person or action which is impulsive and careless
Exodus 20:7. Reckless use of God's name forbidden
Numbers 30:6. Careless vow
Judges 9:4. Hiring miserable men
Proverbs 14:16. Reckless fool
Ecclesiastes 5:3. Multiplying words
Habakkuk 1:6. Babylonians sent as judgment
Zephaniah 3:1, 4. Reckless prophets
Matthew 12:36. Careless words accounted for
Luke 15:13. Reckless lifestyle
2 Timothy 3:4. Reckless living in the latter days

▶ Reckoning *(avenge, punish, retribution)*

The avenging of one's past mistakes
Genesis 9:5. Demanding life
Genesis 42:22. Payment for bloodshed
Numbers 35:12. Safety from reckoning
Psalm 59:5. Reckoning the nations
Isaiah 1:24. Avenging opponents
Matthew 24:51. A place among the hypocrites
Luke 12:46. Severely punishing a servant
1 Corinthians 4:21. Preferred attitude
2 Corinthians 10:6. Ready to punish

▶ Recommend *(advocate, commend, endorse)*

To speak on behalf of someone or something with regard to a propitious future
Ecclesiastes 8:15. Enjoy life.
Matthew 19:11–12. Following suggestions, if possible
Acts 16:20–21. Advocating trouble
2 Corinthians 3:1–2. Letter of recommendation
2 Corinthians 4:2. Recommended by the truth
2 Corinthians 10:12. Folly of self-measurement
2 Corinthians 10:18. Seek recommendation from the Lord.
2 Corinthians 12:11. Recommending God's workers

▶ Recompense *(compensate, repay, reimburse)*

A punishment of proportionate response to the seriousness of the crime
Deuteronomy 32:35. Doomsday
Psalm 91:8. Fatal vision
Isaiah 34:8. Year of recompense
Isaiah 61:8. Repaying injustice
Isaiah 66:6. Terrible sound of the Lord's vengeance
Jeremiah 25:14. Repaying evil deeds
Jeremiah 51:56. The Lord is a God of recompense.
Hosea 9:7. Days of recompense present
Revelation 22:12. Vengeance coming soon

▶ Reconciliation *(appeasement, placation, reunion)*

The restoration of relationship through the removal of enmity
Matthew 5:23–24. Reconciling before making an offering
Acts 7:26. Reconciling two men
Romans 5:8. Demonstration of God's love
Romans 5:10–11. Reconciled while we were enemies
2 Corinthians 5:18–19. Ministry of reconciliation
2 Corinthians 5:20. Be reconciled with God.
Ephesians 2:14–16. Reconciling Jews and Gentiles
Colossians 1:20–22. Reconciled to God through Christ

James 4:4. Reconciling worldly relationships with God

▶ Reconnaissance *(covert, explore, survey)*

Strategic information-gathering in order to decide a future course of action

Numbers 21:32. Using spies to ascertain information

Joshua 2:23. Information gathering

Judges 18:2. Spying out the land

1 Samuel 26:4. Keeping the king under close watch

2 Samuel 10:3. Planning destruction

Psalm 5:8. Skilled enemy

Psalm 54:5. Deliverance from spies

Luke 20:20. Seeking to betray Jesus

Galatians 2:4. Spying out our Christian freedom

Hebrews 11:31. Welcoming a spy and obeying God

▶ Reconstruct *(rebuild, renovate, restore)*

The rebuilding or restructuring of something after an initial creation and/or destruction

Numbers 32:34. Rebuilding a city

2 Chronicles 33:3. Rebuilding high places of false worship

Ezra 1:5. Rebuilding the Lord's temple

Ezra 5:13. Cyrus gives permission for the rebuilding of Israel's temple

Galatians 2:18. Folly of reconstituting the law

Galatians 6:15. New creation!

▶ Recreation *(fun, leisure, pleasure)*

An activity done for the sake of enjoyment

Deuteronomy 27:7. Enjoying God's presence

Judges 16:25. Comedian

Nehemiah 8:16–17. Enjoying the Feast of Booths

Job 21:11. Children playing

Psalm 104:26. Animals at play

Proverbs 1:11–12. Mischievous recreation

Ecclesiastes 2:1–2. Personal recreation

Zechariah 8:5. Playing children

Matthew 11:16–17. Bad reactions

▶ Recruit *(conscript, draft, enlist)*

To enlist others for service of some kind, typically military service

Exodus 3:1–22. Moses recruited by God to deliver Israel

1 Samuel 14:52. Enlisting strong men, fit for war

2 Samuel 8:3–4. Recruiting new forces

1 Kings 20:25. Recruiting an army

Matthew 23:15. Great pains to recruit so few

Acts 12:20. The negotiator

2 Timothy 2:4. Pleasing the one who enlists you

▶ Rectitude *(goodness, righteous, virtue)*

Behavior or patterns of thinking that are morally upright

Leviticus 11:44–45. God's holiness as our basis for holiness

Deuteronomy 6:18. Called to do what the Lord considers good

Psalm 37:27. Avoid evil, do good.

Matthew 5:20. The impossibility of salvation by morality

Romans 13:14. Called to live like Christ

1 Corinthians 15:33. Corrupting company

1 Timothy 5:1–2. Instructions for correcting morality within Christian community

Titus 2:7. Called to set an example in purity

1 Peter 2:12. Evangelistic morality

1 Peter 3:10–11. Turning from evil

▶ Recuperation *(heal, recover, restore)*

Recovery or rest from a previous illness or action

Exodus 34:21. Resting one day of the week

2 Kings 1:2. Recovering from an injury

Psalm 23:3. Renewed soul

Isaiah 38:16. Prayer for health

Matthew 11:29. Finding rest in Jesus

Mark 10:51. Asking for recuperation of sight
Luke 22:32. Post-recovery task
John 11:12. Regenerating rest
2 Corinthians 4:16. Daily renewed

▶ Red *(color, crimson, scarlet)*

A rich blood-like color

Genesis 25:25. Born red (play on words in the Hebrew)
Genesis 25:30. Red meat
Exodus 26:1. Red yarn used in making the tabernacle
Joshua 2:18. Red cord signals protection.
2 Samuel 1:24. Ornate clothing
2 Kings 3:22. Water turns red.
Proverbs 23:31. Red wine
Isaiah 1:18. Sins like scarlet
Matthew 16:2. Indication of weather
Matthew 27:28. Jesus dressed in red cape
Revelation 17:3. Bright red beast

▶ Red Sea *(sea, water)*

A long narrow body of water which divides modern Africa from Arabia

Exodus 13:18. Heading towards the sea
Exodus 14:21. Moses parts the sea.
Exodus 15:19. Egyptians swept up in the water
Exodus 23:31. Borders of God's people
Deuteronomy 1:40. Constant reminder of the place of God's deliverance
Psalm 106:9. Moses leads the way.
Hebrews 11:29. Faith to cross the sea

▶ Redeemer *(savior, rescuer, liberator)*

Someone who delivers or protects others from evil

Leviticus 25:25. Redeemer of land
Ruth 3:9. Close relative
Ruth 3:12. Closest redeemer
Job 19:25. My redeemer lives
Psalm 19:14. The Lord my defender
Psalm 78:35. Remembering the defender
Isaiah 41:14. Help from God
Isaiah 47:4. The Lord of hosts
Jeremiah 50:34. Strong defender
Acts 7:35. Redeemer because of angels

▶ Redemption *(deliverance, ransom, saving)*

The deliverance of something or someone from a malevolent circumstance

Exodus 21:30. Paying a ransom
Leviticus 25:24. Redemption of land
Psalm 111:9. Redemption for God's people
Luke 21:28. Redemption drawing near
Romans 3:23–25. Redemption in Christ
Romans 8:23. Awaiting redemption of our bodies
1 Corinthians 1:30. Christ, our redemption
Ephesians 1:7. The forgiveness of sins through Christ's blood
Ephesians 4:30. Sealed for a coming day
Hebrews 9:12. Eternal redemption secure

▶ Refine *(purify, test, treat)*

A common process of purifying metals to increase their worth and quality

1 Chronicles 29:4. Refined silver decorum
Job 28:1. Gold refinery
Psalm 12:6. Pure promises of the Lord
Proverbs 17:3. Hearts purified through fire
Jeremiah 6:27. Refining God's people
Jeremiah 9:7. People in need of refining
Daniel 11:35. Future time of refinement
Zechariah 13:9. Refined and repentant
Malachi 3:3. Refining the priesthood
Revelation 1:15. Glowing like bronze in the furnace

▶ Reflect/Reflection *(consider, meditate, think)*

Disciplined thinking or meditation upon a particular topic or event

Psalm 1:2. Delight in the law
Psalm 48:9. Pondering God's mercy
Psalm 77:12. Considering one's actions
Psalm 119:15. Studying the ways of God
Psalm 119:23. Stressful study
Psalm 119:148. Nocturnal reflection

Psalm 143:5. Remember what God has done.
Proverbs 27:19. Heart reflection
Luke 12:27. Reflection on God's provision
Hebrews 10:24. Encouraging others to love

▶ Reform *(amend, correct, improve)*

Changes in regular structure or practice that represent improvement

1 Samuel 7:3–4. Removing idols
2 Kings 18:4. Removing illegal worship cites
2 Chronicles 19:11. Reforms under the chief priest
2 Chronicles 29:35. Worship reformed
2 Chronicles 31:5–6. Reforming tithing
Nehemiah 12:27. Reforms complete

▶ Refuge *(protection, safety, shelter)*

Literally referring to fortifications or cities that offer protection

Numbers 35:11–12. Cities of refuge
Deuteronomy 32:37. Where has our refuge gone?
2 Samuel 22:3. My refuge, shield, and strength
Psalm 5:11. Rejoicing in our refuge
Psalm 18:2. God our refuge
Psalm 46:1. Help in times of trouble
Proverbs 14:26. Confidence in fear of the Lord
Isaiah 25:4. Help for the poor and needy
Jeremiah 17:17. Refuge on a day of disaster
Zephaniah 3:12. Refuge in the Lord's name
Hebrews 6:18. Holding on to confidence in God

▶ Refugees *(ex-patriots, persecuted)*

People who have been driven from home and country due to wars, persecutions, and/or disasters

Numbers 21:29. Family members becoming refugees
Isaiah 16:3. Do not betray refugees.
Isaiah 43:14. Bringing back the Babylonian refugees
Jeremiah 44:14. Very few refugees will return from Egypt.
Jeremiah 49:5. Refugees will not be gathered.
Ezekiel 24:26–27. Speaking with refugees
Obadiah 14. Be merciful to refugees.
Obadiah 17. Rest and habitation for refugees

▶ Refute *(disprove, invalidate, rebuke)*

Generally involves not only the pointing out of false teaching or ideas, but the correction of them

Job 32:12. No one refuted Job.
Matthew 18:15. Refuting a wrong action
Luke 3:19. Rebuking Herod's actions
Acts 18:28. Refuting from the Scriptures
1 Timothy 5:20. Refuting sinful leaders
2 Timothy 4:2. Pointing out errors of doctrine
Titus 1:9. Correcting those who oppose the word
Titus 2:15. Authority of leadership
Jude 15. Convicting the ungodly
Revelation 3:19. Correction and discipline

▶ Regeneration *(new birth, renewal, salvation)*

The concept of regeneration is found throughout the NT, particularly related to the idea of Christian conversion or "new birth."

John 1:12. Children of God
John 3:3–5. Being born from above
2 Corinthians 5:17. New creation in Christ
Galatians 6:15. What really matters
Ephesians 2:5. Alive in Christ
Titus 3:5. Renewal in the Spirit
James 1:18. Life through the word of truth
1 Peter 1:3. Confidence of new life
1 Peter 1:23. Born of imperishable seed
1 John 5:1. Belief that Jesus is the Messiah

▶ Regicide *(killing, murder)*

The killing of the king

Joshua 10:28. Israel kills the king of Makkedah.
Joshua 10:33. Joshua kills King Horam of Gezer.

Joshua 11:10. Killing the king by sword
2 Samuel 1:16. Punishing regicide
2 Kings 12:20. Joash killed by his own officials
2 Kings 14:5. Revenge for regicide
2 Kings 15:10. Consolidating kingship
Esther 2:21. Plotting to kill the king
Daniel 5:30. King Belshazzar killed
John 19:15. Calling for the murder of the King of Kings

▶ Regret *(contrition, remorse, repentance)*

Expressing remorse for one's present circumstances
Genesis 6:6. Regretting creation
Numbers 12:11. Regretting foolish sin
Judges 11:30–40. Regretting a rash vow
1 Samuel 15:11. Regretting making Saul king
Ezekiel 16:63. Forgiveness for everything committed
Matthew 14:8–9. Regretting a promise
Matthew 27:3. Judas regrets betraying Jesus.
2 Corinthians 7:10. No regrets
Revelation 1:7. Some will mourn the second coming

▶ Regulation(s) *(law, precept, rule)*

A law or precept decreed by an authority
Exodus 12:43–49. Passover rules
Leviticus 18:30. Following the Lord's instructions
Numbers 9:3. Festival regulations
1 Kings 2:3. Mosaic regulations
1 Chronicles 29:19. Following God's request for building the temple
Ezekiel 43:18. Altar regulations
Luke 1:6. Following the Lord's regulations perfectly
Romans 8:4. Meeting God's standards
Hebrews 9:1. Priestly regulations
Hebrews 9:10. Outmoded regulations

▶ Rehabilitate *(heal, invigorate, restore)*

The restoration of health and wellness
Luke 10:25–37. Samaritan's care
John 11:38–44. Lazarus raised from the dead
Acts 20:7–12. Paul rehabilitates Eutychus.

▶ Reign *(kingship, rule, sovereign)*

The ruling activity of an earthly king or of God
1 Samuel 13:1. Saul's kingship
2 Samuel 5:4–5. David's reign
1 Kings 11:25. Rival reign
Psalm 93:1. The Lord is king.
Isaiah 52:7. God rules as king.
Micah 4:7. Eternal reign
Luke 1:33. Unending kingdom
1 Corinthians 15:25. All things under Christ's control
Colossians 3:1. Life hidden with exalted Christ
Revelation 11:15. Heavenly kingdom
Revelation 20:4. Millennial reign

▶ Reinstate *(reinstall, reinstitute, restore)*

The restoration of someone or something to a prior condition or status
Genesis 40:13. Restoring a position of prominence
Deuteronomy 30:2–3. Faithfulness and prosperity
2 Samuel 8:3. Military control restored
2 Kings 8:6. Restoring what is due
2 Chronicles 24:13. Restoring God's temple
Job 42:10. Job reinstated
Psalm 51:12. Joy reinstated
Psalm 126:4. Fortunes restored
Isaiah 58:12. History reinstated
Amos 9:14. Israel reinstated
Nahum 2:2. Glory reinstated

▶ Rejection *(despise, nullify, set aside)*

To set aside, dismiss, or nullify something that appeared to be valid
Judges 2:20. Rejection of God's promises

R

1 Samuel 8:7. Total rejection
Psalm 60:1. Rejection and restoration
Matthew 21:42. Rejected stone
Luke 7:30. Rejecting John's baptism
John 12:48. Rejecting God's words
Romans 11:15. Israel's current rejection
1 Corinthians 1:19. Earthly intelligence rejected
1 Thessalonians 4:8. Rejecting human and divine authority
1 Timothy 5:12. Rejecting Christian faith
1 John 2:22–23. Rejecting the Father and the Son

▶ Rejoice *(delight, joyful, praise)*

To feel or show great delight to someone or something
Deuteronomy 16:11. Enjoyment
Psalm 19:8. God's law makes the heart rejoice.
Psalm 32:11. Finding joy in the Lord
Isaiah 66:10. Joyous day for Jerusalem
Zephaniah 3:14. Cause for celebration
Matthew 5:12. Rejoicing in heavenly reward
Luke 10:21. Joy-filled prayer
Galatians 4:27. Barren woman can rejoice.
Philippians 4:4. Called to joyfulness in the Lord
Revelation 19:7. Joy of marriage of the lamb

▶ Relationship(s) *(family, friend, friendship)*

An emotional and intellectual (and perhaps sexual) connection between two people wherein each functions to help meet the relational needs of the other
Judges 21:1–6. Tribe of Benjamin among the twelve tribes
Ruth 1:16. Committing to a family relationship
1 Kings 3:1. Alliance by marriage
Song of Songs 4:9. Two young lovers
Matthew 12:46–50. Priority of kingdom ministry over family
Luke 14:26. Prioritizing relationships
John 19:26–27. Forging new family relationships
Ephesians 5:22. Wife's relationship to husband
Ephesians 5:25. Husband's relationship to wife
James 2:23. Friend of God
1 John 3:1–2. God's children

▶ Relaxation *(leisure, rest, unwind)*

Resting from the worries and work of one's regular schedule
Deuteronomy 33:12. Protected by God
1 Samuel 16:23. Relaxed by David's music
Mark 6:31. Jesus and the apostles desire rest.
Luke 12:19. Taking life easy
2 Corinthians 7:5. Working without rest
Hebrews 3:11. Never entering God's rest

▶ Relevance *(applicable, meaningful, pertinent)*

A teaching or idea which is extremely applicable or meaningful to the person or cause at hand
John 3:16. Ultimate relevance
John 20:30–31. Record of Jesus' life for our belief
Romans 11:14. Means to save some
Romans 15:4. Purpose of things written in the past
1 Corinthians 9:22. Cultural relevance
1 John 2:26. Correction from those who deceived you

▶ Reliability *(dependable, faithful, trustworthy)*

Quality or consistency that can be depended upon no matter what the circumstances
Deuteronomy 32:4. God's reliability
Nehemiah 13:13. People who could be trusted
Psalm 93:5. Reliability of the Lord's testimony
Psalm 119:142. Reliable teachings
Isaiah 25:1. Faithful history
Jeremiah 6:16. Following a reliable path
2 Timothy 2:11. Death with Christ, life with Christ

Titus 3:8. A trustworthy statement
Hebrews 2:2. Reliable message
1 John 1:9. God is faithful and reliable.

▶ Relief *(comfort, consolation, reassurance)*

Reassurance and rest from the pressures of a stressful situation

Genesis 5:29. Relief from pain and work
1 Samuel 16:23. Soothing music
Job 32:20. Asking for relief
Psalm 146:9. Relief to orphans and widows
Psalm 147:6. Relief to the oppressed
Isaiah 14:3. Day of relief
Lamentations 3:56. Hear my cry.
2 Corinthians 8:13. Balancing relief with hardship
2 Thessalonians 1:7. God-given relief from suffering

▶ Religion(s) *(belief, faith, sect)*

The melding of belief and practice concerning God or the gods

Jeremiah 10:3. Idol religion
Acts 4:12. Salvation through Jesus alone
Acts 9:2. Followers of the way of Christ
Acts 26:5. Strictest party of Jewish religion
Galatians 1:13–14. Extremely religious
Colossians 4:11. Religious converts
James 1:26. Worthless religion
James 1:27. Essence of pure religion

▶ Reluctance *(doubt, hesitation, unwillingly)*

An unwillingness or hesitation in carrying out a particular task

Deuteronomy 10:10. Reluctant to destroy
2 Samuel 12:4. Unwilling to use one's own property
Isaiah 30:9. Reluctance to listen to the Lord
Matthew 1:19. Reluctance to cause shame
Matthew 15:32. Not willing to send people away hungry
2 Corinthians 9:7. Do not give reluctantly.

▶ Remarriage *(matrimony, nuptials, wedding)*

Getting married again

Genesis 25:1. Abraham marries after Sarah dies.
Deuteronomy 24:1–2. Regulations for remarriage
Ruth 4:10. Ruth remarries.
Hosea 2:7. Returning to the better husband
Romans 7:1–3. Circumstances for remarriage
1 Corinthians 7:8–9. Guidelines for widows
1 Timothy 5:11. Remarriage for widows

▶ Remedy(ies) *(cure, treatment, medicine)*

A medication or treatment for an ailment

Genesis 37:25. Imported medicine
Proverbs 17:22. Home remedy
Jeremiah 30:13. When medicine fails
Jeremiah 46:11. (Metaphorical) Medicines come from Egypt.
Ezekiel 27:17. Valuable commodity
Matthew 10:8. Curing diseases
Luke 8:43. Failed medication

▶ Remember this *(memory, recall, recollect)*

Likely used as a rhetorical device (much like "listen up!"), the instruction to "remember this" serves to draw attention to the coming instruction or message.

Exodus 13:3. Remember this day.
Nehemiah 13:22. Remember this purity.
Psalm 74:18. Remember this scoffer.
Isaiah 46:8–9. Remember this . . . I am God.
2 Corinthians 9:6. Planting for a large harvest
James 1:19. Remembering to listen carefully and speak hesitantly

▶ Remnant *(chosen, elect, people)*

Significant to OT theology, the notion of the remnant refers to those whom God acts repeatedly on behalf of.

Genesis 45:7. God's action to save a remnant
2 Kings 19:31. Remnant judged
2 Chronicles 36:20. Remnant carried into exile
Isaiah 7:3. Shear Jashub means "a remnant shall return"
Jeremiah 23:3. A remnant returns.
Micah 2:12. Gathering a remnant
Zephaniah 2:7–9. Remnant vengeance
Romans 9:27. A remnant will be saved.
Romans 11:5. A chosen remnant

▶ Remuneration *(payment, salary, wages)*

Payment made for a work or service
Exodus 32:30. Moses makes a payment for sin
Numbers 35:31. Refusing payment for a criminal
Judges 3:15. Paying taxes
1 Samuel 18:25. An unusual payment
Ezra 6:8. Full payment made so that work is not interrupted
Isaiah 65:7. Repaying the sins of ancestors
Matthew 18:25. Unable to make a payment
Romans 6:23. Payment for sin is death.
Philippians 4:18. Grateful for missionary support
James 5:4. Warning to those who hold back payment
1 Peter 1:18–19. Good and bad payments

▶ Renewal *(creation, new creation, regeneration)*

The state of updating, repairing, or regenerating something that already exists into something new
Judges 6:25–26. Building a new worship site
Psalm 19:7. Teachings which renew the soul
Psalm 104:30. Renewing the earth
Isaiah 44:3. Renewing the land
Ezekiel 36:26. New heart and new spirit
Zephaniah 3:17. Renewal of love
2 Corinthians 4:16. Daily renewal
2 Corinthians 5:17. Renewed creation
Colossians 3:10. New person
Titus 3:5. New birth and spiritual renewal

▶ Renounce *(abandon, deny, relinquish)*

Words or actions which effectively demonstrate one's abandonment of a formal ideal or goal
Psalm 89:39. Covenant promise renounced
Matthew 26:70. Peter denies Jesus
Luke 8:45. Denying touching Jesus
Luke 9:23. Renouncing the world, following Jesus
Acts 3:13. Jesus rejected by his people
1 Timothy 5:8. Actions which renounce Christian faith
2 Timothy 2:12. Renounced by God
Titus 1:16. Actions which deny God
2 Peter 2:1. Judgment for renouncing the Lord
1 John 2:22–23. Rejecting Jesus as Messiah

▶ Repair *(fix, mend, restore)*

To fix or mend something that is distressed or broken
Joshua 9:5. Sole repair
1 Kings 11:27. Fixing the wall
2 Kings 12:5–6. Priests failing to repair the temple
2 Chronicles 35:20. Josiah repaired the temple.
Nehemiah 3:4. Numerous repairs
Nehemiah 4:7. Wall repair
Proverbs 29:1. Beyond repair
Jeremiah 19:11. Effect of coming judgment
Ezekiel 13:5. Unprotected on the day of battle
Amos 9:11. Repairing the tabernacle

▶ Repentance *(change of mind, return, turn)*

Literally meaning "to change one's mind," repentance refers to the action of turning from a present course of action or thought to a drastically different course.
Exodus 32:12–14. Reconsidering a decision
Job 42:6. Repenting of words
Jeremiah 18:8. Change of plans

Jonah 3:9. Seeking repentance
Matthew 4:17. Changing thoughts and actions
Matthew 21:29. Change of mind
Luke 19:8. Repenting of a cheating lifestyle
Acts 2:38. Preaching repentance
Romans 2:4. God's grace and kindness leads to repentance.
2 Corinthians 7:8–10. Distress which causes repentance
2 Timothy 2:25. Allowed by God
2 Peter 3:9. Prolonged opportunity for repentance
Revelation 9:20. Stubbornly refusing repentance

▶ Repetition *(reiteration, restatement, retelling)*

The action of restating or retelling something which has already taken place
Exodus 19:7. Moses repeats God's words to the people.
Deuteronomy 6:7. Learning through repetition
1 Samuel 20:28. Repetitive nagging
Proverbs 26:11. Repeating sinful patterns
Jeremiah 46:16. Pattern of sin
John 5:18. The repeated claim of divinity
Hebrews 6:1–2. Repeating basic teachings

▶ Report(s) *(announce, communicate, describe)*

A communicative act, typically spoken, wherein one relays something they have seen, heard, or accomplished
Genesis 24:66. Detailing actions
Numbers 13:26. Initial reports
1 Samuel 2:24. Bad report
2 Samuel 24:9. Reporting census figures
Ezra 5:7–8. Report to the king
Proverbs 22:20–21. Receiving an accurate report
Matthew 2:8. Birth announcement
Mark 6:30. Apostles report to their master.
Acts 15:27. Delegates sent to report decision
1 Thessalonians 1:9. Reporting faithfulness
1 John 1:2. Reporting about eternal life

▶ Reprehensible actions resulting in quick deaths *(mortal sin)*

Actions which warrant swift action from God in judgment
Genesis 19:24–26. Lot's wife disobeys the messenger and dies.
Genesis 38:9–10. Failure to perform the rights of a brother
Numbers 3:4. Death in the Lord's presence at an unholy sacrifice
Acts 5:1–11. Ananias and Sapphira mislead and die.

▶ Representative(s) *(ambassador, messenger, missionary)*

A person or persons who function as ambassadors or messengers, speaking and representing the presence and authority of someone else
Exodus 18:19. Priests are people's representative to God.
Numbers 1:44. Leaders representing their tribal families
2 Samuel 2:15. Representatives of Benjamin
Ezra 10:14. Leaders representing the community
Ezekiel 23:4. Symbolic representation
Luke 19:14. Representatives following Jesus
2 Corinthians 5:20. Ambassadors for Christ
2 Corinthians 8:23. Church representatives
Ephesians 6:20. Christ's imprisoned representative
Philippians 2:25. Cared for by church representative
Hebrews 5:1. Function of chief priest

▶ Reprimand *(see Discipline; Reproach)*

▶ Reproach *(contempt, disgrace, insult)*

An expression of disapproval or judgment on account of one's actions
Psalm 79:4. Reproach to our neighbors
Isaiah 25:8. Reproach removed

Ezekiel 22:4. Dishonored because of idols
Joel 2:19. Fixing reputation among the nations
Matthew 5:11. Blessed through reproach
Matthew 27:44. Reproaches from the cross
Romans 15:3. Reproaches which fell upon Christ
Hebrews 10:33. Public reproach
Hebrews 13:13. Enduring Christ's disgrace
1 Peter 4:14. Insulted, yet blessed

▶ Reprobate *(dross, refuse, unfit)*

An object that is rejected and worthless
Jeremiah 6:30. Useless metal
Ezekiel 22:19–20. Worthless because of sin
Romans 1:28. Given over to immoral mindset
Romans 9:22. Patience with objects headed for destruction
1 Corinthians 9:27. Disqualified from reward
2 Timothy 3:8. Corrupt minds and counterfeit faith
Titus 1:16. Unfit to do anything good

▶ Reproduction *(see Procreation)*

▶ Reptile *(crocodile, frog, snake)*

A cold-blooded animal distinguished by dry, scaly skin
Genesis 3:1. Slippery serpent
Exodus 7:10–12. Magic performed
Exodus 8:2–3. Plague of frogs
Psalm 78:45. Remembering the plague of frogs
Isaiah 11:8. Dangerous reptiles, dangerous times
Ezekiel 29:3. Crocodile in the Nile
Luke 10:19. Snakes and scorpions
Acts 28:3. Paul bitten by a snake
Romans 1:23. Glory exchanged for an image
Romans 3:13. Lips like poisonous snakes

▶ Reputation *(fame, name, renown)*

A common opinion about someone or something, their reputation or fame
Genesis 6:9. Man of integrity
1 Samuel 18:30. David's reputation in battle
Proverbs 22:1. Good name and respect
Daniel 5:12. A good reputation
Matthew 1:19. Protecting Mary's reputation
John 13:35. Reputation
Acts 10:22. Approved by God
Acts 22:12. Well-respected man
Romans 16:19. Reputation for obedience
Galatians 1:23–24. Convert's reputation
3 John 12. Good reputation

▶ Request *(appeal, petition, prayer)*

To make an appeal or petition to an authority in order that a certain action might be accomplished
1 Samuel 1:27. Request granted
1 Samuel 28:8. An unusual request
1 Chronicles 4:10. Prayer of Jabez
Ezra 7:6. Heeding every request
Esther 7:3. Esther's request before the king
Psalm 20:5. The Lord fulfills requests.
Mark 15:6. Request for release
Luke 14:18–19. Making excuses
Ephesians 6:18. Prayer requests
2 Thessalonians 2:1–2. Apostolic request
1 John 5:15. God listens to our requests.

▶ Requirement(s) *(commands, law, testimony)*

Typically associated with aspects of God's law, requirements refer to practices which are obligatory for God's people.
Numbers 6:21. Instructions for the Nazirites
Joshua 7:11. Sinfully ignoring God's requirements
Zechariah 3:7. Effects of following the Lord's requirements
Acts 15:28. No additional requirements
Romans 2:15. Requirements written on our hearts
Romans 8:4. Meeting God's standards
Hebrews 7:16. Human requirements met
Hebrews 7:18. Former requirements now rejected

▶ Rescue *(deliver, heal, save)*

Used literally of the need to deliver someone from a dangerous or stressful circumstance

Genesis 14:14–16. Abraham rescues Lot.

Esther 7:3. Esther saves her people.

Isaiah 31:5. Rescuing Jerusalem

Jonah 1:17. Rescued from the sea, by a fish

Matthew 6:13. Rescue us from evil.

Matthew 8:25–26. Rescued from the storm

Luke 1:74. Promise of rescue

Romans 15:31. Rescued from unbelievers

Colossians 1:13. Rescued from the power of darkness

2 Peter 2:7. God rescued Lot.

▶ Resentment *(animosity, bitterness, indignation)*

Bitterness or indignation caused by one's sense of feeling treated unjustly

Genesis 16:4–5. Sarai's contempt for Hagar

1 Samuel 1:10. Praying, yet resentful

1 Kings 21:4–6. Visibly upset

Proverbs 3:11. Desiring discipline from the Lord

Proverbs 31:6. Easing the pains of resentment

Ecclesiastes 5:17. No way to live

Matthew 20:15. Resenting generosity

Romans 3:13–14. Attitudes of the sinful nature

Colossians 3:21. Family relationships

▶ Residence *(abode, home, house)*

The place where one lives, their home

Joshua 2:19. Safety and responsibility in the home

Judges 18:31. God's dwelling place

2 Kings 11:6. Guarding the king's residence

Daniel 4:30. Royal palace

Matthew 2:11. Commoner's house

Matthew 12:45. Permanent residence of evil spirits

Acts 23:35. House arrest in Herod's palace

1 Corinthians 16:19. Patrons' house

▶ Resilience *(flexible, strong, tough)*

The quality of being strong and able to recover quickly from tiring work

2 Corinthians 11:27. Tireless working

Ephesians 3:16. A prayer for resilience

Philippians 4:12–13. Living in any circumstance

1 Timothy 1:12. Working with Christ's strength

▶ Resist(ance) *(fight, opposition, struggle)*

A willing act of defiance or opposition to an idea or person

Leviticus 26:21. Resistance and punishment

Ecclesiastes 4:12. Group resistance

Acts 7:51. Resisting the Holy Spirit

Acts 26:14. Attempting to resist God

Romans 9:19. Who can resist God?

Romans 13:2. No resisting government

1 Corinthians 10:13. Resisting temptation

Hebrews 12:4. Resistance, but not to the point of death

James 4:7. Resist the devil.

1 Peter 5:9. Resisting the adversary

▶ Resolute *(adamant, purposeful, resolved)*

An attitude of purposeful determination

Exodus 7:13. Stubborn heart

2 Chronicles 32:5. Resolutely working

Hosea 11:7. People determined to turn away from God

Luke 9:51. Determined to accomplish

John 4:38. Following others in working hard

1 Corinthians 15:58. Resolute work

Galatians 4:11. Wasted hard work

James 4:2. Resolute decisions

▶ Resource(s) *(assets, money, wealth)*

A supply of material or immaterial assets which may be drawn upon to enhance the quality of one's life

Psalm 52:7. Trusting in wealth instead of God

Luke 8:3. Using resources to support ministry

Luke 14:33. Called to give up everything

Acts 2:42. Sharing resources with others

Acts 5:1–2. Withholding possessions

2 Corinthians 12:14. Not needing possessions

Philippians 4:17. Desiring resources for others

Hebrews 10:34. Missing resources

▶ Respect *(admire, esteem, regard)*

The feeling or treatment of others in accordance with standards of honor, esteem, or admiration based upon social status, achievements, or abilities

Exodus 20:12. Respecting parents

Leviticus 19:32. Respecting the elderly

Deuteronomy 18:21–22. Prophets who deserve no respect

Nehemiah 8:5. Respect for God's Word

Proverbs 23:22. Respecting the opinion of parents

Malachi 2:4–5. Standing in awe of a good name

Romans 13:7. Paying respect where it is due

Ephesians 5:33. Respect within marriage

1 Thessalonians 5:13. Thinking highly of church leaders

1 Timothy 5:1–2. Respectful speech toward elders

1 Peter 2:17. Mutual respect

▶ Response *(answer, rejoinder, reply)*

Although typically referring to verbal or written replies to a prior action, response can also indicate an intellectual or emotional reaction.

Joshua 1:16. Response to good leadership

1 Samuel 3:4. Samuel responds to God's calling.

John 2:23. Reponses to Jesus' miracles

John 8:30. Response to Jesus' teachings

John 10:27. Responding to the shepherd's voice

Acts 6:7. Massive response to the gospel message

Galatians 2:2. Traveling in response to a revelation

2 Thessalonians 1:8. Refusing to respond to the Good News

1 Peter 1:8. Response of faith

1 John 5:10. Bad responses to Christian message

▶ Responsibility *(duty, function, job)*

A duty or task which is entrusted to someone

Genesis 38:8. Responsibility, according to Levirate marriage

Ruth 4:5. Assuming responsibility as a kinsman-redeemer

Proverbs 20:16. Holding others responsible

Ezekiel 45:17. Responsible for the whole nation

Jonah 1:12. Responsible for a violent storm

Acts 20:26. Personal responsibility

1 Corinthians 11:27. Responsibility related to the Lord's supper

Galatians 6:5. Assuming responsibility

Ephesians 3:2. Responsibility of preaching

Hebrews 1:2. Son's role in the universe

▶ Rest *(ease, peace, relaxation)*

Rest is used in two senses within the Bible. First, rest from activity or second, used theologically to refer to a time and/or a place when God's people will receive rest from their toils or enemies.

Genesis 2:3. Works of creation, time to reign and rest

Deuteronomy 12:10. A land of peace

Psalm 95:10–11. Wandering without finding rest

Isaiah 57:2. Promise of rest

Daniel 12:13. Rest which is to come

Matthew 11:28. Rest found in Jesus

Mark 6:31. Seeking rest from ministry

2 Thessalonians 1:7. Relaxation from intense lifestyle

Hebrews 4:11. Striving to enter God's rest
Revelation 6:9–11. Fullness of rest

▸ Restitution *(compensate, restore, return)*

Restoration of an item to its rightful owner; giving something equivalent

Exodus 22:5–6. Making restitution for lost property
Exodus 22:11–12. Repayment for a stolen animal
Numbers 5:7. Paying back the person you have wronged
Psalm 116:12. Futility in seeking to repay God
Matthew 16:27. Repayment based upon actions
Matthew 18:34. Repaying all that is owed
Romans 11:35. The Lord owes no one anything.
Romans 12:19. Leave vengeance to God.
1 Thessalonians 5:15. Returning good instead of evil
Philemon 19. Taking responsibility for repayment

▸ Restless *(anxious, troubled, stirred)*

A situation of high anxiety or troubled thoughts generally caused by worry or boredom

Psalm 42:5. Restless soul
Psalm 55:2. Restless thoughts
Jeremiah 2:23. Restless animal
Matthew 6:34. Tomorrow's worries can wait.
Luke 12:25. Worry and quality of life
Philippians 4:6. Presenting anxious thoughts to God
James 3:8. Restless evil

▸ Restoration *(healing, peace, reestablish)*

Bringing back to former condition or position

Genesis 20:17. Health restored
Jeremiah 27:22. Restored from exile
Daniel 9:25. Restoration of Jerusalem
Matthew 12:13. Healing the sick
Matthew 17:11. Coming restoration
Acts 1:6. Time of Israel's restoration?
Acts 3:21. Future restoration
2 Corinthians 13:11. Aiming for restoration with others

▸ Restraint *(moderation, restriction, self-control)*

Controlled or kept within limit

Genesis 8:2. Judgment restrained
1 Samuel 3:13. Actions not restrained
1 Samuel 25:34. Restrained by the Lord
Proverbs 17:27. Exercising self-restraint
Isaiah 48:9. Restraining anger
Mark 5:2–3. Uncontrollable man
Acts 14:18. Unrestrained crowd
1 Corinthians 7:35. Sexual restraint
2 Thessalonians 2:6–7. Man of lawlessness now restrained
2 Peter 2:16. Prophet's words restrained

▸ Restriction *(see Restraint)*

▸ Result(s) *(consequence, effect, outcome)*

A consequence or effect of a previous course of action

Romans 1:20. No excuses
Romans 5:16. Resulting from one man
Romans 6:22. Holy living
Romans 11:11. Result of constant stumbling
Ephesians 2:8–9. Salvation is not a result of your own work.
Philippians 1:22. Work which produces results
Colossians 1:6. The Good News producing results
James 1:11. Result of the hot sun
1 Peter 1:7. Result of trials and suffering

▸ Resurrection of Christ *(life after death, revitalization, Risen Christ)*

The victory of Jesus Christ over sin and death through the power of God

Matthew 28:1–7. Angel proclaims the resurrection of Christ.
Mark 8:31. Predicting the resurrection

R

Acts 2:24. Raised by the Father
Romans 1:4. Demonstration that Jesus is the Son of God
Romans 4:25. Justification wrought through the resurrection
Romans 6:5–6. United in life and death
1 Corinthians 6:14. Ensures resurrection of believers
1 Corinthians 15:4. Risen, just as the Scriptures predicted
1 Corinthians 15:20. Firstfruits of the general resurrection
Ephesians 1:20. Raised and exalted
Philippians 3:10–11. Faith in the resurrection
Colossians 3:1. Effects of Christ's death
1 Peter 1:3. Regeneration through the resurrection
1 Peter 3:21. Jesus Christ, who came back to life

▶ Resurrection of Christians *(eternal life, life after death, renewal)*

The NT teaches that one day everyone will rise, the just to life with Christ and the unjust to judgment.

Matthew 22:31–32. God of the living
John 5:29. Resurrection for life and judgment
John 11:24. The day when all come back to life
John 11:25. Jesus brings others back to life.
Romans 6:5–6. United in life and death
2 Corinthians 4:14. Brought back to life with Christ
Philippians 3:10–11. Faith in the resurrection
Colossians 2:12. Died and raised with Christ
1 Thessalonians 4:14. Returning with Jesus
Hebrews 6:2. Basic teachings of the church
1 John 3:2. Becoming like Christ

▶ Retaliation *(retribution, revenge, repayment)*

To return a previous assault or attack with an attack of similar proportion

Exodus 21:23–25. Eye for an eye
Deuteronomy 19:18–19. Punishment for planned retaliation
Esther 7:10. Ironic death
Psalm 58:10. God will avenge
Proverbs 24:29. Repaying unjust actions
Matthew 5:38–41. Upping the ante
Romans 12:17. Not repaying evil
2 Thessalonians 1:6–7. Relief from suffering when Christ comes
1 Peter 3:9. Do not return evil with evil

▶ Retirement plans *(withdrawal, stop working)*

Departing from work for reasons of age, and the plans thereafter

Numbers 20:26. Passing on the priesthood
Deuteronomy 34:7. Working into old age
Joshua 13:1. Nearing the end of life
Joshua 14:10–11. Strong and fit
Ecclesiastes 6:1–2. Life that cannot be enjoyed
Daniel 5:30–31. An age fit to rule
Zechariah 8:4. In the land of promise
Luke 2:36–37. A prophetess in old age
1 Timothy 5:5–7. Caring for one's immediate family

▶ Retreat *(fall back, retire, withdraw)*

Typically used in combat situations, when one person or group is forced to withdraw due to being outnumbered or outmanned

Psalm 6:10. Terror of defeat
Psalm 9:3. Moment before death
Psalm 44:10. Robbed and looted by the enemy
Psalm 56:9. Protected by God
Psalm 129:5. Removing enemies of Zion
Isaiah 44:25. Conveyers of worldly knowledge retreat.
Jeremiah 21:2. Consulting the Lord

▶ Retribution *(punishment, retaliate, vengeance)*

Punishment received in response to a perceived wrong

Genesis 9:5–6. Death penalty
Exodus 21:23–25. Eye for an eye
Numbers 11:1. Punished by fire

2 Chronicles 7:20. People and temple rejected
Ezra 9:13. Receiving less punishment
Jeremiah 25:13–14. Making good on threats
Luke 1:18–20. Zechariah made a mute
Acts 5:1–11. Ananias and Sapphira
Acts 12:18–19. Punished for allowing a prisoner to escape
1 Thessalonians 4:6. The Lord punishes.
Hebrews 2:2. Just retribution
Jude 7. Example of eternal punishment

▶ Retrospect *(recall, reflect, remember)*

To recall or rehash past actions
Psalm 48:9. Reflecting on God's mercy
Psalm 77:6. A song of reflection
Psalm 77:12. Recalling God's actions
Psalm 119:27. Reflecting upon God's miracles
Psalm 119:148. Joyful reflection
Psalm 143:5. Considering what God has done
Isaiah 46:8. Introspection
Lamentations 1:22. Recalling rebelliousness
Hebrews 10:32. Recall the past.
Revelation 3:3. Remember the message.

▶ Returning *(coming home, replace, restore)*

Understood literally in contexts of travel and arriving at one's home
Amos 4:11. Failure to return to the Lord
Zechariah 1:3. Promise upon Israel's return
Matthew 24:42. Alertness on the day of return
Luke 2:20. Returning to work
Luke 15:20–22. Prodigal son returns.
Luke 17:15. Returning healing with praise
Luke 24:33. Returning to Jerusalem
1 Peter 2:25. Returning to the shepherd
2 Peter 2:21. Folly of turning from grace to sin
2 Peter 3:4–5. Promise of God's return

▶ Reunion *(friendship, together, union)*

The gathering of people or persons after a period of separation
Genesis 33:4–5. Jacob and Esau reunited
Genesis 45:4–5. Joseph and his brothers
Genesis 46:29. Father and son reunited
2 Samuel 14:33. Joab reunites with the king
Luke 15:20–22. Family reunites.
2 Corinthians 5:20. Be reunited with God.
2 Corinthians 12:20–21. Afraid of the reunion
1 Thessalonians 4:16–18. Believers reunite.
2 Timothy 1:17. Searching for a friend

▶ Revelation *(apocalyptic, disclosure, word)*

Refers to the disclosure of information
Luke 2:32. Revealer of salvation
Romans 16:25. Source of strength
1 Corinthians 1:7. Awaiting the full revelation of Christ
1 Corinthians 14:26. Source of spiritual growth
Galatians 1:12. Personal revelation of Christ
Galatians 2:2. Traveling because of a revelation
Ephesians 1:17. Spirit of revelation
Ephesians 3:3. Understanding of God's mystery
1 Peter 4:13. Joy at Christ's final revelation
Revelation 1:1. Written revelation of Jesus Christ

▶ Revenge *(punish, satisfy, vengeance)*

The action of returning hurt or harm for injustices suffered at the hands of someone else
Leviticus 26:25. Divine revenge
Joshua 10:13. Taking an opportunity for revenge
2 Kings 9:7. Plotting revenge
Isaiah 34:8. Vengeance is the Lord's.
Jeremiah 51:36. Revenge against Babylon
Micah 5:15. Anger toward the nations
Acts 5:28. Accused of taking revenge
Acts 7:24. Revenging one's kinsman
2 Thessalonians 1:8. Revenging those who disavow God

Hebrews 10:30. Only God has the right to vengeance.
Revelation 19:2. Final vengeance

▶ Reverent/Reverence *(awed, devoted, respectful)*

Displaying a deep sense of awe and respect
Exodus 3:5. Moses on holy ground
Joshua 5:15. Joshua standing on holy ground
2 Kings 18:4. Destroying an object of superstitious reverence
Psalm 5:7. Bowing in reverence
Psalm 33:8. Standing in awe of God
Psalm 46:10. Knowing God
Psalm 51:17. Sacrifice pleasing to God
Isaiah 8:13. Revering the Lord
Isaiah 57:15. God renews the humble
Habakkuk 2:20. Silent before God

▶ Revival *(renewal, vital, zealous)*

A work of restoring and improving spiritual life with God
Genesis 4:26. Revival during Seth's life
Nehemiah 8:12. Joyful celebration
Psalm 79:4–9. Outcries from judgment
Psalm 80:14. Asking for God to stir
Joel 2:28. Promise of God's Spirit
Zechariah 2:10–12. Conversion of many nations
Acts 2:17–21. Spirit poured out
Acts 4:32. Living in harmony with one another
1 Corinthians 1:2. People everywhere who call on his name

▶ Revolution *(mutiny, rebellion, uprising)*

A political or social uprising which attempts to overthrow a current societal structure, typically by force
Judges 9:26–36. Squashing a revolution
Ezra 4:19. Long history of political revolution
Luke 21:9. Wars and revolutions rumored
Luke 23:2. Jesus accused of being a revolutionary
John 18:40. Calling for the freedom of a political revolutionary
Acts 21:38. Starting a revolution

▶ Reward(s) *(honor, payment, prize)*

A form of compensation that is either merited or earned
Exodus 20:12. Reward for honoring one's parents
Isaiah 3:10–11. Rewards in proportion to actions
Isaiah 49:4. Reward is with God.
Jeremiah 32:19. Rewarded every day
Luke 6:22–23. Blessed through persecution
1 Thessalonians 2:19. Converts
1 Timothy 5:18. Rewarded for work
Hebrews 10:35. Keeping confident in God's rewards
James 1:12. Crown of life
2 John 8. Carefully maintaining one's work
Revelation 22:12. Works-based rewards for believers

▶ Riches in Christ *(blessings, grace, riches)*

A figurative image used primarily by Paul
Galatians 2:20. Alive in Christ
Ephesians 1:7. Set free from our sins
Ephesians 2:13. Brought near by Christ's blood
Ephesians 3:7–9. Riches in Christ shared with all
Ephesians 4:32. Forgiveness in Christ
Colossians 1:22. Removing sin, fault, and blame
Colossians 3:3. Life hidden with Christ
Titus 3:4–7. Confidence in God's kindness
Hebrews 10:14. Set apart for God
1 Peter 1:5. Guarded by God's power

▶ Riddle(s) *(mystery, pun, rhyme)*

A statement or question which requires clever thinking or resourcefulness to answer
Numbers 12:8. Speaking plainly
Judges 14:12–14. Samson shares a rhyming riddle.
1 Kings 10:1. Testing wisdom with riddles

Psalm 49:4. Explaining a riddle through song
Ezekiel 17:2–18. Ezekiel commanded to share a riddle
Daniel 5:12. Solver of riddles
Habakkuk 2:6. Ridiculing riddles
John 16:29. Speaking plainly and not with riddles
1 Corinthians 13:12. Seeing darkly

▶ Ridicule *(contempt, despise, mock)*

The mockery, derision, or scorning of someone or something
Exodus 32:25. God's people ridiculed
2 Chronicles 29:8. Lord's anger with his people
Psalm 102:8. Name used as a curse
Psalm 123:4. Suffering a good deal of ridicule
Isaiah 51:7. Do not be discouraged.
Jeremiah 29:18. Cursed people
Hosea 7:16. Ridiculed in exile
1 Peter 2:12. Living well in spite of persecution
1 Peter 3:9. Do not ridicule others.
Jude 18. Ridiculers in the last days

▶ Right *(dextral, direction, side)*

Denoting a specific side or location of which the opposite is left
1 Samuel 6:12. Veering neither right nor left
Psalm 110:1. Sit at the highest position (i.e., my right hand).
Isaiah 62:8. Swearing an oath
Matthew 5:30. Leading you to sin
Matthew 5:39. Slapping on the right cheek
Mark 16:5. Location
John 21:6. Fish finder
Romans 8:34. At God's right hand, interceding for us
Galatians 2:9. Right hand of fellowship
Hebrews 1:3. Exalted to the right hand of God
Revelation 1:17. Right hand

▶ Righteous *(honorable, just, virtuous)*

The attribute of being morally upright and just
Genesis 7:1. The Lord saves a righteous man.
1 Samuel 12:7. Remembering the Lord's righteous acts
Job 4:17. Is righteousness attainable?
Psalm 37:29. Righteous inherit the land.
Habakkuk 2:4. Righteous will live by faith(fulness).
Malachi 3:18. Differences between righteous and wicked demonstrated
Matthew 23:35. Murdering a righteous person
John 17:25. Praying to the righteous Father
2 Corinthians 9:9. Righteous care for the poor
Ephesians 4:24. A new person

▶ Righteousness of God *(approval, justification, righteous)*

God's standard of righteousness, which is Himself
Genesis 18:25. God will act fairly.
Deuteronomy 32:4. Fair and faithful God
Psalm 19:8. Correct precepts
Isaiah 45:19. Speaking what is right
Romans 1:17. Revealed in the Good News, through faith
Romans 3:5. God's righteousness demonstrated through our unrighteousness
Romans 3:21. Manifest through Christ
Romans 10:3. Ignoring God's righteousness
2 Corinthians 5:21. Gained through Christ
James 1:20. Anger cannot produce righteousness.

▶ Rights *(eligible, entitlement)*

Something which someone is entitled to based upon their birth or their socio-political status
Genesis 25:31. Selling the rights of the firstborn
Ruth 4:6. Surrendering family rights of inheritance
1 Samuel 8:11. Rights of the king
Job 27:2. Rights taken away
Psalm 82:3. Protecting rights of the poor
Isaiah 10:2. Injustice performed

Jeremiah 32:8. Redemption of land
Malachi 3:5. Judgment on those who deny basic rights
1 Corinthians 9:12. Rights of an apostle
1 Corinthians 9:15. Suspending rights
Hebrews 12:16. Foolishly surrendering earthly rights

▶ Ring(s) *(decorum, jewelry, seal)*

A round piece of jewelry, typically worn on the hand or in the nose
Genesis 24:22. Gold nose ring
Genesis 38:18. Signet ring
Esther 8:2. Royal signet ring
Esther 8:8. Seal of authenticity
Hosea 2:13. Decorum used to attract lovers
Luke 15:22. Status symbol within family
James 2:2. Worn by the rich

▶ Rioting *(disturbance, turmoil, uproar)*

A (violent) disturbance of the peace by a crowd
Matthew 26:5. Avoiding a riot
Matthew 27:24. Riots breaking out as Pilate deliberates
Mark 15:7. Rioting rebel
Acts 17:5. Jews riot against Paul and Silas.
Acts 19:40. Inciting a riot
Acts 21:31. All Jerusalem rioting
2 Corinthians 6:4–5. Enduring hardships

▶ Risk(s) *(danger, gamble, jeopardize)*

A situation which poses an immediate threat of danger
Judges 5:18. Risking one's life
1 Samuel 19:5. David's risky kill
2 Samuel 17:17. Risking being seen
2 Samuel 23:17. Lives lost in battle
Lamentations 5:9. Risking life for food
Daniel 3:28. Risky business
Acts 19:31–32. Calculated risk
Acts 19:40. Risking arrest
Romans 16:4. Risking life to save Paul
Philippians 2:30. Suffering intense persecution

▶ Ritual(s) *(ceremony, observance, rite)*

A religious practice or ceremony in which prescribed actions are carried out in sequence
Numbers 31:19. Cleansing with ritual water
1 Kings 18:28. Pagan rituals
1 Chronicles 16:1–2. Ritual worship initiated at Jerusalem
2 Chronicles 30:24. Priestly purification ceremonies
Isaiah 66:17. Strange rituals
John 2:6. Rituals of purification
Acts 21:26. Purification ceremony at the temple
Hebrews 9:6. Priests perform ritual duties.
Hebrews 9:10. Ritual sacrifices no longer required

▶ Rival(s) *(contending, competing, opposing)*

A person or group competing for the same objective
Exodus 20:5. God does not tolerate rivals.
Leviticus 18:18. No rival wives
1 Samuel 1:6. Cruelly treating a rival
1 Kings 5:4. Blessed with no rivals
1 Kings 11:14. Solomon's rival
Ecclesiastes 4:4. Folly of rivalry
Romans 13:13. Living without rivalry
2 Corinthians 12:20. Church is no place for rivalry.
1 Timothy 6:3–4. Avoiding unhealthy desires
James 3:16. Indicative of disorder

▶ River(s) *(current, stream, water)*

A large stream of flowing water
Genesis 2:10. River flowing from the heart of Eden
Genesis 2:13–14. Rivers in the paradise land
Exodus 7:19. Rivers turned to blood
Deuteronomy 2:37. On the banks of the Jabbok
2 Kings 5:12. Pure water
Isaiah 18:1. Beyond the rivers of Sudan
Isaiah 66:12. Peace like a river
Jeremiah 47:2. An overflowing river

Ezekiel 47:5–12. River flowing from the temple
Revelation 22:1. River of life

▶ Road rage *(anger, irrational, fury)*

Unsafe and agitated travel, typically used metaphorically or in scenes of battle
Lamentations 3:11. Unsafe travel

▶ Road(s) *(path, street, way)*

A path on which one travels
Numbers 20:19. The main road
2 Kings 3:8. Desert road
Matthew 2:12. Travel plans
Matthew 7:13. Wide road to destruction
Mark 10:17. Meeting on the road
Mark 11:8. Triumphal entry
Luke 10:30. Dangerous place
Acts 8:26. Major highway
Acts 8:36. Traveling along the road
Acts 9:27. Saul saw Jesus on the road.

▶ Robbery *(burglary, stealing, theft)*

The action of stealing someone else's personal property, generally through the use of force
Exodus 22:2–3. Catching a thief
Leviticus 19:13. Forbidden activity
Judges 9:25. Ambush
Job 24:16. Nighttime robbery
Jeremiah 7:11. Den of thieves
Hosea 6:9. Lying in wait
Matthew 27:38. Robbers crucified with Jesus
Luke 10:30. Lurking along the road
Luke 19:46. Temple turned into a den of thieves
John 10:1. Predator
2 Corinthians 11:26. Travel danger

▶ Robe *(clothing, garment, tunic)*

A long outer-garment which wraps around the body
Genesis 37:3. A special robe given as a gift
Exodus 28:4. Priestly robes
Joshua 7:21. Expensive robe
1 Samuel 15:27. Robe torn
Jonah 3:6. Disrobing in fear
Mark 16:5. Bright white robe
Luke 15:22. Sign of opulence
Luke 23:11. Dressing Jesus in a kingly robe
John 19:23. Dividing up Jesus' clothes
Revelation 1:13. Long robe
Revelation 6:11. Martyrs clothed in robes of white

▶ Rock(s) *(boulder, mountain, stone)*

In addition to a very literal use of rock(s) in the Bible, they are used symbolically to refer to security, defense, and refuge.
Deuteronomy 32:37. Rock of refuge
2 Samuel 22:32. God is a rock.
Psalm 40:2. Unshakable foundation
Psalm 118:22. Rejected stone
Isaiah 8:14. Stumbling stone
Isaiah 28:16. Precious cornerstone
Matthew 16:18. Peter, the rock
Mark 15:46. Tomb covering
Romans 9:33. Stone of offense
1 Corinthians 10:1–4. Christ was the rock

▶ Rod *(scepter, staff, stick)*

Although appearing in a variety of contexts in the Bible, "rod" has the basic meaning of a thin, straight object.
Genesis 38:18. Carried by men of rank
Exodus 4:2. Shepherd's staff
Exodus 4:20. Moses' staff
Exodus 7:12. Divination staff
2 Kings 18:21. Trusting a broken rod
Psalm 23:4. Courage and comfort
Isaiah 28:27. Threshing stick
Zechariah 8:4. Old person's cane
Revelation 11:1. Measuring stick

▶ Rodent(s) *(hare, mice, rats)*

A type of gnawing mammal typically known for having strong, sharp teeth
Leviticus 11:6. Unclean food
Leviticus 11:29. Unclean animals

Isaiah 2:20. Throwing items to rodents
Isaiah 66:17. Eating rodents

▶ Roman(s) *(authority, imperium)*

The New Testament world was under Roman rule.

Luke 2:1. Ordering a census in Palestine
Luke 20:22–25. Roman rights defended
John 11:48. Fear of the Romans
John 19:15. Loyalty demanded
Acts 17:6–7. Roman interventions at Thessalonica
Acts 22:27. Roman citizenship
Romans 13:4. Government as God's servant
2 Corinthians 11:24–25. Beaten by Roman officials

▶ Romance *(adoration, love, passion)*

The emotional excitement and intrigue associated with being in love

Genesis 2:23. Perfect mates for life
Genesis 25:19–20. Isaac's bride
Genesis 29:10–11. Rachel makes Jacob sob.
Deuteronomy 21:11. Strange customs
Ruth 3:9. Female proposition
2 Samuel 13:1–4. Infatuation
Proverbs 30:18–19. Mysteries of romance
Song of Songs 1:15. Romantic words
Song of Songs 2:14. Listening to a sweet voice

▶ Roman Road(s) *(path, road, way)*

Travel in the ancient world improved greatly under Roman rule. Elaborate and far-reaching road systems were developed in order to aid military travel and postal routes.

Acts 9:3. Saul confronted on the Roman road
Acts 20:13. Traveling on a Roman road from Troas
Acts 28:15. Paul travels on Via Appia.
Galatians 1:17. Paul's travels between Jerusalem and Damascus

▶ Rooftop adventures *(excitement, risk, thrill)*

Actions and activities which take place on the roof

Joshua 2:6. Hiding spies
Judges 3:20. Hearing a message from God
Judges 16:27. Rooftop party
2 Samuel 11:2. A bathing beauty
Jeremiah 48:38. Mourning from the rooftops
Matthew 24:17. Day of woes
Mark 2:4. Lowering a man through the roof
Acts 10:9. Praying on the roof

▶ Rooster(s) *(bird, fowl, hen)*

A domesticated, male bird. Although each of the Gospels record this event, only selections from Matthew's Gospel have been included.

Proverbs 30:29–31. Animal which walks with dignity
Matthew 26:34. Jesus predicts Peter's betrayal and the rooster crow
Matthew 26:74–75. The rooster crows.

▶ Roots *(foundation, origin, source)*

The foundation of a plant which grows underground, providing sustenance and strength to the plant

Proverbs 12:3. Roots of the righteous
Isaiah 11:10. Root of Jesse
Hosea 9:16. People like dried-up roots
Matthew 3:10. Total destruction
Matthew 13:6. Shallow roots
Romans 11:16–18. The root and the branches
Colossians 2:7. Sink your roots in.
1 Timothy 6:10. Money the root of all kinds of evil
Hebrews 12:15. Do not allow bitterness to take root.
Revelation 22:16. Root of David

▶ Rope *(cable, cord, line)*

A length of cord created by smaller cords being twisted together

Exodus 28:24. Priestly decorum
Numbers 3:37. Ropes for the tent
Joshua 2:15. Rappelling down a wall
Judges 16:12. Breaking free from the ropes
2 Samuel 8:2. Measuring device
Job 41:1. Fishing metaphor
Ecclesiastes 4:12. Cord of three strands
Isaiah 3:24. Rope belt
John 2:15. Weapon
Acts 27:17. Reinforcing ropes

▶ Rose of Sharon *(flower, plant, rose)*

A flower believed to have grown in the valleys of the Sharon plain

Song of Songs 2:1. Flower of the Sharon plain

▶ Royalty *(king, noble, queen)*

A member of a noble, royal family; especially a queen, king, prince, or princess

1 Samuel 26:15. Attempted royal assassination
2 Samuel 3:6. The royal family
1 Kings 9:1. King Solomon's building projects
2 Kings 11:1. Trouble in the royal family
1 Chronicles 29:25. Royal honor
Esther 1:9. Royal banquet
Jeremiah 52:13. Destruction of the temple and palace
Ezekiel 17:13. Royal family
Daniel 2:14–15. Royal vanity
1 Peter 2:9. Royal priesthood of believers

▶ Ruins *(debris, remains, wreckage)*

The wreckage which remains after a substantial destruction of property

Leviticus 26:33. Country in ruins
Deuteronomy 13:16. Pile of ruins
Joshua 8:28. Ai burned and left in ruins
2 Chronicles 36:21. A land lying in ruins
Job 3:14. Fleeting worldly kingdoms
Job 30:14. Crawling out from ruins
Psalm 9:6. Impending judgment on enemies
Lamentations 5:18. Zion lies in ruins
Amos 9:14. Promise of a city restored
Malachi 1:4. Rebuilding the ruins

▶ Rules *(commands, edicts, regulations)*

A set of principles or regulations meant to be followed

Exodus 12:43–49. Rules for Passover
Exodus 15:25. Rules to live by
Leviticus 26:46. Rules given at Sinai
1 Kings 3:3. Living under the king's rule
2 Kings 17:40. Making up your own rules
Ezekiel 5:6. Ignoring God's laws and rules
Matthew 15:9. Following human rules
Acts 22:3. Ancestral rules
2 Timothy 2:5. Playing by the rules
Hebrews 13:9. Rules concerning food

▶ Rumor(s) *(gossip, hearsay, speculation)*

A story in circulation of uncertain truth

Exodus 23:1. Never spread false rumors.
Numbers 14:13–16. Circulating rumors
Nehemiah 6:10–13. False rumor
Job 28:20–22. Rumor concerning wisdom
Psalm 15:1–3. Telling the truth
Jeremiah 51:46. Do not lose heart over rumors.
Mark 13:7. Wars and rumors of wars
John 21:22–23. Rumor caused by misunderstanding

▶ Running *(jog, race, sprint)*

Running is used literally of quick-paced foot movement.

Genesis 18:7. Abraham runs to the herds.
Genesis 24:20. Caring for animals
1 Samuel 20:36. Running to fetch arrows
Psalm 19:5. Champion eager to run
Isaiah 59:7. Quickly pursuing evil
Joel 2:4. Galloping horses
Matthew 27:48. Running to meet a dying need of Jesus
Luke 15:20. Prodigal's father runs to his son.
Luke 24:12. Running to Jesus' tomb
1 Corinthians 9:24. Running to win
Hebrews 12:1. Running God's race

▶ Ruthless *(cruel, heartless, merciless)*

An attitude of sheer cruelty

Job 6:23. Asking for deliverance from a ruthless tyrant

Psalm 37:35. Wicked person

Psalm 54:3. Seeking one's life

Isaiah 13:11. Ruthless arrogance ended

Isaiah 25:3. Ruthless nations will fear you.

Romans 1:29–31. Acting cruel

2 Timothy 3:1–3. Ruthless people in the latter days

▶ Sabbath *(holiday, observance)*

A day of rest commanded by God for His covenant people

Genesis 2:2–3. Resting after the completion of creation work

Exodus 16:23. Preparing for the day of worship

Exodus 20:11. Setting apart a day as holy to the Lord

Exodus 31:13. Sign of covenant with God

Deuteronomy 5:15. Remembering former life as slaves

Isaiah 58:13–14. Finding joy in the Lord

Matthew 12:4–5. Priestly work permitted

Matthew 12:12. Lawful practices on the Sabbath day

Mark 2:27–28. Sabbath was made for people.

Mark 6:31. Jesus sees value in rest.

▶ Sackcloth *(clothing, goat hair, sack)*

A cloth made of coarse black goat hair and used to make sacks, worn by those who are mourning and as a sign of repentance

Genesis 37:34. Sign of mourning

2 Samuel 3:31. Mourning the death of a king

Nehemiah 9:1. Penitence for sins

Isaiah 3:24. Cheap, unpleasant clothing

Lamentations 2:10. Mourning nation's disaster

Joel 1:13. Priests called to mourn

Matthew 11:21. Sign of repentance

Revelation 6:12. Goat's hair which is black in color

▶ Sacrament *(baptism, grace, Lord's Supper, ritual)*

An outward, visible sign of an inward spiritual blessing

Mark 10:38–39. Following Christ in both life and death

Luke 22:20. Lord's Supper

Acts 2:41–42. Baptism and the breaking of bread together

Romans 6:3. Baptized into Christ's death

1 Corinthians 10:16. Sharing in the blood and body of Christ

1 Corinthians 11:25. Drinking in remembrance

▶ Sacred *(blessed, consecrated, holy)*

That which is dedicated to God or connected to religious order and purposes

Exodus 30:29. Dedicated for a holy purpose

Leviticus 26:31. Sacred space

Deuteronomy 12:5–6. Sacred practices

1 Chronicles 16:22. Holy peoples

1 Chronicles 16:42. Musicians playing sacred songs

Micah 5:13. So-called sacred monuments

Matthew 23:16–17. Sacred temple

1 Timothy 1:9. Is nothing holy or sacred?

▶ Sacrifice *(gift, offering)*

A gift or offering, typically an animal, which is presented in the temple as a sacrifice of atonement

Exodus 3:18. Traveling to offer sacrifices

Exodus 29:25. Sacrifice by fire

Leviticus 2:1. Grain offering

Leviticus 3:1. Fellowship offering

Leviticus 4:23. Sin offerings

Leviticus 8:28. Burned on the altar

Numbers 29:6. Regular offerings of God's people

1 Samuel 2:28. Levites chosen to offer sacrifices

Ezekiel 20:28. Idolatrous offerings

Malachi 3:8. Cheating God of offering money

Matthew 9:13. God desires mercy, not sacrifice

Mark 12:33. Love of neighbor more important than offerings

Romans 12:1. Bodies as living sacrifices

Ephesians 5:2. Christ gave his life as an offering

Philippians 2:17. Suffering and sacrifice of Paul

Hebrews 7:27. Once for all sacrifice
Hebrews 10:26. No sacrifice remains if we go on sinning
1 Peter 2:5. Spiritual sacrifices acceptable to God

▶ Sacrilege *(blasphemy, desecration, profanity)*

Misusing or violating something which is considered sacred
Leviticus 10:1. Offering an authorized sacrifice in the temple
Numbers 25:1–2. Illicit sex and eating idol meat
2 Chronicles 24:7. Worshiping Baal in the Lord's temple
Psalm 74:18. Godless fools who despise the Lord's name
Isaiah 66:3. Choosing to pursue detestable things
Daniel 5:2. Using the temple's finery
Daniel 11:31. Setting up an abomination in the temple
Matthew 21:13. House of prayer turned into den of thieves
Matthew 26:65. Accusing Jesus of sacrilege
1 Corinthians 11:20–21. Turning Lord's Supper into excuse for gluttony

▶ Sadducees *(elders, lawyers, rulers)*

One of four identifiable Jewish sects who were opposed to Jesus and His ministry
Matthew 3:7. Dangerous group
Matthew 16:11–12. Yeast of the Pharisees and Sadducees
Luke 20:27. Denying the resurrection
Acts 4:1–2. Annoyed at apostles' teaching concerning Jesus
Acts 23:6. Paul on trial before the Sadducees and Pharisees

▶ Sadness *(despair, sorrow, unhappiness)*

Demonstrating feelings of sorrow or despair
Esther 9:31. Purim commemorates sadness.
Psalm 46:10. Letting go of earthly concerns
Ecclesiastes 7:1–4. Enjoying sad disposition
Isaiah 60:20. Days of sadness drawing to a close
Isaiah 65:14. Cries of sadness and depression for enemies of God
Zephaniah 3:17. Renewed by God's love
Matthew 11:17. Although a funeral song was played, no sadness
Luke 22:45. Sad sleep
John 16:6. Filled with sadness
2 Corinthians 7:10. Distress leading to change of heart
1 Peter 1:6–7. Temporary suffering and troubles
Revelation 21:4. Sadness ended

▶ Safety *(peace, protection, welfare)*

Comfort of knowing that one is protected and watched over, shielded from dangerous risk; at peace in body and mind
Job 11:18. Resting confidently in safety
Job 18:14. Dragged from safety
Psalm 12:5. The Lord provides safety for those who desire it.
Psalm 59:16. Rejoice in God's strength.
Psalm 91:2. Refuge and fortress
Isaiah 8:14. Safety from all nations
Isaiah 14:30. No safety from God's judgment
Ezekiel 28:26. Ezekiel's vision of comfort and safety
Acts 17:10. Safety in the synagogue
Acts 27:24. Safe sailing granted
Romans 8:38–39. Nothing can separate us from the love of God.
1 Peter 1:5. Guarded by God's power through faith

▶ Saffron *(flavor, spice)*

An exotic spice and food coloring derived from the crocus plant
Song of Songs 4:13–14. Delicacies of paradise

▶ Sagacity (see *Wisdom*)

▶ Sailing *(boating, cruising, transportation)*

The action of sailing in a boat for the purpose of transportation, trade, or pleasure

Psalm 107:30. Sailing through a quiet storm
Isaiah 42:10. Singing at sea
Ezekiel 27:28–29. Fearful sailors
Jonah 1:5. Frightened sailors cry out to gods.
Luke 8:23. Sleeping in a storm
Acts 13:4. Sailing around the Mediterranean
Acts 27:27–44. Shipwreck
Revelation 18:17. Wealth of the captain is destroyed.

▶ Saint(s) *(holy, holy one, virtuous)*

A designation used in the Bible for those who are considered sacred

Psalm 16:3. Those who live holy lives
Psalm 30:4. Saints sing praise.
Psalm 34:9. Saints who fear the Lord
Daniel 7:18. Saints of the Most High
Matthew 27:52. Vision of saints risen from the dead
Romans 1:7. God's holy people
Ephesians 1:1. Faithful saints
Ephesians 3:8. Least of the saints
Hebrews 6:10. Helping God's holy people
Revelation 14:12. Call for endurance
Revelation 18:24. Slain saints

▶ Salary *(compensation, pay, wages)*

A pre-arranged monetary compensation for services rendered

Numbers 18:11–13. Priestly salary
Deuteronomy 23:18. Unpleasing salary
Luke 3:14. Be satisfied with pay.
John 4:36. Cheerful salary
Philippians 4:10–19. Sharing with the apostle Paul in a time of need
1 Thessalonians 2:9. Working without salary
1 Timothy 5:17–18. Pay a generous salary to those who teach God's Word.
Titus 3:14. Using salary wisely
James 5:4. Injustice of unpaid salaries

▶ Salt *(flavor, preservation, spice)*

A highly useful preservative and something to add flavor to food

Genesis 19:26. Lot's wife turned into column of salt.
Deuteronomy 29:23. Poisons the ground
Judges 9:45. Destruction of the ground
Job 6:6. Flavor enhancer
Matthew 5:13. Salt of the earth
Mark 9:50. Do not lose your flavor.
Colossians 4:6. Speech seasoned with salt
James 3:12. Salt water does not produce fresh water.

▶ Salutations *(see Greetings)*

▶ Salvation *(deliverance, Savior)*

All humanity's need to be delivered from the punishment of death for sin

Exodus 14:13. The Lord will save today.
Exodus 15:2. The Lord is my Savior.
Psalm 35:9. Joy in God's salvation
Isaiah 12:2. The Lord is my salvation.
Romans 6:23. Free gift of God
Romans 13:11. Salvation draws near.
Ephesians 1:13. Good News of your salvation
Ephesians 2:8. Saved by grace through faith
Philippians 2:12. Working out salvation with fear and trembling
1 Thessalonians 5:9. God's will for salvation
Hebrews 5:9. Source of eternal salvation
Revelation 7:9–10. Salvation song

▶ Samaritan(s) *(Jewish people)*

A mixed Jewish religious group separate from Jerusalem

2 Kings 17:29. Religious syncretism
Matthew 10:5. Warning to stay away from Gentiles and Samaritans
Luke 9:52. Entering into a Samaritan village
Luke 10:33. Samaritan shows mercy and justice.
John 4:9. Woman at the well
John 8:48. Demon possessed
Acts 8:25. Preaching the Good News to Samaritans
Acts 15:3. Joy spreading in Samarian cities

▶ Sanctification *(holiness, regeneration, righteousness)*

The cooperative and progressive work of God in humanity, conforming followers of Christ's image and likeness with respect to holiness and righteous living

Romans 6:13. Doing what God approves of
Romans 7:23–24. Influence of corrupt nature
1 Corinthians 6:11. Made holy
1 Corinthians 6:19. Taking care of God's temple
2 Corinthians 4:6. Living as God's servants
2 Corinthians 7:1. Cleaning up one's life
Galatians 2:20. Living by faith in God's Son
Galatians 5:14. Obedience to God's great commands
Philippians 3:12–14. Living a heavenward life
Colossians 3:9–10. Living as a new person in Christ
2 Thessalonians 2:13. Carrying out redemptive work
1 John 4:7. Loving one another

▶ Sanctimonious *(disingenuous, hypocritical, self-righteous)*

Public demonstration of one's own superior moral fabric

Job 33:9. Pretending to be without sin
Isaiah 58:2. Oblivious nation
Isaiah 65:5. Holier than thou
Matthew 6:5. Hypocrites' prayer
Mark 12:38–40. Scribes who seek admiration
Luke 18:11. False apologizing
Revelation 3:17. Out of touch with reality

▶ Sanctuary *(holy, tabernacle, temple)*

The place where Yahweh is worshipped and where the divine presence resides

Exodus 15:17. Holy place
Exodus 25:8. The tabernacle
1 Chronicles 22:19. The temple
Psalm 102:19. The heavens
Psalm 114:2. Judah and Israel
Mark 14:58. The temple of God
Ephesians 2:21. House of God
Revelation 21:22. No sanctuary in the new creation

▶ Sand *(beach, coast, shore)*

A granular substance found in high supply near most lakes and seas and desert areas

Genesis 22:17. Descendants as numerous as sand
Genesis 49:13. Coastal living
Deuteronomy 33:19. Treasures hidden in sand
Job 6:3. Determinative of weight
Job 29:18. Longevity
Isaiah 10:22. Only a select few shall return as a remnant.
Matthew 7:26. Unstable for building a home
Revelation 20:8. Numerous nations gathering

▶ Sandals *(shoes, soles)*

A foot covering typically made of wooden soles and fastened on with leather straps

Exodus 3:5. Removing sandals on holy ground
Joshua 9:5. Tattered outfits
Ruth 4:7. Completing a contract
Matthew 3:11. Unworthy to remove Jesus' sandals
Matthew 10:10. Unnecessary for disciples' travel
Luke 15:22. Reconstituting a son

▶ Sanhedrin *(council, governing board, officials)*

A council consisting of seventy-one leaders (including the high priest), responsible for judicial and administrative council of the Jews

Numbers 11:16–17. Men chosen to dispense law
Matthew 5:22. A court of justice
Matthew 26:3. Chief priests and elders
Matthew 26:59. Supreme Jewish Court
Mark 15:1. Jewish council
John 11:47. Questioning Jesus
Acts 4:2–3. Silencing the apostles
Acts 6:12–15. Interrogating Stephen

▶ Sanitation *(clean, sanitary)*

Concerned with issues of public health and wellness, particularly concerning public water supplies and the disposal of waste

Exodus 16:19–20. Food which only keeps one day

Leviticus 13:6. Keeping diseased persons at a distance

Leviticus 15:4–7. Male sanitary regulations

Numbers 5:1–3. Separating unclean from clean

Numbers 19:14–21. Instructions for when someone dies in a tent

Deuteronomy 23:12–13. Digging a hole outside the camp

2 Kings 2:19–22. Clean water

Nehemiah 13:9. Cleaning rooms

Ezekiel 16:4–5. Unsterile child

Mark 7:2. Refusing to eat prior to washing hands

▶ Sanity *(faculties, reason, saneness)*

Having the ability to think rationally and clearly in accordance with normal mental health

Job 11:12. Unlikely situation

Job 12:24. No common sense

Isaiah 32:4. Sanity restored

1 Corinthians 1:20–21. Wisdom of this age turned on its head

▶ Sarcasm *(derision, mockery, scorn)*

The skillful, often humorous use of irony and mockery to express contempt

Judges 10:14. Perhaps your gods can save you?

1 Kings 18:27. Elijah mocks Baal's prophets.

Nehemiah 4:1–3. Making fun of the building project

Job 12:2–3. Quick witted

Job 38:19–21. Mocking ignorant people

Jeremiah 10:5. Unafraid of silent idols

Matthew 27:28–29. Mocking the King of Kings

Luke 16:14. Responding with sarcasm

Luke 23:35. Calling upon Jesus to save Himself

Galatians 5:12. Calling upon troublemakers to carry out extreme action

▶ Satan *(Accuser, devil, deceiver)*

The proper name for the ruler of evil spirits; in the New Testament, used as the personal name given to the diabolical creature known as the devil

Job 1:6. The Accuser

Matthew 4:1–3. Wilderness temptation by the devil

John 12:31. Ruler of this world

Acts 26:18. Coming back under God's control

Romans 16:20. Crushing Satan

2 Corinthians 2:11. Aware of Satan's schemes

2 Corinthians 4:4. The god of this world

Ephesians 2:2. Spiritual ruler of this world

2 Timothy 2:26. Under the devil's snare

Hebrews 2:14. Death and the devil destroyed at the cross

1 Peter 5:8. On the prowl

Revelation 12:9. The serpent or snake

▶ Satisfaction *(content, fulfilled, gratified)*

Fulfillment of one's wishes or needs

2 Samuel 3:36. Popular appeal

Psalm 17:15. Satisfied to see the Lord

Psalm 103:4–5. Life full of blessings

Proverbs 10:24. Desires of righteous granted

Luke 9:17. Satisfied with bread

John 15:11. Information leading to joy

Philippians 4:19. Every need met in Christ

James 4:2. Wrong desires

3 John 1:3–4. Good reputation

▶ Satrap(s) *(protector, ruler, subordinate)*

A provincial protector in the ancient Persian empire; a subordinate ruler to the king

Ezra 8:36. King's satraps

Esther 3:12. Provincial governor

Daniel 6:1–3. Daniel's impressive spirit

S

▶ Savage behavior *(untamed, wild)*

Behavior which is wild, untamed, and irrational

Deuteronomy 28:53–57. Men and women given to depravity
Judges 19:22–26. Sexual savagery
Galatians 6:7–8. Reaping what one sows
Revelation 9:8. Savage-looking creatures

▶ Savior *(deliverer, rescuer)*

A deliverer; in the New Testament, the title for Jesus which was indicative of His purpose and work on behalf of the world

Exodus 15:2. The Lord my Savior
Judges 3:9. The judges save Israel.
1 Samuel 14:39. Swearing an oath on the Savior of Israel
Psalm 17:7. Protector of God's people
Isaiah 12:2. God is my Savior.
Isaiah 59:20. A Savior will come to Zion.
Luke 2:11. Christ the Lord is born.
John 4:42. Savior of the world
Philippians 3:20. Savior's return from heaven
Titus 1:4. Peace from Christ the Savior
2 Peter 3:18. Growing in knowledge of the Savior

▶ Scales *(measurement)*

Used literally to speak of honest business deals involving commodities and minerals; metaphorically used to highlight the need for fairness and justice in all of one's dealings

Leviticus 19:36. Using honest scales and weights
Job 31:6. Integrity considered honestly
Psalm 62:9. Common people amount to nothing.
Proverbs 11:1. Dishonesty disgusts the Lord.
Proverbs 16:11. God considers things fairly.
Proverbs 20:23. Double standard
Isaiah 40:15. Nations are as nothing.
Ezekiel 45:10. Honest tools
Daniel 5:27. Weight loss
Amos 8:5. Price inflation
Micah 6:11. Inaccurate weights
Revelation 6:5. Justice came riding in.

▶ Scapegoat *(Azazel)*

One of two goats used in the Day of Atonement cultic practice which was released into the wild as a symbolic picture of the removal of sin from human society

Leviticus 16:8. One goat is the Azazel
Leviticus 16:22. Goat released in a deserted place

▶ Scarecrow(s) *(dummy, protector)*

An object made to appear human and used to keep unwanted pests out of a garden or crop land

Jeremiah 10:5. Protecting cucumber gardens

▶ Scavenger *(forager, rummager)*

An animal that feeds on the decaying flesh of dead animals

Leviticus 11:13. Unclean birds
Job 39:29–30. Found near dead bodies
Psalm 63:10. Bodies left as food for jackals
Jeremiah 7:33. Animals that feed on the dead
Ezekiel 39:17–18. Scavengers eat well.
Luke 17:37. Vultures

▶ Schedule *(plan, program, timetable)*

A plan for carrying out a process on a reasonable timetable

Deuteronomy 16:16–17. Scheduled festivities
1 Kings 9:25. Regularly scheduled sacrifices
Nehemiah 4:21. Continuing work on schedule
Ecclesiastes 3:1–8. A time for all things
Isaiah 25:1. Reliable plans
Isaiah 49:8. Scheduled time
Jeremiah 6:4–5. Scheduled attacks
Luke 4:42–44. Scheduling a longer stay
Acts 18:20–21. Trying to prolong Paul's stay
Acts 20:13. Keeping a trip on schedule

Romans 5:6. Christ's death occurred "at the right time."

Revelation 12:12. The Devil still has time.

▶ Scheme *(see Plan[s])*

▶ Schism(s) *(break, rift, split)*

A split between two groups caused by differing opinions or beliefs

Numbers 14:1–4. Pondering appointing a new leader

Isaiah 7:6. Appointing a competing king

Jeremiah 8:8. Lord's teachings turned into lies

John 3:25. Argument over Jewish ceremony

Acts 19:35–36. An unruly crowd

1 Corinthians 1:12. Division at Corinth over baptism

1 Corinthians 3:3. Corrupt nature leading to quarrels

1 Timothy 1:3–4. Stopping the teaching of false doctrine

2 Timothy 2:14. Quarrels destroy listeners.

Titus 1:10–16. Rebellious converts

▶ School *(academy, education, institution)*

An institution, formal or informal, for the education of children

Genesis 18:19. Family following after the Lord

Leviticus 10:11. Teaching children Mosaic Law

Deuteronomy 11:19. Following the Lord's statutes

Deuteronomy 31:11–12. Learning the fear of the Lord

Judges 8:14. Writing

Matthew 7:29. Learning from the scribes

Acts 19:9. Daily discussions in the lecture hall

▶ Science *(biology, botany, chemistry, zoology)*

The study of the natural world and its inhabitants through basic methods of observation and interpretation

1 Kings 4:33. Botany

Job 9:9. Astronomy

Psalm 8:8. Oceanography

Mark 5:26. Failed medication

Mark 7:19. More scientific explanation

1 Timothy 6:20. Guard against false knowledge.

▶ Scoffing *(see Mockery)*

▶ Scorn *(contempt, disdain, mockery)*

The belief that someone or something is worthless, thus producing feelings of contempt

Genesis 37:19. Deriding the imaginative brother

1 Samuel 17:41–44. Scornful comments from the mighty warrior

Job 34:7. Drinking scorn like water

Psalm 31:11. Scorned by opponents

Psalm 89:41. Object of neighbor's scorn

Proverbs 19:29. Punishment for scorn

1 Corinthians 1:18. Scornful message of the cross

1 Corinthians 1:27–28. Scornful things of the world chosen to shame the wise

Hebrews 11:24–26. Moses scorns his upbringing.

▶ Scorpion *(sting)*

A small arachnid with a jointed poison tail

Deuteronomy 8:15. Poisonous scorpions in the desert

1 Kings 12:11. Severe punishment

Ezekiel 2:6. Do not fear your surroundings.

Luke 10:19. Nothing will hurt the disciples.

Revelation 9:5. Pain of the scorpion's sting

▶ Scourging *(punishment, suffering, whip)*

Inflicting great pain and suffering through beatings or whipping

Judges 8:7. Scourging the body

1 Kings 12:11. Scourging elevated

Isaiah 28:18. Overwhelming scourging

Nahum 3:2. Sounds of scourging

Matthew 27:26. Scourging Jesus
Mark 15:15. Jesus scourged to satisfy the crowd
John 19:1. Whipped

▶ Scribe(s) *(amanuensis, copyist, student)*

A term used to describe an official writer
2 Samuel 8:16. Royal historian
2 Chronicles 24:11. King's scribe employed as public administrator
Ezra 7:6. Ezra's expertise in the Law
Jeremiah 32:12. Jeremiah's scribe: Baruch
Jeremiah 36:26. Baruch and Jeremiah hidden
Mark 9:11. Debating Jesus
Mark 12:28. Scribes seek answers from Jesus
John 5:39–40. Professional students of Scripture

▶ Scripture(s) *(sacred, word)*

God's Word in written form
Exodus 31:18. Written by God himself
Joshua 24:26. Joshua writes in the book of the Law.
Isaiah 30:8. Permanent witness
Jeremiah 30:2. Recording the words of the Lord
Ezekiel 34:1–2. Communication from God
1 Corinthians 14:37. Paul writes the Lord's words.
2 Timothy 3:16. Scripture inspired by God
2 Peter 3:2. Words of prophets and apostles

▶ Scroll(s) *(book, document, writing)*

A rolled piece of parchment used as a writing surface
Exodus 17:14. Writing on a scroll
Deuteronomy 17:18. Recording a copying of the law of the king
1 Samuel 10:25. Writing laws on a scroll
Jeremiah 36:2. Commanded to write in a scroll
Jeremiah 36:13. Public reading of scrolls
Ezekiel 3:3. Prophet commanded to eat a scroll
Zechariah 5:2. Vision of a large, flying scroll
Revelation 1:11. Writing and sending scrolls to seven churches
Revelation 5:5. Lion is worthy to open the scroll.

▶ Sea monster *(fish, leviathan, serpent)*

A monster who lives in the sea
Job 41:1–34. Poetic description of Leviathan's strength compared to the Lord
Psalm 74:14. Leviathan crushed
Psalm 104:26. Playing in the sea
Isaiah 27:1. Leviathan punished
Amos 9:3. Snake of the sea
Jonah 1:17. Large fish swallows up Jonah.

▶ Sea of Galilee *(sea, water)*

A body of water located in Northern Palestine
Deuteronomy 3:17. Borderline of land
Matthew 4:13. Living on the shores of Galilee
Matthew 4:18. Calling fishermen to be disciples
Matthew 16:5. Traveling across the sea
Mark 4:1. Teaching from a boat

▶ Seal(s) *(clay, mark, wax)*

In antiquity, one way of authenticating a letter or message was to seal it with wax or clay and impress a signet.
1 Kings 21:8. Signed, sealed, delivered
Nehemiah 9:38. Marking a document with seals
Esther 3:12. Sealed with king's ring
Isaiah 8:16. Seal the teachings of God.
Matthew 27:66. Seal placed on the entrance to the tomb
John 6:27. Seal of approval
Romans 4:11. Circumcision as seal
1 Corinthians 9:2. Seal of apostleship
Ephesians 1:13. Sealed with the Holy Spirit
Revelation 5:1. Scroll with seven seals
Revelation 6:1. Opening the seals

▶ Seamstress *(see Textile Arts)*

▶ Séance *(meeting, paranormal)*

A meeting at which the living seek to contact the dead

Exodus 22:18. Ridding the land of witches

1 Samuel 9:8–9. Seer now called a prophet

1 Samuel 28:5–25. Calling up the dead

2 Kings 23:24. Josiah cleanses the land of spiritualists.

Isaiah 8:19. Asking God for help

Isaiah 65:11. Flirting with fortune and destiny

▶ Search *(hunt, look for, seek)*

Carefully looking or seeking something out

Job 11:7. God's unsearchable depths

Psalm 53:2. Searching out wisdom

Psalm 139:23. Search my heart and mind.

Proverbs 2:4–5. Searching out wisdom

Jeremiah 29:13–14. Seeking out God wholeheartedly

Luke 14:13. Searching out guests for a banquet

John 5:39. Searching the Scriptures

Acts 17:11. Carefully searching the Scriptures

▶ Season(s) *(period, time of year)*

One of four subdivisions of the year: spring, summer, fall, winter

Genesis 8:22. Perpetual seasons while the earth exists

Leviticus 26:4. Rain and crops in their seasons

Ecclesiastes 3:1–2. A time for and season for all things

Daniel 2:20–21. God changes times and periods of history.

Zechariah 8:19. Season for fasting

2 Timothy 4:2. Be ready at all times.

▶ Seasoning *(flavor, spices)*

Anything added to food in an attempt to enhance flavor

Exodus 30:35. Seasoned with salt

Song of Songs 4:13–14. Various spices and seasoning

Mark 16:1. Spices for anointing a dead body

▶ Seat(s) *(bench, chair, stool)*

A place where one sits and, generally speaking, performs a certain kind of task from

Psalm 1:1. Sitting in the company of mockers

Psalm 113:5. God is seated and ruling on his throne.

Mark 10:40. Silencing an argument about heavenly seating

Luke 11:43. Important seats in the synagogue

Romans 3:25. Mercy seat

2 Corinthians 5:10. Christ's judgment seat

James 2:3. Preferential seating

Revelation 20:4. Thrones for judges

▶ Second coming *(Parousia, rapture, return)*

Used in reference to the bodily return of Christ in the air at the end of the ages

Matthew 24:44. An unexpected time

John 14:3. Jesus promises to come again.

Acts 1:11. Returning in the same way that he left

Philippians 3:20. Eagerly awaiting Christ's coming

1 Thessalonians 4:16. Coming from heaven with a command

Titus 2:12–13. Awaiting our hope

Hebrews 9:28. Appearing a second time to save those who wait

Hebrews 10:25. The day which is drawing near

James 5:8. The Lord is near.

2 Peter 3:10. Coming like a thief in the night

Revelation 1:7. Coming in the clouds

Revelation 22:20. I am coming soon.

▶ Secret(s) *(hidden, private, surprise)*

Something which is unknown or kept hidden from others

Deuteronomy 29:29. God knows all secrets

S

Psalm 51:6. Searching the secrets of a sinful heart
Psalm 94:11. Knowing our thoughts
Proverbs 11:13. Keeping a secret
Luke 8:17. Nothing will be hidden.
Ephesians 1:9–10. Mystery revealed
Revelation 22:10. Message which is to be shared

▶ Secretary *(amanuensis, scribe, writer)*

One who performs the service of writing correspondence
2 Samuel 8:16–17. David's secretary
2 Kings 12:10. King's scribe
2 Chronicles 24:11. King's scribe employed as public administrator
Ezra 7:6. Ezra's expertise in the Law
Isaiah 36:3. Scribe and historian
Jeremiah 37:15. Imprisoned with the secretary
John 5:39–40. Professional students of Scripture
Galatians 6:11. Paul takes up the pen.

▶ Sectarian *(group, sect, section)*

Describing or concerning a sub-group of a large group; a sect
Isaiah 29:13. Divided heart and allegiance
Jeremiah 8:8. Arguing wisdom versus folly
Jeremiah 23:25–26. False prophets
Acts 19:35–36. Worshipers of Artemis
Acts 24:5. Sect of Nazarenes
Acts 24:14. Follower of the way
1 Corinthians 1:11–13. Sectarianism within the body of Christ

▶ Secular *(laity, material, worldly)*

Relating to that which is worldly and non-spiritual
John 2:13–16. Temple secularized
Romans 16:23. Church members in high government positions
1 Corinthians 3:3. Influenced by the corrupt nature
1 Corinthians 15:47–48. Earthly minded
1 Timothy 3:7. Secular reputation
1 John 4:5. Belonging to this world

▶ Security *(defense, protection, safety)*

The quality of being guarded and free from looming dangers and threats
Psalm 32:7. Hidden with God
Luke 17:33. Reverse psychology
John 7:1. Keeping a safe path
John 10:28–29. Gift of eternal life
Romans 8:38–39. True security offered through God's love
Ephesians 6:13. Armor of God
2 Timothy 1:12. Convinced of protection in Christ
Hebrews 12:28–29. A secure kingdom
1 Peter 1:4. Incorruptible inheritance

▶ Sedative (see *Gall*)

▶ Seduction *(attractiveness, charms, tempting)*

The action of tempting someone sexually or intellectually to wander
Exodus 22:16. Seducing a virgin
Job 31:9–10. Quid quo pro
Proverbs 7:21. Charms of a lady
Proverbs 9:13. Seduction and folly
Isaiah 3:16. Women of Zion
Ezekiel 16:25. Seduction with beauty
Daniel 11:32. Flatterer
Mark 13:22. Seductive teachings
Acts 20:30. Distortions of truth
2 Peter 2:14. Seduction of the mind
2 Peter 2:18. Appealing to sexual nature and desires
Revelation 2:20. Misleading God's servants to sexual sin

▶ Seed *(offspring, plant, progeny)*

A small unit of reproduction produced by flower plants
Genesis 1:11. Seed-bearing plants
Genesis 3:15. Enmity between offspring

Psalm 89:4. Offspring established forever
Matthew 13:31–32. Parable of the mustard seed
Mark 4:7–8. Parable of seeds
John 12:24. Death brings life
1 Corinthians 15:35–37. Parallel with bodily resurrection
2 Timothy 2:8. Descendant of David

▶ Seek *(find, hunt, search for)*

The act of searching or attempting to find something or someone

Psalm 69:32. Refreshed hearts
Psalm 105:4. Seek the presence of the Lord.
Proverbs 28:5. Understanding all things
Jeremiah 29:13. Finding and seeking God
Hosea 10:12. Time for seeking the Lord
Matthew 6:33. Seeking the kingdom of heaven first
Matthew 7:7. Ask, seek, knock.
John 8:31. Seeking true discipleship
Romans 3:11. No one seeks God.
James 1:2–4. Seek Christian maturity.
James 4:8. Drawing near to God

▶ Seeker(s) *(Searcher)*

Someone who is actively searching for someone or something

Exodus 33:7. Seeking the Lord
2 Chronicles 31:21. True seeker of God
Psalm 143:6. Outstretched hands
Lamentations 3:21–25. Lord's goodness to those who seek him
John 12:20–22. Seeking to meet Jesus
Romans 3:10–18. Unregenerate heart

▶ Segregation *(separation, set apart)*

The action of setting someone or something apart from others

Numbers 15:15. Laws which also govern foreigners
Nehemiah 13:1. No outsiders admitted into assembly
Luke 9:53–56. Samaritans and Jerusalemites segregated
John 4:9. No associations
John 7:41–43. Division over Jesus
Ephesians 2:14. Christ broke down the wall of hostility between Jews and Gentiles.

▶ Selah *(musical notation)*

Precise meaning of the term is unknown, however most suggest that it is some sort of musical notation.

Psalm 3:2. A strange song
Psalm 46:3. Rushing waters, surging waves
Habakkuk 3:3. Poetic description of God redeeming a remnant

▶ Selection *(choice, election, preference)*

The action of making a choice between one or more options

Numbers 35:11. Selecting cities of refuge
Joshua 4:4. Joshua selects one from each tribe of Israel.
Ezra 8:24. Selecting leaders
Ezekiel 24:4–5. Best selection of meat
John 15:16. Chosen by God
Romans 9:11. Child selected prior to birth
Romans 11:28. Jewish people loved by God
2 Timothy 2:10. All things endured for the sake of chosen
2 Peter 1:10. Labor to make calling sure

▶ Self-centeredness *(see Selfishness)*

▶ Self-control *(discernment, maturity, restraint)*

The ability to control one's emotions, desires, and behaviors and their expression of them in situations

Proverbs 25:28. Image of some who lack self-control
Acts 24:25. Need of self-control
1 Corinthians 7:5. Lack of sexual self-control
1 Corinthians 7:9. Controlling sexual desires
1 Corinthians 9:25. Self-control in training for competition

Galatians 5:22–23. Fruit of the Spirit
1 Timothy 2:9. Dressing with modesty and self-control
1 Timothy 2:15. Saved through childbearing, if self-controlled
2 Peter 1:5–6. Adding self-control to faith

▶ Self-denial *(denial, discipline, sacrifice)*

Denying one's own needs and interests in a sacrificial manner so as to grow in Christian holiness

Matthew 16:24–26. Denying the world
Mark 10:28. Forsaking all things to follow Christ
Romans 8:13. Putting evil activities to death
Romans 14:20–21. Not causing others to stumble over food choices
1 Corinthians 9:19. Self-enslavement for the sake of the gospel
Galatians 5:24. Crucified passions and desires
Colossians 3:5. Putting to death worldly ways
Titus 2:12. Avoiding ungodly lives

▶ Self-destruction *(dangerous, harmful)*

A person or large entity who inflicts harm upon themselves either intentionally as the result of grievous sin, up to and including suicide

2 Samuel 17:23. Suicide
Psalm 55:9–10. City's self-destruction
Ecclesiastes 7:17. Dying before one's time is up
Jonah 1:12. Cast into the sea
John 8:22. Questioning suicide

▶ Self-esteem *(confidence, self-respect, self-worth)*

Confidence and satisfaction in oneself

Job 9:21. Low self-esteem
Proverbs 21:2. God is the judge of human hearts.
Isaiah 5:21. Inflated ego
Mark 12:31. Self-love basis for neighbor love
Romans 12:3. Sober self opinion
1 Corinthians 15:9. Self-deprecation
2 Corinthians 10:12. No self-recommendations
Galatians 6:1. Evaluation and response

▶ Self-examination *(consideration, reflection)*

A reflective examination of one's beliefs and motives

Psalm 139:23–24. Divine examination
Lamentations 3:40. Examining ways
2 Corinthians 13:5. Discern your faith commitment.
Galatians 6:4. Personal comparison
James 1:23–24. Forgetfulness of sin
1 John 3:20–22. Clean conscience

▶ Selfishness *(narcissistic, self-centered)*

Lacking in consideration and concern for others

Psalm 10:3. Boasting in selfish desires
Amos 6:6. Self-indulgent narcissists
Romans 2:7–8. Refusing to believe the truth
2 Corinthians 12:20. Fearful of wayward church
Philippians 3:19. Taking pride in shameful actions

▶ Self-pity *(complaining, grumbling)*

The disposition of unhappiness toward one's personal circumstances expressed through excessive complaining

Job 6:2–3. Grief weighs heavy.
Psalm 73:12–13. No reward
Jeremiah 20:14–15. Cursing day of one's birth
Habakkuk 1:1–3. Prophet cries out against injustice.
Luke 10:40. A sister's complaint
Luke 23:27–28. Self-woe
Philippians 2:14–15. Working without complaint or arguing

▶ Self-righteousness *(convoluted, narcissism)*

The disposition of unfound and uncritical self-appraisal and endorsement causing a looming personal blindness to flaws and personal sins

Proverbs 30:12. Blinded to flaws

Matthew 9:11–13. Pharisees' self-righteousness

Matthew 23:30. Self-righteous attitude

Luke 16:15. Self-justifying actions

Romans 2:1. Self-condemning judgments

1 Timothy 1:9. Laws are intended for the self-righteous.

▶ Self-worth *(see Self-esteem)*

▶ Senses *(sight, smell, sound)*

Faculties which perceive the external stimuli of sight, sound, smell, and touch

Proverbs 20:12. Senses created by God

Ezekiel 12:2. Sensory failure

Matthew 27:34. Bad to the taste

1 Corinthians 15:34. Return to your senses.

1 John 1:1. Experience through the senses

1 John 2:16. Physical senses in a passing world

▶ Sentence *(see Justice; Verdict)*

▶ Separation *(detachment, distinction, segregation)*

Actively creating distinction between one's former way of living and one's new life in Christ

Isaiah 52:11. Clean and unclean separation

Romans 8:38–39. Nothing can separate us from God's love.

Romans 13:12–13. Separating darkness from light

Ephesians 4:22–24. Setting off the old self and putting on the new

Titus 2:11–12. Separation from ungodliness

James 4:7. Resisting the devil

1 John 2:15–17. Living in distinction from the world

▶ Septuagint *(Greek Old Testament, LXX)*

The Greek translation of the Hebrew Bible

Matthew 1:23. Underlying Hebrew source

Matthew 4:4. Underlying Greek source

▶ Sepulcher *(monument, tomb)*

A cave or series of caves used as tombs for the kings of Israel

Genesis 23:20. Hittites sold tomb to Abraham.

2 Kings 21:18. Manasseh's burial in his own palace

2 Chronicles 16:14. Personal tomb for king Asa

2 Chronicles 28:27. Family tomb

Nehemiah 3:16. Repairs on walls and tombs

Isaiah 22:16. Sepulcher on high

Acts 7:16. Abraham's tomb

▶ Seraphim *(angel, celestial being)*

A high order celestial being; an angel

Isaiah 6:2–3. Six-winged angels chanting God's holiness

Isaiah 6:6–7. Angelic encounter

▶ Serendipity *(accident, coincidence, destiny)*

A sudden and favorable unfolding of events

John 4:4–15. An off-chance meeting

Romans 8:28–30. All things work together for good

▶ Sermon *(authoritative message, teaching)*

An authoritative message preached on a biblical subject aimed at moving the hearer's affections and bringing about spiritual change

Matthew 5:1–7:29. Sermon on the M ount

Acts 10:42. Commanded to preach

Acts 13:16–41. Paul's sermon before Israel

Acts 20:7. Late-night Scripture discussion

Romans 1:15. Eager to preach in Rome

Romans 15:20. Preaching the gospel in new places

S

▶ Sermon on the Mount *(see Sermon)*

▶ Serpent *(see Snake[s])*

▶ Servant(s) *(attendant, help, slave)*

Someone who performs duties on behalf of others or in their service

2 Kings 5:22. Master and servants
Matthew 8:8–9. Asking for healing of a servant
Matthew 12:18. Servant of God endowed with the Spirit
Matthew 18:27–28. Unjust master
Luke 16:13. Cannot serve two masters
Romans 1:1. Paul, a servant of Jesus
Philippians 2:7. Christ's role of servanthood
Colossians 1:25. Caring for God's church

▶ Service/Serving Others *(labor, work, slave)*

The action of helping others through the meeting of needs or gracious acts of service

Matthew 25:35–36. Meeting material needs
John 13:12–17. An important lesson in servant leadership
John 16:2. Cost of serving; suffering
John 21:15–17. Service reinstated
Romans 15:1–2. Building up one another's faith
2 Corinthians 11:9. Serving without bothering
Galatians 5:13. Using freedom to serve others through love
Ephesians 6:5–9. Earthly servitude
Colossians 1:24. Filling up what is lacking in suffering
Colossians 3:16. Instructing each other in all wisdom

▶ Seven *(cardinal number, completeness, number)*

Symbolically, a representation of completeness

Genesis 2:2. Resting on day seven
Genesis 29:18. Working seven years for Rachel
Exodus 20:8–11. Sabbath significance
Leviticus 4:6. Dipped in blood seven times
Leviticus 13:4–5. Seven-day isolation
Leviticus 23:6. Seven-day festivals
Deuteronomy 15:1–9. Canceling debts
Joshua 6:3–4. Seven days, seven priests, seven laps
1 Kings 6:38. Seven years building the temple
Matthew 18:22. Forgiveness seventy times seven
Mark 8:8. Seven baskets left over
Revelation 1:4. Seven churches (church universal?)

▶ Sewing *(designing, needlework, stitching)*

The action or craft of sewing textiles into usable products

Exodus 28:5. Linen garments for priests
Exodus 35:35. High fashion, high skill
Ecclesiastes 3:7. Tearing apart and re-sewing
Isaiah 19:9. Textile workers put to shame
Ezekiel 13:17–18. Women who sew magic charms
Matthew 9:16. Patching an old coat
Acts 9:39. Hand-fashioned clothing

▶ Sex *(copulation, intercourse, lovemaking)*

The intimate act of sexual intercourse God intended for husbands and wives to share freely with one another

Genesis 4:1. Adam made love to Eve.
Genesis 4:17. Love and procreation
Ruth 3:8. Sexual proposition
Proverbs 5:18–20. Enjoying sex
Song of Songs 2:15. Sexually aware and ready
1 Corinthians 7:5. Not withholding sex, except to pray

▶ Sexual allegories *(allegory, imagery, fantasy)*

Vivid sexual images conveyed through the means of story meant to illustrate the pleasures of marital sexual relationship

Song of Songs 2:4. His banner over me is love(making)
Song of Songs 6:3. Openness and desire
Song of Songs 7:7–10. Longing for love

▶ Sexual sin *(immorality, sin)*

Sins of immorality associated with extramarital sexual relationship

Leviticus 18:22. Sexual relationships delineated
Ezekiel 16:15. Sex trade
Ezekiel 23:20. Graphic sexual content
Matthew 5:27. Fidelity in sexual relationship
Romans 1:26. Natural sexual relations exchanged for unnatural ones
Romans 13:13. Not given to promiscuous relationships
Galatians 5:19. Corrupt nature and sexual sins
Ephesians 5:5. Sharing in the inheritance of the kingdom
1 Thessalonians 4:1–8. Keeping sexually pure

▶ Shallow actions *(hasty, unthoughtful)*

Exhibiting actions which are inconsistent and unthoughtful with one's stated system of values

Ezekiel 33:31–32. Listening, but not obeying
Mark 4:16–17. Shallow roots
Luke 6:49. Hearing without obeying
John 6:66. Call to commitment
Galatians 1:6–9. Deserting Christ
Ephesians 4:14. Changing beliefs on a whim

▶ Shame *(guilt, humiliation, remorse)*

Feelings of contempt, derision, and humiliation

Proverbs 11:2. Arrogance and shame versus wisdom
Mark 8:38. Ashamed of Christ
Romans 1:16. No shame in the gospel
Romans 6:21. Shaming actions ending in death
1 Corinthians 1:27. Nonsense used to shame the wise
2 Timothy 1:12. Unashamed of suffering
2 Timothy 2:15. Unashamed to teach the Word
Hebrews 12:2. Despising shame
1 Peter 3:16. Ashamed of ridiculing Christians

▶ Share *(allot, divide, inheritance)*

An allotment or inheritance

Exodus 29:28. Portion given to Aaron and sons
Numbers 18:20. Aaron's line will have no property.
Deuteronomy 10:9. God is the possession of the Levites.
Joshua 19:9. Simeon's inheritance
Psalm 73:26. Permanent inheritance
Isaiah 61:7. Double portion of land
Galatians 6:6. Sharing with teachers of God's Word
Philippians 4:15. Sharing with the apostle
1 Peter 4:13. Sharing in Christ's sufferings

▶ Shaving *(cut, trim)*

The action of cutting hair from one's head or beard

Genesis 41:14. Fresh shave
Leviticus 19:27. Growing out bangs and beard edges
Numbers 6:9. Cause of Nazirite to shave
Numbers 8:7. Actions for ceremonial cleanness
2 Samuel 10:4. Shaving half a beard
Job 1:20. Sign of grief
Ezekiel 5:1. Shaving head and beard
Acts 18:18. Hair cut during a vow
Acts 21:24. Shaving heads for a vow

▶ Sheep *(animal, offering, ram)*

A domesticated animal kept for wool, meat, and use in sacrifices; often used in imagery of shepherd and sheep between Christ and His people

Genesis 46:32. Shepherds and flocks
Exodus 12:5. Passover offering
1 Samuel 25:2. Measurement of wealth

Psalm 23:1. The Lord is a shepherd.
Isaiah 53:6. Straying sheep
Matthew 12:11. Rescuing sheep on the Sabbath day
Matthew 26:31. Shepherd will be struck.
John 10:1–3. Sheep hear and respond to the shepherd's voice.
John 10:11. Good shepherd sacrifices for his sheep.
1 Peter 2:25. Lost sheep returning to the shepherd

▶ Shekinah *(glory, presence, resting)*

Refers to the glory of God's presence dwelling and resting on particular places; in the New Testament Jesus is identified as the image of the glory of God dwelling among humanity.
Exodus 13:21–22. Columns of smoke and fire
Exodus 33:9. Descending glory
Ezekiel 9:3. Glory removed from the temple
Ezekiel 43:2–4. Vision of God's glory returning
Hebrews 1:3. Christ the image of God's glory

▶ Shelter(s) *(protection, shade, shadow)*

A place of protection and shade from the elements and storms of life
Deuteronomy 33:27. God is your shelter.
Judges 9:15. Taking shelter in the shade of the king
Ruth 2:12. Protection under the Lord of Israel
Job 24:8. Unsheltered from the storm
Psalm 31:20. Hidden in a shelter
Isaiah 4:6. Protection from the elements
Isaiah 30:2. Seeking shelter in Egypt
Jonah 4:5. Jonah's makeshift shelter

▶ Sheol *(grave, netherworld, pit)*

The underworld or place of the dead
Deuteronomy 32:22. Depths of the earth
Psalm 49:13–14. Punitive aspect to Sheol
Proverbs 9:18. Place of the dead
Ezekiel 31:15. Below the surface of the earth
Luke 16:23. Hades, place of torment
Revelation 1:18. Christ holds the keys to death and hell.

▶ Shepherd(s) *(guides, Jesus, leaders)*

A person who tends and cares for sheep
Exodus 7:9. Miracle with a shepherd's staff
Numbers 14:33. Shepherds for forty years in the wilderness
Psalm 23:1. The Lord is my shepherd.
Isaiah 40:11. Caring like a shepherd for the flock
Jeremiah 3:15. Shepherds after God's heart to lead Israel
Zechariah 11:7. Caring for the sheep that are oppressed
Luke 2:8–9. Shepherds witness angelic hosts.
John 10:11. Jesus is the good shepherd.
Acts 20:28. Shepherds of the church
Hebrews 13:20. Great shepherd of the sheep
1 Peter 5:2. Shepherd your entrusted flock.

▶ Shepherd Tools *(see **Rod; Staff**)*

▶ Shield *(guard, protection)*

An instrument of war, used for protection against enemy attacks both large and small; also used metaphorically for God's protection for His people
Genesis 15:1. God is Abraham's shield.
2 Samuel 1:21. Saul's shield ruined
Psalm 35:2. Asking for protection
Jeremiah 46:3. Preparing for battle
Ephesians 6:16. Shield of faith

▶ Ship(s) *(boats)*

A seaworthy vessel used for transporting people and goods
Numbers 24:24. Ships from Cyprus bringing certain destruction
Judges 5:17–18. Activities on the Mediterranean
2 Chronicles 9:21. Merchant ships
Jonah 1:3–5. Ship Jonah boarded
Matthew 14:22. Crossing over the sea
Mark 4:35–37. Jesus' ship caught in a storm

▶ Shipwreck *(crash, stranded)*

The situation of having one's boat wrecked and unusable due to inclimate weather, difficult navigation, or often both

Ezekiel 27:34. Wrecked at sea

Acts 27:41. Crashing into a sandbar

▶ Shoes *(feet, sandals)*

A foot covering typically made from wood and leather

Deuteronomy 29:5. Long-lasting shoes

1 Kings 2:5. Dressed for war

Psalm 60:8. Tossing in the shoe

Acts 12:8. Be prepared.

Ephesians 6:15. Ready to spread the Good News

▶ Shrewd *(clever, canny, sharp)*

The quality of showing wit quick on the draw and astute powers of judgment

Exodus 1:10. Outsmarting enemies

1 Chronicles 26:14. Insightful counselor

Job 5:12. Shrewd prevented from carrying out plans

Isaiah 5:21. Shrewd in their own sight

Daniel 2:14. Speaking with shrewd judgment

Luke 16:8. Shrewdness commended by dishonest manager

Acts 7:19. Shrewd treatment of Israel

▶ Shrine(s) *(memorial, temple, home)*

The home of a deity which is fashioned by humans

Judges 17:5. Judge's shrine

2 Kings 17:29. Building shrines in illegal places of worship

Isaiah 44:13. Home for an idol

Acts 7:43. Shrine of Moloch

Acts 17:24. God's home is not a human-made shrine.

Acts 19:24. Silver shrines of Artemis

▶ Shun *(avoid, distance)*

Persistently avoiding, ignoring, or rejecting something

Psalm 88:8. Caused my shunning

Psalm 88:18. Beloved and friend shun

Ecclesiastes 9:2. Shunning an oath

Luke 17:33. Shunning the body

▶ Siblings *(brother, sister)*

Offspring who share a common parentage

Genesis 4:8. Sibling rivalry

Genesis 12:13. Treating a wife as a sister

Genesis 27:6. Jacob and Esau

Numbers 6:7. Sibling's death apart from the Nazirit

Acts 22:13. Term of endearment to Saul

1 Peter 5:13. Sister church

▶ Sickness *(disease, illness, weakness)*

Physical ailments or illness with a degree of semi-permanence

Exodus 23:25. Protected from food poisoning

Deuteronomy 28:61. Plagued with sickness

2 Chronicles 21:19. Spilled intestines

Psalm 38:11. Quarantine

Psalm 39:10. Divine affliction

Psalm 91:10. Wellness in the home

Matthew 4:23. Various kinds of sicknesses healed by Jesus

Matthew 9:35. Every sickness healed

Matthew 10:1. Disciples given authority to cure ailments

John 11:4. Sickness which results in God's glory

▶ Siege(s) *(encircle, surround)*

A military tactic which surrounds a city and cuts off all essential supplies and avenues of transportation

Joshua 10:31. Attacking Lachish

1 Kings 15:27. Laying siege against Gibbethon

2 Chronicles 32:10. Siege upon Jerusalem

Jeremiah 10:17. Dwelling under siege

Ezekiel 4:7. Jerusalem blockaded

Ezekiel 24:2. Babylon's siege on Jerusalem

Zechariah 12:2. Jerusalem's fate will also come true in Judah.

▶ Sight *(eyes, glimpse, vision)*

Although frequently used in reference to the faculty of vision, also extended to mean a range of awareness

Genesis 6:11. Corruption of the world visible to God

Exodus 4:11. The Lord gives sight to the blind.

Leviticus 21:20. Ailments barring proximity to the altar

Psalm 116:15. Martyrs a precious sight to God

Proverbs 4:20–22. Keeping God's words in mind

Isaiah 42:7. Sight given to the blind

Matthew 20:34. Jesus restores sight by touch.

Luke 4:18. Summary statement of Jesus' ministry

Luke 18:42. Sight restored by faith

Acts 22:13. Saul's sight restored after three days of blindness

2 Corinthians 5:7. Lives guided by faith and not by sight

2 Corinthians 8:21. Doing what is right in the sight of all

1 Timothy 5:4. Actions pleasing in God's sight

▶ Sign(s) *(signified, symbols)*

A symbol that communicates meaning through what it signifies

Genesis 4:15. Sign of the Lord's vengeance

Genesis 9:12–13. Rainbow as a sign of God's promise

Genesis 17:11. Circumcision as the sign of Abrahamic covenant

Exodus 4:8. Miraculous signs meant to garner allegiance

Exodus 12:13. Blood on the house is a sign of protection on Passover.

Numbers 14:11. God expects remembrance of His signs.

Deuteronomy 4:34. God's demonstration of numerous signs

2 Kings 20:8–9. Sign of Hezekiah's healing

Psalm 74:9. No signs, no prophets

Isaiah 7:14. The sign of a virgin birth

Matthew 12:38. Desiring a miraculous sign from Jesus

Matthew 24:3. What will be the sign of Christ's second coming?

Matthew 26:48. The sign of a kiss marks betrayal.

John 2:11. Jesus' first miraculous sign

Acts 2:19. Signs in the sky

Romans 15:19. Ministry accompanied by amazing signs

2 Thessalonians 3:17. Paul's own handwriting a sign of authenticity

Revelation 1:1. Message communicated by symbols

▶ Signal(s) *(gesture, sign, wave)*

A gesture, sound, or action which serves to convey information or instructions to onlookers

Numbers 10:2. Trumpets used to signal breaking camp

Judges 20:38. Smoke signal

Proverbs 6:13. Various signals

Isaiah 5:26. Flag raised as a signal to attack

Isaiah 49:22. Hand signals relief

Jeremiah 6:1. Raising a flag signaling disaster

Matthew 26:48. Signaling betrayal

▶ Signet ring *(mark, seal, signature)*

A small seal used as a mark of authenticity

Genesis 38:18. Signet ring

Esther 8:2. Royal signet ring

Esther 8:8. Seal of authenticity

Daniel 6:8–9. Marks a royal signature

Daniel 6:17. Seal marked on stone using a signet ring

Haggai 2:23. God's people will be a seal.

▶ Silence *(peace, quiet, tranquil)*

The absence of sound

Numbers 17:5. Silencing complaints

Job 11:3. Empty talk which silences

Psalm 8:2. Silencing the enemy

Psalm 65:1. Awe in Zion

Psalm 115:17. Death

Isaiah 47:5. Waiting in silence and darkness

Jeremiah 51:55. Babylon silenced

Daniel 11:18. Commander who silences insults

Romans 16:25. Mystery kept in silence revealed in Jesus Christ

1 Timothy 2:11. An instruction for orderly worship

1 Peter 2:15. Need to silence ignorance

Revelation 8:1. Heavenly action ceases for half an hour!

▶ Silver *(coins, metal, money)*

A shiny, silver precious metal

Exodus 20:23. Do not fashion gods of silver or gold.

Leviticus 5:15. Commercial transaction

Numbers 7:13. Silver plate and bowl

Proverbs 3:14. Wisdom greater than silver

Proverbs 17:3. Refining silver in the crucible

Malachi 3:2–3. Enduring on the day of judgment

Luke 10:35. Two silver coins as payment

Acts 19:24. Silver shrines

James 5:3. Corroded silver

▶ Simile *(comparison)*

Figure of speech comparing two unlike things, often introduced by *like* or *as*

Psalm 1:3. Righteous like a well-fed tree

Psalm 5:12. Surrounded like a shield

Psalm 17:8. Hidden and protected

Psalm 131:2. Contented soul

Isaiah 1:9. Destruction similar to Sodom and Gomorrah

Hosea 5:10. Pouring out fury

Luke 11:44. People like unmarked graves

▶ Simplicity *(easy, effortless, simple)*

The quality of being easy to understand and carry out

Psalm 119:130. Your Word sheds light and guides the simple.

Psalm 131:1. Concerned with only simple things

Matthew 11:25. Truths revealed to children

Acts 2:46. Single purpose

Romans 6:19. Speaking humanly

2 Corinthians 1:12. Living by God's grace, not human wisdom

▶ Sin(s) *(transgression, immorality, wrong)*

An overt transgression against God's covenant which creates enmity between a human and God

Genesis 20:6. Prevented from sinning against God

Joshua 7:11. Israel's sin of apathy

1 Samuel 19:4. Sins against humanity

Psalm 38:3. No peace because of sins

Psalm 51:3–4. Sins against God

Isaiah 1:18. Our sins are bright red.

Matthew 9:2. Jesus forgives sins.

Matthew 26:28. Jesus' blood poured out for sins

Luke 17:3–4. Correcting and forgiving a sinful believer

John 5:14. Stop sinning to prevent future harm.

John 9:2–3. Sin does not cause handicap.

Romans 3:23. All have sinned.

1 Corinthians 6:18. Sexual sins against one's own body

1 John 3:4. Sin is disobedience.

▶ Sincerity *(honesty, genuine, trustworthy)*

Actions which are free from false pretense or hypocrisy

2 Corinthians 2:17. Sincere message

Colossians 3:23–24. Working unto the Lord

1 Timothy 1:5. Sincere faith

James 3:17. Wisdom from above

1 Peter 1:22. Sincere love that comes from obeying the truth

1 John 3:18. Love demonstrated, not simply stated

▶ Singing *(song, music, voice)*

The action of making music sounds with one's voice

Exodus 15:1. Moses' song to the Lord after the Red Sea

Nehemiah 13:5. Commodities belonging to Israelite singers
Psalm 95:1. Sing with joy.
Psalm 108:1. Making music with all your soul
Psalm 149:5. Singing in bed
Isaiah 30:29. Happy hearts in song
Luke 19:37–40. Singing stones
Ephesians 5:19. Musical conversation
Colossians 3:16. Sing with gratitude in your hearts.
James 5:13. Sing when you are happy.

▶ Sinner *(evildoer, wrongdoer, transgressor)*

Anyone who commits even one sin against God and His standards for holiness
Ecclesiastes 9:18. Destruction of one sinner
Isaiah 6:5. A man of unclean lips
Luke 7:37–39. Sinful woman pours perfume on Jesus.
Luke 15:1–7. Jesus leaves the ninety-nine for a sinner.
Luke 19:1–10. Zacchaeus the tax collector
Romans 3:10–11. All are sinners.
Romans 5:8. Christ died for sinners.
1 Corinthians 6:9–10. Types of sinners

▶ Six *(cardinal number, number)*

Significant in reference to six days of work with Sabbath rest on the seventh day; pattern also seen in reference to the Jubilee year
Genesis 1:31. Day six
Leviticus 25:3. Preparing for Jubilee
John 2:6. Six stone jars
John 12:1. Six days prior to Passover
James 5:17. Three years and six months
Revelation 4:8. Six-winged seraphim
Revelation 13:18. Mark of the beast

▶ Skepticism *(unbelief, doubt)*

When person doubts the status quo or questions the world as they see it
Genesis 17:17. Doubting God's promise
Genesis 19:14. Lot's warning not heeded
Psalm 78:32. Discontinued belief in miracles
Mark 9:24. Help my unbelief.
Luke 1:18–20. Desiring proof of an angelic claim
Luke 24:9–11. Doubting the women's story
John 1:45–46. Questioning goodness from Nazareth
John 7:5. Brothers' unbelief
John 12:37. Closed hearts to Jesus' miracles

▶ Skill(s) *(talents, abilities, gifts)*

An above average ability to carry out a task or perform a certain job
Exodus 28:3. Textile artists
Exodus 31:1–6. Masters of the minerals
1 Chronicles 22:15–16. Workers of stone
2 Chronicles 2:13–14. Skillful son
Daniel 1:3–4, 17. Skilled and trained in divination
Romans 12:6–8. Differing spiritual gifts
1 Corinthians 12:28–31. Unique skill sets for the body of Christ
1 Peter 4:10. Stewarding God's good gifts

▶ Skipping death *(skipping out, taken up)*

Individuals who have not tasted physical death because of God's intervention in their lives, taking them up to heaven
Genesis 5:24. Taken by God
2 Kings 2:11–12. Elijah taken up into heaven by windstorm

▶ Slander *(falsehood, maliciousness)*

The action of falsely representing someone in such a manner as to damage their reputation
Exodus 23:1. Never speak false rumors.
Deuteronomy 5:20. Tell the truth in testimony.
Psalm 101:5. Slanderer destroyed
Proverbs 10:18. Spreading slander like a fool
Proverbs 11:9. Ruining a neighbor with godless talk
Ephesians 4:31. Speaking well
Titus 3:2. Unbefitting of believers
James 4:11–12. Byproduct of slandering each other

1 Peter 2:1. Ridding all slanderous communication

▶ Slaughter *(death, murder, pogrom)*

Large-scale killing of people in a violent manner

Joshua 6:21. People will die.

2 Kings 21:16. Manasseh's vicious pogrom

Isaiah 37:36. Angel of the Lord slays.

Daniel 8:5–7. Symbolic vision of slaughter

▶ Slave(s) *(servant, vassal)*

The legal property of someone else, typically enslaved for a seven-year period

Deuteronomy 23:15–16. Treatment of a lost slave

2 Chronicles 8:9. Israelites not enslaved

Jeremiah 34:8–11. Slaves set free and then re-enslaved

John 8:34. Slave to sin

Romans 6:6–23. Slavery to sin ended

Ephesians 6:5–8. Household codes

Titus 2:9. Living under the authority of an earthly master

1 Peter 2:18. Obeying earthly masters

2 Peter 2:19. All are enslaved to something.

▶ Slavery *(institution, servant)*

The condition of being a slave and under the power of an authority

Exodus 1:8–14. Backbreaking labor

Leviticus 25:44–46. Slaves from foreign nations

Galatians 4:7. No longer slaves, but children of God!

Galatians 5:1. Enjoying the benefits of freedom

▶ Sleep *(nap, rest, relaxation)*

The condition of being at rest, allowing both mind and body to refresh for the next day's events

Genesis 15:12. Abram's deep sleep

Psalm 4:8. Peaceful sleep

Psalm 127:2. God's provision while sleeping

Proverbs 6:10–11. Slumbering and napping

Proverbs 20:13. Nocturnal tendencies

Ecclesiastes 5:12. Sleep after work is sweet.

Jonah 1:5–6. Prophet asleep in the storm

Matthew 8:23–25. Sleeper in a storm

1 Thessalonians 4:14. Bringing back those asleep in the Lord

▶ Slingshot *(weapon, sling)*

A leather tool used for slinging rocks moderate distances with a high decree of accuracy

Judges 20:16. Left-handed slingers

1 Samuel 17:40, 49–50. David's famous kill

Proverbs 26:8. Like slinging a stone

▶ Sluggard/Sloth *(bum, lazy)*

A person characterized by extreme laziness and procrastination

Proverbs 6:6–9. Learning from ants

Proverbs 13:4. Craving food, but having none

Proverbs 18:9. Laziness is like stealing.

Proverbs 26:14–16. A turning door, moving but going nowhere

Isaiah 56:10. Loving sleep

Jeremiah 48:10. Curse on those who neglect the Lord's work

2 Thessalonians 3:6–12. Living disciplined lives

Hebrews 6:12. Leaving laziness behind

▶ Smiling *(beaming, grinning)*

A warm, pleasant expression of happiness and satisfaction in one's countenance

Numbers 6:24–26. God's blessing

Job 9:27. Change of expression

Job 29:24. Surprising smile

Psalm 80:3. Restore with a smile

Proverbs 31:25. Smiling about future

▶ Snacking *(eating, food)*

The action of consuming small amounts of food between meals or "on the go"

1 Samuel 17:17. Feeding family

Proverbs 24:13. Tasty honey

Ecclesiastes 9:7. Enjoying eating and drinking

Luke 6:1. Picking a snack while walking

1 Corinthians 10:31. All things for God's glory

▶ Snake(s) *(asp, serpent, viper)*

A slithering reptile known for its venomous bite and connection with the garden of Eden

Genesis 3:1–14. Cunning serpent

Exodus 4:1–12. Signs in Egypt

Numbers 21:8–9. A bronze snake

Jeremiah 8:17. Snakes that cannot be charmed

Matthew 7:9–10. Giving good gifts to children

Matthew 23:33. People like snakes

Luke 10:19. Nothing will hurt the disciples.

Acts 28:3. Paul's strange bite

Revelation 20:2. Christ's overpowering the ancient snake

▶ Snakebites *(bite, injury, illness)*

Bites incurred from snakes; especially dangerous ones

Numbers 21:6–7. Snakes biting Israelites

Ecclesiastes 10:11. Charmed snake still biting

Amos 5:19. Snakebite at home

Acts 28:3. Paul's brush with a snake

▶ Sneezing *(tickle, sniffle)*

A sudden involuntary expulsion of air through the nose and mouth

2 Kings 4:35. Sneezing fit

▶ Snow *(flakes, snowfall)*

The season of wetness coupled with reduced atmospheric temperature leading to frozen water vapor

2 Samuel 23:20. Memorable day

Job 37:6. Directing weather

Job 38:22. Storing snow and hail

Proverbs 26:1. Wrong seasons

Isaiah 1:18. Sins made white like snow

Jeremiah 18:14. Lebanon never without snow

▶ Soap *(clean)*

A substance use for cleaning

Jeremiah 2:22. Lasting stains from wickedness

Malachi 3:2. Cleansing soap

Matthew 27:24. Pilate washes hands of this situation.

▶ Sober *(dry, sensible, serious)*

Someone who is not addicted to much alcohol, using it either with extreme moderation or not at all

Leviticus 10:9. No wine for Levites in the tent of meeting

Numbers 6:1–3. Instructions for Nazirites

Proverbs 31:4–5. Kings and rulers should remain sober.

Isaiah 5:11. Drinking early in the day

Romans 13:13. Living soberly

Romans 14:21. Avoiding actions which cause doubts in others

1 Thessalonians 5:6–8. Moderation

1 Timothy 3:2–3. Sobriety

▶ Social justice *(equity, fairness, morality)*

Actions which promote justice and liberation from oppression for all, especially orphans and widows

Leviticus 19:15. Administering justice fairly

Deuteronomy 15:1–18. Canceling debts

Proverbs 21:3. Justice preferred to sacrifices

Isaiah 1:17. Seek justice.

Jeremiah 22:3. Treating foreigners, orphans, and widows well

Micah 6:8. Do justice, love mercy, live humbly with God.

Zechariah 8:16–17. Dispensing justice in truth

James 1:27. Pure religion = caring for orphans and widows

James 2:2–3. Treating all men equally

1 John 3:17–18. Demonstrating love through action

▶ Sodomy *(copulation, unnatural)*

Unnatural sexual activity which is typically practiced in homosexual relationships

Genesis 19:5. Homosexual men

Leviticus 18:22. Forbidden intercourse

Leviticus 20:13. Worthy of death

Romans 1:27. Unnatural relations

Jude 7. Recalling the fate of Sodom and Gomorrah

▶ Soldier(s) *(fighter, military, serviceman)*

Someone who serves in the military

Numbers 1:45–46. Eligible soldiers

1 Samuel 14:52. Saul's enlistment policy

2 Chronicles 17:13–15. Commander forces

Ephesians 6:10–17. Armor of God

2 Timothy 2:3–4. Suffering as a soldier of Christ

▶ Solicitation *(implore, request, solicit)*

The action of asking in hopes of attaining a specific need or request

2 Kings 4:3. Requesting items from neighbors

John 16:7. Christ goes, the Spirit comes.

Acts 3:2–3. Soliciting handouts

James 1:5. Asking the generous God

1 John 5:14. Confidence in God's provision

▶ Solitude *(alone, isolation, seclusion)*

Status of being alone, typically to spend time in prayer

Matthew 14:23. Sneaking away to pray

Mark 1:35. Up before the dawn

Mark 6:31–32. Seeking solitude and rest

Luke 5:16. Seeking solitude and prayer

Luke 22:41. Stopping to pray

▶ Solo(s) *(song, performance, vocal)*

A performance done without the aid of accompaniment

Exodus 15:21. Miriam's song to the Lord after victory

1 Samuel 2:1. Hannah's song

Luke 1:46–55. Mary's Magnificat

▶ Son(s) *(child, heir)*

Relating to one's parental relationship between an adult and a male child

Genesis 17:16–19. God will provide an heir.

Genesis 22:2. Testing Abraham

Genesis 37:3. Son born in old age

Exodus 2:1–2. Birth of Moses

Luke 15:11–32. Parable concerning sons

John 3:16. God's "one of a kind" Son

1 John 4:14. Father sent his Son as Savior of the world.

▶ Son of God *(God's Son, sonship, children of God)*

One of Jesus' many titles; how the Father addressed Him at His baptism; also carries the connotation of both inheritance rights and relationship, two aspects available to all who believe in Jesus

Genesis 6:4. Sons of God, the Nephilim

Matthew 3:17. Baptism of Jesus

Mark 1:1. The Good News concerning the Son of God

Luke 3:38. Jesus' genealogy traced back to Adam, first son of God

Romans 1:4. Declared Son of God in his nature

Romans 8:14. Those guided by the Spirit are God's children.

Romans 8:19. Coming revelation of God's children

Galatians 2:20. Life through believing in God's Son

Ephesians 4:13. United in faith in God's Son

1 John 4:15. Spiritual blessings for declaring that Jesus is the Son of God

▶ Son of Man *(Savior)*

A messianic name taken from the book of Daniel which Jesus often applied in referring to Himself

Daniel 7:13. Son of Man coming on the clouds

Matthew 8:20. Son of Man is without home.
Matthew 10:23. Son of Man will come.
Matthew 12:8. Authority over the Sabbath
Matthew 12:32. Words against Son of Man forgiven
Matthew 12:40. The sign of Jonah given to the Son of Man
Matthew 17:12. Son of Man must suffer.
Mark 14:21. Predictions of death
John 3:13–14. Son of Man came from heaven.
Acts 7:56. Heaven opened up, Son of Man on the throne!

▶ Son of man *(human, Ezekiel)*

A title frequently given to the prophet Ezekiel likely in reference to human weakness
Psalm 8:4. Human son
Ezekiel 2:1. Prophet Ezekiel's frequent designation
Daniel 8:17. Daniel's infrequent designation

▶ Song(s) *(music, singing)*

A poetic set of words set to music
1 Samuel 18:6. Song and dance
1 Kings 4:32. Sagacious poet
Psalm 32:7. Songs of salvation
Psalm 100:2. Entering Lord's presence in song
Isaiah 52:9. Lord will reclaim Jerusalem
Ephesians 5:19. Spiritual music
Colossians 3:16. Christ's word dwelling richly in you
James 5:13. Singing when happy

▶ Sophistry *(fallacy, deception)*

Misleading or misguided argumentation intentionally presented to bring about confusion
Genesis 3:1–7. Misrepresenting the argument
Matthew 4:1–11. Satan attempts to mislead Jesus.
2 Corinthians 2:11. Cognizant of Satan's scheming
2 Corinthians 11:3. Careful not to be lured

▶ Sorcery *(divination, magic)*

The use of magic in seeking to manipulate an outcome
Exodus 7:11. Egyptian magicians
Leviticus 19:26. Consulting fortunetellers
Numbers 24:1. Balaam and omens
Deuteronomy 18:10. Divinatory practices forbidden in Israel
2 Kings 17:17. Child sacrifice
Isaiah 47:12. Casting spells and magic
Ezekiel 13:18. Judgment on those involved in magic trade
Daniel 1:20. Divination in Babylon
Acts 8:9. Simon the magician
Acts 19:19. Burning up books of the occult

▶ Sorrow *(grief, sadness)*

A deep feeling of loss caused by overwhelming suffering or sadness experienced
Psalm 6:7. Grief-filled eyes
Psalm 119:28. Drowning in tears
Ecclesiastes 1:18. Wisdom and sorrow
Isaiah 51:11. Day of no sorrow
Isaiah 53:3–4. Man of sorrows
Jeremiah 8:18. Sick at heart
Jeremiah 31:13. Sorrows turned to joy
Mark 14:34. Great anguish
Romans 9:2–3. Paul's heartache over his kinsmen
2 Corinthians 7:10. Distressed

▶ Soul *(emotional, moral)*

The inner being and essence of a person, also understood as moral and emotional faculties
Deuteronomy 4:29. Loving God with heart and soul
Joshua 22:5. Serving God with heart and soul
1 Samuel 1:15. Outpouring of Hannah's soul
Job 33:28. Freed soul
Psalm 23:2–3. Peaceful pastures, renewed soul
Psalm 35:9. Finding joy in God alone

Psalm 42:2. Thirsting for the living God
Mark 8:36. Gaining the world, losing one's soul

▶ Soul-winning *(winsome, converting)*

Evangelistic efforts undertaken to win converts to Christianity
Matthew 28:19. Great commissioning
Acts 15:3. Bringing great joy to all believers
Romans 10:1. Desiring salvation for Jewish people
Galatians 2:8–9. Divine labor and resources
1 Peter 2:25. Lost sheep return to the shepherd.

▶ Sound doctrine *(orthodox, truthful)*

Teachings that conform to the core teachings of Scripture as pertains to the life, death, and resurrection of Jesus Christ
1 Corinthians 15:3. Matter of first importance
1 Timothy 1:10. Accurate teachings
1 Timothy 4:16. Life and teaching able to save
2 Timothy 4:3. Time when sound teaching will no longer be endured
Titus 1:9. Devoted to the message
Titus 2:1. Living according to sound teaching

▶ South *(direction, down)*

The compass direction opposite north
Genesis 13:14–15. Looking in all directions
Numbers 2:10. South-side armies
1 Kings 6:8. Temple architecture
1 Chronicles 26:15. Representing south side
Job 9:9. Creator of stars in the southern hemisphere
Ezekiel 20:46–47. Burning the whole land
Daniel 11:17. Diplomatic efforts with the southern king
Luke 11:31. Queen (Sheba) from the south
Acts 8:26. Heading south on the road

▶ Sovereignty *(omnipotence, providence, power)*

God's complete and total exercise of power over His creation; God is both able and willing to accomplish His holy will in the world.
Genesis 18:14. Nothing is too hard for the Lord.
Psalm 24:8. The Lord is strong and mighty.
Jeremiah 32:17. Sovereign of heaven and earth
Daniel 7:27. All power and greatness belong to God.
Matthew 19:26. All things possible with God
Ephesians 3:20. One who works abundantly more than we can imagine
1 Timothy 6:15. King of Kings, Lord of Lords

▶ Sow *(plant, scatter, spread)*

Planting or scattering seed in preparing for harvest time
Psalm 126:5. Sowing a harvest
Proverbs 11:18. Honest work
Ecclesiastes 11:6. Discerning where to sow
Matthew 6:26. Birds that do not sow
Matthew 13:3–39. Sowing seeds in various locales
Luke 8:8. Seeds planted in good earth
1 Corinthians 15:42–43. Body is planted
Galatians 6:7–8. Reaping what one sows
James 3:18. Sowing peace

▶ Spain *(country)*

A country Paul intended to visit, according to Romans
Romans 15:24. En route to Spain
Romans 15:28. Visiting on the way to Spain

▶ Sparrow *(bird, worthless)*

A bird sold very cheap and mentioned among offerings made by those who are in extreme poverty

Psalm 84:3. Sparrows finding a home
Proverbs 26:2. Fluttering bird
Luke 12:6–7. Sparrow's worth versus humans
Luke 13:19. Birds that nested

▶ Speech *(words, talking)*

The verbal expression of thoughts, ideas, and passions in a rhetorically satisfying manner
Genesis 11:1. Common world language
Exodus 4:10. Bad communicator
Psalm 19:2–3. Listening to the stories of day and night
Proverbs 22:11. Gracious speech
Mark 9:17. Demon silences speech
2 Corinthians 8:7. Growing in teaching proficiency
1 Timothy 4:12. Setting example in speech and behavior
1 Peter 3:10. Practicing guarded speech

▶ Spice(s) *(flavor, salt)*

Variety of vegetable substances used to add flavor or preserve food
Genesis 37:25. Exotic materials from Gilead
Genesis 43:11. High-quality products
Exodus 30:34. Frankincense
1 Kings 10:2. Queen of Sheba's entourage of camels and spices
2 Chronicles 9:1. Various spices
Song of Songs 6:2. Bed of spices
Matthew 23:23. Tithing spices at harvest, yet neglecting justice!
Mark 16:1. Spices to anoint a dead body

▶ Spider(s) *(bugs, insects)*

An eight-legged insect known for spinning beautiful webs which serve in the process of catching food
Job 8:14. Fragile home
Isaiah 59:5. Hazardous home life

▶ Spinster *(older woman, single)*

An unmarried older woman who is perceived to be beyond the normal years for marriage
Psalm 78:63. Virgins hear no music of weddings.
1 Corinthians 7:27–28. Remain as you are.

▶ Spiritism *(spiritualism)*

System of religious practice interested in necromancy and divination
1 Samuel 28:7. Consulting the dead
Acts 8:9–11. Actively interested in magic and divination

▶ Spiritual disciplines *(holiness, prayer, fasting)*

Christian disciplines which help increase holiness and strengthen faith
Daniel 9:3. Prayer and fasting
Matthew 4:2. Prolonged fasting
Matthew 6:16–18. Instructions for fasting
Luke 5:33. Frequently fasting
Philippians 4:8. Honorable things
2 Timothy 2:15. Teaching the word of truth correctly
Hebrews 10:25. Gathering together

▶ Spiritual gifts *(gifts, blessings, anointing)*

Unique spiritual blessings which God grants through the indwelling work of the Spirit for the growth of the church
Romans 12:3–8. Differing gifts
1 Corinthians 12:1–2. Not for unbelievers
1 Corinthians 13:13. These three remain.
1 Corinthians 14:1–2. Pursuing love
Ephesians 4:11–12. Christian servants
1 Peter 4:10. Managing God's gifts

▶ Spiritual growth *(growth, disciplines, grace)*

Growth which results from the practicing of spiritual disciplines
Romans 12:2. Following what is good, pleasing, and perfect
Ephesians 4:16. Growing in Christian unity
Ephesians 4:23. New attitudes in Christ
Philippians 1:6. Perseverance of faith

2 Timothy 1:7. Spirit of power, love, and good judgment
James 5:16. Confession of sins to one another
1 Peter 2:2. Desirous for God's Word
2 Peter 3:18. Growing in the knowledge of Christ the Savior
3 John 1:2. Peace in mind and body

▶ Spiritual rebirth *(**see Born Again**)*

▶ Spiritual thirst *(hunger, longing, yearning)*

The intense expressions of "thirsting for God" found in the Bible truly demonstrate the joy experienced in seeking God with all one's might.
Psalm 42:2. Spiritual thirst for God
Psalm 63:1. Longing for God
Psalm 84:1–2. A longing soul
Psalm 143:6. Outstretched hands
John 4:13–14. Living water
John 7:37. Coming to Jesus for a drink
Revelation 21:6. Water of life
Revelation 22:17. Invitation to all who are thirsty

▶ Spirituality *(spirit, soul, transcendence)*

An astute awareness of spiritual matters in all of life, discernment to judge spiritual teachings, and the prophetic voice to share and bless others with it
1 Corinthians 2:13–14. Spiritual teachings rather than intellectual arguments
1 Corinthians 10:3–4. Eating and drinking from Christ
Galatians 5:16. Living according to the spiritual nature
Colossians 1:9. Spiritual wisdom and insight into God's will
2 Thessalonians 2:13. Life springs with spiritual devotion.
1 Timothy 4:14. Developing a spiritual gift
1 Peter 4:6. Earthly life contrasted with spiritual life
3 John 1:2. Knowledge of good spirituality

▶ Spoils of war *(booty, loot, plunder)*

Those things which are taken from a conquered people by their captors in the wake of a military loss
Genesis 34:29. Houses looted, women and children taken
Exodus 3:22. "Borrowing" wealth from Egypt
Numbers 31:11. City looted
Deuteronomy 20:14. The Lord grants the spoils of war.
1 Samuel 30:19. Nothing was missing upon David's return.
2 Chronicles 14:14. Much to take
Psalm 119:162. Priceless treasure
Isaiah 53:12. Dividing the prize with the strong
Amos 3:10. Collecting profit in palaces
Luke 11:22. Taking weapons and loot

▶ Spring *(season) (new life, season)*

The time following the wet season when new life begins to emerge
Deuteronomy 11:14. Rain in the fall and spring produces new grain.
2 Samuel 11:1. Time when kings head out to battle
1 Kings 20:22. Preparing for a spring attack
2 Chronicles 36:10. Returning from Jerusalem with temple loot
Job 29:23. Spring showers
Jeremiah 5:24. Autumnal rain, spring rain
Zechariah 10:1. Asking at the right time
James 5:7. Time farmers wait for

▶ Springs *(water) (fountain, source, water)*

Sources of fresh, drinkable water which provide necessary life sustenance
Genesis 7:11. Deep springs of the earth bursting open
Genesis 24:43–44. Rebekah's hospitality
Deuteronomy 8:7. Rivers and streams that will not run dry
2 Chronicles 32:4. Finding abundant water

Psalm 107:33. Reversal of fortunes
Isaiah 35:7. Springs bursting from dry ground
Isaiah 41:18. God's transformative power
Isaiah 49:10. Neither hungry nor thirsty again
Revelation 7:17. Springs that fill with the water of life
Revelation 21:6. Fountain filled with the water of life

▶ Spy(ies)/Spying *(competitor, enemy, watchful)*

People sent out "below the radar" to ascertain information about a stated objective
Genesis 42:9–14. Brothers, not spies
Deuteronomy 1:22. Spying out the land ahead of time
Joshua 2:1. Joshua's spies and Rahab
Joshua 6:23. Rahab and family spared
2 Samuel 10:3. Destroying a city
Luke 20:20. Religious spies watching Jesus
Galatians 2:4. Spying out Christian freedom
James 2:25. Recalling Rahab

▶ Stability *(faithfulness, firm, steadiness)*

Used literally of one's steadiness in walking and figuratively of strong and faithful foundation from which one operates
Exodus 17:12. Stabilizing Moses
Deuteronomy 20:1–2. Stable forces
Psalm 91:1. Protection from God
Proverbs 28:2. Wisdom to provide national stability
Proverbs 29:4. King's presence
Isaiah 33:6. Foundation in place for a solid future
Colossians 1:23. Continuing on without straying from the solid foundation
2 Peter 3:17. On the lookout, maintaining spiritual stability

▶ Staff *(instrument, tool, utensil)*

A rod or scepter used in various professions
Exodus 4:1–4. Shepherd's staff
Exodus 7:19. Plagues called upon
Numbers 17:3. Staff for each tribe
1 Samuel 14:27. Honey-dipped staff
1 Samuel 17:40. Shepherd's stick
Psalm 23:4. Rod and staff provide courage.
Isaiah 14:5. Staff of the wicked broken
Zechariah 11:7–14. Caring for sheep with Favor and Unity
Matthew 10:10. No need for a walking stick
Hebrews 1:8. God's scepter for justice
Hebrews 9:4. Ark contains Aaron's staff that budded.

▶ Standard *(excellence, level, quality)*

A measure or model used in making comparative evaluations which seeks to bring about uniformity and fairness
Leviticus 19:35. Standard weights and measures
Numbers 1:52. Standard tribal family flag
2 Samuel 14:26. Royal standard
2 Chronicles 3:3. Standard form of measurement
Ezekiel 11:12. Standards of law disobeyed
Daniel 5:27. Placed on the scale and found to be lacking
John 8:15. Judging each other according to human standards
1 Corinthians 1:26. Run of the mill when you were called
2 Corinthians 10:2. Human motives

▶ Star(s) *(celestial bodies, heavens)*

Used literally of heavenly lights (actual stars) which are visible on a clear night; figuratively in what a star refers to or communicates symbolically
Genesis 1:16. God's creation of light
Genesis 15:5. Uncountable stars
Genesis 37:9. Joseph's strange dreams
Deuteronomy 4:19. Astral worship forbidden
Judges 5:20. Stars at war in the heavens
Psalm 147:4. Stars numbered and named
Isaiah 34:4. Rolled up like a scroll

Matthew 2:9. Wise men follow a star.

Philippians 2:15. Shining like stars in the world

▶ Status *(circumstance, condition, position)*

One's current standing with regard to a project, position, or life in general

1 Samuel 19:7. Status returned

Proverbs 27:23. Awareness of flock's condition

1 Corinthians 7:20. Remaining in a current position or context

1 Corinthians 7:24. God-given circumstances

Galatians 4:14. Illness presenting difficulties

Philippians 4:12. Working with every circumstance

Jude 6. Position of authority lost

▶ Status symbol(s) *(example, guide, model)*

A person with significance derived from worldly accomplishments and wealth; viewed as an example to be imitated

Genesis 24:35. Abundant riches

Deuteronomy 8:17. Wealthy and strong

1 Samuel 17:25. Elevating social status through marriage

Esther 1:20. Husbands' status elevated by decree

▶ Statutes *(decrees, regulations, requirements)*

Intimately connected with Torah, "statutes" typically denote generic references to the law of God and its regulations.

1 Kings 3:3. Solomon's regard for David's rules but not the Lord's statutes

1 Kings 11:34. God's faithfulness on account of David's faithfulness

Psalm 19:7. Perfect teachings

Psalm 119:2. Blessed are those who obey the Law.

Luke 1:6. God's regulations

▶ Steadfast *(committed, faithful, loyal)*

The quality of being firmly and resolutely committed to a person, purpose, or cause

1 Samuel 22:14. Who will be faithful like David?

1 Kings 8:23. Promises made and kept

Psalm 51:10. Faithfulness in spirit

Psalm 57:7. Confident heart

Isaiah 26:3. Perfect peace through pleasing protection

1 Peter 5:10. Support in the midst of suffering

▶ Steadfast love *(enduring mercy, grace, love)*

The loving-kindness of God associated with the mercy and hope of His people

Exodus 15:13. Salvation and a holy dwelling

Numbers 14:19. Forgiveness and the steadfast love of God

Deuteronomy 7:9. Merciful to generations of those who love the commands

1 Chronicles 16:34. Mercy endures forever.

Nehemiah 9:17. God's compassionate mercy

Psalm 13:5. Joyful heart in your salvation

Psalm 44:26. Rescue your people on account of your mercy.

1 John 3:16. Christ's life given for us

▶ Stealing *(burglary, robbery, theft)*

The unlawful taking of another's property, typically by stealth

Exodus 20:15. Do not steal.

Exodus 22:7–8. Thieves caught and punished

Matthew 6:19. Earthly treasures will be stolen.

Matthew 27:64. Tomb raiders?

John 10:10. Difference between a thief and a shepherd

John 12:6. Judas, the thief

Romans 2:21. Correlating deed and action?

Ephesians 4:28. Quit stealing, work hard.

1 Thessalonians 5:2. Day which comes like a thief in the night

Titus 2:9–10. Honest workers

▶ Steps *(incline, path, stairs)*

A series of small, flat surfaces which gradually incline

Exodus 20:26. Sage advice

2 Kings 20:9–10. Shadow defies physics.

2 Chronicles 9:11. An ornate royal palace

Job 23:11. Following footsteps

Ecclesiastes 5:1. Watching one's step at the temple

Acts 21:40. Speaking on the steps of the barrack

1 Peter 2:21. Following the footsteps of Christ in suffering

▶ Steward *(manager, overseer)*

One who oversees the affairs of the home and is responsible for the effective running of a household

Genesis 43:19, 24. Joseph's hospitability

2 Samuel 16:1. Steward of many men and animals

Luke 8:3. Administrator of Herod's household

Luke 12:42. Faithful, skilled manager

Luke 16:8. Dishonest manager

▶ Stewardship *(authority, responsibility)*

The task of responsibly overseeing the actions of someone or something as an appointed manager to that realm

Deuteronomy 12:11. Stewarding God's gifts

Matthew 23:23. Bad stewards

Mark 12:41–43. Surprising example of extreme stewardship

1 Corinthians 9:17. Entrusted with stewardship

Ephesians 3:2. Responsibility to share God's kindness

Colossians 1:25. Stewardship of God's message

1 Timothy 1:4. Distractions from stewardship of faith

▶ Stiff-necked (see *Stubborn*)

▶ Stingy *(mean, miserly, parsimonious)*

Ungenerous and unwilling to spend or give money for any reason

Proverbs 23:6. Avoid the food and company of a stingy person.

Proverbs 28:22. Stingy person's get-rich-quick plan

Jeremiah 6:13. Eager for dishonest gain

1 Corinthians 5:10. Living between two worlds

1 Timothy 3:8. Deacons must not be stingy.

▶ Stoicism *(philosophy)*

A philosophy noted for its ideals of high standard of personal conduct, sense of duty without delight, and asceticism

Acts 17:18. Stoic philosophers

Philippians 2:6–9. Self-abnegation

Philippians 4:11. Contentment in all circumstances

▶ Stomach ailments (see *Indigestion*)

▶ Stones *(mountains, pebbles, rocks)*

A hard, organic material of variable size, used for architectural purposes, writing surfaces, and weaponry

Exodus 23:24. Crushing sacred stones

Exodus 28:9–21. Working with minerals

Deuteronomy 27:5. Stone altar

Deuteronomy 27:8. Writing on stones

Joshua 4:20–21. Stones of remembrance

Joshua 8:32. Copy of Moses' Teaching

1 Kings 7:10. Laying a foundation

Ecclesiastes 3:5. Scattering and gathering

Matthew 3:9. Confidence in God's work

John 20:1. Tombstone was removed.

1 Peter 2:6. Chosen stone in Zion

▶ Stoning *(martyr, persecute, punishment)*

A torturous form of capital punishment prescribed for particular offenses

Exodus 21:29. Stoning a deadly bull

1 Samuel 30:6. David's distress

John 10:33. Threats of stoning on the charge of blasphemy

Acts 7:59. Stephen's death

Acts 14:19. Paul stoned nearly to death.
Hebrews 11:37. Deaths in the great cloud of witnesses

▶ Storm(s) *(weather, wind, tempest)*

A violent atmospheric disturbance, typically involving winds, rain, thunder, and lightning
Exodus 9:24. The perfect storm
Job 30:22. Tossed around in a storm
Psalm 55:8. Seek shelter.
Proverbs 10:25. Righteous have lasting shelter
Isaiah 25:4. Sheltered from rain and heat
Matthew 8:24–26. Jesus calms the storm.
Acts 27:13–15. Storms at sea
2 Peter 2:17. False teachers blowing in the wind like whims

▶ Storytelling (see *Parable[s]*)

▶ Stranger(s) *(newcomer, outsider, visitor)*

Someone who is in a strange and foreign land
1 Chronicles 29:15. Resident aliens
Psalm 54:3. Attacked by strangers
Ezekiel 16:32. Adulterous wife prefers strangers.
Zechariah 7:14. Scattered among the nations
Hebrews 11:13. Living as a stranger on the earth
Hebrews 13:2. Be hospitable to the house of believers.
1 Peter 1:1. Temporary residents
3 John 5. Faithfulness to guests

▶ Strategy *(plan, plot, program)*

A plan of action designed to achieve a large-scale goal
2 Kings 18:20. Taking and receiving advice for war
Proverbs 24:6. Waging war with the right strategy
Isaiah 8:10. Battle ready
Acts 20:3. Plotting to kill Paul
Acts 25:3. Plotting ambush

▶ Stream(s) *(fountain, river, water)*

A small, flowing river
Exodus 7:19. Streams turned to blood
Leviticus 11:9–10. Swarming animals and creatures
Deuteronomy 8:7. Land with underground streams
Job 29:6. Buttermilk and olive oil
Psalm 1:3. Growing like a well-planted tree
Isaiah 19:6. Streams emptied and dried up
John 7:38. Streams of living water will flow from within believers.

▶ Strength *(might, muscle, power)*

Used in reference to the raw power of animals and human beings
Exodus 15:2. The Lord is my strength.
Deuteronomy 3:28. Words of strength
Deuteronomy 6:5. Loving God with all your strength
Judges 16:17. Secret strength
2 Samuel 22:33. Armed with strength
Isaiah 33:2. Be the strength of your people.
Isaiah 40:31. Those who wait on the Lord will be strengthened.
Mark 12:33. Commanded to love God with full strength
Acts 16:5. Churches strengthened in faith
Philippians 4:13. Strengthened through Christ to do all things

▶ Stress *(anxiety, pressure, strain)*

Mental and emotional pressure resulting from highly demanding circumstances, often causing physical duress
Psalm 34:19. Righteous delivered from troubles
Psalm 54:4. God is my helper.
Psalm 62:1. Waiting calmly for God
Proverbs 12:25. Anxiety weighs down, kind words lift up.
Matthew 6:34. Forgetting about tomorrow's worries
1 Corinthians 1:8–9. Strength from God when it is needed
1 Peter 5:7. Trusting God with anxiety

▶ Strife/Striving *(bitterness, conflict, quarreling)*

Anger and bitterness verbally expressed over an important point of conflict

Proverbs 30:33. Producing strife

Ecclesiastes 2:22. Anxious striving

Habakkuk 1:3. Strife is at hand

Romans 1:29. Life of strife

Galatians 5:15. Criticism and personal attacks

Ephesians 4:31. Ridding life of bitterness

1 Timothy 6:4. Unhealthy desire to mix words

1 Peter 2:23. Verbal and physical attack

▶ Stripes (see *Flogging*)

▶ Struggle *(fight, scuffle, wrestle)*

Physical fighting, constraining and wrestling; figuratively, difficult and challenging situations which require proportionate amounts of exertion

Genesis 32:28. Jacob wrestled with God.

Exodus 2:13. Moses interrupts two fighting men.

Hosea 12:3. Recalling Jacob's life of struggle

Romans 15:30. Join in Paul's struggles by praying for him.

Ephesians 6:12. Divine and spiritual warriors

Philippians 1:30. Similar struggles

Hebrews 12:4. Struggling, but not to the point of death

▶ Stubborn *(arrogance, prideful, stiff-necked)*

The quality of being fixed and unshakable in one's opinion, in spite of counterpoints and the use of logic and reason

Exodus 32:9. Stubborn people

Exodus 34:9. Stubborn people seeking forgiveness

Deuteronomy 9:6. Misunderstanding God's gracious blessings

2 Kings 17:14. Family continuity

Nehemiah 9:17. Attempting to return to Egypt

Psalm 78:8. Rebellious generation with disloyal hearts

Mark 3:5. Closed minds even while healings take place

Acts 7:51. Stubborn and heartless like one's ancestors

▶ Student(s) *(disciple, follower, learner)*

Used in reference to persons who are studying either formally or informally under an instructor

1 Chronicles 25:8. Music students

Ezra 7:10. Diligent student

Jeremiah 32:33. Student backsliding

Daniel 1:17. Wisdom and proficiency in understanding Babylonian literature

Matthew 10:24–25. Student/teacher relationships

Mark 4:34. Explaining all things to the disciples

Acts 18:24. Study of the Scriptures

Galatians 6:6. Sharing with teachers of God's Word

▶ Study *(meditation, research, reflection)*

The disciplined undertaking of the acquisition of knowledge through research, reflection, meditation, and studying under someone

Psalm 119:4. Principles to be studied and followed

Ecclesiastes 1:13. Brilliant yet miserable

Ecclesiastes 12:12. Endless writing of books and exhaustion from too much study

John 5:39. Source of life discovered in the study of Scripture

2 Timothy 2:15. Rightly handling the word of truth

1 Peter 2:2–3. Craving the milk of God's Word

▶ Stumble *(trip, fall, sway)*

Conveys the act of tripping or falling in a literal sense; frequently found in contexts of judgment and sin

Leviticus 26:37. Unable to withstand against one's enemies

1 Chronicles 13:9. Oxen stumbling on the threshing floor

Psalm 119:165. Lasting peace without stumbling

Isaiah 5:27. Prepared and ready for action

Daniel 11:35. Temporary setbacks

Hosea 14:9. Rebels stumble over the Lord's righteous ways.

John 11:9–10. Walking during the day versus walking at night

Romans 9:32–33. Stumbling over the stumbling stone

Romans 14:20. Causing others to stumble over food issues

▶ Subjection *(subjugation, oppression, domination)*

Used actively in reference to forceful domination and situations of military conquest; used passively with the nuance of willful subjugation of oneself to an authority

1 Samuel 7:1. God's authority through the ark

Luke 10:17. Demons obey disciples of Jesus.

Romans 13:1. Obeying government as placed by God

1 Corinthians 15:28. All things subjugated to Christ

Philippians 2:9–11. Christ honored above all the earth

Titus 3:1. Willful subjugation to government

Hebrews 2:5. Under the angels' control

1 Peter 2:13. Be subject to government

1 Peter 3:1. Wives under authority of their husbands

▶ Submission *(yielding, consent, compliance)*

The action of willingly accepting and genuinely following the leadership and initiative of another

1 Chronicles 29:24. Loyalty pledged to King Solomon

1 Corinthians 15:28. All will submit to Christ.

1 Timothy 2:11. Submissive learning

Titus 3:1. Submitting to and helping government officials

Hebrews 5:7. Submissive to the Father

Hebrews 13:17. Submission to leadership is for your good.

1 Peter 3:1. Wife's submission to husband's authority

1 Peter 3:22. Christ's authority and the submission of angels, rulers, and powers

1 Peter 5:5. Submission to spiritual leaders

▶ Substitution *(atonement, exchange, replacement)*

Someone or something that acts in the place of another

Leviticus 27:10. Discerning a worthy sacrifice

Matthew 20:28. Son of Man gave his life as a ransom.

Acts 1:21. Choosing a substitute for Judas

2 Corinthians 5:21. A great exchange

1 Peter 3:18. Righteous for the unrighteous

1 John 2:2. Payment for the sins of the whole world

1 John 4:10. Love demonstrated through payment of sin

▶ Success *(victory, triumph, winner)*

The accomplishment of an aim or purpose followed by the reaping of positive results

Genesis 24:12. Prayer for success

Genesis 39:3. Joseph's success in all things and advancement

Deuteronomy 20:4. The battle belongs to the Lord.

Joshua 1:8. Success and prosperity found through internalizing the Law

1 Samuel 18:14. Success in the Lord

Psalm 118:25. Begging for protection and military success

Proverbs 16:3. Trusting God

Luke 10:17. Successful ministry

1 Corinthians 3:6–7. Sharing in God's success

James 1:10. Successful business leading to humility

S

▸ Successor *(heir, inheritor, usurper)*

Someone who steps in, filling a leadership void, either through death or consolidation of power

1 Kings 1:48. David and Solomon

1 Kings 11:43. Solomon succeeded by Rehoboam

2 Kings 16:20. Hezekiah succeeds Ahaz.

1 Chronicles 3:16. Family lineage

1 Chronicles 29:28. Death of David, rise of Solomon

Ecclesiastes 2:12. Difficult shoes to fill

Daniel 11:20. Kingly succession

▸ Suffering *(hardship, distress, misery)*

Undergoing hardship for a cause; to experience great pain, duress, and hardships

Exodus 3:7. God's people suffering in Egypt

Job 2:13. Suffering immense personal loss

Psalm 22:24. God hears the cries of the oppressed.

Isaiah 53:3. Coming one who will be rejected, and despised

Lamentations 1:12. Seeing the suffering of others

Mark 5:34. Relieved from suffering illness

Romans 5:3. Boasting in suffering because it produces endurance

Romans 8:18. Present sufferings are insignificant compared to future glory.

Colossians 1:24. Filling up what is lacking

James 5:10. Following the example of the prophets

1 Peter 2:19. God is mindful of those who suffer on his behalf.

▸ Sufficient/Sufficiency *(enough, ample, adequate)*

The quality of being enough or adequate; able to stand up to an expectation

Isaiah 40:16. Insufficient for a sacrifice

Romans 15:18–19. Sufficient boldness to Gentiles

2 Corinthians 2:16. Who is qualified to testify about this?

2 Corinthians 3:5. Sufficiency from God

2 Corinthians 9:8. Sufficiency in God

2 Corinthians 12:9. Grace is sufficient.

1 Thessalonians 3:9. Sufficient thanks cannot be made.

Hebrews 7:26–27. A sacrifice sufficient for all time!

▸ Suicide *(death, self-murder)*

The willful taking of one's own life

Genesis 27:46. Contemplating the value of one's life

1 Samuel 31:4. Saul finishes the job.

2 Samuel 17:23. Death and a "suicide note"

1 Kings 16:18. Death by fire

Matthew 27:5. Judas commits suicide.

Acts 1:18. Strange manner of death

Acts 16:27. Jailor's near-death experience

▸ Summer *(dry season, warm season)*

The warmest, driest season of the year

Genesis 8:22. Perpetual changing of days and seasons

Psalm 32:4. Strength fading in the heat of summer

Proverbs 10:5. Wise living in season

Proverbs 26:1. Right element, wrong season

Proverbs 30:25. Ants storing food

Jeremiah 8:20. Harvest not enough

Luke 21:30. Signs of summer

▸ Summons *(order, directive, command)*

A written or oral request to appear before an authority

Numbers 22:37. Questioning a summons

Psalm 50:1. Commanding the days

Isaiah 45:3. Summoned by name

Isaiah 55:5. Summoning a new nation

Daniel 3:13. Youths summoned before the king

Acts 24:2. Paul summoned before leaders

▸ Sun *(sunshine, daylight, beams)*

The glowing orb which rises daily and shines upon the land, providing light and warmth

Genesis 37:9. Cosmically involved dream

Exodus 16:21. Hot sun melts away Israel's food.

Deuteronomy 4:19. Do not worship the sun.

Joshua 10:12–13. Joshua asks the Lord for an omen.

Psalm 72:17. An enduring name

Psalm 113:3. Praise God in all places.

Ecclesiastes 1:9. Nothing new under the sun

Mark 4:6. Scorching sun

Ephesians 4:26. Settling disputes before the sun goes down

Revelation 7:16. Sun's heat ineffective with living water

▶ Sunday *(see Sabbath)*

▶ Sunrise *(dawn, daybreak, first light)*

The earliest moments of the day when the rays of the sun first break through the darkness in the eastern sky

2 Samuel 23:4. Like morning light

Psalm 113:3. Praise to the Lord

Isaiah 13:10. Sun rises in darkness.

Habakkuk 3:4. Bright like the sun

Mark 16:2. Dawn's early light

▶ Sunset *(twilight, dusk, evening)*

The last light of day before the sun sets in the western sky

Genesis 15:12. Falling into a deep sleep at sundown

Exodus 17:12. Steady until sunset

Exodus 22:26. Returning property before sunset

2 Chronicles 18:34. Death at sundown

Malachi 1:11. A great name over all the earth

Mark 1:32. Healing after hours

▶ Superiority *(supremacy, dominance)*

A position of supreme status or preeminence

1 Corinthians 2:1. Not a superior speech

Hebrews 1:1–14. Son is superior to the angels.

Hebrews 8:6. Work of the priesthood is superior.

▶ Supernatural *(miracles, signs, wonders)*

Suspension of the natural laws of physics in a manner that demonstrates the in-breaking of the kingdom of God through Jesus Christ

Matthew 12:38. Seeking a sign

Matthew 14:20. Multiplying the bread with plenty to spare

Luke 5:24. Healing a paralyzed man

Luke 11:16. Signs from heaven

John 2:18. Seeking to see a miracle

John 10:37. Jesus does what His Father does.

Acts 2:22. Worker of miracles, wonders, and signs

Acts 3:6. Causing a man to walk

1 Corinthians 15:46. Spiritual aspects come second.

▶ Superstition(s) *(myth, legend, unfounded belief)*

Excessive spiritualism to the extent of refusing to see God's working in and through time and space

Isaiah 2:6–22. Eastern influences

1 Timothy 1:4. Myths

1 Timothy 4:7. Avoiding godless myths

2 Timothy 4:4. Refusing the truth

Titus 1:14. Jewish myths

▶ Supervisor(s)/Supervision *(manager, overseer, governor)*

An overseer, typically in a managerial role

2 Kings 22:9. Giving money to the workers

2 Chronicles 34:17. Paying builders

Nehemiah 3:5. Nobles unwilling to be supervised in work

Nehemiah 11:11. Supervising God's temple

Daniel 1:11a. Supervisor over Daniel

Matthew 20:8. Manager of the vineyard

Titus 1:7. Appointed by God

S

▶ Supplication *(see Ask/Seek/Knock)*

▶ Supply *(see Provision)*

▶ Suppression *(persecution, ill treatment, subdue)*

The action of stopping or minimizing someone or something from completing an objective

1 Samuel 7:13. Philistines suppressed
1 Chronicles 17:10. Enemies crushed
2 Chronicles 13:18. Victory through trusting the Lord
Nehemiah 9:24. Canaanites subdued
Psalm 17:13. Plea for help from God
Isaiah 45:1. Cyrus, God's anointed
Mark 5:4. Demon possession that cannot be subdued
Romans 1:18–32. Unrighteous suppression of the truth
1 Thessalonians 5:19. Do not quench the Spirit.

▶ Supremacy *(authority, mastery, sovereignty)*

The status of being ultimate in existence, power, and worth

Mark 9:7. Christ supreme
John 1:1–2. Christ with God prior to creation
1 Corinthians 8:6. One God, One Lord
Philippians 2:9–10. The preeminent Christ
Colossians 1:15–18. Supremacy of Christ
Hebrews 1:4. Greater than the angels
Revelation 1:5. Faithful witness

▶ Surrender *(concede, yield, submit)*

The action of submission and ceased resistance prior to the outbreak of war

Joshua 20:5. Do not surrender one wrongly accused.
Psalm 37:7. Surrender to the Lord.
Psalm 41:2. At the mercy of the enemy
Jeremiah 21:9. Surrender to Babylon.
Luke 9:23. Surrendering life itself
Romans 12:1–2. Surrendering of self to God
1 Corinthians 13:3. Surrendering possessions
James 4:7. Surrendered to God's authority

▶ Surveying *(observing, viewing, inspecting)*

Careful and critical inspection of someone or something, often followed by a report of findings

Exodus 39:43. Inspecting the work of the people
Joshua 18:4. Surveying the new land
Job 5:24. Clean inspection
Job 7:18. Surveyor of all things
Proverbs 5:21. Ways seen by the Lord
Ecclesiastes 2:11. Life surveyed: pointless
Amos 7:17. Survey says: judgment

▶ Survivor(s) *(remainder, remnant)*

Someone who has lived through circumstances in which most others have died

Exodus 2:1–10. Moses survives in the Nile.
Numbers 14:38. Two return.
1 Samuel 11:11. Scattered survivors
1 Samuel 18:11–12. Two close calls
Luke 14:31–32. Considering survival rates
Luke 15:16. Surviving on scraps

▶ Suspicion *(intuition, doubt, distrust)*

An unconfirmed feeling that something is possible, likely, or true

Numbers 5:14. Jealous spouse
Numbers 20:12. No trust
2 Samuel 10:3. Suspicious of David
Proverbs 3:5. Suspicious of one's own understanding
Isaiah 36:15. Creating suspicions
Matthew 14:31. Have faith.
1 Timothy 6:4. Arguments which cause suspicion
2 Peter 1:19. Confirmed words

▶ Sustenance *(nourishment, food, rations)*

Food or drink that functions as a source of nourishment and strength to partakers

Genesis 1:29–30. Food for every creature
Genesis 9:15. Sustenance restored
1 Kings 18:4. Obadiah feeds hidden prophets.
Proverbs 22:9. Blessing due to generosity
Proverbs 30:25. Putting away food for later use
Matthew 6:11. Daily sustenance
2 Thessalonians 3:8. Working for food

▶ Swearing *(oath, curse, covenant)*

Accepting an undertaking or confirming a not yet known fact by the offering up of an oath
Genesis 21:23–24. Abraham swears an oath.
Genesis 50:5–6. Honoring one's father by carrying out an oath
Leviticus 19:12. Do not swear by God's name.
Jeremiah 4:2. Words to make an oath by
Daniel 12:7. An oath by the one who lives forever
Matthew 5:34. Do not swear "by heaven."
James 5:12. Letting yes be yes, no be no

▶ Sweetness *(sugary, sweetened, honeyed)*

The quality of being sweet to the taste
Exodus 15:25. Water that became sweet
Judges 14:18. Samson's riddle
Psalm 19:9–10. Lord's decisions are always in good taste.
Psalm 119:103. Promises which are sweet to the taste
Revelation 10:10. Sweet scroll turns to bitterness.

▶ Sword(s) *(knife, blade, saber)*

A sharp weapon used in warfare; figuratively used as a symbol of strength and might
Genesis 3:24. Angels to guard with flaming sword
Deuteronomy 33:29. Sword to aid in victory
1 Samuel 13:19. Weapon makers not found among the Hebrews
1 Samuel 17:39. Weighed down by another man's sword
1 Kings 3:24–25. Sharp wisdom
Matthew 26:47. Angry mob
Romans 8:35. Can sword separate us from the love of Christ?
Hebrews 4:12. Double-edged sword which is the Word

▶ Sword of the Spirit *(spiritual weapon, Word)*

The Word of God
Ephesians 6:17. Armor of God
Hebrews 4:12. Word which is sharper than a sword
Revelation 1:16. Word of God likened to a sword

▶ Sycamore *(tree, shade, fig tree)*

An arboricultural specimen which highly resembles a fig tree
1 Kings 10:27. An abundant tree
Psalm 78:47. Trees destroyed
Amos 7:14. A fig farmer
Luke 19:4. Catching a glimpse of Jesus

▶ Symbolism *(emblem, representation, allegorical)*

Communication which occurs at two levels: (1) through the literal words; (2) through what those words signify symbolically
Genesis 9:12–13. Rainbow as a sign of God's promise
Genesis 17:11. Circumcision as the sign of Abrahamic covenant
Exodus 4:8. Miraculous signs meant to garner allegiance
Numbers 2:2. Flag symbolizing household tribe
Numbers 14:11. God expects remembrance of signs.
Deuteronomy 4:34. God's demonstration of numerous signs
Ezekiel 20:12. Sabbath given as a sign
Matthew 24:3. What will be the sign of Christ's second coming?
Luke 2:12. Jesus is a sign.
Acts 2:19. Symbols in the sky
Revelation 1:1. Message communicated by symbols

S

▶ Sympathy *(compassion, pity, concern)*

Compassionate concern for the misfortune of others

1 Chronicles 19:2. Returning kindness for kindness

Psalm 69:20. Desiring sympathy

Jeremiah 16:5. Unsympathetic

Daniel 1:9. Sympathy from a high level official

Joel 2:14. Compassion reconsidered

Mark 6:34. Sympathy for the sheep

Luke 10:33. Samaritan's concern for an abject man

▶ Synagogue *(temple, House of God, sanctuary)*

House of worship that was set up remotely to allow worship practices to continue even though Jews were not at the true temple of Jerusalem

Matthew 4:23. Teaching in the synagogue

Matthew 6:2. Seeking acclaim in public

Mark 5:35–36. Call to belief in the synagogue

Mark 12:38–39. Careful to watch out for officials

Mark 13:9. Persecution in the Jewish courts

John 12:42. Fear of the Pharisees

Acts 6:9. Visitors from another synagogue

Acts 9:20. Preaching Christ in the synagogue

Acts 14:1. Belief and conversion in the synagogue

▶ Syncretism *(blending, merging)*

The blending of Israelite religion with elements of pagan religions from the larger surrounding culture

Deuteronomy 17:17. Allowing foreign wives to change one's heart

1 Kings 13:33. Illegal worship sites constructed

▶ Syro-Ephraimite War *(battle, war)*

A war occurring during the early years of Isaiah's ministry (c.a. 735 BCE)

Isaiah 7:1–12. Isaiah's instructions from the Lord

▶ Syrophoenicians *(Greeks, Canaanites)*

Inhabitants of Phoenicia, which during the New Testament era was located in the Roman province of Cilicia and Syria. These people lived northwest of Israel and were closely related to the Canaanites.

Matthew 15:21–28. Canaanite woman, from Syrophoenicia

Mark 7:24–30. Syrophoenician woman asks Jesus for help.

▶ Tabernacle *(dwelling, home, temple)*

Home or dwelling; the tent structure which God commanded His people to build for Him while they were wandering in the desert

Exodus 25.9. Tabernacle to be made
Exodus 28:43. Tent of meeting
Leviticus 9:23–24. God's place of earthly residence
Leviticus 16:2–3. Entering the holy place
Deuteronomy 23:18. House of the Lord
1 Kings 8:4. Ark brought into God's temple
Ezekiel 37:26–27. God's desire for a permanent dwelling with His people
Romans 3:25. The mercy seat of God
Hebrews 9:8. Making a way into the holiest place

▶ Tabernacles, Feast of *(booths, ingathering)*

A celebration commemorating the annual harvest and remembering Israel's days following the Exodus

Leviticus 23:34. Seven-day festival
Leviticus 23:43. Remembering temporary dwellings
Numbers 29:13. Stipulations for sacrifice
Deuteronomy 16:13. Preparing grain and making wine
Deuteronomy 16:14. Festival of joy
Zechariah 14:17. Associated with rain and crops
John 7:37. Jesus in the temple during the festival

▶ Table *(counter, furniture, surface)*

An article of furniture used for various purposes within the home, tabernacle, or temple

2 Samuel 9:12–13. Symbol of acceptance and peace
1 Kings 7:48. Temple table
2 Kings 4:10. Furniture in a guest room
Psalm 23:5. Place of sustenance
Proverbs 9:2. Wisdom sets her table.
Matthew 15:27. Place of dining
Luke 22:27. Seating and status at the table
John 2:15. Moneychangers' table
Acts 16:34. Preparing a table for guests
1 Corinthians 10:21. The Lord's table

▶ Tablet *(sign, stone, writing)*

A writing surface used to record information

Exodus 24:12. Stones given to Moses
Exodus 31:18. Inscribed by God
Deuteronomy 10:3–5. Tablets placed in the ark
Proverbs 3:3. Tablet of the heart
Isaiah 8:1. Drawing a large sign
Isaiah 30:8. Record keeping
Jeremiah 17:1. Recording the sins of God's people
Habakkuk 2:2. Recording a vision large enough for all to see
Luke 1:63. Zechariah reduced to writing
2 Corinthians 3:3. Letter of recommendation
Hebrews 9:4. The tablets which recorded the promise

▶ Tact *(diplomacy, empathy, thoughtfulness)*

Sensitivity in working and dealing with others in the midst of difficult circumstances

2 Samuel 2:4–5. Appointing leaders
Job 32:4–6. Keeping silent
Proverbs 15:1. Stilling anger
Ecclesiastes 8:5–6. Right way and time to act
Isaiah 50:4. Learning how to encourage the weary
Mark 12:34. Responding to critics
Ephesians 4:15. Speaking the truth in love
Colossians 4:6. Planning out words
Hebrews 5:2. Dealing gently with others
James 1:19–20. Tactful demeanor

▶ Tactics (see *Strategy*)

▶ Taking a stand *(standing firm, unyielding)*

Making a decision that is difficult or defining for one's life without yielding to pressure

Joshua 24:15. Choose today whom you will serve.

2 Chronicles 20:17. Standing firm in position

Ezra 7:18. Conforming to the will of God

Isaiah 46:8. Take courage.

Matthew 4:20–22. Deciding to follow Jesus

Mark 1:15. Choosing to follow the kingdom of God

1 Corinthians 16:13. Firm in the faith

Galatians 5:1. Firm in the benefits of freedom

Ephesians 6:13. Taking a stand during evil days

Philippians 4:1. Stand firm in the Lord.

Colossians 1:10. Living worthy lives

▶ Talent(s) *(aptitude, gift, skill)*

God-given skill or aptitude in a particular field

Genesis 4:21. Family talent

Exodus 4:10–12. Talent overlooked

Psalm 90:17. Asking for success in all things

Isaiah 44:11. Mortal artists

Daniel 1:3–4. Healthy, virile men

Romans 11:29. Gracious gift giving

Romans 12:6–8. Using God-given gifts

1 Corinthians 7:7. Special gifts for each person

Hebrews 2:4. Gifts given by the Spirit

1 Peter 4:10. Stewarding God's gifts

▶ Talkativeness *(long-winded, verbose, wordy)*

Expressing the tendency to talk too much or more than is needed

Job 8:2. Long-winded

Proverbs 26:24–26. Speaking wickedness in the community

Ecclesiastes 5:2. Limiting words

Ecclesiastes 5:6. Holding mouth back from sin

Jeremiah 5:13. Windbag prophets

Acts 17:18. Babbling fool

2 Corinthians 11:1. Putting up with foolishness

James 1:19. Be slow to speak.

▶ Target(s) *(bull's-eye, goal, mark)*

An object of attack, typically used in reference to target practice

1 Samuel 20:20. Shooting arrows

Job 6:4. Divine arrows find their target.

Psalm 58:7. Missing the mark

Lamentations 3:12. Shooting arrows at targets

Hosea 7:16. Weapon failure

▶ Task(s) *(duty, job, work)*

A job or body of work to be undertaken

Exodus 5:13. Daily tasks

Exodus 36:4. Various tasks performed

Numbers 4:19. Assigning tasks

Numbers 4:49. Moses assigns tasks for the tabernacle.

1 Kings 2:25. King assigns tasks.

1 Chronicles 16:7. Singing songs

2 Chronicles 26:18. Holy tasks

Ezra 10:4. Tasks of obligation

Psalm 104:23. Tedious tasks

John 5:36. Tasks given by the Father

Hebrews 6:2. Set apart for work

▶ Taste *(flavor, palate)*

The sensation of flavor experienced while eating or drinking food

2 Kings 4:40. Gross tasting meal

Job 6:6. Tasteless food

Psalm 34:8. Taste and see the Lord is good.

Song of Songs 2:3. Sweet tasting fruit

Lamentations 3:15. Bitter drink

Matthew 5:13. Tasteless salt

Matthew 27:34. Bad to the taste

Matthew 27:48. Tasting bitter wine-vinegar

John 2:10. Tasty wine

Acts 23:14. Tasting food before a kill

Colossians 2:21. Basic etiquette

▶ Tattoo(s) *(design, marking)*

A mark or design made on the body through puncturing the skin and inserting a dye

Leviticus 19:28. Tattooing forbidden

Isaiah 44:5. Writing the Lord's name on the body
Ezekiel 9:4. Marking persons throughout the city

▶ Taunt(s) *(insults, mocking, ridicule)*

A remark made for the purpose of provoking anger and insult
Judges 8:15. Harboring insults
2 Samuel 21:21. Taunting Israel
Psalm 42:10. Enemies that taunt
Psalm 79:12. Taunting neighbors
Psalm 102:8. Constant torment
Isaiah 14:4. Mocking the king of Babylon
Jeremiah 42:18. Ridicule in exile
Lamentations 3:63. Object of taunt
Micah 2:4. A day of coming taunt
Zephaniah 2:10. Insults against the people of the Lord

▶ Tax(es) *(charge, fee, tariff)*

An obligatory payment made to a governing authority, typically based on annual income or production
Genesis 47:13–14. Joseph collects money.
1 Samuel 8:15. Taking a tenth of harvest
2 Kings 23:35. Taxing according to wealth
Ezra 7:24. Tax exemption for clergy
Nehemiah 5:4. Borrowing money to pay taxes
Esther 10:1. Levying a tax on the country
Matthew 17:27. Jesus pays a tax.
Matthew 18:17. Treating someone like a tax collector
Luke 2:1–2. Taxes and census
Luke 20:25. Paying what emperor demands
Romans 13:6–7. Paying taxes

▶ Tax collector(s) *(publican, sinners)*

Refers to one who worked for the Roman government levying taxes
Matthew 5:46. Tax collectors' etiquette
Matthew 9:11. Jesus eating with tax collectors
Matthew 11:19. Friend of tax collectors
Matthew 18:17. Heathens and tax collectors
Matthew 21:32. Tax collectors believed Jesus.
Mark 2:16. Questioning eating with sinners
Luke 3:12. Tax collectors coming to be baptized
Luke 3:13. Being honest

▶ Teacher *(educator, instructor, rabbi)*

Someone who instructs others in wise living; often used of one who teaches God's law and is called by the name of "Rabbi"
Psalm 32:8. The Lord will instruct.
Isaiah 28:26. Taught by God
Malachi 2:6. Good teaching
Matthew 22:16. Truth teller
Mark 12:32. Teaching the truth of God
Luke 6:40. Student is not better than teacher.
John 14:16–17. The indwelling Spirit
Acts 8:30–31. Philip teaches the Ethiopian eunuch.
Acts 11:26. Saul and Barnabas teaching in Antioch
1 Thessalonians 4:9. Taught to love by God
2 Timothy 4:3. False teachers
James 3:1. Not many should become teachers.
1 John 2:27. Taught through Christ's anointing

▶ Teaching *(education, instruction, training)*

Ideas or instruction given from an authority for the purpose of wise living
1 Samuel 12:23. Teaching and discerning goodness
Psalm 143:10. Instruction in God's will
Proverbs 3:1. Remembering the teachings of wisdom
Malachi 2:6. Truth-filled teaching
Matthew 22:33. Amazing the crowds
Acts 5:42. Refusing to stop teaching the Good News
Romans 12:7. Using gifts of teaching
Romans 16:17. Teaching bad doctrine

1 Timothy 4:13. Instructions for public worship
1 Timothy 5:17. Honoring those who teach the Word of God well
2 Timothy 3:16. Useful Scripture

▶ Teamwork *(see Cooperation)*

▶ Tears *(crying, sobbing, weeping)*

The salty-liquid secretion from the eyes during times of intense physical or emotional pain

1 Samuel 20:41. David weeps.
Job 16:16. Physical signs of weeping
Psalm 126:5. Crying during planting, rejoicing during harvest
Jeremiah 9:1. Crying for the deceased
Lamentations 2:11. Miserable mourning
Matthew 26:75. Bitter weeping of a betrayer
Luke 19:41. Weeping over the city
2 Corinthians 2:4. Heart-felt message
Philippians 3:18. Crying over enemies of the cross
Revelation 21:4. Every tear wiped away

▶ Teenage rebellion *(defiance, opposition, revolt)*

Youthful wandering from God's path for one's life

Job 24:13. Straying from God's paths
Proverbs 5:9–10. Effects of bad choices
Proverbs 17:11. Searching out evil
Luke 15:11–32. Rebelling against family
1 Timothy 4:12. Setting an example
2 Timothy 2:22. Avoiding youthful lusts

▶ Teen idols *(philanderers, young men)*

Dashing young men who each find love in unique (and sometimes unwanted) places

Genesis 39:6–7. Potiphar's wife and Joseph
1 Samuel 9:2. Saul: tall, dark, handsome
1 Samuel 16:12. David's dashing good looks
Song of Songs 1:16. Handsome young lover

▶ Teens *(see Youth)*

▶ Teeth *(chew, eating, mouth)*

The pearly white enamel coated structures found in the mouths of most mammals; used for chewing and biting

Genesis 49:12. Bright white teeth
Job 4:10. Teeth knocked out
Psalm 37:12. Gritting of teeth
Proverbs 30:14. Sharp teeth
Lamentations 3:16. Grinding teeth with gravel
Daniel 7:7. Large iron teeth
Joel 1:6. Strength of a mighty nation
Zechariah 9:7. Flossing
Matthew 8:12. Extreme pain
Revelation 9:8. Teeth like a lion

▶ Temper *(anger, fury, rage)*

The tendency to be stirred to anger easily

Deuteronomy 19:6. Avenging death
Nehemiah 5:6. Very angry
Psalm 6:1. Divine temper
Psalm 30:5. Anger only for a moment
Psalm 86:15. God is slow to anger.
Proverbs 14:29. Foolishness of a short temper
Proverbs 22:24. Avoiding bad-tempered people
Daniel 3:19. Showing anger
Hosea 11:9. God's temper calmed
2 Corinthians 12:20. Fearful of bad tempers in the church
James 1:19–20. Do not be quick to anger.

▶ Temperament *(character, disposition, nature)*

The character or disposition of a living thing

Proverbs 14:16–17. Cautious living
Proverbs 16:32. Even-tempered
Proverbs 25:28. Self-control
Proverbs 29:11. Controlling emotions
Ecclesiastes 7:9. Anger is typical of fools.
Matthew 5:22. Answering for anger
James 1:19–20. Quick to listen, slow to speak

▶ Temperance *(abstinence, prohibition, restraint)*

Moderation and self-restraint from frequently misused commodities or activities; especially food, drink, and sex

1 Samuel 21:4–5. Abstinence
Proverbs 23:20–21. Avoid drunks and gluttons.
Proverbs 23:30–33. Drunkenness
Isaiah 28:1–2. Arrogant drunks destroyed
Amos 2:12. Forcing Nazirites to drink wine
Matthew 5:39. Exercising temperance in conflict
1 Timothy 3:3. Requirement for eldership
1 Timothy 3:11. In control of mind and body

▶ Temple *(house, sanctuary, tabernacle)*

God's house of worship built in Jerusalem by King Solomon. The first temple was destroyed 586 B.C. by the Babylonians. The second temple was rebuilt in 516 B.C. and it remained until A.D. 70.

2 Chronicles 3:17. Solomon builds the temple.
Psalm 79:1. God's temple lying in ruins
Zechariah 6:12–13. Eschatological temple
Matthew 12:6. Jesus is greater than the temple.
Matthew 21:13. House of prayer
Matthew 27:51. Curtain of the temple torn
John 2:19–21. Temple of the body
1 Corinthians 3:16–17. Warning against destroying God's temple
Ephesians 2:21. Symbol of Christian unity
Revelation 3:12. A pillar in God's temple
Revelation 21:22. God as the temple

▶ Temporal *(fleeting, passing, transient)*

Related to one's experience of the passing of time

Genesis 24:35. Earthly blessings
Exodus 23:25. Blessing sustenance
Deuteronomy 33:29. Temporal blessing
Job 5:17. Temporary scolding
Luke 6:24. Earthly comforts
John 17:13. Short time in this world
Philippians 4:6–7. Trusting God
1 Peter 3:14. Temporary suffering

▶ Temporary *(interim, nonpermanent, short-term)*

Something which is short-lasting or impermanent

2 Samuel 11:11. Temporary shelters
Psalm 39:5. Shortness of life
Psalm 49:10. The end of life
Psalm 78:39. Transient human life
Psalm 103:14. Humans are but dust.
Isaiah 2:22. Trusting worthless people
2 Corinthians 4:17–18. Seen versus unseen
James 4:14. Unknown lifespan
1 Peter 1:6. Temporary suffering
1 Peter 1:13. Ready for action

▶ Tempt *(entice, induce, persuade)*

The act of enticing or alluringly persuading someone to do something which, although attractive, is dangerous or self-destructive

Deuteronomy 13:6. Temped to worship other gods
1 Kings 11:2. Foreigners will tempt to false worship.
Matthew 4:7. Never tempt the Lord.
1 Corinthians 7:5. Sexual temptation
2 Timothy 2:22. Lusts which tempt the young
James 1:13. God tempts no one.

▶ Temptation *(allurement, desire, seduction)*

A sinful desire which is highly attractive in the short run, but destructive in the long run

Matthew 4:1. Jesus' wilderness temptation
Matthew 26:41. Temptation to sleep and sin
1 Corinthians 10:13. Temptations common to all
Galatians 6:1. Helping others out of temptation

Ephesians 6:16. Protection against temptation

1 Thessalonians 3:5. Caving to temptation?

Hebrews 2:18. Jesus' experience of temptation

Hebrews 4:15. Temptation in all the same ways

James 1:12. Enduring temptation

James 4:7. Resisting the devil

2 Peter 2:9. Help in time of temptation

▶ Temptress *(femme fatal, prostitute, seductress)*

A woman who tempts someone to do something, typically involving sexual invitation

Genesis 3:6. Sharing in original sin

Judges 16:1–2. Samson goes to bed with a prostitute.

2 Samuel 11:2–3. David and Bathsheba

1 Kings 11:1–2. Solomon's love of foreign women

1 Kings 21:25. Listening to evil advice

Job 2:9–10. Tempting a husband to blaspheme

Proverbs 5:3–5. An adulterous woman

Isaiah 3:16. Seductive glances

Ezekiel 13:18–19. Controlling women

Mark 6:22. Seductive, yet pleasing dancing

▶ Ten *(completeness, decade, number)*

Used literally as a numeral figure (one greater than nine), or metaphorically as a number of completeness or wholeness

Exodus 20:3–17. God gave Moses ten commandments.

Exodus 34:28. Ten Commandments

1 Samuel 1:8. Hyperbolic number

Daniel 1:20. Ten times more

Matthew 25:1. Ten virgins

Matthew 25:28. Ten talents

Luke 17:12. Ten lepers

Luke 19:16–17. Ten times, ten cities

Revelation 2:10. A complete time of suffering

Revelation 17:3. Woman with ten horns

▶ Ten Commandments *(see Ten)*

▶ Tenacity *(determination, persistence, resoluteness)*

The quality of being persistent and determined to accomplish something or maintain the status of something

Joshua 24:14. Serving the Lord with integrity

Judges 8:4. Pursuing an enemy

Job 2:2–3. Satan's persistent trouble-making

Job 14:7–9. Determined growth

Proverbs 30:24–28. Persistence of small species

Hebrews 12:1–3. Resolute group

James 5:11. Enduring suffering

▶ Tenderness *(affection, devotion, love)*

Demonstrating affection, concern, or loyalty toward someone through words and actions

Deuteronomy 28:54. Losing love and feeling

Deuteronomy 28:56. Woman loses her tender side.

Proverbs 4:3. A tender child

Proverbs 27:25. Small, fragile growth

Proverbs 31:26. Wisdom of tender instruction

Matthew 24:32. Tender branches in the summer

▶ Tension *(anxiety, stress, worry)*

Mental or emotional strain which often leads to physical pain

Psalm 55:22. Freedom from tensions

Psalm 68:19. God carries daily burdens.

Ecclesiastes 11:10. Get rid of bodily troubles.

2 Thessalonians 3:16. Peace in the midst of strife

James 4:2. Quarrelling and fighting rather than asking

1 Peter 5:7. Turning over anxious thoughts to God

▸ Tent(s) *(domicile, temporary home)*

A collapsible, portable structure of cloth or skins which can be assembled at will

Genesis 4:20. New form of domicile
Genesis 9:21. Noah in his tent
Genesis 26:17. Isaac travels with tents.
Exodus 16:16. Traveling and staying in tents
Numbers 1:50. The tabernacle
Numbers 16:26. Tents of the wicked
1 Kings 8:66. Place of habitation
Luke 9:33. Peter attempts to set up tents.
Acts 18:2–3. Tentmakers by profession
Hebrews 9:2. Remembering the former tent and covenant

▸ Tent making *(independent, self-supporting)*

Coming from the life of the apostle Paul, "tent making" refers to those who engage in mission and ministry of church while earning their own living.

Acts 18:2–3. Paul's profession as a tentmaker
Acts 20:34–35. Self-supporting
1 Corinthians 4:12. Working to the point of exhaustion
1 Corinthians 9:1–2. Paul's freedom because he works
1 Thessalonians 2:9. Working both night and day
2 Thessalonians 3:8–10. Setting an example to follow
1 Timothy 5:17–18. Paying your instructors well

▸ Terminal illness *(deadly, fatal, mortal)*

Sickness that results in a death or near-death experience

2 Kings 8:8–9. Questioning the length of one's life
Mark 5:26–29. Worsening condition
Luke 7:2. Sick to the point of death
John 11:13–15. Lazarus's terminal illness
Acts 9:37. Sickness causing death
Galatians 4:14. Paul's difficult illness
Philippians 2:26–27. Major sickness prevented

▸ Territory *(land, possession, region)*

An area of land under national or local jurisdiction

Genesis 9:27. Prayer for expanded territory
Numbers 20:21. Guarding a territory
Joshua 1:2–3. Taking a new territory
1 Chronicles 4:10. Prayer of Jabez
Psalm 111:6. Territories shifting power
Proverbs 30:24–28. Small species with territory
Zephaniah 2:5–6. Land designation
Mark 5:17. Begging Jesus to leave their territory
Acts 13:50. Cast out of a territory

▸ Terrorism *(insurgence, revolution, violence)*

The use of violence and scare tactics to advance a political cause

Judges 1:7. Cruel revenge
Song of Songs 3:8. Terrors of the night
Jeremiah 6:25. Enemies on the prowl
Jeremiah 49:29. Terror is all around.
Luke 21:12–13. Treating others unfairly on account of Christianity
Acts 17:5–6. Trying to kill innocent men
Acts 21:38. Terrorists in the desert

▸ Testimony *(attestation, declaration, evidence)*

A formal piece of evidence which seeks to demonstrate the veracity of something

Exodus 23:1. Never give false testimony.
Numbers 35:30. Testimony of several witnesses required
Psalm 19:7. The Lord's testimony is dependable.
Matthew 19:18. Recalling the commandments
Matthew 24:14. Spreading testimony to all nations
Mark 14:55. Digging for false testimony
Acts 22:17–18. Testimony rejected
2 Thessalonians 1:10. Message received
1 Timothy 6:12. Testimony of a good life

1 John 5:9. God's testimony compared with human testimony
1 John 5:11. Eternal life in the Son
Revelation 1:2. Testimony about Jesus

▶ Testing *(challenge, trial)*

Trials or ordeals which forge character-defining moments and decisions which demonstrate one's true allegiances
Genesis 22:1–14. Testing of Abraham
Exodus 17:2. Testing the Lord
Deuteronomy 13:3. Testing the heart condition
Jeremiah 6:27. Jeremiah's task for the people of God
Romans 8:28. All things work for good
1 Corinthians 10:13. Limits of God's testing
2 Corinthians 8:8. Testing love
Colossians 1:11. Enduring all things
James 1:12. Blessed for endurance
1 Peter 1:6–7. Testing of faith
Revelation 3:10. Coming time of testing

▶ Tetrarch(s) *(client-king, official, ruler)*

Used in reference to a ruler who governs over "one-fourth" of a region
Matthew 14:1. Herod and Jesus
Luke 3:1. Numerous leaders
Acts 13:1. Herod

▶ Textile arts *(cloth, designer, fabric)*

The practice of working with fabric in various capacities, but specifically in designing clothing
Exodus 28:5. Linen garments for priests
Exodus 35:35. High fashion, high skill
Deuteronomy 22:5. Strange fashion tendencies
Joshua 2:6. Flax
Isaiah 19:9. Textile workers put to shame
Ezekiel 27:12–14. Trading various items for textile merchandise
Acts 9:39. Hand-fashioned clothing
Acts 16:14. Worker in purple dye

▶ Thankfulness *(see Gratitude)*

▶ Thanksgiving *(see Gratitude)*

▶ Theocracy *(God-ruled, kingdom)*

Governed by God
Deuteronomy 17:15–20. Rules for appointing a king over Israel
Judges 8:23. The Lord will rule.
1 Samuel 8:5–9. God's people request a human king.
John 18:36. Kingdom not of this world

▶ Theology *(study of God)*

Disciplined thinking and study of God through reflection on the Word of God
Psalm 119:15. Reflecting on God's law and ways
Ephesians 3:4–6. Mystery revealed through reading of the Word
2 Timothy 3:16. Inspiration of Scripture
2 Peter 3:14–15. Some theology is difficult to understand.

▶ Theophany *(appearance, manifestation, revelation)*

A visible manifestation of God on earth
Genesis 32:22–30. Jacob wrestles with God.
Exodus 3:2–4. The burning bush
Exodus 24:16–18. Fire on the mountain
Deuteronomy 31:14–15. God's presence as Joshua takes over
Judges 5:23. Messenger of the Lord
Matthew 1:23. God with us
Matthew 17:1–3. Transfigured on the mountain
Luke 3:22. All the Trinity present
Acts 9:3–5. Theophany of Christ

▶ Thief *(criminal, robber, stealer)*

Someone who steals another person's property, typically through covert plans without the use of force
Exodus 22:2. Tough luck for thieves
Psalm 50:18. Bad class of people
Proverbs 6:30. Stealing to eat

Jeremiah 2:26. Ashamed when caught
Zechariah 5:3. Thieves forced away
Matthew 24:43. Catching a thief
John 10:1. Breaking and entering
John 10:10. Jesus' ministry contrasted with a thief
1 Thessalonians 5:2–4. Day that will come like a thief in the night
Revelation 3:3. Be alert!

▶ Thinking/Thoughtful *(intelligent, reasonable, sensible)*

Those faculties of the mind which aid in precise thinking and logical decision-making
Proverbs 12:8. Praised for intellect
Jeremiah 31:33. God's action to change his people
Ezekiel 11:5. God's knowledge of the human mind
Matthew 9:4. Followers with evil thoughts
Romans 12:2. Changing patterns of thinking
1 Corinthians 14:20. Be mature thinkers.
2 Corinthians 10:5. Arrogance
Philippians 3:15. Mature faith and mature thinking connected
Philippians 4:8–9. Focusing on honorable things
Colossians 3:2. Keeping eternal perspective
1 Peter 1:13. Ready for action

▶ Thirst *(desire, dehydration)*

A longing or need for a drink; also used metaphorically of a desire for something
Psalm 42:1–2. Soul thirsting
Amos 4:7–8. Staggering from thirst
Matthew 5:6. Thirsty for God's approval
Matthew 25:37. Opportunity for Christian service
John 4:15. Asking for living water which quenches thirst
Romans 12:20. Meeting the needs of an enemy
Revelation 7:16. No longer thirsty
Revelation 21:6. Drinking from the fountain of life

▶ Thirty *(cardinal number, number)*

Significant because it denoted the general age at which one would enter priestly ministry
Genesis 18:30. Abraham's request drops to thirty
Numbers 4:23. Beginning age for priestly ministry
Judges 12:9. Round numbers
1 Samuel 13:1. Appointed king at thirty
2 Samuel 23:13. A famous group of thirty men
1 Kings 1:8. David's thirty men
Proverbs 22:20. A grouping of wisdom sayings
Matthew 13:8. Thirty times more than needed
Matthew 27:3. Thirty pieces of silver was the price of betrayal.
Luke 3:23. Jesus' ministry began when he was around thirty years old.
John 2:6. Jars holding up to thirty gallons

▶ Thorn(s) *(barb, prickle, spike)*

A tree, bush, or vine which has sharp-pointed projections coming off its stem
Genesis 3:18. The ground is cursed.
Matthew 7:16. Identifying marks of false prophets
Mark 4:18–19. Hearing the Word but being choked out
2 Corinthians 12:7. Paul's thorn in the flesh
Galatians 3:13. Christ took the curse.
Hebrews 6:8. Worthless product of the earth

▶ Thoroughness *(complete, exhaustive, meticulous)*

The quality of detailed precision and attention to all details
Genesis 11:3. Proper preparation of materials
Exodus 21:19. Healing a wound
Joshua 8:34–35. Reading all that Moses had commanded
Nehemiah 6:1. An excellent rebuild
Psalm 51:2. Washing from guilt

Proverbs 7:2. Complete protection
Jeremiah 6:9. Picking a vineyard
Ephesians 5:15–16. Making the most of opportunities
Philippians 1:6. Seeing it through to completion

▶ Threat(s) *(remarks, ultimatums, warnings)*

A statement of intended action to induce pain, incur injury, or otherwise hostile action
Exodus 32:14. Reconsidered threat
Psalm 73:8. Threats to oppress
Proverbs 13:8. Not heeding threats
Isaiah 25:5. Threats reduced
Luke 3:14. Never threaten to get money.
Luke 23:5. Accused of stirring up a rebellion
Acts 4:29. Speaking boldly in the face of threats
Acts 9:1. Murderous threats
Ephesians 6:9. Treating slaves with respect
1 Peter 2:23. Christ made no threats.

▶ Three *(cardinal number, fullness, number)*

Most significant biblically, representing fullness or completeness
Genesis 6:10. Noah's three sons
Deuteronomy 14:28. Sharing one-tenth every third year
Deuteronomy 16:16. Entering the temple three times a year
2 Samuel 24:12–13. Three-day plague
1 Kings 18:34–35. Soaking an altar three times
Matthew 12:40. Three days and nights
Matthew 28:19. Trinity
Mark 8:31. Resurrection
2 Corinthians 13:1. Verified by two or three witnesses

▶ Threshing *(crushing, grinding, separating)*

The action of preparing grain by beating it from its husks on a threshing floor
Genesis 50:10. Mourning on the threshing floor
Leviticus 26:5. Provision through all seasons
Numbers 18:27. Slight contributions
Ruth 3:7. Sleeping on the threshing floor
Jeremiah 51:33. Symbol of judgment
Hosea 9:1–2. Immorality on the threshing floor
Habakkuk 3:12. Trampling the nations
1 Corinthians 9:9–10. Receiving a share of your work

▶ Thrift *(see Stewardship)*

▶ Thrive *(bloom, flourish, prosper)*

To grow quickly and fully
Leviticus 26:4. Growing at the right time
Joshua 1:8. Teachings which bring prosperity
Jeremiah 12:1. Why do the wicked thrive?
Ezekiel 17:9–10. The thriving vine of Israel
Zechariah 8:12. Thriving produce
3 John 1:2. Praying for spiritual well-being

▶ Thunder *(roar, rumble, storm)*

The loud cracking sound associated with lightning storms, often used to signify a thunderous sound
Exodus 19:16. Thunder on the mountain
1 Samuel 7:10. God's thundering presence
1 Samuel 12:17. Sent by God
Psalm 77:18. Sights and sounds of a storm
Psalm 104:6–7. The voice of God
John 12:28. A voice from the heavens
Revelation 6:1. The living creature's voice

▶ Tidings *(information, news, reports)*

Information or news which is communicated through a messenger
Isaiah 52:7. God rules as king
Isaiah 61:1. Good tidings to the humble
Jeremiah 23:16–18. Listen only to news from the Lord.
Ezekiel 33:21. Bad tidings
Nahum 1:15. Messenger proclaims good news.
Luke 2:10–12. Birth announcement

Acts 11:22. News from Antioch
Romans 10:15. Bringing glad tidings
1 Thessalonians 3:6. Messenger brings news.

▶ Time *(age, chronology, eternity)*

The point or period during which something occurred

Genesis 1:3–5. God created time.
Genesis 8:11. Time of evening
Psalm 9:9. Troubled times
Psalm 31:15. Time is in God's hands.
Jeremiah 31:1. A time of covenant faithfulness
Mark 1:15. Appointed time to repent
Romans 3:26. God's approval at the present time
Romans 16:25. Revealing what has been kept silent for ages
Galatians 4:4. Fullness of time

▶ Timidity *(fearful, frightened, nervous)*

Lacking in courage or confidence when interacting with others

Numbers 17:12–13. Doubting vitality
1 Samuel 3:15–16. Timid response
Job 29:10. Hushed voices
Psalm 124:1–5. Timidity in battle
John 12:42–43. Concerned for people's opinion
Acts 5:13–14. Timid to join the movement
1 Corinthians 2:3. Weak presence
2 Corinthians 10:1. Timid in the body, bold when away
1 Thessalonians 5:14. Cheer up the discouraged.
2 Timothy 1:7. Not from God

▶ Timing *(discernment, planning)*

Discernment over when an action or event should occur

Psalm 37:23–24. Divine timing
Psalm 119:126. Time for action
Ecclesiastes 3:1–8. A time for all things
Ecclesiastes 3:11. God's perfect timing
Isaiah 49:8. Timing of God's answer
Haggai 1:2–5. Rebuilding the temple of the Lord
Luke 22:52–53. Bad timing
Romans 5:6. Timing of God's salvation

▶ Tireless *(energetic, enthusiastic, vigorous)*

Demonstrating great energy and enthusiasm in accomplishing tasks

Judges 8:4. Persistently pursuing
Judges 15:16. Tireless work
Ecclesiastes 9:10. Working with great might
Isaiah 40:29–31. Strength from the Lord to run and not grow weary
Isaiah 65:22. Seeing the benefits of hard work
John 5:17. Working without rest
Romans 12:11. Serve the Lord with energy.
Colossians 4:5. Making every opportunity count
2 Thessalonians 3:6–7. Disciplined life

▶ Tithing *(tenth, stewardship)*

Practice of giving one-tenth of one's livelihood to God

Genesis 14:18–20. Abram gives Melchizedek one tenth of his things.
Leviticus 27:30. Firstfruits of produce belong to the Lord.
Numbers 18:28. Providing for Aaron
Deuteronomy 14:22. Saving one-tenth of crops
Proverbs 3:9–10. Giving the best to the Lord
Ezekiel 44:30. Contributions for the priesthood
Malachi 3:10. Blessing for obedience
Luke 11:42. Tithing alone does not please God.
2 Corinthians 9:6. Planting the seeds of God's harvest
Hebrews 7:5. Priests collect from their own people.

▶ Today *(see **Present**)*

▶ Togetherness *(harmony, fellowship, unity)*

The state of being harmonious with others in fellowship and unity of purpose and goals

T

Exodus 23:2. Avoiding mob mentality
Deuteronomy 18:9. Sticking together as a nation and avoiding pagan practices
Nehemiah 4:6. Teamwork
Psalm 34:3. Praising God's name together
Proverbs 27:17. Sharpening others intellectually
Matthew 18:20. Unity in God's name
Romans 8:28. Working out for good and glory
1 Corinthians 1:10. Be unified.
2 Corinthians 6:14. Togetherness forbidden
Colossians 2:2. Unified in love

▶ Token(s) *(emblem, sign, symbol)*

A sign or symbol which serves to signify a more abstract idea or concept, generally calling it to memory in a tangible way

Genesis 9:12–13. Rainbow
Genesis 17:11. Circumcision as a sign of the covenant
Exodus 12:13. Emblem of protection on the doorposts
Exodus 16:32. Storing manna as a remembrance
Ruth 4:7–8. Publicly approved contract

▶ Tolerance *(acceptance, patience)*

An acceptance or willingness toward the opinions and actions of others

Exodus 23:9. Tolerating foreigners
Numbers 11:4–6. Intolerance for food
Psalm 123:3–4. Dealing with ridicule
Nahum 1:3. Lord's patience
Matthew 9:10. Eating with the lost
Matthew 17:17. Putting up with a twisted generation
Mark 9:38–39. Tolerating competition
Romans 14:1–8. Differences of opinion
Romans 15:1. Patience with the weaker Christians
Philippians 1:17–18. Tolerating strange competition
2 Timothy 2:10. Tolerating all things

▶ Tomb *(burial, grave)*

A large, underground chamber used for burying the dead

Genesis 23:6. Sharing the best tomb with a mighty leader
Deuteronomy 34:6. Unknown grave
2 Kings 21:26. Tomb made for a king
2 Chronicles 16:14. Ornate tomb decorum
Isaiah 22:16. Digging one's own grave
Matthew 28:1–10. Strange happenings at the tomb of Jesus
Mark 16:1–7. The empty tomb of Jesus

▶ Tomorrow *(day, time)*

A time in the immediate future; the day following today

Exodus 8:10. Day of the Lord's judgment
Numbers 11:18. Prepared for tomorrow
1 Kings 20:6. Warning about tomorrow's judgment
Proverbs 27:1. No bragging about tomorrow
Isaiah 22:13. Enjoying today, dying tomorrow
Matthew 6:34. Forgetting about tomorrow's worries
James 4:13–14. Tomorrow's business

▶ Tongue(s) *(glossa, language, speaking in tongues)*

Supernatural manifestation of speech in a language not known to the speaker

Mark 16:17. Miraculous sign accompanying belief
Acts 2:4–6. Spirit-given ability to speak
Acts 10:46. Non-Jews speaking in various languages
Romans 8:26–27. Groaning expressed through the Spirit
1 Corinthians 12:10. Gift of speaking in tongues
1 Corinthians 14:1. Pursuing spiritual gifts
1 Corinthians 14:2–4. Foreign languages versus spiritual languages
1 Corinthians 14:5. Speaking and interpreting for the church

▶ Tool time *(gadget, instrument, machine)*

A device which is easily manipulated by the hands and increases the function of productivity of one's work

Numbers 4:14. Shovels
1 Samuel 13:20. Plowshare
2 Samuel 12:31. Saws, hoes, and axes
2 Chronicles 24:12. Metal workers
Isaiah 44:13. Measuring tools
Jeremiah 10:4. Hammer and nails
Jeremiah 18:3. Potter's wheel

▶ Torment *(agony, judgment, torture)*

Physical and mental suffering inflicted on someone
Psalm 60:3. Tormented existence
Psalm 137:9. Killing children
Lamentations 5:11–13. Tortuous work
Ezekiel 11:8. Instruments of torture
Amos 1:3. A crushed people
Matthew 18:34. Handed over to torture until payment could be made
Luke 16:22–23. Torment in hell
1 John 4:18. Fearful of punishment
Revelation 9:5. Pain of torture without the release of death
Revelation 20:10. Tortured with the devil

▶ Torture *(abuse, persecute, torment)*

Practice of inflicting significant degrees of pain on others in the hopes of ascertaining information or carrying out a punishment
Judges 16:5. Seeking to torture Samson
Job 15:20. Wicked person tortured
Jeremiah 38:19. Torturous capturers
Matthew 8:29. Demons cry out.
Matthew 18:34. Handed over to be tortured
Luke 16:23. Constant torture
Hebrews 11:35. Believers brutally tortured
2 Peter 2:8. Days like torture

▶ Totalitarianism *(autocratic, dictatorial, tyrannical)*

Relating to a governing body that is dictatorial or tyrannical in nature
1 Kings 12:9–11. Adding to the people's burden from the king
Ecclesiastes 4:1. Oppressors hold all the power.
Isaiah 26:13. Anti-totalitarian
Romans 13:1. Governments established by God
1 Peter 2:13–14. Submitting to governing officials
Revelation 13:5. Acting and speaking for a short time

▶ Touch *(brush up against, feel, press)*

Come in close contact with; feel
Genesis 3:3. Forbidden fruit
Leviticus 5:2. Touching an unclean body
Numbers 19:13. Touching a dead body
Matthew 8:3. Healing a leper
Matthew 20:34. Restoring sight
Mark 10:13–16. Jesus holds little children.
Luke 22:51. Healing a flesh wound
1 Corinthians 7:1. Good not to touch a woman
Colossians 2:21. Matters of opinion

▶ Tower(s) *(fortification, steeple, wall)*

A tall narrow building typically used in fortifying a city
Genesis 11:4. Tower of Babel
2 Chronicles 26:9–10. Building multiple towers
2 Chronicles 27:4. Fortification
Nehemiah 3:11. Repairing towers in Jerusalem
Psalm 18:2. God is a stronghold.
Proverbs 18:10. The name of the Lord
Song of Songs 4:4. Body like a tower
Ezekiel 26:4. Destruction of walls and towers
Habakkuk 2:1. Standing guard

▶ Town(s) *(city, township, urban)*

An urban area with defined boundaries and socio-political structure
Judges 10:4. Owner of thirty small towns
Ruth 1:19. Excitement in a small town
Job 29:7. Sitting in the town square
Ecclesiastes 9:14. Small town attacked and overpowered

T

Isaiah 1:21. Faithful town wanders

Matthew 9:35. Traveling through towns and villages

Acts 21:22. News travels fast in small town.

▶ Trade *(business, commerce, transaction)*

The buying and selling of goods and services

Genesis 24:10. Traveling to the city to trade

1 Kings 9:26–27. Sea merchants

1 Kings 10:14–15. High profits

1 Kings 10:28–29. Purchasing horses from Egypt

Proverbs 20:14. Bragging about a bargain

Ezekiel 27:12–25. Extensive trading practices

Matthew 25:14. Entrusting money to wise investors

Acts 16:14. Lydia's trade

Acts 18:3. Tent making

▶ Tradition(s) *(customs, observances, practices)*

The transmission of certain customs and practices between generations

2 Chronicles 35:25. Tradition in the making

Esther 9:26–27. Purim established

Matthew 15:2. Breaking with ancestral tradition

Mark 7:8. Abandoning the commandments to follow human traditions

Mark 7:13. Traditions which destroy the authority of God's Word

Acts 24:6. Violating tradition

1 Corinthians 11:2. Following Christian traditions

Galatians 1:14. Following the traditions of Jewish ancestry

Colossians 2:8. Following human traditions

2 Thessalonians 2:15. Hold firm to new traditions.

2 Thessalonians 3:6. Do not associate with those who break tradition.

▶ Training *(guidance, instruction, teaching)*

The process of teaching someone a predetermined idea or skill

Genesis 14:14. A small army of trained men

Numbers 27:18–23. Preparing Joshua for leadership

Judges 3:1–2. Training in the art of war

1 Chronicles 5:18. Skilled fighters ready for war

Proverbs 22:6. Training a child

Proverbs 22:15. Role of punishment in training

Matthew 11:1. Instructions for the twelve disciples

2 Timothy 3:16. Scripture's usefulness in training in righteousness

Titus 1:6. Training up a solid family

Titus 2:12. Avoiding ungodly living

▶ Traitor *(betrayer, backstabber, deserter)*

Someone who willfully betrays a friend or cause

2 Kings 17:4. Traitor tossed in prison

Esther 2:23. Traitors impaled

Psalm 59:5. No pity on traitors

Psalm 119:158. Denying God's promise

Isaiah 21:2. Preparing for war

Isaiah 24:16. Increasing treachery and betrayal

Isaiah 33:1. Coming judgment on traitors

Luke 22:3–6. Judas the traitor

2 Timothy 3:4. Pursuing pleasure rather than God

▶ Traits *(see Attributes of God; Character)*

▶ Tranquility *(see Peace)*

▶ Transfiguration *(manifestation, revelation)*

The revelation or manifestation of Christ's glory on the mountainside

Matthew 17:1–8. Theophany up on a mountain

Mark 9:2–8. Jesus' appearance changes.

Luke 9:28–36. Peter tries to set up three tents.

▶ **Transformation** *(alteration, change, conversion)*

A thorough and dynamic change in the content and quality of one's being

John 3:1–8. Born from above

Acts 1:8. Powerful witness for God's kingdom

Acts 19:18–19. Sudden changes of lifestyle

Romans 12:2. Changing patterns of thinking

2 Corinthians 3:18. Consistently conformed into the image of Christ

2 Corinthians 5:17. New creation

Ephesians 5:8–10. Walking in light instead of darkness

Colossians 2:20–23. Transferred powers for discerning life in Christ

1 Timothy 1:12–14. Transformed manner of living

Hebrews 4:12. Power of God's word

1 Peter 1:14. Transformed lives of obedience

1 John 2:29. New birth

▶ **Transgression** *(see Sin[s])*

▶ **Transient** *(brief, impermanent, temporary)*

Something which is short-lived or impermanent

Genesis 24:35. Earthly blessings

Numbers 14:35. Meeting an end shortly

Job 5:17. Temporary scolding

Psalm 49:10. Temporality of life

Luke 6:24. Earthly comforts

John 17:13. Short time in this world

Philippians 4:6–7. Trusting God

1 Peter 3:14. Temporary suffering

▶ **Transition** *(conversion, progression, transformation)*

The period of time where change and progression happens

Genesis 12:1–9. God drastically alters Abram's life.

Joshua 1:1–2. Leadership transition

Proverbs 27:24. Period of transition

1 John 2:8. Fading darkness, brightness rising

▶ **Translation** *(converting, rendering)*

The process of translating the words of one communicative act into another language in the hopes of conveying faithful meaning

Isaiah 36:11. Speaking in an understandable language

Acts 2:6. No need for translation

▶ **Transmutation** *(alteration, change)*

The process of taking on another form

Exodus 3:2–4. Theophany of God in a bush

John 3:3–6. You must be born again.

1 Corinthians 15:49. Man from earth, man from heaven

2 Corinthians 5:17. New creation

Galatians 6:15. What matters is being new creation

▶ **Transportation** *(movement, transit, travel)*

The action of transit or travel between locations

Genesis 37:25. Ishmaelite caravan

Judges 12:14. Family entourage

2 Kings 2:11–12. Fiery chariots

Psalm 68:17. God's countless chariots

Song of Songs 3:9. Royal carriage

Isaiah 19:23. International coastal highway

Isaiah 49:11. Mountains turned into roads

Jeremiah 51:13. Port cities

▶ **Trap(s)** *(deception, pitfall, snare)*

A device which catches and retains someone or something

Genesis 14:10. Trapped in the pits

Exodus 23:33. Trapped into serving false gods

Deuteronomy 7:25. Idol traps

Psalm 9:15. Trapped and taking others down
Psalm 25:15. Rescued from the traps
Psalm 66:11. Trapped in a net
Matthew 22:15. Attempting to trap Jesus
2 Corinthians 11:29. Apostolic empathy
Galatians 6:1. Helping someone get unstuck
1 Timothy 3:7. Avoiding the devil's traps
1 Timothy 6:9. Harmful desires
James 1:14. Tempted and lured by desires

▶ Travel *(explore, journey, tour)*

The action of journey between two locations; from place to place
Numbers 9:23. Traveling at the Lord's will
Numbers 10:35. Praying for protection in travel
1 Samuel 17:20. Departing early
2 Chronicles 15:5. Travel turmoil
Isaiah 59:8. Injustice on the highways
Matthew 2:12. Changing travel plans
John 4:6. Weary from the journey
John 7:1. Avoiding dangerous paths
Romans 15:24. En route to Spain
2 Corinthians 1:15–16. Extensive travel plans

▶ Treachery *(betrayal, disloyalty, unfaithfulness)*

A characteristic or action which is marked by unfaithfulness, deception, and lies
Judges 16:18–19. Treacherous woman
2 Samuel 3:27. Unsuspecting murder
2 Samuel 4:5–7. Senseless murder
Nehemiah 6:2–4. Avoiding a harmful plot
Esther 3:8. Suggesting genocide
Jeremiah 9:4–5. Committing numerous forms of treachery
Matthew 2:7–8. Plotting treachery
Luke 17:1. Treachery of treacheries
Luke 20:20–26. Plotting to hand Jesus over

▶ Treason *(rebellion, sedition, treachery)*

Crime of betraying one's local ruling authority through subverting the government structure and/or attempting to kill government leaders
1 Samuel 24:11. No harm meant
2 Kings 11:14. Athaliah shouts "treason."
Ezra 4:19. City with many guilty of treason

▶ Treasure *(riches, valuables, wealth)*

An object or objects that are very valuable
1 Kings 14:26. Temple treasures plundered
Proverbs 8:17–18. Riches, honor, wealth, and righteousness
Proverbs 15:16. Fear of the Lord preferred
Matthew 2:11. Presenting gifts to Jesus
Matthew 6:19. Stop accumulating earthly wealth.
Mark 10:21. Selling possessions and storing up things in heaven
Luke 12:34. Heart and treasure aligned
2 Corinthians 4:7. Treasures in jars of clay
Colossians 2:3. Hidden treasures in Christ
Hebrews 11:26. Treasures of Egypt compared with Christ's treasures

▶ Treasurer *(financial planner)*

An appointed official who oversees the expenditure of money of local authorities
Ezra 1:8. Working underneath the king
Romans 16:23. Erastus, the city treasurer

▶ Treaty(ies) *(agreement, contract, settlement)*

A formal agreement between two nations, typically stipulating terms of peace, trade, or travel
Genesis 21:32. Treaty at Beersheba
Exodus 23:32. Never make treaties with false gods.
Deuteronomy 7:2. Treaties forbidden
Joshua 9:6. Foreigners demand a treaty with Israel.
Judges 2:2. Treaties forbidden due to syncretism
Ezekiel 17:13–14. Forced treaty
Hosea 12:1. Treaties with foreign nations
Amos 1:9. Not honoring terms of treaty

▶ Tree(s) *(marker, material, plant)*

A woody perennial plant growing various sizes and extremely useful in the production of buildings, weapons, and boats

Genesis 1:11–12. Vegetation and sustenance
Genesis 13:18. Boundary marker
1 Kings 5:6–7. Cutting down Cedars of Lebanon
Psalm 92:12–13. People who are planted and flourish
Isaiah 44:12–17. Making idols from cedar wood
Matthew 3:10. Removing unfruitful trees
Matthew 21:8. Ground covered with palm branches
Luke 13:19. Large tree from a tiny seed
1 Peter 2:24. Jesus hung upon a "tree."
Revelation 18:12. Construction material

▶ Tree of Life *(life, rejuvenating, revitalizing)*

One of the two special trees which God placed in the Garden of Eden with Adam and Eve; a source of perpetual life and youth
Genesis 2:9. Beautiful trees in the middle of the garden
Genesis 3:22. Cut off from the tree of life
Proverbs 3:18. Role of wisdom in life
Revelation 2:7. Eating from the tree of life
Revelation 22:2. River feeding the tree of life in the New Jerusalem

▶ Tree of the Knowledge of Good and Evil

One of two trees in the garden of Eden; fruit of this tree off-limits to Adam and Eve
Genesis 2:9. Beautiful trees in the middle of the garden
Genesis 2:17. Forbidden to eat from this tree
Genesis 3:6–7. Eating of the tree and immediate effects
Genesis 3:22. Cut off from the tree of life

▶ Trespass *(see Sin[s])*

▶ Trial(s) *(afflictions, persecution, suffering)*

A situation which tests one's patience, strength, and resoluteness
Psalm 46:1. God is our refuge.
Habakkuk 3:17–18. Happiness in God despite circumstances
Luke 17:25. Rejection by kinsmen
Romans 5:3. Boasting in sufferings which produce endurance
Romans 8:28. All things work for good.
Romans 12:12. Patience in affliction
2 Corinthians 1:4. Comforting those who suffer
2 Corinthians 12:9. Power made perfect in weakness
James 1:2. Joy in the midst of trials
1 Peter 1:6–7. Testing of faith
1 Peter 3:17. Suffering for doing good

▶ Tribe(s) *(nation, people)*

A group of people having a common character, occupation, or interest; the nation of Israel was comprised of twelve tribes
Genesis 49:1–28. Last testimony of Israel
Joshua 7:16–18. Joshua calls upon the tribes.
Matthew 19:28. Believers will judge the twelve tribes.
Philippians 3:5. Paul's heritage from the tribe of Benjamin
Hebrews 7:14. Jesus from the tribe of Judah
James 1:1. God's dispersed people
Revelation 7:4. Sealed from every tribe

▶ Tribulation *(see Persecution)*

▶ Tribute *(money, payment, tax)*

A tax imposed by a governing authority on subjects of the land
Exodus 30:12. Paying the Lord for ransom
Numbers 31:28–29. Tribute given to God
Matthew 17:24–27. Jesus' contribution questioned
Matthew 22:17. What is the correct policy?
Romans 13:6. Instructed to pay tribute to the government

▶ Trinity *(Godhead)*

Word used to describe the truth that the one true God describes Himself in terms of three all-powerful, all-knowing, and all-present persons—Father, Son, Holy Spirit

T

Matthew 28:19. Father, Son, Spirit
John 1:14. The incarnation
John 10:30. Unity of Father and Son
John 14:16–17. Another helper from God
1 Corinthians 8:6. One God, one Lord
1 Corinthians 12:4–6. Spirit, Lord, and God correlated
2 Corinthians 13:14. Trinitarian thanksgiving
Ephesians 1:3, 7, 14. Paul's Trinitarian prayer

▶ Triumphal entry *(riding into Jerusalem)*

Jesus' entry into Jerusalem at the beginning of the week preceding his death
Zechariah 9:9. Jerusalem's king will come riding on a donkey.
Mark 11:4–5. Acquiring the donkey
Mark 11:9–10. Praises sung by the crowd
Mark 11:11. Approaching the temple courtyard

▶ Trouble *(difficulty, problems)*

A cause of worry, inconvenience, or mild stress
Judges 10:14. Crying out to false gods in trouble
1 Samuel 28:15. Saul's serious trouble
Psalm 10:1. Where is God in times of trouble?
Psalm 34:19. Rescued from troubles
Psalm 138:7. Walking into trouble
Proverbs 16:27. Plotting trouble
Acts 8:3–4. Saul troubles the church.
1 Corinthians 10:25. Untroubled conscience
Galatians 6:17. No more troubling the faithful apostle
James 5:13. Pray when you are troubled.

▶ Trouble causers *(enemies, false prophets, false teachers)*

Those who infiltrate the church with false doctrines and stir up the people of God
Colossians 2:4. Countering false arguments
2 Timothy 4:14–15. Naming opponents
Titus 3:10. Have nothing to do with false teachers.
1 Peter 4:15. Suffering should be legitimate.
2 Peter 2:1–2. False teachers and destructive teachings
1 John 4:3. Spirit of antichrist

▶ Troubled women *(problematic women)*

Bible-time women with either too much time on their hands or who try to solve their problems on their own
Genesis 16. Sarai
Genesis 30. Rachel and Leah
Genesis 39:6–20. Potiphar's wife
2 Samuel 11:2–5. Bathsheba

▶ Trumpet(s) *(horn, instrument)*

A curved instrument made from a ram's horn
Exodus 19:16–17. Loud blast from the ram's horn
Leviticus 25:9. Indicating Jubilee year
Joshua 6:16. Signaling attack
Judges 3:27. Summoning Israel to battle
Nehemiah 4:18. Enemy warning system
Psalm 81:3. Marking the new moon festival
Joel 2:1. Announcing the day of the Lord
Matthew 24:31. Returning at the trumpet call
Hebrews 12:18–19. Trumpet blast heard from Sinai
Revelation 1:10. Voice like a trumpet

▶ Trust *(believe, faithful, trustworthy)*

To rely or depend upon, with the nuance of feeling confident and safe in one's trust
2 Kings 18:5. Hezekiah's trust in Yahweh
Psalm 28:7. Receiving help from the Lord
Psalm 56:3. Fearful, yet trusting
Proverbs 3:5–6. Trusting in the Lord's direction
Isaiah 12:2. Confidence in God
Isaiah 26:3. God protects those who trust Him.
Jeremiah 17:7. Blessed is the one who trusts in the Lord.
Romans 8:28. Trusting in God's good plan

2 Corinthians 1:9. Suffering to learn trust in God

Philippians 3:3–4. Folly of trusting in physical qualifications

2 Timothy 1:12. Trusting through suffering

▶ Trustworthy *(dependable, faithful, reliable)*

The quality of faithfulness or dependability; able to be trusted and relied upon

2 Samuel 7:28. God's trustworthy words

1 Chronicles 9:22. Appointed because of trustworthiness

Nehemiah 9:13. Fearing God

Psalm 33:4. The Lord's character

Psalm 111:7. God's law is trustworthy.

Proverbs 11:13. Able to keep a secret

Proverbs 14:5. Telling the truth

Daniel 6:4. Trustworthy character

1 Corinthians 4:2. Required of management

1 Timothy 3:11. Wives of church leaders

Titus 1:9. Teaching the trustworthy message

Revelation 1:4–5. Jesus Christ, the trustworthy one

▶ Truthful *(faithfulness, fidelity, trustworthiness)*

The quality of being accurate and truthful

Genesis 42:16. Determining the character of Joseph's brothers

Psalm 31:5. God of truth

Psalm 57:3. Mercy and truth sent forth

John 1:14. Full of grace and truth

John 3:21. Living in the light

John 4:24. Worship God in spirit and truth

John 5:31–32. True testimony about Jesus from the Father

John 8:32. Truth will set you free.

John 17:17. Words of truth

Galatians 2:5. Broadcasting the message of truth

Ephesians 4:24–25. Actions that reflect commitment to the truth

1 John 1:6. Telling the truth about one's relationship with God

1 John 4:6. Spirit of truth listens to God's messengers.

▶ Tunic(s) *(clothing, garment, wardrobe)*

A loose-fitting garment which hangs down to one's knees

1 Samuel 17:38. Battle tunic

Job 30:18. Grabbed by the garment

Daniel 3:21–22. Clothing and men untouched in blazing fire

Matthew 5:40. Generosity in settling legal disputes

Matthew 10:10. Packing light for a trip

Luke 6:29. Sharing all things

John 19:23. Seamless tunic

Acts 9:39. Hand-fashioned clothing

▶ Turkey *(Asia Minor, province, region)*

Used in reference to the modern country Turkey; much of Paul's second missionary journey took place in what is now modern-day Turkey

Acts 16:6. Paul travels through Asia Minor (modern Turkey).

▶ Turning one's cheek *(passive, patience, peacemaker)*

Ignoring an insult

Lamentations 3:30. Taking a fill of insults

Matthew 5:39. Presenting both cheeks

Luke 6:29. Offering both cheeks for striking

▶ Twelve *(dozen, number, wholeness)*

Number that signifies completeness

Genesis 35:22. Jacob's twelve sons

Genesis 49:28. Twelve tribes of Israel

Exodus 24:3–4. Twelve stone pillars representing the twelve tribes

Numbers 1:44. Adding up total figures

1 Kings 11:30. Garment torn into twelve to represent the tribes

Ezekiel 47:13. Vision of land reapportioned

Matthew 10:1. Twelve disciples

Acts 6:2. Twelve apostles designated ministry duties

James 1:1. Twelve tribes still distinct

Revelation 7:5–8. Twelve thousand sealed from each tribe

T

▶ Twins *(double, duplicate)*

The circumstance when two children (or animals) are born at the same birth

Genesis 25:21–26. Jacob and Esau born

Genesis 38:27–30. Strange birth phenomenon

Song of Songs 4:5. Admiring a lover's beauty

Hosea 12:3. Recalling the birth of the twins

John 20:24. Thomas the twin

▶ Tyrant(s) *(dictator, oppressor)*

A cruel and oppressive ruler who exercises control in unreasonable and destructive ways

Exodus 1:14. Driven by tyrants

Job 6:23. Ransomed from a tyrant

Job 27:13. Inheritance of tyrants

Psalm 37:35. Acting wicked

Ecclesiastes 4:1. Sad status of oppression in the world

Isaiah 13:11. Coming end of arrogance

Isaiah 14:4. Tyrant's attacks have ended.

Isaiah 29:20. Wrongdoers will meet their end.

Isaiah 49:25. The Lord will fight your enemies.

Jeremiah 15:21. Rescuing from wickedness

▶ UFOs *(mysterious object)*

Technically no UFOs (unidentified flying objects) are mentioned in the Bible. Below are listed a few common "proof texts" generally construed to be about UFOs.

2 Kings 2:11. Elijah carried up to heaven in a fiery chariot

Jeremiah 10:2. Omens in the sky

Ezekiel 1:15–21. Ezekiel's vision of a chariot wheel

Revelation 9:13–16. Bringing about destruction upon humanity

▶ Ultimatum(s) *(demands, requests, threats)*

A final request or demand which, if denied, will result in the swift action of retaliation

Exodus 8:21. Making ultimatums against Egypt

Deuteronomy 20:10. Offering peace before an attack

Joshua 24:15. Choose this day

1 Kings 20:39. Threat of loss

2 Chronicles 35:21. Stop now, or else

Psalm 13:3. Need to be restored

Jeremiah 38:21–22. Refusing to surrender

▶ Unanimity *(agreed, harmonious, united)*

Two or more people who have come to an understanding or agreement

Job 22:21. Harmonious with God

Psalm 133:1. Living in harmony with family

Daniel 2:9. Agreeing on a phony story

Matthew 28:12. Leadership agrees on a devious plan

John 17:21. Unity like God's unity

Acts 4:32. Believers living in agreement

Acts 15:28. Consensus between God and man

Romans 12:16. At peace with one's surroundings

Romans 15:5. Granted by God

Galatians 2:9. Agreement over apostolic division of labor

Ephesians 4:3. Maintaining unity through the Spirit

Philippians 2:2. Caused by love

1 Timothy 1:11. Unanimity between the Law and the gospel

1 Peter 3:8. Rules for life in community

1 John 5:8. Three witnesses agree.

▶ Unashamed *(indifference, honor, pride)*

Feeling or acting without guilt or embarrassment

Genesis 2:25. Naked and unashamed

Job 11:3. Talking without shame

Psalm 22:5. Trust without shame

Psalm 34:5. Faces not covered with shame

Psalm 119:6. No shame in studying the commandments

Isaiah 29:22. No more shame in Jacob

Isaiah 54:4. No cause for fear

Luke 9:26. Need to be unashamed of the Son of Man

Romans 1:16. Not ashamed of the gospel

Romans 9:33. Believers will not be put to shame.

2 Corinthians 7:14. No shame in bragging about others

Philippians 1:20. Desiring to be without shame

2 Timothy 1:8. Unashamed of Christ

1 Peter 4:16. Praising God on account of suffering for his name

▶ Unaware *(ignorant, unknowing, unmindful)*

Without knowledge or foresight of a present or future situation

Job 13:23. Asking for an awareness of one's sins

Ecclesiastes 5:1. Fools' unawareness

Ezekiel 45:20. Making peace over sins of unawareness

Hosea 4:6. Destroyed because of ignorance

Matthew 24:39. Ignorance of impending judgment

Luke 2:43. Parents unaware of leaving Jesus behind
Acts 10:4. God is not unaware.
1 Corinthians 4:4. Apostle is not unaware.
2 Corinthians 1:8. Awareness of ministry and suffering
2 Corinthians 2:11. Not unaware about Satan's plans
1 Thessalonians 4:13. No awareness about death
Hebrews 13:2. Unaware of hospitality to angels

▶ Unbelief *(disbelief, doubt, rejection)*

Refusing to accept what is true; in the New Testament, the word for unbelief is literally a negated form of the word "faith."

Genesis 17:17. Doubting God's promise
Exodus 4:1. Moses questions the Lord.
Exodus 5:2. Pharaoh's defiance
Judges 2:10. Unbelieving generation
2 Chronicles 15:3. Years of rebellion
2 Chronicles 15:13. Unbelief quashed
Matthew 9:23–24. Doubting Jesus' words
Matthew 13:58. Miracles put on hold
John 12:37–40. Unbelief in spite of miracles
Romans 3:3. Acting out of unbelief
Romans 4:20. Faith without doubt
Romans 11:20. Israel's unbelief
Romans 11:23. Turning from unbelief
1 Timothy 1:13. Acting in ignorance
Hebrews 3:12. Careful not to develop unbelieving heart

▶ Unbeliever(s) *(nonbeliever, unfaithful)*

Someone who does not believe that Christ Jesus is Lord

Matthew 17:17. Unbelieving generation
Luke 12:46. Unfaithful people
John 20:27. Thomas called to stop doubting
Acts 26:8. Many who refuse to believe the resurrection
1 Corinthians 6:6. Bad conduct in front of unbelievers
1 Corinthians 7:12–15. Instructions for uneven marriages
1 Corinthians 10:27. Respecting requests and customs of unbelievers
1 Corinthians 14:22–24. Place of spiritual gifts
2 Corinthians 4:4. Minds blinded to Christ
2 Corinthians 6:14–15. Believers are not to be yoked with unbelievers.
1 Timothy 5:8. Conduct worse than an unbeliever
Titus 1:15. Corrupt in mind and conscience
1 Peter 2:12. Influencing unbelievers by gracious living
1 Peter 4:3–4. Leaving unbelieving ways behind

▶ Unceasing *(continuous, endless, incessant)*

An action or actions which are without end

Nehemiah 9:19. God's compassion
Psalm 119:20. Desiring God's laws
Isaiah 14:6. Incessant attacks
Jeremiah 15:18. Unending pain
Daniel 7:9. The Ancient One
Nahum 3:19. No relief from endless evil
Romans 9:2. Endless heartache over Israel's rejection of Jesus
1 Corinthians 13:8. Love never ends.
Ephesians 1:16. Consistent thanksgiving
Colossians 1:9. Constantly praying
Colossians 2:18. Incessant speaking
1 Timothy 1:3–4. Idle occupations
Revelation 4:8. Unceasing praise

▶ Uncertainty *(debatable, incalculable, unknown)*

Doubting or questioning a present or future course of action

Genesis 15:1–3. Abraham's uncertainty of God's promise
Exodus 5:22–23. Uncertain outcome
Judges 6:12–13. Uncertain times
Proverbs 3:5–6. Trusting in God in times of uncertainty
John 8:45–47. Basis of uncertainty

John 13:22. Uncertain teaching

Acts 17:23. Uncertain which god is being worshiped

1 Corinthians 9:26. Living a life in faith

1 Corinthians 14:8. An uncertain call to battle

1 Timothy 6:17. Confidence in worldly things

Hebrews 11:1–3. Assured through faith

Jude 22–23. Showing mercy toward doubters that they might be saved

▶ Unchangeable *(established, fixed, immutable)*

In reference to God's character, the immutable nature of God's being, purposes, and promises

Numbers 23:19. God does not waver like humanity.

1 Samuel 15:29. The resolute mind of God

Psalm 33:11. Plans which endure through the generations

Psalm 102:25–27. God remains the same.

Isaiah 46:9–11. God's plans stand.

Malachi 3:6. The Lord does not change.

Ephesians 1:4. Election prior to the creation of the world

Hebrews 13:8. The unchangeable Christ

James 1:17. The Father's constancy

1 Peter 1:20. Preexistent lamb

▶ Unclean *(ceremonially unclean, defiled, impure)*

Actions or people who are not in keeping with God's rules and standards for holiness and purity in certain physical and moral ways

Leviticus 10:10. Priests' duty of teaching what is unclean

Leviticus 18:24–25. Land made unclean through people

Leviticus 20:3. Exclusion from the community

Numbers 35:33. Prohibition against murder

2 Chronicles 23:19. Nothing unclean allowed in the temple

2 Chronicles 36:14. Desecrated temple

Psalm 106:38. Murder and idolatry

Isaiah 52:11. Run away from impurity.

Ezekiel 22:26. Priests failing to discern unclean from clean

Matthew 10:1. Unclean spirits

Matthew 23:27. Unclean on the inside

Acts 10:14. Peter's abstinence from all things unclean

Acts 10:28. All are declared clean.

2 Corinthians 6:17. Unbelief and unclean

2 Corinthians 12:21. Sexual sin

▶ Unction *(anointing, baptism)*

The anointing of God's people in Christ for service among the body of Christ

1 John 2:20. Gift of knowledge

1 John 2:27. Christ's anointing teaches all things.

▶ Undeniable *(beyond doubt, indisputable, unquestionable)*

Something that is beyond doubt or dispute

Matthew 28:1–7. The tomb is empty.

Mark 14:30–31. Peter's denial

John 20:26–28. Thomas's undeniable proof

Acts 4:16. Undeniable miracle

Acts 19:36. Reality that cannot be denied

Hebrews 7:7. Important bless the unimportant

1 John 1:1–2. Heard, seen, revealed

▶ Underestimation *(diminish, understate, undervalue)*

Undervaluing or diminishing someone or something, judging them to be less capable or valuable than they actually are

Numbers 13:17–33. Underestimation of strength

1 Samuel 17:42–43. David underestimated

Proverbs 30:24–28. Small, yet wise

Matthew 6:19–21. Valuing earth above heaven

Matthew 13:57. Jesus undervalued in his hometown

John 1:46. Something good from Nazareth

Romans 4:20. God's promises not underestimated

1 Corinthians 6:20. Valuing the body

Philippians 4:13. All things possible through Christ

1 Peter 1:18–19. Living in proportion to God's sacrifice

▶ Underprivileged *(see Poor, the; Poverty)*

▶ Under scrutiny *(examination, inspection, probing)*

The passive action of being under examination or inspection

Leviticus 13:5. Priest's examination of unclean persons

Psalm 33:13. God sees all things.

Proverbs 5:21. Ways of humanity seen by God

Matthew 12:10. Scrutinizing Jesus

Matthew 16:1. Testing Jesus

Luke 6:7. Keeping a close eye on Jesus

Luke 20:20. Spies sent to catch Jesus

2 Corinthians 13:5. Self-examination

Galatians 2:4. Spying out Christian freedom

▶ Understanding *(compassion, intellect, mind)*

Faculties of reason and logic related to discerning information in order to make a sound judgment

1 Kings 3:11–12. Asking for understanding

Job 11:12. Difficulty of understanding for some

Psalm 119:32. Understanding increased through the commandments

Psalm 147:5. No limit to the Lord's understanding

Proverbs 2:6. Wisdom from the mouth of God

Proverbs 3:5. Trusting in the Lord's understanding

Isaiah 11:2. Spirit of understanding

Jeremiah 10:12. Heavens created through God's understanding

Mark 12:33. Loving God with heart and mind

Luke 2:47. Stunning understanding

1 Corinthians 1:10. Seek unity in understanding.

Colossians 2:2. Riches in understanding Christ

1 Peter 3:7. Understanding with wives

1 John 5:20. Understanding the Father through his Son

▶ Undivided *(agreement, unified, whole)*

The quality of being in agreement with someone or something in a way that produces a harmonious environment

1 Samuel 12:14. King and kingdom united

1 Samuel 14:7. Agreement

Nehemiah 8:1. People united as one

Amos 3:3. Two in agreement

John 13:34–35. Mark of discipleship

Acts 2:44–45. Undivided in community and purpose

2 Corinthians 13:11. Living in peace

Ephesians 2:14. Wall of hostility broken

Colossians 2:2. United in love

Titus 1:4. Common faith

▶ Unexpected *(abrupt, sudden, unanticipated)*

An event or occurrence which happens suddenly and not in accordance with one's expectations

Psalm 64:7. Sudden death

Isaiah 28:21. God's mysterious deeds

Isaiah 29:5. Enemies fall quickly.

Matthew 24:44. Jesus' return will be unexpected.

Acts 16:26–28. A violent quake, no jail break

Acts 22:6. Recalling a drastic conversion experience

Acts 28:5–6. Unexpected result of a snake bite

1 Thessalonians 5:3. Destruction coming like labor pains

▶ Unfairness *(biased, injustice, unbalanced)*

The attitude or action of treating someone without due consideration to justice and equity

Genesis 16:5. Sarai's complaint
Exodus 21:8. Treating a foreign wife unfairly
Psalm 82:2. Questioning God's judgments in a time of distress
Psalm 92:15. The Lord is never unfair.
Proverbs 28:8. Unfair business dealings
Ezekiel 18:25. Turning the table on an accusation
Malachi 2:9. Misapplied teachings
Matthew 20:13. Sticking with an agreement
Acts 7:24. Stopping unfair treatment
Romans 3:5. God's fairness
Romans 9:14. Making an unthinkable claim
1 Peter 2:18. Obeying an unfair master

▶ Unfaithful *(adulterous, untrue, wandering)*

Having a heart and/or actions which wander from one's commitments and values
Numbers 14:35. Life ending in destruction
Judges 8:33–34. Turning to foreign gods
Ezra 10:2. Unfaithful to God
Ezekiel 12:2. Living among rebellious people
Hosea 5:7. Unfaithful to the Lord
Hosea 9:1. Vivid depiction of Israel's sin
Matthew 5:32. Appearance of unfaithfulness
Matthew 12:39. Desiring signs from God
Romans 3:3. God's faithfulness cannot be negated.
2 Timothy 2:13. Unfaithfulness, faithfulness
James 4:4. Friend of the world
Revelation 21:8. Destined for the lake of fire

▶ Unfit *(unqualified, unsuited)*

The failure to meet an expected standard of quality or response
Isaiah 52:3. Unfit price
Matthew 10:37–38. Unfit for discipleship
Matthew 22:8. Unfit to attend
Acts 13:46. Unfit for the preaching of the Word
Acts 27:12. Unfit place to spend winter
2 Corinthians 3:5. Unqualified for service
Titus 1:16. Unfit to do anything good

▶ Unforgiveness *(backsliding, falling, relapse)*

A person's own relapsing into sinful living and rejection of God
Numbers 15:30. Excluded from God's covenant people
Deuteronomy 17:12. Disobedience to God's servants
Hebrews 6:4–6. Deserted Christ
Hebrews 10:26. No sacrifice remains.
2 Peter 2:20. Entanglement with the world
1 John 5:16. Sin which leads to death

▶ Unhappiness *(abject, dejected, sorrowful)*

The condition or feeling of being sorrowful or dejected
Genesis 40:7. Unhappy prisoners
Judges 10:16. Stopping Israel's unhappy condition
Job 3:20. Life is bitter.
Proverbs 31:7. Drowning sorrows
Ecclesiastes 1:13. Weighed down
Ecclesiastes 4:8. Deprived of good things
Mark 10:22. Unhappy news
Romans 3:16. Persistent suffering

▶ Unicorn *(see Wild ox)*

▶ Unique *(distinct, rare, special)*

Someone or something which is rare and/or distinct from the normal patterns in the world
Genesis 1:27. Distinct from the rest of creation
Job 23:13. God is one of a kind.
Job 33:23. A special messenger
Psalm 139:13. Uniqueness of the Creator
Song of Songs 6:9. A unique woman
Jeremiah 1:5. Unique and set apart
Zechariah 14:7. A unique day
John 3:16. God's unique Son

▶ Unity *(accord, harmony, oneness)*

Living and practicing harmonious existence among humanity and before God

U

Psalm 133:1. Living in harmony
Proverbs 16:7. Unity with God and humanity
Zephaniah 3:9. All serving God with one purpose
Matthew 18:19. Agreement on earth and heaven
John 14:20. Unity in God
John 17:10. United in purpose
John 17:21. Unity modeled after God's unity
Acts 2:44–45. All things in common
Romans 12:10. Devoted to family
Romans 15:5. Gracious gift of harmony in life
1 Corinthians 1:10. United in understanding
1 Corinthians 1:12–13. Christ is the unifying factor.
Galatians 3:28. Unity in Christ
Ephesians 4:3. Unity through the Spirit
Ephesians 5:31–33. Marital unity
Colossians 2:2. United in love through riches in Christ
Colossians 3:14. Unity through love
Titus 1:4. Common faith
1 Peter 3:8. Living in unity

▶ Universe *(cosmos, creation, world)*

All the existing matter in the cosmos which has been created by God
Genesis 1:1–2. God created
Psalm 8:3–4. Man in relation to the universe
Psalm 102:25. Heavens are the work of God's hands.
Matthew 24:29. Powers of the universe
Acts 17:24. All things created by God
Colossians 1:16. All things created for God
Hebrews 1:2–3. The Son's role in creation
2 Peter 3:10. Universe destroyed
2 Peter 3:12. Elements of the universe destroyed

▶ Unkind acts *(affliction, persecution, violence)*

Actions which are malicious and ill-conceived
Genesis 15:13. God's people oppressed in foreign land
Exodus 1:8–12. Oppression under Egypt
Deuteronomy 26:7. God hears the cries of the oppressed.
Judges 10:8. Bad leaders
Psalm 9:9. The Lord is a stronghold.
Psalm 146:7. Justice for the oppressed
Proverbs 31:20. A righteous woman
Isaiah 1:17. Doing good
James 2:6. Rich oppressing the poor

▶ Unmarried *(bachelor, single, unattached)*

The condition of never having been married, or being single after a marriage ends
Leviticus 21:2–3. Caring for an unmarried sister
Numbers 30:6–7. Unmarried woman's vows
Judges 21:12. Many unmarried
2 Chronicles 36:17. Unmarried men not spared
Luke 20:34–35. Unmarried in the next world
Acts 21:9. Philip's unmarried daughters
1 Corinthians 7:8. Paul's singleness
1 Corinthians 7:11. Time to remain single
1 Corinthians 7:32–34. Unmarried ministry blessing

▶ Unpardonable Sin *(unbelief, unforgivable)*

Rejection of the Holy Spirit
Matthew 12:31–32. Speaking against the Holy Spirit
Mark 3:28–29. Guaranteed truth
Luke 12:10. Dishonoring the Holy Spirit
Hebrews 6:4–6. Deserting Christ

▶ Unprepared *(surprised, unready)*

Not ready or unable to deal with something
Ecclesiastes 9:12. Unprepared for a coming time
Malachi 3:1. Clearing a way for the future
Matthew 24:38–39. Unprepared for the flood
Luke 14:26. Not ready to be a disciple
Luke 21:34. Drunk and unprepared
1 Corinthians 3:2. Unprepared for solid food
2 Corinthians 9:4. Caught unprepared

▶ Unproductive *(barren, infertile, unfruitful)*

Used primarily in reference to land which is fruitful or women who are infertile

Leviticus 26:20. Hard work, yet no fruit
Psalm 68:6. Unproductive land
Isaiah 5:10. Unproductive vineyard
Isaiah 32:10. No harvest
Isaiah 54:1. Barren women given cause for rejoicing
Hosea 9:16. Unproductive people
Mark 11:13. Fig tree's unproductiveness
Luke 23:29. Blessing on barren women

▶ Unresponsive *(dumb, idle, slow)*

Idle or dull to a message

Leviticus 5:1. Responsive to testimony
Job 19:7. Calling out with no response
Isaiah 6:10. People made like their idols
Jeremiah 2:30. Unresponsive to correction
Jeremiah 25:3–4. Ignoring the words of the prophets
Jeremiah 25:7. Idol-makers becoming idle
Ezekiel 12:1–2. Failure to hear
Matthew 11:20–24. Unresponsive cities denounced
Revelation 2:16. Fate of an unrepentant heart

▶ Unrighteousness *(injustice, unfair, ungodliness)*

Wicked or ungodly actions or thoughts which are indicative of unbelievers

Job 27:7. Treated like an unrighteous person
Isaiah 55:7. Unrighteous called to the Lord
Jeremiah 22:13. Dishonest gain
Ezekiel 28:15. Exceptional behavior, then sin
Luke 18:6. Crying out against an unrighteous judge
Romans 1:18. God's anger revealed against unrighteousness
Romans 2:8. Refusing to believe
Romans 3:5. Human unrighteousness demonstrates God's righteousness.
Romans 6:13. Unholy use of the body
1 Corinthians 6:9–10. Unrighteous deeds
2 Thessalonians 2:12. Delighting in what displeases God
1 Peter 3:18. Christ's sufferings for our unrighteousness
2 Peter 2:9. Immoral persons held for punishment
1 John 1:9. Cleansed from all unrighteousness

▶ Unsaved (see *Unbeliever[s]*)

▶ Unseen *(concealed, hidden, invisible)*

Not being visible or revealed, but hidden or concealed

Exodus 33:20–23. God's unseen face
2 Samuel 17:17. Need to be unseen
Job 33:21. Unseen flesh and bones
Psalm 77:19. Footprints missing
Isaiah 66:19. Glory unseen
John 1:18. No one has ever seen God.
John 5:37. Voice unheard, form unseen
Acts 26:16. Bearing witness to what you have seen
Romans 8:25. Hope for what we do not see
1 Corinthians 2:9–10. Unseen revealed to those who love God
2 Corinthians 4:18. Eternality of the unseen
Colossians 1:15. Christ, image of the invisible God
1 Timothy 1:17. Invisible God
Hebrews 11:3. Seen made by the unseen
1 Peter 1:8–9. Loving Christ, even though you have not seen him

▶ Unselfishness *(charitable, generous, selfless)*

The quality of putting the needs of others in greater priority than personal needs

Genesis 13:6–9. Abram shares land with Lot.
1 Samuel 30:24. Sharing supplies
2 Samuel 19:29–30. Valuing life over land
2 Kings 4:8–10. Unselfishly caring for God's workers
Nehemiah 5:14–15. Fear of God
Psalm 119:36. Valuing the Law rather than selfish gain

U

Acts 9:36. Dorcas's charitable service
Romans 15:1–2. Caring for the concerns of others
1 Corinthians 10:33. Doing what's best for others
2 Corinthians 8:9. Christ's unselfishness
2 Corinthians 13:9. Mutual dependence
Galatians 6:6. Sharing with those who teach
Philippians 2:3. Acting humbly and valuing others
2 Timothy 2:10. Enduring difficult things for other believers

▶ Unshakable *(determined, purposeful, resolute)*

Highly fixed, determined, and unwavering in purpose or process

Jeremiah 32:17–21. Surety of God's work
Jeremiah 32:27. Nothing is too hard for God.
Habakkuk 3:19. Trusting in God's strength
Matthew 16:18. Hell shall not prevail against the church.

▶ Untruth *(see Lying)*

▶ Unusual deaths *(death, strange)*

Deaths which occur in strange and irregular circumstances

Genesis 19:26. Look of death
Exodus 14:27–28. Swept up in the sea
Numbers 16:28–33. Swallowed up in the ground
Numbers 16:35. Consumed by fire
Joshua 10:11. Large hailstones
Judges 4:21. Hammering a tent peg
Judges 15:16. Massacre with a donkey's jawbone
Judges 16:30. Building collapses
1 Samuel 4:18. Falling over in a chair
2 Samuel 20:10. Intestine-spilling death
1 Kings 3:19. Death by smothering
2 Kings 7:17. Trampled to death
Matthew 14:8. Asking for John's head on a platter
Luke 13:4. Crushed by a building

▶ Unwillingness *(hesitant, reluctant, resistance)*

Resistance to a stated plan or purpose

Genesis 3:6. Unwilling to obey
2 Chronicles 36:16. Unwilling to accept God
Psalm 81:11. Unwilling to listen
Proverbs 5:12. Hating discipline
Isaiah 65:12. Unwilling to live wisely
Jonah 1:1–3. Unwilling to obey God's directive
Zechariah 7:12. Unwilling to listen
Matthew 22:3. Unwilling guests
Matthew 23:37. Rejection of God's protection
2 Peter 3:9. Unwilling to come before the time is right

▶ Upper room *(second floor, upstairs)*

A large, second-floor room of a wealthy patron, typically used for entertaining and lodging guests

Judges 3:20a. Message from the roof
1 Samuel 9:25. Saul's place of slumber
1 Kings 17:19. Son carried upstairs
Daniel 6:10. Praying in the upper room
Mark 14:15. Preparing the upper room for Passover
Acts 1:13. Withdrawing to the upper room
Acts 9:37. Dead body stored in an upper room

▶ Urgency *(critical, desperate, serious)*

The status or situation of requiring action immediately

Exodus 12:11. Eating with urgency
1 Samuel 21:8. King's urgent business
2 Samuel 15:14. Fleeing for life
Psalm 70:5. Come without delay.
Ecclesiastes 9:10. Urgency of work
Isaiah 62:1. Working swiftly on behalf of Zion
Matthew 28:7–10. Urgently proclaim: "He is risen!"

Luke 14:21. Announcing release for the poor, blind, and lame

Acts 17:10–11. An urgent message

1 Corinthians 7:29–31. Living in urgent times

Ephesians 5:15–16. Seizing opportunities because the days are evil

Colossians 4:5. Wise living

▶ Useless *(futile, pointless, vain)*

Falling short of an objective, or failing to provide useful aid or provision

2 Kings 18:20. Useless advice

Proverbs 26:7. Useless words

Hosea 7:16. People compared to a useless tool

Hosea 8:8. God's people become useless.

Romans 4:14. Faith and promise made null?

Ephesians 5:11. Avoiding useless works

1 Timothy 1:6. Unfruitful discussions

Philemon 11. Slave becomes useful.

Hebrews 7:18. Useless requirements rejected

James 2:20. Useless faith

▶ Usurp *(expropriate, seize, take possession)*

The acquisition of an unwarranted position of power or prominence, often by force

2 Kings 15:10. Strategic kill

2 Kings 15:30. Hoshea assumes the throne.

2 Chronicles 23:1. Plotting overthrow

1 Timothy 2:12. Usurping authority

Revelation 3:11. Holding steadily to the crown

▶ Vacillation *(fluctuate, indecisive, undecided)*

Alternating between one or more positions

1 Samuel 15:29. Unchanged mind

1 Kings 18:21. Vacillating between God and Baal

2 Kings 22:19. Change of heart

Psalm 125:1. Unshaken trust in God

Jeremiah 18:10. Conditional plans

Ezekiel 21:26. The times are changing.

Joel 2:13–14. Reconsidering plans

Jonah 3:10. Plans for destruction changed

2 Corinthians 1:17. Not vacillating

▶ Vagabond(s) *(fugitive, nomad, wanderer)*

One who perpetually travels from place to place without home or work

Genesis 4:12. Wandering on the earth

Psalm 109:10. Children who wander and beg

Proverbs 6:11. Need arising like a vagabond

Acts 19:13. Traveling spiritual groups

▶ Valiant *(see Bravery; Courage)*

▶ Validity *(believable, credible, reasonableness)*

Used in reference to whether a message or idea is considered believable or reliable

John 8:16. Judgment validated by God

2 Thessalonians 1:9–10. Day of validation

1 Timothy 2:6. Validity of God's message for all time

1 Peter 1:8–9. Belief validated

1 John 5:10. Message invalidated

1 John 5:13. Purpose of this message

▶ Valley(s) *(basin, gully, depth)*

A low plain surrounded by mountains

Genesis 26:17. Moving into the valley

Deuteronomy 8:7. Refreshing valley

Joshua 11:17. Strategic land

Psalm 84:5–6. Valley of blessings

Psalm 104:8. Mountains high, valleys low

Isaiah 22:1. The valley of Vision

Isaiah 41:18. Replenishing valley

Luke 3:5. Leveling of the land

John 18:1. Crossing over the valley

▶ Value(s) *(beliefs, ideas, judgments)*

Foundational ideas or beliefs which serve as a guide for life

Psalm 52:7. Trusting wealth, not God

Isaiah 5:20. Misguided values

Haggai 1:2–3. Building homes rather than the temple

Luke 7:2. Valued life

▶ Vanity *(breath, futility, temporality)*

Metaphorical reference that carries with it the sense of temporality and futility

2 Chronicles 26:16. Success-inspired pride

2 Chronicles 32:24–25. Pride and humility

Proverbs 21:24. Blinding arrogance and conceit

Proverbs 30:8. Keeping vanity away

Ecclesiastes 1:2. All is vanity!

Isaiah 5:21. Vanity of self-inflation

Jeremiah 10:3. Worthless religion

Jeremiah 50:11–12. Conqueror brought low

Hosea 12:8. Wealth equated with righteousness

Luke 11:43. Seeking honorable positions

2 Corinthians 10:12. Self-comparison

1 Timothy 6:3–4. Vanity of speech

▶ Vanquished *(conquer, defeat, pogrom)*

A thorough defeat of one's opposition

Genesis 6:13. Vanquishing the earth

Genesis 14:7. Conquering an entire territory

Numbers 21:30. Total destruction

Deuteronomy 4:3. God's devastation of idol worshipers

Joshua 13:1. Much left to be conquered

Job 32:13. Defeated by God

Isaiah 49:19. Land lying in ruins

Galatians 1:13. Attempting to vanquish the church of God

Philippians 3:19. Self-destruction

2 Peter 3:16. Destruction of those who distort the truth

▶ Variety *(change, diversity, variation)*

The quality of being diverse in comparison to normal expectations

2 Chronicles 16:14. Various spices

Matthew 4:24. Numerous diseases and ailments healed by Jesus

Matthew 22:42. Variety of opinions about the Messiah

1 Corinthians 12:4–6. Variety of gifts in the church

▶ Vegetable(s) *(crop, food, plant)*

A cultivated crop used as a food source

Deuteronomy 11:10. Cultivated crops

2 Samuel 17:27–28. Beans served to troops

2 Samuel 23:11–12. Lentils

1 Kings 21:2. Purchasing a garden

Isaiah 1:8. Farmer hut

▶ Vegetarian *(meatless, vegan)*

Someone who does not eat meat, and in extreme cases does not consume any animal products

Numbers 11:5. Cucumbers, garlic, and onion from Egypt

Proverbs 15:17. More important to have love than rich foods

Daniel 1:8–16. Diet of vegetables

Romans 14:2. Strong and the weak

▶ Vengeance *(payback, revenge, retribution)*

Revenge exacted for an injury or wrongdoing

Genesis 4:15. Promised vengeance for killing Cain

Leviticus 19:18. Never get revenge (on your own initiative).

Numbers 31:3. Settling a score with Midian

Deuteronomy 32:35. Satisfying vengeance

1 Samuel 25:39. Vengeance returned

2 Samuel 14:11. Avenger of blood

Psalm 94:1. God of vengeance

Isaiah 59:17–18. Righteous vengeance

Ezekiel 25:14. Israel as an instrument of revenge

Romans 12:19. Vengeance belongs to God.

2 Thessalonians 1:7–8. Christ will avenge those who deny the Good News.

Revelation 6:10. Apocalyptic revenge

▶ Venom *(poison, toxin)*

A poisonous fluid secreted by snakes and other animals which is highly potent and life-threatening to humans

Deuteronomy 32:33. Deadly poison

Job 20:13–14. Food turns to venom in the stomach.

Psalm 58:4. Dangerous enemies

Psalm 140:3. Waiting to strike

Romans 3:13. Venomous words

▶ Verdict *(adjudication, justice, ruling)*

A decision rendered over a civil, criminal, or religious dispute

Deuteronomy 17:9. Asking priests for a verdict

Psalm 17:2. Verdict from God

Psalm 58:1. Questioning the king's verdicts

Psalm 76:8. Verdict sent from heaven

Lamentations 3:59. Seeking just recompense

Zechariah 8:16. Commanded to seek justice

Matthew 26:66. Assigning the death penalty

Romans 5:16. Verdict on one, verdict on all

Romans 5:18. One verdict brings about righteousness.

2 Peter 2:3. Long-standing verdict

▶ Versatility *(adaptable, adjustable, flexible)*

One's ability to adapt and assimilate to a new environment or situation

Acts 15:22–29. Versatile beliefs and practices in the church

Acts 17:22. Paul addresses the Areopagus.
1 Corinthians 1:7. Lacking in no good gifts
1 Corinthians 9:22. The adaptable man
2 Peter 3:9. Patience not slowness

▶ Vice *(see Crime[s]; Sin[s])*

▶ Victim *(injured, innocent, sufferer)*

A person or thing who has been disturbed, injured, or killed as a result of an action

Numbers 23:24. Preying on a victim
Deuteronomy 21:1–6. Instructions for finding a murder victim
Psalm 10:8–10. Waiting to prey on the next victim
Psalm 109:25. Victim of insults
Proverbs 7:26. Many victims
Isaiah 59:15. Turning from evil
Jeremiah 14:16. Catastrophe victims
Lamentations 4:9. Victims compared
1 Timothy 3:7. Devil's victim

▶ Victory *(success, supremacy, triumph)*

The supremacy of God in all things

Exodus 14:13–14. "The Lord is fighting for you."
1 Samuel 17:47. Victories determined by God
Isaiah 42:24–25. Handed over to destruction
Jonah 2:9. "Victory belongs to the Lord."
1 Corinthians 15:54–57. "Death, where is your victory?"
Ephesians 6:16. Victory over the evil one
1 John 5:4–5. Victory over the world through faith
Revelation 7:9–10. "Salvation belongs to our God!"

▶ Vigorous *(healthy, robust, vibrant)*

A quality or condition of good health, energy, and vibrancy

Exodus 1:19. Midwives lie about Hebrew women.
Deuteronomy 34:7. Virile until death
Job 20:11. Losing life
Job 21:23. Death in the prime of life
Job 30:2. Vigor is gone.
Job 33:25. Youthful vigor
Psalm 38:19. The strength of the enemy
Isaiah 59:10. No zest for life

▶ Vindication *(absolve, acquit, exonerate)*

The exoneration or acquittal of responsibility or blame from someone

Genesis 20:16. Sarah vindicated
Deuteronomy 32:36. The Lord vindicates his people.
Job 6:29. Job's vindication on the line
Psalm 35:24. Vindication according to righteousness
Isaiah 50:8. Nearness of God
Jeremiah 51:10. God wrought vindication.
Ezekiel 36:23. Holiness of God's name vindicated
1 Timothy 3:16. Vindicated by the Spirit

▶ Vindictiveness *(revenge, spite, vengeance)*

Demonstrating a strong and irrational desire for revenge

Judges 16:21. Vindictiveness toward Samson
1 Samuel 14:24. Saul desires revenge on his enemies.
1 Samuel 31:8–10. Vindictiveness toward the dead
2 Kings 9:7. Plotting revenge
Micah 5:15. Anger toward the nations
Acts 5:28. Accused of taking revenge

▶ Vine, the *(Israel, Jesus)*

Plant whose stem requires support; often used in reference to God's people, Israel

1 Kings 4:25. Security
Psalm 80:8. Symbol of Israel
Psalm 128:3. Wife as a fruitful vine
Jeremiah 2:21. God's people
Joel 1:11–12. Withering vines a symbol of destruction

Habakkuk 3:17–18. Happiness despite bad circumstances
Zechariah 8:12. Vines will grow again.
Matthew 26:29. Fruit of the vine
John 15:1–4. Jesus the true vine
Revelation 14:18–19. Harvesting grapes image of the final judgment

▶ Vineyard *(garden, vinery, vines)*

Place where grapevines grow; symbol of wealth and blessing

Genesis 9:20. Noah plants a vineyard.
Exodus 22:5. Rules for replacing damaged goods
Exodus 23:11. Social welfare
Numbers 18:12. Firstfruits belong to God.
1 Samuel 22:7. Sign of wealth
2 Kings 5:26. Trading goods
Proverbs 24:30–31. Cultivating the vineyard
Isaiah 5:7. God's people are his garden of delight.
Matthew 20:1–16. Parable of the vineyard laborers
Matthew 21:28–32. Parable of sons working in the vineyard
1 Corinthians 9:7. Eating from your own vineyard

▶ Violence *(disturbance, fighting, hostility)*

Strong, disturbing behavior generally involving physical force and damaging of things or people

Genesis 6:11. World of violence
Genesis 49:5. Weapons of violence
Psalm 35:11–12. Repaid with evil
Isaiah 53:9. No violence committed
Isaiah 59:6. Societal injustice
Jeremiah 6:7. Cries of violence from Jerusalem
Ezekiel 7:11. Violence as a means of judgment
Acts 5:26. Minimal force
Acts 21:35. Mob mentality
Acts 27:41. A violent storm

▶ Virgin *(chaste, unmarried, untouched)*

A person, typically a woman, who has never had sexual relations

Genesis 24:16. An attractive virgin
Genesis 34:1–4. Dinah violated
Deuteronomy 22:13–21. Requiring proof of virginity
Judges 21:12. Large gathering of virgins
2 Samuel 13:2. Protecting a virgin's honor
Job 31:1. Promised not to look with lust
Isaiah 7:14. A virgin will conceive.
Isaiah 47:1. Virgin princess of Babylon
Matthew 1:23. Mary conceives Jesus.
Luke 1:27. Angelic visit to the virgin Mary
1 Corinthians 7:28. Concerns of a young virgin
2 Corinthians 11:2. God's people betrothed to Christ

▶ Virgin birth *(incarnation, miracle)*

Teaching that Jesus was conceived in the womb of his mother Mary by a miraculous work of the Holy Spirit and not by a human father

Isaiah 7:14. Promise made
Matthew 1:18–25. Pregnant by means of the Spirit, not Joseph
Luke 1:34–35. Mary's sexual chastity
Galatians 4:4–5. Jesus' incarnation

▶ Virtue(s) *(goodness, morality, righteousness)*

Behaviors or patterns of thinking which demonstrate godly characteristics of holiness and morality

Ruth 3:11. A woman of character
Proverbs 12:4. A husband's crown
Proverbs 31:10. Virtuous wife
Philippians 4:8. Virtue list
Titus 2:3. Examples of virtue
1 Peter 2:9. Sharing God's virtues
2 Peter 1:3. Virtue through God's power
2 Peter 1:5. Adding virtue to faith

▶ Vision *(appearance, apparition, dream)*

A vivid appearance or interaction with God in a dreamlike state

Numbers 12:6. Communicating through visions to prophets
1 Samuel 3:15. Samuel's fear of the vision
Isaiah 1:1. Isaiah's vision
Ezekiel 12:27. A far-off vision?
Daniel 2:19. Daniel's visions explain reality.
Matthew 17:9. Transfiguration
Luke 1:22. A vision in the temple silences Zechariah.
Acts 9:10. Visionary calling
Acts 10:9–16. Peter's visionary experiences
2 Corinthians 12:1. Visions and revelations from the Lord

▶ Visitation *(appearance, manifestation, return)*

A time of judgment which is yet to come
Luke 19:44. Unknown day of visitation
1 Peter 2:12. Glory to God on the day of visitation

▶ Vocalist(s) *(singer, vocal, voices)*

A singer or group of singers who recite and perform music for the purpose of entertainment or praise
Exodus 15:1–21. God's people sing of deliverance.
Judges 5:11. Singing of God's victories at the wells
Psalm 33:1–3. Sing a new song.
Psalm 100:1–2. Entering God's presence with song
Psalm 118:15. Righteous break into song.
Psalm 149:1–3. Music of praise
Acts 16:25. Silas and Paul singing in prison
Revelation 14:3. New song before the throne

▶ Vocation *(calling, job, work)*

Any trade, profession, or occupation; a calling to a particular work
Psalm 68:6. Productive lives
Proverbs 16:3. Entrusting work to God
Romans 11:29. God's calling on someone
1 Corinthians 1:26. Consider your calling.
1 Corinthians 10:31. Working for God's glory
1 Corinthians 16:9. Opportunity for effective work
Colossians 3:17. Work in the name of the Lord.
Colossians 3:23. Working wholeheartedly
Titus 3:14. Examples of productive lives
Philemon 6. Effective faith sharing
2 Peter 1:8. Increasing knowledge and productivity

▶ Voice(s) *(communication, expression, utterance)*

Sound or communication produced through the vocal chords
Genesis 4:10. Voice of the dead cries out.
Genesis 21:6. Voices of laughter
Exodus 3:18. Listening to the prophetic voice
Judges 9:7. Shouting from the mountaintops
1 Samuel 15:14. Vocal sounds of animals
Isaiah 65:19. Rejoicing over Jerusalem
Matthew 3:17. A voice from heaven
Mark 1:3. A voice crying in the desert
John 10:4–5. Following the voice of the shepherd
Galatians 4:20. Desiring to change the tone of voice

▶ Volunteer(s) *(availability, offer, service)*

Someone who willingly offers up their services for a cause
Judges 5:2. Men vowing to fight for Israel
1 Samuel 22:2. Banding together
2 Chronicles 17:16. Volunteering to serve the Lord
Psalm 110:3. Volunteer army
Acts 28:30–31. Paul lives at his own expense.
1 Corinthians 9:17. Spreading the Good News willingly

▶ Vomit *(regurgitate, sickness, spit up)*

The unwanted release of previously consumed matter; metaphorically, to cast out, exile
Leviticus 18:25. Allusions to exile
Leviticus 18:28. Promise of exile

Leviticus 20:22. Called to obey
Job 20:15. Riches swallowed up and expelled
Proverbs 23:8. Ruining a nice time
Proverbs 25:16. Do not eat too much.
Proverbs 26:11. Acting like a fool
Isaiah 19:14. Drunk and disorderly
Isaiah 28:8. Vile condition
Jeremiah 25:27. Drinking to forget
Jeremiah 48:26. Wallowing in filth
2 Peter 2:22. Proverbs coming true

▶ Voting *(choose, decide, elect)*

A formal indication of one's choice between two or more options
Numbers 27:16. Appointing new leadership
Deuteronomy 17:14–15. Picking a king
Matthew 27:15–26. Barabbas selected over Jesus
Acts 26:10. Voting for death

▶ Vow(s) *(oath, pledge, promise)*

A promise made in the name of God or gods, thus heightening the level of commitment
Genesis 28:20–22. Jacob's vow to God
Numbers 30:3–5. Father's role in daughter's vow
Judges 11:30–31. Rash vow
1 Samuel 1:11. Vowing a future son's service
Jonah 1:16. Sacrifices and vows attempted to appease God
Acts 18:18. Paul cuts his hair at the end of a vow.
Acts 21:23. Fulfilling a vow

▶ Voyage *(expedition, journey, trip)*

A journey undertaken by way of the sea
Proverbs 30:18–19. Difficult voyage
Jonah 1:4–6. Trouble on the high seas
Acts 16:11. Direct voyage
Acts 21:7. Completing a voyage
Acts 27:10. A voyage with heavy losses
Revelation 18:17. Cargo lost

▶ Vulnerability *(availability, susceptible, weak)*

Used negatively of susceptibility to attacks and pressure and positively in terms of emotional and physical availability. In the New Testament, the early church's vulnerability with each other allowed for the mutual meeting of needs and the growth of the Christian church.
Acts 2:42–45. Being the body together
1 Corinthians 12:10. Sharing spiritual gifts in community
Galatians 6:1. Being helpful without being vulnerable
Philemon 6. Vulnerability in community
James 5:20. Restored from a vulnerable position

▶ Wages *(payment, revenue, salary)*

Payment(s) made for services rendered

Genesis 31:8. Animals paid as wages

Deuteronomy 24:14–15. Do not withhold pay.

Judges 17:10. Money paid for priestly service

Matthew 20:1–2. Paying a day's wage

Mark 1:20. Hired help

Luke 6:23. Reward in heaven

Luke 10:7. Workers deserve their pay.

Romans 4:4. Something that is earned

Romans 6:23. Wages of sin

1 Corinthians 9:14. Earning a wage from gospel ministry

2 Corinthians 11:8. Mishandling wages

1 Timothy 5:18. Paying what is due

1 Peter 5:2. Serving out of desire, not greed

2 John 8. Preserving one's wages

▶ Waiting *(remain, rest, stop)*

Staying in one place or delaying an action until a given point of time

Genesis 8:10. Noah waiting in the ark

Judges 3:25. Waiting for a ruler who wouldn't come

2 Kings 7:3. Waiting for death?

Job 30:26. Waiting for good

Psalm 5:3. Waiting on the Lord

Psalm 37:7. Waiting patiently

Lamentations 3:25. Good things come to those who wait.

Mark 9:9. Waiting to tell about the Son of Man

Mark 15:43. Awaiting God's kingdom

Acts 1:4. Waiting in Jerusalem

Romans 3:25–26. God waited to deal with sins.

Romans 8:19. Creation eagerly waiting

1 Corinthians 1:7. Awaiting Christ's revelation

1 Corinthians 4:5. Wait until the Lord comes.

Hebrews 6:15. Abraham waited patiently.

1 Peter 3:20. God's patience in the days of Noah

▶ Waiting in the wings *(accession, waiting, succession)*

A modern idiom referring to the period of waiting for one's future office or ministry to begin

Leviticus 8:33. Prolonged ordination ceremony

Joshua 1:1–2. Joshua takes over for Moses.

1 Kings 1:20. Who shall succeed?

Acts 25:1. Festus assumes duties.

▶ Walk *(manner of life, walking)*

Used to describe the action of walking in a literal sense; metaphorically refers to following God in faith

Deuteronomy 1:36. Walking through the land

Joshua 14:9. Land your feet traversed

Habakkuk 3:19. Walking on the path

Matthew 9:5. Commanded to get up and walk

John 8:12. Following after Jesus

Acts 3:8–9. Walking again

Romans 6:4. Walking in newness of life

2 Corinthians 5:7. Walking by faith and not sight

Galatians 5:16. Way of living

Ephesians 2:2. Following worldly ways

1 Peter 5:8. An opponent on the prowl

1 John 1:6–7. Walking in darkness and light

2 John 4. Walking in the truth

▶ Wall(s) (see *City walls*)

▶ Wallowing *(lull, splash, wade)*

Kick about, splash, or dwell in a dirty substance such as mud, vomit, or blood

2 Samuel 20:12. Wallowing in blood

Jeremiah 48:26. Residing in vomit

Ezekiel 16:6. Kicking around in blood

Ezekiel 16:22. Youthful days
Ezekiel 27:29–30. Wallowing in ashes
2 Peter 2:22. Returning to the mud

▶ Wander *(abandon, drift, stray)*

Aimlessly moving around, typically on account of one's proclivity toward sin

Numbers 32:13. Wandering forty years in the desert
2 Kings 21:8. Conditional promise that God's people will not wander again
Psalm 59:15. Wandering to find food
Psalm 119:10. Asking for sustaining power
Proverbs 5:6. Path of folly
Isaiah 35:8. Off the beaten path
Isaiah 63:17. Asking for God's guidance
Jeremiah 4:1. Perceiving God's distance from a sinful people
Jeremiah 31:22. Unfaithful wanderers
Ezekiel 14:11. Looking forward to a day
Hosea 9:17. Rejecting God
Amos 8:12. Aimless wandering
Zechariah 10:2. Led astray by false idols

▶ Wanton behavior *(see Lascivious behavior, Lust, Sin[s])*

▶ Wants *(desires, lacking, need)*

To be in short supply of or lacking something desirable

Exodus 16:16–18. Gathering double portion to meet the wants of the Sabbath
Mark 10:21. Something's missing
Luke 10:34. Attending to the wants of a wounded man
1 Corinthians 9:11. Payment in the form of earthly goods
1 Corinthians 16:17. Coworkers filling the void
2 Corinthians 8:14. Balance of needs
Philippians 4:12. Living in either circumstance
Colossians 1:24. Filling up what is lacking
1 Thessalonians 3:10. Needs supplied for faith
Hebrews 4:1. Promise has not been found lacking.

▶ War *(battle, conflict, fighting)*

Armed conflict between two opposing forces, typically national or tribal

Exodus 15:3. The warrior Lord
Judges 4:14. Lord leads into battle
Judges 7:18. Battle horn
1 Samuel 17:45. God of the army of Israel
2 Samuel 5:23–24. Dependence on God
1 Kings 22:19. Ready for battle
2 Chronicles 20:15. Battle belongs to the Lord
Psalm 18:34. Hands trained for battle
Psalm 46:9. Wars ended
Isaiah 42:15. Effects of war
Jeremiah 21:5–6. Fury and rage
Micah 4:3. Future peace
Matthew 24:6. Wars and rumors of wars
Matthew 26:52. Put away your sword.
Ephesians 6:10–20. Spiritual warfare
1 Timothy 1:18. Continuing to fight the noble war
1 Peter 2:11. Under attack from sinful desires
Revelation 16:16. Armageddon

▶ Wardrobe *(see Clothing)*

▶ Warning(s) *(alert, caution, notice)*

Statements which provide cautionary notice regarding an unpleasant future circumstance

Exodus 9:20. Heeding the Lord's warning to Pharaoh
Deuteronomy 32:46. Warning to obey teachings
2 Samuel 22:16. Powerful warning
1 Kings 2:3. Obeying the law
Nehemiah 9:34. Ignoring the Lord's gracious warning
Job 36:10. Seeking to reorient lives
Proverbs 15:31–32. Heeding a warning
Jeremiah 6:8. Judgment to be poured out
Mark 6:11. Visual sign of warning
1 Corinthians 10:11. An example and warning to learn from
2 Corinthians 13:2. Warning about a future visit

▸ Warrior *(mighty one, powerful one, soldier)*

A brave or experienced soldier, typically one who is more impressive than his or her contemporaries

Genesis 10:8–9. Nimrod, mighty warrior of the earth
Exodus 14:4. Plotting the Lord's victory
Joshua 1:14. Best soldiers protect family.
Judges 6:12. Gideon equipped with the Lord
2 Samuel 23:8–9. David's mighty men
Psalm 24:8. God is a strong warrior.
Psalm 45:3. Preparing for battle
Isaiah 3:25. Widowed wives of warriors
Isaiah 42:13. The Lord marches out.
Jeremiah 51:30. Babylon's warriors fail.
Daniel 11:3. Warrior-king who is to come
Revelation 6:2. Victorious warrior on a white horse
Revelation 19:17–18. Destroyed by birds of prey

▸ Washing *(cleaning, laundering)*

The cleaning or laundering of clothing or a human being

Genesis 49:11. Washing garments
Exodus 2:5. Attempted bathing
Exodus 19:10. Preparing to be set apart
Leviticus 6:27. Washing blood out of clothes
Numbers 8:7. Ceremonial cleaning
Deuteronomy 21:6. Washing hands
2 Samuel 19:24. Grungy meeting
Psalm 51:2. Requesting spiritual cleansing
Isaiah 1:16. Metaphor for human condition in sin
Jeremiah 2:22. Stains which cannot be washed
Acts 16:33. Washing wounds
Acts 22:16. Washing away of sins
1 Corinthians 6:11. Washed and made holy through Christ
1 Timothy 5:10. Hospitable care for guests
Hebrews 10:22. Washed with cleansing water

▸ Watchfulness *(focus, guard, protect)*

The close observation of someone or something

1 Samuel 1:12. Eli watches Hannah.
Job 10:12. Life preserving
Isaiah 27:3. The Lord's watchful eye
Matthew 24:42. Alertness
Matthew 26:41. Prayer during the night
Mark 13:33. Waiting and watching for the Lord
Acts 20:31. Alertness for false doctrine
1 Corinthians 16:13. Conscientious Christians
Colossians 4:2. Attentive in prayer
1 Peter 5:8. Clarity of mind

▸ Watchman/Watchmen *(guard, lookout scout)*

Persons who are appointed to stand guard and watch over a specific location

2 Samuel 18:24–25. The king's watchman
Job 7:20. Big brother
Psalm 127:1. Need for an alert guard
Isaiah 21:6–8. Lookout for enemies
Ezekiel 3:17. Prophet is a watchman over God's people.
Daniel 4:13. Heavenly guardian

▸ Water *(drink, river, stream)*

The essential drink for sustaining human life; metaphorically, spiritual life-giving

Genesis 1:6. Separating waters above and below
Genesis 7:11–12. Floodgates opened
Exodus 7:17. Nile water contaminated
Exodus 17:6. Water from a rock
1 Kings 17:1. Elijah controls the water supply.
Psalm 23:2. Sign of peace and refreshment
Jeremiah 2:13. God the source of life-giving water
Jeremiah 14:3. Empty cisterns
Lamentations 5:4. Water rations
Ezekiel 26:19. Cosmic waters of judgment

W

Joel 1:20. Dry streambeds
Amos 8:11. Indication of spiritual need
Zechariah 14:8. Waters of blessing flowing from Jerusalem
Matthew 23:25–26. Spiritual cleansing
Luke 7:44. Washing Jesus' feet
John 4:14. Thirst-slaking water
John 7:37–38. Streams of living water flowing from people
1 Corinthians 10:1–2. United by baptismal waters
Revelation 7:17. Led to springs of water of life
Revelation 21:6. Fountain filled with life-giving water already flowing

▸ Way, the *(Christianity)*

One of the earliest designations for the Christian church
Isaiah 40:3. The way of the Lord
Matthew 7:14. Few find the way.
John 14:6. I am the way.
Acts 9:2. Attempts to arrest followers of the Way
Acts 19:9. Speaking evil of the Way
Acts 19:23–25. A great disturbance
Acts 22:4. Paul's testimony
Acts 24:14. An alleged religious sect
Romans 6:4. Newness of life
Galatians 5:25. Way of the spiritual nature
Ephesians 5:2. Walking in love
Colossians 2:6. Walking in Christ
2 Peter 2:2. The way of truth

▸ Weakness *(delicate, frailty, sickness)*

The condition or status of being frail and without strength, energy, or charisma
Luke 5:15. Physical illness
Luke 13:11–12. Longstanding weakness
John 11:4. God glorified through weakness
Romans 6:19. Weakness of the corrupt nature
1 Corinthians 2:3. Weak in presence
1 Corinthians 15:43. Weakness of the human body
2 Corinthians 12:10. Paradoxical strength
Hebrews 4:15. Christ sympathizes with our weaknesses.
Hebrews 11:33–34. Strength in times of weakness

▸ Wealth *(money, storehouse, treasure)*

An abundance of possessions, either material or spiritual, which one possesses
Genesis 2:11–12. Earth's wealth
Deuteronomy 6:10–12. Promise of prosperous land
Deuteronomy 7:25. The snare of wealth
1 Samuel 2:7. Given by God
2 Samuel 8:9–12. Plundered wealth dedicated to God
2 Chronicles 9:22. Solomon's immense wealth
Job 1:3. Job's wealth
Psalm 39:6. Accumulating wealth
Psalm 119:14. Joy in God's law over riches
Proverbs 3:9–10. Honoring the Lord with wealth
Ecclesiastes 2:11. Pointless accomplishments
Jeremiah 17:11. Loss of wealth
Haggai 2:8. Commodities which belong to God
Matthew 6:19–21. Storing up treasure in heaven
Luke 6:20. Blessed are the poor.
Ephesians 1:7–8. Riches of God's grace poured out
Philippians 4:19. Needs met through Christ
1 Timothy 6:9. God and money difficult to balance
James 1:10. Exalting in humble circumstances
Revelation 2:9. Richness in Christ

▸ Weapon(s) *(bow, sword, tool)*

An item specifically designed to inflict pain even to the extent of death
1 Samuel 13:19–20. No blacksmiths in Israel

1 Samuel 17:45. God stronger than great weapons in a champion's hand
2 Samuel 22:35. Shooting a bow
Psalm 35:3. Spear to block the way
2 Corinthians 10:4. Arguments as powerful weapons
Ephesians 6:17. Sword of the Spirit
Hebrews 4:12. Double-edged sword

▶ Weary *(exhausted, fatigued, tired)*

Showing extreme tiredness on account of physical exertion or poor sleep habits

Exodus 17:12. Moses grows weary.
Deuteronomy 25:18. Attack on the weary
2 Samuel 17:2. A weary opponent
Job 3:17. Place of rest for the weary
Psalm 69:3. Exhaustion from crying out to God
Isaiah 28:12. Rest for the weary
Matthew 11:28. Call to the weary
Galatians 6:9. Do not grow weary of doing good.
2 Thessalonians 3:13. Maintaining strength to do what is right
Hebrews 12:3. Remember Jesus in your weariness.
Revelation 2:3. Persecution endured on account of Christ's name

▶ Weather *(elements, rain, storm)*

The atmospheric elements in a given place at a given time

Genesis 8:1–2. Control of the winds
Leviticus 26:4. God sends rain at the right time.
Joshua 10:11. Large hailstones win the battle.
Job 37:3. God directs lightning.
Psalm 29:10. Control over the flood
Psalm 78:47. Hail and frost
Isaiah 29:6. Various drastic weather patterns
Jeremiah 10:13. Rain and lightning controlled by God
Jeremiah 24:10. Judgment through famine
Matthew 16:2–3. Red sky at night
Mark 4:39–41. Jesus stills the storm.

▶ Weaving *(see Textile arts)*

▶ Wedding(s) *(celebration, feast, marriage)*

Marriage ceremony and subsequent celebration

Genesis 34:12. Paying the dowry
Esther 2:18. Massive banquet
Psalm 45:9. Taking a new queen
Song of Songs 3:9–11. Opulent wedding day
Isaiah 61:10. Dressed for the wedding
Jeremiah 2:32. God's people like a forgetful bride
Joel 2:16. Wedding night disturbed
John 2:1–10. Miracle at a wedding
Revelation 18:23. No more brides and grooms
Revelation 21:9. The bride of Christ

▶ Weed(s) *(flower, plant, wild)*

A wild, unwanted plant that is competing for nutrients with cultivated plants

Proverbs 24:31. Overgrown land
Isaiah 5:6. Wasteland that will not be pruned
Hosea 9:6. Sign of judgment and loss of wealth
Hosea 10:8. Illegal worship sites will be overgrown.
Matthew 13:25–30. Weeds planted among wheat

▶ Weeks, Feast of *(Feast of Harvest, Pentecost)*

One of three major Israelite festivals celebrated annually, also known as Feast/ Festival of Harvest and Pentecost in the New Testament

Exodus 23:16. Harvest celebrating firstfruits
Numbers 28:26. Festival of Weeks
Acts 2:1. Pentecost, fifty days after Passover
Acts 20:16. Celebrating Pentecost in Jerusalem
1 Corinthians 16:8. Paul's plans for Pentecost

▶ Weeping *(anguish, crying, tears)*

Intense crying or anguish

W

Numbers 11:10. God's people weeping in their tents

Deuteronomy 34:8. Weeping for Moses' death

Ezra 10:1. Weeping over the temple

Psalm 30:5. Weeping night, joyful morning

Isaiah 65:19. No more weeping in the new creation

Matthew 8:11–12. Weeping and gnashing of teeth

Mark 5:38–39. Weeping over a child

John 20:11–13. Mary weeps at the tomb.

Revelation 18:15. Mourning over torture

Revelation 21:4. No more tears

▸ Weight(s) *(measurement, poundage, scales)*

Variety of measuring tools used in commodity trading and payment

Genesis 23:16. Weighing out silver

Deuteronomy 25:13. Weights carried

1 Samuel 17:5. Heavy armor scales

2 Samuel 12:30. A heavy crown

2 Kings 18:14. Demanding a sizable weight of precious metal

Proverbs 16:11. God uses honest scales and weights in his judgments.

Micah 6:11. No toleration for dishonesty

John 12:3. Pouring a pound of pure nard

John 19:39. Much myrrh and aloe

▸ Welcome *(greeting, salutation)*

Greeting someone upon meeting them

Matthew 10:14. How to deal with a city that is not welcoming

Matthew 25:43. Unwelcoming to stranger

Acts 18:27. Welcoming Apollos in Greece

Romans 14:1. Welcoming less mature Christians into your midst

Romans 15:7. Accepting each other in a Christlike manner

Romans 16:2. A warm Christian welcome

2 Corinthians 6:17. Unwelcome with unbelievers, welcome with God

Colossians 4:10. Welcoming Christian brothers from other churches

Hebrews 11:31. Rahab's treatment of Joshua's spies

3 John 10. Wrongly refusing the welcoming of new believers

▸ Well(s) *(cistern, pit, water)*

A crevice in the ground, either naturally occurring or manmade, which collects and stores water

Genesis 21:25. Disputing over a precious commodity

Genesis 37:24. Joseph dropped in a cistern

Numbers 21:17–18. Springs of water

1 Chronicles 11:17–18. Public well

Psalm 40:2. Deliverance from the pit

Jeremiah 38:6. Jeremiah tossed into an empty well

John 4:6. Waiting by Jacob's Well

James 3:11. Illustrating hypocrisy

▸ West *(direction)*

The direction from which the sun sets

Genesis 13:14. Looking in every direction

Exodus 10:19. Strong western wind

Deuteronomy 11:30. Mountains to the west of the Jordan

Joshua 1:4. Western border

1 Chronicles 9:24. Gatekeepers on four sides

2 Chronicles 32:30. Water tunnel west of Jerusalem

▸ Wheel(s) *(disk, rolling, round)*

A round object which spins around an axle allowing for easy movement for the purpose of transportation, irrigation, or craftsmanship

1 Kings 7:32–33. Bronze stands made to look like chariot wheels

Ecclesiastes 12:6. Water wheel

Jeremiah 18:3. Potter's wheel

Jeremiah 47:3. Thundering sound of chariot wheels

Ezekiel 23:24. When chariots and wagons attack
Daniel 7:9. Throne with wheels of fire
Nahum 3:2. Enemy approaching

▶ Whirlwind *(storm, thunderstorm, windstorm)*

A violent windstorm; also refers to a sudden attack and thus, symbolizes judgment

2 Kings 2:11. Elijah taken to heaven in a windstorm
Job 27:20. Storms in the night
Job 38:1. The Lord speaks from the storm.
Isaiah 5:28. Sudden attack
Isaiah 66:15. The Lord's terrible return
Hosea 8:7. Reaping a bad storm

▶ Whisper *(mumble, murmur, softly)*

A soft, breathy way of speaking which preserves confidentiality

2 Samuel 12:19. Whispering bad news
1 Kings 19:12. God's presence in a still, small whisper
Psalm 31:13. Rumors
Psalm 62:9. Meaningless breath
Isaiah 8:19. Garbled truth
Jeremiah 20:10. Fears rising
Matthew 10:27. Making the whispers public
John 11:28. Softly sharing a message

▶ White *(bright, pure, radiant)*

Symbolic color, representing purity or radiance associated with God's glory

2 Chronicles 5:12. Levite musicians dressed in white linen
Psalm 51:7. White as snow
Isaiah 1:18. White like wool
Daniel 7:9. White clothing and hair
Matthew 17:2. Appearance white as light
Revelation 3:18. White clothes
Revelation 7:14. White robes washed in the blood of the lamb

▶ Wicked *(depraved, evil, sinful)*

Not merely a quality of malignance, but evil or sinfulness which is active and persistent

Genesis 6:5. Lord's wrath welling up against evil humanity
Numbers 16:26. Wicked men under judgment
Psalm 18:20–21. Wickedly turning from God
Proverbs 15:26. Evil people with evil thoughts
Jeremiah 17:9. Beware of the evil mind.
Matthew 16:4. Evil people seek a sign.
Mark 7:21–23. Evils which come from within
Romans 1:29. Evil lives
Ephesians 6:16. Extinguishing the evil one's arrows
Colossians 1:21. Evil actions which alienate from the life of God
1 John 2:13. Victory over the evil one is won.
1 John 3:12. The evil child Cain

▶ Widow(s) *(survivor, woman)*

A woman who has lost her husband, yet has not remarried

Exodus 22:22. Never exploit widows.
Deuteronomy 26:12. Money goes to widows.
Ruth 1:3–5. Three widows
2 Samuel 20:3. Living like widows amidst the king
2 Kings 4:1. Widow's money troubles
Job 27:15. Widows who do not cry
Psalm 68:5. God cares for the fatherless and the widow.
Jeremiah 15:8. Judgment coming, many widows soon
Ezekiel 44:22. Regulations for priests
Luke 21:1–4. Widow's generous offering
1 Timothy 5:3–5. Honoring widows
James 1:27. Essence of true religion

▶ Wife(ves) *(partner, spouse, woman)*

A woman who is married to a man

Genesis 2:24. Man and wife united

Genesis 4:19. Early acceptance of polygamy
Exodus 21:10. Caring for the first wife
2 Samuel 6:20. Undermining wife
2 Chronicles 11:21. Favored wife
Job 2:9–10. Wife's bad advice
Proverbs 12:4. Crown of husband
Matthew 19:8–9. Grounds for divorce
1 Corinthians 7:3–5. Satisfy each other
Ephesians 5:22. Under husband's authority
Ephesians 5:25. To be cherished as Christ loves the church
1 Timothy 5:14. Encouraging younger widows to remarry

▶ Wild ox *(bovine, bull, cow)*

A non-domesticated male or female cow
Deuteronomy 33:17. Symbol of power
Job 39:9–10. Untamable
Psalm 29:6. Poorly treated animal

▶ Wiles *(ploys, schemes, tricks)*

Elaborate and devious trickery employed to manipulate an outcome otherwise not expected or deserved
Genesis 27:36. Jacob's trickery
Numbers 25:18. Plotting trickery
Job 5:13. God catches the wise in their tricks.
Proverbs 12:2. The Lord condemns schemers.
Luke 20:23–26. Jesus sees through opponents' schemes.
Acts 13:10. Tricks and schemes against God's people
1 Thessalonians 2:3–5. No wiles in spreading the Good News

▶ Will, the *(determination, mind, resolution)*

That faculty of reasoning by which a person makes choices in accordance with what seems most reasonable and best
Mark 3:35. Acting in accordance with God's desire
Luke 22:42. Human and divine will
Luke 23:25. Will of the crowd
John 1:13. New birth not according to human willing
Romans 12:2. Determining God's will for your life
Ephesians 2:3. Following corrupt nature
Ephesians 6:6. Desiring what God desires
Colossians 4:12. Growing to maturity according to what God wants
1 Thessalonians 4:3. Following God's will for sexuality
Hebrews 10:36. Endurance to follow through with what God wants
1 Peter 3:17. God's will to suffer
2 Peter 1:21. Human will subservient to divine will

▶ Wind *(air, breath, breeze)*

The natural movement of air in the atmosphere in the form of a current
Exodus 14:21. East wilderness wind
1 Kings 18:44–45. Westward wind and rain
Psalm 107:25. Voice controlled wind and waves
Proverbs 25:23. North wind brings rain.
Isaiah 21:1. Tempestuous South wind
Isaiah 40:7. The Lord's breath
Jeremiah 49:36. Four winds from the four corners
Ezekiel 37:9. Breath of life
Daniel 7:2. Winds which stir up the sea
Amos 4:13. Created by God
Acts 27:14–15. Northeaster causes Paul's shipwreck.

▶ Window(s) *(aperture, opening, slit)*

An opening in a building or wall which allows for the admittance of fresh air and light
Genesis 7:11. The windows of heaven
Genesis 26:8. Abimelech sees more than he bargained for.
Joshua 2:15. Rappelling down the city wall from the window
2 Kings 1:2. King Ahaziah falls and hurts himself.
2 Kings 9:31–33. Jezebel thrown to her death

Joel 2:9. Entry point of thieves

Malachi 3:10. Windows of heaven opened for blessings

Acts 20:9. Nodding off

2 Corinthians 11:33. Paul narrowly escapes.

▶ Wine *(alcohol, strong drink, vino)*

An alcoholic drink made by fermenting the juice of grapes

Exodus 29:40. Wine offering used in sacrifices

Leviticus 10:9. Priests must be completely sober when they enter the tent.

Numbers 6:3. No grape products for Nazirites

2 Samuel 16:2. Nourishing tired travelers

Nehemiah 2:1. Cup bearer

Esther 1:7–8. Social drinking

Psalm 104:15. Gladdens the heart

Proverbs 21:17. Expensive tastes

Ecclesiastes 2:3. Drowning of sorrows

Song of Songs 4:10. Love preferred to wine

Mark 2:22. New wine in new wineskins

Luke 21:34. Avoid drunkenness.

John 2:1–11. Jesus turns water into delicious wine.

Ephesians 5:18. Drunkenness forbidden

1 Timothy 5:23. Aiding in wellness

Titus 1:7. Overseers should only drink in moderation.

▶ Wing(s) *(extension, pinion)*

Feathered limb of bird, typically used for flying; metaphorically used to speak of care, concern, protection, and swift action

Genesis 1:21. God created winged creatures.

Exodus 25:20. Wings of the cherubim

Deuteronomy 32:11. Swift action

Ruth 2:12. Refuge under the wings of God

Ruth 3:9. Marriage proposal

Job 39:13. Ostrich wings

Psalm 17:8. Hidden in the shadow of God's wings

Psalm 36:7. Mercy and care

Psalm 68:13. Wings of a dove

Psalm 91:4. Shielded by God

Jeremiah 48:40. A swift attack

Ezekiel 10:21. Ezekiel's angelic vision

Ezekiel 16:8. Protection and covenant keeping

Malachi 4:2. Healing in his wings

▶ Winking *(batting, blink, gesture)*

Closing and opening of an eye quickly which may indicate flirtation, joking, or even hostility

Psalm 35:19. Actions toward an enemy

Proverbs 6:13. Malicious actions

Proverbs 10:10. Causing heartache

Proverbs 16:30. Plotting something

Isaiah 3:16. Flirting with eyes

▶ Winnowing *(dividing, preparing, separating)*

Separating the chaff from the grain by throwing it up in the air with a shovel; often used to metaphorically described God's action of judging others

Ruth 3:2. Boaz on the threshing floor

Psalm 1:4. Wicked are like husks in the wind.

Isaiah 21:10. Winnowing of God's people

Isaiah 30:24. Winnowed with forks and shovels

Jeremiah 4:11–12. Coming judgment

Jeremiah 51:2. God's people will judge Babylon.

Matthew 3:12. Working with wheat

▶ Winter *(season, wet)*

Season in the Middle East characterized by rainstorms which roll in off the Mediterranean Sea

Genesis 8:22. Ongoing seasons

Psalm 74:17. Seasons created by God

Isaiah 28:25. Storing wheat for the winter
Jeremiah 36:22. A warm fire in the middle of winter
Amos 3:15. Winter houses destroyed
Zechariah 14:8. Waters flowing all season long
Matthew 24:20. Difficult time for travel
John 10:22. A winter festival
Acts 27:12a. Harbor not a good place to dock for winter
1 Corinthians 16:6. Paul considers spending the winter.

▶ Wisdom *(experience, knowledge, morality)*

A category or quality of knowledge which is both moral and intellectual; a way of life for those who earnestly desire to live according to God's standards
2 Chronicles 9:23. Impressive wisdom
Job 11:6. Need for true wisdom
Psalm 90:12. Asking for aid to grow in wisdom
Psalm 111:10. Fear of the Lord is the beginning of wisdom.
Proverbs 10:23. Wisdom and understanding
Proverbs 13:10. Taking the advice of others
Matthew 13:54. Amazing wisdom of Jesus
Acts 6:3. Spiritually wise chosen to serve
Romans 11:33. Attribute of God
1 Corinthians 2:6–7. Mystery of God's wisdom
1 Corinthians 3:18. Worldly wisdom
Ephesians 1:17. Desire for a spirit of wisdom
Ephesians 5:15. Wise living
Colossians 1:9. Prayer for spiritual wisdom
Colossians 2:23. Having the appearance of wisdom
Colossians 3:16. Wisdom of the word of Christ
Colossians 4:5. Wise living among unbelievers
James 1:5. God's generosity to those who ask for wisdom

▶ Wise men *(see Magi)*

▶ Wishing *(desire, dream, hope)*

A strong, heartfelt desire for something which is either unreasonable or difficult to attain
Ezra 5:7. Well wishing
Job 11:5. Wishing to hear God's voice
Psalm 145:16. God satisfies wishes of the living
Acts 16:19. Loss of monetary hope
Romans 9:3. An anguished apostle's wish
1 Corinthians 14:5. Desire for the church
Galatians 4:20. Wishing to be present
Revelation 3:15. A wish for God's people

▶ Witchcraft *(divination, magic, sorcery)*

A means of attaining and discerning information and manipulating an outcome
Exodus 22:18. Ridding the land of witches
Leviticus 19:31. Witchcraft forbidden
1 Samuel 15:23. Rebellious magic
2 Chronicles 33:6. Grotesque actions
Isaiah 19:3. Egyptians turn to false means of knowledge.
Micah 5:12. Judgment against divination
Nahum 3:4. Judgment and destruction

▶ Withdrawn *(isolation, separation)*

Isolating oneself, if only for a time, from the public and often to solitude
Lamentations 2:3. Withdrawing strength
Ezekiel 9:3. God's glory departing from the temple
Daniel 11:30. Abandoning the holy promise
Hosea 5:6. The Lord withdrew.
Luke 5:16. Prayer and isolation

John 5:13. Jesus withdraws from the crowd.
Acts 15:38. John Mark's withdrawal

▶ Withholding *(hold back, keep, retain)*

Refusing to give or holding back something
Genesis 23:6. Nothing withheld
Exodus 22:29. Not withholding the best from God
Deuteronomy 24:14. Forbidding of withholding payments
Psalm 40:11. Need for compassion
Isaiah 32:6. Actions of fools
John 20:23. Giving or withholding forgiveness
1 Corinthians 7:5. Do not withhold sex within marriage.

▶ Witness *(observer, testimony, truth)*

An onlooker who provides testimony concerning a past or present event
Joshua 22:27. Remembrance of witness
Ruth 4:7. Witness of a matter
1 Samuel 12:5. God is my witness.
Proverbs 14:5. Trustworthiness
Jeremiah 32:10. Many sign a deed.
Mark 14:63. No more witnesses needed
Acts 1:8. Called to be witnesses of Jesus
Acts 7:58. Witnesses begin stoning.
Acts 26:16. Paul is appointed to be a witness.
Romans 1:9. God as witness
Hebrews 12:2. Witness to Jesus' life
1 Peter 5:1. Witness of Christ's sufferings
Revelation 1:5. The faithful witness

▶ Woe(s) *(distress, misery, sorrow)*

An onomatopoeia outburst which expresses emotional pain or anguish on account of an impending situation
1 Kings 13:30. Cries when a man of God is buried
Isaiah 1:4. Anguish concerning the nation
Isaiah 5:8. Woes to those who aimlessly buy
Jeremiah 22:18. No mourning of the king
Ezekiel 13:3. Woe against false prophets
Matthew 11:21. Woe to cities who have rejected Jesus
Matthew 23:13–33. Woe against the Pharisees
Matthew 24:19. Woe to pregnant women
Matthew 26:24. Woe to Judas
1 Corinthians 9:16. Personal woe if the Good News is not preached
Jude 11. Woe against those who follow patterns of sin
Revelation 8:13. Expressions of coming judgment

▶ Wolf(ves) *(animal, dog, predator)*

A large carnivorous animal which preys on smaller animals and incites fear in shepherds
Isaiah 11:6. Wolves will live with lambs.
Jeremiah 5:6. Destroyed by a wolf
Ezekiel 22:27. Leadership like wolves
Habakkuk 1:8. A quick animal
Zephaniah 3:3. Judges like wolves
Matthew 7:15. Dressed in sheep's clothing
Matthew 10:16. Dangerous animal
Acts 20:29. Unsparing animal

▶ Woman *(female, lady, wife)*

A wife or person of the female gender
Genesis 2:23. Taken out of man
Exodus 2:16. Tending sheep
Exodus 15:20. The prophetess Miriam
Exodus 35:26. Women at work
Judges 1:13–15. Negotiating a land deal
Judges 4:4–5. Deborah's wisdom as a prophetess
Ruth 4:11. Strong women of Israel
Psalm 68:11. Women announcing good news
Proverbs 12:4. Husband's crown
Isaiah 19:16. Weaker sex
Luke 8:2–3. Women patrons of Jesus
Romans 16:1–2. Phoebe's help in advancing the gospel
1 Corinthians 11:3. Relationship to husband
1 Corinthians 11:8–9. Created for man
1 Corinthians 14:33–34. Paul's instruction on women teaching

Ephesians 5:25. To be loved like the church
1 Timothy 2:11–12. Learning in silence
1 Timothy 5:11. Sexual longing
Titus 2:3–5. Instructions for older women
1 Peter 3:7. Weaker vessel

▶ Wonders *(astonishment, miracle, sign)*

Extraordinary deeds of God or an apostle; has a positive sense
Genesis 18:14. Nothing is too hard for the Lord.
Exodus 3:20. Miracles performed in Egypt
Deuteronomy 28:59. Terrible plagues
Joshua 3:5. The Lord will do miracles.
Psalm 9:1. Speaking of the Lord's wonders
Psalm 71:17. Remembering God's miracles
Matthew 24:24. False wonders
John 4:48. Need to see miracles
Acts 2:19. Miracles in the sky
2 Corinthians 12:12. Wonders which prove apostleship
Hebrews 2:4. Words verified through wonders

▶ Word of God *(Bible, Scripture, Word)*

God's written Word which is recorded in the Christian canon
Exodus 31:18. Inscribed by God
Deuteronomy 31:9–11. Moses records portions of the law.
Isaiah 30:8. Permanent witness
Jeremiah 30:2. Recording the words of the Lord
1 Corinthians 14:37. Paul writes the commands of the Lord.
2 Timothy 3:16. Scripture inspired by God
2 Peter 3:2. Words of prophets and apostles

▶ Word, the *(Jesus, logos, message)*

A spoken message or deed; in the New Testament also refers to Jesus as "the Word" of God
Deuteronomy 12:32. Obeying and maintaining the Lord's command
Psalm 103:20. Spoken orders
Isaiah 40:8. The enduring word
Isaiah 55:11. God's word is effective.
Jeremiah 2:31. Considering the word of the Lord
Mark 2:2. Speaking God's word
John 1:1–2. Jesus the Word of God
Acts 6:2. Ministers of God's word
Acts 13:26. The message of salvation
Romans 10:8. The word is near.
1 Corinthians 1:18. Message of the cross
Galatians 6:6. Learning from and sharing God's Word
Ephesians 1:13. The message of truth
Ephesians 6:17. Word of God as a sword
Hebrews 6:5. Goodness of God's word
Revelation 19:13. The risen Lord

▶ Words *(communication, speaking)*

Oral communication spoken between one or more parties
Mark 10:24. Stunning words
John 16:29. Teaching with plain words
Acts 20:35. Remembering the words of the Lord
Romans 16:18. Flattering words
2 Corinthians 9:15. Speechless
Ephesians 6:19. Praying for the right words
1 Thessalonians 4:18. Words of comfort
1 Timothy 5:1. Avoiding harsh words
1 Peter 4:11. Speaking God's words
1 John 3:18. Empty words
Revelation 21:5. Faithful and true words

▶ Work *(job, labor, vocation)*

Exertion of physical energy or intellectual faculties in order to accomplish a given purpose, typically as a paid vocation
Exodus 1:13–14. Hard physical work
Nehemiah 5:16. Best efforts
Psalm 90:17. Seeking success in work
Proverbs 14:23. Benefit from hard work
Ecclesiastes 3:13. Work is a gift from God.
2 Corinthians 11:27. Intense work schedule

2 Thessalonians 3:10. Working and eating
2 Timothy 4:5. Devotion to work

▶ World, the *(cosmos, earth, sphere)*

Biblically, a place of hostility and opposition toward God

Romans 3:19. Everything judged
Romans 4:13. Inheriting the whole world
Romans 5:12. Sin entered the world through one person.
1 Corinthians 1:21. Unable to recognize God's wisdom
2 Corinthians 7:10. Worldly distress
Galatians 4:3. Slaves to worldly principles
Ephesians 2:12. Apart from God
Colossians 2:8. Worldly traditions
1 John 2:2. Sins of the whole world

▶ Worldliness *(corruption, flesh, material)*

The quality of being caught up in worldly ways

Genesis 6:11–12. Corruption
Luke 16:8. Cleverness
1 Corinthians 1:26. Human standards
1 Corinthians 3:3. Living according to human standards
2 Corinthians 10:4. Weapons of the world
Philippians 3:19. Minds set on earthly things
Colossians 3:2. Set minds on things above.
Colossians 3:5. Put sinful ways to death.
Titus 2:12. Training against worldliness
1 Peter 2:11. Desires of the corrupt nature
Jude 19. Physical things, not spiritual things

▶ Worm(s) *(larva, maggot)*

A small creeping animal typically associated with death and decay

Exodus 16:20. Manna becomes full of worms.
Deuteronomy 28:39. Worms destroy crops.
Job 25:6. Man compared to a worm
Isaiah 14:11. Consumed by maggots and worms
Isaiah 51:8. Destroyer of goods
Jonah 4:7. God's control of a worm
Mark 9:48. Consumed by worms, but not dying

▶ Wormwood *(bitter, drink, poison)*

A woody shrub noted for its intense bitterness

Deuteronomy 29:18. Bitter poison
Proverbs 5:3–4. Kiss of an adulterous woman
Jeremiah 23:15. Given by God
Lamentations 3:15. Bitter drink
Lamentations 3:19. Compared with suffering
Revelation 8:11. Star named Wormwood

▶ Worry *(anxious, panic, stressed)*

The overwhelming sense of panic or anxiety caused by one's sense of loss of control over circumstances in life

Genesis 45:20. Do not worry about possessions.
Psalm 73:12. Why are the wicked without worry?
Proverbs 1:33. Living without worry
Isaiah 28:16. Believing in God's promise
Matthew 6:28. Worrying about needs
Matthew 6:34. Do not worry about tomorrow.
Luke 10:41. A woman's worries
Luke 12:11. Keeping worry in perspective
Acts 20:10. Calming the worries of others
Philippians 4:6. Presenting requests to God

▶ Worship *(homage, honor, praise)*

The activity and attitude of glorifying God in His presence in both heart and voice

Exodus 34:14. Commanded to worship God alone
Psalm 29:2. Worshiping God's great name
Psalm 95:6–7. Worship our Creator.
Isaiah 19:21. Sacrificial worship
Matthew 2:2. Coming to worship baby Jesus
Matthew 15:9. Pointless worship

Luke 1:46–47. Magnifying God
John 4:23–24. Worshiping in spirit and truth
Acts 7:7. Future time of true worship
Romans 1:25. Worshiping creature rather than Creator
Ephesians 1:12. To the praise of His glory
Colossians 3:16. Singing unto God
Hebrews 10:22. Drawing near to God
Jude 25. Doxology
Revelation 4:10. Elders' endless worship

▶ Worth *(cost, price, value)*

The quality of having value intrinsically as a creation of God or benefit due to natural value
Esther 5:13. No value added
Psalm 119:72. Valuable teachings
Proverbs 31:10. A wife of strong character
Isaiah 40:23. Reduced value
Lamentations 4:2. Worth of God's children
Matthew 6:26. Of greater worth
Mark 12:42. Worthy sacrifice, yet low worth

▶ Worthless *(cheap, inferior, valueless)*

Having no real value or worth
Deuteronomy 32:21. Idols are worthless.
Psalm 127:1–2. Worthless work
Ezekiel 13:6–9. Worthless prophetic visions
Romans 1:28. Acknowledging God thought to be worthless
1 Corinthians 15:17. Situation where faith would be worthless
Ephesians 4:17. Futile thinking
Philippians 3:7. Worthless compared with Christ
Titus 3:9. Worthless words
James 1:26. Worthless religion
1 Peter 1:18. Worthless life of ancestors

▶ Wound(s) *(injuries, hurts, pain)*

An injury to the body which causes damage to the tissue and requires treatment
Psalm 38:5. Untreated wounds
Psalm 147:3. God bandages our wounds.
Proverbs 27:6. Friendly fire
Isaiah 53:5. By his wounds we are healed.
Jeremiah 30:17. God promises to heal Zion's wounds.
Luke 10:33–34. Samaritan treats a wound.
Acts 16:33. Jailer cares for prisoner's wounds.
1 Peter 2:24. Healed by the wounds of Christ

▶ Wrath of God *(anger, justice, righteousness)*

God's holy and just anger that will be poured out against all ungodliness
John 3:36. Result of rejecting the Son
Romans 1:18. Revealed against the ungodly
Romans 2:7–8. Anger and fury toward those who refuse to believe the truth
Romans 5:9. Saved from wrath by Christ's blood
Ephesians 5:6. Failing to obey God
Colossians 3:6. Certain sins provoke God to anger.
Revelation 14:19. Agents of God's wrath

▶ Wrestling *(fight, games, grappling)*

The sport of grappling with an opponent in an attempt to pin them down
Genesis 32:24–26. Jacob wrestles with God.
Ephesians 6:12. Wrestling with spiritual forces

▶ Writing *(letters, script, words)*

The practice of recording ideas through the use of letters, symbols, or pictures
Deuteronomy 27:8. Commanded to write carefully and clearly
Joshua 8:32. Joshua records teachings.
1 Chronicles 28:19. God's written plan
Jeremiah 8:8. Scribes who turn teachings into lies
Jeremiah 36:6. Dictation
Habakkuk 2:2. Clearly writing a vision
Luke 1:3–4. Undertaking a noble writing project
John 8:6–8. Jesus writes in the sand.

Acts 18:27. Letters of commendation
2 Corinthians 10:10. Strong letters
Galatians 6:11. Paul takes up the pen.
Revelation 1:10–11. Write on a scroll.

▸ Wrong/Wrongdoing *(error, mistake, sin)*

A sinful act which offends the holiness and righteousness of God

Exodus 34:7. Continued patience of God
Leviticus 4:3. Making atonement for wrongdoing
Deuteronomy 32:4. God does no wrong.
Nehemiah 1:7. Calling out public wrongs
Proverbs 3:29. Do not plot wrongdoing.
Matthew 18:21–22. Forgiving those who do wrong
1 Corinthians 13:4–5. Love does not keep track of wrongs.
Colossians 3:25. Reciprocating wrong
Hebrews 1:9. Loving what is right, hating what is wrong
1 John 1:9. Cleansed from every wrong
1 John 5:17. Various kinds of wrongdoing

▶ Yahweh *(Adonai, God, Jehovah)*

The Hebrew name for God par excellence; denotes the holy, personal, Creator and sustainer of the world

Genesis 2:4. Yahweh is the true Creator God.

Exodus 6:3. Personal God

Exodus 12:50–51. Yahweh brings Israel out of Egypt.

Exodus 33:18–19. Glory associated with God's name

Leviticus 11:44. Yahweh's holiness a standard for human holiness

Deuteronomy 4:24. Jealousy of Yahweh

Judges 5:11. Divine warrior

1 Samuel 2:7. The sovereign God

Psalm 8:1. Majestic name

Psalm 33:21. Trust in God's holy name

Psalm 102:15. Glory of the Lord's name

Isaiah 30:27. Yahweh comes to judge.

▶ Year of Jubilee *(forgiveness, homecoming, sabbatical)*

Marked every fiftieth year by the release of every debt, holdings of land, and the freeing of slaves

Leviticus 25:10. Setting aside the fiftieth year

Leviticus 25:11–12. Eating spontaneous, uncultivated crop

Leviticus 25:13–14. Slaves set free

Leviticus 27:16–24. Returning property to an original owner

Numbers 36:4. Awaiting the year of jubilee

▶ Yeast *(leaven)*

The leavening agent of bread; metaphorically refers to a catalyst for multiplying good or evil

Exodus 12:15. Removing yeast during Passover

Matthew 13:33. Kingdom of heaven is like yeast.

Matthew 16:6. Symbol of hypocrisy

1 Corinthians 5:6–8. Illustration using yeast

Galatians 5:9. The effects of even a small amount of yeast

▶ Yield *(deliver, give, permit)*

Commonly used to refer to the transaction or transference of an object

Genesis 1:11. The earth yields crops for eating.

Genesis 4:12. Ground cursed because of the fall

Numbers 20:8. Yielding water from the rock

Deuteronomy 13:8. Not yielding to certain people

2 Chronicles 30:8. Yielding to the Lord

Hosea 10:1. Israel like a vine which yields fruit

Matthew 13:23. Someone who bears good fruit

Matthew 27:50. Yielding up his spirit

Galatians 2:5. Not yielding to false teachers

Hebrews 12:11. Yielding peace from discipline

James 3:12. Like yields like.

Revelation 22:2. Yielding various fruits

▶ Yom Kippur (see *Atonement)*

▶ Youth *(adolescence, juvenile, young)*

The early stages of one's life which precede maturity or adulthood

1 Samuel 2:26. Growing and gaining favor

1 Samuel 9:2. Handsome young man

2 Kings 2:23–24. Mocking youth

2 Chronicles 13:7. Youthful inexperience

2 Chronicles 26:1. Young king

Job 32:4. Youth must wait.

Psalm 71:5. Youthful faith

Psalm 119:9. Keeping life pure from youth

Proverbs 20:29. Young men's strength

Isaiah 9:17. Ungodly youth

Jeremiah 1:6–8. Young prophet called

1 Timothy 4:12. Do not look down on the young.

2 Timothy 2:22. Youthful lusts

1 Peter 5:5. Respecting spiritual leadership

1 John 2:13. Victory won

Z

▶ Zeal *(devotion, earnestness, passion)*

Biblically, refers to fervor in either a positive or negative sense

John 2:17. Zeal for God's house

Romans 10:2. Deep, but misguided, devotion

2 Corinthians 7:7. Zeal for seeing Paul

2 Corinthians 9:2. Enthusiasm leading to action

2 Corinthians 11:2. Zealous like God

Galatians 1:14. Fanatical for ancestral tradition

Philippians 3:6. Zeal for the law

Hebrews 10:27. Zealous fury of God

▶ Zealot(s) *(activist, enthusiast, fanatic)*

In the technical sense, a sect of Judaism known for religious enthusiasm, political activism, and social retreat

Luke 6:15. Simon the Zealot

Acts 5:37. Led by Judas of Galilee

Acts 22:3. A religious zealot

▶ Zion *(citadel, hill, Jerusalem)*

Refers to the hill or mount on which the city of David was built after it was captured from the Jebusites; may also refer to Jerusalem in general, or true Israel in particular

Psalm 9:11. Place of the Lord's enthronement

Psalm 87:2. The Lord loves Zion.

Isaiah 1:27. People of Zion pardoned by the Lord's justice

Isaiah 4:3. Those left in Zion will be called holy.

Jeremiah 8:19. The Lord's presence in Zion

Lamentations 1:4. Zion deserted

Joel 3:16. Victory again in Zion

Micah 4:2. Teachings which go out from Zion

Matthew 21:5. Jesus entering Zion

Romans 9:33. A rock in Zion

Romans 11:26. Savior will come from Zion.

Hebrews 12:22. City of God

Revelation 14:1. Picture of heavenly Zion